Francis I

To Sonia

Francis I

R. J. KNECHT

Reader in French History
University of Birmingham

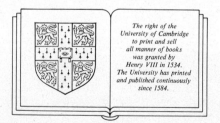

The right of the
University of Cambridge
to print and sell
all manner of books
was granted by
Henry VIII in 1534.
The University has printed
and published continuously
since 1584.

CAMBRIDGE UNIVERSITY PRESS

Cambridge
London   New York   New Rochelle
Melbourne   Sydney

Published by the Press Syndicate of the University of Cambridge
The Pitt Building, Trumpington Street, Cambridge CB2 1RP
32 East 57th Street, New York, NY 10022, USA
296 Beaconsfield Parade, Middle Park, Melbourne 3206, Australia

First published 1982
First paperback edition 1984

Printed in Great Britain at the
University Press, Cambridge

Library of Congress catalogue card number: 81–12197

British Library cataloguing in publication data
Knecht, R. J.
Francis I.
1. France – History – Francis I, 1515-1547
I. Title
944'.028   DC113
ISBN 0 521 24344 0 hard covers
ISBN 0 521 27887 2 paperback

Contents

Plates

Figures

Preface

THIS BOOK is an attempt to fill a gap. There is at present no up-to-date scholarly history of the reign of Francis I in any language.* Why has a monarch so familiar to the thousands who visit the châteaux of the Loire each year been so neglected by scholars? Two possible explanations may be offered: the contempt for *l'histoire événementielle* shared by many French historians of the present generation and the absence of any corpus of printed sources for the reign comparable with the *Letters and Papers of Henry VIII*. Francis has been the subject of much serious scholarship over the years: his relations with foreign powers, military campaigns, artistic and scholarly patronage, fiscal reforms, religious policy and interest in overseas enterprise have all been seriously examined; but the results of this research are to be found mainly in specialist articles and monographs; no attempt has been made recently to cover all these aspects in a single volume.

My treatment of Francis is not biographical, but historical. Biography has its own rules, which cannot always be reconciled with those governing sound historical practice: its success depends on a completeness which the available documentary evidence may not permit. This is particularly true of a king in an age of personal monarchy. There is no possible comparison between the life of a constitutional ruler whose administrative competence is clearly circumscribed and that of a theoretically absolute monarch who set no limits to his own authority. Francis was ultimately responsible for everything that took place in his name. In the absence of documentation capable of illuminating sufficiently the decision-making process at the highest level of government, the only

---

* Owing to an unfortunate delay for which neither my present publisher nor myself is responsible, this claim requires a qualification. Jean Jacquart's *François Ier*, which has recently appeared in France, is an excellent synthesis. I am glad to see that we agree on most matters of substance. As one would expect from the author, his treatment of the economic and social background is particularly strong. He is less informative on the life of the king, the political history of the last ten years of the reign, artistic patronage and overseas expansion.

way open to the biographer who is unwilling to resort to conjecture is to turn historian and take an all-embracing view of the monarch's role.

For the sake of clarity, I have treated the reign analytically within a broadly chronological framework. This method has enabled me to focus on a number of aspects which might easily have got lost in a straight narrative. My conventions are as follows: rulers and places are given the commonly accepted English version of their names (e.g. 'Francis', not 'François'; 'Lyons', not 'Lyon'); otherwise, French names and titles are in their original form (e.g. Henri, duc d'Orléans). I have translated most quotations and modernized the spelling of sixteenth-century English. Dates are New Style throughout.

Many friends and colleagues have assisted my work. Their contribution in respect of particular topics is acknowledged, where appropriate, in the footnotes. Here I wish to record my more substantial debts: to John Bright-Holmes for his patience and kindness over many years; to Miriam Hodgson for guiding my first steps; to Germaine Ganier for her interest, generosity and countless acts of kindness; to Jack Scarisbrick and Eric Ives for valuable advice and help on many occasions; to Richard Bonney, who read the completed typescript, for suggesting a number of corrections and improvements; to René and Suzanne Pillorget for helping to make my visits to Paris so enjoyable and keeping me in touch with academic life across the Channel; and to John Grenville and Ragnhild Hatton for their help and encouragement in the difficult business of changing publishers. Among the librarians who have helped me, I wish to single out Leslie Brierley of the University of Birmingham and Colin Bailey of the Barber Institute of Fine Arts, Birmingham; and among archivists, Monique Langlois of the Archives Nationales in Paris. My gratitude, too, goes to Christopher Allmand, Henry Cohn, Cecil Clough, Christopher Dyer, Rodney Hilton, Michael Mallett, Hamish Miles, John Rogister, Hamish Scott and Ellis Waterhouse for help of various kinds. Research for this book has been made possible by generous grants from the British Academy and the University of Birmingham. I warmly thank Doreen Leigh for typing my manuscript, not once but twice, with unfailing accuracy and good humour. Finally, my greatest debt is to my wife, who has put up with 'Francis' for nearly twenty years; her criticisms have spared me many errors and her encouragement has helped me to finish.

R.J.K.

Leamington Spa
March 1981

Abbreviations

A. du M.	Annales du Midi
A.N.	Archives Nationales, Paris
A.R.	Archiv für Reformationsgeschichte
Arch. Stor. It.	Archivio storico italiano
Barrillon	Le journal de Jean Barrillon, secrétaire du chancelier du Prat, ed. P. de Vaissière, 2 vols. (1897–1899)
B.H.R.	Bibliothèque d'humanisme et Renaissance
B.I.H.R.	Bulletin of the Institute of Historical Research
B.L.	British Library, London
B.N.	Bibliothèque Nationale, Paris.
B.S.H.P.F.	Bulletin de la Société de l'histoire du Protestantisme français
C.A.F.	Catalogue des actes de François 1er, 10 vols. (1887–1910)
Champollion-Figeac	Captivité du Roi François 1er, ed. A. Champollion-Figeac (1847)
C.S.P. Span.	Calendar of State Papers, Spanish, ed. G. A. Bergenroth, P. de Gayangos and M. A. S. Hume, 12 vols. (London, 1862–95)
C.S.P. Ven.	Calendar of State Papers, Venetian, ed. R. Brown, C. Bentinck and H. Brown, 9 vols. (London, 1864–98)
D.B.F.	Dictionnaire de biographie française
Decrue, i	Anne de Montmorency, grand maître et connétable de France à la cour, aux armées et au conseil du roi François 1er (1885)
Decrue, ii	Anne de Montmorency, connétable et pair de France sous les rois Henri II, François II et Charles IX (1889)
Desjardins	Négociations diplomatiques de la France avec la Toscane, ed. A. Desjardins, 6 vols. (1859–1886)
Doucet	Doucet, R., Etude sur le gouvernement de François 1er dans ses rapports avec le Parlement de Paris, 2 vols. (1921–6)

Doucet, *Institutions*	Doucet, R., *Les institutions de la France au XVIe siècle*, 2 vols. (1948)
du Bellay	*Mémoires de Martin et Guillaume du Bellay*, ed. V.-L. Bourrilly and F. Vindry, 4 vols. (1908–19)
Econ. H.R.	*Economic History Review*
E.S.R.	*European Studies Review*
F.H.S.	*French Historical Studies*
Florange	*Mémoires du Maréchal de Florange dit le jeune adventureux*, ed. R. Goubaux and P. A. Lemoisne, 2 vols. (1913–24)
G.B.A.	*Gazette des beaux arts*
Granvelle, *Papiers d'état*	*Papiers d'état du cardinal de Granvelle*, ed. C. Weiss, 9 vols. (1841–52)
Guiffrey	*Cronique du roy Françoys Premier de ce nom*, ed. G. Guiffrey (1860)
Herminjard	*Correspondance des réformateurs dans les pays de langue française*, ed. A. Herminjard, 9 vols. (Geneva, 1886–7)
Imbart de La Tour	Imbart de La Tour, P., *Les origines de la Réforme*, 4 vols. (1905–35)
Isambert	*Recueil général des anciennes lois françaises*, 29 vols. (1827–33)
J.B.P.	*Le journal d'un bourgeois de Paris sous le règne de François Ier (1515–1536)*, ed. V.-L. Bourrilly (1910)
J.W.C.I.	*Journal of the Warburg and Courtauld Institutes*
Kaulek	*Correspondance politique de MM. de Castillon et de Marillac, ambassadeurs de France en Angleterre 1537–42*, ed. J. Kaulek (1885)
Le Glay	Le Glay, *Négociations diplomatiques entre la France et l'Autriche*, 2 vols. (1845)
L.P.	*Letters and Papers, Foreign and Domestic, of the Reign of Henry VIII*, ed. J. S. Brewer, J. Gairdner and R. H. Brodie, 21 vols. (London, 1862–1910)
Michaud et Poujoulat	J.-F. Michaud and J.-J.-F. Poujoulat, *Nouvelle collection de mémoires*, 1st ser., vol. v (1836)
Ordonnances	*Ordonnances des rois de France: règne de François Ier*, 9 vols. (1902–75)
R.D.B.V.P.	*Registres des délibérations du Bureau de la Ville de Paris*, 3 vols. (1883–6)
Rev. d'hist. écon. et soc.	*Revue d'histoire économique et sociale*
Rev. d'hist. mod. et contemp.	*Revue d'histoire moderne et contemporaine*
R.H.	*Revue historique*
R.H.E.F.	*Revue de l'histoire de l'église de France*
Ribier	Ribier, G., *Lettres et mémoires d'Estat des roys,*

	princes, ambassadeurs et autres ministres sous les règnes de François Ier, Henri II et François II, 2 vols. (1666)
R.Q.H.	*Revue des questions historiques*
St.P.	*State Papers of Henry VIII,* 11 vols. (London, 1830–52)
Versoris	*Livre de raison de Me Nicolas Versoris, avocat au Parlement de Paris, 1519–1530,* ed. G. Fagniez (1885)

All references to *C.A.F.* and *L.P.* are to document numbers, not pages, unless otherwise stated.

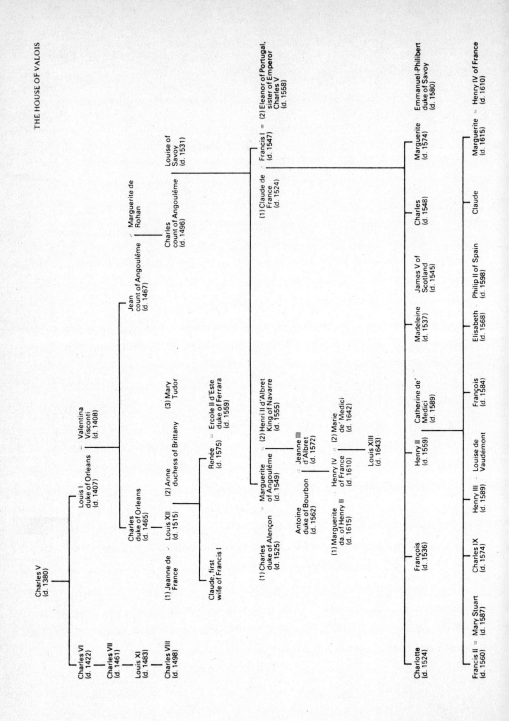

Childhood and youth

THE SMALL TOWN of Cognac stands on the left bank of the river Charente in the midst of a fertile and undulating countryside in western France. To most people it means only one thing, the finest brandy, but it has another claim to fame, for it was the birthplace of King Francis I, the 'knight-king' (*roi-chevalier*) and 'father of letters' (*père des lettres*). The castle in which he was born is now the warehouse of a distillery.

Francis was a scion of the house of Angoulême, a cadet branch of the royal house of Valois, which was founded by Jean, comte d'Angoulême, the second son of Louis I, duc d'Orléans, and of Valentina Visconti, daughter of the last duke of Milan of that name.

At the age of thirteen, Jean was sent as a hostage to England, where he remained for thirty-two years. In 1415 he was joined by his elder brother Charles, duc d'Orléans, the poet of the *Rondeaux*, who had been taken prisoner at Agincourt. Jean shared his brother's literary tastes, and, after his return to France in 1445, he built up a fine library in his château at Cognac. He was not, however, a rich man, having had to sell part of his estates in order to pay his ransom.[1]

Jean was succeeded in April 1467 by his second son, Charles, who was only seven years old. In 1478 there was some question of his marrying Mary of Burgundy, but King Louis XI betrothed him instead to his two-year-old niece Louise, daughter of Philip, count of Bresse, a younger son of the duke of Savoy. Philip became duke in 1496, but died in the following year. Having lost her mother, Marguerite de Bourbon, when she was only seven, Louise was brought up by her aunt, Anne de Beaujeu, Louis XI's daughter, who shared the regency of France with her husband, Pierre, during Charles VIII's minority. Charles d'Angoulême tried to escape the matrimonial fate prescribed for him by Louis XI by taking part in an aristocratic revolt, called *la Guerre folle*, in 1487. He assembled an army in Saintonge, but was crushed 'like a waffle between two irons'. The price of his submission was his marriage to Louise on 16 February 1488.[2]

[1] *D.B.F.*, ii. 1219–21.
[2] *Ibid.*, ii. 1202–3.

Though Charles was twenty-eight years old in 1488 and Louise only twelve, their marriage proved, by all accounts, reasonably happy; no harsh word was ever heard to pass between them.[3] Yet the count did have two mistresses, Antoinette de Polignac and Jeanne Comte. By the first he had two daughters, Jeanne and Madeleine, and by the second another daughter, Souveraine. In the fifteenth century, however, illegitimacy did not carry the stigma that it has since acquired. Louise apparently accepted her husband's infidelities with perfect equanimity. She brought up his bastards along with her own children, and took Antoinette de Polignac as her companion.

Charles had two children by Louise: Marguerite, who was born on 11 April 1492, and Francis (François), who was born two years later, on 12 September.[4] The latter owed his Christian name to Francis of Paola, an Italian hermit, who had been called to France in 1482 to save the life of King Louis XI. Although he failed in this mission, he was persuaded to settle in France, where he soon gained the reputation of being a miracle-worker.[5] He specialized in getting divine assistance for the production of heirs and heiresses, and male children who came into the world as a result of his intercession were usually named after him. Louise had called on the hermit at Plessis-lez-Tours soon after her marriage and had been told by him not only that she would have a son but that he would become king of France. This showed a truly prophetic insight, since in 1494 the odds were heavily weighted against Francis ever reaching the throne. He was only the cousin of the reigning monarch, Charles VIII, the next in line of succession to the throne being Louis II, duc d'Orléans. Only if both were to die without male issue would Francis become king. Females, of course, were debarred from the throne by the Salic law.

Charles d'Angoulême never became politically significant; he was an easy-going, weak person whose chief redeeming feature was a love of literature and art. In spite of his limited means, he continued to build up the library at Cognac, and his entourage included Robinet Testard, a talented illuminator of manuscripts, Jean de Saint-Gelais, the official historian of Louis XII's reign, and his brother, Octavien, the poet.

On an exceptionally cold winter's day in 1495 Charles left Cognac to go to court, but he was taken ill that same night at Châteauneuf. Louise called several doctors and 'attended on him day and night as tenderly and humanely as the poorest wife might nurse her husband'.[6] Her devotion, however, proved unavailing; on 1 January 1496 the count died, leaving a

---

[3] P. Paris, *Etudes sur François Premier* (1885), i. 28.
[4] Michaud et Poujoulat, v. 87.
[5] G. Roberti, *Francesco di Paola* (Rome, 1915).
[6] Paris, i. 27

will in which he appointed Louise as the guardian of his children.[7] But, as she was only nineteen and the minimum legal age for guardianship was twenty-five, Louis d'Orléans, the children's nearest male kinsman, claimed their guardianship for himself. Louise, however, opposed him by invoking a local custom of Angoumois, which fixed the age of guardianship at fourteen. The dispute was submitted to the Grand Conseil and a compromise reached: Louise was allowed to retain the custody of her children, while the duc d'Orléans was appointed their honorary guardian. In practice, this meant that Louise could not transact any important business without the duke's prior knowledge and approval. It was also stipulated that he would get full custody of the children and their property in the event of Louise remarrying.[8]

Charles VIII died childless on 8 April 1498 and was succeeded on the throne by Louis d'Orléans, who became Louis XII. As the new king was also childless, Francis became heir presumptive to the throne. Louis granted him an annuity of 8,000 *livres* and, in 1499, created the duchy of Valois for him out of the patrimony of the house of Orléans. He also confirmed Louise's guardianship of her children and invited her to bring them to the court at Chinon, where he entertained them with an almost paternal show of affection. One week later, however, he entrusted them to the custody of Pierre de Rohan, seigneur de Gié and marshal of France, who took them first to the château of Blois, then to that of Amboise. Gié was a middle-aged widower, second only in political importance to Georges d'Amboise, archbishop of Rouen. In 1503 he took as his second wife Charlotte d'Armagnac and assumed her late father's title of duc de Nemours. Being ambitious, he doubtless regarded his custody of the heir to the throne as a unique opportunity for self-advancement. As he had been appointed by word of mouth, his duties are not precisely known, but presumably he was expected to ensure Francis's safety. To this end, he purchased the captaincy of Amboise, establishing there a company of twenty-five archers under a lieutenant called Roland de Ploret. Gié also exercised some control over Louise's household. Thus, he dismissed Jean de Saint-Gelais and others who had served the countess and her late husband for many years, replacing them by his own creatures. Although Gié was often at court, he did visit Amboise from time to time; he would then dine at Louise's table and accompany her son to church or on outings.

Louise deeply resented any restriction of her independence. She slept in the same room as her children, and would allow only certain ladies to be

---

[7] *Procédures politiques du règne de Louis XII*, ed. R. de Maulde La Clavière (1885), pp. 716–22.

[8] *Ibid.*, pp. 723–7.

present at her *lever* and *coucher*. No gentleman was admitted, and Ploret was only allowed as far as her chamber door when he came each morning to escort Francis to mass. One day, however, he delegated this duty to a subordinate called du Restal, who, finding the door shut, simply broke it down. Louise was understandably furious. She obtained du Restal's dismissal, but was foiled in her efforts to get rid of Gié as well. The king ordered Francis's removal from her room at night so that Gié's men might keep watch over him at all times.[9]

It seems that Louise was allowed a free hand in the education of her children and that she took her duties seriously.[10] In keeping with her motto, *libris et liberis*, she commissioned books specially for them. They included a work on ancient mythology, called *Commentaire sur le livre des échecs amoureux*, and a dialogue on penance. A history book and an atlas, now at the Bibliothèque Nationale in Paris, may have been used by Francis as a child.[11] He learnt Italian and Spanish from his mother and was taught biblical history and Latin by François Demoulin and François de Rochefort. Francis may also have had lessons with Christophe de Longueil, the Flemish humanist, but the 'new learning' did not play an important part in his education. Ironically enough, the future 'father of letters' was a poor Latinist.[12] Guillaume Budé wrote his *Institution du prince* in French because he knew that Francis would not read it if it were in Latin.[13]

But Francis's education, whatever its shortcomings, was regarded by contemporaries as unusually enlightened. Florange, who was brought up with Francis, believed that no prince had been better taught,[14] and even as discriminating an observer as Castiglione, author of *The Book of the Courtier (Il Cortegiano)*, was favourably impressed by him when he visited the court of Louis XII. 'I believe', says Count Lodovico in *The Book of the Courtier*, 'that for all of us the true and principal adornment of the mind is letters; although the French, I know, recognize only the nobility of arms and think nothing of all the rest; and so they not only do not appreciate learning but detest it, regarding men of letters as basely inferior and thinking it a great insult to call anyone a scholar.' To which the Magnifico Giuliano replies: 'You are right in saying that this error has

9   *Ibid.*, pp. xiii–cxxxi.
10 The presence of a few salacious books in her library hardly warrants Guizot's severe judgment that she gave her son 'neither principles, nor moral examples'. Paris, i. 37.
11 B.N., MSS. fr. 143, 2794, 5709.
12 Paris, i. 37; *Procédures politiques*, pp. 233–41.
13 C. Bontems, L. P. Raybaud, and J. P. Brancourt (eds.), *Le prince dans la France des XVIᵉ et XVIIᵉ siècles* (1965), p. 7.
14 Michaud et Poujoulat, v. 7.

prevailed among the French for a long time now; but if good fortune has it that Monseigneur d'Angoulême, as it is hoped, succeeds to the throne, then I believe that, just as the glory of arms flourishes and shines in France, so also with the greatest brilliance must that of letters. For when I was at that Court not so long ago, I set eyes on this prince . . . and among other things I was told that he greatly loved and esteemed learning and respected all men of letters, and that he condemned the French themselves for being so hostile to this profession.'[15]

'Nobility of arms', however, was not overlooked in Francis's education. Florange's memoirs contain a vivid account of Francis and his young companions at Amboise disporting themselves in the open. They played an Italian game called *l'escaigne*, in which a large inflated ball was hit with a bat shaped like a stool with legs filled with lead. Francis excelled in archery and in hunting deer and other animals with nets. He and Florange also used to fire darts from a small gun or *serpentine* at a target fixed to a door. Another Italian game was played in pairs: Francis and Anne de Montmorency versus Florange and Philippe Chabot de Brion. A ball 'as large as a barrel and filled with air' was hit with a piece of tin lined with felt and strapped to the forearm. Being tall and strong for his age, Francis was particularly successful in this game, which required both skill and strength. He and his friends also used to besiege and defend model forts; and, as they grew up, they wore armour and took part in jousts and tournaments.[16] Inevitably, there were accidents. On 25 January 1502 Francis was carried off by his mount, much to the anguish of Louise, who recorded the incident in her journal. At Fontevrault, on 6 August 1508, he was struck on the forehead by a stone.[17] Such accidents were to punctuate much of his life.

In January 1499 Louis XII, having divorced his first wife, Jeanne de France, married Charles VIII's widow, Anne, duchess of Brittany. This was, of course, a matter of grave concern for the house of Angoulême, for Anne, who was only twenty-two years old, could reasonably be expected to produce a son, who would inevitably displace Francis as heir to the

[15] B. Castiglione, *The Book of the Courtier*, tr. G. Bull (Harmondsworth, 1967), p. 88. The passage in question may not have been disinterested, for Francis had some involvement in the creation of the *Courtier*. About late 1515 or early 1516 Castiglione interpolated in the first draft of his work the claim that Alfonso Ariosto at the behest of the king had urged him to continue working on it. This claim was dropped from a later draft, which served as the basis for the first printed text (1528). For a full discussion of this problem see C. H. Clough, 'Francis I and the Courtiers of Castiglione's *Courtier*', *E.S.R.*, viii (1978), 23–70.

[16] Michaud et Poujoulat, v. 6–7.

[17] *Ibid.*, v. 88.

throne. Her first child by Louis, however, was a daughter, Claude, born at
Romorantin on 13 October 1499, who was for eleven years the only child
in the royal nursery and the pivot of Louis XII's matrimonial diplomacy.
Though plain in looks, she was a desirable match because her dowry
comprised the Orléans patrimony, the duchy of Brittany and the French
claims to Asti, Milan, Genoa and Naples. If the kingdom were to remain
united, it was essential that she should marry the heir to the throne.
Consequently, in April 1500, her father made a secret declaration nullifying in advance any other match.[18] In the following year, however, the
Archduke Philip the Fair, son of the Emperor Maximilian, requested
Claude's hand for his infant son, Charles of Luxemburg, and Louis
granted his request in the hope that Maximilian would, in return, give
him the investiture of Milan. Anne of Brittany welcomed the marriage as
a means of preserving her duchy's independence of France. A marriage
treaty was accordingly signed on 10 August, and soon afterwards the
archduke and his wife came to Blois to see their prospective daughter-in-
law. It was on this occasion that Francis made his first official appearance
as heir to the throne.[19]

In September 1504 Francis celebrated his tenth birthday, and his
mother had a medal struck for the occasion. This shows, on one side, the
boy's head in profile, wearing a bonnet, and, on the other, a salamander
in the midst of flames with the motto *Notrisco al buono, stingo el reo*. Every
visitor to the châteaux of the Loire knows Francis I's salamander, which
adorns so many fireplaces, chimney-stacks and other architectural features; fewer, one may safely assume, are familiar with the origin of the
emblem or its significance. The fallacy that a salamander can go through
fire unscathed, extinguishing it at the same time, can be traced back to the
works of Aristotle and other scholars of antiquity. Contrary to popular belief, Francis was not the first to use the salamander in the midst
of flames as an emblem; it had already been used by his father and
paternal grandfather. The significance of the half-Latin, half-Italian
motto *Nutrisco et extinguo* has given rise to much discussion. In its
complete form (as on the medal of 1504) it can be translated as: 'I feed
upon the good (fire) and put out the evil one' (i.e. 'I am burning with
lawful zeal, faith, a desire for peace and love, and I put out guilty zeal,
harmful and destructive passions, unjust war and lust'). The salamander, which was often amusingly represented in the ceremonial
entries of Francis I, was seen either swallowing fire or spitting water. Its

---

[18] *Procédures politiques*, p. 135.
[19] J. S. C. Bridge, *History of France from the Death of Louis XI* (Oxford, 1921–36), iii.
      208–14.

1   The salamander amidst flames. Reverse of a medal of Francis of Angoulême as duc de Valois (1504).

third attribute – that of being able to live through fire – made it also a symbol of endurance.[20]

Louis XII fell seriously ill in 1504, and in the absence of his chief minister, the cardinal of Amboise, who had gone to Rome, the government passed into the hands of Marshal Gié, Francis's governor, whose views on Breton independence were in direct opposition to the queen's. He feared that, if the king died, Anne would return to her duchy, as she had done after the death of her first husband; only this time she would take her daughter Claude with her so as to frustrate any chance of the latter marrying Francis. Whether or not Gié actually tried to prevent such an eventuality is uncertain; what is clear is that, after Louis had recovered his health, Gié was accused by Pierre de Pontbriant, a servant of Louise of Savoy, of having attempted a *coup d'état* during the king's illness. Somewhat reluctantly, the king ordered an enquiry during which Louise

[20]   A.-M. Lecoq, 'La salamandre royale dans les entrées de François 1er', in *Les fêtes de la Renaissance*, iii, ed. J. Jacquot, and E. Konigson, (1975), pp. 93–104.

confirmed all Pontbriant's allegations. Gié, she claimed, had planned to carry her son off to the castle at Angers, he had talked of the need to collect boats on the Loire, had pressed her to allow his son to sleep in the same room as Francis, and had recommended some of his servants to him. Eventually, Gié was sent for trial on more than a hundred charges. He admitted that he had always wanted the marriage of Claude and Francis, but denied all the other charges. Pontbriant's allegations, he claimed, were lies inspired by Louise, who wanted to be avenged for certain measures he had taken by order of the king. In February 1506, Gié was acquitted of high treason but found guilty of 'certain excesses and faults'. He was suspended as marshal of France, fined and banished from court.[21] He was also replaced as Francis's governor by Artus Gouffier, seigneur de Boisy, whose younger brother Guillaume, seigneur de Bonnivet, now joined Francis's circle of friends.[22]

In April 1505 Louis XII again fell ill and, on 31 May, made his will. He ordered Claude and Francis to be married as soon as possible, notwithstanding his obligations to Philip the Fair; appointed a council of regency, which included the queen and Louise of Savoy; and bequeathed to Claude the Orléans patrimony, including Blois, Genoa and Milan. He also forbade her to leave the kingdom on any pretext whatever. Queen Anne showed her disapproval of these arrangements by retiring to her duchy after the king's recovery. Louis, in the meantime, visited Amboise and took Francis with him to Plessis-lez-Tours. His council took steps to ensure that his will would be properly executed. Thus, the captains of the *gendarmerie* had to promise in writing that they would serve Francis and Claude 'without excepting anyone here or outside the kingdom'. On 8 October the cardinal of Amboise was entrusted with the 'total administration' of Francis, duc de Valois, until his majority.[23]

Before Francis and Claude could be married, however, it was necessary to repudiate the treaty of Blois, in which she had been promised to Charles of Luxemburg. This Louis did not mind doing, since he had now been given the investiture of Milan. But, under the treaty, Burgundy, Milan and Asti were to be forfeited to Charles if his marriage to Claude were broken off by Louis, Anne or Claude herself. The king overcame this difficulty by shifting the responsibility for his breach of faith on to his subjects. In April 1506 an assembly of notables, including representatives of the 'good towns' and universities, was summoned to Tours. The deputies were received by the king on 14 May and their spokesman, Thomas Bricot, made a speech. He began by acclaiming Louis as 'Father

21 *Procédures politiques*, passim.
22 Paris, i. 36; Barrillon, i. 5.
23 C. Terrasse, *François Ier: le roi et le règne* (1945–70), i. 39–40.

of the people' on account of the stable peace and sound justice which he had given them. Then, as the deputies fell upon their knees, Bricot came to the point. 'Sire', he said, 'we are come here to proffer a request for the general welfare of your kingdom. Your humble subjects beg that it may please you to give your only daughter in marriage to my Lord Francis here present, who is France's son (*tout français*).' The king, apparently much moved by these words, promised to give them careful consideration. Five days later the delegates were told that he had granted their request. They were asked to swear in return that they would see the marriage carried out when the children came of age, and to recognize Francis as their sovereign lord should Louis die without male issue. Before returning home they witnessed the betrothal of the royal children.[24] This was performed by the cardinal of Amboise on 21 May in the great hall of the château of Plessis-lez-Tours, the marriage contract being signed on the following day.[25]

On 3 August 1508 Francis left his mother to settle permanently at court.[26] He was nearly fourteen years old, the age at which in France a youth was traditionally deemed capable of assuming the full responsibility of kingship. But he could not yet be certain of reaching the throne. In April 1510 Queen Anne became pregnant for the seventh time. The king prayed for a son, but on 25 October he was given a second daughter, called Renée.[27] In 1512 Anne did produce a son, but he died almost immediately. Louise, who set great store by the unimpeded advancement of her son, expressed her relief in her diary. 'Anne, queen of France', she wrote, 'gave birth to a son on 21 January, the feast of St Agnes; but he was unable to prevent the exaltation of my Caesar, for he was still-born.' The king now abandoned hope of perpetuating his line, and Francis became popularly known as 'Monsieur le Dauphin'. He was admitted to the king's council and appointed captain of a hundred *lances*.[28] In September 1512 he was given command of the army of Guyenne, but being too young and inexperienced to be left in charge of operations, he was accompanied by Odet de Foix, seigneur de Lautrec, who bore the title of *lieutenant-général*. The task facing the army was the reconquest of the small kingdom of Navarre, which Ferdinand of Aragon had overrun recently. But the ensuing campaign was a fiasco. The French, after trying

---

[24] J. Russell Major, *Representative Institutions in Renaissance France, 1421–1559* (Madison, 1960), pp. 122–4.

[25] J. d'Auton, *Chronique de Louis XII*, ed. R. de Maulde La Clavière (1889–95), iv. 44ff; *Procédures politiques*, pp. 221–2.

[26] Michaud et Poujoulat, v. 88.

[27] In 1528 she married Ercole d'Este, who became duke of Ferrara in 1534. She became a patron of the Reformation. See C. J. Blaisdell, in *A.R.*, lxiii (1972), 196–226.

[28] *Procédures politiques*, p. 314.

unsuccessfully to prevent the duke of Alba from retreating to Pamplona, laid siege to the town as winter closed in upon them. Francis was only marginally involved in these operations, his responsibility being to cover Bayonne. Nor did he see the campaign through to the end: early in November, after leading an unsuccessful diversionary attack on San Sebastian, he disbanded his troops and returned to court. Later that month, the French raised the siege of Pamplona and retreated north-wards, leaving behind their sick and wounded and even their precious artillery. Francis's first experience of real warfare had been anything but glorious, but the following year had worse in store.[29]

In June 1513 the French in north Italy suffered a crushing defeat at Novara at the hands of the Swiss. In September, after they had been driven out of the peninsula, the Swiss swept into Burgundy as far as the walls of Dijon. The local commander, La Trémoïlle, had to sign a humili-ating treaty, which Louis XII subsequently refused to implement. Mean-while, the king of England, Henry VIII, and his ally, the Emperor Maxi-milian, invaded Picardy and laid siege to Thérouanne. A force of French cavalry was routed at Guinegatte as it tried to bring supplies to the beleaguered garrison. The action became known as the 'Battle of the Spurs' because the French fled from the field so fast. Louis XII, who was at Amiens at the time, sent out another force under Francis and the duc de Bourbon, but it could not save Thérouanne, which capitulated on 23 August. A month later the much more important town of Tournai also fell into English hands.

On 9 January 1514 Anne of Brittany died, leaving the way to the throne clear for Francis.[30] It was still possible, of course, for the king to remarry, but Francis was fairly confident on this score. 'Even if the king should commit the folly of marrying again', he said, 'he will not live for long: any son he may have would be a child. This would necessitate a regency and in accordance with the constitution the regent would be me.'[31]

Although Francis was not yet allowed any share in policy-making, he acquired political significance as people began to regard him as Louis XII's likely successor. Foreign ambassadors, in particular, tried to win his friendship. On 13 March he signed a truce with Ferdinand of Aragon at Louis's request.[32] Ferdinand was anxious to follow this up with a mar-riage between his grandson and Princess Renée, hoping that her dowry would include Milan and Naples. This was acceptable to Louis, but not to Pope Leo X, who did not wish to see Ferdinand more powerful in Italy. His envoy in France decided to enlist Francis's help. 'I have spent a long

[29] P. Boissonnade, *Histoire de la réunion de la Navarre à la Castille* (1893), pp. 379ff.
[30] Florange, i. 146–9; *Procédures politiques*, pp. 338–40.
[31] *Procédures politiques*, pp. 353–4.   [32] *Ibid.*, p. 342.

time with him', he wrote, 'pointing out the dangers and explaining that he would be the chief sufferer, having regard to the position for which God intends him. With suitable arguments I have convinced him that the affair should not be allowed to go on. His views are sound and he has done some good. I am especially commissioned by him to tell His Holiness that his one desire is to do him service, and that, if he ever attain the station to which he may peradventure be called, he will give an unequivocal manifestation of his respect for and devotion to Holy Church.'[33]

The death of Anne of Brittany also facilitated the marriage of her daughter, Claude, with the heir to the throne. This was celebrated at Saint-Germain-en-Laye on 18 May. The ceremony was extremely simple, as the court was still in mourning for the queen. Francis came from Paris, bringing with him only a bed, a bolster and a blanket, while Claude arrived from Blois with hangings of white damask for the bed. Both wore mourning at the nuptial service, which was attended by few guests; even Louise of Savoy was absent.[34] She would probably have preferred a more attractive daughter-in-law, for Claude was 'very small and strangely corpulent'. She also had a bad limp. But she was all sweetness, affability and piety. An ambassador remarked that her 'grace in speaking greatly made up for her want of beauty'. Whether or not Francis appreciated these qualities, he had reason to feel delighted with his marriage: he assumed the title of duke of Brittany, and, on 20 May, seemed like a changed man to the Venetian ambassador. 'Henceforth', he declared, 'I shall be kept informed of everything; and nothing but good will come of this; I promise you that I will speak frankly to the king as I have not dared to do so far.'[35]

In May 1514 Francis clearly expected shortly to become king. Louis XII's health had been failing for some time, and now that his queen had died the chance of his acquiring a son and heir must have seemed extremely remote. On 7 August, however, he signed two treaties with Henry VIII: the first left Thérouanne and Tournai in English hands and provided for the resumption of Henry's French pension, while the second laid down that Louis would marry Henry's sister, Mary. Public opinion was shocked that a girl of eighteen, universally acclaimed for her looks, should be married off to a gouty dotard of fifty-three, but Mary apparently accepted her fate with composure, having been assured by her brother that she would be free to choose her next husband. She was, moreover, prepared to put up with a great deal to be queen of France.[36]

33 Desjardins, ii. 601–6.
34 *Procédures politiques*, p. 358; Florange, i. 151–3; du Bellay, i. 39–40.
35 *Procédures politiques*, p. 360.
36 C.S.P. Ven., ii. 196; L.P., i (pt 2), pp. 1343, 1351.

Louis and Mary were married at Abbeville on 9 October, and, after their first night together, the old king 'seemed very jovial and gay and in love', boasting that 'he had performed marvels'.[37] But Francis had doubts about the king's virility. Two days after the wedding he said to Florange: 'I am happier and more at ease than I have been for years, for I am certain, unless I have been told lies, that the king and queen cannot possibly have a child.'[38] Within a short time Louis began to show signs of wear and tear. The clerks of the *Basoche*, who specialized in ribald farces at the expense of the 'establishment', put on a play in which he was shown being carried off to Heaven or Hell by a filly given to him by the king of England.[39] His health would certainly not allow him to be a *gentil compaignon* to Mary. Soon after the Christmas festivities he fell seriously ill and was confined to his room at the palace of the Tournelles in Paris. 'He sent for Monsieur d'Angoulême', writes Florange, 'and told him that he was very ill and would not survive, whereupon the said lord comforted him as best he could . . . and, after fighting hard against death, he died on New Year's Day and the weather that day was worse than had ever been seen. . . . The king being dead, Monsieur d'Angoulême put on mourning as the nearest person to the crown, and coming to the palace in haste, informed all the princes and ladies of the kingdom, especially his mother, Madame Louise. It was a splendid New Year's gift, I must say, for he was not the king's son, and for your information the said seigneur d'Angoulême was born on New Year's Day and acquired the kingdom of France on New Year's Day.'[40]

Florange was wrong about Francis's birthday, but his insistence on 1 January as a memorable date in the annals of the house of Angoulême is echoed in Louise of Savoy's *Journal*. 'On the first day of January', she writes, 'I lost my husband and on the first day of January my son became king of France.'[41]

[37]   *C.S.P. Ven.*, ii. 207–11; Florange, i. 154–9.
[38]   Florange, i. 160.
[39]   *Ibid.*, i. 163. *Basoche* was a name given to the Palais de Justice. Its clerks were ill-disciplined young men, whose farces and morality plays provided the only comic element in the French theatre before the Renaissance. For an account of the activities of the *Basoche* and of measures taken to restrict them under Francis I see H. G. Harvey, *The Theatre of the Basoche: The Contribution of the Law Societies to French Mediaeval Comedy* (Cambridge, Mass., 1941), pp. 228–31.
[40]   Florange, i. 163–4.
[41]   It has been argued, not very convincingly, that Louis XII died on 31 December 1514, not 1 January 1515. See H. Hauser, 'Sur la date exacte de la mort de Louis XII et de l'avènement de François Ier', *Rev. d'hist. mod. et contemp.*, v (1903–4), 172–82. For the argument in favour of 1 January see Bridge, *History of France*, iv. 267–83.

King of France

'KINGSHIP IS the dignity, not the property, of the prince.' These words, spoken by Philippe Pot at the Estates General of 1484, embody the theory of royal succession in France at the close of the Middle Ages. The king was not free to dispose of the crown as if it were a piece of private property; whatever his own wishes might be, he was bound to be succeeded by his nearest male kinsman. 'The crown is not strictly hereditary', wrote the jurist du Moulin, 'for the new king is not the heir of his predecessor, and does not succeed him in the possession of his goods or in the heritage abandoned by the deceased, but he succeeds to the crown by right of blood in accordance with the Salic law.'[1] It was on the basis of this principle that Francis of Angoulême secured the throne on the death of Louis XII. His right to do so was unimpeachable, yet his accession has been described as 'in a certain measure a *coup d'état*', because he proclaimed himself king regardless of the fact that Mary Tudor might still produce a son by the late king.[2] But it was a clearly established principle that 'the king never dies'; he was to be followed immediately by his eldest son or nearest male kinsman. This ruled out the possibility of an interregnum, so that Francis's accession cannot be regarded as unconstitutional. It would only have been so if Mary had given birth to a son and Francis had refused to stand down.

While preparations were being made for the funeral of Louis XII, which took place at Saint-Denis on 12 January 1515, Francis had to attend to much urgent business. In theory, he was not obliged to honour any of his predecessor's obligations: he was not bound to settle Louis's debts or to recognize officials he had appointed or the liberties and privileges he had conceded to towns and corporations. In practice, however, a new king usually confirmed former grants of offices, privileges and the like in return for appropriate fees. Thus, on 2 January Francis confirmed members of the Parlement of Paris and of the other 'sovereign

[1]   Doucet, *Institutions*, i. 81.
[2]   H. Hauser, 'Sur la date exacte de la mort de Louis XII et de l'avènement de François Ier', *Rev. d'hist. mod. et contemp.*, v. (1903–4), 179.

courts'. Five days later he did the same in respect of members of the provincial parlements and *chambres des comptes*. Among distinguished members of the old regime who were kept in office were Charles de Rohan, comte de Guise and *grand échanson de France*; Louis de La Trémoïlle, the king's lieutenant-general in Burgundy; and, above all, Florimond Robertet, who has been fairly described as 'the father of the secretaries of state'.[3] 'He governed the entire kingdom', wrote Florange, 'for since the death of the legate of Amboise he was the man closest to his master . . . he was undoubtedly one of the most intelligent and able men I have ever seen and it is to his credit that, as long as he was in charge of the affairs of France, they fared marvellously.'[4]

Continuity, however, was not all that was required of the new king; the administration also needed an infusion of new blood. On 7 January Francis appointed Antoine Duprat to the office of chancellor of France, which had been vacant since 1512. The chancellor was the head of the judicial administration and also had vast administrative responsibilities. He attended the king's council regularly, taking the chair in the king's absence, he explained royal policy to the Parlement, of which he was the official head, and, as custodian of the king's great and secret seals, he authenticated royal enactments. His principal assistants were the eight *maîtres des requêtes de l'hôtel*, who, in spite of their name, had little to do with the royal household.[5]

Like so many successful Frenchmen of his day, Duprat hailed from Auvergne. The son of a merchant of Issoire, he had entered the legal profession and had worked his way up from the parlement of Toulouse to that of Paris, becoming its first president. He had won the favour of Anne of Brittany by his prosecution of Marshal Gié and, after her death, had entered the service of Louise of Savoy. It was doubtless with her backing that he now obtained the chancellorship at the age of fifty-two.[6] Duprat was hard-working and shrewd, but also ruthless and grasping. He became universally unpopular.

Another office that was vacant when Francis came to the throne was the constableship of France. The constable, who, like the chancellor, was appointed for life, was considered the most important of the 'great officers' of the crown. His duties were exclusively military and included the enforcement of discipline among the troops, the supervision of army

3   Barrillon, i. 2–4; *C.A.F.*, i. 17, 26; v. 5675.
4   Florange, i. 152; *C.A.F.*, v. 15674–5. The development of the office of secretary of state is examined by N. M. Sutherland, *The French Secretaries of State in the Age of Catherine de Medici* (London, 1962).
5   Doucet, *Institutions*, i. 104–9.
6   Barrillon, i. 7–9; *Ordonnances*, i. no. 4; A. Buisson, *Le chancelier Antoine Duprat* (1935), pp. 17–68.

supplies, the appointment of commissioners of musters, the authorization
of military expenditure and the allocation of troops to garrison towns. In
time of war, it was customary for the constable to command the army in
the king's absence and the vanguard in his presence. On ceremonial
occasions, it was his privilege to carry the king's naked sword. On 12
January 1515 Francis appointed Charles III, duc de Bourbon, his most
powerful vassal, to the office.[7] He was twenty-five years old, handsome
and could already boast of a distinguished military record, having fought
bravely against the Venetians at Agnadello in 1509 and against the Swiss
in 1513.[8] In addition to being constable, Bourbon was governor of
Languedoc and *grand chambrier de France*.

The marshals of France, though subordinate to the constable, were on
a par with dukes and peers and were entitled to address the king as
'my cousin'. At Francis's accession, they numbered only two: Stuart
d'Aubigny and Gian-Giacopo Trivulzio, a member of an old Milanese
family who had entered the service of the French crown in 1495.[9] Francis
soon created two new marshals: Odet de Foix, seigneur de Lautrec, who
belonged to a cadet branch of the house of Foix, and Jacques de Chabannes, seigneur de Lapalisse, a veteran of the Italian wars.[10] On being
appointed marshal, Lapalisse relinquished the office of grand master
(*grand maître*) of France, which was given to Francis's former governor,
Artus Gouffier, seigneur de Boisy.[11]

Francis did not forget his relatives and friends in distributing favours.
Jean Barrillon, whose diary is an important source for the early part of the
reign, states that the king handed over to his mother the money obtained
from the confirmation of office-holders. Her county of Angoulême was
raised to ducal status in February 1515 and she was also given the duchy
of Anjou, the counties of Maine and Beaufort-en-Vallée and the barony of
Amboise.[12] Her half-brother, René, who was usually called 'the great
bastard of Savoy', was appointed *grand sénéchal* and governor of
Provence. Francis's brother-in-law, Charles, duc d'Alençon, was officially
recognized as 'the second person in the kingdom' and made governor of
Normandy. The house of Bourbon also benefited from the king's largesse.
The *vicomté* of Châtellerault, which belonged to François de Bourbon,
the constable's brother, was turned into a duchy, and the county of
Vendôme, belonging to Charles de Bourbon, was raised to the same

[7] *Ordonnances*, i. no. 13; Doucet, *Institutions*, i. 112–13.
[8] A. Lebey, *Le connétable de Bourbon* (1904), pp. 31–43; Barrillon, i. 15–16.
[9] C.A.F., v. 15664.
[10] Barrillon, i. 4; B. de Chantérac, *Odet de Foix, vicomte de Lautrec* (1930), pp. 13–25.
[11] C.A.F. i. 13; Doucet, *Institutions*, i. 122–3.
[12] Barrillon, i. 4, 16; *Ordonnances*, i. nos. 20, 21.

level.[13] Guillaume Gouffier, seigneur de Bonnivet, who had been one of Francis's companions at Amboise, received an annuity of 1,000 écus.[14]

By the sixteenth century, the coronation or *sacre* at Rheims was no longer considered by jurists essential to the exercise of kingship. The king ruled from the moment he succeeded to the throne, and his regnal years were reckoned accordingly, yet the *sacre* remained important as a symbol of the supernatural quality of kingship and the close alliance that existed between church and state.[15]

Francis left Paris for Rheims on 18 January accompanied by his mother, the princes of the blood and a host of lords and dignitaries. The queen, however, had to stay behind because she was pregnant.[16] The royal procession arrived at Rheims on 24 January and was received by the archbishop, Robert de Lenoncourt, and other prelates. The next morning, Francis, who had spent the night at the archbishop's palace, was escorted by the bishops of Laon and Beauvais to the cathedral, where the nobility of the kingdom had already gathered. Wearing a gown of white damask over a shirt and tunic of white silk, he advanced along the nave, which had been adorned with gorgeous tapestries. He took his seat in the choir opposite the archbishop's throne, and the peers disposed themselves on either side of him. The archbishop then went to the cathedral porch and received the Holy Ampulla – a vessel containing the oil for the king's anointing – at the hands of the abbot of Saint-Rémi.[17]

The coronation service began with the oath. Standing over the Gospels, the king solemnly promised to promote peace in Christendom, to protect Christians against injuries and iniquities, to dispense justice fairly and mercifully and to expel heretics from his dominions. This was followed by the anointing, the most important part of the whole ceremony. Thrusting his hand through specially contrived openings in the king's tunic and shirt, the archbishop anointed his body with a chrism similar to that used for a bishop's consecration. This conferred on the king an almost sacerdotal character. Although no French king ever claimed the right to

---

[13] C.A.F., i. 106, 108; v. 15661; *Ordonnances*, i. nos. 28, 31, 32. This Charles de Bourbon was not the constable.
[14] C.A.F., v. 15669.
[15] Doucet, *Institutions*, i. 87–8.
[16] T. Godefroy, *Le cérémonial françois* (1649), i. 245–53; M. Sanuto, *Diarii* (Venice, 1887), xx. cols. 22–34; Barrillon, i. 17.
[17] According to legend, a dove had brought the ampulla from heaven on the day of Clovis's baptism. When not in use, it was kept at the abbey of Saint-Rémi, Rheims. Some people believed that it was filled miraculously before each coronation; others, that the level of oil remained constant or registered fluctuations in the health of the reigning monarch. See M. Bloch, *Les rois thaumaturges* (1961), p. 224.

celebrate mass, he did take communion in both kinds, a privilege other-wise enjoyed only by priests.[18]

The king then discarded his garments and put on his coronation robes: a blue gown embroidered with gold fleur-de-lis and the great cloak or *soccus*. According to a fourteenth-century treatise by Jean Golein, this part of the ceremony signified the king's rejection of the 'worldly estate' and his adoption of the 'royal religion'. Golein attributed to the *sacre* the same regenerative force as baptism.[19] The king also received from the arch-bishop the royal insignia: the sword, the ring, the sceptre and the hand of justice. The sword, which symbolized the king's military power, was blessed by the archbishop. The king then placed it on the altar before handing it to the duc de Bourbon, who carried it upright during the rest of the ceremony.

The scene was now set for the coronation proper. At a call from the chancellor, the peers, dukes and counts clustered around the king and helped the archbishop place the heavy crown of Charlemagne upon his head. They then escorted him to a throne raised on a platform above the screen. Removing his mitre, the archbishop made a low bow, embraced the king and cried out three times: 'Vivat Rex in aeternum!' After the peers had also acclaimed him, the trumpets blared out, the organ roared and the entire congregation shouted: 'Vive le roi!' This was followed by the singing of the Te Deum and by high mass. At the offertory, the king made the customary presentation of a silver loaf, a silver pitcher filled with wine and thirteen pieces of gold. His crown was removed and replaced by a smaller one, and his robes, too, were taken from him. He then returned in procession to the archbishop's palace, in whose great hall he dined with the peers of the realm.[20]

From Rheims Francis went to the shrine of Saint-Marcoul at the priory of Corbeny in the Aisne valley.[21] The pilgrimage was closely connected with his thaumaturgical powers. Early in the Middle Ages the idea had de-veloped that the king of France was endowed with the miraculous power of healing the sick. The only other Christian ruler to claim this power was the king of England. In time, it became restricted to the curing of scrofula, a disease more repulsive than dangerous and subject to periods of re-mission. Originally it was assumed that the king derived his power of healing from his anointing, but about the twelfth century an obscure

[18] *Ibid.*, p. 194.
[19] *Ibid.*, pp. 197–8.
[20] B.L., Harley MS. 3462 contains a long account of Francis I's coronation (fols. 202b–214b). I owe this reference to the kindness of Professor John Shearman.
[21] Barrillon, i. 23.

Norman saint, called Saint-Marcoul, posthumously acquired the reputation of curing scrofula, presumably as a result of a pun on his name (*mar* = bad; *cou* = neck). By the late Middle Ages it had become customary for the kings of France to visit his shrine immediately after their coronations in order to reinforce their own thaumaturgical powers through his intercession. This soon led to the idea that the king owed his power of healing to the saint, not to his anointing.[22]

The royal pilgrimage to Corbeny was a well-regulated affair. The monks went in procession to meet the king, who received the saint's skull from the prior. Then, after carrying the relic to the church and praying before the shrine, the king retired to the *pavillon royal*, a part of the monastery reserved for his use. Next day he healed a number of scrofulous people: touching their sores and tumours with his bare hands, he made the sign of the cross over each one and said: 'The king touches you and God cures you.' Each then received two small silver coins.[23]

From Corbeny Francis visited the shrine of the Black Virgin at Notre-Dame de Liesse. Then, after stopping for a few days at Compiègne, he went to Saint-Denis, burial-place of his royal predecessors, where he confirmed the abbey's privileges and underwent another, less elaborate, coronation. Finally, he made his entry into Paris, which had taken almost a month to prepare. On 15 February the mayor (*prévôt des marchands*) and aldermen (*échevins*), the representatives of the seventeen trade gilds and the members of the Parlement and other sovereign courts met the king at La Chapelle-Saint-Denis and escorted him back to a crowded and jubilant capital. First to enter the city were the *gens de ville*. Then came the *gens du roi,* some wearing the late king's badge of the crowned porcupine, others Francis's salamander and motto. They were followed by the marshals of France and the grand master, all of them resplendent in suits of cloth of silver and gold, and by the gentlemen pensioners and others wearing the king's colours. The obese figure of Chancellor Duprat appeared next, preceded by his staff; a horse carried the great seal in a blue velvet coffer. After a flurry of pages, musicians and heralds came four gentlemen carrying respectively the king's hat, cloak, sword and helmet. These were followed by members of the royal household. Only then did Francis appear, radiant in a suit of silver cloth and a white hat with flashing jewels. As he bounded forward on his horse, he threw fistfuls of gold and silver pieces into the crowd lining the processional route. Behind him rode the princes of the blood and other nobles. The rear of the procession was made up by the two companies of the *Cent-gentilshommes* and by 400 archers. The procession led to Notre-Dame,

[22] M. Bloch, pp. 261–6; Florange, i. 169–70.   [23] M. Bloch, p. 281.

where the king attended a solemn service of thanksgiving. This was followed by a splendid banquet at the royal palace, and the day ended with dancing and an entertainment staged by the clerks of the *Basoche*. Thereafter jousts and tournaments were held for several days in the rue Saint-Antoine. On 11 March the municipal government (*bureau de la ville*) gave Francis an elaborate statue in solid gold of his patron saint.[24]

The prophecy of Francis of Paola had come true: Francis of Angoulême had become king. But what did kingship mean to a Frenchman living in the early sixteenth century, and by what means was it exercised?

France was still to a large extent a feudal country in which many towns, corporations and individuals enjoyed a measure of autonomy. All these bodies regarded themselves as parties to a contract, which laid down mutual obligations and excluded total submission to the king. But there also existed a school of thought which favoured royal absolutism. Its chief exponents were the royal jurists, who found in Roman law the idea of absolute power vested in one man and of subjects equally subservient to him. The doctrine of absolutism also received support from the Christian concept of the monarch as God's vicegerent on earth. The king, it was claimed, had the right to legislate, to dispense justice, to revoke all lawsuits to his court, to levy taxes and to create offices. He could at any time annul any concession which detracted from his authority; no fief could be held for ever, and local privileges could survive only if the king chose to renew them at his accession. The authority of Cicero was invoked to show that the king was entitled to sacrifice private interest to the public good.[25]

But absolutism was liable to different interpretations. While the Parlement of Paris admitted that authority resided in the king's person, it did not believe that he was free to dispose of the kingdom as he liked. He was its administrator, not its owner, and was bound to observe the so-called 'fundamental laws' governing the succession to the throne and preservation of the royal demesne. The Parlement's view implied a distinction between the sovereign as an ideal and permanent being and the fallible human being who actually occupied the throne. It believed that the interests of the ideal sovereign needed protection from the possible consequences of the king's human weaknesses. Its magistrates, in other words, saw themselves as the agents of an ideal monarchy, not as the slaves of the reigning monarch, and frequently compared themselves to the senators of ancient Rome.[26]

[24] *R.D.B.V.P.*, i. 221–2; M. Félibien, *Histoire de la ville de Paris* (1725), ii. 933–4; Godefroy, i. 266–78.   [25] Doucet, *Institutions*, i. 73–7.
[26] G. Zeller, *Les institutions de la France au XVIᵉ siècle* (1948). pp. 82–4; Doucet, i. 21–2.

Two main currents of absolutist thought, then, existed in France in the early sixteenth century: a moderate one, which advocated a close collaboration between the king and the sovereign courts, and an extreme one, according to which the king alone had the right to govern. The two trends may be illustrated by the writings of a distinguished churchman, Claude de Seyssel, and of a leading humanist scholar, Guillaume Budé.

Though born in the duchy of Savoy, Seyssel had served the French crown over many years as a councillor, administrator and diplomat and had been rewarded for his services with the see of Marseilles. In 1515 he decided to retire to his diocese, but before doing so he wrote a treatise called *La monarchie de France* for the new king, Francis I. Seyssel was above all a realist: instead of advocating radical changes, he accepted the world as he found it and offered remedies suitable for immediate application. Like Machiavelli, he treated politics as a science independent of morality and religion. His realism is exemplified by his attitude to war: knowing that he would not extinguish the king's bellicose proclivities, he abstained from pacifism and merely tried to discourage him from war by showing that it was easier to conquer a territory than to keep it. As an Aristotelian, Seyssel valued moderation in a constitution and admired the French monarchy because he believed it to be tempered by aristocracy. He did not, however, identify the aristocratic element with the nobility, but only with the sovereign courts. The greatness of the kings of France, in his opinion, stemmed from their willingness to accept three restraints on their authority: religion, justice and *police*. By acting as a devout son of the church, curbing judicial abuses and remembering his coronation oath the king could prevent monarchy from degenerating into tyranny.[27]

The purpose of Budé's *L'institution du prince*, written towards the end of 1518, was to bring the author to the king's notice by entertaining and instructing him. Like many of his contemporaries, Budé believed that a knowledge of history was essential to political success. He tried to guide Francis in the right direction by stringing together, sometimes rather clumsily, stories from Scripture and from ancient histories. While sharing Seyssel's high regard for monarchy, he was prepared to allow the nobility only privileges, not a share of authority. As for ordinary people, Budé dismissed them contemptuously as politically inept, citing the expulsion of Themistocles from Athens as evidence of their inability to recognize

---

[27] C. de Seyssel, *La monarchie de France*, ed. J. Poujol (1961), pp. 29–46, 91–221 (tr. J. H. Hexter as *The Monarchy of France*, ed. D. R. Kelley (New Haven, Conn., 1981). See also J. H. Hexter, *The Vision of Politics on the Eve of the Reformation: More, Machiavelli, and Seyssel* (London, 1973), pp. 204–30; N. O. Keohane, *Philosophy and the State in France: The Renaissance to the Enlightenment* (Princeton, N.J., 1980). pp. 32–42; Quentin Skinner, *The Foundations of Modern Political Thought* (Cambridge, 1978), ii. 260–1, 264–5.

real worth. Because of his conviction that royal authority was vested in the king alone, Budé attached an enormous importance to his education. He advised the king to listen to wise counsellors, to respect his predecessors' ordinances, to safeguard the freedom and prosperity of his subjects and to abstain from war. Budé admitted, however, that the king was free to reject this advice, the only limit on his absolute power being the judgment of posterity.[28]

From the beginning of his reign Francis showed a strongly authoritarian disposition. He did not consider himself bound by tradition and believed that he had the right to depart from existing ordinances, institutions and methods of government. The concept of a feudal state, comprising semi-autonomous elements, had no place in his political thinking, and on several occasions he rejected the parallel, which the Parlement liked to draw, between itself and the Roman Senate. The king was supported in his authoritarianism by the chancellor, Duprat, who as a former *parlementaire* was well qualified to deal with any resistance from this quarter. He denied that the court had any right to oppose the king's wishes. 'We owe obedience to the king', he declared in 1518, 'and it is not for us to question his commands.' All authority, he said, including the Parlement's, came from the king; otherwise the kingdom would be an aristocracy, not a monarchy.[29] But how far could the king implement his wishes? What kind of machinery of government did he have at his disposal?

Among the various organs of central government in early-sixteenth-century France three stand out as particularly important: the king's council or Conseil Etroit, the Grand Conseil and the Parlement of Paris. All three had once formed part of the Curia Regis and were still closely related in theory. In practice, however, they were separate institutions with essentially different functions. The Conseil Etroit was the supreme policy-making body in the state, consisting of the monarch himself and his advisers. There were no limits to its competence, though it tended to concentrate on political and administrative matters. No specialization existed among its members, but there was an inner ring which the king would consult on matters of particular importance or requiring absolute secrecy, such as foreign affairs. Although ultimately responsible for financial policy, the council tended to leave technicalities to the king's fiscal officials.[30]

The Grand Conseil was an exclusively judicial body which had taken

28 C. Bontems, L. P. Raybaud and J. P. Brancourt (eds.), *Le prince dans la France des XVIe et XVIIe siècles* (1965), pp. 1–139; Keohane, pp. 58–61; Skinner *passim*.
29 Doucet, i. 49.
30 Doucet, *Institutions*, i. 131–6; F. Decrue, *De consilio regis Francisci I* (1885).

over part of the work formerly exercised by the king's council: it investigated complaints against royal officials, intervened in conflicts of jurisdiction between other courts and could revoke enactments that the Parlement had registered. It also acted as a court of appeal and of first instance for a wide range of legal cases. Though its procedure was fairly simple and comparatively cheap, the court had one great disadvantage for suitors: like the Conseil Etroit, it still followed the king on his travels about the kingdom. Consequently, its records had to be carried around, and suitors were obliged to change their lawyers as it moved from place to place. Because of its proximity to the king, the Grand Conseil was more susceptible to his influence than the Parlement of Paris and was often used by him to bend the law in his own interest.[31]

The Parlement of Paris, which had 'gone out of court' in the thirteenth century, was permanently based in the royal palace on the Ile-de-la-Cité. It comprised several chambers, the most important being the Grand' Chambre. Originally the Parlement's *ressort* or area of jurisdiction had been the whole kingdom, but as the latter had been enlarged a number of provincial parlements were added. By 1515 there were six of these: Toulouse, Grenoble, Bordeaux, Dijon, Rouen and Aix-en-Provence. Yet the Parlement of Paris retained control of two-thirds of the kingdom: it was responsible for the whole of northern France, excluding Normandy, as far south as the Lyonnais and Upper Auvergne. Within this area it judged in the first instance all *cas royaux* (i.e. offences against the king's person, rights and demesne), ranging from treason and *lèse-majesté* to rape and highway robbery. At the same time, it was a court of appeal from lesser royal and seigneurial tribunals.

But the Parlement was much more than a court of law. It issued decrees regulating such matters as public hygiene or the upkeep of roads, bridges and quays; it ensured that Paris received enough corn and fuel; it controlled the quality, weight and price of bread; fixed wages and hours of work; penalized shoddy workmanship; and intervened in academic affairs. Not even the church escaped its vigilance: no papal bull could be applied in France if it had not been registered by the Parlement. The court also kept an eye on the conduct of royal officials in the provinces.

Finally, the Parlement played a significant role politically by ratifying royal legislation. If it found an enactment satisfactory, this was registered and published forthwith; if not, the Parlement submitted remonstrances to the king, either verbally or in writing, whereupon he would either modify his enactment or issue a *lettre de jussion*, ordering the court to register it as it stood without further delay. Such a move might lead to

---

[31] Doucet, *Institutions*, i. 202–6; Zeller, pp. 189–90.

more remonstrances and more *lettres de jussion*. In the end, if the Parlement remained obdurate, the king would come to the court and personally supervise registration of the enactment. This ceremony, called a *lit-de-justice*, implied a temporary resumption by the king of the authority he had delegated to the Parlement. Only the Grand' Chambre could register royal enactments or issue decrees (*arrêts*). Though its official head was the chancellor of France, its effective head was the first president, who was assisted by three other presidents and about thirty lay and clerical councillors.[32]

Local government in early-sixteenth-century France was far from neat and precise. There were eleven provincial *gouvernements*, but they did not cover the whole of France: large areas of the centre and west were excluded, presumably because they ranked as royal apanages. Nor were the boundaries of the *bailliages* and *sénéchaussées* clearly defined, because a running battle was still going on between the king's officials and the agents of the various seigneurs.[33] Yet, in spite of tax and other anomalies, a system of local government did exist, and it played an essential role in the growth of royal authority.

At the head of the hierarchy of local officials was the provincial governor, who was always a high-ranking nobleman, enjoying the king's favour and commanding a large clientele among the aristocracy of his province. His duties were not exclusively military, as was once supposed, but he tended to intervene in local affairs only in an emergency; he would then enforce law and order, keep royal officials up to the mark and co-ordinate their efforts. A governor seldom resided in his province, as he usually held a military command or an office requiring attendance at court. His local duties were normally carried out by a lieutenant, who might himself employ a deputy.[34]

Below the governors were the *baillis*, who were also mostly recruited from the nobility and invariably appointed by the king. As they often held military posts and were seldom trained in the law, their duties, apart from summoning the feudal levy (*ban et arrière-ban*), were usually exercised by

[32] On the role of the Parlement of Paris see E. Maugis, *Histoire du Parlement de Paris*, 3 vols. (1913–16); J. H. Shennan, *The Parlement of Paris* (London, 1968).
[33] Though *bailliages* were mainly in the north and west and *sénéchaussées* in the south and east, there were exceptions to this rule: e.g. the *sénéchaussée* of Boulogne (north) and the *bailliage* of Vivarais (south). In any case, the two names were synonymous. Subdivisions of the *bailliages* and *sénéchaussées* were given all kinds of names in different parts of France: e.g. *prévôtés, châtellenies, vigueries, jugeries*.
[34] G. Zeller, 'Gouverneurs de provinces au XVIᶜ siècle', *R.H.*, clxxxv (1939), 225–56; R. R. Harding, *Anatomy of a Power Elite: The Provincial Governors of Early Modern France* (New Haven and London, 1978).

a deputy (*lieutenant-général*) chosen by the king from a list of three locally elected candidates, who was assisted by three or four *lieutenants-particuliers*. The *bailliage* was a sort of parlement in miniature with an equally wide competence within a much smaller area. It employed a fairly large staff, including a *procureur du roi*. The *bailli* or his deputy also presided over an assembly of local people (*conseil de bailliage*), who were not paid for their services; their role was purely advisory, the power of decision being vested in the chairman. The officials of a *bailliage* were not well paid, but they could charge fees for certain services and often received gifts. Their income, in other words, reflected their zeal, and many were more absolutist than the king. There were, all told, about eighty-six *bailliages*, each one being on average slightly smaller than a modern French département.[35]

A link between the central government and the *bailliages* was provided by the *maîtres des requêtes de l'hôtel*, who helped the chancellor of France run his department. One of their duties was to go on tours of inspection (*chevauchées*) of the provinces, and they had the power to preside over the tribunals of the *bailliages* and deal with complaints against royal officials. If they found anything seriously wrong, they were supposed to report back to the king's council. They thus had a key role to play in the development of centralized government in France. But it is unlikely that they visited the provinces often, as they were too few in number and had heavy duties at the centre of government. The temptation to compare them with the *intendants* of a later period should, therefore, be resisted.[36]

The most complex and probably the least efficient part of French government at this time was the fiscal administration, which we shall examine when dealing with Francis I's fiscal reforms.[37]

France in 1515 was still at a comparatively early stage of her national development. A national consciousness can be found in the writings of humanists such as Robert Gaguin and Valéran de Varennes and also at a more popular level, yet France still lacked well-defined frontiers, a common language and unified legal system. Her eastern border was so blurred in places that certain villagers did not know to which nation they belonged and exploited this confusion to evade taxes and the law. In so far as this frontier existed at all, it followed roughly the rivers Scheldt, Meuse, Saône and Rhône from the North Sea to the Mediterranean.

---

[35] G. Dupont-Ferrier, *Les officiers royaux des bailliages et sénéchaussées* (1902); A. Bossuat, *Le bailliage royal de Montferrand, 1425–1556* (1957); B. Guénée, *Tribunaux et gens de justice dans le bailliage de Senlis à la fin du Moyen Age* (Strasbourg, 1963).
[36] Doucet, *Institutions*, i. 154–9; Zeller, *Institutions*, pp. 115–17.
[37] See below, ch. 8.

People who lived west of this line were vassals of the French king; those to the east were subject to the Holy Roman Emperor. French suzerainty over Artois and Flanders, however, was purely nominal, effective control of these areas having passed into the hands of the house of Burgundy. Further east, the frontier cut across the duchy of Bar so that its ruler, the duke of Lorraine, did homage for one half to the king of France and for the other to the emperor. In the south, Dauphiné and Provence were still not regarded as integral parts of the kingdom, because they were situated east of the Rhône: the king was obeyed as Dauphin in the one and as count in the other. The south-west border of France more or less followed the Pyrenees, avoiding Roussillon, which belonged to Aragon, and the small kingdom of Navarre, ruled by the house of Albret. Within France, there were three foreign enclaves: Calais belonged to England, the Comtat-Venaissin to the papacy and the principality of Orange to the house of Chalon. A few great fiefs also survived, notably the duchy of Brittany, which did not become officially part of the kingdom till 1532, and the large Bourbon demesne in central France.[38]

The surface area of France in 1515 was far smaller than it is today: 459,000 square kilometres as against 550,986. Yet it must have seemed enormous to people living at the time, given the relative slowness of their system of communications. The speed of travel by road in the sixteenth century may be assessed by consulting a famous guidebook published by Charles Estienne in 1553.[39] It was possible to cover fifteen to sixteen leagues in a day when the terrain was flat, fourteen when it rose gently and only eleven to thirteen where it rose steeply. Thus it would normally have taken two days to travel from Paris to Amiens, six from Paris to Limoges, seven and a half from Paris to Bordeaux, six to eight from Paris to Lyons and ten to fourteen from Paris to Marseilles.[40]

By modern standards France in the early sixteenth century was also very thinly populated. No precise figures can be given because of the paucity of documentary evidence: there is no general census for this period, and relatively few parish registers survive. These relate mainly to Provence and north-west France, and are often in poor condition: they do

---

[38] Zeller, *Institutions*, pp. 1–9; H. Stein and L. Legrand, *La frontière d'Argonne* (1905).

[39] C. Estienne, *Le guide des chemins de France de 1553*, ed. J. Bonnerot, 2 vols. (1936).

[40] R. Mousnier, *Etudes sur la France de 1494 à 1559* (Cours de Sorbonne, 1964), pp. 9–13. These figures are theoretical optima. 'In the sixteenth century all timetables were completely dependent on the weather. Irregularity was the rule.' F. Braudel, *The Mediterranean and the Mediterranean World in the Age of Philip II*, tr. S. Reynolds (London 1972–3), i. 360.

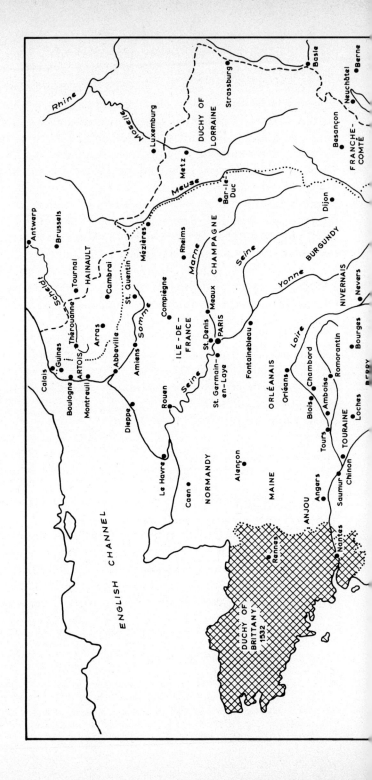

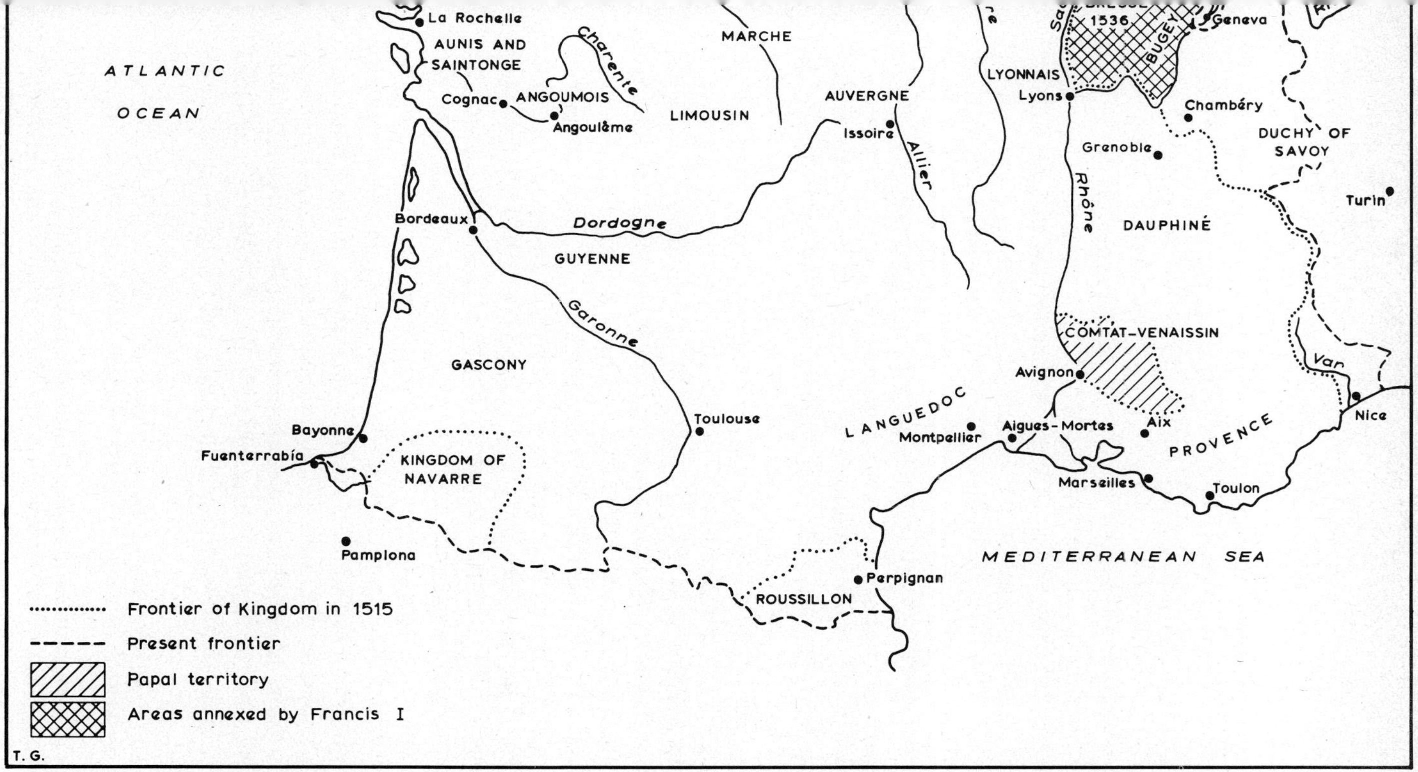
La Rochelle
AUNIS AND SAINTONGE
ATLANTIC
OCEAN
Cognac
ANGOUMOIS
Angoulême
Charente
MARCHE
LIMOUSIN
AUVERGNE
Issoire
Allier
LYONNAIS
Lyons
1536
BUGEY
Geneva
Chambéry
DUCHY OF SAVOY
Grenoble
Turin
Rhône
DAUPHINÉ
Bordeaux
Dordogne
GUYENNE
Garonne
GASCONY
COMTAT-VENAISSIN
Avignon
Var
Nice
Toulouse
LANGUEDOC
Montpellier
Aigues-Mortes
Aix
PROVENCE
Bayonne
Fuenterrabía
KINGDOM OF NAVARRE
Marseilles
Toulon
Pamplona
MEDITERRANEAN SEA
Perpignan
ROUSSILLON
Frontier of Kingdom in 1515
Present frontier
Papal territory
Areas annexed by Francis I
T. G.

2 Map of France, *c.* 1515–47.

not provide complete baptismal lists, seldom record burials and mention marriages only occasionally. The population of France has been estimated at more than 19 million in 1494, but this is almost certainly an exaggeration; it was about that figure in 1700 and therefore is unlikely to have exceeded 15 million two centuries earlier.[41] But, if the population was small by present-day standards, it was growing. Seyssel, in his history of Louis XII's reign, states that the increase in population might be seen from the towns and the fields. 'Many big towns', he writes, 'which had become half-deserted and empty are today so crowded that it is difficult to find room in them to build new houses. While some have grown, others have thrown out suburbs almost as large as themselves, and throughout the kingdom new, large and sumptuous buildings are under construction ... The fields, too, clearly indicate growth in population, for many areas which had turned into waste or woodland are now cultivated or occupied by villages and houses to such an extent that a third of the kingdom has been brought under cultivation in thirty years, especially in this reign.'[42] This description is supported by statistical evidence for certain areas: a village with only 100 inhabitants in 1467 had 300 in 1503; another with only one inhabitant in 1467 had 260 half a century later. Many parish churches were enlarged under Louis XII to accommodate larger congregations.[43]

The population growth was accompanied by a trend towards linguistic unity. Modern French is descended from *langue d'oïl*, a dialect spoken in northern France during the Middle Ages; in the south, *langue d'oc* was used. In about 1450 the frontier between the two linguistic zones ran from the Bec d'Ambès in the west to the col du Lautaret in the east, passing through Limoges, the Cantal and Annonay. South of this line even educated people used the local idiom or Latin; French was spoken by feudal magnates only when addressing the king. After 1450, however, the situation began to change rapidly. As the French monarchy asserted its authority following the expulsion of the English, the *langue d'oïl* began to make deep inroads in the south-west. The parlements of Toulouse, Bordeaux and Aix used it, and noblemen from the south who took up offices at court adopted it. They continued to speak it when they returned home and communicated the habit to their servants. By 1515 the expansion of the French language southward was in full swing, at least in so far as

[41] Mousnier, pp. 14–27; P. Goubert, 'Recent Theories and Research on French Population between 1500–1700', in D. V. Glass and D. E. C. Eversley (eds.), *Population in History* (London, 1965), pp. 456–73.
[42] C. de Seyssel, *Histoire singulière du roy Louis* (1558), pp. 59–60.
[43] J. S. C. Bridge, *History of France from the Death of Louis XI* (Oxford, 1921–36), v. 25.

upper-class usage was concerned; only Gascony, Provence and a few smaller areas needed to be won over.[44]

Another area where unification was less than complete was the law. During the Middle Ages each province, each *pays* and often each locality had its own set of customs. Louise of Savoy, as we have seen, invoked a custom of Angoumois to retain the guardianship of her children in 1496. Broadly speaking, Roman law prevailed in the *pays de langue d'oc*, while customary law held sway in the *pays de langue d'oïl*, but patches of customary law existed in the south and Roman law did penetrate the north to a limited extent.

For a long time customs were fixed by practice only and were, therefore, susceptible to continual change. This made for flexibility, but also uncertainty. So, from the twelfth century onwards charters were drawn up listing the customs of individual lordships or towns. The first serious attempt at a more general codification was made by Charles VII, but no real progress was made until Charles VIII set up a commission in 1495. It was under Louis XII, however, that codification really got under way. The permanent commission lapsed and the king nominated two commissioners for each area. One of these was Antoine Duprat, the future chancellor, who was chosen to codify the customs of Auvergne. In each *pays coutumier* an assembly of representatives of the three estates was called to draw up a code, which was then scrutinized by the commissioners. Those parts of the code which met with general approval were promulgated at once, while the rest were referred to the decision of the appropriate parlement. Within a few years a large number of customs were printed, and the process was to continue under Francis.[45]

France was also becoming more prosperous in 1515. The need to feed her growing population stimulated the recovery of her agriculture from the extensive destruction caused by the Hundred Years' War. In many areas, especially in the north-west and south-west, villages had been wiped out and cultivated land had gone to waste. The reconstruction began in earnest about 1470 and continued till about 1540. It was left to the initiative of individual lords, who had to overcome enormous difficulties. On countless estates nothing was visible except 'thorns, thickets and other encumbrances'; the old boundaries had disappeared and people no longer knew where their patrimonies lay. The task of compiling new

---

[44] A. Brun, *Recherches historiques sur l'introduction du français dans les provinces du Midi* (1923). Most meridional peasants continued to speak *occitan* until well into the nineteenth century. For the situation in Dauphiné in the sixteenth century see E. Le Roy Ladurie, *Carnival: A People's Uprising at Romans, 1579–80*, tr. M. Feeney (London, 1980), p. 46.

[45] Shennan, *Parlement of Paris*, pp. 50–3; Buisson, *Le chancelier Antoine Duprat*, pp. 70–96.

censiers and terriers was expensive and time-consuming. There was also an acute shortage of labour, and lords had to offer substantial concessions to attract settlers to their lands: serfs were emancipated and concessions of all sorts granted to freemen. As a result of these developments the peasants were generally better off than before; some were even able to buy vacant lands and build up holdings. It was the seigneurial class, not the peasantry, which was economically hard-pressed at this time.[46]

In the towns, too, reconstruction was under way at the time of Francis's accession. Security helped to boost trade and industry, and the tempo of trade grew brisker under the stimulus of a gentle rise in prices. All over France a demand arose for the establishment of markets and fairs under royal licence: no fewer than 344 were set up between 1483 and 1500. When a fair was set up it was given privileges in order to attract merchants: foreign money was allowed to circulate freely, the goods of aliens were guaranteed against seizure and distraint, and the *droit d'aubaine*, whereby an alien's inheritance was liable to forfeiture to the crown, was set aside. Some fairs were exempt from entry or exit dues and sometimes special judges were appointed to hear the suits of merchants, thereby sparing them the delays of ordinary justice. By 1515 most big towns and many smaller ones had fairs.[47] The four annual fairs of Lyons attracted many foreigners, especially Italians, Germans and Swiss, and were also important for the development of banking. Though banks had existed in France since the thirteenth century, if not before, it was only in the fifteenth that they became important as agencies of credit and exchange. They fixed themselves at Lyons because of the large amount of business transacted there, and threw out branches in other trading centres. Use of the bill of exchange almost eliminated the need to transport large amounts of cash, and the Lyons fairs became a regular clearing-house for the settlement of accounts. At the same time, the bankers took money on deposit, lent it at interest and negotiated letters of credit. The crown was one of their best customers: Charles VIII's Italian expedition had been financed by the Lyons bankers.[48]

No statistics exist for the volume of French overseas trade in 1515, but it had certainly recovered from its stagnation during the Hundred Years' War. The annexation of Provence in 1481 was an event of major sig-

[46]   M. Bloch, *French Rural History* (London, 1966), pp. 21–63, 112–49; G. Duby and A. Wallon (eds.), *Histoire de la France rurale*, ii (1975); E. Le Roy Ladurie and M. Morineau, *Histoire économique et sociale de la France*, i (1450–1660), pt 2, *Paysannerie et croissance* (1977), pp. 483–689.
[47]   Bridge, v. 261–8.
[48]   R. Doucet, 'La banque en France au XVIe siècle', *Rev. d'hist. écon. et soc.*, xxix (1951), 115–23; M. Brésard, *Les foires à Lyon au XVe et au XVIe siècles* (Lyons, 1914), pp. 238–93; M. Vigne, *La banque à Lyon du XVe au XVIIIe siècle* (Lyons, 1903).

nificance for French trade in the Mediterranean: though Marseilles was unable to wrest the monopoly of the Levantine trade from Venice, it established useful links with the ports of the Ligurian coast, Tuscany, Catalonia, Sicily, Rhodes and the Barbary coast. With a single exception, its chief merchants were Italians who turned to the Lyons bankers for capital.[49] The French Atlantic and Channel ports also recovered in the late fifteenth century and carried on an active trade with England, Spain, the Netherlands and Scandinavia.[50] Land communications being so poor, harbours developed, not only along the west coast, but also along navigable rivers, even far inland. As many as 200 ships might be seen at any time along the quays at Rouen. By far the most important port of the south-west was Bordeaux, which was visited each year by the English wine fleet.[51]

The expansion of trade was related to industrial growth. The most important French industry was cloth-making, which was centred in the north but was also becoming entrenched in other areas, notably Languedoc. An important development, apart from the introduction of the fulling-mill, which facilitated the production of cheaper cloth, was the establishment of a luxury cloth industry, first at Tours, then at Lyons. Previously, cloths of gold and silver and silks had been imported at a high cost from Italy and the east. Mining also received official encouragement at this time, if only to remedy the acute shortage of silver: people were authorized to prospect in many parts of the country, but mainly in the centre. German miners were invited to settle in France on favourable terms. This movement in turn stimulated the metallurgical industries: pots and pans of copper and tin came into general use, and a passion for objects of gold and silver seized the nobility and rich bourgeoisie. Printing grew rapidly at the end of the fifteenth century: the first press was set up in Paris in 1470 and in Lyons in 1473. By 1500 more than thirty towns had presses, and in 1515 there were more than a hundred printing houses in Lyons alone. Originally, the workers and their materials were German; later they were recruited locally.[52]

The revival of trade and industry was accompanied by significant social changes. While some noblemen were finding it difficult to make both ends meet, many bourgeois were making fat profits and lending money at interest. In exchange for loans, the nobles pledged their lands, and, if they

---

[49] R. Collier and J. Billioud, *Histoire du commerce de Marseille*, iii (1480–1599) (1951), 3–165.

[50] E. Trocmé and M. Delafosse, *Le commerce rochelais de la fin du XVe siècle au début du XVIIe* (1952).

[51] R. Boutruche, *Bordeaux de 1453 à 1715* (Bordeaux, 1966), pp. 113–38.

[52] Bridge, v. 195–211, 230–42.

failed to redeem them, a change of ownership followed. At the same time, bourgeois lent money to the crown and purchased offices which carried social dignity. This was not the first time the bourgeoisie had risen, but the phenomenon was now on a larger scale than before. Several leading figures of Francis I's reign were *nouveaux riches*, like Thomas Bohier, a merchant turned civil servant who acquired the lordship of Chenonceaux from an impoverished aristocratic family. Within industry a similar gulf began to appear between the wealthy entrepreneur, who could afford to acquire expensive machinery and employ skilled labour, and the small man who had only his labour to sell. This gulf was particularly noticeable in the printing industry, where the journeymen formed associations in the guise of confraternities to defend their interests.

Despite the military disasters which had cast a shadow over the last years of Louis XII, France in 1515 was a land rich in promise. The widespread devastation caused by the Hundred Years' War was being repaired slowly but surely: the population was growing, land was being reclaimed, trade was gathering momentum and industry was acquiring new techniques. If the seigneurial class was under pressure economically, the peasantry, which formed the bulk of the population, was better off than before. Though prices were tending to rise, the phenomenon known to historians as the Price Revolution had not really begun: what inflation there was helped to stimulate the economy. Among the bourgeoisie growing prosperity was reflected in the rise of certain families to positions of influence in church and state. France was also becoming more unified: few of the great medieval fiefs remained, and, if the legal system remained bewilderingly varied, an attempt was at least being made to streamline it. The French language was being adopted by all the king's subjects. Within the sphere of government, however, there was less cause for complacency: views were divided as to the nature of royal authority, and the fiscal administration was incompatible with efficient government; the king could not hope to live within his means, particularly if he became involved in war. The future, then, was not quite cloudless. It remained to be seen whether Francis would choose a path of peaceful consolidation or one of military adventure.

3

Marignano

(1515)

WITHIN THE first year of his reign Francis invaded Italy in pursuit of a
dynastic claim to Milan inherited from his great-grandmother, Valentina
Visconti. His action, however, did not mark a departure in French foreign
policy: it was a continuation of the Italian wars begun by King Charles
VIII in 1494. It was once fashionable to regard these wars as the first
manifestation of the aggressiveness inherent in the modern nation-state,
but their motivation was essentially traditional. The kings of France were
not seeking to round off natural frontiers or to gain economic advantages,
but to affirm territorial and dynastic rights. Charles VIII also had the idea
of using Italy as a base from which to launch a new crusade against the
Infidel. He was encouraged in his policy by Italian political exiles, who
hoped to regain all that they had lost in their homeland with the help of
French arms. Later, under Francis I, other motives came into play, notably the desire to keep the Holy Roman Emperor out of the peninsula.
And behind the king there was the French nobility, avid for personal fame
and booty.

Italy at the end of the fifteenth century was, of course, a tempting prey
to a comparatively large, powerful and united neighbour, consisting, as it
did, of a large number of more or less independent states, different in size
and constitution, which could be played off against each other. The most
important were Venice, Milan, Florence, the States of the Church and
Naples. The Venetian republic, though threatened by the westward expansion of the Ottoman empire, was then at the height of its power: in
addition to an extensive territory on the mainland, it controlled lands
along the Adriatic's eastern seaboard, in the Aegean and the eastern
Mediterranean. Its monopoly of trade with the Levant was only temporarily disrupted by the opening up of the Cape route to the Far East by the
Portuguese. The Venetian constitution was the most stable in Italy, being
vested in an aristocratic oligarchy and exercised through an admirably
balanced system of elected councils. To the west, in the Lombard plain,
lay the duchy of Milan, which the house of Visconti had created out of a
collection of cities. It was now ruled by the house of Sforza, under which it

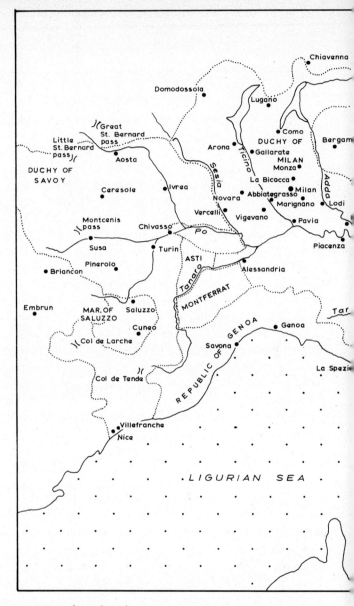

3 Map of north Italy, *c.* 1515–47.

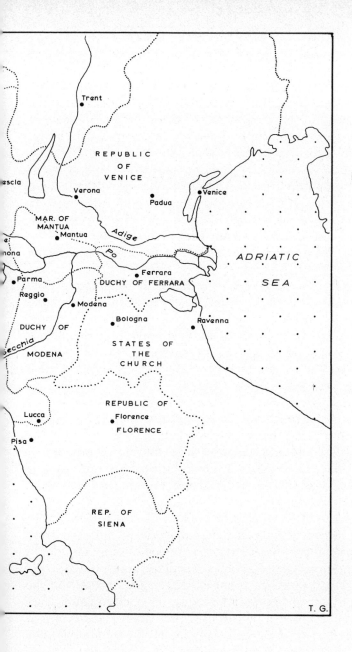

REPUBLIC
OF
VENICE

Trent

Verona
Padua
Venice

MAR. OF
MANTUA
Mantua

Adige

Po

escia

nona

Parma

Reggio

Ferrara

DUCHY OF FERRARA

Modena

Bologna

Ravenna

DUCHY OF

secchia

MODENA

STATES OF
THE
CHURCH

ADRIATIC

SEA

REPUBLIC OF
Florence
FLORENCE

Lucca

Pisa

REP. OF
SIENA

T. G.

continued to prosper economically. A strong Milan was regarded by other Italian powers as a necessary bulwark against foreign invasion and a check to Venetian expansion. Florence was theoretically ruled by a popular government, but effective authority lay in the hands of the Medici family. Although weak militarily, the republic enjoyed a considerable influence among the Italian states because of the Medici's extensive banking connexions and genius for diplomacy. The States of the Church stretched diagonally across the Italian peninsula from the Tiber to the Po and comprised a number of virtually autonomous towns and districts. The city of Rome was continually disturbed by the rivalries of its leading families, while dreams of republican self-government still stirred among its inhabitants. A principal aim of the Renaissance popes was to establish their authority firmly throughout their territories, but to do this they often needed to resort to nepotism. Naples, the only feudal monarchy in the peninsula, was a land of large estates ruled by turbulent barons. It was divided into two parts: Sicily belonged to the house of Aragon, while Naples and the mainland were ruled by an illegitimate branch of the same house. Notable among the lesser states of Italy were the duchy of Savoy, sitting astride the Alps and under the shadow of France; the republic of Genoa, which had lapsed into political insignificance as a result of domestic squabbles; and the duchy of Ferrara, serving as a buffer state between Venice and the States of the Church.

After 1454 peace was more or less maintained in Italy by a skilful policy of equilibrium among the principal states, but this was upset in 1494 by the armed intervention of Charles VIII of France, who founded his ambitions on earlier French successes in the peninsula. The house of Anjou had once reigned in Naples and that of Orléans had intermarried with the Visconti of Milan. The French invasion precipitated a revolution in Florence and the overthrow of the Medici. Naples fell into French hands, but the formation of a coalition against Charles forced him to return home. He narrowly escaped defeat at Fornovo, and the army which he had left behind in Naples was soon wiped out by disease. In 1499 his successor, Louis XII, led another expedition across the Alps. He gained control of Milan and Genoa, but foolishly signed a treaty for the partition of Naples with Ferdinand of Aragon. This led to conflict between the two occupying powers, and in 1504 the whole of Naples passed under the Aragonese crown. Four years later Louis allowed himself to be drawn into a coalition against Venice engineered by Pope Julius II. Once Venice had been defeated, the pope devoted all his energies to getting the French expelled from Italy. With the military assistance of the Swiss he drove them out of the peninsula, and an attempt by Louis to stage a comeback in 1513 ended disastrously. The Swiss, after routing the French at Novara, swept into Burgundy and laid siege to Dijon. They withdrew only after La Trémoïlle, the local commander, had signed a humiliating treaty, which Louis subsequently refused to ratify.

By January 1515 France had lost all her Italian territories. The house of Sforza had been restored to power in Milan in the person of Maximilian Sforza, Genoa was an independent republic, and the whole of Naples belonged to Aragon. A twofold responsibility thus weighed upon Francis I at the start of his reign: he had to regain the ground lost by his predecessors and avenge the military disasters recently suffered by French arms. Old commanders whose reputations had been tarnished and young noblemen who had yet to prove their valour looked to him for satisfaction. And he seemed endowed with all the necessary qualities of mind and body. His youthful spirit and powerful physique fitted him perfectly for a life of action: he had only to complete the preparations begun by Louis XII.

Francis immediately entered into negotiations with his more powerful neighbours with a view to neutralizing them. The most important was Charles of Luxemburg, a shy and unprepossessing youth of fifteen. He was the son of the Archduke Philip the Fair and the grandson of the Emperor Maximilian and Ferdinand of Aragon. On his father's death, in 1506, he had inherited the territories of the house of Burgundy (Franche-Comté, the duchies of Luxemburg and Brabant and the counties of Flanders, Holland, Zeeland, Hainault and Artois) as well as a claim to the duchy of Burgundy, which France had annexed in 1477. Although of cosmopolitan blood, Charles was a Burgundian by birth and upbringing. As a child, he had read Olivier de La Marche, the panegyrist of Charles the Bold, under whom Burgundy had been one of the most powerful states in Europe, and he grew up obsessed with the idea of rebuilding his mutilated inheritance. In 1515, however, his policy was determined by Guillaume de Croy, lord of Chièvres, the leader of the traditionally francophil Walloon aristocracy. Francis was therefore able to secure his neutrality without difficulty. In the treaty of Paris (24 March 1515) Charles was promised the hand of Princess Renée, Louis XII's daughter, whose dowry was to include the duchy of Berry and 200,000 ducats.[1]

Henry VIII, king of England, was the very reverse of shy and unprepossessing. Twenty-four years old, he lived 'with huge, extroverted ebullience . . . revelling in spectacular living' and was considered handsome by contemporaries.[2] He was an excellent sportsman, a good linguist, an accomplished musician and a competent amateur theologian, but also unstable, vain, jealous and cruel. He was most anxious not to be outshone

---

[1] *Ordonnances*, i. 147–72.
[2] J. J. Scarisbrick, *Henry VIII* (London, 1968), p. 16.

by the new king of France, yet was not anxious at this stage to pick a quarrel with him.[3] Having recently tasted victory on the continent, Henry was content for the present to enjoy himself and to leave policy-making in the capable hands of his minister, Thomas Wolsey. His first move was to send Charles Brandon, duke of Suffolk, to congratulate Francis on his accession. But there was also another motive behind the duke's mission: he was expected to obtain possession of the jewels given to Mary Tudor by her late husband, Louis XII, and to exploit Francis's desire to recover Tournai, which the English had captured in 1513.[4] The French, however, argued that the jewels had been given to Mary as queen of France and could not be taken out of the realm; they also recalled a promise made at the marriage that Tournai would be handed back unconditionally. In the end, Francis agreed to pay 200,000 *écus* to Mary as the moiety of her dowry, but he failed to return all her plate and jewels. On 5 April the treaty of London, which was due to expire one year after Louis XII's death, was given a new lease of life, but Francis took no chances: he sent John Stuart, duke of Albany, heir presumptive to the Scottish throne, who had long been resident in France, back to Scotland to stir up trouble there for the English.[5]

Within Italy itself, Francis's diplomacy met with only limited success. The Venetians agreed to help him militarily in return for assistance against the Emperor Maximilian, and the Genoese reverted to their former allegiance to France in exchange for certain local concessions.[6] But the other powers showed no inclination to co-operate with France. The Swiss, in particular, had not forgotten Louis XII's refusal to ratify the treaty of Dijon; nor were they prepared to give up the territories ceded to them by Sforza or the pension which they received from him in return for their armed protection.[7] From the French standpoint this was unfortunate, as the Swiss had become the leading military power in Europe. Their

---

[3]　See Henry's well-known conversation with the Venetian Pasqualigo inviting a comparison between his looks and Francis's. *C.S.P. Ven.*, ii. 1287.

[4]　The courteous exchanges between Henry and Francis concealed a web of intrigue about Mary Tudor's future. She complained to Suffolk that Francis had been importunate 'in divers matters not to her honour'. A. F. Pollard concluded that he had 'forced his attentions upon the beautiful widow'. It is more likely that he tried to prevent her marrying Charles of Luxemburg or some other potentially dangerous prince. It was certainly with his encouragement that she and Suffolk were secretly married in Paris. By placing the duke in his debt, he probably hoped to gain an influential friend at the English court. Pollard, *Henry VIII* (London, 1913), p. 81; *L.P.*, ii. 70, 80, 105–6; Florange, i. 164–7; Barrillon, i. 12–13, 54–5.

[5]　*Ordonnances*, i. 224–47; Barrillon, i. 54; A. Teulet, *Relations politiques de la France et de l'Espagne avec l'Ecosse au XVIᵉ siècle* (1862), i. 1–3.

[6]　*Ordonnances*, i. 260–2; Barrillon, i. 61–2.

[7]　Barrillon, i. 57.

confederation was made up of thirteen cantons whose common policy was determined by a diet which met at regular intervals. Although they profited from cattle-breeding, the transit of goods through their territory and certain industries, they were heavily dependent on the hire of their manpower to other European states. Few nations in the early sixteenth century could afford to keep up permanent armies on a large scale. Mercenaries were, therefore, in great demand, and the Swiss pikemen were the best. Their victories over the Burgundians in the 1470s had shown that wars could no longer be won by cavalry alone.

The Swiss were not alone in standing by Sforza in 1515. He was also supported by Ferdinand of Aragon, who did not wish to see any change in the Italian situation which might endanger his hold on Naples, and by the new pope, Leo X, who wished to avoid a repetition of the events of 1494, which had precipitated the overthrow of his Medici relatives in Florence. He was also afraid of losing the towns of Parma and Piacenza, which Sforza had ceded to him. As for the Emperor Maximilian, he was at war with Venice and was not prepared to negotiate with her ally, the king of France. On 17 July 1515 the duke of Milan, the pope, the king of Aragon and the emperor formed a league for the defence of Italy.

The French army in 1515

The most important military task facing Francis in 1515 was to raise a large force of infantry. His standing army, though the largest in western Europe, consisted almost entirely of cavalry. The *compagnies d'ordonnances*, known collectively as the *gendarmerie*, were made up of aristocratic volunteers grouped into units or *lances*, each comprising a man-at-arms, two archers and a variable number of auxiliaries. The man-at-arms was heavily clad in armour, while the archers wore only light protection. Both categories fought with lances, though in 1515 some men had bows and crossbows. There were eight horses per *lance*: four for the man-at-arms and two for each archer. The usual number of *lances* in a company was fifty or sixty, and each company was commanded by a captain of high social rank or his lieutenant, for a captain might command several companies at once. A system of terminal musters kept a check on the numerical strength of the companies, and their wages were paid at the same time. The duty of providing the *gendarmerie* with fodder, billets, fuel, candles, salt and vinegar was borne by the garrison towns; other necessities had to be bought, but the troops usually preferred to pillage the countryside.

Alongside the *gendarmerie* and modelled upon it were the troops of the king's household: the Scottish archers, the *Cent gentilshommes*, consisting of two companies of a hundred men each, and three companies of

French archers. In wartime the crown could raise additional cavalry by summoning the *ban et arrière-ban* or feudal levy. Every vassal was bound to give military service to the king in proportion to the value of his fief. Thus a tenant holding a fief worth 500 *livres* a year would be expected to supply one fully equipped man-at-arms with two auxiliaries, while a lesser one might be required to supply only a single archer. A tenant who, for reasons of age or health, could not give personal service paid a tax related to the value of his fief. Actually, many categories of people enjoyed exemption from the *ban et arrière-ban*. Those who were liable to serve attended musters held by the *baillis* and *sénéchaux*; they were grouped into companies of fifty men-at-arms and a hundred archers, each under a captain and subordinate officers. The entire force was commanded by a captain-general. Although the *ban et arrière-ban* continued to be called from time to time in the sixteenth century, it was not of great military value: its duration of service was strictly limited and, as young noblemen joined the *compagnies d'ordonnances*, it was increasingly made up of older men with inferior horses and equipment.[8]

For infantry the king of France depended on volunteers, known as *aventuriers*, recruited by captains holding a commission from him. Thus, in 1515, he instructed Pedro Navarro to raise a force of 8,000 Gascons, Basques and Roncalois.[9] Gascony and Picardy were the main recruiting grounds of native volunteers, who were formed into companies 500 strong under veteran captains. Wearing a leather jerkin and a light helmet, they were armed with a pike, halberd, crossbow or arquebus. During the early sixteenth century the crossbow was gradually superseded by the arquebus, whose heavy bullet was a distinct asset, in spite of its limited range of barely 400 metres. The infantry was mustered on a monthly basis and paid less than the cavalry.

Foreign mercenaries were also employed by the king of France. Until 1510 he had been able to call on the Swiss, but now that they were employed by the enemy he had to look elsewhere. In 1515 he raised 23,000 German landsknechts, including the famous 'Black band' from Guelders, comprising 12,000 pikemen, 2,000 arquebusiers, 2,000 men armed with two-handed swords and 1,000 halberdiers.[10] The landsknechts terrorized their homeland in peacetime and were prepared to fight for the emperor's enemies in wartime. Their tactics were closely modelled on those of the Swiss, but they were less well disciplined, as their

[8] A. Spont, 'Marignan et l'organisation militaire sous François Ier', *R.Q.H.*, n.s., xxii (1899), 59–77; P. Contamine, *Guerre, état et société à la fin du Moyen Age* (1972).
[9] Barrillon, i. 58–9.
[10] F. Lot, *Recherches sur les effectifs des armées françaises des guerres d'Italie aux Guerres de Religion, 1494–1562* (1962), p. 42.

captaincies went to the highest bidder, not the best soldier. Though extremely brave, they would often exploit a crisis to extort more money from an employer.

The French artillery in 1515 was second to none. From the mid-fifteenth century important changes had taken place in the designing of guns, mere size having been abandoned in favour of portability and accuracy of fire. Pioneers of this trend were the French brothers Jean and Gaspard Bureau, whose guns had blasted the English out of the castles of Normandy and Guyenne in the 1450s. When Charles VIII invaded Italy in 1494 the Italians were surprised by the new features of the French ordnance. Their guns, Guicciardini noted, were 'lighter and all cast in bronze . . . were drawn by horses with such dexterity that they could keep up with the marching speed of an army . . . shot at very short intervals . . . and could be used as usefully in the field as in battering walls'. But if the new French guns seemed highly mobile by comparison with the clumsy bombards of the early fifteenth century, they were not particularly manoeuvrable by modern standards; European field artillery was characterized by a low degree of mobility and a poor rate of fire till the mid-seventeenth century. Guns continued to be more effective against masonry than against men, and the absence of any standardization made the supply and transport of ammunition difficult and wasteful. In 1515 the French artillery was made up of about sixty guns of many calibres.[11]

The Marignano campaign

On 26 June Francis informed the 'good towns' of his kingdom that he was about to leave for Italy and that his mother would be regent in his absence. He also obtained from his queen the formal cession of her claim to Milan, and on 29 June he slipped away from Amboise quietly before daybreak.[12] Passing through Bourges and Moulins, he made his way to Lyons, where a most elaborate entry awaited him on 12 July. Among the tableaux performed on this occasion by members of the city's leading families was one showing the king and his companions defending Peace against Sforza and the Swiss bear; another showed him as Hercules gathering fruit in the garden of the Hesperides.[13]

Francis spent nearly three weeks at Lyons putting the finishing touches

[11]   C. M. Cipolla, *Guns and Sails* (London, 1965), pp. 28–9; P. Contamine, 'L'artillerie royale française à la veille des guerres d'Italie', *Annales de Bretagne*, lxxi (1964), 221–61.
[12]   Claude was pregnant at the time. Barrillon, i. 64.
[13]   J. Chartrou, *Les entrées solennelles et triomphales à la Renaissance (1484–1551)* (1928), pp. 32–3.

to his invasion preparations. On 15 July he appointed his mother regent in his absence, but her authority was limited, since the chancellor took the great seal with him to Italy.[14] At the end of the month Francis joined his army at Grenoble. Meanwhile, his enemies prepared to defend Italy. Between 12,000 and 15,000 Swiss troops were sent to the Milanese. On 17 July the duke of Milan, the pope, the king of Aragon and the emperor formed a defensive league, and 1,500 papal horse under Prospero Colonna were sent to Piedmont to assist the Swiss, who had no cavalry of their own. Assuming that the French would cross the Alps either by the Mont-Genèvre or Montcenis pass, the Swiss posted themselves in the Val Chisone and Val di Susa.[15] Francis was thus faced with the choice of either fighting his way through them or finding an alternative and undefended route into Italy. On the advice of Marshal Trivulzio, who was familiar with the country, he chose the Col de Larche, a pass normally crossed only by local peasants and their animals. To remove obstacles and bridge torrents, 1,200 sappers were sent ahead of the army. By 11 August they had completed their work and the vanguard under Bourbon began to cross the mountains. It emerged a few days later in the plain of Piedmont near Cuneo, and on learning that the papal cavalry under Colonna was close by at Villafranca, three companies of men-at-arms fell upon the town. Colonna was taken completely by surprise and captured along with 300 of his men.[16] The Swiss were thus deprived of cavalry support.

In the meantime Francis set out from Guillestre with the rest of the army. In spite of the work of the sappers, however, he did not find the crossing of the Alps easy. 'We are in the strangest country that any of us has ever seen', he wrote to his mother, 'but I hope to reach the plain of Piedmont with my army tomorrow. This will be a great relief to us, as we are finding it irksome to wear armour in these mountains; most of the time we have to go on foot, leading our horses by the bridle.' On the Italian side of the mountains the descent was so precipitous that horses and mules slipped and fell into ravines, while guns had to be dismantled and their parts lowered on ropes. A Venetian eyewitness thought nothing comparable had happened since Hannibal's crossing of the Alps.[17]

On reaching the plain of Piedmont, Francis advanced rapidly eastwards, stopping only half a day in Turin, the capital of the duchy of

---

14 *Ordonnances*, i. 262–8.
15 P. Pieri, *Il Rinascimento e la crisi militare italiana* (Turin, 1952), p. 514.
16 Barrillon, i. 79–80; du Bellay, i. 63–5; Florange, i. 176–80.
17 Barrillon, i. 65–6, 78, 82–3; F. Mignet, *La rivalité de François 1er et de Charles-Quint* (1875), i. 77–8. Not all the French artillery was carried across the Col de Larche: the heavier guns were taken over the Mont-Genèvre pass.

Savoy, and a day at Chivasso to enable his baggage to catch up. The king tried to gain the confidence of the local population by imposing a strict discipline on his troops. He forbade the infantry to enter towns which had opened their gates and intervened personally wherever incidents were brought to his notice. Thus he persuaded some landsknechts, who had entered Novara in search of loot, to return to their camp, and fell upon some French adventurers who were up to mischief at Trecate, killing some of them. On another occasion, Francis suffered the indignity of falling off his horse as he was pursuing some delinquent soldiers. One of them stopped to help him remount before running off to join his companions. The king gave up the chase and later tried to find his benefactor so as to reward him, but no one came forward. The Swiss, meanwhile, finding themselves outflanked, retreated from the Alpine passes, which they had been guarding, to the western shore of Lake Maggiore, leaving a trail of damage in their wake.[18]

Despite his hankering after martial glory, Francis was prepared to consider a peaceful settlement of his claims. Prompted by the duke of Savoy, he sent his uncle René to treat with the Swiss at Vercelli. He offered them a large subsidy if they would acquiesce in his occupation of Milan and promised them military support in the future. Francis was even willing to compensate their ally, Sforza, for the loss of his duchy. At first the Swiss seemed ready to talk, but, after a treaty had been drafted, they asked for a new round of negotiations to take place at Gallarate. This time René of Savoy was joined by Marshal Lautrec, while the duke of Savoy acted as mediator.[19] But Francis did not allow these talks to affect his strategy: he continued his advance eastward, crossing the Ticino on 31 August. At Bufalora he was met by a deputation from Milan with an offer of victuals and the promise of a friendly welcome to the city. Francis reacted cautiously to this move. He merely sent a reconnaissance party under Trivulzio towards Milan, while he himself began a semicircular movement to the south of the city, pitching his camp successively at Abbiategrasso, Binasco and Lachiarella. His aim was to link up with the Venetian army under Bartolomeo d'Alviano, which was stationed at Lodi. The king's caution was justified, for the Milanese were split into two factions: the Ghibellines were ready to submit to him, but the Guelfs wanted to resist. As Trivulzio approached Milan, the Guelfs came out in force, compelling him to withdraw.[20]

On 9 September Francis received the text of a new treaty negotiated with the Swiss at Gallarate. In return for a subsidy of one million gold *écus*, of which 150,000 were to be paid at once in cash, they agreed to give

[18] Barrillon, i. 83–7, 90–3, 109.   [19] *Ibid.*, i. 87–91, 93.   [20] *Ibid.*, i. 99–102.

up all their Milanese territories except Bellinzona. Sforza was to receive the duchy of Nemours as compensation for Milan along with a company of fifty men-at-arms and the hand of a French princess of royal blood. Francis was to be allowed to raise as many troops as he liked in Switzerland in return for an annual subsidy of 2,000 *livres* to each canton. If the Swiss went to war for themselves, he was to help them with cavalry and artillery provided he did not need them himself.[21] Though stiff, these terms were acceptable to Francis for the sake of gaining Milan and the valuable asset of Swiss military support in the future. Within ten hours he had collected the sum of 150,000 gold *écus* from his entourage and sent it under armed escort to Gallarate.[22] On 10 September, pending ratification of the treaty, he moved his camp to Marignano (now Melegnano) and sent Louis d'Ars to take possession of Pavia. That same evening Alviano called on Francis at his camp. In spite of the treaty, the king stressed the need for vigilance and urged the Venetians to cover his rear from a possible attack by a Hispano-papal army that had assembled at Piacenza.[23]

Once again Francis's caution was justified, for the Swiss, like the Milanese, were sharply divided in their attitude to the French. While the men of Berne, Fribourg and Solothurn voted to go home, those of the eastern and central cantons refused to accept the treaty of Gallarate, which threatened to deprive them of their hold on Lombardy. In the end, a majority of Swiss decided that it would be shameful to give up the fruits of their victories in 1512 and 1513 without a fight. This was the gist of a speech delivered by Cardinal Schiner to a mass meeting of Swiss troops outside the Franciscan convent in Milan on 13 September.[24] A minor skirmish with a French reconnaissance party outside the city precipitated a decision. The leaders of the war party claimed that the French were approaching Milan in force. Church bells summoned everyone to arms and about midday the Swiss swarmed out of the city like hornets from a nest. Most of them wore no hats, shoes or armour; eight small guns made up their artillery. Cardinal Schiner and 200 papal horse followed in the rear. In order to take the French by surprise the Swiss carried no drums. They marched briskly and in silence towards the enemy, throwing up a cloud of dust into the clear blue sky.

The French camp was situated near San Giuliano, a village about five kilometres north of Marignano. It was flanked on the west by the road

21   *Ordonnances*, i. 286–92.
22   Barrillon, i. 108.
23   Pieri, p. 515.
24   For different versions of this speech see F. Guicciardini, *The History of Italy*, tr. A. P. Goddard (London, 1763), vi. 347–52; Barrillon, i. 114–15.

from Milan to Lodi and on the east by the river Lambro. The intervening terrain was marshy and intersected by many ditches. The camp itself was divided into three parts: the van, commanded by the constable of Bourbon, was nearest Milan. It comprised, first, the artillery, which was protected in front by a ditch and a line of marksmen and, on its flanks and rear, by 10,000 French infantry; secondly, a huge square of 10,000 landsknechts; and thirdly, 950 men-at-arms. The centre or 'battle', which was situated at Santa Brigida, about a kilometre further south, comprised another block of 9,000 landsknechts and the flower of the French *gendarmerie* under the king. Finally, the rearguard was three kilometres further south. It comprised only cavalry and was under Francis's brother-in-law, Charles d'Alençon.[25]

The alarm was sounded in the French camp after a party of sappers working on the approaches to Milan had reported seeing a cloud of dust in the direction of the city. Bourbon immediately sent a warning to the king, who passed it on to his brother-in-law. As usual, the Swiss pikemen advanced in an echelon of three compact squares, each containing 7,000 or 8,000 men. The first square came into contact with the French about 4 p.m. With irresistible force it broke through the line of sharpshooters and crossed the ditch protecting the French guns. The French infantry dispersed, leaving the gunners isolated. After a pause, which the Swiss used to consolidate their position, the landsknechts moved forward and the two gigantic squares of pikemen collided. Again the Swiss broke through and a counter-attack by the French cavalry was thrown back. As the first Swiss contingent began to grow tired, the second moved up to give it flanking support. By now it was night, but the moon shed enough light for the fighting to continue. The Swiss attacked again, and this time the second square of landsknechts held firm, while Francis and the *gendarmerie* tried to outflank the enemy. About midnight, however, the moon vanished, plunging the field into complete obscurity. The two armies broke apart; as the French rallied to shrill trumpet calls, the Swiss responded to the bellowing of their great war-horns, the *Bull of Uri* and the *Cow of Unterwalden*. Only a ditch and a distance of ten metres separated the two camps. Indeed, so close were they to each other that skirmishing went on throughout the night.

Contemporary accounts differ as to how the king spent the night: some say he snatched sleep on the limber of a gun, others that he remained saddled and armed. He certainly reorganized his army during the night in

---

[25] On the battle of Marignano see H. Harkensee, *Die Schlacht bei Marignano* (Göttingen, 1909), passim; Pieri, pp. 516–24; G. Treccani degli Alfieri, *Storia di Milano*, viii (Milan, 1957), 181–4; F. L. Taylor, *The Art of War in Italy, 1494–1529* (Cambridge, 1921), pp. 101, 111, 123–5.

preparation for the resumption of the battle next day. The rearguard was brought forward to form a single line with the centre and the remnants of the vanguard. The extremities of the line were set back slightly to avert the danger of encirclement. Meanwhile, Duprat wrote three important letters for the king: the first, to Lautrec, instructed him not to hand over the 150,000 *écus* to the Swiss at Gallarate; the second, to Alviano, urged him to bring the Venetian army without delay; and the third, to Louis d'Ars, ordered him to guard Pavia in case he, Francis, should need to retreat there.[26]

The battle was resumed at dawn, between 4 and 5 a.m. The Swiss modified their tactics in response to the new French formation. Instead of advancing behind each other, as on the previous day, the three squares of pikemen moved alongside each other so as to engage the entire French line, but they reserved their main effort for the French left. The French right, under Bourbon, managed to repulse the first Swiss square, which had been weakened by its losses of the previous day. In the centre, the Swiss were more successful: braving the fire of the French guns, they crossed the ditch, scattered the infantry and forced back the landsknechts; but they had to retreat across the ditch after being charged by Francis and the *gendarmerie*. 'The king', writes Barrillon, 'did his duty well and did not spare himself. He was struck three times by a pike and his life would have been seriously threatened if he had not been well protected by his armour.'[27] It was on the left that the Swiss were most successful at first: they overwhelmed the French guns, scattered the infantry and lunged into the landsknechts, who fought back heroically. The French cavalry came to their assistance, as did some artillery and cavalry from the centre and right, a move paralleled on the Swiss side. About 8 a.m., as the French left began to collapse, shouts of 'San Marco! San Marco!' announced the arrival of the Venetians. This revived French spirits.[28] They mounted a counter-attack and by 11 a.m. the Swiss had been routed. As they filed back into Milan, some without a limb, others carrying their wounded companions on their backs, an eyewitness was reminded of the wretched creatures in the ninth pit of Dante's *Inferno*.[29]

[26] Du Bellay, i. 71; Michaud et Poujoulat, v. 596; Barrillon, i. 122; Pieri, p. 518.

[27] Barrillon, i. 122.

[28] Harkensee (pp. 97–101) attaches little significance to the Venetian intervention, but S. Frey (*Le guerre milanesi* (fasc. 2 (Berne, 1936) of *Storia militare svizzera*, ed. R. M. Feldmann and H. G. Wirz (12 vols., Berne, 1915–36)), p. 391) believes that it transformed the imminent victory of the Swiss into a defeat, a view shared by Pieri (p. 519). Although Francis failed to mention the Venetians in his official account of the battle, he nevertheless showed them his gratitude. Barrillon, i. 127.

[29] Barrillon, i. 124; Florange, i. 197; du Bellay, i. 74; 'Storia di Milano da Giovanni Andrea Prato, 1499–1519', *Arch. Stor. It.* iii, (1842), 343.

The aftermath of Marignano

Marshal Trivulzio, a veteran of seventeen battles, described Marignano as a 'battle of giants' beside which the others seemed but 'children's games'. It had certainly been a bloody affair. The grave-diggers reported that they had buried 16,500 bodies, but the exact number of French and Swiss losses is unknown. Each side made absurd claims. Francis claimed that 22,000 Swiss had been killed and only 4,000 Frenchmen. In fact, the losses were probably more evenly balanced. Many French noblemen are known to have lost their lives; their bodies were embalmed and taken to France for burial on their estates.[30] Never again, Francis wrote, would the *gendarmerie* be called 'hares in armour'. He also singled out for praise Galiot de Genouillac, master of the artillery, whose guns had slowed down the Swiss attack by tearing open large gaps in their ranks.[31] Another hero of the day was Pierre du Terrail, seigneur de Bayard. Legend has it that the king crowned his victory by having himself knighted on the battlefield and chose Bayard to perform the ceremony on account of the outstanding valour which he had shown. Though knighthood had lost most of its social significance, it retained a certain archaic glamour.[32]

The immediate result of the battle of Marignano was the capitulation of Milan. A deputation from the city made its submission to the king at Chiaravalle, on 16 September. But Sforza surrendered the castle only on 4 October after a siege. Francis promised him a pension on condition that he would settle permanently in France.[33] He died in Paris, in May 1530, and was given a splendid funeral. Francis entered Milan in triumph on 11 October 1515 and remained there until the end of the month, when he moved to Vigevano, leaving the city in the hands of Bourbon and Duprat. The latter was appointed chancellor of Milan in addition to his existing office, and Jean de Selve, first president of the parlement of Bordeaux, became vice-chancellor. The senate set up originally by Louis XII, which consisted of French and Italian members, was revived. As for the people of Milan, they were asked to pay a heavy fine for their 'great rebellions and acts of disobedience' and to surrender hostages.[34]

Francis did not try to chase the Swiss out of north Italy, for he was anxious to gain their friendship. No important ruler in the sixteenth

---

[30] They included François de Bourbon, the comte de Sancerre, the prince de Talmont and the seigneurs de Bussy and d'Humbercourt. Lot, *Recherches sur les effectifs*, p. 44; Spont, 'Marignan', pp. 72–3; Barrillon, i. 125; M. Sanuto, *Diarii* (Venice, 1879–1903), xxi. col. 97.

[31] Michaud et Poujoulat, v. 595–7.

[32] *Le loyal serviteur*, ed. J. Roman (1878), p. 246; S. Shellabarger, *The Chevalier Bayard: A Study in Fading Chivalry* (London, n.d.), pp. 291–2.

[33] *Ordonnances*, i. 294–300.   [34] Barrillon, i. 160–3.

century could afford to neglect them; as Charles V once said, the 'secret of secrets' was to win them over. Thus in October Francis dispatched an embassy to Switzerland to thank the cantons which had pulled out of the war and offer them his mediation in their dealings with the others. He wanted *carte blanche* to hire troops in their territories and an undertaking that they would not serve his enemies in future, and, since cash was the only language they understood, he empowered his envoys to distribute bribes totalling 12,000 *écus* and to promise a million more. On 7 November the treaty of Geneva was signed with ten cantons, but after the diet of Zürich had refused to ratify it, only eight made peace with France, while the rest offered their services to the emperor.[35]

No one felt more anxious after the battle than Pope Leo X, who had backed the wrong horse. He was afraid that Francis would follow up his victory by marching on Florence and unseating his Medici relatives, and, in the hope of averting this disaster, sent Lodovico di Canossa, one of his most esteemed diplomats, to the king with an offer of peace and friendship. Leo, in fact, had nothing to fear, for Francis wanted his friendship. The pope was more than a spiritual ruler: he controlled a sizable territory in central Italy, he could effectively rally other powers to aid or hinder a foreign invader and he could authorize a secular ruler to tax his clergy. Recent history had shown that the French could hope to establish a permanent foothold in Italy only with papal co-operation. Even after Marignano, Francis's position in the peninsula was precarious: the Swiss were intent on revenge and the emperor and the king of England might well join them. The threat of such a coalition made it all the more urgent for Francis to gain the pope's support or at least to neutralize him. What is more, as suzerain of Naples, Leo had its investiture in his gift. Thus a treaty was speedily arranged between Francis and the pope: in exchange for Parma and Piacenza, Francis gave the duchy of Nemours and a large pension to Leo's brother Giuliano, and another pension to his nephew Lorenzo. This, however, was only a first step. The two rulers needed to settle many other questions, notably the abrogation of the Pragmatic Sanction of Bourges of 1438, which the papacy had been demanding for some time. They therefore agreed to meet in December at Bologna.[36]

Francis left Milan on 3 December and, travelling very fast down the Via Emilia, reached Bologna on the 11th, three days after the pope. He was given accommodation in the Palazzo Pubblico immediately beneath Leo's apartments, an arrangement which betokened mutual trust and provided an ideal setting for secret negotiations. Their first encounter, however, was a formal one. Francis and his suite were conducted into a

[35] *Ibid.*, i. 142–6, 148–59; *Ordonnances*, i. 304–12.
[36] *Ordonnances*, i. 300–4; Barrillon, i. 141–2.

great hall, where the pope, corpulent and short-sighted, sat surrounded by his cardinals. After walking up to the papal throne through a dense crowd of spectators, the king doffed his cap, genuflected three times and kissed the pope's hand and foot. Leo bade him rise, and embraced him. Each then made a short speech, after which Duprat delivered an address in Latin. It began with an extravagant eulogy of the house of Medici and the pope, its most illustrious member, and went on to show how the king had crossed the Alps and run the gauntlet of the Swiss in order to do homage to the Vicar of Christ. Then, after more formalities, Leo led Francis by the hand into another room where the serious talking began.[37]

Though shrouded in secrecy, the negotiations at Bologna were evidently much concerned with Italian affairs. Francis, it seems, asked the pope to join him against the king of Aragon, but Leo asked for a delay of sixteen months, when his alliance with Ferdinand was due to expire. He did, however, hint at the possibility of Francis being given Naples on Ferdinand's death, if in return he would support the Medici in Florence. Leo agreed to hand over Reggio and Modena to the duke of Ferrara on certain conditions, but turned a deaf ear to Francis's intercession on behalf of the duke of Urbino, who had broken his fealty to the Holy See. Agreement was reached on the need for a crusade against the Turks, Francis being given permission to levy a tenth on the French clergy towards this end. But the most important decision taken at Bologna was to substitute a Concordat for the Pragmatic Sanction of Bourges. Details of the new agreement were left to be worked out by legal experts, Duprat acting for the king and the cardinals of Ancona and of Santi Quattro Coronati for the pope.[38]

The conference lasted four days. On 13 December the pope celebrated high mass in San Petronio, the largest church in the city. Francis did not take communion, though forty of his followers did so. During the service a Frenchman publicly confessed that he had fought Julius II and defied his excommunication, whereupon Francis and several others admitted the same offence and begged the pope for absolution, which he promptly conceded. At a consistory on the following day Adrien Gouffier, brother of Admiral Bonnivet, was created a cardinal. On 15 December Leo gave Francis a magnificent cross of solid gold containing a piece of the true cross; it had belonged to Julius II and was valued at 15,000 ducats. The king's gifts to the papal entourage gave less satisfaction, the pope's master

[37] Barrillon, i. 164–73; Le Glay, ii. 85–90; L. von Pastor, *The History of the Popes*, tr. F. I. Antrobus and R. F. Kerr (London, 1891–1933), vii. 134–7. See also B.L., Harley MS. 3462, fols. 197b–199a.
[38] Pastor, vii, 141–6; Barrillon, i. 173–4.

of ceremonies, in particular, being offended by his gratuity of 100 gold *écus*.[39]

Francis returned to Milan for Christmas and on 7 January presided over a meeting of the senate during which a Milanese lawyer appealed for his clemency in the name of his fellow citizens. Replying for the king, Duprat announced that he had decided, in spite of their past misdeeds, to remit the fine that had been imposed on them, to release their hostages and to allow their exiles to return and resume their property. The citizens expressed their gratitude by swearing an oath of fealty to the king. Next day he appointed Bourbon as his lieutenant-general in the duchy and left for home, confident in the knowledge that the lilies were once again growing in Italian soil.[40]

[39]   Pastor, vii, 138–40; Le Glay, ii. 88.
[40]   Barrillon, i. 177–86; Sanuto, xxi. cols. 448–9; C.A.F., v. 16093.

4

The Concordat of Bologna

ONE OF THE main tasks facing Francis on his return home in 1516 was to win acceptance by his subjects of the Concordat of Bologna. The relationship between church and state in France was one of close mutual dependence. Whilst the king solemnly promised at his coronation to uphold ecclesiastical privileges, the church, on its part, deferred to his authority in various ways: no capitular election could be held without his permission and a successful candidate had to swear allegiance to him before he could be consecrated; the king was entitled to summon and preside over an assembly of French prelates; he could also intervene in diocesan affairs. But, if the relationship between church and state in France was clear, the papacy's share in that relationship was highly controversial. Did the church in France owe obedience primarily to the king or to the pope? Was the pope free to interfere in its affairs regardless of the king's wishes? These were some of the questions that had been at the root of the great struggle between King Philip IV and Pope Boniface VIII at the close of the thirteenth century. In the bull *Clericis laicos* (1296) Boniface excommunicated any ruler who taxed the clergy without papal permission; Philip retaliated by banning the export of money to Rome. As a result, the bull was revoked in so far as it applied to France, but in 1301 its doctrine was reaffirmed; the pope claimed not merely spiritual but also temporal authority over Christendom. In 1302 he proclaimed in the bull *Unam Sanctam* that obedience to the Holy See was essential to salvation. When the king appealed to a general council of the church, Boniface excommunicated him, releasing his subjects from their allegiance to him. The quarrel reached its climax when French agents broke into the papal palace at Anagni and humiliated the pontiff, who died soon afterwards. His successors annulled the sentences passed on Philip, acknowledging that the Holy See had no authority over the king of France and no right to interfere in the government of his kingdom.

This, however, was not the end of the rivalry between the French crown and the papacy. In the late fourteenth century Christendom found itself in the curious situation of having to choose between two rival popes. The

French church proposed that both should resign so that another might be elected. When Benedict XIII refused, the king of France suspended his allegiance for five years; in 1407 he issued two ordinances, which are normally regarded as marking the birth of Gallicanism.[1] They pledged royal support in future for the maintenance of the ancient liberties of the church governing ecclesiastical appointments and forbade payments to the Holy See arising out of its interference in beneficial affairs. These principles were affirmed in another ordinance of March 1418 and again in the famous Pragmatic Sanction of Bourges of July 1438.[2] This was a royal edict embodying decisions taken by an assembly of the French church that had met at Bourges under the presidency of King Charles VII after Pope Eugenius IV had broken off relations with the council of Basle. It asserted that a general council of the church was superior in authority to the pope, upheld the decision of the council of Basle that elections to major benefices should be restored, safeguarded the rights of those traditionally authorized to appoint to lesser benefices, severely curtailed the payment of annates to Rome and endorsed the disciplinary reforms of the council. As the Pragmatic Sanction conformed exactly with the Parlement's views, it was registered without difficulty.

The papacy was deeply offended by the Pragmatic Sanction – 'this thorn driven into the eye of the church' – and during the remainder of the fifteenth century it continually pressed for its abrogation. The Parlement refused to give way, but King Louis XI saw that he could make political capital out of the Sanction. In 1462, he revoked it so as to gain papal support for his policies in Italy; when the pope failed to satisfy him, he reverted to a Gallican position. Then, in 1472, he signed a Concordat with Sixtus IV, allowing him a half share of appointments to French benefices. Three years later, Louis again fell out with the pope, so the Sanction was reaffirmed by an assembly of the French church. The papacy continued to demand its revocation, and, in December 1512, supporters of the Sanction were ordered to appear before the fifth Lateran council.[3]

In addition to manipulating the Sanction, the French crown put pressure on the Holy See by playing on its fear of a general council. The doctrine that a council was superior in authority to the pope was an important element in Gallicanism. France was the cradle of conciliarism. It was at the suggestion of a French cardinal that the council of Constance had issued the decree *Sacrosancta* to the effect that it derived its

[1]   V. Martin, *Les origines du Gallicanisme* (1939), vol. i.
[2]   N. Valois, *Histoire de la Sanction Pragmatique de Bourges sous Charles VII* (1906), passim.
[3]   R. Aubenas and R. Ricard, *L'église et la Renaissance, 1449–1517* (1951), pp. 56–7, 70–2, 78–81.

authority directly from Christ and that everyone, including the pope, should obey it. Even after the Holy See had triumphed over the conciliar movement, the theory of conciliar supremacy continued to have adherents in France. It was kept alive by a general desire for church reform and by an increase of anti-papal feeling generated by the administrative methods of Sixtus IV. In the fifteenth century 'Gallican France was the real stronghold of the strict conciliar theory and the University of Paris its citadel.'[4] In 1511 Louis XII retaliated against the anti-French policies of Julius II by calling a council. It met at Pisa and suspended the pope, but he cleverly took the wind out of its sails by calling the fifth Lateran council, which received much wider support.[5]

By the sixteenth century, then, Frenchmen were generally opposed to papal interference in the administration of their church. But what of royal interference? There is much evidence that the crown already controlled the Gallican church to a considerable extent in the fifteenth century. In theory, the church was governed according to the Pragmatic Sanction, but it lacked the cohesion necessary to withstand external pressures. Consequently, the electoral freedom of chapters often succumbed to force and bribery. In these circumstances, the monarchy could easily determine the outcome of elections. Louis XI freely appointed to bishoprics and abbeys from 1471 onwards: if the chapters resisted, he simply imposed his nominees on them. The scope of the *régale* was so enlarged at this time that the king was also able to appoint to many archdeaconries, canonries and prebends. A demand by the Estates General of 1484 that the Pragmatic Sanction be strictly observed was disregarded: by 1515 royal control of the ecclesiastical hierarchy was an acknowledged fact.[6] This was shown in the instructions given to René of Savoy when he was sent to negotiate with the Swiss: 'and if the brother of the said Maximilian [Sforza] wishes to become a churchman, the king will obtain benefices in his kingdom for him'.[7] In March 1515 Mondot de La Marthonie acknowledged the king's control of church appointments by asking that it should please him 'to provide *gens de bien* of good life and sufficient years to bishoprics, archbishoprics and prelacies and likewise good men of religion to the monasteries of his kingdom and dominions'.[8]

Any restriction of papal authority in France was a source of satisfaction

4 H. Jedin, *A History of the Council of Trent*, tr. E. Graf (London, 1957–61), i. 32.
5 *Ibid.*, i. 106–12; A. Renaudet, *Le concile Gallican de Pise–Milan* (1922), passim.
6 Imbart de La Tour, ii. 211; A. Renaudet, *Préréforme et humanisme pendant les premières guerres d'Italie, 1494–1517* (1953), p. 5; G. Loirette, 'La première application à Bordeaux du Concordat de 1516: Gabriel et Charles de Grammont (1529–30)', *A. du M.*, lxviii (1956), 317.
7 Barrillon, i. 89.
8 Renaudet, *Préréforme et humanisme*, p. 578.

to the Parlement of Paris, believing as it did that the king should be master in his own house. It was firmly committed to the principles of the Pragmatic Sanction and instinctively hostile to any ultramontane move by the crown. But Francis, as we have seen, was anxious at the start of his reign to improve his relations with the Holy See: the main objective of his foreign policy was to restore French rule in Milan and Naples. To acquire a permanent foothold south of the Alps, however, he needed papal co-operation. This had been the lesson of recent events: Louis XII had been successful in Italy only as long as he had enjoyed the support of Alexander VI and Julius II; when the latter had turned against him, he had been driven out of the peninsula. The pope was a significant temporal power: he controlled the overland route from the north to Naples, could rally other powers to aid or hinder a foreign invader, and could authorize a secular ruler to tax his clergy. Moreover, as suzerain of Naples, he alone could confer its investiture. Thus Francis needed the pope's friendship for several good reasons. This is what Duprat tried to make the Parlement understand in April 1515, when it was asked to ratify the powers of the papal legate, Canossa: 'It was a question', he explained, 'of gratifying the pope for good reasons and to achieve things of the utmost importance which cannot be disclosed to everyone.'[9] But the Parlement was not interested in the king's foreign ambitions and viewed with suspicion his efforts to draw nearer to Rome. It agreed to ratify Canossa's powers on condition that no harm would be done to the Pragmatic Sanction or the liberties of the French church.[10]

The Holy See, however, wanted not merely acceptance of its legates, but the complete repudiation of the Pragmatic Sanction. On this basis alone would it seriously envisage a political arrangement with France. By winning the battle of Marignano, it is true, Francis had strengthened his negotiating position, but he still could not dictate his terms to the papacy, for his position in north Italy remained precarious: the Swiss were intent on revenge, while the emperor and the king of England were ready to support them. This threat of a new coalition made it all the more urgent for Francis to neutralize the pope or, better still, win his support. For more than half a century French kings had put pressure on the Holy See by either manipulating the Pragmatic Sanction or threatening to call a general council. Only the first alternative was available to Francis: after the fiasco of Pisa he would merely have exposed himself to ridicule had he resorted to the conciliar cudgel. So the Pragmatic Sanction had to be revoked, even at the price of causing bitter resentment among his Gallican subjects. As the principal court of law in the realm, the Parlement

---

[9]   *Ibid.*, p. 579.   [10]   Doucet, i. 71–2.

favoured the existing regime, which restricted appeals to Rome, while the university of Paris had a vested interest in a system which reserved a third of vacant benefices to graduates. The king, on the other hand, had little to lose by revoking the Sanction: his effective control of most church appointments was unlikely to be reduced by a restoration of papal authority in France.

There was great anxiety among members of the Parlement while the Concordat was still being negotiated. The first president, La Marthonie, warned his colleagues, on 26 December, that the king was preparing to substitute a system of nominations for elections to benefices. Francis, for his part, tried to allay the court's suspicions. He appointed one of its members, Roger Barme, to discuss certain procedural details with the Holy See without, however, showing him the text of the Concordat. The king also pointed out that, if the Concordat were not signed, the Lateran council would abolish the Pragmatic Sanction on its own authority. This argument, however, failed to win any substantial support among the *parlementaires*. The barrister Jean Bochard spoke for the majority when he condemned the papacy's efforts to destroy the Sanction and urged his colleagues to defend it.[11]

The Concordat, which was approved by Leo X on 18 August 1516, consisted originally of three bulls: *Pastor aeternus*, which abolished the Pragmatic Sanction; *Divina providente gratia*, which promulgated the Concordat; and *Primitiva illa ecclesia*, which contained its text.[12] Bishops, abbots and priors, who in the past had been elected by chapters, were henceforth to be nominated by the king and instituted by the pope, though an exception was made of churches that had been given the privilege of electing their superiors by the papacy. Benefices vacated at the curia or which remained vacant beyond a certain time were to be filled by papal, not royal, nomination. It was also laid down that nominees to lesser benefices should indicate their real value in their letters of appointment. Ostensibly, this was to check pluralism; in reality, it pointed to the resumption of annates, which the Pragmatic Sanction had virtually abolished. The Concordat was ratified by the Lateran council on 19 December, Francis being allowed six months in which to secure its registration by the French parlements.

On 5 February 1517 the king came before the Parlement of Paris, accompanied by high-ranking ecclesiastics, canons of Notre-Dame and representatives of the university. The purpose of this exceptional gathering was to explain the Concordat. Speaking first, the chancellor, Duprat, who could reasonably claim to be its architect, explained that the king

[11]   *Ibid.*, i. 81–3; *Ordonnances*, i. no. 90.
[12]   *Ordonnances*, i. no. 91.

had done all in his power to save the Pragmatic Sanction, but papal demands had been too powerful. If Francis had tried to resist them, his kingdom would have been placed under an interdict, and this would have given its foreign enemies justification to invade it and carve it up among themselves. If, on the other hand, he had given way without negotiating, the French church would have fallen under the tyranny of Rome, and the abuses that had been swept away by the council of Constance would have returned. By securing the Concordat, he had achieved a settlement in the best interest of the kingdom and its universities. The king's intention was to submit it in due course to an assembly of clergy and notables, after which he would send it to the Parlement for registration. The object of the present meeting was to give the court due notice so that it should raise no difficulty when eventually it would receive the Concordat. Francis then added a few strong words of his own. He criticized the court for acting beyond his orders in recent lawsuits, and hinted darkly that it would be well advised to show more compliance in respect of the Concordat. The king's short speech was followed by a debate. Then Cardinal de Boisy, speaking for the clergy, asked that an assembly of the Gallican church be called to examine the Concordat before it was ratified. Francis retorted that unless the clergy yielded he would send them to Rome to discuss the Concordat with the pope. He was better pleased by the Parlement's reply, vague as it was, that it would satisfy both God and the king.[13]

On 21 March 1517 another meeting was held in Paris, this time of fifty-two representatives of the 'good towns'. It had been called by the king, ostensibly to seek advice about ways of enriching the kingdom, but Duprat's speech to the delegates was concerned less with economic matters than with the Concordat. Clearly, the meeting was an attempt to force the Parlement's hand by mobilizing an influential section of public opinion. The Concordat, Duprat explained, was a bilateral convention aimed at preserving the regime of the Pragmatic Sanction. True, capitular elections had been abolished, but only because they had become corrupt; the king hoped eventually to restore them in a purer form. What the delegates made of all this is not known.[14]

The papal bulls embodying the Concordat were brought to Paris at the end of April by Canossa, the papal nuncio, and on 13 May Francis issued letters patent demanding its execution. Once again he attempted to justify it on the basis of the events which had led up to it. He claimed that he had

---

[13]   B.N., MS. fr. 10900, fol. 3a–b; Doucet, i. 84–7.
[14]   They were invited to send proposals in writing after consulting 'the larger and wiser part' of the inhabitants of their respective towns. When these eventually reached Paris, they were dropped unopened into a large leather bag and quietly forgotten. Barrillon, i. 275–83, 302–4.

succeeded in saving all that mattered of the Pragmatic Sanction except for the elective principle, which he had been reluctantly forced to surrender to the pope. He did not ask for the publication of *Pastor aeternus*, presumably because he felt that revocation of the Pragmatic Sanction was implicit in the Concordat. But the Parlement disobeyed his command. On 29 May, therefore, he sent the duc de Bourbon, Chancellor Duprat and the seigneur d'Orval to remind the court of the urgent necessity to register the Concordat.[15] Duprat repeated his arguments of four months before, but the court was not handed the full text of the Concordat until 5 June, when Guillaume Roger, the *procureur général*, and Le Lièvre, the *avocat du roi*, drew attention to its weaknesses, notably its attack upon the liberties of the Gallican church and the resumption of annates, which, they argued, would drain the kingdom of money. The court set up a twelve-man commission to examine and report on the Concordat, which it proceeded to do in a most leisurely fashion. On 21 June, seeing that no action had yet been taken by the Parlement, the king ordered it to register the Concordat forthwith and René of Savoy to sit in on its debates. This attempt to intimidate the court provoked an instant reaction: two councillors, La Haye and Dorigny, were sent to the king at Nampont, in Picardy, with an explanation of the delay in registering the Concordat, a request for the rescinding of the king's order to René of Savoy and an offer to send representatives whenever the king should wish to be informed of the court's proceedings.

The delegates were admitted to the king's presence after he had dined. Leading them to a window recess, he invited them to speak, whereupon La Haye unburdened himself with many excuses and humble protestations. Francis seemed ready to accept the excuse that the Parlement had only recently received the text of the Concordat, but he made no secret of his irritation with its members. Some, he admitted, were 'worthy men' (*gens de bien*), but others were 'madmen' (*une bande de folz*). He intended, he said, to be no less a king than his predecessors and, like them, to be obeyed, and complained that comparisons between himself and Louis XII, the so-called 'father of justice', were both offensive and unfair. He reminded the delegates that Louis had banished two *parlementaires* for their disobedience, adding that he himself was ready to do likewise. René of Savoy, Francis insisted, would attend the Parlement's debates and submit a detailed report; as for the Concordat, it would be registered. As La Haye attempted to remonstrate, the king exclaimed angrily: 'He will be there and you may tell that to the court!' On being asked if he would receive remonstrances over the Concordat, Francis replied that his uncle

---

[15] *Ibid.*, i. 306–7.

would let them know his wishes in due course. The audience then came to an abrupt end as the king walked away to join a group of courtiers in another part of the room.[16]

On 13 July the Parlement agreed to let René of Savoy attend its debates. Unfortunately, these are not described in the court's registers. If Duprat is to be believed, the chief *parlementaires* were willing to accept the Concordat but were overruled by clerics with a vested interest in the existing regime. Be that as it may, the Parlement firmly refused, on 24 July, to register the Concordat and proclaimed its loyalty to the Pragmatic Sanction. In the event of the king persisting in his determination, the court demanded that an assembly of the Gallican church be called. It also declared itself willing to hear an appeal from the university of Paris, which had already made known its opposition to the Concordat, and from any other French university. Finally, it invited René of Savoy to give the king an account of all that he had heard, especially concerning the 'great evils and inconveniences' that would flow from the Concordat, and offered to send another deputation to Francis should he require a fuller statement of its opinions.[17]

Though startled by the Parlement's stand, Francis agreed to receive its representatives. Three were promptly selected, but they were detained in Paris for various reasons. Nothing more happened until 22 December, when an angry reminder from the king prompted the court to appoint two new delegates, André Verjus and François de Loynes. They reached Amboise on 13 January, when they were told by the grand master, Boisy, that Francis was in two minds about keeping them waiting as long as he had been left in suspense. This, however, would only have delayed further the Concordat's registration. Two days later, therefore, the *parlementaires* were asked to draw up a memorandum which the king might study before seeing them. They accordingly produced a document, comprising 116 articles and an appendix, which is the only surviving record of the Parlement's detailed objections to the Concordat.

The memorandum begins with a criticism of the Concordat on three principal counts: first, the implicit restoration of annates; secondly, the evocation of major ecclesiastical causes to the Roman curia, and thirdly, the abolition of elections to benefices in favour of nominations. All benefices, it asserts, will become liable to papal taxation once the elective system has been abolished, and gold and silver will be drained away from the kingdom. The removal of 'major causes' from the local ecclesiastical courts will open the door to large-scale papal interference in the affairs of the Gallican church. The abolition of elections, too, will profit only the

---

[16]   A.N., X^{1a} 1519, fols. 205r–206r; Doucet, i. 89–95.
[17]   A.N., X^{1a} 1519, fol. 222r; Doucet, i. 95–7.

Holy See: even if royal nominations to major benefices are allowed, there are enough loopholes in the Concordat to enable the pope to advance his own creatures. He has no right to deprive the French church of its immemorial right of free election, based as it is on Scripture, the decrees of church councils and royal ordinances. The replacement of elections by nominations, far from removing abuses, will open the way to a permanent system of simoniacal annates. Here, the memorandum timidly points to the danger of royal interference in church affairs: a king may easily succumb to pressures from his advisers, acting in the interest of their friends.

The second part of the memorandum challenges the legality of the abrogation of the Pragmatic Sanction. Does not *Pastor aeternus* threaten the king's subjects with confiscation, revoke the Sanction, which is a royal ordinance, and refer back to Boniface VIII's bull *Unam Sanctam*, that supreme statement of papal superiority over kings? The abrogation of the Sanction must inevitably entail the repudiation of the doctrine of conciliar supremacy over the pope. It cannot be valid, since the French church has not been formally summoned to appear before the Lateran council; nor can the decisions of one pope override those of the two councils of Constance and Basle. Two courses are open to the king: he can either persuade the pope to call a general council or he can himself summon an assembly of the Gallican church to acquaint it more fully with this whole business. In an appendix, the memorandum criticizes Duprat's arguments justifying the Concordat. The king, it asserts, has no superior *in temporalibus* and therefore does not need to fear that his kingdom will be delivered to his enemies; should the pope venture upon such a course, the king has enough power to defend himself. The memorandum concludes that the Concordat is directed 'against the honour of God, the liberties of the church, the king's honour and the public good of his kingdom'.[18]

Francis, after acquainting himself with the memorandum, asked the chancellor to reply, and Duprat grasped eagerly this opportunity to criticize the Parlement. The gist of his reply is as follows: in difficult times the Parlement invariably says that all is badly administered and badly directed; if its wages are delayed by as much as a quarter owing to sheer necessity, then 'all is going badly and the king's treasury is being robbed' ('tout va mal et les finances sont desrobées'). Opposition to the Concordat is the work of churchmen with a stake in the old corrupt system and of routinists who cannot be troubled to operate a new one. The agreement would already have been registered if it had only been seriously examined and discussed by the Parlement. Its criticisms of the Concordat are

---

[18] B.N., MS. fr. 10900, fols. 5b–6a; n. ac. 8452, no. 133; Doucet, i. 99–106.

childish and capable of frightening only women and small children. Its refusal to register it has struck at the very roots of royal authority; it is an attempt by the Parlement to imitate the Roman Senate and to force the king to account for his actions. The kingdom is not an aristocracy, but a monarchy in which decisions are taken by a few and the rest have only to obey. The Parlement itself owes its authority to the king, and not so long ago its powers were reviewed annually; having submitted remonstrances, its duty is to obey the king once he has made known his decision. The idea that Francis had exaggerated the perils facing the kingdom in 1516 is a nonsense. Under Louis XII the Lateran council had begun the indictment of the Pragmatic Sanction, and the pope had formed a powerful coalition against France. This had brought ruin to the kingdom and the loss of Tournai and Thérouanne. Francis wants to avoid a repetition of these disasters. It is true, of course, that he holds his kingdom of God alone and would have resisted a papal onslaught, but this would have damaged his subjects and his own financial situation. Although the coalition was smashed at Marignano, the situation remains precarious: the emperor and the kings of Spain and England are still hostile, while the Swiss are looking for a chance to strike back. Although Francis tried to save the Pragmatic Sanction, he has been forced to choose between submission and schism; yet he has skilfully managed to persuade the Lateran council to swallow the substance of the Sanction in the form of a Concordat, the only major difference between them being the abolition of elections. Francis has defended the interests of the Gallican church by securing an exemption for privileged churches; he would have liked to do even more and is still hoping to bring back the old system.

Duprat then takes a closer look at the elective system. Its abolition is regarded by the Parlement as an infringement of the Gallican liberties; but what, he asks, are these liberties? Where do they come from? He, for one, does not believe in their existence. What is more, he thinks the elective system has been thoroughly discredited by quarrels, acts of violence and lawsuits, perjury and simony and the unworthiness of those elected. Such an intolerable system needs to be replaced by one better suited to modern conditions. Elections have not got the backing of divine law; they are simply an administrative matter, which the pope has a perfect right to change as he thinks fit; he is not bound to obey conciliar decrees, since his authority is superior and his decision has, in any case, been endorsed by the Lateran council. Leo has also been extremely generous: instead of reserving all nominations to himself, as he might have done, he has given most of them to the king, while respecting the privilege of election held by certain churches. Francis will not misuse his right of nomination, as the Parlement has insinuated, nor will he allow the pope to encroach upon it;

benefices will not remain vacant long enough for the pope to intervene, and the king will see to it that his nominees are not rejected by the pope on grounds of insufficiency. As for annates, Francis dislikes them as much as the Parlement does. The demand for a statement of the true value of benefices should not be seen as a first step towards their resumption; it is simply intended to facilitate the allocation of benefices.[19] Nor is it true to suggest that the present system of ecclesiastical jurisdiction is to be changed; the Concordat has, in fact, guaranteed its survival. Whatever its imperfections may be, it is surely better to live with it in harmony with the pope and the rest of Christendom than schismatically with the Pragmatic Sanction, which a general council has condemned. Finally, Duprat sees no reason for calling another such council, from which the Sanction could expect no other treatment. As for an assembly of the Gallican church, the king's intention has always been to call one, but the Concordat ought to be judged by its results; it should, therefore, be registered first by the Parlement.[20]

Duprat's memorandum was meant to provide the king with a stock of arguments for his audience with the two delegates of the Parlement. This took place on 28 February. Francis began by asking Verjus and de Loynes if they wished to add anything to their own memorandum. They asked to see the chancellor's reply, but the king refused. When they insisted, he launched into a violent diatribe. It had taken a hundred people seven months, he stormed, to produce a memorandum to which his chancellor had replied in just a few days. There would be only one king in France, and what had been done in Italy would not be undone in France; he would see to it that no Venetian Senate was set up in his kingdom. The Parlement, he declared, should limit its activity to judicial matters. 'Look to justice', he snarled; 'it is as badly administered as it was a hundred years ago', and he threatened to turn the court into a nomadic institution and make it 'trot after him like those of the Grand Conseil'. Finally, he criticized the Parlement's recruitment and reception of new members. A heated argument ensued, as Verjus and de Loynes attempted to reply, but it was soon cut short by the king. 'Go!' he said, 'leave tomorrow without fail.' The two representatives tried once more to justify the Parlement's conduct, but Francis would not listen. 'Go!' he repeated, 'go tomorrow morning, early.' After they had returned to their lodgings, the *parlementaires* were instructed to hasten their departure. They begged for a delay, as the river Loire was in flood, but were warned by the grand

---

19 Annates were specifically mentioned in a bull of 1 October 1516, which Francis submitted to the Parlement after the Concordat had been registered, thereby giving the lie to Duprat's statement. Doucet, i. 133.

20 A.N., J. 942; Doucet, i. 106–15.

master that if they had not left by 6 a.m. next day they would be thrown
into a pit and left there for six months.[21]

The king's attitude posed a serious challenge to the Parlement, for he
was, in effect, disputing its right to intervene in matters of state. On
6 March, six days before Verjus and de Loynes reported back, he sent his
first chamberlain, La Trémoïlle, to the court with a demand for the
immediate registration of the Concordat, failing which he threatened to
give effect to certain secret measures. It was rumoured that he planned to
set up a new parlement at Orléans.[22] La Trémoïlle came before the court
on 15 March and repeated the arguments in support of the Concordat,
emphasizing the king's determination to call the Parlement to order as he
would his other subjects and servants. Francis, he said, had repeated these
words more than ten times in a quarter of an hour and had uttered vague
threats should the court fail to obey. This had the desired effect. On the
following day, the *avocat général*, Le Lièvre, presented the observations
of the *gens du roi* to the court. The Concordat, he pointed out, was a
contract only between the king and the pope, and the rights of the
Gallican church were intact, since it had not been a party to the agreement. Nor was it necessarily a definitive convention; Louis XI had suspended the Pragmatic Sanction only to revive it subsequently. This might
happen again in the case of the Concordat. For these reasons, Le Lièvre
continued, he and his colleagues were ready to waive their opposition to
the Concordat and allow its publication on two conditions: first, the
words *de expresso mandato regis iteratis vicibus facto* must be added to
the formula of registration as an indication of duress; secondly, it must be
made clear that the publication did not entail abrogation of the Pragmatic
Sanction.

The recommendation of the *gens du roi*, despite its conditions, was
nothing less than a total surrender: they abandoned the idea of calling a
general assembly of the Gallican church, which would have seriously
embarrassed the crown, and sacrificed their political principles and the
Gallican liberties for the sake of their own safety. The Parlement nevertheless accepted their advice, albeit with some modifications. On
18 March, after another debate, it confirmed its *arrêt* of 24 July and laid
down conditions for the publication of the Concordat. In addition to the
formula proposed by Le Lièvre, it stipulated that the publication should
take the form of a royal ordinance in the presence of 'an important
person' ('quelque gros personnage') nominated by the king. The court
also decided that it would continue to judge cases in accordance with the
Pragmatic Sanction. But La Trémoïlle, suspecting another attempt at

[21]   B.N., MS. fr. 10900, fols. 6a–7b.
[22]   Barrillon, ii. 79–80.

procrastination, refused to refer the court's decision back to the king; he insisted on immediate compliance with Francis's request and again uttered vague threats. The Parlement, seeing the risk involved in further resistance, decided to publish the Concordat, but, at the same time, it drew up a secret protestation repudiating its responsibility for this action and affirming its determination to adhere to the Pragmatic Sanction in judging future beneficial lawsuits. Having thus salved its conscience, it registered the Concordat on 22 March, inserting the formula indicating duress. Two days later it disclaimed responsibility for the registration in a second secret protestation.[23]

The Parlement had no sooner given way than the university and clergy of Paris began to agitate against the Concordat. The university was determined to uphold the Gallican principles enunciated by its teachers in the past and the reforms they had carried through. Despite an assurance by Jacques Olivier, first president of the Parlement, that the university's privileges would not suffer as a result of the Concordat's registration, the doctors were afraid that benefices would henceforth fall into the hands of rich courtiers rather than poor graduates. They decided to forbid the printing of the Concordat, to lodge an appeal against it to a future general council and to suspend their lectures. At a meeting on 27 March they drew up an appeal to a future council, which rejected the Concordat on three grounds: first, it had been devised by a body without proper authority; secondly, it had cancelled decisions taken by earlier church councils; and thirdly, it had been published without the consent of the university and other interested parties. The appeal, which was printed and widely circulated, blamed papal greed, not royal policy, for the Concordat. At the same time, a memorandum attacking the agreement was distributed to preachers in the capital to provide them with ammunition for their Lenten sermons, posters to the same effect being put up in colleges and public places. Meanwhile, the Parisian clergy also manifested its discontent. A deputation of churchmen led by the dean of Notre-Dame went to the Parlement on 22 March with a demand to see the text of the Concordat, and also for an assembly of the Gallican church to be called. They threatened to oppose the Concordat's execution unless these demands were met.

On 4 April Francis ordered the Parlement to see to the printing of the Concordat and to enquire into the recent disturbances at the university. He complained of 'evil and dangerous persons who cause others to do what they themselves do not dare to do openly' and threatened to act 'in a way that would be remembered for ever'. Eight days later, seeing that the

---

[23] A.N., X[1a] 1520, fols. 116–18, 120, 122, 126; B.N., MS. fr. 10900, fols. 7b–12a; Doucet, i. 118–23.

court had as yet taken no action, the king appointed two commissioners to investigate the university. This provoked more trouble among the students, and the Parlement ordered twelve college principals to keep better discipline. It declined, however, to register a royal edict threatening to banish the university or to suspend its privileges if it continued to meddle in state affairs. During the summer several people associated with the university's appeal to a general council were arrested, and another commission was set up to try them. They were soon released, however, their case being referred to the king's judgment; but it was never mentioned again. Having obtained what he wanted, Francis presumably felt that it would be wise not to reawaken Gallican feeling by making a martyr of the university.[24]

What was the long-term significance of the Concordat? Historians have argued that it destroyed the independence of the Gallican church and conferred so many advantages on the king of France that he was never tempted thereafter to break with Rome.[25] These claims cannot be accepted without serious reservations. First, the king's effective control of ecclesiastical appointments in France was, as we have seen, considerable even before the Concordat. What it did was to increase that control by giving the king the *right* to appoint to major benefices, whereas previously he had acted in defiance of the Pragmatic Sanction of Bourges. Secondly, some important churches in France were allowed to continue electing their superiors. They lost this privilege only in 1532 as a result of a new agreement between the king and Pope Clement VII.[26] Thirdly, the Concordat included a number of safeguards against the abuse of royal power. The pope reserved to himself the right to set aside any royal nominee whose qualifications fell short of the canonical requirements. A bishop, for example, had to be at least twenty-seven years of age and an abbot twenty-three. True, the king, in exercising his right of nomination, often disregarded these requirements, and the pope very rarely objected.[27] But

---

[24] Doucet, i. 125–39; C.-E. du Boulay, *Historia Universitatis Parisiensis* (1665–73), vi. 88–92; Barrillon, ii. 79–84; *C.A.F.*, i. 814; v. 16782.

[25] 'The French monarchy was fated to remain Catholic. What had it to gain from going Reformist? In the all important business of appointing to bishoprics and wealthy abbeys, the king of France, under the Concordat of 1516, was as much Head of the Church as Henry VIII of England.' J. E. Neale, *The Age of Catherine de' Medici* (London, 1943), pp. 14–15.

[26] This privilege was sometimes disregarded by the king. Thus, when the chapter of Troyes tried to hold an election in November 1518 on the strength of it, Francis compelled it to accept his nominee. Also in 1518 Jean de Magedeleine, abbot-elect of Cluny, was ousted by Aymar Gouffier, the king's protégé. J. Thomas, *Le Concordat de 1516; ses origines, son histoire au XVIe siècle* (1910), ii. 349ff; iii. 105–6; Imbart de La Tour, ii. 479–80.

[27] Martin Fournier became archbishop of Tours at twenty-three, Louis de Husson bishop

this is no reflection on the Concordat; it simply means that it was badly enforced. Indeed, it can be legitimately argued that the French church after 1516 suffered less from the Concordat than from its distorted application.

It is not difficult to see why the papacy connived at this state of affairs. While the Concordat undoubtedly helped to buttress royal absolutism by legalizing and extending the scope of royal patronage, it was also a triumph for the papacy. The authority of the Holy See, which the Pragmatic Sanction had so drastically undermined, was now restored to its full splendour. Conciliarism had been overthrown, and, at least in theory, the papacy once more held sway over the French church. The thorn had been removed from the eye of the church; annates and appeals could now reach Rome unimpeded. The Concordat, in short, was not just a feather in the king's cap; it was also a jewel added to the papal tiara. Having gained so much from it, the pope would have been foolish to quibble over the details of its application. Francis, on his part, was never inclined to repudiate it although he did not gain as much from it in terms of papal support for his policies in Italy as he had hoped. Had he repudiated it, he would have humiliated himself in the eyes of the Gallican opposition and lost the domestic advantages that he had gained from the agreement. Even if the bargain he had struck with the pope at the expense of Gallican liberties did not quite live up to his political expectations, it was nonetheless a bargain worth keeping.

of Poitiers at eighteen, Gabriel le Veneur bishop of Evreux at fourteen and Charles de Guise archbishop of Rheims at nine. Nor was the king particularly concerned about the education or morals of his nominees: thus, Thomas Duprat became a bishop because of the services given to the king by his brother, the chancellor. Charles de Villiers was appointed to Limoges because he belonged to a 'great and noble house' that had served the crown well. Thomas, iii. 184–5, 204. See also M. M. Edelstein, 'The Social Origins of the Episcopacy in the Reign of Francis I', *F.H.S.*, viii (1974), 377–92, and M.C. Peronnet, 'Les évêques de l'ancienne France' (unpublished thesis, University of Lille, 1977), vols. i–ii. The latter states that Francis found 104 bishops in office at the time of the Concordat (i. 435) and that he had altered the entire episcopate by 1540 (i. 440). He also notes that it was only from 1591 that a candidate underwent scrutiny by the papal nuncio in France; previously the only mechanism for enforcing the Concordat's conditions was the papal veto. I am grateful to Dr R. Bonney for drawing my attention to this work.

5

The uneasy peace

(1516–20)

MARIGNANO did not mark the end of the war in Italy. The Venetians and the Emperor Maximilian were still fighting over Brescia, and the French sent an army to help their allies. Meanwhile, in Austria, Cardinal Schiner, who had escaped from the field at Marignano, was urging the emperor to invade the duchy of Milan and restore the Sforzas to power in the person of the duke of Bari. Maximilian was assured that, if the Milanese people were given the chance, they would rise against the French. He could also count on the support of the Swiss cantons that had been defeated at Marignano, and for money could turn to the king of England, whose jealousy had been aroused by Francis's victory.[1] In October 1515 Henry sent his secretary, Richard Pace, to Switzerland to raise an army against the French, while he himself toyed with the idea of leading a new expedition across the Channel.[2] Another ruler who might have been interested in joining a coalition against France was Ferdinand of Aragon, but he died on 23 January 1516, leaving his kingdom to his grandson, the Archduke Charles.

The death of Ferdinand seriously altered the balance of power in Europe. The Archduke Charles, who already ruled the Netherlands and Franche-Comté, suddenly acquired the kingdoms of Castile, Aragon and Naples. He became overnight France's most powerful neighbour and the ruler of territories in which she had an interest. Francis had inherited the Angevin claim to Naples, and as soon as Ferdinand died he ordered the archives of the counts of Provence to be searched for evidence in support of his title.[3] The actual investiture of Naples was in the gift of its suzerain, the pope, who had given Francis to understand that he might support his claim. Another potential trouble-spot was Spanish Navarre, which Ferdinand had wrested from its king, Jean d'Albret, in 1512. It had since been annexed to Castile, and Jean looked to the king of France for help in regaining it. As duke of Burgundy, Charles had implicitly recognized Albret's claim; but he was unlikely to do so now that he had become king of Castile. It seemed equally improbable that he would voluntarily

---

[1] Barrillon, i. 126n.   [2] *L.P.*, ii. 1095.   [3] Barrillon, i. 195.

renounce Naples, which had become an integral part of the Aragonese empire in the Mediterranean.

But, early in 1516, Charles still had to take possession of his Spanish kingdoms, and there were signs that this might not prove an altogether smooth process. There were powerful forces at work in Aragon and Castile which favoured a return to separate rulers, while the authority of the Castilian monarch was being challenged within his own kingdom by turbulent grandees and towns. Only the speedy arrival of Charles in Spain could assure him of a relatively trouble-free succession, and this required the friendly collaboration of France. On 13 August, therefore, he signed the treaty of Noyon with Francis. This substituted Francis's infant daughter, Louise, for Princess Renée as Charles's future bride and added Naples to her dowry. Pending completion of the marriage, Charles undertook to pay Francis 100,000 gold *écus* per year as a tribute for Naples, thereby implicitly recognizing his claim. He also conditionally promised to give satisfaction to Jean d'Albret's widow, Catherine.[4] The treaty has been described as 'nothing but an outward show'.[5] It was certainly unsatisfactory in that Charles, who was now seventeen, could hardly be expected to wait for a bride still in her cradle; nor were the Spanish authorities likely to regard Naples as an acceptable dowry for her. But it enabled Charles to establish his authority in Spain without interference from France, and Francis to consolidate his position in Italy. The treaty also effectively undermined Henry VIII's plan for a new coalition against France.

The 'perpetual peace' of Fribourg (29 November 1516)

Early in March 1516 Maximilian arrived at Trent with an army 15,000 strong; he advanced rapidly southward, relieving Brescia. The French retreated, first to the river Adda, then to Milan, where Bourbon posted guards in all the belfries and imprisoned or executed any citizen whose loyalty was suspect. On 24 March the French garrison was reinforced by 8,000 Swiss from the cantons that had signed the peace of Geneva. This dashed Maximilian's hopes of a swift victory; after waiting two days at Marignano, he suddenly decamped, leaving his troops behind.

The emperor's ignominious flight helped Francis in his efforts to reach a settlement with the Swiss cantons. He resumed negotiations with them in May, and, on 29 November, the so-called perpetual peace was signed at Fribourg.[6] Francis agreed to pay the Swiss a war indemnity of 700,000

---

[4]   *Ordonnances*, i. 409–30.
[5]   K. Brandi, *The Emperor Charles V*, tr. C. V. Wedgwood (London, 1939), p. 76.
[6]   *Ordonnances*, i. 477–93. The treaty remained in force till the reign of Louis XVI; hence its nickname.

écus (400,000 for the siege of Dijon; 300,000 for the recent Milanese expedition). They were also to receive 300,000 *écus* in exchange for the castles of Lugano and Locarno and fortresses in the Valtelline. Finally, an annual subsidy of 2,000 francs was promised to each canton. The Swiss, for their part, undertook not to serve anyone against the king in France or his duchy of Milan. Expensive as it was, this agreement was less than Francis had hoped for: he had wanted a full alliance and had only got a defensive one. Yet, it was no mean achievement, for it meant that, in future, he would be able to hire Swiss mercenaries instead of fighting them.

The peace of Cambrai (11 March 1517)

Even after the emperor's flight from Italy, England continued its intrigues against France. In October 1516 a league was signed in London, Maximilian being promised a large subsidy for the defence of Verona. But on 3 December he signed another treaty in Brussels in which he agreed to give up Verona in return for 200,000 gold crowns to be paid equally by France and Venice. He also agreed to meet Francis at Cambrai at Candlemas, but, the time being too short, ambassadors were sent instead.[7] In the treaty of Cambrai, of 11 March 1517, Francis, Maximilian and Charles of Spain agreed to help each other if attacked, and to join in a crusade. These terms, however, were for public consumption only. Secret clauses provided for the partition of Italy at the expense of the Venetians.[8] It is difficult, however, to believe that this scheme was ever seriously contemplated by Francis, for it would have marked a return to Louis XII's disastrous policy of taking a traditional enemy into partnership. It remained a dead letter, as Francis had reserved to himself the right to implement it only if his alliance with Venice broke down, whereas this was confirmed on 8 October.[9]

The peace of Cambrai rounded off the first phase of the Italian wars, and Francis could feel reasonably satisfied with the results of his foreign policy to date: in the course of a spectacular military campaign he had shown his personal valour, avenged the disasters of 1513 and exploded the myth of Swiss invincibility. The emperor had been made to look ridiculous in the eyes of Europe. Milan and Genoa were once more under French rule and the pope seemed subservient. By a skilful use of diplomacy, Francis had acquired the monopoly of Swiss recruitment in the future and sabotaged Henry VIII's plan for a new league against France. England was now isolated, and already there were signs of her coming

---

[7] *Ordonnances*, i. 494–502.   [8] *Ibid.*, ii. 7–18.   [9] *Ibid.*, ii. 164–8.

round to a more conciliatory attitude: in July 1517 an agreement was reached with her concerning maritime disputes.[10]

To the average Frenchman the year 1517 offered a welcome respite from war. 'There was great peace and tranquillity in the kingdom of France', wrote Barrillon, 'and no noise or rumour of war, division or partisanship. Merchants plied their trade in perfect safety as well on land as on sea. Frenchmen, Englishmen, Spaniards, Germans and all other natives of Christendom traded peacefully together. This was a great favour bestowed by God on Christendom.'[11]

Peace came at a time when Christendom desperately needed to unite against the westward expansion of the Ottoman Turks. Under Mehmet II they had captured Constantinople, penetrated far into the Balkans and expelled the Venetians from Euboea. Now, under Selim the Grim, they were again advancing: having conquered Syria in August 1516, they invaded Egypt early in the following year. 'It is time', Leo X declared, 'that we woke from sleep lest we be put to the sword unawares.'[12] In November 1517 the Sacred College proposed a new crusade to be led by the emperor and the king of France with other powers participating in accordance with their individual resources. It was hoped that Francis would respond favourably to the proposal, particularly as Leo had recently allowed him to levy a clerical tenth and given his consent to the marriage of his own nephew, Lorenzo, to a French princess of royal blood. But Francis did not reply till 23 December. Moreover, he asked to control the crusade funds and to be allowed to raise another tenth three years in advance. The replies sent by the emperor and the king of Spain were equally disappointing, yet Leo did not give up his plan. In March 1518 he proclaimed a five-year truce among all Christian powers and sent out four cardinals to the principal courts of Europe to rally support for the crusade. But, as they soon discovered, no one was really interested in it. Although the seriousness of the Turkish threat was generally recognized, other problems seemed more urgent to the princes of western Europe.[13]

The treaty of Noyon had become a millstone around the neck of Charles of Habsburg now that he had taken possession of his Spanish kingdoms. He could not afford to pay Francis the annual tribute of 100,000 *écus* for Naples and showed little inclination to compensate Catherine d'Albret for the loss of Navarre.[14] In February 1518 the Castilian Cortes left him in no doubt as to where his duty lay: the deputies

10 *Ibid.*, ii. 126–30. 11 Barrillon, i. 273.
12 L. von Pastor, *The History of the Popes*, tr. F. I. Antrobus and R. F. Kerr (London, 1891–1933), vii. 218.
13 *Ibid.*, vii. 223–54. 14 Le Glay, ii. 147.

offered to sacrifice their lives and property for the defence of Navarre, describing it as 'the principal key to Spain'. Charles assured them that he did not intend to give it up and, in August, he persuaded Germaine de Foix, Ferdinand's widow, to hand over to him her claim to the kingdom. Yet even now Charles's authority in Spain was not sufficiently secure for him to risk an open breach with France; he also remained under the influence of Chièvres and other Flemish councillors, traditionally friendly to France. Thus, far from repudiating the treaty of Noyon, he assured Francis of his good intentions. He even asked for the king's daughter, Charlotte, to be substituted for her sister, Louise, who had recently died, as his prospective bride under the treaty.[15]

On 1 May 1519 a conference opened at Montpellier to examine the differences outstanding between Francis and Charles. The French delegation was led by the grand master, Boisy, and the Spanish one by Chièvres. Alain d'Albret, regent of Navarre, sent representatives to press the claim to the kingdom of his grandson, Henri. But the conference got off to a bad start: Boisy fell ill on the first day, leaving his colleagues, Bishop de Poncher and President Olivier, to negotiate on their own. After squabbling over the agenda, the conference soon turned into an acrimonious debate on the lawful ownership of Navarre. Albret's representatives claimed that his ancestors had held it for four centuries and that Charles would commit a grave injustice if he failed to hand it back. The Spaniards, for their part, argued that it belonged to Charles by right of inheritance and gift. They tactlessly recalled that it had been annexed by Ferdinand of Aragon after the pope had excommunicated Jean d'Albret for conniving at Louis XII's schism. This provoked a sharp rejoinder from the French. 'Never', they declared, 'had the king of France ceased to be a very Catholic and very Christian sovereign; never had he been infected with the leprosy of schism!' Chièvres then proposed a cash indemnity for Henri d'Albret. This, however, was unacceptable to the French, who decided that they might as well go home.[16] The death of Boisy on 10 May gave them a convenient pretext. 'The said death', writes du Bellay, 'was the cause of great wars . . . for if they had finished their talks Christendom would certainly have remained at peace until now; those who subsequently had charge of affairs cared less for the peace of Christendom than did the said Chièvres and the grand master.'[17]

The Montpellier conference had been doomed from the start, for neither side had approached it in a conciliatory spirit. Nor were Boisy and

---

[15]   P. Boissonnade, *Histoire de la réunion de la Navarre à la Castille* (1893), pp. 508–29.
[16]   *Ibid.*, pp. 532–9; Le Glay, ii. 450–4.
[17]   Du Bellay, i. 95. Florange believed that the death of Boisy was responsible for the deaths of 200,000 men. Florange, i. 257.

Chièvres as influential as they had once been: the former's health had been failing for some time, while the latter was being superseded by Charles's brilliant new chancellor, Mercurino di Gattinara, who was no friend of France.[18] What is more, circumstances had arisen since the treaty of Noyon which far outweighed in importance mere differences of personality. On 12 January 1519 the Emperor Maximilian, Charles's paternal grandfather, had died, throwing open the contest for the succession to the Holy Roman Empire.

The imperial election

Although the empire had been in Habsburg hands for a long time, it was an elective, not hereditary, dignity. The emperor was chosen by seven electors: the archbishops of Mainz, Cologne and Trier, the king of Bohemia, the elector-palatine, the duke of Saxony and the margrave of Brandenburg. They were under no obligation to choose a member of the house of Habsburg or even a German, so that it was possible for the king of France to stand for election. Indeed, towards the end of 1516, the archbishop of Trier's chancellor and Ulrich von Hutten, the eminent humanist who had recently entered the service of the archbishop of Mainz, visited the French court and formally committed their respective masters to vote for Francis at the appropriate time. Another German who promised the king his support was Franz von Sickingen, the redoubtable knight, who could raise an army of 20,000 men at the drop of a hat.[19] In June 1517 Francis signed a treaty with Joachim of Brandenburg. This laid down that Princess Renée would marry the margrave's son and that an indemnity of 75,000 *écus* would be paid to Joachim for Renée's renunciation of her parental inheritance. The margrave, for his part, promised to vote for Francis at the next imperial election.[20] A similar undertaking was entered into by the elector-palatine. Francis therefore had reason to believe that a majority of electors favoured his candidature. Other German princes who accepted pensions from him included the dukes of Lorraine, Guelders, Brunswick-Lüneburg and Holstein.

The empire attracted Francis on two counts. Though based in Germany, it was a supranational dignity, the secular counterpart of the papacy, and therefore had enormous international prestige. Earlier

---

[18] Boisy told the Spanish envoy in June 1518 that his influence with the king was less than it had been five or six years earlier. Le Glay, ii. 143–4.

[19] Barrillon, i. 251–2. Sickingen received a pension of 3,000 francs from Francis and a chain worth 3,000 *écus*. Florange i. 233–4.

[20] *Ordonnances*, ii. no. 123.

French kings also had toyed with the idea of becoming emperor.[21] But there was another, more practical, reason for Francis's interest in the matter. He knew that Maximilian, passionately dedicated as he was to the idea of the universal mission of the Habsburg dynasty, wanted to be succeeded by his grandson Charles, who already ruled the Netherlands, Franche-Comté, Spain and Naples. Should this happen, Charles would become indisputably the most powerful ruler in Christendom. As suzerain of Milan, he might try to wrest the duchy from Francis, and, should he go to Italy to be crowned emperor by the pope, he might be tempted to drive the French out of the peninsula. By offering himself as candidate Francis hoped to avert this danger. 'You understand', he wrote, 'the reason which moves me to gain the empire, which is to prevent the said Catholic king from doing so. If he were to succeed, seeing the extent of his kingdoms and lordships, this could do me immeasurable harm; he would always be mistrustful and suspicious, and would doubtless throw me out of Italy.'[22]

Francis failed to see that the German electors were interested less in his success than in promoting a contested election. An imperial election, though it was supposed to be conducted with the highest integrity, offered marvellous opportunities for bribery and corruption. Provided the candidates were wealthy enough, the electors could hope to build up large fortunes for themselves by selling their votes to the highest bidder. This was mainly why they invited Francis to join the contest; that he should have allowed himself to be thus exploited says little for his political judgment. Maximilian, on the other hand, was all too well acquainted with the seamy side of German political life. He urged his grandson to impress the electors with his munificence and treated with scorn an offer by Charles of 300,000 ducats. 'If you wish to gain mankind', he wrote, 'you must play at a high stake. Either follow my counsel and adopt my suggestions or abandon any chance of bringing this affair to a termination satisfactory to our wishes and creditable to our fame. It would be lamentable if, after so much pain and labour to aggrandize and exalt our house and our posterity, we should lose all through some pitiful omission or penurious neglect.'[23] Taking this advice to heart, Charles sent more money to Germany, and at Augsburg, in August 1518, Maximilian managed to bribe five electors into promising to vote for his grandson.

[21] M. François, 'L'idée d'empire en France à l'époque de Charles-Quint', *Charles-Quint et son temps* (1959), p. 25; G. Zeller, 'Les rois de France candidats à l'Empire', *R.H.*, clxxiii (1934), 273–311, 497–534.

[22] L. Schick, *Un grand homme d'affaires au début du XVI siècle, Jacob Fugger* (1957), p. 163.

[23] *L.P.*, iii, p. iv.

Only the francophil archbishop of Trier and the incorruptible duke of Saxony resisted his efforts. But the emperor had no sooner died than the electors invited new bids from the candidates.

As the Habsburgs began to marshal their resources, Francis sent envoys to the electors and to the king of Poland, who was expected to vote in place of his young nephew, the king of Bohemia. To co-ordinate and expedite their efforts, he also dispatched Admiral Bonnivet, the seigneur d'Orval and Charles Guillart, first president of the Parlement, to Lunéville in Lorraine. They were empowered to send envoys in the king's name, to read and reply to their dispatches and to promise money to the electors and others who might be useful.[24] They soon moved to Coblenz, carrying with them 400,000 crowns in cash. The greed of some of the electors, especially the archbishop of Mainz and his brother, Joachim of Branden-burg, shocked the French envoys, but Francis seemed prepared to go to any lengths to win their votes. 'I want the marquis Joachim', he wrote, 'to be made drunk with all things.'[25] He brushed aside Guillart's suggestion that persuasion might be preferable to bribery. 'If I had only to deal with the virtuous', he explained, 'or with those who even pretend to a shadow of virtue, your advice would be expedient and honest; but in times like the present, whatever a man sets his heart upon, be it the papacy, be it the empire or anything else, he has no means of obtaining his object except by force or corruption.'[26]

Francis certainly pursued his imperial ambitions with determination and vigour, but he did not give enough attention to lesser German nobles. Thus he alienated Robert de La Marck, lord of Sedan, by disbanding his company of men-at-arms in August 1517, and his brother, Everard, bishop of Liège, by opposing his promotion to the purple; in April 1518 they both undertook to serve Charles. Sickingen also deserted Francis after his pension had been cut off for some offence committed against Milanese merchants. In exchange for an annuity from Charles he took up a command in the army of the Swabian League.[27] This had been set up to resist Ulrich, duke of Württemberg, who had sacked Reutlingen soon after Maximilian's death. His duchy was completely overrun and he had to take refuge in the county of Montbéliard. This episode did much harm to the French cause in Germany, where it was believed, albeit wrongly, that Francis had instigated the duke's aggression.[28] With Ulrich's defeat,

---

[24] Barrillon, ii. 120–1. In his memoirs, Florange does not mention Guillart and exagger-ates his own role in the campaign. Florange, i. 244–5.

[25] 'Je veux qu'on soulle de toutes choses le marquis Joachim.' F. Mignet, *La rivalité de François 1er et de Charles-Quint* (1875), i. 197.

[26] *L.P.*, iii, p. x.

[27] Florange, i. 238–43; Le Glay, ii. 207.

[28] Le Glay, ii. 189, 193, 205, 219.

the army of the Swabian League was left in virtual control of south Germany. Francis was prompted to assemble an army on the borders of Champagne, but this merely created the impression that he was planning to seize the empire by force. The Swiss at the diet of Zürich asked him to desist and even to withdraw from the election altogether; Cardinal Schiner prophesied a torrent of bloodshed if the king persisted with his policy.[29]

The imperial election was bound to alter significantly the balance of power in Europe, and no one was more aware of this than Leo X. As temporal ruler of the States of the Church, he had no cause to feel enthusiastic about either candidate, since each held lands in Italy. Of the two, Charles was the more dangerous to the papacy, for he already ruled Naples; by becoming emperor he would acquire fiefs in north Italy and gain a stranglehold on the States of the Church in the middle. From the thirteenth century it had been an axiom of papal policy to try always to keep Naples and the empire in separate hands. Indeed, Charles on becoming king of Naples had taken an oath endorsing this principle. Ideally, Leo would have liked to see the election of a German prince without territorial possessions in Italy. By March 1519, however, he had come to understand that the effective choice lay between Francis and Charles; he decided, therefore, to support the former as the lesser evil. He sent a nuncio to Germany to work against Charles and authorized Francis to promise a legateship to the archbishop of Mainz and red hats to the archbishops of Cologne and Trier in return for their votes. Leo's intervention, however, did Francis more harm than good, for his legates made themselves thoroughly unpopular in Germany by suggesting that Charles was not even eligible for the empire.[30]

Francis was better placed initially than his rival to win the election. He was nearer Germany and allowed his agents to act as they thought best; Charles, on the other hand, was far away in Spain, and expected his representatives to obtain his permission before conceding anything. The French also managed to create the impression that they had inexhaustible funds at their disposal. 'In this affair of the empire', wrote a Habsburg agent, 'we must not haggle at any fixed sums. Fresh disbursements will be constantly required, as these devils of Frenchmen scatter gold in all directions.'[31] In fact, Francis had difficulty raising money. He tried unsuccessfully to raise loans in Genoa and Lyons, and also failed to borrow 100,000 crowns from Henry VIII; hence Bonnivet's remark that even if it rained gold in England, the French would not get so much as 'a piece . . .

[29] Florange, i. 253–4; L.P., iii. 173.
[30] Schick, pp. 164–5; Pastor, History of the Popes, vii. 272–83.
[31] L.P., iii, p. xiii.

to set upon a bonnet'. Yet Francis did obtain a loan of 360,000 crowns from Italian bankers in London.[32] He also raised money at home by selling royal lands and offices. In May 1519 he seized the inheritance of the grand master, Boisy.[33] By such means, he was able to regain some of the ground lost at Augsburg: the margrave and the elector-palatine promised to vote for him, and the archbishop of Cologne hinted that he might do so too.[34]

Raising enough money was not Francis's only problem; it also had to be sent to Germany, which was in a state of turmoil. Law and order had broken down in many areas, and roads were being closely watched by thieves and robbers. The normal and safe way to transfer large amounts of cash from one country to another was by bill of exchange, but Francis was denied this facility by the German banks, whose own long-term interests were best served by supporting the Habsburgs. Thus Jacob Fugger, the great Augsburg banker, refused to accept a bill of exchange for 300,000 gold crowns from the king despite the offer of a tempting commission, while he agreed to place more than half a million florins at Charles's disposal. In February 1519 the town council of Augsburg, acting under pressure from the Swabian League, forbade any merchant to transfer money from France to Germany under pain of death, and other towns in Germany and the Netherlands followed suit.[35] Francis was, therefore, obliged to send ready cash. On 30 May Richard Pace, Henry VIII's agent, reported that Francis was sending 'money comptable without bills of exchange' through the see of Trier.[36] It was also said that sacks containing large amounts of French gold were attached to boats and dragged along the Rhine. The archbishop of Trier certainly carried French money intended for the archbishop of Cologne and king of Bohemia when he travelled up the Rhine to Frankfurt.[37]

Money was not the only decisive factor in the election; German public opinion was also crucial. Habsburg agents used sermons and illustrated broadsheets to stir up a deep hatred of everything French. They suggested that the money Francis was paying out in bribes had been obtained by tyrannical means. Charles's agents were instructed to inform the Germans 'through preaching or otherwise of the condition of the French people, especially of the great demands made upon them, of the innovations and expedients by which they are daily fleeced, how in a single year'

---

[32] Schick, p. 169; A. Spont, *Semblançay (? – 1527): la bourgeoisie financière au début du XVIᵉ siècle* (1895), p. 166; *L.P.*, iii. 161, 385.

[33] Barrillon, ii. 142. Boisy's widow and son received the lordships of Sézanne and Montmorillon as compensation.

[34] Mignet, ii, 188–96.

[35] Schick, p. 170; Le Glay, ii. 244, 249.

[36] *L.P.*, iii. 274.   [37] Schick, p. 170.

three clerical tenths have been levied and other things which may help to bring them [Francis's agents] into disrepute and contempt'.[38] Francis tried to counter this propaganda by claiming that he would be better able to defend Christendom against the Turks than his rival. In a letter to the bishop of Brandenburg, Duprat laid stress on Charles's youth and on the distance separating Spain from Germany, which would prevent him from attending to either. 'Furthermore', he wrote, 'the customs and way of life of the Spanish people are not only different from, but clean contrary to, those of the German people. The French nation, on the other hand, is like the German in almost every respect, since it has sprung from it, namely from the Sicambri, as is described by the ancient historians.'[39] Such arguments, however, carried no weight with the Germans. It was dangerous, Pace reported, to speak one good word of a Frenchman in Germany; he himself was almost thrown out of Frankfurt after he had been mistaken for one.[40]

On 8 June the electors gathered in Frankfurt, the only absentee being the king of Bohemia, who was represented by his chancellor. Under the Golden Bull, which regulated the electoral procedure, no foreigner was allowed to remain in the city. So Bonnivet, wearing disguise and under the assumed name of 'Captain Jacob', had to watch the proceedings from the castle of Rüdesheim.[41] The atmosphere in Frankfurt was hardly conducive to calm and impartiality: the summer heat was intense and plague was rife. Outside the city, the army of the Swabian League stood waiting. The electors were told that this was for their protection, but they were also made to understand that their safety depended on their choosing the right man. No Frenchman, Henry of Nassau declared, would enter Germany except on the points of spears and swords.[42] Francis's cause was evidently hopeless, and, at the eleventh hour, the pope performed a characteristic *volte-face* by agreeing conditionally to the union of the imperial and Neapolitan crowns. Even Francis saw the futility of further effort on his part: on 26 June he withdrew from the election and instructed his agents to support either Joachim of Brandenburg or Frederick of Saxony.[43] No one, however, was prepared to vote for the margrave, and Frederick refused to be considered. On 28 June, therefore, Charles was elected unanimously. As wild rejoicing greeted the news throughout Germany, Bonnivet and his colleagues took to their heels and, with the help of the archbishop of Trier, managed to give the slip to the men of La Marck and Sickingen, who had been on the lookout for them.[44]

[38] *Ibid.*, p. 169.   [39] Barrillon, ii. 126–40.   [40] *L.P.*, iii. 297.
[41] Barrillon, ii. 143.   [42] *L.P.*, iii. 326.   [43] Pastor, vii. 285–6.
[44] Bonnivet retired to Plombières for a cure. He was apparently suffering from syphilis and stayed away from court for three months. He was reported to be 'sore sick and not

The result of the election was known at the French court on 3 July. It cannot have been a surprise; yet Francis was evidently disappointed. He had wasted a lot of money and had been cheated by the electors who had once invited him to stand. He retired to Fontainebleau and 'sought relaxation and consolation in hunting'. Later he put a brave face on his defeat. He told Sir Thomas Boleyn that he was much indebted to God for having spared him all the trouble that he would have incurred by becoming emperor.[45]

The imperial election was followed by a period of international readjustment. The immediate future was reasonably predictable: Charles would go from Spain to Germany to be crowned as King of the Romans at Aachen; he would then go to Italy for his imperial coronation by the pope. This was something Francis was most anxious to prevent, not so much through pique at his recent defeat as because of the likely repercussions on his position in Italy. In the summer of 1519, therefore, he sent an envoy to the pope, who was equally apprehensive about the domination of Italy by the house of Habsburg. In a secret treaty, signed on 22 October, Francis promised to defend the States of the Church against Charles and the pope's insubordinate vassals (i.e. the duke of Ferrara), while Leo pledged himself to defend the interests of France with temporal and spiritual weapons, and to deny Charles the investiture of Naples in conjunction with that of the empire. No new league, however, was formed, as Venice refused to be drawn into a coalition against Ferrara.[46]

The Field of Cloth of Gold

As France and Spain seemed set on a collision course, there was a marked improvement in Anglo-French relations. Bonnivet led an embassy to England in July 1518 accompanied by more than eighty 'young fresh galants of the court of France'.[47] The English government, having been left high and dry by the treaty of Cambrai, welcomed the opportunity of forging a new diplomatic link; Wolsey, in particular, was working for a multilateral treaty of peace. This was achieved on 2 October, when England and France signed a treaty binding all the great powers and more

like to recover', but, on 14 October, Thomas Boleyn saw him at Orléans 'leap up and down of his mule as well as he was wont to do'. On 22 October he was appointed governor of Dauphiné in place of Boisy. Florange, i. 261; Barrillon, ii. 145, 150; *L.P.*, iii. 468.

[45] Louise of Savoy claimed that Francis had spent only 100,000 crowns on the election; in fact, he had spent at least four times as much. *L.P.*, iii. 352, 416; Barrillon, ii. 146–7; Michaud et Poujoulat, v. 91.

[46] Barrillon, ii. 147–8; Pastor, viii. 1–4, 8.

[47] E. Hall, *Henry VIII*, ed. C. Whibley (London, 1904), i. 168.

than twenty lesser ones to perpetual peace. Any party to the treaty who came under attack was to be defended by the rest acting together. On 4 October a number of subsidiary treaties were signed: Tournai was to be handed back to France in return for an indemnity of 600,000 gold *écus*, payable in annual instalments of 50,000 *livres*. Eight French noblemen would be sent to England as hostages, pending final settlement. Another indemnity of 12,000 *livres* would be paid to Wolsey as compensation for the loss of his see of Tournai. Another treaty provided for the marriage of the Dauphin with Henry's daughter Mary, and, at a ceremony at Greenwich on 5 October, Bonnivet slipped a ring on her finger in the name of her prospective husband. Other treaties dealt with the suppression of piracy by subjects of both countries and envisaged a meeting between Henry and Francis before 31 July.[48] In December an English embassy, led by the earl of Worcester, visited Paris, and was magnificently entertained for a month; on 9 February Tournai was formally handed over to Marshal de Châtillon.[49]

During the election campaign for the Holy Roman Empire, Henry VIII had secretly opposed Francis's candidature while tentatively putting himself forward as a third candidate. Outwardly he had pretended to support Francis, but the latter had not been deceived. Reports of Henry's intrigues had reached him from his agents in Italy and Spain; Bonnivet had even been able to eavesdrop from behind a tapestry during an interview between Henry's agent and the margrave of Brandenburg. Yet Francis kept any resentment to himself; he pretended to be grateful to Henry for his support, even calling his second son after him.[50]

One result of the election was to enhance England's international significance. Whereas in the past there had been four major powers in Europe – France, Spain, England and the Empire – now there were only three, Spain and the Empire having become united in the person of Charles. Of these, France and the new Habsburg state seemed of roughly equal weight, so that England found herself in a peculiarly influential position: 'her alliance would bestow dominance, while her neutrality could, in theory, guarantee peace'. It was in pursuit of this 'policy of imbalance', as it has been called, that Wolsey revived the idea mooted in the treaty of 1518 of a meeting between his master and Francis.[51] In January 1520 Francis took the unusual step of appointing Wolsey as his

[48] *Ordonnances*, ii. 165–9.
[49] A tournament on 22 December was followed by a memorable banquet in the courtyard of the Bastille. One of the eight hostages taken home by the English ambassadors was Anne de Montmorency, the future constable. *L.P.*, ii. 4652; Hall, i. 173–4; Florange, i. 227–30; Barrillon, ii. 114–15; *J.B.P.*, pp. 64–7; du Bellay, i. 97–8.
[50] *L.P.*, iii. 289, 306; J. J. Scarisbrick, *Henry VIII* (London, 1968), pp. 99–103.
[51] Scarisbrick, p. 81.

commissioner to arrange the meeting, and, on 12 March, the cardinal produced a draft treaty, which the two monarchs subsequently ratified. This laid down that they would meet near Guines early in June and take part in 'a feat of arms'.[52]

The Anglo-French rapprochement was viewed with anxiety by Charles, who was preparing at this time to leave Spain for Germany. He decided to stop in England on the way in the hope of either persuading Henry to break off his meeting with Francis or creating so much suspicion of him in France that the Anglo-French meeting would stand little chance of success. Charles could count on the support of his aunt, Catherine of Aragon, Henry's queen, and of most Englishmen, who preferred him to the king of France, if only because he controlled the Netherlands, with which they had close commercial ties. In fact, many observers believed that Wolsey was the only Englishman who really wanted the meeting with Francis. But Charles needed more time to get to England. He asked Henry, therefore, to postpone his meeting with Francis; but the latter refused on the grounds of his wife's pregnancy. A postponement, he explained, would preclude her attendance. In fact it proved unnecessary, for Charles, thanks to a favourable wind, managed to reach Dover in record time. He and Henry spent three days together in May and agreed to meet again in the near future.[53]

Although the emperor's visit to England caused uneasiness in France, it did not disrupt the elaborate preparations for the Anglo-French meeting. These had been entrusted to two commissioners, who decided that the kings should meet in the Val Doré, a shallow valley situated on English soil halfway between Guines and Ardres. This was artificially reshaped to improve its symmetry and a sumptuous tent set up nearby. The commissioners also fixed on a site for the 'feat of arms', which, when completed, comprised stands for spectators, small wooden houses in which the kings were to put on their armour, and a 'tree of honour', on which the shields of the jousters were hung. Accommodation was a major headache for the organizers of the Field of Cloth of Gold, for Ardres had been sacked in the war of 1513–14 and Guines castle was partly in ruins. An attempt was made to repair both, but it was realized from the start that many people would have to sleep in tents. The French pitched three or four hundred in a meadow outside Ardres: they were covered with velvet and cloth of gold, emblazoned with the arms of their owners and surmounted by pennants or golden apples. Francis's tent, being taller than the rest, was supported by two ship's masts lashed together. It was covered with cloth of gold and at the top was a life-size statue of St

52 Hall, i. 182–7.
53 *L.P.*, iii. 637, 672, 681, 725–8, 733, 788–9; *C.S.P. Ven.*, iii. 50, 53.

Michael, carved in walnut. An eyewitness described the French tents as
more magnificent than 'the miracles of the Egyptian pyramids and the
Roman amphitheatres'.[54] But many people were impressed even more by
the temporary palace erected by Henry near Guines. This had walls of
timber painted to look like brick and many large windows. Even Leonardo da Vinci, an Italian commented, could not have done better.[55]

Henry and his court crossed the Channel on 31 May and arrived at
Guines on 5 June, slightly later than the treaty had stipulated. Meanwhile,
Wolsey called on Francis at Ardres and on 6 June signed a treaty with him.
This reiterated France's obligation to pay one million gold crowns to
Henry in two annual instalments and stipulated that the pension was to
be prolonged indefinitely should the marriage between the Dauphin and
Princess Mary take place. Wolsey and Louise of Savoy were to collaborate
in an effort to settle the differences between England and Scotland.[56] The
two kings met for the first time on 7 June, the feast of Corpus Christi.
They and their escorts set off simultaneously from their respective camps
at a signal fired by guns at Guines and Ardres. Then, after the two
processions had come to a standstill on opposite sides of the Val Doré, a
fanfare sounded, and the kings, detaching themselves from their companies, rode towards a spot marked by a spear at the bottom of the
valley.[57] As they drew near to each other, they spurred their mounts as if
to engage in combat, but instead doffed their hats and embraced. They
then retired to the tent nearby, where they were joined by Wolsey and
Bonnivet, while Dorset and Bourbon guarded the entrance. What happened inside the tent is not known for certain. Wolsey, it seems, read out
certain diplomatic documents (presumably the treaty just signed), and a
polite altercation followed over Henry's claim to the French throne. The
ministers then withdrew, leaving the kings alone; about an hour later they
came out into the open and presented their nobles to each other. Refresh-
ments were consumed by all, and as darkness fell the kings returned to
their respective quarters.[58]

The 'feat of arms' began officially on 9 June when the kings, accompanied by their courtiers, went to the lists and displayed their

---

[54] Work on the French tents began at Tours in February and continued till June. The
      operation, which involved a large labour force, was supervised by Galiot de Genouil-
      lac, Grand Master of the Artillery. The accounts are in B.N., MS. fr. 10383. See also
      J. G. Russell, *The Field of Cloth of Gold* (London, 1969), pp. 23–31.
[55] *Ibid.*, pp. 31–46.
[56] *L.P.*, iii. 869–70; Hall, i. 194–5; *C.S.P. Ven.*, iii. 62, 73, 87; *Ordonnances*, ii. no. 257.
[57] The Field of Cloth of Gold derived its name from the expensive clothes worn by the
      nobles and their servants. 'Many', writes du Bellay, 'carried their mills, forests and
      meadows on their backs.' Du Bellay, i. 102.
[58] Hall, i. 195–200; *C.S.P. Ven.*, iii. 60, 67.

horsemanship.[59] The shields of the 'challengers' were hung up on the 'tree of honour', and those of the 'comers' on railings at its foot. Next day, being Sunday, there was no jousting: instead, Francis dined with Catherine of Aragon at Guines, and Henry with Queen Claude at Ardres. The joust, which began on 11 June, offered the ladies an opportunity to show off their finery: the queens arrived on the field in richly covered litters, their ladies on palfreys and their servants in waggons. The 'feat of arms' comprised three sorts of contest: jousting at the tilt, tournament in the open field and combat on foot at the barriers. In the tournament, which began on 20 June, the challengers faced their opponents in pairs, not singly as in the jousts; and in the foot combat at the barriers, which ended the 'feat of arms', the contestants fought in pairs with puncheon spears, swords and two-handed swords. The kings earned high praise for their martial qualities, but, contrary to common belief, they did not fight each other; as 'challengers' in the joust they fought against teams of noblemen. A royal wrestling match, however, may have taken place. According to Florange, the kings were drinking together one day, when Henry challenged Francis, who instantly threw him to the ground, using a trick called 'tour de Bretagne'.[60] The English records are understandably silent about this incident. The Field of Cloth of Gold was punctuated by many banquets, dances and mummings, which need not be described here. One incident, however, deserves a mention. On about 17 June Francis, casting aside etiquette, rode to Guines early one day and surprised Henry in his bedchamber. Calling himself Henry's prisoner, he helped him on with his shirt and accompanied him to mass. Henry was apparently so impressed by this demonstration of trust that he reciprocated a few days later by bursting into Francis's room at Ardres as he was getting out of bed.[61] On 23 June Wolsey celebrated mass at a temporary altar on the tournament field. He was assisted by a papal legate, three cardinals and twenty-one bishops, music being provided in alternation by the choirs and organists of the two royal chapels. At the end of the service, Pace made a speech in Latin pointing to the great benefits both nations could expect from the meeting. Wolsey than conferred the pope's blessing on the two kings and granted a plenary indulgence and absolution to everyone present. The congregation then sat down to an *al fresco* meal, which was followed by a display of foot combat with spears and swords. On 24 June, each queen

[59] For a full treatment of the meeting see Russell, pp. 81–181; S. Anglo, *Spectacle, Pageantry and Early Tudor Policy* (Oxford, 1969), pp. 124–69.

[60] Florange, i. 272. Michelet's claim that the incident had 'incalculable consequences' for Anglo-French relations is mere conjecture, like much else in his work. J. Michelet, *Histoire de France*, x. *La Réforme* (n.d.), 137–8.

[61] Hall, i. 208; Florange, i. 268–70; *C.S.P. Ven.*, iii. 50, 77–8, 90.

gave a ring as a tournament prize to the other's consort. Then came the sad farewells. Louise of Savoy told some foreign ambassadors that the kings had parted with tears in their eyes, intending to build in the Val Doré a chapel dedicated to Our Lady of Friendship and a palace where they might meet again each year.[62] Francis left Ardres on 25 June and returned in haste to Saint-Germain-en-Laye, where his queen gave birth to a daughter on 10 August.[63] Henry, meanwhile, met Charles V in Gravelines. They agreed to hold a conference in Calais and undertook not to make a separate treaty with France in the meantime.

The Field of Cloth of Gold has been described as 'the most portentous deception on record', but the Anglo–imperial agreement, which followed immediately afterwards, was not necessarily a betrayal of Francis; it was consistent with Wolsey's ambition to impose a Christian peace by holding the balance between Francis and Charles.[64] Peace, however, depended not so much on England's neutrality as on the willingness of her two more powerful neighbours to sink their differences, and this, unfortunately, was wanting. As a Venetian ambassador reported to his government, 'these sovereigns [i.e. Francis and Charles] are not at peace; they adapt themselves to circumstances, but hate each other very cordially'.[65]

[62] *C.S.P. Ven.*, iii. 50, 93, 95.
[63] Madeleine, who married James V of Scotland in 1536.
[64] A. F. Pollard, *Henry VIII* (London, 1913), p. 142; Scarisbrick, pp. 79–81.
[65] *C.S.P. Ven.*, iii. 119. This is sometimes mistakenly taken to refer to Henry and Francis.

6

The king and his court

WHAT KIND OF man was Francis I? The English chronicler Edward Hall described him as 'a goodly prince, stately of countenance, merry of chere, brown coloured, great eyes, high nosed, big lipped, fair breasted and shoulders, small legs and long feet'.[1] Less succinct, but equally vivid, is a description by Ellis Griffith, a Welshman in Henry VIII's service, who saw the king at the Field of Cloth of Gold. Francis, he writes, was six feet tall. His head was rightly proportioned for his height, the nape of his neck unusually broad, his hair brown, smooth and neatly combed, his beard of three months' growth darker in colour, his nose long, his eyes hazel and bloodshot, and his complexion the colour of watery milk. He had muscular buttocks and thighs, but his legs below the knees were thin and bandy, while his feet were long, slender and completely flat. He had an agreeable voice and, in conversation, an animated expression, marred only by the unfortunate habit of continually rolling his eyes upwards.[2]

A number of early portraits of Francis bear out these descriptions. One at Chantilly shows him wearing a black cap, wide-necked shirt, slashed doublet and fur-trimmed cape. His oval face is framed by neatly combed chestnut hair, reaching down to the nape of his neck; the eyebrows are thin and the eyes hazel, almond-shaped and widely spaced; the nose is long, the mouth large with full lips and the chin well defined beneath a nascent beard. A drawing at Leningrad clearly shows Francis's cleft chin. In the well-known half-length portrait attributed to Jean Clouet the king is shown with a full growth of beard. His fondness for fine clothes finds expression in his suit of silk with gold embroidery and his black velvet hat with a white plume and jewels.[3]

Contemporaries often remarked on Francis's eloquence and charm of

---

[1] E. Hall, *Henry VIII*, ed. C. Whibley (London, 1904), i. 200.
[2] P. Morgan, 'Un chroniqueur gallois à Calais', *Revue du Nord*, xlvii (1965), 199. For the original Welsh text see *Bulletin of the Board of Celtic Studies*, xviii (1960), 326–7. I am indebted to Dr P. Morgan of University College, Swansea, for drawing my attention to this source.
[3] P. Mellen, *Jean Clouet* (London, 1971), pp. 49–50.

manner, but it seems that he was shy. 'If a man speak not to him first', wrote Sir Thomas Cheyney, 'he will not likely begin to speak to him, but when he is once entered, he is as good a man to speak to as ever I saw.'[4] There were few things he enjoyed more than a good conversation: he would talk easily on almost any subject, though his knowledge was sometimes superficial; it was the form, rather than the content, of what he said that impressed listeners. Francis was also a good writer. The letters he wrote to his mother during his first Italian campaign are spontaneous and vivid, and some of his poems have an emotive sincerity rare in French poetry of the early sixteenth century.[5] But Francis was, above all, a man of action, who was happiest, it seems, when riding to hounds, tilting in a joust or performing in a masque at court. No joyful occasion at court was complete without such entertainments. Mock battles, reminiscent of those fought by Francis and his friends as children, continued to be a favourite pastime. A most elaborate one took place at Amboise, in April 1518, when 600 men led by the king and the duc d'Alençon defended a model town, complete with a moat and gun battery, against an equal number led by the dukes of Bourbon and Vendôme. 'It was the finest battle ever seen', wrote Florange, 'and the nearest to real warfare, but the entertainment did not please everyone, for some were killed and others frightened.'[6] Another mock siege, held at Romorantin in 1521 as part of the Epiphany celebrations, almost brought the reign to an untimely end. A party of courtiers led by the king attacked a house occupied by the comte de Saint-Pol. As Francis tried to force open the door, one of the defenders dropped a burning log on his head from an upstairs window. The king

---

[4] L.P., iii. 2050.
[5] Francis I's poetry is a subject of great complexity. Many poems attributed to him are now known to have been written by other contemporary poets. Altogether it seems that 205 poems (including *rondeaux, chansons, ballades, épitres, épitaphes* and many shorter poems) can be safely attributed to him. None survives in his own hand or is dated, but most seem to date from before 1535. No collection of Francis's poems was published in his own lifetime or for 300 years afterwards. That edited by A. Champollion-Figeac (*Poésies de François 1er* (1847)) is quite unreliable. The best modern edition is by Dr June E. Kane ('Edition critique de l'œuvre du roi François 1er', unpublished Ph.D. thesis, University of Liverpool, 1977). This rests on a careful examination of many contemporary manuscripts, including B.N., MSS. fr. 879, 1723, 2372, 3940, 25452; Musée Condé, Chantilly, MSS. 520, 521; Bib. de l'Arsenal, MSS. 3458, 5109. The most important of these manuscripts is B.N., MS. fr. 25452, which belonged originally to Guillaume du Bellay, to whom it may have been given by the king himself. I am much indebted to Dr Kane for allowing me to consult her thesis and also to Professor C. A. Mayer of Liverpool for his valuable help in respect of Francis's poetry. A number of poems attributed to Francis were set to music in his own day, mainly by composers in the royal service, such as Sermisy, Janequin and Sandrin. It is unlikely, however, that Francis himself composed. See *The New Grove Dictionary of Music and Musicians*, ed. S. Sadie (London, 1980), vi. 794.
[6] Florange, i. 225–6.

was knocked senseless and for several days his life was in danger.[7] Francis's love of violent sport made him particularly accident-prone: in September 1519 he was almost blinded when he struck a branch while hunting in a forest near Blois, and, in February 1523, he suffered a dangerous injury below the knee after being thrown from his horse.[8]

Hunting was the chief pastime of the French aristocracy when it was not engaged in war. It could take the form of hunting with dogs (*vénerie*) or birds of prey (*fauconnerie*), both forms being represented in the organization of the court. Whereas Louis XII had favoured falconry, Francis preferred riding to hounds.[9] A contemporary illumination shows him chasing a stag in a forest, surrounded by his pack of hounds, his favourite huntsman at his side.[10] In April 1520 Sir Richard Wingfield sent to Henry VIII the following account of a boar hunt at the French court:

soon after three o'clock the said afternoon he [Francis] went to hunt for the wild boar, and caused me to go with him, which boar was killed after such manner as here follows. When he came to the place, in which the boar lay, there was cast off one hound only to him, the which incontinently had him at the bay, and then immediately was thrown off upon a twenty couple of hounds, with three or four brace of mastiffs let slip, all which drew to the bay, and there plucked down the poor boar, and the king, with divers others, being afoot, with their boar spears had dispatched him shortly; and then the king himself, after their fashion, cut off the right foot of the said boar, which done he mounted to horseback, and passed through the forest to have seen a flight to the heron, at the request of M. de Lautrec, unto which disport I assure Your Grace he has no more affection than Your Highness has. Notwithstanding, the said Seigneur de Lautrec with divers others, do what they can possible to fashion one appetite to be in him, which shall be hard for them to bring about, after my conceit.[11]

Francis well deserved the title of 'père des veneurs' given to him in a treatise of 1561.[12] He extended the practice of trapping game by means of large nets and increased the number of huntsmen attached to the court. It was during the reign also that they began to specialize, some being assigned to the greyhounds, others to the white dogs and so on.[13]

In hunting, as in war, Francis displayed great physical courage. During

---

[7] Barrillon, ii. 179; Michaud et Poujoulat, v. 92.
[8] Michaud et Poujoulat, v. 91. On 18 February Sir Robert Wingfield, writing to Wolsey from Malines, reported that Francis had recovered consciousness after being in a coma for two days, but was paralysed on one side 'in so much that, as touching his own person, either in wit or activity for the war, he is not like to do any great feat'. *L.P.*, iii. 2833, 2846.
[9] G. Zeller, *Les institutions de la France au XVIe siècle* (1948), p. 103.
[10] B.N., MS. fr. 13429.
[11] *St.P.*, vi. no. 27, pp. 57–8. I have modernized the spelling.
[12] M. Devèze, *La vie de la forêt française au XVIe siècle* (1961), ii. 57n.
[13] Zeller, *Institutions*, p. 103.

celebrations at Amboise in June 1515 he was dissuaded from fighting a duel with a wild boar only by the combined entreaties of his queen and mother. The boar was pitted instead against dummies in the courtyard of the château, all the exits being blocked. But the boar, after tearing the dummies to pieces, battered its way up a staircase leading to a loggia where the king and his courtiers had assembled to watch the sport. Panic seized the spectators, but Francis, showing as much composure 'as if he had seen a damsel coming towards him', faced the boar and transfixed it with his sword.[14]

Women played an important part in Francis's life, though much that has been written on the subject is mere fantasy. It has been alleged that he had a mistress at the age of ten, that his relations with his sister were incestuous, that he built Chambord to be near one of his mistresses and so on.[15] None of these stories merits serious attention. That is not to say that Francis's life was irreproachable. He had the reputation of being dissolute, and he may have had syphilis as early as 1524.[16] There is evidence, too, that, about the time of his accession, he was having an affair with the wife of Jacques Disomme, an eminent Parisian barrister, and Mary Tudor also complained that he had been 'importunate with her in divers matters not to her honour'.[17] But the truth cannot be sifted from the gossip. Even the king's first official mistress, Françoise de Foix, comtesse de Châteaubriant, remains a shadowy figure. We do not know when the king met her for the first time or when he jilted her. A number of love letters and poems attributed to her and Francis are singularly uninformative and may not be genuine. Françoise seems to have had little or no political influence. She has been held responsible for the appointment of her three brothers, Odet, Thomas and André, to important military commands, but this cannot be proved. Odet had already become a marshal of France by April 1518, when the king and the countess allegedly met for the first time.[18]

[14] P. Paris, *Etudes sur François Premier* (1885), i. 44–7.
[15] Many scabrous stories about Francis can be traced back to the works written in the late sixteenth century by authors associated with the house of Bourbon, who had an interest in discrediting the king. For a list of these stories and an attempted refutation of them see Paris, i. 4–25. The legend of Francis's incestuous love for his sister originated in the eighteenth century and received support in the nineteenth from F. Génin, who misinterpreted one of Marguerite's letters, and from Jules Michelet. For its repudiation see P. Jourda, *Marguerite d'Angoulême* (1930), i. 63–4.
[16] In August 1524 it was reported that Francis was sick 'of his own French disease'. *L.P.*, iv. 606.
[17] With reference to Madame Disomme, there is an interesting correlation between a story told by Marguerite d'Angoulême in the *Heptaméron* (ed. M. François (1942), pp. 203–6) and an entry in *J.B.P.*, pp. 14–15. For a discussion of this see Jourda, ii. 778–9. On Mary Tudor see A. F. Pollard, *Henry VIII* (London, 1913), p. 81.
[18] Paris, i. 118–71.

Three women were pre-eminent at the court of Francis during the first decade or so of the reign: his mother, his sister and his wife. Louise of Savoy, being only in her forties and free from the normal domestic commitments of a wife, was able to devote herself largely to her son's service. She was given a powerful voice in government and served as regent twice, in 1515 and 1524, when Francis led his armies to Italy.[19] Even when he was at home, her influence, particularly on foreign affairs, was considerable. Wolsey referred to her several times as 'the mother and nourisher of peace'.[20] In October 1521 the English ambassador in France advised the cardinal to write to Louise in the hope that she might persuade her son to accept a truce. 'I have seen in divers things since I came hither', he wrote, 'that when the French king would stick at some points, and speak very great words, yet my Lady would qualify the matter; and sometimes when the king is not contented he will say nay, and then my Lady must require him, and at her request he will be contented; for he is so obeissant to her that he will refuse nothing that she requireth him to do, and if it had not been for her he would have done wonders.'[21]

The king's sister, Marguerite, was intelligent, vivacious and physically quite attractive. When she was still a child Louis XII tried to marry her off, first to Arthur, Prince of Wales, then to his younger brother, the future Henry VIII. But their father, Henry VII, was not interested at first in such a match, for it was uncertain that Marguerite's brother would become king of France. In 1505, however, Henry changed his mind and asked for Marguerite's hand for his younger son, then for himself. This time it was Louis who was not interested, while Marguerite said that she hoped to find a suitable husband without having to cross the sea. On 2 December 1509 she married Charles, duc d'Alençon, but it seems that she did not find happiness.[22] The marriage proved childless, and Marguerite, perhaps as an escape from her wretchedness, began to devote herself to pious meditation and good works.[23] In June 1521 she sought the spiritual guidance of Guillaume Briçonnet, bishop of Meaux, a leading reformer within the church: she corresponded with him regularly for three years and through his teaching became acquainted with the ideas of Jacques Lefèvre d'Etaples.[24] She also began to write religious poems, which Simon du Bois published in 1531. Even after her marriage,

---

[19] G. Jacqueton, *La politique extérieure de Louise de Savoie* (1892), pp. 3–10.

[20] J. J. Scarisbrick, *Henry VIII* (London, 1968), p. 92; *L.P.*, iii. 1696.

[21] *L.P.*, iii. 1651.

[22] Jourda, i. 12–16, 31–2.

[23] L. Febvre, *Autour de l'Heptaméron: amour sacré, amour profane* (1944), p. 33.

[24] The correspondence, consisting of 123 letters (59 from Marguerite), is in B.N., MS. fr. 11495. See G. Briçonnet and Marguerite d'Angoulême, *Correspondance (1521–24)*, ed. C. Martineau and M. Veissière, 2 vols. (Geneva, 1975–9).

Marguerite was often at court. She shared her mother's interest in foreign affairs and was frequently mentioned by foreign ambassadors in their dispatches.

As for Queen Claude, she was renowned for her sweet, charitable and pious nature, and, if her looks fell short of the king's ideal, she gave him no cause for complaint on other grounds: over a period of nine years she bore him no fewer than three sons and four daughters. Such intensive childbearing naturally precluded her from any active share in public life, yet she was allowed one brief moment of glory: her coronation at Saint-Denis on 10 May 1516 and her entry into Paris, two days later, were comparable in magnificence to the king's.[25] Unfortunately, Claude's life was short. She died at Blois on 26 July 1524 after a brief illness; and it seems that Francis, who had gone to repulse an imperial invasion of Provence, was genuinely upset. 'If I could bring her back with my life', he said, 'I would gladly do so.' Because of the war, Claude's funeral had to be postponed. Meanwhile, her body was embalmed and laid to rest in a chapel at Blois, where it allegedly performed miracles.[26]

Louise, Francis's first child, was born at Amboise on 19 August 1515, while he was in Italy. He did not rejoice at the news of her birth, as he had been hoping for a son. In the following year, on 23 October, he suffered another disappointment when Claude produced another daughter. She was called Charlotte after the king of Spain, whose ambassador held her over the font at her baptism. In November 1517 Francis walked from Amboise to the shrine of St Martin at Tours to pray for a son, and he was duly rewarded on 28 February 1518 when a Dauphin was born at Amboise. A tide of Te Deums swept through the cathedrals of the kingdom and a rash of bonfires erupted in the towns. So many people flocked to see the prince that Francis had to instruct his chamberlain to admit only members of the royal family or people equipped with a written permit. The baptism of the Dauphin, who was called François like his father, was deferred until Easter to allow for the preparation of 'great triumphs'. The king's second son was born at Saint-Germain-en-Laye on 31 March 1519 and christened Henri after the king of England. On 10 August 1520 Claude produced another daughter, Madeleine. Francis's third son, Charles, was born at Saint-Germain on 22 January 1522, and was followed, on 5 June 1523, by a fourth daughter, Marguerite. Out of all these children only two, Henri and Marguerite, outlived their father.[27]

[25] C. Terrasse, *François 1er: le roi et le règne* (1945–70), i. 125–8.
[26] Jourda, i. 90; Florange, ii. 148–9; Guiffrey, p. 41.
[27] Barrillon, i. 86, 249; ii. 78, 122, 173; Michaud et Poujoulat, v. 89–90; *J.B.P.*, pp. 92, 101, 139; *L.P.*, iii. 289, 306.

The court

The court of France was, of course, much larger than the king's family circle: it comprised his household, the separate households of members of his family and an amorphous mass of hangers-on. Though less magnificent than the court of the dukes of Burgundy, it had nevertheless become by the fifteenth century an important political institution.[28] Whoever had the king's ear shared to some extent in his power.[29] Impoverished nobles went to court in the hope of obtaining offices, pensions and other royal favours, a process which received a boost in the early sixteenth century as inflation began to depress the value of the aristocracy's landed revenues. The king, on his part, welcomed a trend which increased the nobility's dependence on his authority. His 'absolutism' rested essentially on this arrangement.

By 1523 the king's household (*hôtel du roi*), the essential nucleus of the court, comprised 540 officials, more than twice the number inscribed on the payroll of Louis XI's household in 1480. The sixty or so categories of officials included a confessor, almoners, chaplains, doctors, surgeons, an apothecary, barbers, stewards, gentlemen of the chamber, valets, ushers, bread-carriers (*panetiers*), cup-bearers (*échansons*), carvers, squires, grooms, pages, secretaries, a librarian, quartermasters, porters, musicians, sumpters, coopers, spit-turners, sauce-makers, pastry-cooks, tapestry-makers and laundresses. By 1535 the number of officials had increased to 622, and this growth was reflected in the wage bill, which went up from 65,915 *livres* in 1517 to 214,918 *livres* in 1535.[30]

The absence of any major household ordinance for the reign of Francis suggests that he was broadly satisfied with the structure of the household as he found it. His only important innovation was the creation of the *gentilshommes de la chambre* in 1515. Previously the king's most intimate companions had been called *valets de chambre*. By 1515, however, the term *valet* had become so debased in estimation that Francis decided to give his aristocratic companions a title better suited to their social eminence.[31] The gentlemen of the chamber were his constant companions: they had direct access to his presence and followed him everywhere. But they did not all attend at the same time; they had a duty roster, and

---

28 *Comptes de l'hôtel des rois de France aux XIVe et XVe siècles*, ed. L. Douët-d'Arcq (1865), pp. i–xiii.

29 P. S. Lewis, *Later Medieval France* (London, 1968), pp. 121–4.

30 B.N., MS. fr. 2953, fols. 1r–20r; MS. fr. 7853, fols. 255r–262r; A.N., KK. 98, fols. 1r–25v. For some interesting statistics concerning the personnel of each department in Francis's household see B.N., MS. fr. 7853, fols. 339ff.

31 J. du Tillet, *Recueil des roys de France leurs couronne et maison* (1602), ii. 295–6; C. Loyseau, *Cinq livres du droit des offices* (1610), p. 430.

were often employed as ambassadors, which could take them away for considerable periods of time. The effective head of the chamber was the first gentleman of the chamber (*premier gentilhomme de la chambre*), an office held for much of the reign by Jean de La Barre, comte d'Etampes and *prévôt* of Paris. His duties included looking after the crown jewels, holding money for the king's private use and signing contracts for work on royal châteaux.[32] The wages paid to household officials were modest enough – 1,200 *livres* per annum was the norm for a gentleman of the chamber – but the perquisites which they could pick up on the way were considerable. La Barre was richly rewarded with gifts of land, offices and royal revenues.

In addition to the *hôtel du roi*, the court included four special departments: the *argenterie*, which was responsible for the purchase of clothes and furniture; the *écurie* (divided into the *grande* and *petite écuries*), which looked after the king's horses, besides employing a large staff of messengers (*chevaucheurs*); and the *vénerie* and *fauconnerie*, which shared the task of organizing the royal hunts.

Modelled on the king's household, though smaller in size, were those of the queen, the king's mother and the royal children. In 1523 the latter had a staff of 240, including 5 chamberlains, 9 stewards and some 20 pages.

The court also comprised a military section made up of independent units created at different times, the oldest being the *garde écossaise*, founded by Charles VII, which traditionally supplied the king's bodyguard. The *archers de la garde* or *garde du roi* consisted of three companies of a hundred men each, the last being a creation of Francis I. Then there were the *Cent-Suisses*, set up by Charles VIII, and the *Deux cent gentilshommes de l'hôtel*. Except for the Swiss, all these troops were mounted.

Law and order at court was maintained by the *prévôt de l'hôtel* and his staff of three lieutenants and thirty archers. He could punish crimes committed in any royal residence or within five miles of the king's person. When the court was on progress, it was the *prévôt*'s duty to ensure adequate supplies, by requisition if necessary, and to prevent unscrupulous victuallers overcharging.

The finances of the household were administered by the *chambre aux deniers*, whose annual budget was subject to the approval of the *chambre des comptes*. But the king's privy purse (*menus plaisirs*) escaped this control.

Many people not actually on the staff of the court had to attend there frequently on state business. They included councillors, *maîtres des requêtes*, notaries and secretaries. They were allowed to eat under the

---

[32] C.A.F., i. 3086; vi. 20613; vii. 26407.

king's roof and were collectively known as *domestiques et commensaux du roi.*[33]

Finally, there were numerous hangers-on, including merchants and artisans, who were exempt from tolls and gild regulations in return for an undertaking to serve only the crown. Under Louis XII they had numbered about 100; Francis raised their number to 160 in March 1544. Among the hangers-on were the *filles de joie suivant la cour,* who, in accordance with an ancient custom, received a New Year gift of 20 *écus* from the king.[34]

Overall control of the household was vested in the *Grand Maître,* who was also an important minister of the crown. One of his duties was to introduce foreign ambassadors to the king's presence. Other senior court officials included the *Grand Ecuyer* (Master of the Horse), who controlled the royal stables and carried the king's sword on ceremonial occasions; the *Grand Veneur* and *Grand Fauconnier,* who organized the king's hunts; the *premier médecin* and the *Grand Aumônier* (grand almoner), who looked after his bodily and spiritual needs respectively.[35]

The court of Francis I was not only larger than its predecessors; its manners were also more polished, at least on the surface, a change directly related to the growth of Italian influence. As the king of France became a key political figure south of the Alps, Italians sought his aid or protection. Among those who attached themselves permanently to his entourage were Marshal Gian-Giacopo Trivulzio and Galeazzo da San Severino, the Master of the Horse.[36] But the traffic between France and Italy was not one-way only: Frenchmen were given many opportunities, as soldiers, diplomats or administrators, of observing Italian life and manners at close quarters. They found that women in Italy were considered an essential adornment of court society and that close attention was given to literature and the arts. In the light of this experience, the French court became more refined. Sophistication, however, entailed extravagance, particularly with regard to buildings, clothes and entertainment. Frenchmen tried to emulate Italians, often at the risk of ruining themselves, and many looked to the king's favour and munificence to rescue them from the consequences of their prodigality. This was grist to the mill of contemporary satire. Criticism of court life was not new, but it became wider in scope and more barbed in the sixteenth century.

[33] Zeller, *Institutions*, pp. 96, 100–9.
[34] *C.A.F.*, iv. 11551; viii. 29836.
[35] Zeller, *Institutions*, pp. 102–3; R. Doucet, *Les institutions de la France au XVIe siècle* (1948), i. 123–7. Doucet's account of the *grand chambrier* and *grand chambellan* is misleading. Cf. Loyseau, pp. 416, 421–2.
[36] E. Picot, 'Les italiens en France au XVIe siècle', *Bulletin italien*, i (1901), 92–137.

Extravagance was criticized not simply as lack of thrift, but as a sign of physical and moral decay.[37]

Not enough, unfortunately, is known about the day-to-day life of Francis's court, but it seems to have had an established routine. The day began with the king's *lever* in the presence of the principal courtiers and distinguished guests. He would then hold a council meeting and deal with dispatches and other paperwork. Mass would follow at about 10 a.m.; then lunch, during which the king might be read to aloud. Immediately afterwards, foreign ambassadors or deputations would be admitted to his presence. The afternoon was usually left free for hunting or some other open-air activity. In the evening Francis would sup with his family and perhaps offer an indoor entertainment, such as a ball or masque. He was reported as saying that it was necessary to give a ball at least twice a week to live at peace with his subjects, who liked to be kept merry and engaged in some exercise.[38]

Except when an outbreak of plague forced the king to shut himself up in his room, as in October 1520, he was very accessible. The preamble of an ordinance of 1523 states that 'a greater conglutination, bond and conjunction of true love, pure devotion, cordial harmony and intimate affection have always existed between the kings of France and their subjects than in any other monarchy or Christian nation'.[39] This may have been propaganda, but access to the court was certainly easy: anyone who was decently dressed or could claim acquaintance with a member of the royal entourage was admitted, sometimes with unfortunate consequences. In November 1530 Francis complained of ornaments being stolen from his chapel, as well as silver plate and clothes belonging to himself among others. In future, such thefts were to be punished by death regardless of the value of the objects stolen.[40]

In one important respect the French court in the early sixteenth century did not differ from its predecessors: it remained peripatetic. Indeed, as the kingdom grew larger and more peaceful, the court travelled more extensively than in the fifteenth century. 'Never during the whole of my embassy', wrote a Venetian ambassador, 'was the court in the same place for fifteen consecutive days.'[41] But this was exceptional; Francis's movements, as one would expect, were seasonal. In the winter and spring, when the roads were little better than quagmires, he tended to stay put.

[37] P. M. Smith, *The Anti-courtier Trend in Sixteenth Century French Literature* (Geneva, 1966), pp. 57–97.
[38] *Lettres de Catherine de Médicis*, ed. H. de La Ferrière-Percy (1880–95), ii. 90ff.
[39] Zeller, *Institutions*, p. 97.
[40] *Ordonnances*, vi. no. 547.
[41] *Relations des ambassadeurs vénitiens sur les affaires de France*, ed. N. Tommaseo (1838), i. 107–11.

The peripatetic nature of Francis's court was more than a feudal survival: in an age of increasing royal centralization it was vitally important for the monarch to know his kingdom at first hand and to establish personal contact with his subjects. Francis's wanderings were anything but haphazard. Early in his reign he systematically visited many French provinces: Provence in 1516, Picardy in 1517, Anjou and Brittany in 1518, Poitou and Angoumois in 1519, Picardy again in 1520 and Burgundy in 1521. He then became involved in a war with the emperor, so that his movements henceforth were mainly determined by military exigencies. With the return of peace in 1526, however, he resumed his progresses, and, even when his health declined seriously, he continued to roam about his kingdom at regular intervals.[42]

Though Francis's movements were often related to the political or military situation, they were also inspired by more mundane considerations. Travel provided him with opportunities to go hunting. Nothing, it seems, pleased him more than to shed cares of state and vanish, sometimes for days on end, into some deep forest with a few friends of both sexes. He did not enjoy city life, and one can well understand why: by comparison with the cramped and unwholesome conditions of any major town in sixteenth-century France the lure of the countryside of the Loire valley or the Ile-de-France must have been wellnigh irresistible.

Yet Paris was too important politically and economically for the king to ignore it.[43] He did not, as is so often imagined, spend most of his time among the châteaux of the Loire or at Fontainebleau. He visited Paris more often than any other town in his kingdom; he went there at least once in every year of his reign except 1525 (when he was a prisoner in Spain), 1526, 1541 and 1547. He spent a total of more than a month in Paris in each of seventeen years and less than ten days in four. Admittedly, he was not often there in the summer. In the course of his reign he spent a total of only thirty-one days in Paris during August.[44] He stayed there usually in the winter or the spring.

Parisians probably viewed the occasional visits of the court with misgivings. An immature streak in Francis's character found an outlet (but only at the beginning of his reign) in senseless pranks at the expense of the citizens. In May 1517 he and his courtiers shocked the Parisians by riding through the streets almost daily, disguised and masked, and frequenting houses of ill-repute.[45] Two years later some distinguished English visitors were invited to take part in a similar sport. They 'rode daily disguised

[42] *C.A.F.*, viii. 417–20.
[43] *Paris: fonctions d'une capitale*, ed. G. Michaud (1962), pp. 157–8.
[44] These figures are based on the king's itinerary in *C.A.F.*, viii. 411–548.
[45] *J.B.P.*, p. 49.

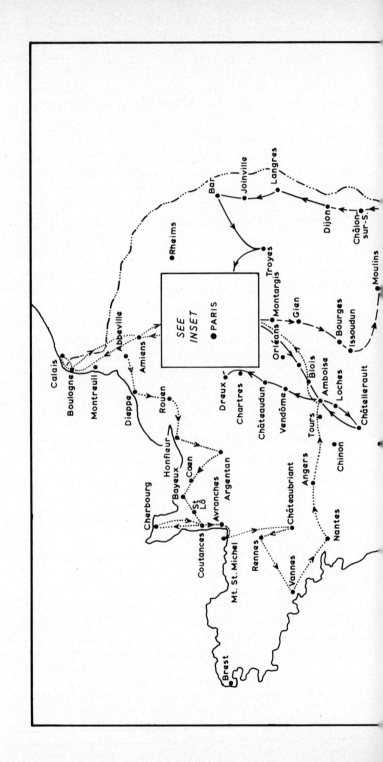

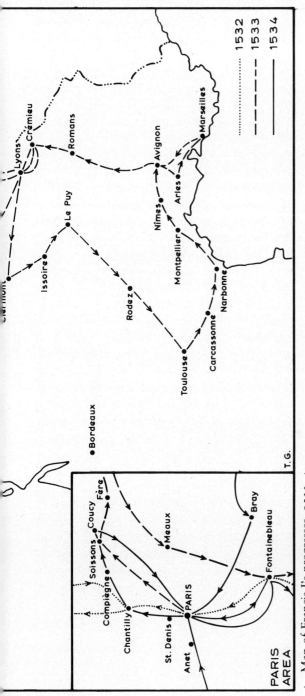

4   Map of Francis I's progresses, 1532–4.

through Paris throwing eggs, stones and other foolish trifles at the people which light demeanour of a king was much discommended and jested at'.[46] Could anything express more eloquently the contempt of the courtier for his social inferiors?

In the course of his progresses Francis visited many churches and monasteries and inspected fortifications, castles and harbour installations. At Marseilles in 1516 he took a trip out to sea to look at a rhinoceros which the king of Portugal was sending as a gift to the pope.[47] Whenever Francis visited an important town for the first time he was given an *entrée joyeuse*. This was a most effective form of royal propaganda. Neither royal proclamations nor official tracts could move the hearts of the people as deeply as ceremonies in which the king appeared in person amidst a *décor* carefully designed to project his personality and the nature of his rule. Impressive as it was, a coronation or royal funeral was seen only by relatively few subjects; an entry had the advantage of being repeated several times within a reign and in a variety of places. Furthermore, it was organized by the townspeople themselves so that they were more closely identified with the mystery of kingship. But this could be rudely dispelled. In 1518, for example, the captain of Brest had to pay 100 gold *écus* 'following artillery accidents during the king's entry . . . as indemnity to the wounded and widows of the deceased'.[48]

From a comparatively simple affair in which the townspeople had offered victuals and sometimes fodder to the king, a royal entry had become by the end of the Middle Ages a magnificent spectacle with religious and political overtones. The king was met outside the town by the citizens, wearing colourful liveries, and escorted into it to the accompaniment of trumpeters and other musicians. The presentation of gifts, which might be money or some costly *objet d'art*, was preceded by an exchange of oaths: the king promised to maintain the town's privileges, and the inhabitants to obey him. After receiving the town keys, the king rode through it in procession under a rich canopy or *dais* along a route that had been carefully prepared in advance. The road surface was usually covered with sand or rushes, and tapestries were hung over the façades of the houses. By the early sixteenth century roadside theatricals had become the rule. The procession culminated in a service of thanksgiving at the town's main church followed by a banquet and jollification lasting well into the night.[49]

One of Francis's most spectacular entries was at Lyons in July 1515, on

[46] Hall, *Henry VIII*, i. 175.
[47] Barrillon, i. 193.   [48] C.A.F., v. 16800.
[49] B. Guénée, and F. Lehoux, *Les entrées royales françaises de 1328 à 1515* (1968), pp. 7–8.

the eve of his first invasion of Italy. As he approached the city he was greeted by a ship towed across the Saône by a white stag. This was to remind him of the legend of Clovis, to whom a stag had indicated a ford by which he might pursue his enemies. The gateway of the city was decorated with a Tree of Jesse and a salamander, flanked by figures representing Lyons and Loyalty. At intervals along the processional route, which had been decorated with the king's colours, young women stood on columns, each holding a letter of his name. Between them, *tableaux vivants* were performed by members of the city's leading families: one showed Francis defending Peace against the duke of Milan and the Swiss bear; in another he appeared as Hercules gathering fruit in the garden of the Hesperides. It was on this occasion, too, that a mechanical lion, designed by Leonardo da Vinci originally for the city of Florence, performed for the king.[50]

The reign of Francis marks an important transition in the development of the royal entry in France. Whereas in 1515 the symbolism of its *tableaux vivants* was still essentially medieval, by 1547 this had incorporated many classical features. The transition was gradual, with medieval and classical ideas existing side by side or even overlapping; but as from 1530 the latter began to dominate. Instead of being acclaimed as a second David or Solomon, Francis was now hailed as a new Caesar. Allegories inspired by such medieval works as the *Roman de la Rose* or the *Songe du Vergier* were displaced by the idea of the Roman triumph. The chariot, the equestrian statue and the triumphal arch began to figure among the entry's ceremonial trappings, albeit in association with the Carolingian and Trojan legends.[51]

Moving the court was like moving an army. According to Cellini, 12,000 horses were used to transport it, and this was an exceptionally low figure. In peacetime, when the court was complete, 18,000 horses were used.[52] Dr Taylor, the English ambassador who witnessed the court's arrival in Bordeaux in 1526, reported that stabling had been provided for 22,500 horses and mules.[53] Nor were these the only animals 'suivant la cour'. Many dogs and birds were attached to it, as well as a lion and a lynx.[54] Often, of course, the court – or at least its more important members – travelled by water. Thus in March 1534 the sum of 627 *livres*

[50] J. Chartrou, *Les entrées solennelles et triomphales à la Renaissance (1484–1551)* (1928), pp. 26–7, 32–3, 37; Terrasse, *François 1er*, i. 85–8; C. Pedretti, *Leonardo da Vinci; The Royal Palace at Romorantin* (Cambridge, Mass., 1972), p. 2.

[51] Chartrou, pp. 49, 62, 69.

[52] *The Life of Benvenuto Cellini Written by Himself*, tr. J. A. Symonds, ed. J. Pope-Hennessy (London, 1949), p. 264.

[53] *L.P.*, iv (pt 1), 1938.   [54] *C.A.F.*, viii. 30314.

was paid to several men and horses 'who have taken the king's great boat and that of his kitchens from Paris to Melun'.[55]

The court's baggage train was enormous: it could include furniture, gold and silver plate, and tapestries. Only royal châteaux that were frequently visited by the court were kept furnished; the rest remained empty from one visit to the next. In the autumn of 1533, when Francis met Pope Clement VII at Marseilles, the sum of 4,623 *livres* was spent on moving the court's furniture, plate and tapestries.[56]

Feeding the court could be a problem. Thus in May 1533 the Venetian ambassador reported as follows from Lyons:

This town cannot accommodate so many men and horses, and this has caused a great scarcity of all things and most especially of lodgings, bread, corn, stabling; and the quantity of bread sold for one French *sou*, equal to rather more than three *marchetti*, is so small, that I never remember to have got less for three *marchetti* in Venice, however great the scarcity may have been there. The poor people eat very coarse and bad bread; corn has trebled in price; and should the court remain here some days longer, the cost will become unbearable.[57]

Finding accommodation for the court was also difficult. Wherever possible Francis stayed in one of his own châteaux or accepted the hospitality of one of his courtiers. Sometimes, however, there was no château; he would then put up at an abbey or an inn, and his followers would seek lodgings in the neighbourhood. This was often a frantic scramble. The bishop of Saluzzo complained of the way in which an isolated house with only a few rooms would be found for the king and the ladies, while the rest of the court were left to find shelter up to six miles away.[58] Sometimes they were reduced to pitching tents. The most famous occasion on which this was done was the Field of Cloth of Gold; normally, however, less magnificent tents were used. As Cellini discovered, the hardships imposed on the court's rank and file could be severe. 'Sometimes', he writes, 'there were scarcely two houses to be found and then we set up canvas tents like gipsies, and suffered at times very great discomfort.'[59] It was partly with a view to solving this accommodation problem that Francis embarked on his spectacular building programme.

[55]   *Ibid.*, ii. 7047.
[56]   B.N., MS. fr. 10390, fol. 33r. An inventory drawn up in 1551 by the heirs of Guillaume Moynier, 'tapissier ordinaire du Roy et gardes des meubles à Fontainebleau', contains objects acquired or inherited by Francis and already listed in an earlier inventory of 1542. They include 213 tapestries, almost all of which are described as 'finely woven in the Brussels manner'. Unfortunately, most of them were destroyed by order of the Directoire in 1797 so as to recover the gold threads. See S. Schneebalg-Perelman, 'Richesses du garde-meuble parisien de François 1er: inventaires inédits de 1542 et 1551', *G.B.A.*, 6th ser., lxxviii (1971), 253–304.
[57]   *C.S.P. Ven.*, iv (1527–33), no. 902.   [58]   Terrasse, iii. 23–4.   [59]   *Cellini*, p. 264.

Blois and Chambord

The early sixteenth century was marked by an outburst of architectural activity all over France, motivated by both functional and aesthetic considerations. Until the mid-fifteenth century the houses of the French aristocracy had been built for defence rather than comfort: they had thick walls, few windows, massive angle towers, machicolations, portcullises and moats filled with water. However, with the return of domestic peace after the Hundred Years' War, the need for such military features disappeared. They were not abandoned overnight, but were now treated mainly as decorations and status symbols. The nobility began to rebuild their homes essentially with an eye to comfort: large mullioned windows appeared in the walls, the angle towers were reduced to graceful turrets and the machicolations became a sort of frieze. At the same time, the Italian campaigns brought the French nobility into contact with Renaissance architecture, and if they lacked the necessary education to grasp its basic principles, they nevertheless responded to its decoration and imported into France such classical features as columns, pilasters, pediments, and medallions, which they applied to the façades of buildings that remained Gothic in structure.[60] A pioneer of this trend was King Charles VIII, who, on his return from Naples in 1495, set a team of Italian craftsmen to work at Amboise. Another was Georges, cardinal d'Amboise, who added Italianate features to his château at Gaillon in Normandy.[61]

Under Francis, the classical influence ceased to be merely decorative and began to determine the structure of buildings. His earliest architectural activities were centred on the Loire valley: at Amboise, where he had spent much of his childhood; at Romorantin, which belonged to his mother; and at Blois, which was the property of his first queen. It is tempting to connect these early activities with the last three years of Leonardo da Vinci's life, which were spent at Amboise. Leonardo's connection with the French court antedated Francis's reign: he had been employed as a painter by Louis XII and as an architect by Galeazzo da San Severino and Charles d'Amboise. But it was only in 1516 that he came to France at the invitation of Francis and settled at the manor of Cloux, near Amboise.

There has been much speculation as to the nature and scope of Leonardo's work for the king of France. One theory is that he was commissioned to build a new palace for the king's mother at Romorantin. The evidence for this consists in part of eighteenth-century descriptions and

---

[60] F. Gébelin, *Les châteaux de la Renaissance* (1927), pp. 5–16; A. Blunt, *Art and Architecture in France, 1500–1700* (Harmondsworth, 1957), pp. 3–13.
[61] R. Weiss, 'The Castle of Gaillon in 1509–10', *J.W.C.I.*, xvi (1953), 1–12, 351.

a map pointing to the remains of an unfinished building, probably of the
early sixteenth century, and, in part, of sketches by Leonardo in the
'Codex Atlanticus'. One of these is the ground plan of a château, flanked
on one side by a road and on the other by a river. The road is described as
'strada d'Ambosa' (road to Amboise) and has been identified with the
present rue des Capucins at Romorantin, which runs parallel to the river
Saudre. Carlo Pedretti, who has made a close study of the Romorantin
project, suggests that it was 'most probably carried to the stage of a
wooden model' and that it was part of an ambitious scheme for a new
city. Be that as it may, the project had been abandoned by 1519. Various
explanations have been offered: the swampy nature of the soil, an
epidemic of plague and the death of Leonardo. Whatever the reason, his
project, if it was ever seriously contemplated, was never put into effect.
Nor can his responsibility be proved for such building as was carried out
at Romorantin under Francis.[62]

Leonardo has also been claimed as the architect of the château of
Chambord, but again the evidence is tenuous.[63] Any direct participation
by him in the actual building can be ruled out, since work on the château
began about September 1519, four months after his death. It also took a
very long time: the marshy soil hampered the laying of the foundations,
and all work was interrupted during the Pavia campaign and Francis's
captivity. In fact, the château was built mainly after 1526, and the
decoration of the upper storeys was not completed till about 1540. By the
time it was finished it was already out of fashion.

The overall plan of Chambord is essentially medieval, consisting of a
square keep, flanked by four round towers from which run lower buildings with towers at the corners. The whole was originally surrounded by a
moat. But the plan of the keep was new to sixteenth-century France: it is
divided into four parts by a Greek cross, the arms of which lead from the
entrances to a double spiral staircase in the middle. This arrangement
leaves a square space in each corner, subdivided into a unit or *appartement* of three rooms. It is generally agreed that this plan is of Italian origin
and related to that of the villa at Poggio a Caiano, which Giuliano da
Sangallo built for Lorenzo de' Medici. Sangallo visited France in 1495, but
returned to Italy soon afterwards and died in Florence in 1516, so he
cannot have been directly responsible for Chambord; but he left behind a
pupil, Domenico da Cortona.[64]

[62] Pedretti, *Leonardo*, passim.
[63] L. H. Heydenreich, 'Leonardo da Vinci, Architect of Francis I' *Burlington Magazine*,
      xciv (Oct. 1952), 277–85; M. Reymond and M.-R. Reymond, 'Léonard de Vinci,
      architecte du château de Chambord', *G.B.A.*, i (1913), 337.
[64] P. Lesueur, *Dominique de Cortone, dit Le Boccador* (1928).

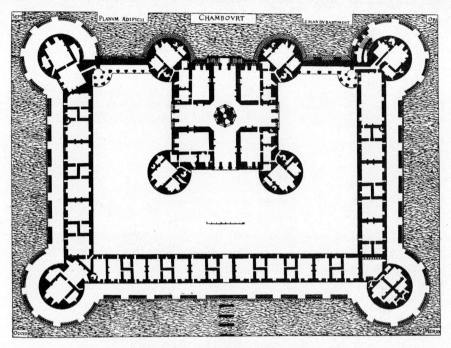

5 Plan of the château of Chambord.

In 1531 Francis ordered payment of 900 *livres* to Domenico for wooden models of various buildings, including Chambord, made over the previous fifteen years.[65] According to André Félibien, the seventeenth-century architect and historian, Francis commissioned several designs before he began to build Chambord. Such designs, including a wooden model for the keep at Chambord, could still be seen in Blois in the late seventeenth century. The model has since disappeared, but Félibien has left us some drawings of it. No one knows who made the model, but Domenico da Cortona is a likely candidate. But if the model seen by Félibien was an early design submitted to Francis for his approval, then whoever put up Chambord chose to depart from it in several respects. The arrangement of the façades is quite different, as is the staircase within the keep: whereas the model shows a straight staircase within one arm of the Greek cross, the actual château has a double-spiral staircase at the central crossing.[66]

[65] L. de Laborde, *Les comptes des bâtiments du roi (1528–1571)* (1878–80), ii. 204.
[66] Gébelin, pp. 69–71. Leonardo da Vinci has been suggested as the inspiration behind the staircase in the model. J. Guillaume in 'Léonard de Vinci, Dominique de Cortone et l'escalier du modèle en bois de Chambord', *G.B.A.*, i (1968), 93–108, points to the originality of this staircase and its affinity with one of Leonardo's sketches. He also suggests that, far from being forgotten, it influenced the straight staircases at the

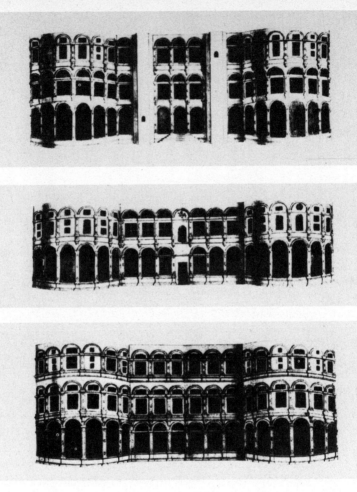

6   Drawings by A. Félibien of a wooden model of a château, possibly a project for the keep at Chambord.

Oddly enough, given the enormous effort and expense which went into the construction of Chambord, it seems to have been little used by Francis. [67] His itinerary, covering the thirty-two years of his reign, lists

châteaux of Challuau and La Muette, which were built for Francis in the 1540s by Pierre Chambige.

[67]   According to a seventeenth-century source (*Jodoci Sinceri itinerarium Galliae* (Lyons, 1616)), Chambord was built by 1,800 workmen over a period of twelve years. The total cost from 1526 until the death of Francis I is given by Félibien (*Mémoires pour servir à l'histoire des maisons royalles et bastimens de France* (1874), p. 32) as 444,570 *livres 6 sous 4 deniers.*

Chambord for a total of only thirty-six days.[68] This figure, however, may be misleading. Chambord was probably not intended to be anything more than a glorified hunting pavilion set in the midst of a huge forest, and we know that when the king went hunting he tended to leave most of the court behind, sometimes for several days, and to be accompanied simply by the gentlemen of his privy chamber and what became known as his 'privy band of ladies'. After a hard day's hunting, he liked to relax, away from the cares of state, in an agreeable silvan setting. This surely was the purpose of Chambord: it was a retreat from Blois, where chivalric fantasy was given play. Tradition has it that when the king and his male companions were out hunting, the ladies gathered on the terraced roof, itself an Italianate touch. It is necessary to make a distinction between châteaux intended for the whole court and what might be described, in the words of Edward Hall, as 'houses of solace and sport', where the king and only a handful of choice companions would gather.

Three châteaux were favourite residences of the court for prolonged periods during the first part of Francis's reign: Amboise, Blois and Saint-Germain-en-Laye. Amboise had been the scene of much building activity, involving Italian workmen, during the reign of Charles VIII. This was continued by Louis XII and Francis, but little remains of their work.[69] A far more impressive survival is the wing built by Francis at Blois. This narrowly escaped destruction in the early seventeenth century, when Gaston d'Orléans planned to rebuild the whole château in the classical style of his day. Shortage of money happily prevented him from accomplishing his purpose, so that the château as it now stands offers four distinct styles reaching back to the Middle Ages. The building accounts show that Francis began work at Blois in June 1515 and continued till the death of his first queen in 1524. His wing was not built *ex novo* as a unified whole, but around an existing medieval building: the 'façade of the loggias' added fifteen feet to the width, turning the old outside wall into an inner one. An exterior spiral staircase on the courtyard side serves to attenuate an awkward rhythmic change in the articulation of the façade. Much has been written on the ornamentation of the 'façade of the loggias', which seems to have been the work of French master masons whose high technical skill was, as yet, not matched by any deep understanding of the rules of classical architecture. Their inspiration, it is generally agreed, was Bramante's work at the Vatican palace; by taking this as his model, Francis showed his desire to keep abreast of fashion as it was set in Rome.[70]

[68] C.A.F., viii. 411ff.   [69] Gébelin, pp. 37–9.
[70] *Ibid.*, pp. 55–62; Blunt, pp. 9–10; F. Lesueur and P. Lesueur, *Le château de Blois* (1914–21), pp. 76–105.

The example set by Francis as a patron of Renaissance architecture was enthusiastically followed by his courtiers. When Thomas Bohier, *général des finances*, acquired the lordship of Chenonceaux in February 1513, he demolished the old castle, except a tower which he kept for his treasure and muniments, and built an elegant residence in the Renaissance style on the foundations of a water-mill. In 1518 more than 400 workmen were toiling, day and night, on the foundations of Azay-le-Rideau, home of another fiscal official, Gilles Berthelot, the king's secretary, between 1514 and 1524; Le Lude was rebuilt at the same time by Jacques de Daillon, the king's chamberlain, while Oiron was begun by Artus Gouffier, the grand master. Chancellor Duprat was building the château of Nantouillet in 1521, and three years later Anne de Montmorency set to work on the long gallery at Chantilly.[71] All over France the early sixteenth century was marked by a frenzy of building comparable with that which England was to experience later in the century when Elizabeth's courtiers erected country houses on a lavish scale.

[71]   Gébelin, pp. 51, 65, 75, 81, 141–2, 153, 155.

7

The loss of Milan

(1520–2)

CHARLES OF HABSBURG was crowned King of the Romans at Aachen on 23 October 1520. Two days later Pope Leo X allowed him to use the title 'Roman Emperor elect'; to become a full-fledged emperor, Charles needed to be crowned by the pope in Italy. But there were problems needing his attention elsewhere, notably the beginnings of the Lutheran Reformation in Germany, the revolt of the *comuneros* in Spain and the intrigues of the king of France.

Francis had hoped to forestall the emperor by going to Italy himself in the autumn of 1520, but perhaps because of his mother's health (she suffered a severe attack of gout, which would have prevented her acting as regent), he remained in France.[1] What is more, early in the New Year he himself was the victim of a serious accident which put his life at risk. Two months elapsed before he fully recovered.[2] Yet even during his convalescence he plotted against the emperor. Early in February he was visited at Romorantin by Robert de La Marck, lord of Sedan, who agreed to serve him in return for a lump sum of 10,000 *écus*, an annuity and twenty-five men-at-arms.[3] Soon afterwards La Marck sent his defiance to Charles and invaded Luxemburg. Francis openly dissociated himself from this action, but few were deceived. 'Though it is called Messer Robert's act', wrote Fitzwilliam, the English ambassador, 'it is done by Frenchmen and at the King's charge.'[4] Francis also took advantage of the revolt of the *comuneros* to reconquer Spanish Navarre for the house of Albret. The small kingdom was virtually defenceless in May, when it was invaded by a French army under André de Foix, seigneur de Lesparre. He captured Saint-Jean-Pied-de-Port without firing a shot, and at Pamplona only the castle offered any resistance.[5]

It is unlikely that Francis intended these moves to be the opening shots

---

[1] Barrillon, ii. 176; *L.P.*, iii. 1100.
[2] See above, ch. 6. Cf. *L.P.*, iii. 1183.
[3] *L.P.*, iii. 1176; du Bellay, i. 107–12; *Fragments de la première Ogdoade de Guillaume du Bellay*, ed. V.-L. Bourrilly (1905), pp. 21–36.
[4] *L.P.*, iii. 1176.
[5] Barrillon, ii. 186.

of a full-scale war with the emperor; he probably meant only to draw his attention away from Italy. But he seriously underestimated Charles's capacity to strike back. On 1 April Philibert Naturelli, the imperial ambassador in France, delivered a strong protest to Francis, accusing him of using La Marck and Henri d'Albret to make war on Charles and warning him of the serious consequences of this policy. On 14 April Francis vigorously denied the charge. Not only had he given no help to La Marck, he affirmed; he had actually forbidden his subjects to serve him. As for Henri d'Albret, if it were true that he had gone south to reconquer his kingdom, then he was only doing his duty, for Navarre had been wrongfully taken from his parents. If Francis were asked for assistance by Henri, it would be difficult for him to refuse. In conclusion, the king accused Charles of looking for a pretext to stop paying the tribute he owed for Naples, and declared his intention of defending himself.[6]

As the king of France and the emperor accused each other of starting a war, they evidently looked to Henry VIII, who, under the treaty of London, was bound to assist whichever of the two rulers was under attack. Henry, however, was unprepared for war, and merely offered his arbitration. Charles immediately accepted it, but Francis refused, after keeping Henry's ambassadors waiting for three days.[7] Meanwhile, the military situation took a dangerous turn for him. In April an imperial army under Henry of Nassau threw La Marck out of Luxemburg and, after overrunning his lordship of Sedan, took up a threatening posture on France's northern border.[8] In Navarre, Lesparre alienated the local population by calling himself viceroy and administering the kingdom as if it were a French province. What is more, he foolishly penetrated Castile just as the revolt of the *comuneros* was being crushed. He soon had to beat a hasty retreat and, on 30 June, was heavily defeated at Ezquiros. Within a few days the whole of Spanish Navarre had reverted to Castilian rule.[9]

In Italy, too, Francis faced trouble. Leo X was tired of his alliance with France, which had brought him more irritation than profit. Francis was always making demands upon him and giving nothing in return; he had been unforthcoming in respect of Parma and Piacenza and had continued to treat the duke of Ferrara as an ally. For several reasons Leo began to think that the emperor would be a more useful ally: as the ruler of Spain and Naples, he was more directly interested in resisting the Turks, and his

6   Barrillon, ii. 180–2; Le Glay, ii. 468–72.
7   *L.P.*, iii. 1303.
8   Du Bellay, i. 120–2.
9   *Ibid.*, i. 104–6; Barrillon, ii. 186–7. The *comuneros* were defeated at Villalar on 23 April.

co-operation was also necessary to the suppression of Lutheranism in Germany. So, on 29 May, after a long period of hesitation, Leo signed a treaty with Charles. The emperor promised to restore Parma and Piacenza to the Holy See, help the pope against the duke of Ferrara and take the house of Medici under his protection. Leo, for his part, promised to crown Charles emperor in Rome and assist him against the Venetians. He also signified his willingness to invest Charles with Naples.[10]

But the treaty was kept secret until the pope was given a suitable occasion for overthrowing his alliance with France. He did not have to wait long. In June, Thomas de Foix, seigneur de Lescun, who had been left in charge of Milan during the absence of his brother Lautrec, entered the States of the Church with an armed force in pursuit of some Milanese rebels. Denouncing this violation of papal territory, Leo proclaimed his intention of allying himself with the emperor.[11] On 28 June he was confirmed in his attitude by a disaster which befell the French garrison in Milan. Lightning struck an ammunition store in the castle, causing a tremendous explosion and the deaths of about 300 French troops.[12] Leo acclaimed the event as a divine punishment on the French and next day made public his treaty with Charles. He accepted from the emperor the white mare which was the traditional token of investiture to Naples. Soon afterwards the pope and the emperor formed a league with the marquis of Mantua and the Florentines, command of its army being given to Prospero Colonna. On 13 July, after several unsuccessful attempts to win back the pope, Francis issued a manifesto complaining of his ingratitude. He also banned the dispatch of all ecclesiastical revenues from his kingdom to Rome, boasting that 'he would ere long enter Rome and impose laws on the pope'.[13] At the end of July he struck at the Florentine bankers in France by levying ransom from them under pain of imprisonment or confiscation of their property. The Lyons bankers alone paid 100,000 *livres*.[14]

Lautrec returned in the meantime to Milan, where he was joined by 10,000 Swiss troops; but he only had enough money to pay for 6,000. Francis advised him to use all the troops, but sent him no money. To make matters worse, the Swiss asked for extra pay as a reward for their swift response to the king's call for help. In order to satisfy them, Lautrec had to borrow from his friends and sell his own valuables, including his collar of

[10] L. von Pastor, *The History of the Popes*, tr. F. I. Antrobus and R. F. Kerr (London, 1891–1933), viii. 35–6.
[11] *Ibid.*, viii. 42–3.
[12] Barrillon, ii. 189–90; *J.B.P.*, pp. 110–11.
[13] Pastor, viii. 46; *J.B.P.*, p. 95.
[14] A. Spont, *Semblançay* (1895), p. 174; *J.B.P.*, pp. 88–9.

the order of St Michael. He repeatedly implored Louise of Savoy and Robertet to persuade the king to send him money, but without success.[15]

The Calais conference (1521)

By the summer of 1521 Francis had good reason to review his policy: La Marck had received a sound drubbing and northern France was under threat of invasion. Navarre was once more in Castilian hands, the pope had turned imperialist and the French occupation of Milan was precarious. The English ambassador noted a distinct change of mood at the French court. 'For about half a year past', he wrote, 'they would by their words have overrun all the world, and cared for nothing save our master; and by as much as I can see, they would now have peace with all their hearts.'[16]

On 9 June Francis decided, after all, to accept Henry VIII's offer of arbitration and, on 20 July, he sent a delegation led by Duprat to a conference at Calais under Wolsey's chairmanship. He was hoping, it seems, to draw back with honour from the dangerous course on which he had embarked, but he wanted peace with the emperor, not a truce which would simply give Charles a breathing space for solving his own domestic problems. But the imperial chancellor, Gattinara, who led the imperial delegation at Calais, argued cogently against a settlement with France. Using the analogy of the conflict between the seven deadly sins and the ten commandments, he showed that if there were good reasons for making peace with France, there were even better ones for continuing the war.[17] Gattinara came to Calais with the specific aim of proving that France had broken the peace as the first step towards an Anglo-imperial alliance.

Wolsey's role at the conference has perplexed historians. Was he genuinely looking for peace or committed in advance to England entering the war on the emperor's side? His behaviour certainly did not inspire confidence among the French delegates.[18] On 6 August, two days after their arrival, he announced his departure for Bruges, ostensibly with a view to persuading the emperor to empower his representatives at Calais to conclude a peace treaty. But the real purpose of his journey, as we now know, was to conclude an Anglo-imperial alliance. Under this treaty, which was signed on 23 August, Henry was to declare war on France if the present hostilities were not ended by the following November. A joint campaign led by him and the emperor would be mounted in May 1523.

15   B. de Chantérac, *Odet de Foix, vicomte de Lautrec* (1930), pp. 56–62.
16   *L.P.*, iii. app. 29.
17   Le Glay, ii. 473–82.
18   Barrillon, ii. 205–16.

Henry's daughter Mary was substituted for Francis's daughter Charlotte as Charles's prospective bride.[19] The Bruges conference has been called 'a monument of perfidy worthy of Ferdinand the Catholic', but a less severe judgment is called for. It is clear that the terms of the Anglo-imperial alliance had not been worked out in advance, for it was preceded by some hard bargaining at Bruges, which detained Wolsey rather longer than he had expected. Nor did Charles get all he wanted from the treaty. He would have liked England to enter the war immediately, but Wolsey secured a respite for his master. Moreover, he persuaded Charles to empower his representatives at Calais to negotiate a truce with France, thereby opening up the possibility of ending the war by November, in which case England's obligation to enter it would lapse.[20]

On 20 August, however, eight days before Wolsey's return to Calais, the emperor launched an all-out attack on France's north-east border. An army under the command of Henry of Nassau and Franz von Sickingen, after capturing Mouzon, laid siege to Mézières. Bayard, who commanded the garrison, proudly rejected Nassau's call to surrender, saying that he and his men would leave the town only across a bridge of enemy corpses. This was no idle boast. For three weeks Nassau battered the walls of Mézières with his artillery, but the town's heroic resistance deterred him from risking an assault.[21] Francis was thus allowed a respite in which to assemble a relief force at Rheims. On 26 August he informed his envoys at Calais that 9,500 Swiss troops had arrived in France and that 3,000 more were on the way. He had summoned the *gendarmerie* of Burgundy and the military personnel of his household, in all some 700 men-at-arms. Vendôme had been ordered to gather 10,000 infantry and 200 cavalry near Saint-Quentin and Laon, and Bourbon to come to Rheims with 6,000 infantry and 200 cavalry.[22]

As long as the fate of Mézières hung in the balance, Wolsey kept up the pretence of arbitration at Calais. The arguments on both sides of the conference table, he declared, were so weighty that he found it difficult to decide who deserved his master's aid. He advised Henry to allow the English wine ships to sail to Bordeaux as usual in the autumn as a means of allaying French suspicions. But the French grew restive as the talks at Calais dragged on without getting anywhere. Their impatience turned to

---

[19] *L.P.*, iii. 1508.
[20] For contrasting interpretations of Wolsey's policy see A. F. Pollard, *Henry VIII* (London, 1913), pp. 145–6 and J. J. Scarisbrick, *Henry VIII* (London, 1968), pp. 83–9. See also J. G. Russell, 'The Search for Universal Peace: The Conferences at Calais and Bruges in 1521', *B.I.H.R.*, xliv (Nov. 1971), 162–93.
[21] Du Bellay, i. 139–42; Barrillon, ii. 264n.
[22] Barrillon, ii. 253 n. 2.

anger when Ardres, which had been left unfortified as a result of English objections, was sacked on 9 September by an imperial raiding party. Francis instructed Duprat to leave Calais unless Wolsey pressed him to remain. Even at this stage the king had not given up hope of a settlement, but his sister was less optimistic. 'See ye not', she asked Fitzwilliam, 'how the cardinal is ever treating for peace almost to the day of battle?'[23] Without mutual trust the Calais conference became little more than a farce, even normal diplomatic civilities being forgotten. For example, when Duprat wagered his head if it could be proved that his master had acted in collusion with La Marck, Gattinara retorted that he would rather have a pig's head, which at least would be worth eating. Absurd claims were also advanced by both sides. Thus Gattinara argued that Charles could lawfully claim the whole of France, since Pope Boniface VIII, in the thirteenth century, had deposed Philip the Fair in favour of Albert of Austria![24]

Late in September, however, the tide of war again turned, this time in France's favour. On 23 September a small French force under the seigneur de Lorges managed to bring supplies to the garrison at Mézières, so that Nassau's hopes of reducing the town by starvation were dashed. Three days later, knowing that Francis was in the offing with a large army, the count lifted the siege and began to retreat towards Hainault, leaving a trail of destruction behind him. The sack of Aubenton by his men caused much indignation in France and was, according to du Bellay, 'the origin of the great cruelties committed in wars for the next thirty years'.[25] Elsewhere, too, the French chalked up successes. In north Italy Lautrec relieved Parma, while on the Franco-Spanish border Bonnivet accomplished an even more notable feat. On 19 October he captured Fuenterrabía, commonly regarded as 'the key to Spain', after a siege of only twelve days.[26]

These French victories inevitably made an impact on the talks at Calais, for Wolsey had no wish to see his master dragged into the war on the losing side. On 4 October he informed Duprat and his colleagues that the emperor and the pope were prepared to sign a conditional truce of eighteen months, but Francis was even less interested in a truce now that success was smiling upon his arms. He was also anxious to use the army he had assembled with so much effort. 'Ye see what charge I am at', he explained to the English ambassador, 'and also how my men eat up my subjects, wherefore I will march on straight, and live upon their countries

23   *Ibid.*, ii. 262n; *L.P.*, iii. 1544, 1552, 1581.
24   Granvelle, *Papiers d'état*, i. 184; Barrillon, ii. 267.
25   Du Bellay, i. 145–52; Barrillon, ii. 263–4.
26   Chantérac, pp. 61–2; du Bellay, i. 154–8.

as they have done on mine.'[27] His plan was to march to the relief of Tournai, now under siege by the imperialists, and give them battle on the way if they tried to stop him. But a sudden change in the weather frustrated his intentions. Torrential rain brought his advance into Hainault almost to a standstill, and, as most of the villages in his path had been destroyed by the enemy, his troops began to suffer appalling hardships. 'Their horses', wrote Fitzwilliam, 'waste sore away by stabling without, and men weary and sick very fast; and for my part, I had never worse journey in all the wars that ever I had been in.'[28]

On 22 October, as the deadline laid down at Bruges for ending the war drew near, Wolsey made a last attempt to secure a truce. The earl of Worcester and the bishop of Ely called on Francis at his camp near Valenciennes, but they found him difficult to deal with. He feared that the emperor would use a truce to marry the king of Portugal's daughter, pacify Spain, raise money and win over France's allies; he would then resume the war. On 23 October, however, Francis missed a unique opportunity of ending the war rapidly. Hearing that the emperor was at Valenciennes, he tried to draw him out by crossing the Scheldt near Bouchain. Most of his army had already crossed the river by the time the imperialists arrived on the scene. They were far fewer than the French and could have been easily routed, but a mist concealed their precise strength from the king, who, after discussing the matter with his captains, cautiously decided not to attack. 'That day', writes du Bellay, 'God placed the enemy in our hands and our refusal to accept him has since cost us dear; he who refuses what God offers through good fortune cannot get it again when he asks.'[29]

By 27 October Francis had lost any chance of relieving Tournai before the winter. He agreed, therefore, to a truce of eighteen months on three conditions: Charles was to promise not to go to Italy in the meantime; he was to allow Francis to revictual and fortify Tournai; and he was to acknowledge Francis's suzerainty over Flanders and Artois. A few days later he reduced his terms by asking only for the right to revictual Tournai, but he absolutely refused to include in the truce the Milanese rebels, whom he regarded as his own subjects. Duprat, meanwhile, advised Francis not to sign a truce, but to use the winter to gather funds for the war and wear down the enemy by a 'guerre guerroyable', or 'dribbling war'. This, he believed, would oblige Charles to sue for peace, whereas a truce would merely be 'the wetnurse of a bigger war'.[30]

27 *L.P.*, iii. 1631, 1651. On 4 October Francis reviewed his Swiss troops at Attigny and marched with them pike in hand.
28 *L.P.*, iii. 1698.   29 Du Bellay, ii. 161–3.
30 Barrillon, ii. 315–16.

As winter closed in and the talks at Calais dragged on, Francis set out to inflict as much damage as he could on Hainault. 'Here', it was reported, 'is the most piteous destruction of towns and spoiling of so fair a country as never have been seen among Christian men.' Charles accused Francis of setting fire to everything and cutting off the fingers of small children.[31] But this was the king's last throw before the winter. On 1 November he began to retreat towards Arras, a move that prompted the emperor to remark that Francis need not have led his army in person just to burn a few villages; this could have been left to a lieutenant. On 10 November at Amiens the king disbanded his army. He posted the *gendarmerie* to various towns of Picardy and sent home the Swiss, save for 2,000 whom he kept to garrison Abbeville. Tournai was left to fend for itself; at the end of the month, it surrendered with Francis's permission.

At this juncture, Francis proposed a truce that would exclude the war in Italy, from which he expected to hear good news.[32] But again disappointment lay in store for him. Lautrec had been obliged to disband part of his army owing to lack of funds; as a result, he was unable to resist an autumn offensive launched by Colonna. He shut himself up in Milan and prepared for a long siege, but his cruel administration of the city, particularly the execution of Cristoforo Pallavicini, an elderly and respected citizen, aroused the indignation of the inhabitants. The imperialists were thus assured of a friendly welcome when they broke through the city's defences on 19 November. Leaving a garrison in the castle, Lautrec retreated first to Como, then to Cremona, where he planned to spend the winter with the rump of his army. The fall of Milan was quickly followed by the expulsion of the French from other cities in the duchy.[33]

The Calais conference, meanwhile, came to an end. Francis's willingness to sign a truce was enough to deter the emperor from doing so. Even Henry VIII began to quibble over it. Wolsey complained that he had been 'sore tempested in mind by the untowardness of the chancellors and orators on every side, putting so many difficulties and obstacles to condescend to any reasonable conditions of truce and abstinence of war that he had found no rest by day or by night'. It was with profound relief, therefore, that he wound up the talks. The French delegation left Calais on 22 November; two days later, Wolsey signed the treaty of Bruges. England was now definitely committed to entering the war on the emperor's side in the following year.[34] Francis used the winter to replenish his coffers in preparation for a new campaign.

[31] *L.P.*, iii. 1715, 1727.
[32] *Ibid.*, iii. 1733; Barrillon, ii. 324–7.
[33] Du Bellay, i. 191–202; Chantérac, pp. 63–70.
[34] *L.P.*, iii. 1728, 1802.

By 1522 Frenchmen were heartily tired of war. 'To hear how the rich and poor lament the war', wrote Fitzwilliam, 'would grieve any man's heart.'[35] But Francis would not give up until he had recovered Milan. In December he had sent an embassy to Switzerland to ask for 16,000 more troops. All the cantons except Zürich complied, but the price they demanded was high. A deal, however, was concluded and the troops set off for Italy almost at once.[36] Francis would doubtless have liked to go himself, but he needed to guard against a possible English invasion of his kingdom. In January he inspected the coastal defences of Normandy and saw his new ship, *La Grande Françoise*, at Le Havre.[37] Henry VIII's pension was stopped, and the duke of Albany returned to Scotland. But, as Francis wanted to concentrate his efforts in Italy, he kept up an outward show of friendship towards England. Robertet told the English ambassador that Henry's pension had only been delayed, and Francis explained that Albany had slipped away against his wishes. Louise of Savoy played her part in this comedy of deceit. She told Cheyney that she would rather never see her son again than see his friendship with England broken.[38]

The battle of La Bicocca (27 April 1522)

The sudden death of Pope Leo X on 1 December 1521 put an entirely new complexion on the situation in Italy. As the flow of money from the papal treasury to Colonna's army dried up, the French were able to reorganize themselves, while enemies of the Medici everywhere in Italy raised their heads. Much, however, depended on the outcome of the conclave which opened on 27 December. Francis was not especially hopeful as to its outcome. 'It is hardly the custom in Rome', he wrote, 'to cast votes under the inspiration of the Holy Ghost.' He warned that if Giulio de' Medici, leader of the imperial faction in the Sacred College, were elected, he would sever his allegiance to the Holy See.[39] The choice of the cardinals in the event fell not on Medici, but on Adrian of Utrecht. Even so, the French reaction was hostile, for Adrian was Charles V's old tutor and regent in Spain. Louise of Savoy said that Charles might as well call himself pope, while Francis at first refused to recognize the new pope, calling him 'the emperor's schoolmaster'. But French sympathizers in Rome took a different view of the election. Cardinal Trivulzio thought Adrian the best man

[35] *Ibid.*, iii. 1971.   [36] Decrue, i. 22.
[37] On 28 February 1521 Francis ordered payment of 2,875 *livres* for the completion of this ship (*Ordonnances*, iii. no. 281). The mainmast was not yet up on 18 August 1522 (*L.P.*, iii. 2446).
[38] *L.P.*, iii. 1946, 1992, 1994, 2036, 2059.
[39] *Ibid.*, iii. 1947, 2203.

for France among the possible candidates, and the French ambassador stressed the new pope's personal reputation. He pointed out also that it would take Adrian six months to travel from Spain to Italy, so that he would not be able to obstruct Francis immediately, even if he were so inclined.[40] Adrian VI, in fact, turned out to be one of the better Renaissance popes; a humble, devout and simple man, he approached his duties in a truly Christian spirit, though his stark austerity offended many people who had become used to a worldly papacy. From the beginning, he denied that he owed his election to Charles and refused to join the league against France. His chief aim was to pacify Christendom and unite its rulers against the Turks, who were threatening Rhodes, the last Christian bastion in the eastern Mediterranean. But Adrian's concern was not shared by the secular rulers of Christendom, least of all by Francis, who subordinated everything to the recovery of Milan. 'We are ready', he told Adrian, 'to make a peace or truce and to come with great power against the Turk, provided Milan which is our patrimony is returned to us.'[41]

In March Lautrec, who had received 16,000 Swiss reinforcements during the winter, laid siege to Milan but, finding it too strongly defended, turned against Pavia instead, thereby enabling Francesco Sforza to reinforce Colonna's garrison in Milan. Francis, who was watching the situation from Lyons, was greatly upset by this; he denounced his captains in Italy as worthless and announced that he would go there himself to put things right.[42] But he was overtaken by events. Soon after Sforza's arrival, Colonna came out of Milan and threatened Lautrec's rear by occupying the Certosa of Pavia, whereupon the marshal lifted the siege of Pavia and marched north to Monza. Colonna followed him at a safe distance, eventually taking up a position in the grounds of a country house called La Bicocca some three miles north-east of Milan. He fortified his camp with deep ditches, an earthen rampart and artillery platforms. Lautrec realized that it would be sheer madness to attack it, but he was not a free agent: he depended on the loyalty of his Swiss troops, who by now had become thoroughly disgruntled with the campaign. Their rations were dwindling fast and part of their pay was overdue. Tired of marching and counter-marching to no apparent purpose, they threatened to go home unless they were given action at once. Lautrec pleaded with them: he explained that their pay had only been delayed and pointed to the formidable strength of the enemy camp. But the Swiss would not listen. On 27 April, therefore, he sent them into action.

The result of the battle of La Bicocca was a foregone conclusion. The

[40]   Pastor, *History of the Popes*, ix. 32–3.
[41]   F. Mignet, *La rivalité de François 1er et de Charles-Quint* (1875), i. 354.
[42]   *L.P.*, iii. 2176.

Swiss pikemen made a frontal attack on Colonna's camp, while Lescun's cavalry tried to outflank it. But the Swiss were met by a fierce artillery barrage, and those who managed to get as far as the rampart of the imperial camp were picked off by Colonna's arquebusiers. Some 3,000 Swiss were allegedly killed, including many captains. Meanwhile, Lescun, who had succeeded in penetrating Colonna's camp, had to withdraw. When Lautrec ordered the Swiss to renew their assault, they refused, leaving him no option but to retire from the field.[43] As he retreated northwards, the Swiss deserted him. They 'returned to their mountains', writes Guicciardini, 'diminished in number, but much more in audacity; for it is certain that the loss they received at Bicocca humbled them to that degree that for several years afterwards they did not show their accustomed vigour'.[44] The Swiss certainly never again tried the headlong assaults with which, in the past, they had swept away enemies of superior strength. Without them Lautrec lacked the infantry necessary to retain control of Lombardy. After a vain attempt to hold on to Lodi, he returned to France, bitterly disappointed and angry. His brother, Lescun, surrendered Cremona soon afterwards, and the French defeat was completed on 30 May, when Genoa capitulated. Francis's reaction to these events can be imagined. He had been hoping each day for news of a victory beyond the Alps, and planning to cross them himself within a fortnight. Now he had lost virtually everything in Italy; only the castles of Milan and Cremona remained in his hands.

A frigid reception awaited Lautrec when he returned to France. For several days Francis refused to see him, but, according to du Bellay, the marshal was eventually given the chance to explain his conduct. He blamed his defeat on the fact that his repeated calls for money had remained unanswered. The king replied that he had sent him 400,000 *écus*, but Lautrec denied that this money had ever reached him. Semblançay, the king's chief financial minister, was asked for an explanation. He confirmed that the king had ordered the money to be sent, but revealed that as it was awaiting dispatch it had been seized by Louise of Savoy. Whereupon Francis called on his mother and accused her angrily of having lost him Milan, but she hotly rebutted the charge; the only money she had taken, she said, were her own savings. Semblançay nevertheless insisted on the truth of his version of what had happened. The king, therefore, decided to hold an enquiry.[45] Du Bellay's account, unfortunately, does not stand up to scrutiny. Lautrec had not been starved of money. His *gendarmerie*, it is true, had not been paid for more than a

---

[43] Chantérac, pp. 70–7; du Bellay, i. 224–31.
[44] F. Guicciardini, *The History of Italy*, tr. A. P. Goddard (London, 1763), vii. 352.
[45] Du Bellay, i. 233–4.

year, but the wages owed to the Swiss had been duly sent. Nor was there a rift between Semblançay and Louise at this time. Moreover, Lautrec's complaint was not among the charges brought against Semblançay in 1524.[46] But du Bellay's story, even if it is a misrepresentation, is an interesting illustration of the contemporary view of Francis's fiscal methods and his mother's rapacity.

[46]   Spont, *Semblançay*, p. 188.

8

Penury and reform

FRANCIS WAS extravagant by nature: he liked beautiful clothes and fine buildings, was generous to relatives and friends and revelled in costly sports and entertainments. Above all, he threw himself from the start of his reign into a wildly expensive foreign policy, so that by 1517 he had already acquired a debt of nearly 4 million *livres*. His prodigality, however, was not the sole cause of his financial difficulties: the complicated tax system and cumbersome fiscal administration he had inherited had much to answer for.

The fiscal administration 1515–23

Broadly speaking, there were two kinds of royal revenue in early-sixteenth-century France: the 'ordinary' revenue (*finances ordinaires*), which the king drew from his demesne, and the 'extraordinary' revenue (*finances extraordinaires*), which he got from taxation. The extraordinary revenue owed its name to the fact that originally it had been levied only for a special purpose and for a limited period, usually in wartime. By the sixteenth century, however, it consisted of regular taxes levied in times of peace and war. The 'ordinary' revenue comprised not only feudal rents, which were fixed and predictable, but also a wide range of variable dues owed to the king as suzerain. Thus he inherited from bastards, from persons who died intestate and from foreigners who died on French soil (*droit d'aubaine*); he received the usual profits of justice and the property confiscated from criminals, such as false-coiners and traitors; he also got a share of the produce of French mines and levied tolls on roads and rivers.

The 'extraordinary' revenue was made up of three main kinds of tax: the *taille*, the *gabelle* and the *aides*. The *taille* was the only direct tax. It was levied each year, the amount being fixed by the king's council, and it could be supplemented by a surtax or *crue de taille*. There were two sorts of *taille*: the *taille réelle*, which was a land tax payable by all irrespective of social rank, and the *taille personnelle*, which fell mainly on land owned by non-privileged commoners. Of the two kinds of *taille*, the first was obviously the fairer, but it was found only in a few areas, including Provence and Languedoc. The nobility and clergy were exempt from the *taille*, but it does not follow that the rest of society had to pay it, for many professional groups (e.g. royal officials, military personnel, municipal officials, lawyers, university teachers and students) were exempt. What is more, a large number of towns (the so-called *villes-franches*), including Paris, were exempt. Thus, if the whole peasantry was *taillable*, the same was not true of the bourgeoisie.

The *gabelle* was a tax on salt. By the late Middle Ages the salt trade had become so important in France that the crown decided to share in its profits by controlling the distribution and sale of salt. But royal control was strongest in the northern and central provinces (*pays de grandes gabelles*), which had constituted the royal demesne of King Charles V. Here, the salt was taken to royal warehouses (*greniers*), where it was weighed and left to dry, usually for two years. It was then weighed again and taxed before the merchant who owned it was allowed to sell it. He was also restricted as to where he could sell it and the amount of profit he could make. In order to prevent illicit trading in salt, of which there was a great deal, the crown introduced the system of *sel par impôt*, whereby every household had to purchase from a royal *grenier* enough salt for its average needs. This burden, however, was less onerous in the sixteenth century than later in the Ancien Régime. Outside the *pays de grandes gabelles* the salt tax was levied in different ways. In the west of France (*pays de quart et de quint*) it was a quarter or a fifth of the sale price, while in Languedoc and adjacent lands it was a sort of tariff levied not when the salt was sold but as it passed through royal warehouses situated at various points along the Mediterranean coast near the areas of production.

The *aides* were levied on various commodities sold regularly and in large quantities. The rate of tax was one *sou* per *livre* on all merchandise sold either wholesale or retail, except wine and other beverages, which were taxed both ways. An important *aide* was the levy on livestock raised in many towns. The *aide* on wine was called the *vingtième et huitième*. But indirect taxation, like the *taille*, was subject to local variations. For a number of reasons too complex to recite here, several parts of France were exempt from the *aides*. Some provinces (Languedoc and Provence) paid neither.

How were taxes collected? The usual procedure in respect of the *taille* was for the leading men of a parish to elect from among themselves an assessor and a collector. The assessment, once completed, was read out in church by the local priest; a week later the parishioners paid their taxes to the collector as they left church. The assessor and collector were not inclined to be lenient, as they were liable to be imprisoned or to have their property confiscated if the sum collected fell below the anticipated amount. Indirect taxes were usually farmed by the highest bidder at an auction.[1]

The most lucrative tax was the *taille*, which amounted to 2.4 million *livres* out of a total revenue of 4.9 million at the beginning of Francis's reign. It was followed by the *aides*, which brought in about a third of the *taille*. As for the *gabelle*, it was bringing in 284,000 *livres* (about 6 per cent of the total revenue) in 1515.[2]

In the early sixteenth century the king of France had more control over the purses of his subjects than any other monarch in western Europe. The origin of his power went back to the reign of Charles VII, who in 1440 began to levy the *taille* without the consent of the Estates General. But even in the sixteenth century the king's power over taxation was not absolute, for he continued to seek the consent of local representative bodies. The most important of these were the provincial estates, which survived in Normandy, Provence, Dauphiné, Languedoc, Brittany, Burgundy and a few smaller areas. Consent to taxation, however, did not carry the right to refuse the *taille* or even to negotiate about it; only increases and surtaxes were negotiable. The main function of the provincial estates, it seems, was to learn what was expected of them by way of additional help to the king, and even in this respect their powers were severely limited. What was perhaps more important to them than the actual burden of tax was its allocation (*répartition*) to the various provincial subdivisions; but only in Languedoc, Burgundy and Provence were they able to control this process; in other *pays d'états* it was handled by royal commissioners. Thus the amount of consultation which took place at the provincial level was not particularly important, and the same was true of town assemblies. Towns that were free of the *taille* could petition the king only if he asked them for a 'forced loan'.[3]

The fiscal administration at the beginning of Francis's reign, like the tax system, had not changed since the reign of Charles VII. It comprised two distinct administrations corresponding with the two kinds of revenue. The first, called the *Trésor*, was responsible for the 'ordinary' revenues. It was headed by four *trésoriers de France*, who had very wide powers. They could farm out parts of the demesne or have them managed by royal

---

[1] G. Jacqueton, *Documents relatifs à l'administration financière en France de Charles VII à François Ier (1443–1523)* (1891), pp. v–ix; M. Wolfe, *The Fiscal System of Renaissance France* (New Haven and London, 1972), pp. 304–65.

[2] A. Spont, 'La taille en Languedoc, de 1450 à 1515', *A. du M.*, ii (1890), p. 369; Wolfe, pp. 99–100, 340; L. S. Van Doren, 'War Taxation, Institutional Change and Social Conflict in Provincial France – The Royal *Taille* in Dauphiné, 1494–1559', *Proceedings of the American Philosophical Society*, cxxi, 1 (Feb. 1977), 70–96.

[3] Wolfe, pp. 25–66.

officials under their control. All royal acts concerning the demesne needed their endorsement (*attache d'entérinement*) before they could be put into effect. Each *trésorier* was responsible for one of four areas (*charges*), called respectively Languedoïl, Languedoc, Normandy and Outre-Seine et Yonne, but these areas did not cover the whole kingdom; provinces which fell outside were subject to a different regime. The *trésoriers* were not *officiers comptables*, that is to say, they supervised the collection and disbursement of revenues, but did not handle them; this task was left to subordinate officials, called *receveurs ordinaires*, who were each responsible for one of the subdivisions of the *bailliages* and *sénéchaussées*. The receiver-general for all revenues from the demesne was the *changeur du Trésor*, who was based in Paris, but only a very small proportion of them ever reached him; for the crown normally settled debts not included in its regular budgets by means of warrants (*décharges*) assigned on a local treasurer. This avoided the expense and risk of transporting large quantities of cash along dangerous roads, while passing on the recovery costs to the creditor.

The four *généraux des finances*, who were in charge of the 'extraordinary' revenues, had virtually the same powers as the *trésoriers de France*, each being responsible for an area, called a *généralité*. But a more complex organization was needed to deal with the 'extraordinary' revenues than the 'ordinary' ones. In so far as the *taille* and the *aides* were concerned, the *généralité* was divided into *élections*, each of which normally coincided with a diocese. There were eighty-five *élections* at the start of the sixteenth century, but they did not cover the whole kingdom. Generally speaking, there were no *élections* in areas which had retained their representative estates (*pays d'états*). The *élection* took its name from the *élu*, whose main function was to make regular tours of inspection (*chevauchées*) of his district, checking its ability to pay taxes and the dependability of his subordinates. He examined claims of tax exemption, judged disputes arising out of the assessment or levy of taxes, and was among the first to advance money to the king in an emergency. He would, of course, reimburse himself later out of the king's revenues. There were usually two *élus* per *élection*, who were assisted by a *greffier* and a *procureur royal*. In each *élection*, too, there was a *receveur de la taille* and a *receveur des aides*, though these offices were often held by the same person.

The personnel responsible for the administration of the *gabelles* varied from one part of the country to another according to the different kinds of salt tax. In the *pays de grandes gabelles* each *grenier* was under a *grenetier*, assisted by a *contrôleur*, while in the *pays de quart et de quint* the tax was farmed out by commissioners. In Languedoc, the *grènetiers* and *contrôleurs* were supervised by a *visiteur général des gabelles*.

Standing on the same hierarchical level as the *changeur du Trésor* and performing the same duties, though in respect of the 'extraordinary' revenue instead of the 'ordinary' one, were the four *receveurs généraux des finances*, one for each *généralité*.

The two fiscal administrations which we have just examined were not entirely separate, for the *trésoriers de France* and *généraux des finances* (known collectively as *gens des finances*) were expected to reside at court whenever they were not carrying out tours of inspection in their respective areas. They formed a financial committee, which met regularly and independently of the king's council, and were empowered to take certain decisions on their own. They also attended the king's council whenever important financial matters were discussed. But their most important duty was to draw up at the start of each year a sort of national budget, called *état général par estimation*, which was based on the accounts (*états au vrai*) sent in from each fiscal district. The payment of expenses foreseen in the *état* required no special authorization from the king, but that of other expenses needed letters patent from the king (*acquits*) addressed to the *trésoriers* or *généraux* and the latter's endorsement in the form of an *attache d'entérinement*.[4]

Francis I's fiscal policies 1515–21

Francis incurred some very heavy expenses from the start of his reign. He had to pay for Louis XII's funeral, his own coronation and Mary Tudor's journey to Abbeville in 1514. But his principal expenditure (estimated at 1.8 million *livres*) was on the preparations for the first Italian campaign. Even after he had won the battle of Marignano, Francis promised 100,000 gold *écus* to Maximilian Sforza as compensation for his duchy. In August 1516 Charles of Habsburg agreed to pay 100,000 gold *écus* per annum to Francis as a tribute for the kingdom of Naples, and this encouraged the king to be even more reckless with his money, as did the pope's permission to levy a clerical tenth. In November 1516 he promised enormous sums to the Swiss cantons in the peace of Fribourg and a month later agreed to pay another large sum to the Emperor Maximilian. By June 1517 Francis had accumulated a debt roughly equal to his regular annual income, yet, in 1518, he paid Henry VIII 600,000 gold *écus* for the return of Tournai. The imperial election, in 1519, cost him 400,000 *écus* and the Field of Cloth of Gold, in 1520, at least 200,000 *livres*.[5]

In June 1517 the king's council decided to levy supplementary taxes

---

[4] Jacqueton, *Documents*, pp. ix–xvii.
[5] A. Spont, *Semblançay* (1895), pp. 120–64.

worth 1,100,043 *livres* in an attempt to reduce the government's deficit of
3,996,506 *livres*.[6] Certain items of expenditure were also cut out of the
budget. In 1520 Francis set up commissions of enquiry aimed at discovering commoners and churchmen who had acquired fiefs without paying
the proper dues. These were of three kinds: the *franc-fief*, a fine on
commoners buying noble land; the *droit d'amortissement*, a lucrative fee
on land falling into 'mortmain' (i.e. transferred to the 'dead hand' of an
ecclesiastical community); and the *nouveaux acquêts*, a fine on land
acquired by ecclesiastical bodies and other permanent associations
which, for some reason, had been excused the *amortissement*. Francis
also set about extending the *gabelle* to areas hitherto exempt from it. He
applied it to Anjou in 1517, but when he tried soon afterwards to do the
same in Brittany, he met with so much local opposition that he had to give
up the idea.[7]

On the evidence of the central records it seems that Francis did not
substantially change either the burden or the structure of French taxes in
the course of his reign. His income from them rose from just under 5
million *livres* in 1515 to over 9 million in 1546, an annual average of less
than 2.2 per cent over thirty-two years. The *taille* rose most in absolute
terms: from about 2.4 million in 1515 to some 5.3 million in 1547. The
rate of the *gabelle* in north and central France trebled, but over the whole
kingdom its value was only about 700,000 *livres* in 1547 as compared to
less than 400,000 in the early part of the reign. Although little dependable
information exists on the *aides* and other indirect taxes, they allegedly
rose from about 1.2 million to 2.15 million. Revenues from the demesne,
on the other hand, did not rise at all. Many lordships escheated to or were
seized by the crown, but they were given away almost at once. Tolls,
chancery rights, feudal dues and the rest brought in about 400,000 *livres*
at the end of the reign, almost exactly the same as in 1523.[8] The only tax

---

[6] *Ibid.*, p. 141.
[7] *C.A.F.*, i. 845–52, 1142, 1237–40, 1258, 1387.
[8] Wolfe, pp. 99–100. But as L. S. Van Doren demonstrates in his study of the *taille* in
Dauphiné ('War Taxation', pp. 93–4), conclusions about the taxing-power of the
monarchy should not be based solely on information derived from documents drawn
up in Paris. Most war taxation in Dauphiné would not have been recorded in such
documents, 'for military costs paid in the first instance by individuals and communities
were reimbursed from provincial levies that were imposed with all the legal force of
royal tailles without actually being destined for the king's coffers. In 1537 and 1538,
for example, the monarchy received no taille payments from Dauphiné because Francis
had waived the dons et octrois; yet the "extraordinary" parcelles during those two
years totaled more than 662,000 livres. If similar systems were used in other provinces
through which troops often passed, then the fiscal power of the central government,
exercised in ways that left few traces in Paris, was much greater than has been
supposed.'

created by Francis was the *solde des 50,000 hommes*, which was imposed on walled towns in 1543 to help pay for the king's army.[9]

It was outside his regular income that Francis innovated most. Taxation, however effective in terms of yield, was slow to collect, and, because of the system of *décharges*, only a small proportion ever reached the king's central treasury. Francis was consequently starved of cash for emergencies and forced to resort to expedients from the start of his reign: he borrowed from bankers and private individuals, imposed forced loans on towns, alienated crown lands and sold offices and titles of nobility. Unlike other sixteenth-century rulers, however, he did not devalue the currency to any significant extent.[10]

It has been suggested that the kings of France seldom borrowed from foreign bankers in the century that followed the Hundred Years' War.[11] But Francis did borrow quite heavily from the Italian bankers of Lyons even at the start of his reign. In 1515 he borrowed 300,000 *écus* from them, granting them in return the farm for ten years of the duties on cloth imported into Lyons.[12] Four years later he borrowed 360,000 *écus* from the Italian bankers in London to help pay for his campaign in the imperial election. In 1520, he obtained more loans totalling 550,000 *livres* from the Italian bankers of Lyons and London.[13] Francis also borrowed large sums from private individuals, and, in 1520, he seized the inheritance of the grand master, de Boisy.[14]

Although many French towns were exempt from the *taille*, they were often asked for forced loans, which could be more burdensome than the *taille*. In 1515 and 1516, for example, Francis asked for sums ranging from 1,500 *livres* to 6,000 *livres* each from Toulouse, Lyons, Troyes and Angers.[15] Paris was asked for a gift of 20,000 *livres* to help defend the kingdom against the Swiss.[16] Sometimes a town was reimbursed for a loan made to the crown by being allowed to levy a local tax, or *octroi*. In July 1516, for instance, Paris was given permission to levy a tax on wine until

---

[9]   In 1522 the most important walled towns were each asked to pay the *solde* of 1,000 infantry and the less important one of 500. In 1538 the *solde des 20,000 hommes de pied* was imposed on the towns as a whole. G. Zeller, *Les institutions de la France au XVIᵉ siècle* (1948), p. 259.

[10] In June 1545 the imperial ambassador Saint-Mauris warned his government that 10,000 crowns had been melted down and mixed with copper etc. to produce 150,000 crowns. These had been paid to the troops that de Lorges was taking to Scotland. *C.S.P. Span.*, viii. additions no. 82; *L.P.*, xx (pt 1), 1069.

[11] Wolfe, p. 64.

[12] Spont, *Semblançay*, p. 122.

[13] R. Doucet, *L'état des finances de 1523* (1923), p. 6.

[14] *C.A.F.*, i. 268, 327, 372, 461, 817, 1263, 1328 etc.

[15] *Ibid.*, i. 233, 283, 467, 1218.

[16] *R.D.B.V.P.*, i (1499–1526), 222.

it had recovered the 20,000 *livres* it had advanced to the king.[17] This was, in effect, an extension of the practice of allowing towns to use local taxes for some worthwhile purpose, such as the repair of walls. But Francis was not content to let towns administer such revenues (*deniers communs*) independently. In March 1515 he created officials called *contrôleurs des deniers communs* and, in July, ordered each town to declare the true value of its revenues. These measures caused much consternation, nowhere more so than in Paris, where the local government successfully resisted the appointment of the *contrôleur*. But this was at the price of granting the king another subsidy of 20,000 *livres*.[18]

Francis also borrowed heavily from his own tax officials. These were invariably recruited from men of substance, not only so that they should be less tempted to cheat the king and his subjects, but also because they were expected on occasion to lend him money. If for some reason the tax yield was lower than expected or expenses higher, a tax official would be asked to advance money out of his own pocket. In return, he would receive a warrant to reimburse himself out of the following year's tax receipts or would be granted a salary increase. This was how taxes were 'anticipated'.[19]

Another expedient much used by Francis was the alienation of crown lands by gift or sale. This was repeatedly opposed by the Parlement of Paris as a breach of the 'fundamental law', which proclaimed the inalienability of the royal demesne. The Parlement also pointed to the adverse effects on the king's 'poor subjects' of any diminution of his 'ordinary' revenue. But Francis would not give way, and, in the end, his alienations were always ratified, albeit under protest. In April 1517, it is true, he resumed all royal lands which he and his predecessors had alienated, but this was an empty gesture; soon afterwards he issued letters of exemption to past recipients of these lands.[20]

Two fiscal expedients which became notorious under Francis were the sale of titles of nobility and the sale of royal offices. The exact number of letters of ennoblement issued by the king is not known because of a fire which destroyed the Chambre des Comptes and its archives in 1737. But, as far as we know, only 183 such letters were issued in the course of the reign, of which 153 were sold. They cost between 100 and 300 gold *écus* before 1543 and considerably more afterwards.[21]

But if Francis showed some restraint in selling titles of nobility, it was he who turned the sale of offices into a system. He sold offices directly to

[17] C.A.F., i. 496.
[18] *Ibid.*, i. 163, 310; *R.D.B.V.P.*, i. 223–36; *J.B.P.*, p. 7.　　　　　[19] Wolfe, p. 65.
[20] Doucet, i. 60–3; C.A.F., i. 102, 115, 379, 578, 648, 676, 742.
[21] J.-R. Bloch, *L'anoblissement en France au temps de François Ier* (1934), pp. 152–97.

bourgeois, who were anxious to acquire the social status attached to them or gave them away as rewards for services rendered or as reimbursement for loans, leaving the recipients free to sell them if they wished. Francis also sold *résignations* and *survivances*, which enabled office-holders to nominate their successors. In the long run, these practices created a serious social situation in which offices tended to become the monopoly of a limited number of families.[22] In addition to selling existing offices, Francis also created a large number which he then put on the market. Here again he was opposed by the Parlement. In 1515, for example, it amended a royal ordinance creating *enquêteurs* in all the *bailliages* so as to reduce the number. But the Parlement was most obstructive when its own interests were at stake. In theory, the king was supposed to choose the Parlement's councillors from a list of candidates submitted by the court, but in practice he often imposed his own nominees.[23]

Semblançay

An important figure in the fiscal administration during the early years of Francis's reign was Jacques de Beaune, baron de Semblançay. The son of a rich merchant of Tours, he had entered the royal administration through Anne of Brittany's household. In 1515 de Beaune was *général* of the Languedoïl, and, as such, played a leading part in gathering funds for Francis's first Italian campaign. From September 1515 until January 1516 he collaborated closely with the regent, Louise of Savoy, being in frequent attendance at her council. In December 1515 she gave him the barony of Semblançay.

After the king's return from Italy in January 1516, Semblançay continued to attend his council whenever financial matters came under discussion. Then, on 27 January 1518, he was appointed *général* attached to the king's person: in other words, he was given the powers of a *général des finances* without any particular geographical responsibility. This meant in practice that he became the chairman of the financial committee of the king's council and kept the *état-général* and *états particuliers*.[24] At the same time Semblançay was put in charge of the accounts of the households of the king, queen and royal children, just as he was already responsible for Louise of Savoy's privy purse.

It was, however, as an agent of credit that Semblançay was probably

---

[22] R. Mousnier, *La vénalité des offices sous Henri IV et Louis XIII* (2nd edn, 1971), pp. 35–92.

[23] Doucet, i. 65–8; E. Maugis, *Histoire du Parlement de Paris* (1913–16), i. 136–86.

[24] He was not given authority over the other *généraux*. It is, therefore, wrong to describe him as a *surintendant des finances*. This office did not exist under Francis I.

most useful to the crown, for, in addition to being a civil servant, he ran his own banking business and was closely related to many leading financiers of the day. His private fortune was such that he could borrow more easily than the king, whose credit inspired less confidence.[25]

The financial crisis of 1521–3

Although Francis resorted to fiscal expedients from the start of his reign, it was only in 1521, after he had gone to war with the emperor, that the gulf between his revenues and expenses became almost unbridgeable. For war had become very expensive, a particularly heavy burden being the hire of Swiss mercenaries. 'These people', wrote Montmorency, 'ask for so much money and are so unreasonable that it is almost impossible to satisfy them.'[26] Yet, as long as Francis lacked an efficient native infantry, he could not do without them.

At the beginning of 1521 Semblançay had in his keeping 300,000 *écus*, which the king had received from Charles V as part of the Neapolitan pension; he also had 107,000 *livres* belonging to the queen mother. When, on 10 April, Louise implored the baron to do everything possible to help her son out of his difficulties, he naturally assumed that she meant him to use her savings as well as her son's. Between 25 April and 15 May he placed 200,000 *livres* at Francis's disposal, but this sum fell far short of the king's immediate needs. On 29 May, therefore, his council decided to raise 187,500 *livres* by alienating crown lands. But this too was inadequate. An *état de l'extraordinaire*, drawn up on 6 June, called for 480,000 *livres* immediately and 220,000 *livres* in each of the following three months.[27] On 13 September Semblançay informed the king that he had only enough money left for one month and urged him to fight a 'good battle' in the meantime.[28]

The war, however, dragged on through the winter, and Francis had to resort to yet more expedients. He decided to raise 120,000 *livres* by creating twenty councillorships in the Parlement of Paris. He gave as an excuse the need to speed up justice, but his mother frankly admitted that the real reason was her son's need of money. She told the Parlement that he would drop his proposal if the court could think of another way of raising the same sum. But the Parlement disliked meddling in financial matters; it therefore resorted to procrastination and eventually gave way.[29] Among other offices created by the king in 1522 were sixteen *commissaires examinateurs* and forty *notaires* at the Châtelet of Paris,

[25] Spont, *Semblançay*, passim.   [26] Decrue, i. 22.
[27] Spont, *Semblançay*, pp. 170–3; *C.A.F.*, i. 1353.
[28] Spont, *Semblançay*, p. 176.   [29] Barrillon, ii. 308–14; Doucet, i. 160–4.

twenty councillors in the parlement of Dijon, twenty *serjents* in the *sénéchaussée* of Guyenne and a *procureur du roi* in every *bailliage*.[30]

Crown lands worth 200,000 *livres* were alienated in February 1522 'to put the kingdom in a state of defence', and the *taille* of 1523 was anticipated to the tune of 1,191,184 *livres*. Unpaid expenses amounting to 2,638,855 *livres* were passed on to the budget for the following year.[31] The king also called on a number of towns to pay for a specified number of infantry. At a meeting at the Hôtel de Ville in Paris he asked for 500. While the Parisians debated the matter, he went to Rouen and persuaded its inhabitants to pay for 1,000. He then returned to the capital and shamed it into doubling its contribution.[32]

Following England's entry into the war in May, Francis made even heavier demands on his subjects. The clergy in particular were badly hit. The king seized the treasure of Rheims cathedral, some statues of the apostles in gold at Laon cathedral and a magnificent silver grille given by Louis XI to the abbey of St Martin at Tours.[33] Many *droits d'amortissement* were levied, and, in December, a subsidy of 1,200,000 *livres* was demanded from the clergy to pay for 30,000 infantry during six months.[34]

An important innovation dating from the same year was the system of public credit, known as the *rentes sur l'Hôtel de Ville de Paris*. On 22 September 1522 the government raised a loan of 200,000 *livres* from the Parisian public against the security of the revenues of the municipality. Each contributor to the loan was assured of a life annuity or *rente*, carrying a rate of interest of $8\frac{1}{3}$ per cent, which was to be paid out of the revenue from a number of local taxes. As the interest payments were entrusted to municipal officials sharing the same social background as the potential lenders, the system was based on a fair measure of mutual trust. Parisians showed little enthusiasm for the new scheme, yet they were duly paid till the end of the reign. The *rentes* of 1522 have been acclaimed as the start of a new era in financial history, yet Francis used them sparingly. The next issue, for only 100,000 *livres*, was not floated till 1536. More *rentes* were sold in 1537 and 1543, bringing the total amount for the reign as a whole to 725,000 *livres*, slightly more than one year's yield from the *gabelles*.[35]

[30] C.A.F., i. 1479, 1528, 1644.
[31] C.A.F., i. 1472; Doucet, *L'état des finances de 1523*, p. 8.
[32] J.B.P., pp. 102–4; C.A.F., i. 1495.
[33] C.A.F., i. 1584–5; J.B.P., p. 135; Spont, *Semblançay*, p. 190; L.P., iii. 2522. The silver grille yielded 60,800 *livres*, which were used to pay for Albany's expedition to Scotland.   [34] C.A.F., i. 1627, 1647–8, 1681–2, 1685, 1713.
[35] P. Cauwès, 'Les commencements du crédit public en France: les rentes sur l'hôtel de ville au XVIᵉ siècle', *Revue d'économie politique*, ix (1895), 97–123; B. Schnapper, *Les rentes au XVIᵉ siècle* (1957), pp. 151–4; Wolfe, *Fiscal System*, pp. 91–3.

Despite all these expedients, Francis was virtually bankrupt in 1523. The *état-général des finances* for that year estimated a total revenue of 5,155,176 *livres* and a total expenditure of 5,380,269 *livres*, leaving a deficit of only 226,069 *livres*. In fact, the situation was far worse, for the officials who had drawn up the *état* were extraordinarily careless: they quoted amounts wrongly, were inaccurate in their sums (sometimes by as much as 100,000 *livres*) and failed to allow for emergencies. They overestimated the king's normal income by 1,961,369 *livres*; yet they also failed to take into account supplementary taxation, such as *crues de taille* and clerical tenths, which in 1523 brought in about 4,641,257 *livres*. Thus the total income, not allowing for the yield from expedients, was 7,835,064 *livres*. Unfortunately for Francis, his expenses were also much greater than anticipated by his officials. They amounted to 8,650,333 *livres*, so that the real deficit for 1523 was 815,269 *livres*. And this is only an approximation; the gap between the king's needs and his resources was almost certainly far wider.[36]

Commission de la Tour Carrée

By the beginning of 1523 there was no money left in the royal coffers, not even from expedients, to meet the costs of the war. The king therefore began to look for new sources of revenue. He suspected that many of the officials responsible for the collection of *deniers casuels* (i.e. revenues not anticipated in the *état-général*) had kept some of this money for themselves and decided to make them disgorge it.[37] On 17 January he set up a commission to examine their accounts and to punish any dishonesty on their part. The commissioners were drawn from the Parlement and Chambre des Comptes. By the end of January 1523 they had examined a number of fiscal officials, notably Guillaume Preudomme, *receveur-général* of Normandy, whose accounts were approved, and Jean Prévost, *commis à l'extraordinaire des guerres*, who was sent to prison.[38]

Not even Semblançay, who had done so much to help the king out of his difficulties, was spared by the commissioners. Indeed, he was the principal object of royal suspicion. But the only fault detected by the commissioners in his accounts was a failure to distinguish clearly between the king's purse and that of Louise of Savoy. This was true particularly of the Neapolitan pension, which had changed hands twice: the king had

---

[36] Doucet, *L'état des finances de 1523*, pp. 9–26.
[37] Louise of Savoy wrote in her diary, 'In 1515, 1516, 1517, 1518, 1519, 1520, 1521, 1522, my son and I were continually robbed by the *gens de finances* without being able to do anything about it.' Michaud et Poujoulat, v. 90.
[38] C.A.F., i. 1730; Doucet, i. 180–4.

given it to his mother, who had then given it back to help pay for the war. Semblançay had entered it among the king's receipts; the commissioners thought it should have appeared among Louise's receipts. After the baron had amended his accounts, they showed that he had lent the king 1,574,342 *livres* and been repaid 662,994 *livres*. Louise's receipts, on the other hand, were now put at 760,267 *livres* and her expenses at 53,000 *livres*. In other words, Semblançay now owed Louise 707,267 *livres*, while the king owed him 911,348 *livres*. Since Louise's money had been used exclusively in her son's interest, Semblançay suggested, not unreasonably, that Francis should repay her directly; alternatively he asked for permission to defer settlement of Louise's debt until he had been reimbursed by the king. On 27 January 1525 the commission gave its verdict: Francis was to settle his debt to Semblançay, which by then amounted to 1,190,374 *livres*, while Semblançay was to pay back 707,267 *livres* to Louise. The baron, however, was given permission to defer settlement of his debt to Louise until the king had supplied him with a *décharge* in respect of the Neapolitan pension.[39]

In short, the commission had failed to uncover any serious dishonesty on Semblançay's part. The only fault that could be imputed to him was the failure to distinguish clearly between the king's purse and that of his mother, but, as the baron himself repeatedly stated, they had always insisted on their purses being identical.

The *Trésor de l'Epargne*

The Commission de la Tour Carrée was only part of a more ambitious scheme to change the fiscal administration handed down by Charles VII. For it was necessary not only to discover and punish corrupt officials, but also to reform or even abolish those institutions which had given their dishonesty scope. Among the king's revenues, those most likely to suffer from corrupt practices were the irregular ones, which were collected and handled in an *ad hoc* way by a large number of officials. Clearly some sort of centralization was needed to ensure that these revenues were properly collected, used and accounted for. But this was not all. Bitter experience had taught Francis the need to build up a reserve of cash, which might be used, in wartime, to meet sudden and unexpected demands and, in peacetime, to buy back parts of the royal demesne that he had been forced to alienate.

The first step taken towards achieving these objectives was the creation on 18 March 1523 of an entirely new official, called *trésorier de l'Epargne*

---

[39] Doucet, i. 186–201; Spont, *Semblançay*, pp. 208–28.

et receveur-général des parties casuelles et inopinées des finances with powers to collect and disburse all the king's revenues other than those from the demesne and regular taxation. Alone among the king's financial officials, he was not subject to the supervision of the *trésoriers* and *généraux*, an independence which he affirmed by taking his oath of office to the king alone. The man appointed to this new post was Philibert Babou, *trésorier* of Languedoïl.[40]

Babou could expect to receive seven kinds of *deniers casuels* in 1523: namely, two and a half tenths that the clergy had agreed to pay as a composition for the *droits d'amortissement*, a contribution of 35,100 *livres* per quarter granted in 1521 by the *villes franches* for the upkeep of infantry in wartime, a loan of 50,000 *livres* and a supplement of 4 *sous* per *livre* demanded of all office-holders, loans from private individuals, the profits from the sale and resignation of offices, and various irregular revenues, domainial and non-domainial, such as fines imposed by the Commission de la Tour Carrée. Unfortunately, it is impossible to put even an approximate total figure on these revenues, as only a tattered fragment of Babou's register for 1523 survives. This shows that he received only 900,000 *livres* from the clergy instead of 1,185,221 *livres*, as expected. Even so, the amount of cash he received during 1523 cannot have been negligible.

The next important step in the reform of the fiscal system was taken by Francis on 28 December, when he greatly increased the powers of the *trésorier de l'Epargne*.[41] He was now to receive *all* the king's revenues after deduction of customary local expenses. He was also empowered to make payments on the authority of royal warrants without the endorsement of the *trésoriers* and *généraux des finances*. This, however, placed too heavy a burden on Babou's shoulders. In June 1524, therefore, he was made responsible only for revenues from the demesne and from taxation (henceforth called the *finances ordinaires*), while a second official, the *receveur des parties casuelles*, was given charge of the rest (henceforth called the *finances extraordinaires*).

How well did the new system work? According to the preamble of the edict setting up the *trésorier des parties casuelles* (9 July 1524), it had already proved extremely successful. The king claimed that he had been spared the need to cut back on wages and pensions and had even managed to clear many debts. But apparently the reforms did not quite achieve all that had been expected of them, for money did not reach the *trésorier de l'Epargne* (at Blois in the first instance) as fast or as plentifully as Francis had hoped. This is indicated by the fact that the old system of disburse-

---

[40] C.A.F., i. 1780.   [41] *Ibid.*, i. 1953; *Ordonnances*, iii. 318–24.

ment was not completely abandoned. In 1528 only about a quarter of the payments effected by the Epargne were in cash; the rest were in *décharges* assigned on local treasurers. But even a quarter was an advance on the old system, and the fact that all payments were now authorized by a single official instead of a dozen meant that the king had more control over the way in which his money was spent. He was also in a better position to know how much cash he had at his disposal for emergencies, as the *trésorier de l'Epargne* had to report to the king's council each week on the state of his holdings. Another important effect of the reforms was the destruction of the influence of the *trésoriers de France* and *généraux des finances*. Their offices were not abolished, for as they were venal the king would have had to refund their purchase price, but their powers were drastically reduced. They continued to make the rounds of their respective districts, but ceased to have any say in policy-making. This was now firmly in the hands of the king and his council.[42]

[42] G. Jacqueton, 'Le Trésor de l'Epargne sous François 1er, 1523–1547', *R.H.*, lv (1894), 1–43; Wolfe, pp. 77–86.

9

Humanism and heresy

FRANCE, LIKE OTHER parts of Christendom, was afflicted by a serious religious malaise at the end of the Middle Ages. This was manifested most clearly in the decay of the church. Prelates tended to live luxuriously far from their flocks, and the lower clergy in poverty and ignorance. The monastic ideal, too, was often disregarded; instead of living in common according to the rules of their orders, monks often kept rooms of their own, where they entertained relatives and friends. Many were seen wandering about the streets of Paris in low company. Public opinion was shocked by the violence, insubordination and coarseness of the mendicant friars, who competed fiercely with parish clergy in administering the sacraments or officiating at funerals. The registers of the ecclesiastical courts for this period contain innumerable instances of clerical violence, drunkenness and immorality.[1]

Yet the condition of the church, deplorable and widely condemned as it was, did not produce scepticism among the people in general. New churches were built and new forms of devotion invented, like the Stations of the Cross and the Rosary. Pilgrimages remained as popular as ever, and no one thought of making a will without including a number of pious bequests. Religious books formed the bulk of the printers' output, and art continued to dwell on sacred themes.[2] True, there was much anticlericalism, but this, far from denoting any loss of faith, stemmed rather from a sharpened awareness of the discrepancy between the Christian ideal and the way of life of many of its professional exponents. Yet the huge popularity of private prayer may have been largely due to the fact that many people were no longer deriving spiritual satisfaction from the teaching of the church. The late Middle Ages witnessed a remarkable flowering of mysticism best exemplified by the Brethren of the Common Life, a movement that originated in the Netherlands at the end of the fourteenth century.[3] Their influence was carried to France by John

---

[1] A. Renaudet, *Préréforme et humanisme à Paris pendant les premières guerres d'Italie* (1953), pp. 10–11.
[2] L. Febvre, *Au cœur religieux du XVIᵉ siècle* (1957), pp. 27–37.
[3] M. Aston, *The Fifteenth Century* (London, 1968), pp. 157–61.

Standonck, who came to Paris to study theology and eventually became head of the Collège de Montaigu. In this capacity, he introduced a curriculum based on the study of Scripture, the church fathers and the *Imitation of Christ*; he also tried to instil a truly Christian humility in his students by means of a harsh discipline. Standonck's activities, however, were not confined to his college. He also tried to reform the French church, but failed to obtain the support of the state and therefore achieved no lasting results. When he died in 1504, the Collège de Montaigu passed under the direction of Noël Béda. Though it acquired more students under the new regime, it lost its mystical character and ceased to be a centre of reform.[4]

The growth of mysticism in the late Middle Ages was also a by-product of an important philosophical revolution, namely the triumph of Nominalism over Realism as a method of interpreting Aristotelian thought. By destroying the validity of universal concepts, Nominalism had cut away the foundations of natural theology. The existence of God and the immortality of the soul ceased to be rationally demonstrable, and revelation had to be accepted with unreasoning submission. Theology consequently became an arid subject and its practitioners, notably the doctors of the Sorbonne or faculty of theology of the university of Paris, mere pedantic quibblers. There was, however, another side to the coin: once reason had been banished as a means of knowing God, contemplation came into its own as an alternative.[5]

Humanism

The triumph of Nominalism did not go unchallenged. From the mid-fifteenth century onwards humanism began to take root in Paris, one of its earliest exponents being Guillaume Fichet, who, in addition to setting up a printing press in the cellars of the Sorbonne, published a number of classical and humanistic texts. Medieval schoolmen were not, of course, ignorant of the works of antiquity, but they approached them in a limited way: in reading Virgil or Cicero, for example, they were content to look for moral precepts or confirmation of their own Christian preconceptions. Fichet's approach to the classics was more perceptive. Thus he drew from his study of Plato the lesson that consciousness of the invisible world of ideas may be achieved through the appreciation of beauty. Poetry and art consequently assumed the character of a divine revelation, and all the works of antiquity, even those that seemed most pagan, suddenly became respectable. An implication of this Platonic approach was for Christian dogma to become more acceptable rationally. Beauty served to bridge the

---

[4] Renaudet, passim. Also his *Humanisme et Renaissance* (Geneva, 1958), pp. 114–61.
[5] D. Knowles, *The Evolution of Medieval Thought* (London, 1962), pp. 328–30.

gulf between faith and reason which Occam's remorseless logic had created.

Fichet was not allowed to work in peace. Such was the enmity of the Nominalists towards him that in 1472 he fled to Rome.[6] But he left behind a number of pupils, including Robert Gaguin, who gathered a circle of friends sharing his admiration of the ancient world. They were helped to discover correct Latin usage by Italian scholars like Beroaldo, Balbi and Andrelini, who, in addition to their teaching, produced editions of classical texts. In 1476 George Hermonymos, a refugee from Sparta, settled in Paris as a teacher and a scribe. But all this humanistic activity was only a beginning: for all their interest in the ancient world, Fichet and Gaguin still regarded scholastic philosophy, particularly that of Duns Scotus, as the only true philosophy. By comparison with books of chivalry and works of scholasticism, the number of classical texts published at this time was still very small.[7]

The first Frenchman to break away significantly from the scholastic tradition was Jacques Lefèvre d'Etaples. Like many others of his generation, he was profoundly disturbed by the state of religion, and in 1472 thought of entering a reformed monastery; but he decided that he could serve religion more effectively by remaining in the world as a teacher. He began to devote himself to the restoration of Aristotelianism by replacing the pedestrian and often misleading translations of the schoolmen. He also wrote commentaries on the *Ethics, Politics* and *Economics* and prepared paraphrases of nearly all Aristotle's works.[8] But Lefèvre's enthusiasm for Aristotle was deeply permeated by mysticism. Along with Ficino and Pico della Mirandola, both of whom he had met in Italy, he believed that beyond Aristotelian logic lay another, more mysterious, world of forces and spirits accessible only to a privileged few capable of absorbing esoteric knowledge. After being attracted to Neoplatonism, he turned to the religious philosophy of Dionysius the Areopagite. Above all, he succumbed to the spell of Nicolas of Cusa, who held that the supreme and unimaginable reality can only be intuitively received through ecstasy.[9] But Lefèvre wanted to reform not only the teaching of philosophy in Paris, but also that of theology. It was high time, he felt, to get away from the interminable and sterile discussions of Peter Lombard's *Book of Sentences* and to study the neglected works of earlier writers. In 1509 he published an edition of the Psalter with a commentary in which

[6] Renaudet, *Humanisme et Renaissance*, pp. 83–9.
[7] *Ibid.*, pp. 114–26. [8] *Ibid.*, pp. 130–55.
[9] *Ibid.*, pp. 207–8; E. F. Rice, 'Humanist Aristotelianism in France', in *Humanism in France at the End of the Middle Ages and in the Early Renaissance*, ed. A. H. T. Levi (Manchester, 1970), p. 143.

theological questions were deliberately set aside and the inner life stressed. Three years later he published an edition of St Paul's Epistles. In short, Lefèvre became a Christian humanist.

The greatest exponent of Christian humanism was, of course, Erasmus of Rotterdam, who came to Paris in 1495. He entered the Collège de Montaigu to study theology, but his real interest lay in the study of classical literature. He joined Gaguin's circle of friends, and in 1499 published a small collection of ancient proverbs. This contained some of the earliest Greek printing by a French press and marked the beginning of a gigantic project for the rehabilitation of classical literature, which was to occupy Erasmus for the rest of his life. But his enthusiasm for the classics did not lessen his appreciation of the Christian legacy; quite the contrary. After making the acquaintance of John Colet in England in 1499, he set out to place the wisdom of the ancients at the service of the interpretation of Christianity and, in his *Enchiridion militis Christiani*, indicated the place of secular learning in the training of the Christian mind: the study of the classics, poetry and philosophy was to be simply the prelude to that of Scripture.[10]

Humanism, then, was established in France long before the reign of Francis, so that the claim, advanced by Jacques Amyot in 1559, that it was Francis who 'happily established and began the task in this noble realm of bringing good letters to a new birth and flower' cannot be endorsed.[11] All that he did was to provide the movement with a large-scale patronage, which it had previously lacked. In 1517 he was anxious to show himself not only as a great soldier, but also as a great patron of learning. The time was ripe for such a gesture, as Europe was for once enjoying a spell of peace; Erasmus even hoped that this was the dawn of a new age. Though not a classical scholar himself, Francis enjoyed the company of intelligent, well-educated men. His entourage included several humanists, notably his secretary Guillaume Budé, his doctor Guillaume Cop, his old tutor François de Rochefort, and his confessor Guillaume Petit.

The most important of these men was Budé, who at the age of twenty-three gave up a life of hunting and hard drinking for scholarship. He learnt Greek almost by himself, became something of a recluse and impaired his health by overwork. His two major works were the

[10] M. Mann, *Erasme et les débuts de la réforme française, 1517–1536* (1934), pp. 24–46.
[11] *French Humanism, 1470–1600*, ed. W. L. Gundersheimer (London, 1969), p. 9. The origins of humanism in France have been traced back to the fourteenth century, when the papacy created at Avignon a cultural centre under the aegis of Petrarch whose influence elsewhere in France was extensive and lasting. See F. Simone, *Il Rinascimento francese* (Turin, 1961), and N. Mann, in *Humanism in France*, ed. Levi, pp. 6–28.

Annotationes ad Pandectas (1508) and *De asse* (1515), but his scholarship, though profound, was long-winded and untidy. *De asse*, a treatise on ancient coinage, contains innumerable digressions in which Budé reveals his ardent patriotism by rebutting Italian claims to intellectual hegemony.[12] Like other northern humanists, Budé was a committed Christian and applied his philological expertise to the study of Scripture. But he was also aware of the fundamentally secular assumptions of classical thought, and, unlike Lefèvre, he saw no possibility of compromise between Hellenism and Christianity. In his last book, *De transitu Hellenismi ad Christianismum*, he went so far as to deny the value of ancient philosophy.[13]

At the beginning of Francis's reign the greatest need felt by humanists in France was for an institution devoted to the teaching of Greek and Hebrew. The king's first response to this need was to appoint a Genoese scholar, Agostino Giustiniani, to teach Hebrew in Paris; but, being an incorrigible nomad, he left after only five years. In February 1517 Francis announced his intention to found a college devoted to the study of classical languages.[14] This, however, was not a new idea. In the fourteenth century there had been a move to set up in France an institution where the so-called Oriental languages (i.e. Greek, Hebrew and Arabic) might be taught, but nothing happened until 1457, when Gregorio da Città di Castello began to teach Greek in Paris; but he left after only eighteen months.[15] By the time Francis took up the idea of a classical college, two had been, or were being, set up elsewhere: a college of young Greeks was founded in Rome by Leo X in 1515, and a trilingual one, at Louvain, by Busleiden two years later.

At the instance of Petit and Rochefort, the king decided to invite Erasmus to take charge of his new college and offered him a rich prebend as a bait. Why did he not choose Budé? This question was asked at the time. In January 1519 Christophe de Longueil expressed surprise that the king should have preferred 'a German to a Frenchman, a foreigner to a compatriot and an unknown person to an intimate acquaintance'.[16] Yet the king's choice is understandable. Budé was as good a Greek scholar as Erasmus, possibly even a more profound one, but Erasmus was the only notable scholar who satisfactorily combined the classical and Christian

[12]   L. Delaruelle, *Guillaume Budé* (1907), pp. 58ff, 161–2; D. O. McNeil, *Guillaume Budé and Humanism in the Reign of Francis I* (Geneva, 1975), pp. 3–36.

[13]   R. R. Bolgar, 'Humanism as a Value System', in *Humanism in France*, ed. Levi, p. 204.

[14]   A. Lefranc, *Histoire du Collège de France* (1893), p. 45.

[15]   G. Di Stefano, 'L'Hellénisme en France à l'orée de la Renaissance', in *Humanism in France*, ed. Levi, pp. 31–42.

[16]   D. Erasmus, *Opus epistolarum*, ed. P. S. Allen and H. M. Allen (Oxford, 1906–34), iii. 473.

elements of the Renaissance and whose international reputation was commensurate with the prestige Francis hoped to gain from his foundation. He had already published his *Enchiridion, Adages*, New Testament and *St Jerome*, as well as many other editions of the classics and early church fathers. He was, as Lefèvre d'Etaples said, 'the splendour of letters'.[17]

Budé was not in the least offended by the king's choice. In fact, he wrote to Erasmus on 5 February urging him to accept Francis's invitation. 'This monarch', he wrote, 'is not only a Frank (which is in itself a glorious title); he is also Francis, a name borne by a king for the first time and, one can prophesy, predestined for great things. He is educated in letters, which is usual with our kings, and also possesses a natural eloquence, wit, tact and an easy, pleasant manner; nature, in short, has endowed him with the rarest gifts of body and mind. He likes to admire and to praise princes of old who have distinguished themselves by their lofty intellects and brilliant deeds, and he is fortunate to have as much wealth as any king in the world, which he gives more liberally than anyone.'[18]

Erasmus, though flattered by the king's invitation and tempted by the rich prebend, valued his freedom too much to tie himself to any prince, however generous and enlightened. He was also afraid of offending Charles of Habsburg, from whom he was receiving a pension. On 14 February, therefore, he wrote to Etienne de Poncher, who had brought him the king's invitation, explaining that he could not leave the Netherlands because of his age, health and indebtedness to Charles. He suggested in his place Heinrich Loriti *alias* Glareanus, a young Swiss humanist.[19] In a letter thanking the king, Erasmus expressed his admiration for what seemed to him like the dawn of a new age, but this merely irritated Francis. 'What, then, are Erasmus's intentions', he asked, 'for he does not explain himself clearly?' In April, Budé and the queen's secretary, Germain de Brie, tried to persuade Erasmus to change his mind, but he would not yield. 'France', he replied, 'has always smiled on me, but so far I have been detained by any number of obstacles.'[20]

Seeing that no good would come out of the negotiations with Erasmus, Francis approached John Lascaris, the head of Leo X's college in Rome, whom he had already invited to France in 1515. Lascaris had then refused for fear of offending the pope; this time, he accepted. The scheme for the

[17] M. Mann, pp. 7–8.　　　　　　　　　　　　[18] Lefranc, pp. 48–9.
[19] Erasmus, *Opus epistolarum*, ii. 454–8.
[20] Lefranc, pp. 53–6; M. Mann, p. 7. Late in 1521 or early in 1522 Erasmus met François de Tournon, the young archbishop of Embrun, at Basle and expressed the wish to visit France. This was for reasons of health, not as a result of any new initiative by the king of France. The archbishop got him a safe-conduct, but Erasmus did not use it. See M. François, *Le cardinal François de Tournon* (1951), pp. 29–31.

classical college, however, was not implemented at once. Francis's enthusiasm had waned during the protracted negotiations with Erasmus, and the French humanists were divided as to precisely what kind of college they wanted. Some favoured a trilingual one on the Louvain pattern; others preferred a college of young Greeks on the Roman model. In the end, Francis decided to set up a college in Milan, probably as a first step towards creating a more ambitious one in France. He allocated 10,000 *livres* for it in addition to an annual payment of 2,000 *livres* for the maintenance of twelve Greek students and two teachers, one of Greek, the other of Latin. Lascaris returned to Italy in 1520 and, after finding suitable premises in Milan, moved to Venice, whence he sent agents to Greece to recruit suitable pupils. Pending their arrival, he worked in the library of St Mark's and collected manuscripts for the king of France.[21] It was largely thanks to him that Francis acquired one of the finest collections of Greek manuscripts in western Europe.[22]

Francis's interest in scholarship, though genuine, was easily supplanted by more urgent considerations, such as war, and needed to be kept alive by subtle promptings and reminders. This was where Budé made an important contribution. Much as he detested court life, he put up with it, if only to remind the king from time to time of his promises and obligations to scholarship. One day Budé followed the king into his chamber after he had dined and began a conversation. At the same time he produced a letter from Lascaris, and the king asked to see it. But Budé failed to respond; whereupon Francis snatched the letter, only to find that it was written in Greek. This enabled the humanist to show off 'like a monkey among a crowd of asses'. He proceeded to translate the letter aloud and so impressed the king that he was then able to tell him 'all that seemed opportune and useful'. In January 1521 he took advantage of Francis's narrow escape from death at Romorantin to remind him of his promise to found a college. The upshot was a formal declaration by Guillaume Petit to the Chambre des Comptes on 22 January to the effect that the king intended to set up a college for the study of Greek at the Hôtel de Nesle, in Paris. It was to comprise a chapel with a staff of four canons and four chaplains, and be maintained with the revenues of the chapels of old royal palaces. This represented a watering-down of the king's original scheme, and Budé was disappointed. 'I would not say', he wrote in September, 'that this zeal [the king's] is completely extinguished; I even believe that it will be revived without difficulty, but it is no longer active. I do what I can to rekindle the fire, which is only smouldering at present, but I lack the ability to influence the courtiers, who sometimes

[21]   Lefranc, pp. 63–74.   [22]   Di Stefano, p. 29.

deride my plans and try unfairly to discredit me.' Lascaris, too, had reason to feel despondent, for he received no more money from France after he had spent 2,000 *livres* recruiting young Greeks. He dug into his own pocket to pay for the college in Milan, but in August 1523 informed Montmorency that he would not be able to keep it going after the end of the month. He received no reply; the college was, therefore, dissolved.[23]

Heresy

French humanism was not a purely intellectual movement: as exemplified by the writings of Lefèvre it aimed at reviving religion through a mystical approach to Scripture. To achieve this, however, it required practical assistance from influential churchmen. Generally speaking, of course, the prelates of Renaissance France were not particularly outstanding as spiritual leaders; former civil servants seldom are. But there were exceptions, notably Guillaume Briçonnet, bishop of Meaux, who, on visiting his diocese in 1518, was shocked to find his flock 'starved of divine food' and poisoned by the superstitious claptrap of the local Franciscans.[24] To remedy this state of affairs, he invited Lefèvre to join him and gathered around himself a group of evangelical preachers, who became known as the Cercle de Meaux. They included Gérard Roussel, Guillaume Farel, Martial Mazurier and Pierre Caroli. After dividing his diocese into twenty-six zones, Briçonnet allocated preachers to each of them for Lent and Advent, while he himself preached every Sunday in his cathedral. Inevitably, this was bitterly resented by the Franciscans, whose very livelihood depended on retaining the loyalties of the people. They lost no time in accusing the bishop and his evangelical friends of preaching heresy and looked to the Sorbonne and the Parlement of Paris for support.

Heresy was not unknown in France at the end of the Middle Ages, but, except in Dauphiné and Provence, where there was an infiltration of Waldensianism from the Alpine valleys of Piedmont, it was not in any sense an organized movement.[25] The registers of the ecclesiastical courts contain no evidence of any movement of dissent comparable in scale to the contemporary revival of Lollardy in England. In 1517 Erasmus described France as 'the purest and most prosperous part of Christendom' and the only country not infected with heresy.[26] This state of affairs, however, did not last long. Two years later Lutheranism first made its

23 Lefranc, pp. 75–82.
24 Febvre, *Au cœur religieux*, pp. 145–61; Imbart de La Tour, iii. 110–15.
25 E. G. Léonard, *Histoire générale du Protestantisme* (1961), i. 240–2; see below, ch. 25.
26 M. Mann, p. 23.

appearance in Paris. The earliest indication of its penetration there is a
letter from the Basle printer John Froben, dated 14 February 1519, in
which he informs Luther that he has sent 600 copies of his works to
France and Spain. 'They are sold in Paris', he wrote, 'and are being read
even at the Sorbonne; they meet with everyone's approval.' In May Pierre
Tschudi, a Swiss student, wrote to Beatus Rhenanus from Paris, saying
that Luther's writings were being received there 'with open arms'.[27] What
these writings were we do not know for sure, but they probably included
Luther's Latin works, the *Opera seu lucubrationes* (1518), which enjoyed
great popularity. Even the Sorbonne, it seems, found itself in sympathy
with much of what he said, particularly his vigorous attack on indulgences, and it was presumably because he knew this that he agreed, on
14 July, to refer his recent debate with John Eck at Leipzig to the
university of Paris.[28] A very long time, however, elapsed before its theologians gave their opinion.

The Sorbonne did not receive the full text of the Leipzig debate until
January 1520, and the committee which had been appointed to examine it
got to work very slowly. Although no detailed record of its discussions
survives, it seems that in the autumn the faculty was so divided that no
agreed verdict was possible. But it was able to change its terms of
reference in the light of recent developments in Rome and in Germany.
On 15 June the pope promulgated the bull *Exsurge, Domine*, giving
Luther sixty days in which to recant or suffer excommunication, and,
later in the year, Luther published the three major works which heralded
his breach with the church (*To the Christian Nobility of the German
Nation, The Babylonish Captivity* and *The Freedom of a Christian Man*).
When, eventually, the Sorbonne published its *Determinatio* (15 April
1521) condemning 104 of Luther's propositions, it based its verdict not so
much on the Leipzig articles as on Luther's more recent works, especially
The Babylonish Captivity.[29]

The unusually long time taken by the Sorbonne over the examination
of Luther's works undoubtedly helped to boost their sale in France. For
more than a year they were left to circulate freely, and scholars were
naturally keen to find out why the faculty's theologians were being given
so much food for thought. Their eagerness was increased by the likely
prospect of a ban on Luther's works. This, of course, was not a step which
the Sorbonne could carry into effect on its own. It could condemn a work
as doctrinally unsound, but it needed the co-operation of the Parlement of

[27] W. G. Moore, *La réforme allemande et la littérature française* (Strasbourg, 1930),
      pp. 46–9.
[28] D. Hempsall, 'Martin Luther and the Sorbonne, 1519–21', *B.I.H.R.*, xlvi (1973), 29.
[29] *Ibid.*, pp. 31–6.

Paris, and ultimately the approval of the king, to prevent its publication and sale.

Where did the king stand in the matter of heresy? It is sometimes suggested that he was tolerant towards it until 1534 and then turned against it. This view, however, fails to take into account the extremely complex and fluid ideological situation that existed in France in the 1520s. As the great historian Lucien Febvre so aptly put it, this was a period of 'magnificent religious anarchy', when clear-cut confessions of faith still needed to be worked out.[30] Where, for example, was the boundary between Christian humanism, as manifested by the writings of Lefèvre d'Etaples and the sermons of the Cercle de Meaux on the one hand, and Lutheranism on the other? Both were strongly influenced by the current revival of interest in the writings of St Paul; both were anxious to revivify Christianity through an improved understanding of Scripture, yet they were not identical. Lefèvre came to share many doctrines with Luther. In his *Commentarii initiatorii in IV Evangelia* (June 1522) he stated his belief in justification by faith and denied the effectiveness of the sacraments *ex opere operato*, but he did not accept all Luther's ideas (e.g. his reduction of the number of sacraments) and continued to hope that the church would reform itself. Lutheranism was for him simply one of many sources of spiritual enrichment.[31] But Lefèvre was not the whole Cercle de Meaux; others were prepared to be more radical, notably Farel, who soon embraced Lutheranism.

As far as the Sorbonne was concerned, heresy was simply any deviation, however slight, from its own narrowly scholastic teaching. It had always been opposed to humanism and believed, not altogether wrongly, that it was responsible for Lutheranism. The point was clearly made by Noël Béda, the faculty's syndic. 'Luther's errors', he declared, 'have entered this [kingdom] more through the works of Erasmus and Lefèvre than any others.'[32] This, however, was not a point of view which the king could be expected to share. He was hostile to heresy and shared the view, almost universally held in his day, that religious toleration was incompatible with national unity. The oath which he had sworn at his coronation bound him not only to defend the faith, but also to root out heresy from his kingdom. It did not oblige him, however, to accept any definition of heresy, even that of the Sorbonne, particularly if it clashed with other principles to which he attached importance or with the opinions of close friends and advisers. Francis had already shown an interest in humanism. He had planned to set up a classical college and had invited Erasmus to

30   Febvre, *Au cœur religieux*, p. 66.
31   Renaudet, *Humanisme et Renaissance*, pp. 213–14.
32   Imbart de La Tour, iii. 258 n. 2.

take charge of it. His entourage included several humanists, and his sister, Marguerite, was a disciple of the Cercle de Meaux. She kept up a correspondence with Bishop Briçonnet from June 1521 until October 1524, and through his spiritual teaching imbibed the ideas of Lefèvre.[33] It has even been suggested that Marguerite became a Lutheran. But this is another simplification. She certainly showed an interest in Luther and, like Lefèvre, shared some of his views, but she never committed herself on certain key points of dogma, such as transubstantiation, and, outwardly at least, remained on friendly terms with the papacy. Her religion has been described as neither Catholic nor Lutheran, but as a strange personal mixture concocted over a long period and culled from a variety of sources, including Luther.[34]

The problem that faced Francis, then, was that of eradicating heresy without stifling the intellectual movement he had encouraged. From the first Francis was uncompromisingly hostile to Lutheranism. On 18 March 1521, even before the Sorbonne had published its *Determinatio*, he instructed the Parlement to examine all printers and booksellers and to ascertain that no work had been published without the university's *imprimatur*. There followed consultations between the Parlement and the Sorbonne, which produced an *arrêt* on 13 June, establishing joint control over the book trade in and around Paris. It now became an offence to print or sell any religious work which had not been approved by censors appointed by the Sorbonne. But the Parlement did not find it easy to enforce this decree. In July the Sorbonne complained about the persistent appearance in Paris of printed works, translated from Latin into French, which were offensive to the Catholic faith. More consultations took place, and a new *arrêt* was drawn up. On 3 August a general proclamation was made 'to the sound of trumpets' in the streets of the capital. All booksellers, printers and other persons having Lutheran works in their possession were given one week in which to hand them over to the clerk of the Parlement on pain of a fine of 100 *livres* and imprisonment. A more eloquent testimony of Luther's success in the French capital could not have been given. Within four months it had been found necessary to turn an academic condemnation into a police measure. But even this failed to check the circulation of Lutheran books. In the autumn of 1521, Melanchthon's reply to the *Determinatio* appeared in Paris, only two months

[33] G. Briçonnet and Marguerite d'Angoulême, *Correspondance (1521–1524)*, ed. C. Martineau and M. Veissière (Geneva, 1975–9). In return for his spiritual guidance the bishop expected Marguerite to gain her brother's support for the cause of reform, but he advised her against being too impetuous. 'Cover up the fire for a time', he wrote, 'for the wood you wish to burn is too green.' P. Jourda, *Repertoire analytique et chronologique de la correspondance de Marguerite d'Angoulême* (1930), p. 85.
[34] L. Febvre, *Autour de l'Heptaméron* (1944), pp. 106–22.

after its publication in Germany. It was an immediate success, and the faculty of arts allowed it to circulate freely among its members, much to the Sorbonne's consternation and anger. An attempt by the theologians to muzzle the students of the junior faculty failed, whereupon they sought help from the king. On 4 November he made any breach of the decree of 3 August punishable by banishment.[35]

Sooner or later trouble was sure to break out between the king and the Sorbonne because of their fundamental disagreement over the nature of heresy. Whereas Francis was ready to act against Lutheranism, at least in so far as the censorship of books was concerned, the Sorbonne wanted to use its powers against Christian humanism as well. The first sign of trouble occurred in November 1522, when the king's confessor, Guillaume Petit, complained to the faculty about sermons which Michel d'Arande had been preaching at court. D'Arande was an Augustinian hermit who had become Marguerite d'Angoulême's almoner on Briçonnet's recommendation; he had the reputation among reformers of preaching 'only the pure Gospel'. The Sorbonne began to look into his activities, but when told that it had incurred the king's displeasure by so doing, it proceeded no further. Petit, for his part, disengaged himself by claiming that his words had been misrepresented. D'Arande was thus able to continue preaching as he followed Marguerite on her travels through the kingdom.[36]

By 1523 the Sorbonne and the Parlement had become seriously concerned about the progress of 'heresy' in France. Lutheran books were reported from many parts of the kingdom, and evangelical preachers were increasingly active. The Cercle de Meaux was no exception: Lefèvre published his New Testament, while Mazurier, Caroli and d'Arande preached far and wide. Clearly, censoring books was not enough; it had become necessary to make an example of some of the heretics themselves. On 13 May the home of Louis de Berquin, a young scholar from Picardy, was searched, and on his shelves were found books by Luther, Melanchthon, Karlstadt and von Hutten. There were also works by Berquin himself, which the Sorbonne wished to examine. The king authorized the examination, disclaiming any wish to protect a heretic.[37] If the Sorbonne had been content to restrict itself to Berquin's works, it might not have run into trouble so soon with the king, but it also tried to examine Lefèvre's *Commentarii initiatorii* and some works by Erasmus. This antagonized Francis. On 18 June the dean of the faculty and some of his

[35] D. Hempsall, 'Measures to Suppress "La Peste Luthérienne" in France, 1521–2', *B.I.H.R.*, xlix (1976), 296–9.
[36] Imbart de La Tour, iii. 226–7.
[37] Doucet, i. 336–9; Moore, *La réforme allemande*, pp. 102–4.

colleagues were called before Duprat and warned of the king's displeasure in the presence of Briçonnet and two other bishops. After administering a general rebuke, the chancellor ordered them to submit by 25 June, to a special commission made up of himself and the three bishops, any passages in Lefèvre's work which they deemed heretical.[38] Francis, in other words, forbade the faculty to exercise its traditional right of judging doctrine, at least in so far as Lefèvre was concerned. Rather than let this happen, the Sorbonne decided not to examine the *Commentarii*, but the Parlement none the less banned its sale. The king once again had to intervene. On 11 July he evoked the matter to the Grand Conseil.[39]

Meanwhile, Francis changed his mind about the examination of Berquin's works. On 24 June he forbade the Sorbonne to proceed with it and handed it over to a special commission headed by the chancellor. His letter, however, arrived too late. The Sorbonne had already completed its work. Berquin's works were condemned on 26 June, and about a fortnight later he was invited by the Parlement to retract his views. This he presumably refused to do, for, on 1 August, his incarceration in the Tour Carrée was ordered. Four days later he was sent to the bishop of Paris for trial on a heresy charge. On the same day, Francis evoked the case to the Grand Conseil, but Berquin had already been handed over to the bishop. The Parlement explained to Captain Frédéric, the king's messenger, why it could not comply with his master's command, but the captain insisted on taking Berquin to the king. Eventually, the prisoner was released and nothing more was heard of his trial: he retired to Rambures and resumed his literary activities. His books, however, were burnt outside Notre-Dame.[40]

Preachers, too, came under attack from the Sorbonne in 1523. On 29 July Béda submitted to the faculty twenty-two heretical propositions allegedly contained in sermons by Mazurier and Caroli, two leading members of the Cercle de Meaux. The two preachers denied that the propositions (the so-called *articles de Meaux*) were a true reflection of their teaching and demanded a public debate. The Sorbonne, however, ignored their request. At the end of September the faculty condemned the propositions and ordered Mazurier and Caroli to appear before it. Bishop Briçonnet was asked, at the same time, to put pressure on them to obey. This marked a change of policy by the faculty: whereas in the past it had been content to judge doctrine, now it was encroaching upon episcopal jurisdiction. The two preachers appealed to the Parlement, but without success: on 16 January 1524 Caroli recanted, and was followed on 12 February by Mazurier.[41]

[38] Imbart de La Tour, iii. 228.   [39] Doucet, i. 339.
[40] *Ibid.*, i. 340; *J.B.P.*, p. 142.   [41] Imbart de La Tour, iii. 230–2; Doucet, i. 343.

The Sorbonne's persecution of the two preachers was really an attack on the whole Cercle de Meaux. In August 1523 the faculty debated the pros and cons of translating Scripture. Some of its more liberal members could see nothing wrong with this, but Béda and his friends managed to carry through a resolution condemning as useless and pernicious all editions of Scripture in Greek, Hebrew and French. This move, which was evidently prompted by the recent publication of Lefèvre's New Testament, forced Francis to intervene yet again. In April 1524 he forbade any discussion of Lefèvre's works on the ground that he was a scholar highly esteemed in and outside France.[42] In October 1523 the king also nipped in the bud an attempt by the Sorbonne to condemn Erasmus. The bishop of Senlis, acting on the king's behalf, asked the faculty to submit a signed statement of the errors allegedly contained in Erasmus's works. This new threat to the faculty's jurisdiction in determining matters of faith had the desired effect: the Sorbonne dropped its examination of Erasmus, while refusing, as a gesture of defiance, to sanction publication of his *Paraphrases*.[43]

Francis's attitude to heresy has often been criticized as inconsistent. But it is difficult to see how it could have been otherwise in the 1520s, when heresy itself was so ill-defined. Francis never consciously tolerated heresy; indeed, he repeatedly urged the appropriate authorities to stamp it out. But he was unwilling to treat as heretics all scholars and preachers who advocated a more evangelical religion, particularly if they were attached to his court or had contacts there. In the words of Marguerite d'Angoulême, her brother and mother were determined to show that 'the truth of God is not heresy'.[44] But in the 1520s it was impossible to distinguish clearly between the two. Only by endorsing the Sorbonne's hatred of both Lutheranism and Christian humanism could Francis have combined orthodoxy with consistency.

[42] Doucet, i. 344.   [43] Imbart de La Tour, iii. 232–5.   [44] Herminjard, i. 78.

10

Treason

THE FRENCH DEFEAT in Italy in April 1522 was followed almost immediately by England's entry into the war on the imperial side. At the end of May Charles V visited England on his way back to Spain from the Netherlands. He and Henry VIII entered London on 6 June 'not merely like brothers of one mind, but in the same attire'. They drew up a plan for a joint invasion of France before May 1523, and Henry promised to send a preliminary expedition across the Channel by August 1522. In the meantime, Sir Thomas Cheyney, the English ambassador in France, submitted completely unacceptable truce proposals to Francis. These were predictably rejected, and the ambassador duly took his leave. On 29 May Clarencieux king-of-arms appeared before Francis and his courtiers in the great hall of the archbishop's palace at Lyons and declared war in Henry's name. According to Louise of Savoy, he trembled with fear as he delivered his message; Francis, on the other hand, delighted the assembled company by his eloquence and scornful reply.[1]

Hostilities between England and France began in July, when the earl of Surrey raided Morlaix; but lack of supplies prevented him from doing anything else until September. He then marched out of Calais at the head of an Anglo-imperial army and tried to provoke the French into giving him battle by destroying as much of their countryside as possible. This, however, only earned Surrey a rebuke for his 'foul warfare' from the duc de Vendôme, who defended Picardy. Within a month the English had exhausted their supplies, and, after an unsuccessful attempt to capture Hesdin, they retired to Calais.[2]

The English invasion of Picardy had, in the meantime, provoked a Scottish attack on northern England. Early in September the duke of Albany marched on Carlisle with one of the largest armies ever assembled in Scotland, but he had no hold over his men. The Scots had grown tired of fighting France's wars. When, therefore, Lord Dacre, Warden of the Marches, offered them a truce, they accepted it with alacrity over the head

[1] L.P., iii. 2290, 2292, 2309; Michaud et Poujoulat, v. 92.
[2] L.P., iii. 2362, 2530, 2541, 2560, 2614.

of their commander. Deeply humiliated, Albany slipped back to France, hoping to raise a new army with which to redeem his reputation.[3] In the spring of 1523 there were many rumours that he and Richard de la Pole, Edward IV's nephew who had fled to the continent in 1501, were preparing some great enterprise against England. The earl of Desmond promised in June to start a rebellion in Ireland, and, in August, Francis ordered the payment of 200,000 *livres* to Pole. But for some unknown reason the enterprise never materialized. Five hundred French troops were sent to Scotland in June, but another three months elapsed before Albany followed them with a much larger force.[4]

Francis, in the meantime, prepared to invade Italy, but he had to face a hostile coalition of Italian powers, including his former ally, the Venetians, and Pope Adrian VI. The latter had been deeply distressed by the capture of Rhodes by the Turks in December. On 3 March he called on the Christian princes to sign a peace treaty or a truce as the first step towards a new crusade. Francis replied that, much as he favoured such a move, Milan must be restored to him first. At about the same time, Franco-papal relations were seriously damaged when letters written by Cardinal Soderini, leader of the French faction in the Sacred College, fell into the hands of Cardinal Medici. In these letters Soderini urged Francis to invade Italy, gave details of a planned revolt in Sicily and described the pope as an imperialist. Adrian, indignant that his policy should be misrepresented in this way, ordered Soderini's imprisonment, and Cardinal Medici, who had been living in Florence since the last conclave, returned triumphantly to Rome. Francis interpreted Soderini's disgrace as a hostile act; he also objected strongly to a papal bull of 30 April ordering the princes of Christendom to sign a truce under pain of spiritual censures. The pope, he declared, was forbidden by canon law to impose such a truce. He threatened to set up an antipope and reminded Adrian of the fate that had befallen his predecessor, Boniface VIII, when he had dared to oppose Philip the Fair.[5]

Francis's insolence simply played into the hands of his enemies. Adrian did not abandon his neutrality at once, for reasons which he outlined to the viceroy of Naples. 'I shall not declare myself against France', he wrote, 'because such a step would be immediately followed by the stoppage of all supplies of money from that kingdom, on which I chiefly depend for the maintenance of my Court, and because I know on good authority that the French king would become a protector of the Lutheran heresy and make a

[3] *Ibid.*, iii. 2524, 2532, 2536, 2645.
[4] *Ibid.*, iii. 2755, 2768, 2799, 2870, 3118; *C.A.F.*, i. 1858.
[5] L. von Pastor, *The History of the Popes*, tr. F. I. Antrobus and R. F. Kerr (London, 1891–1933), ix. 174, 185–8, 195, 197–200.

resettlement of the ecclesiastical order in his dominions.'[6] On 18 June, however, Francis forbade the dispatch of all sums of money from his kingdom to Rome; he also dismissed the papal nuncio from his court. These intemperate measures finally drove the pope into the enemy camp: on 3 August Adrian joined the league for the defence of Italy. This, however, was to be his last important political act: he fell ill soon afterwards and, on 14 September, died. A rumour that he had been poisoned by a French agent was disproved by the autopsy.

Francis, in the meantime, completed his preparations to invade Italy. On 23 July he attended high mass at the abbey of Saint-Denis, the saint's relics being, as usual, placed on the high altar for the duration of the forthcoming campaign. Next day the king formally took leave of the Parisians at the Hôtel de Ville. He thanked them for their financial aid and recommended the queen and his mother to them. The court then travelled south to Gien-sur-Loire, where, on 12 August, Louise of Savoy was appointed regent for the second time.[7] She and Queen Claude then went to Blois, while Francis set off for Lyons. So far all had gone according to plan. On about 16 August, however, at Saint-Pierre-le-Moûtier, the king received a letter from Louis de Brézé, *grand sénéchal* of Normandy, warning him of a treason plot by the duc de Bourbon.

Charles III, duc de Bourbon, belonged to the younger branch of the house founded in the fourteenth century by Robert de Clermont, sixth son of King Louis IX. In 1443 the territory owned by this house in central France had been divided between Louis and Charles, the two sons of the duc Jean I, and for a time it looked as if the two branches would go their separate ways. In 1488, however, the lands of the elder branch passed into the hands of Pierre de Beaujeu, who, having no son, bequeathed his property, with the king's permission, to his daughter, Suzanne. Her right of inheritance, however, was challenged by her cousin Charles, head of the younger branch of Bourbon-Montpensier, the future constable. The quarrel was submitted to the Parlement of Paris and an ingenious solution found: Suzanne and Charles were married, the lands of the two branches being thus reunited. In 1521, the Bourbon demesne comprised three duchies, seven counties, two *vicomtés* and seven lordships, forming an unusually compact block of territory in central France, and had its own distinct administration, including a high court of justice. Within his demesne the duke was all-powerful: he could raise troops, levy taxes, dispense justice and summon the estates. He owned several fortresses, and his castle at Moulins was among the largest in France.[8]

[6] *Ibid.*, ix. 201.
[7] *J.B.P.*, pp. 116–17; Versoris, pp. 31–2; *Ordonnances*, iii. 282–9.
[8] Doucet, i. 203–15; A. Lebey, *Le connétable de Bourbon* (1904), pp. 10–24, 122.

Until 1521 Bourbon's relations with the king had been friendly rather than intimate. Francis paid tribute to the constable's valour at Marignano and, in January 1516, appointed him lieutenant-general in Milan. But it seems that Bourbon had to pay his troops out of his own pocket. According to his secretary, Marillac, he did not receive a single *denier* from the royal treasury during the whole of the Marignano campaign. This, however, was nothing new: Louis XII had also failed to pay Bourbon's expenses on several occasions. Yet the duke managed well enough. It was largely due to his efficient administration that the Emperor Maximilian failed to capture Milan in 1516. Soon afterwards the constable was recalled to France and replaced as lieutenant-general by Lautrec. This, however, was nothing more than a formality. Bourbon was warmly received by the king and his mother on his return to France, and thereafter was often at court: in 1517 Francis went to Moulins to be godfather at the christening of Bourbon's short-lived son, in 1518 the constable took part in a tournament to celebrate the Dauphin's birth, in 1519 he and the king celebrated Christmas together at Châtellerault, and in 1520 Bourbon figured prominently at the Field of Cloth of Gold. Thus it is difficult to believe that Bourbon had been systematically persecuted by the king for reasons of jealousy from 1516 onwards, as some historians have suggested.[9]

The first sign of a rift between Francis and the constable occurred in the autumn of 1521 during the campaign against Charles V in northern France.[10] Having assembled a formidable army near Rheims, Francis gave command of the vanguard to Alençon and of the rearguard to Vendôme, while he himself took charge of the 'battle'. This was an unusual arrangement; normally, the constable commanded the vanguard when the king was in charge of the army. Bourbon was apparently offended but concealed his feelings.[11] Yet he captured Hesdin for the king later that year. The reason for the sudden deterioration of the relations between Francis and the constable was almost certainly the death of Bourbon's wife, Suzanne, on 28 April 1521, which raised two issues of fundamental significance: first, the inheritance of the elder branch of the house of Bourbon and, secondly, the constable's remarriage.

Suzanne had made a will in favour of her husband and of any children he might have by another wife, but its validity was challenged by Louise of Savoy, who claimed Suzanne's inheritance as her nearest relative, and by Francis, who argued that it had escheated to the crown. Both claims

---

[9] Lebey, pp. 90–1; Doucet, i. 218.

[10] See above, ch. 7.

[11] 'Some say', wrote Fitzwilliam, 'that Monsieur de Bourbon is not contented that he hath not the vaward, but I know not that of a surety.' *L.P.*, iii. 1651; du Bellay, i. 159.

were submitted to the Parlement of Paris in April 1522, and were naturally resisted by Bourbon and his mother-in-law, Anne de France. But
the king did not wait for the Parlement's verdict to dispose of some of
Bourbon's lands. On 7 October Louise did homage to her son for the
duchies of Bourbonnais and Auvergne, the counties of Clermont, Forez,
Beaujolais and Marche and the *vicomtés* of Carlat and Murat. Soon after
the death of Anne de France on 14 November, Francis also gave some of
her lands and revenues to his mother, and on 10 January 1523 she
received another gift of Bourbon lands from him.[12] These gifts, of course,
contradicted Louise's claim to the Bourbon inheritance, since they implied that this had escheated to the crown. But Francis and his mother
were evidently less concerned with logic than with grabbing part of the
Bourbon demesne. Meanwhile, the lawsuit in the Parlement followed its
normal course. The three counsels concerned – Poyet for Louise, Lizet for
the king and Montholon for Bourbon – argued for and against the
validity of various legal transactions dating back to the fifteenth century.
The historian Roger Doucet, after carefully examining the various arguments, reached the conclusion that 'all the reasons of law and equity
supported the duc de Bourbon' and that the next best claim was the
king's. As for Louise, she could only sustain hers by an arbitrary selection
and interpretation of the documents.[13] The Parlement, unfortunately,
never gave its verdict. On 6 August 1523 the case was adjourned till the
opening of the court's next session on 11 November, but, at the end of
August, it ordered the confiscation of the constable's lands. This decree is
not to be found in the Parlement's registers, but it was almost certainly
issued, for it is mentioned by contemporaries who are normally well
informed. The Parlement may have issued it under pressure from Louise,
who had become regent on 12 August, and deliberately omitted its
registration as a form of protest. Alternatively, it may have been recorded
in a secret register, now lost.[14] But, even allowing for duress, was there
any justification for the drastic action taken by the court in respect of the
Bourbon lands? Before this question can be answered it is necessary to
look at another aspect of the Bourbon case.

The death of Suzanne in April 1521 had raised another major problem:
since she had left no children, her husband needed to remarry in order to
ensure the continuity of his line. Even in Suzanne's lifetime, imperial
agents had hinted at a possible remarriage between him and one of
Charles V's sisters. After her death the hint was turned into a firm offer,
but Bourbon was careful not to rush into a course which would inevitably

---

[12]   C.A.F., i. 1649–5, 1721; vii. 23738; Doucet, i. 227–9.
[13]   Doucet, i. 251–2.   [14]   *Ibid.*, i. 229–44.

alienate the king. Yet he also resisted pressure to marry him off to a French princess of royal blood. Did he reject an offer of marriage from the queen mother, as is often claimed? There is some evidence for this. In May 1523, the imperial ambassador in England reported that Bourbon had quarrelled with the king because he had refused to marry Louise, who was 'much in love with him'.[15] Marillac says nothing about this in his life of Bourbon, but de Laval, who completed his work, does mention a marriage project between the constable and Louise, though he presents it as a completely unsentimental affair by which the king's mother hoped to gain possession of Bourbon's lands.[16] Such a match would certainly have suited the crown. At the age of forty-four, Louise was unlikely to bear children; thus, in the event of her outliving the duke, the Bourbon demesne would eventually revert to the crown. There is evidence, too, that Louise tried to reach some suitable arrangement – perhaps a marriage – with Bourbon before she submitted her claim to his lands. Under the law she should have done so within a year and a day of Suzanne's death, yet she waited until the very last moment, and even had to be given a six months' extension. Such a delay lends substance to the story that her decision to sue the constable was an act of revenge after her advances had been rejected by him.[17]

During the winter of 1522–3 it was rumoured that Francis and the constable had patched up their quarrel. Bourbon, it was reported, would marry Princess Renée and take up a command in Italy.[18] Early in 1523, however, Francis accused him of becoming engaged – presumably to the emperor's sister – behind his back. The story, as reported by the English ambassador in Spain, runs as follows. Bourbon was dining with Queen Claude one day, when Francis burst into the room. As the constable rose to his feet, Francis ordered him to remain seated. 'Senyor', he then asked, 'it is shown to us that you be or shall be married; is it true?' Bourbon denied the charge, but Francis said that he knew that it was true. 'Sir', retorted the duke, 'then you menace and threaten me; I have deserved no such cause', and with these words he returned to his lodging accompanied by 'all the noblemen of the court'.[19] This incident, it seems, ended any hope of an immediate reconciliation with the king. In May Bourbon told his friend, the bishop of Le Puy, that since he could no longer expect fair treatment from the king, he would surrender his sword and collar of St Michael and retire to Germany, where he expected to be joined by more than a thousand French nobles.[20]

---

[15] Quoted by F. Mignet in *La rivalité de François 1er et de Charles-Quint* (1875), i. 380 n. 1, who gives merely 'Vienna archives' as the reference.
[16] Doucet, i. 215–17. [17] *Ibid.*, i. 221–2.
[18] *L.P.*, iii. 2799. [19] *Ibid.*, iii. 2879. [20] Doucet, i. 259.

Bourbon, it has been claimed, became a traitor only after Francis had confiscated his lands. This is true only to the extent that he did not finally decide to sever his allegiance to the king until 7 September 1523. But he had been dabbling in treason for some time before. In August 1522, for example, one year before the decree of sequestration, two of his agents, d'Escars and Lurcy, told the emperor's chamberlain, Beaurain, that their master was ready to rebel with 500 men-at-arms and 10,000 infantry.[21] Henry VIII was keen to accept the offer immediately, but Charles V preferred to wait. By May 1523, however, the emperor was ready to come to some agreement with Bourbon as long as Henry would do likewise. Beaurain went to England and, after securing Henry's co-operation, travelled through the Netherlands to Franche-Comté with powers to negotiate with Bourbon on behalf of both allies. As the constable refused to leave French territory, Beaurain had to go secretly to Montbrison, a castle in Upper Forez, where he met Bourbon and some of his closest associates during the night of 11 July. The talks ended in a treaty signed between Bourbon and Charles V: the duke was promised the hand of one of the emperor's sisters, either Eleanor or Catherine, whose dowry was fixed at 100,000 *écus*; the emperor would invade Languedoc from Spain and place 10,000 landsknechts at Bourbon's disposal. Henry was not a party to the treaty, as his ambassador, Dr Knight, failed to reach Montbrison in time. His role in the plan of campaign was none the less set out: he was to invade Normandy and pay a subsidy of 100,000 crowns to Bourbon.[22]

The constable now began to prepare his rebellion. His plan was to lie low until Francis had crossed the Alps with his army and Henry and Charles had invaded France from two directions. He would then attack Francis from the rear with the help of the landsknechts provided by Charles. Aymar de Prie was to pave the way for this operation by occupying Dijon.[23] But Bourbon was a half-hearted traitor. Even after signing the Montbrison agreement, he still hoped to come to terms with Francis. His advisers, too, were divided as to the best course to follow: some favoured a revolt, others a settlement with the king. Nor did Bourbon get as much aristocratic support as he had hoped. D'Escars, who had once treated with the emperor on his behalf, now refused to co-operate with him, while two Norman nobles, Matignon and d'Argouges, promptly disclosed all they knew of the plot to their confessor, the bishop of Lisieux. He passed the information to Louis de Brézé, who, on 10 August, wrote to the king warning him of the plot.[24] This was the letter Francis received as he travelled south to join his army.

21 *Ibid.*, i. 257–8; *L.P.*, iii. 3030.
22 Doucet, i. 260–4; *L.P.*, iii. 3055, 3123–4, 3154, 3194, 3203; Le Glay, ii. 589–92.
23 Doucet, i. 264–5.   24 *Ibid.*, i. 266–7; B.N., MS. fr. 5770; *L.P.*, iii. 3254.

The king's reaction to Brézé's letter was remarkably cool-headed. He rode with a strong escort straight to Moulins, the constable's chief residence and, finding him in bed seemingly unwell, told him of the warning he had received. Then, pretending not to believe it, he made various promises to Bourbon: he would see to it that his suit in the Parlement was settled amicably; he would increase his pensions, raise him in honour 'as far as it was possible for him to go' and give him the command of the army in his own absence. But the king laid down one essential condition: Bourbon must accompany him to Italy. This put the constable in a quandary: if he refused, the king's worst suspicions would be confirmed; if he accepted, his own plan of campaign would have to be scrapped. In the end, he agreed to follow Francis, but asked for a week's respite so that he might recover his health. This was conceded. Having been assured by his own doctors that Bourbon's illness was genuine, the king resumed his journey to Lyons; but he did not allow the constable to forget his undertaking. On 22 August he sent Perrot de Warty to remind him of it.[25]

Eventually, Bourbon did set out for Lyons, but he travelled very slowly and at La Palisse turned back saying that he was too weak to continue. On 6 September he met Sir John Russell, whom Henry VIII had sent out in place of Dr Knight, at Gayette and formalized his relations with England. He refused to recognize Henry's claim to the French throne, but agreed that it should be referred to the emperor's judgment.[26]

Bourbon's failure to turn up in Lyons convinced Francis of the constable's treasonable intentions. On 5 September, therefore, three of his associates, Jean de Poitiers, seigneur de Saint-Vallier, Antoine de Chabannes, bishop of Le Puy, and Aymar de Prie were arrested in Lyons, while troops under the Bastard of Savoy and Marshal Lapalisse were sent to round up the duke's servants. But no drastic action was yet taken against Bourbon himself; the king merely sent Warty to demand an explanation of his conduct. The constable, in the meantime, retired to his fortress at Chantelle, where, on 7 September, he decided to break with the king. But, as he needed more time to prepare his rebellion, he sent Jacques Hurault, bishop of Autun, to Francis with an offer of loyal service in return for his confiscated property. The bishop, however, was arrested before he could accomplish his mission.

The constable's plight now became desperate. Royal troops were closing in on him, yet he could not count on immediate help from his allies. The 10,000 landsknechts were still too far away to be of use, and neither Henry nor Charles had yet invaded France. The only course open to him was flight. During the night of 7 September, therefore, he left Chantelle

---

[25] Doucet, i. 267–8; B.N., MS. Dupuy 211, fols. 4, 6–7.
[26] Doucet, i. 269; *L.P.*, iii. 3217, 3307.

with a few companions, and a few days later, after following a circuitous route through Auvergne and the Jura, he turned up at Besançon within imperial territory. He wrote to the Swiss cantons on the same day telling them of his decision henceforth to serve the emperor. A few days later, his sister, the duchess of Lorraine, who had tried to bring about a reconciliation between him and Francis, informed the king that she had failed. Bourbon had told her that he was determined to press on with his enterprise. He intended to drive the king into the woods like a wild boar.[27]

Although Bourbon's plot had misfired, its discovery prevented Francis from leading his army to Italy as planned. On 17 September he informed Bonnivet, who had already crossed the mountains, of his decision to stay behind for the present.[28] He remained in Lyons and devoted all his energies to discovering the full extent of the treason plot and bringing its perpetrators to justice. On 11 September, when the constable's whereabouts were still unknown, Francis ordered his arrest and offered a reward of 10,000 écus for his capture.[29] He also set up a commission of four parlementaires to question and try suspects. They were instructed to use torture, if necessary, to find out the names of Bourbon's accomplices and to inflict swift and exemplary punishments on all save the constable, who was to be sentenced by the king. But the commissioners were uneasy about their duties and powers; they believed that the plotters should be tried by the Parlement, but Francis would not listen to their doubts. He threatened to dismiss them unless they showed more zeal.[30]

On 19 September, while Francis was still in Lyons, the duke of Suffolk invaded Picardy with a huge army. His original aim had been to capture Boulogne, but he was persuaded at the eleventh hour to march on Paris instead. His advance was remarkably swift. Within three weeks he had crossed the Somme; by late October he had reached a point only fifty miles away from the French capital.[31] Panic-stricken, the Parisians sent an urgent appeal for help to Francis, who responded by sending Philippe Chabot to reassure them. The king, Chabot said, would willingly sacrifice his life in their defence, and would, if he could not come in person, send his wife, children, mother and all his possessions, knowing that, if he lost the whole kingdom yet retained Paris, he would still be able to recover the rest. Meanwhile, the duc de Vendôme gave instructions for the defence of the capital: a special tax was levied, the francs-archers were called up, trenches dug, chains stretched across the streets and ramparts erected.[32] But all this proved unnecessary, as the English retired of their own accord.

[27]   Doucet, i. 273; B.N., MS. fr. 5109, fols. 87–90.   [28]   B.N., MS. fr. 3897, fol. 244.
[29]   Ordonnances, iii. 297–8.   [30]   Doucet, i. 277–84.
[31]   J. J. Scarisbrick, Henry VIII (London, 1968), pp. 128–30; du Bellay, i. 293–300.
[32]   J.B.P., pp. 146, 148–50; Versoris, pp. 37–9.

The success of Suffolk's campaign depended on the support of England's allies. But Bourbon, instead of leading a rebellion, had fled the country. He tried to raise a force of cavalry in Franche-Comté while waiting for the landsknechts promised by Charles V. Many of these, however, deserted, while the rest invaded Champagne prematurely only to be routed by the comte de Guise. This disaster prevented Bourbon from attempting an invasion of eastern France. Seeing that there was nothing more for him to do in Franche-Comté, he went to Italy, hoping eventually to join the emperor in Spain.[33] As for Charles V's plan to invade Languedoc, it had to be abandoned for lack of money. The prince of Orange recaptured Fuenterrabía instead, but his attack on Bayonne in September was repulsed.[34] Thus Suffolk, instead of being supported by England's allies, was left to fight the war alone. What is more, his Burgundian troops deserted and a sudden cold spell decimated his men and horses. By mid-December his army had retreated, demoralized, to Calais.

Paris had been saved, but not thanks to the king. The inhabitants could legitimately feel that, while Francis had been spending their money in pursuit of his Italian ambitions, they had been left largely defenceless. Their resentment took the form of sympathy for Bourbon, whom they regarded as a man of 'wisdom, virtue and valour', and hatred of the chancellor, Duprat, whose greed they blamed for the constable's treason. These feelings found their expression in many popular songs.[35] But sympathy for the traitor was not confined to the Parisian populace; it was also found among members of the Parlement and probably explains the leniency shown by the court to the duke's accomplices. On 20 December Francis reluctantly agreed to their being tried by the Parlement instead of by the special commission he had set up for this purpose. The prisoners were accordingly moved to Paris, and their trial started soon afterwards. On 16 January 1524 Saint-Vallier was sentenced to death and to the loss of all his property and dignities. It was also decided that he should be interrogated under torture. The other accused, however, were treated much more leniently, presumably because, unlike Saint-Vallier, they had all denounced their more fortunate colleagues, who had fled abroad. Saint-Bonnet was pardoned, de Prie was put under house arrest, and d'Esguières and Brion were each imprisoned for three years. The sentences on d'Escars and Popillon were deferred.

On 17 February Saint-Vallier was stripped of his knighthood, but the judges who had come to interrogate him found him too ill to undergo

33 Du Bellay, i. 290–3; *L.P.*, iii. 3399, 3440, 3455, 3490, 3498.
34 Du Bellay, i. 282–5.
35 E. Picot, *Chants historiques français du XVIe siècle* (1903); B.N., MS. fr. 2200; Champollion-Figeac, p. 375.

torture. He was then taken to the Place de Grève for execution. He mounted the scaffold, made his confession and laid his head on the block, but the axe did not fall, for a messenger suddenly appeared waving a reprieve from the king. Instead of losing his head, Saint-Vallier was to be imprisoned in a cell with an aperture only wide enough to allow the passage of food. The crowd of spectators, though it had been cheated of a bloody spectacle, rejoiced at the reprieve, as did Saint-Vallier himself. He kissed the scaffold, crossed himself several times and returned to his cell 'looking more joyful than when he had left it'. On 1 April he was taken to Loches, where he remained until his release in 1526.[36]

By 4 March, when Francis returned to Paris after an absence of seven months, the citizens had become thoroughly disgruntled. Not only had they been left to face an English invasion alone, they had also suffered an extremely severe winter. Six days of frost in November had wiped out the prospective harvest, as well as many fruit trees and vines; vegetables were almost unobtainable, and, in spite of measures to curb the malpractices of bakers, the price of bread remained high.[37] On 6 March the king addressed a meeting of leading citizens at the Hôtel de Ville. For once he did not ask for money, but tried to justify his policy by presenting himself as the innocent victim of his neighbours' envy and of Bourbon's treachery. He praised the exemplary steadfastness of the Parisians in the recent crisis, thanked them for their support and promised to reward them. 'The king's speech', wrote a chronicler, 'was most acceptable to the bourgeois of Paris, and the people were in part satisfied.'[38]

Two days later Francis went to the Parlement, accompanied by the chancellor, four peers, two bishops and most of the 'great officers', for the opening of the trial *in absentia* of the duc de Bourbon. The *avocat du roi*, Lizet, after reading out the indictment, asked that the duke be immediately sentenced to death and all his property confiscated or that he be arrested or summoned and prosecuted for default, so as to preface the sentence with a regular judicial process. After debating the matter, the Parlement ordered Bourbon's arrest and detention in the Conciergerie,

---

[36] Doucet, i. 299–303; *J.B.P.*, pp. 157–60; Versoris, p. 41. According to the *J.B.P.*, Saint-Vallier had threatened to kill the king, who had allegedly violated his daughter. He would have been beheaded but for the fact that his son-in-law was *grand sénéchal* of Normandy. This is presumably the origin of the story that Saint-Vallier's daughter, Diane de Poitiers, obtained his reprieve by becoming the king's mistress, which provided Victor Hugo with part of the plot of *Le roi s'amuse*, later used by Verdi in his opera *Rigoletto*. More probably, Saint-Vallier owed his reprieve to the fact that it was his son-in-law, Diane's husband, who had warned Francis of the Bourbon conspiracy. Gaillard, *Histoire de François premier* (1766), ii. 247–8.

[37] *J.B.P.*, pp. 155, 160–1.

[38] Versoris, p. 42.

failing which he was to be summoned. His property and titles were, in the meantime, to be seized for the king.

At a *lit-de-justice*, on 9 March, the whole Bourbon affair, not just the duke's trial, came under examination along with other business. After reminding the court of Saint-Vallier's fate, Francis asked for information about Bourbon's other accomplices, who, in his view, deserved exemplary punishment. President de Selve outlined what had been done in each case, but he was interrupted by the chancellor. 'And what of their property?' asked Duprat. 'Have you not confiscated it?' To which the answer was 'no', as the matter in hand was a *rélégation*, which under the law did not allow for confiscation. At this point Francis intervened. It was wrong, he said, for a matter that touched his person and the whole kingdom so closely to be treated like an ordinary civil suit. It was his intention to appoint several worthy persons alongside the existing judges to re-examine the trial of Bourbon's accomplices. Meanwhile, he forbade the prisoners to be moved.[39]

But the king's rebuke did not result in a brisker trial; on the contrary. The judges, knowing that their sentences would be re-examined, showed less zeal than before. Much time was lost, as summonses were pronounced against Bourbon and those of his accomplices who had not yet been rounded up. Francis, for his part, did not follow up the decision announced at the *lit-de-justice* until 16 May, when he added nineteen judges, mostly drawn from the parlements of Toulouse, Bordeaux and Rouen, to those already engaged in the trial. At the same time, he ordered this to be reviewed and forbade the court to publish any new sentences without his knowledge. In reply, the Parlement flatly refused to review its sentences and appointed thirty of its own members to act alongside the nineteen royal commissioners.[40]

Despite repeated admonitions by the king, the Parlement allowed several weeks to pass after the first deadline set for Bourbon's appearance in court before pronouncing the first default against him. As for his accomplices, they were not sentenced until 2 and 7 July. De Prie and Popillon were released on condition that they remained in a town of the king's choice; their property was also returned to them. A similar sentence was passed on d'Escars, though he was confined to a town for two years, because he had recently tried to escape from the Conciergerie.[41] By contrast, savage and unenforceable sentences were passed on all the duke's men who had gone into exile and had failed to answer the court's summonses. The only sentence outstanding was Bourbon's own, which had to await the king's pleasure.

[39] Doucet, i. 306–9.
[40] *Ibid.*, i. 310; C.A.F., v. 17782; J.B.P., p. 161.   [41] J.B.P., pp. 165–6.

Francis was naturally incensed at the Parlement's decisions. Not only had it failed to review its past sentences as he had requested; it had virtually acquitted Bourbon's other accomplices who had been in custody. On 10 July he forbade the court to publish its sentences or to release its prisoners. He warned it that it would hear from him on his return from Italy.[42] But the court was not easily cowed. Two days later it sent him a deputation to justify its conduct. While agreeing not to release its prisoners without his permission, it defiantly announced that all its sentences would be published 'to obviate the murmuring of the people and so that it should not be said that the court denies or conceals justice'.[43] The king, in reply, accused the court of preferring its own wishes to his honour and service and the general good of the kingdom. He again forbade publication of the sentences or the release of the prisoners.[44] A few days later he left Paris to take charge of the campaign that was to end in disaster on the field of Pavia. De Prie and d'Escars remained in prison for the time being; Popillon died in the Bastille on 15 August.

Was Bourbon a second Coriolanus driven into treason by a jealous and ungrateful prince or just a selfish and ambitious plotter? This question has long been debated by historians. Bias and romantic fantasy have often intruded upon the discussion. The duke certainly acted under strong provocation, but his treason was not just the result of a human situation; he had become a feudal anachronism at a time when France was on the point of becoming a nation-state. By eliminating this anachronism, Francis contributed significantly to the unification of his kingdom. But he might easily have failed. Fiscal oppression, food shortages, rising prices, foreign invasion and brigandage caused much popular discontent. Bourbon consequently attracted sympathy. Many people, including perhaps some *parlementaires*, felt that he had been unfairly treated. Why, then, did he fail to lead a national rising? Bad planning was partly to blame, but there were other reasons too. Bourbon, according to Henry VIII, was so dissatisfied with 'the inordinate and sensual governance' of the French king that he was 'much inclined and in manner determined to reform and redress the insolent demeanours of the said king'.[45] But the duke was a malcontent, not a reformer. The wrongs he wanted to avenge were only his own. Furthermore, a rebellion in the sixteenth century needed aristocratic support to succeed. Bourbon expected more than a thousand noblemen to rally to his standard; in the event he was badly let down even by nobles who had encouraged him originally. The nobility had less cause for discontent than any other social group in France, for it was the least affected by the king's fiscal exactions. If discontent existed within its

42 B.N., MS. fr. 5109, fols. 400–1.   43 Doucet, i. 315.
44 B.N., MS. fr. 5109, fols. 401–2.   45 St.P., vi. 103–4; L.P., iii. 2567.

ranks, it would not necessarily erupt into rebellion, for it was one thing to criticize the king and another to take up arms against him. The principle of legitimacy carried overwhelming prestige. Rebellion was a dangerous gamble few were prepared to take.

11

Pavia

(1523–5)

IN SPITE OF Bourbon's treason plot and the English invasion of Picardy, Francis did manage to send an army across the Alps in the late summer of 1523, but instead of leading it himself, he had to hand over his command to Admiral Bonnivet. At first everything went well: after crossing the Ticino on 14 September, the admiral forced Prospero Colonna, the imperial commander, to fall back on Milan, but he then made the fatal mistake of stopping for a few days, thereby giving Colonna a chance to repair Milan's defences. When the French resumed their advance, they found the city so strong that they had no alternative but to blockade it. The severe winter, however, inflicted such hardships on Bonnivet's men that he had eventually to lift the blockade, and retired to Abbiategrasso.[1]

Politically, the winter of 1523–4 was notable for the election of a new pope. Francis tried to bring diplomatic pressure to bear on the conclave, but none of the candidates he supported stood any chance of success. Both favourites, Giulio de' Medici and Pompeo Colonna, were imperialists, and when, after five weeks and several scrutinies, Colonna stood down, Medici's success was assured. He was elected on 19 November and took the name of Clement VII. The result was loudly acclaimed by the imperial ambassador to the Holy See. 'The Pope', he wrote to Charles V, 'is entirely your Majesty's creature. So great is your Majesty's power, that you can change stones into obedient children.'[2] He wrongly assumed that the new pope would necessarily adhere to the policies he had followed as a cardinal. From the start of his pontificate, however, Clement aimed at neutrality. Thus he refused to be drawn into an offensive alliance with the emperor or to subsidize his army in Lombardy. In March 1524 he sent a nuncio on a peacemaking mission to the principal courts, but, as Francis would not accept a truce that included Bourbon, and Charles insisted on exchanging Milan for Burgundy, the mission proved abortive.[3]

[1] Du Bellay, i. 280–2, 285–90, 300–2; B.N., MS. fr. 3897, fol. 244a.
[2] L. von Pastor, *The History of the Popes*, tr. F. I. Antrobus and R. F. Kerr (London, 1891–1933), ix. 253.
[3] *Ibid.*, ix. 257–8.

Early in March 1524 Charles de Lannoy, viceroy of Naples, who had replaced Colonna as the emperor's lieutenant-general in north Italy, advanced across the Ticino threatening Bonnivet's army at Abbiategrasso with encirclement.[4] The admiral, however, managed to extricate himself from this perilous situation, but his army had been hard hit by the winter: it had no ammunition left and only a few victuals. Most of its horses had died, so that the *gendarmerie* were reduced to riding ponies. The army was also hit by plague, and Montmorency, who commanded the van, fell so gravely ill with it that he had to be carried in a litter. Soon afterwards the French suffered heavy casualties as they crossed the river Sesia. Bonnivet, his arm shattered by an arquebus shot, had to hand over his command to the comte de Saint-Pol. On 30 April Bayard, the *chevalier sans peur et sans reproche*, was fatally wounded, also by an arquebus. Legend has it that, as he lay dying, Bourbon came to commiserate with him. 'Monsieur', Bayard allegedly replied, 'there is no need to pity me, for I die as a worthy man; but I pity you, who are serving against your prince, your fatherland and your oath.'[5]

On reaching the Alps, the French went one way, and some Swiss troops, who had joined Bonnivet during his retreat, went another. Their relations were more strained than ever. 'The Swiss', wrote Beaurain, 'swear a great oath never again to serve the French, and the French never to trust the Swiss.'[6] Money, as usual, lay at the root of their quarrel: the Swiss had not yet been paid, but a rumour that they had kidnapped Bonnivet as a security for their wages was unfounded. He accompanied them because of his wound, which prevented him from keeping up with his cavalry. He eventually returned to France, where he slowly recovered. His defeat had been truly crushing. The emperor estimated that only 350 French men-at-arms returned home out of a total of 1,500. Twenty-four guns left by the French in Savoy were added to seventeen already taken by the enemy.[7] Within a few weeks the garrisons at Lodi and Alessandria surrendered, completing the French débâcle.

Encouraged by these events, Henry VIII and Charles V concluded a new treaty on 25 May. Bourbon was to invade France with all possible speed, each prince contributing 100,000 crowns towards the cost of his army. He was to swear allegiance to Henry as King of France; otherwise the latter's contribution was to lapse.[8] On 28 May Wolsey informed Richard Pace, who had joined Bourbon near Turin, that Sir John Russell was on his way with 20,000 *livres* for the duke.[9] Bourbon would not at first swear allegiance to Henry on the grounds that this might alienate his clandestine supporters within France and drive the pope into the French

<hr>

[4] *J.B.P.*, p. 153.   [5] Du Bellay, i. 314.   [6] *L.P.*, iv. 305.

[7] *Ibid.*, iv. 351, 358.   [8] *Ibid.*, iv. 365.   [9] *Ibid.*, iv. 374.

camp. On 25 June, however, he changed his mind. 'I promise unto you upon my faith', he assured Pace, 'that I will by the help of my friends, put the crown of France upon the king our common master's head, or else my days shall be cut off.'[10] He declined, however, to do homage for his duchy to Henry.

On 1 July Bourbon, acting as the emperor's lieutenant-general, led his army across the Var, which marked the frontier between Italy and France. As he waited for his artillery to arrive by sea from Genoa, his galleys were intercepted by the French fleet. Most of them managed to find shelter in the harbour at Monaco, but three ran aground, their precious cargo being saved only after a fierce engagement on the beach in which Bourbon risked his life.[11] Inland, however, his army met with little resistance as it pushed westwards towards Aix, the capital of Provence. The French, under Marshal Lapalisse, were too weak numerically to do anything else than retreat. Town after town capitulated to the invaders. On 7 August the consuls of Aix, led by the seigneur de Pras, surrendered its keys. Two days later Bourbon entered the city and assumed the title of comte de Provence. He had hoped to find money there, but was disappointed, nearly all the wealthy citizens having fled.

So far Bourbon had received little help from his allies. Left to himself, Henry VIII would perhaps have invaded northern France, but Wolsey was very sceptical about Bourbon's chances of success: he could see no sign of an impending revolt in France and believed that the year was too far advanced for an English expedition to be worth while. On 16 August Charles complained that Henry's inactivity was endangering Bourbon's campaign, but he himself was no more helpful: the Spanish army did not move from Catalonia. Thus Bourbon was left to fight the war alone. Even the financial help he received from his allies was inadequate: Russell reached his camp nearly two months after the start of his campaign, and the emperor's subsidy arrived only in dribs and drabs. The duke had, in fact, to borrow from his captains in order to pay his troops.[12]

In about mid-August Bourbon had to decide whether to press on with his advance or lay siege to Marseilles. The town was protected to the south and west by the sea, and to the north and east by fortifications, which Francis had recently strengthened. The garrison consisted of 4,000 troops under Renzo da Ceri and Chabot de Brion; there was also a citizen militia of 8,000 men. The town was well provided with artillery and could, if necessary, invoke the additional fire-power of the French navy. It must have been tempting for Bourbon to bypass such a formidable

[10]   Ibid., iv. 442.
[11]   Ibid., iv. 483; A. Lebey, Le connétable de Bourbon (1904), pp. 237–9.
[12]   L.P., iv. 552.

obstacle, but at the same time he must have seen the danger of penetrating deeper into France without first securing Marseilles, which might then threaten his rear and cut off his supplies. Positive advantages were also to be gained by capturing the city: the French fleet would be deprived of its principal base in the Mediterranean, Bourbon's own communications with Spain and Italy would be improved and other French towns might be induced to capitulate as well. On 19 August, therefore, he laid siege to the city. Four days later his guns opened up a breach in its northern wall, but this was quickly filled in by the defenders with barrels of earth, stones and logs. Bourbon then ordered his sappers to mine the wall, but the citizens countered this threat by hastily digging deep longitudinal trenches. On 2 September the imperialists captured Toulon along with nine guns, which they were able to add to the batteries bombarding Marseilles. This alarming development prompted the defenders to send two envoys to Francis with an appeal for aid.[13]

The king, who had left Blois on 12 July, was with his army near Avignon. It comprised 6,000 Swiss troops and most of the *gendarmerie* that had been guarding Picardy. He received the envoys from Marseilles honourably, and, praising the city's courage and loyalty, promised to come to its assistance soon. For the present, he ordered victuals and 1,500 troops to be sent there by sea.[14] On 21 September Bourbon launched a new attack on Marseilles: having opened up a wide breach in its wall, he ordered his landsknechts to make an assault, but when they saw the obstacles which had been prepared for them beyond the breach they refused to advance. This threw Bourbon into the blackest despair: having been virtually deserted by his allies, he now had to face the disobedience of his own troops. He thought of saving his honour by challenging Francis to battle, but was dissuaded by his captains from such a reckless course. On 29 September, therefore, he lifted the siege and began retreating along the coast. Two days later, as Montmorency gave chase to him with a force of cavalry, Francis regained possession of Aix.[15]

The king could now think of carrying out his long-deferred plan of invading Italy. For several years he had longed to repeat his triumph at Marignano, but he had been forced by circumstances to entrust his armies repeatedly to incompetent or unfortunate deputies. Now the situation was different: the enemy was in headlong flight and Milan lay almost defenceless. Some of the king's councillors advised him to wait until the spring before invading Italy, but he decided to act before the imperialists could reorganize themselves, particularly as the weather was

[13] F. Mignet, *La rivalité de François Ier et de Charles-Quint* (1875), i. 522–30; Lebey, p. 246.
[14] Mignet, i. 539.   [15] *Ibid.*, i. 540–3, 549–51.

exceptionally clement for the time of year. On 17 October he reappointed his mother as regent and immediately afterwards led his army across the Alps in record time.[16] As the French penetrated the Milanese, the imperialists threw garrisons into Pavia and Alessandria but abandoned Milan; they left the city by one gate as the French entered by another. Francis could now choose between the following alternatives: he could pursue the imperialists in an attempt to prevent them digging in at Lodi or he could lay siege to Pavia. He decided in favour of the latter, thereby prompting Pescara to exclaim: 'We were defeated; soon we shall be victorious!'[17] For Pavia was strongly defended. It was enclosed by a wall except on its southern side, where the river Ticino formed a natural line of defence, and the garrison, comprising 6,000 Germans and Spaniards, was commanded by Antonio de Leyva, one of the ablest captains of his day. Having arrived outside Pavia on 26 October, the French began to bombard it on 6 November. Within three days they breached the wall and launched an assault, but this was repulsed with heavy losses. They then tried to divert the Ticino so as to facilitate an assault on the city's southern flank, but torrential rains swept away a dam they had built upstream. Thereafter the siege gradually turned into a blockade punctuated by skirmishes and artillery duels.[18]

Francis's next move has been described as 'the maddest of all the strategical errors for which he and his two predecessors had been responsible'.[19] He detached 6,000 troops from his army and sent them under the duke of Albany to conquer Naples. But the king's madness, as contemporaries easily perceived, was not without method. Albany's expedition probably had two immediate objectives: first, to compel the viceroy of Naples to withdraw from north Italy in order to defend the southern kingdom; secondly, to persuade Clement VII to join the French side in the war.[20] Militarily, the expedition proved a fiasco. Lannoy thought at first that Albany had been sent to escort a convoy of gunpowder sent by the duke of Ferrara to the French king; he tried to intercept him, but allowed him to proceed southwards without further hindrance after Lescun had come to his aid. Had Albany moved faster, he might have conquered Naples, which was seething with popular unrest, but he moved at a snail's pace and allowed himself to become embroiled in Sienese politics.[21] Politically, however, his expedition did help to win over the pope to the French side.

---

[16] *Ordonnances*, iv. no. 380.   [17] Mignet, ii. 9.
[18] L.P., iv. 789, 826, 837, 839–40.
[19] C. Oman, *A History of the Art of War in the XVIth Century* (New York, 1937), p. 191.
[20] L.P., iv. 872.
[21] Ibid., iv. 1010, 1045–6, 1054, 1085, 1102; C.S.P. Span., 1525–26, pp. 28–9.

Clement VII had not so far committed himself openly to either side in the war for fear of prejudicing the rule of the Medici in Florence. In November 1524 he had sent his datary, Gian Matteo Giberti, to both camps with peace proposals, but neither the viceroy of Naples nor Francis had been willing to treat. 'I hope soon to occupy Pavia', the king had declared. 'I have taken all the necessary measures; my supplies are ready and my troops are paid. I am expecting 1,400,000 francs next month and I have summoned fresh troops. I have not crossed the Alps in person or invaded Italy with 30,000 good infantry and the support of a fleet with 6 or 7000 troops on board to stop now. I want nothing less than the entire state of Milan and the kingdom of Naples.'[22] Since neither side wanted an armistice, Clement looked to his own interests. On 5 January 1525, as Albany marched south, the pope signed a treaty with Francis. He bound himself and the Florentines not to support the king's enemies and gave Albany free passage through the States of the Church. Francis, on his part, promised to cede Parma and Piacenza to the pope and to maintain Medici rule in Florence.[23]

Historians have exaggerated the military significance of Albany's expedition. It inevitably reduced the numerical strength available to Francis in Lombardy (although Albany did not leave until a reinforcement of 6,000 Swiss had arrived in the French camp), but the siege of Pavia would have been a serious blunder in any case, since it immobilized the king's army for nearly four months in appalling conditions. Francis was advised by some of his captains to retire to Milan during the winter, but his pride would not let him do so; no king of France, he declared, had ever besieged a town without taking it. At the same time, he underestimated the enemy's endurance, believing that Pavia's garrison would very soon capitulate. Thus he condemned his troops to a wretched winter in the open.[24]

The battle of Pavia (24 February 1525)

The main problem facing the imperial commanders in the winter of 1524-5 was shortage of money. By mid-January this had become so acute that they needed to bring the war to a swift conclusion; otherwise they were likely to have a full-scale mutiny on their hands. The French, however, seemed unwilling to come out and fight. Their main camp on the east side of Pavia was well protected by earthworks and bristled with guns. They also occupied Mirabello, a country seat of the former dukes of

[22] *L.P.*, iv. 826, 837; *St.P.*, vi. 359.
[23] Pastor, *History of the Popes*, ix. 267-8.
[24] *L.P.*, iv. 872, 912, 1053.

Milan, standing in the north-west corner of an extensive walled park, trapezoidal in shape, situated immediately to the north of the city. In order to facilitate movement between the camp and the park, which the French cavalry used for grazing, openings had been made in the park's south wall. The terrain within the park was open and rolling, with clumps of trees and shrubs and many brooks and streams. On 22 January the imperialists tried to draw the enemy out by marching north from Lodi, as if intending to attack Milan, but the French stayed within their camp. So the imperialists veered towards the south-west and, after capturing the village of Sant' Angelo, advanced to within a stone's throw of Francis's camp. For the next three weeks the two armies faced each other across the Vernavola, a small tributary of the Ticino. On 4 February the imperialists tried to storm one of the gates of the park, but were repulsed. The fighting was bitter, no prisoners being taken and no quarter given.[25]

Meanwhile, on the Ligurian coast, an attempt by an imperial army and fleet to recapture the port of Varazzo was successfully repulsed by the French. Moreover, they captured Ugo de Moncada, viceroy of Sicily, and three of his galleys. But this was an isolated success for the French. In Lombardy they suffered a series of setbacks which sapped their numerical strength. The most serious was the sudden departure from Pavia of a force of Grisons, who had been recalled to defend their homeland. Their number, though not known precisely, may have been as large as 5,000. Early in February 1,000 Italian infantry were routed near Alessandria as they were marching to assist the French outside Pavia. On 9 February a small imperial force managed to get through the French lines with a large quantity of gunpowder for Pavia's garrison. Then, on 17 February, Giovanni de' Medici, the famous *condottiere* who had recently entered the service of France, was wounded in a skirmish at Pavia; he retired to Piacenza and was followed by his 'black bands'. Again their number is not known exactly. According to du Bellay, the departure of the 'black bands' and the Grisons deprived Francis of 8,000 troops. Finally, Gian-Lodovico Pallavicini, who had been detailed by Francis to attack Cremona, was defeated and taken prisoner.[26]

By 23 February the efforts of the imperial commanders to draw the French out of their camp had come to naught, so they decided on a new tactic. At about 10 p.m. they moved out of their camp, leaving only a token force behind, and marched northwards alongside the east wall of the park of Mirabello. At midnight they halted at a spot which has not been precisely determined (it may have been at the northern end of the

[25] *Ibid.*, iv. 1064, 1072, 1075.
[26] Du Bellay, i. 332–4, 348–52; *L.P.*, iv. 1064; *Correspondenz des Kaisers Karl V*, ed. K. Lanz (Leipzig, 1844–5), i. 684.

east wall or near the middle of the north wall), and their sappers, using only picks and rams to avoid making too much noise, demolished the wall in three places.[27] This operation took longer than expected; it was dawn by the time the imperial troops began filing into the park in three columns, one through each gap in the wall.

The French, it has been said, were taken completely by surprise by the imperial attack and consequently failed to assemble their army in time to resist it. Some evidence exists to support this view. Florange was ordered by the king to go into action with part of the Swiss and not to wait for the rest to come up from 'the abbeys'.[28] This suggests inadequate preparation on the French side, yet Francis apparently expected a battle. According to Russell, the king had been warned before midnight that the imperialists were planning to attack his camp early next day. He had accordingly drawn up his army in the plain outside, so that the imperialists, instead of finding the French encamped, met them marching towards them in good order with forty guns, which did much damage.[29] This account ties up reasonably well with that of Frundsberg, who commanded some of the imperial landsknechts. As the imperialists entered the park, he states, they were seen by some French cavalry, who promptly fell back to join their fellows. The imperialists attacked them, whereupon Francis came out with all his men-at-arms, light horse, Swiss and landsknechts. His artillery, which was in front, 'shot terribly but did not do much damage'.[30] Yet another account states that Francis had been informed during the night that the imperialists were about to retreat. He had prepared to pursue them and was astonished to see them enter the park so boldly.[31]

The sequel is difficult to determine. Contemporary reports offer little more than glimpses of the battle, while the attempts of military historians to reconstruct it rest largely on guesswork. The broad outlines of the action are nevertheless reasonably clear. As the imperialists regrouped

---

[27] Oman, p. 198; P. Pieri, *Il Rinascimento e la crisi militare italiana* (Turin, 1952), p. 558. For a bibliography on the battle see p. 562n. The standard work on it is still R. Thom, *Die Schlacht bei Pavia* (Berlin, 1907). J. Giono, *Le désastre de Pavie* (1963) is often closer to fiction than history. See also F. L. Taylor, *The Art of War in Italy, 1494–1529* (Cambridge, 1921), pp. 49, 54, 65–6, 68, 79, 101, 126–8, and G. Treccani degli Alfieri, *Storia di Milano*, viii (Milan, 1957), 254–7.

[28] Florange, ii. 224. The so-called five abbeys lay to the east of Pavia within the French camp. Florange shows that not all the Swiss arrived at the end of the battle, as Pieri suggests (p. 561). Some 4,000 from the urban cantons went into action at the beginning; those from the high cantons followed later. This explains why they fled in different directions, some towards Milan, others towards the Ticino.

[29] *L.P.*, iv. 1175.

[30] *Ibid.*, iv. 1123. The fact that the French guns were pointing the right way at the start of the action suggests that the imperial attack did not take them completely by surprise.

[31] *Ibid.*, iv. 1189.

within the park, Francis charged at the head of his cavalry, throwing them into confusion. In doing so, however, he silenced his own guns. At first, the *gendarmerie* carried all before it. The marquis of Sant'Angelo, who commanded the imperial cavalry, was killed, his men being thrown into confusion. 'It is now', Francis shouted to Lescun, 'that I wish to be called duke of Milan!'[32] But he spoke too soon: after the French men-at-arms had broken through the enemy line, they came within range of more than a thousand Spanish arquebusiers, whom the marquis of Pescara had cunningly concealed in copses near the north wall of the park. With their shining suits of armour, plumed helmets and distinctive horse trappings, the French could not have presented easier targets. As the marksmen picked them off one by one, they crashed heavily to the ground, wounded or dead. Others fled terror-stricken from the field, setting a bad example to the Swiss, who followed suit, but the king fought on bravely, even after his horse had been killed beneath him. Meanwhile, the great blocks of infantry on both sides moved into action. The French landsknechts under François de Lorraine and Richard de la Pole fought heroically, but, being heavily outnumbered, they were wiped out almost to a man. By contrast, the Swiss put up a poor showing. Most of them arrived late on the field and, finding themselves sandwiched between the imperial landsknechts and the garrison of Pavia, which chose this moment to sally forth, took to their heels. Many were drowned as they attempted to swim across the Ticino, the bridges having been destroyed. By noon on 24 February, which was appropriately the emperor's birthday, the battle was over. The imperialists had won the day and Francis was their prisoner.

Many accounts exist of the king's capture, some highly romanticized, others less so.[33] It seems that Francis continued to fight on foot after his horse had been killed and was surrounded by a crowd of soldiers, who tried to snatch pieces of his armour as evidence that they had captured him. Eventually, the viceroy of Naples arrived on the scene, and the king surrendered to him. Two points, however, are obscure: at which stage in the battle was Francis taken prisoner and by whom? It has been suggested that he was probably captured much sooner in the action than is commonly supposed. This, however, is contradicted by the contemporary evidence, which indicates that the king was still fighting after the bulk of his army had been crushed.[34] Even at the time, however, the identity of his captor was controversial. Two days after the battle, Henry VIII was informed by the Archduke Ferdinand that Francis had been taken prisoner by La Mothe, Bourbon's steward. When the viceroy subsequently

---

[32] M. Sanuto, *Diarii* (Venice, 1879–1903), xxxviii. 53.
[33] Florange, ii. 231–3; du Bellay, i. 356–7; *L.P.*, iv. 1124, 1131.
[34] Pieri, p. 562n.

claimed the honour of the king's capture, La Mothe went to Spain to acquaint the emperor with the truth and to challenge Lannoy to a duel. Another nobleman, whose name has not been recorded, claimed to have saved the king's life. By his account, Francis was taken prisoner half an hour before the viceroy's appearance on the scene.[35] Florange, in his memoirs, dismisses such claims on the ground that the king refused to give himself up to anyone other than the viceroy.[36]

Francis was lucky to survive the battle, for Pavia was the biggest slaughter of French noblemen since Agincourt. The dead included many of his closest friends and advisers, notably Bonnivet, Galeazzo da San Severino and Lapalisse. Lescun and René of Savoy died of their wounds soon afterwards. The comte de Saint-Pol, who had been badly injured in the face, unexpectedly recovered; he was imprisoned in Pavia castle, but escaped on 15 May after bribing his guards. The bodies of François de Lorraine and Richard de la Pole were found among those of the lands-knechts. Prisoners taken included Henri d'Albret, king of Navarre; Louis, comte de Nevers; Anne de Montmorency; and the seigneurs de Florange, Brion, Lorges, La Rochepot, Annebault and Langey.[37] The only important French nobleman to escape death or capture was the king's brother-in-law, Charles d'Alençon. But, on 15 April, following his return to France, he died, some said of shame, others of sorrow at the loss of his king.[38] About 4,000 prisoners whose status did not command worthwhile ransoms were released on parole; they included Blaise de Monluc, the future marshal of France and memorialist.[39] On the imperial side losses were comparatively small. According to Frundsberg, about 10,000 Frenchmen were killed and only 400 or 500 imperialists. Ferdinand of Austria reported that 14,000 Frenchmen had been killed. But the figures quoted by Russell on 11 March inspire more confidence: he estimated that not more than 400 out of 1,400 French men-at-arms had escaped, that 1,200 men had been killed in addition to the large number drowned in the Ticino, and that 10,000 prisoners had been taken. He put imperial losses at not more than 1,500.[40]

Why was Francis defeated at Pavia? Numerically, it seems, there was little to choose between the two sides at the start of the battle. In mid-January the imperial army comprised 22,000 infantry, 800 men-at-arms

---

[35]   L.P., iv. 1127, 1425. Du Bellay states that Pompérant shielded the king until the viceroy arrived (i. 356).
[36]   Florange, ii. 232–3.
[37]   Ibid., ii. 235–41; du Bellay, i. 357–8; Champollion-Figeac, pp. 85–8.
[38]   J.B.P., p. 198.
[39]   P. Courteault, Blaise de Monluc historien (1908), p. 101.
[40]   L.P., iv. 1123, 1127, 1175.

and 1,500 light cavalry, while the French had between 24,000 and 26,000 infantry, 1,200 men-at-arms and more light cavalry. In the following five weeks, they lost some troops through desertion, but Francis estimated that in the battle he had disposed 26,000 infantry in addition to the men-at-arms and light cavalry.[41] Military historians differ by as much as 10,000 in their estimates of the total numbers involved; they agree, however, that the French were marginally superior in numbers.[42] They certainly had more cavalry and many more guns: fifty-three as against seventeen. But the imperialists had more arquebusiers.

Strategically, the imperialists were better placed than the French on the eve of the battle. True, the latter were strongly entrenched east of Pavia, but their freedom of movement was curtailed by the need to maintain a stranglehold on the city. While the bulk guarded its eastern approaches, the rest formed a ring round it. This explains why many Swiss arrived late on the field, while other French troops never showed up at all. The imperialists, on the other hand, were free to choose where and when to attack without having to look over their shoulders. Their army being divided into two parts (the Pavia garrison and the rest), they were also able to attack the French from two sides simultaneously.

How far was Francis himself to blame for his defeat? Florange criticized him for silencing his own guns at the start of the battle, while modern writers have argued that he made other mistakes as well.[43] The king has been criticized for relying too much on the protection of the wall enclosing the park of Mirabello and for coming into the open to meet the enemy instead of waiting for them in his camp. But he could not have foreseen that the imperialists would risk bottling themselves up within the park, and, once they had entered it, it was surely sensible of him to try to throw them out before they could regroup. The charge of the *gendarmerie*, it should be noted, very nearly succeeded. What altered the course of the action was the timely intervention of the Spanish arquebusiers, who, as far as one can tell, had not entered into the king's calculations at all. This, surely, was his greatest mistake. Although the arquebus had inflicted grievous losses on the French army in recent campaigns, Francis had still not faced up to its challenge. His insouciance, which may have stemmed from a deep-seated contempt for so unchivalrous a weapon, was certainly

---

[41] F. Lot, *Recherches sur les effectifs des armées françaises des guerres d'Italie aux Guerres de Religion, 1494–1562* (1962), pp. 54–5.

[42] The French had 20,000 troops of all arms, according to Oman (p. 197); 31,000, according to Pieri (p. 558).

[43] Florange, ii. 227. 'The king, seeing them repulsed, caused the gendarmerie of the van to advance in front of the artillery, so that it could not fire any more, which was the main cause of the loss of the battle.'

largely responsible for his defeat at Pavia.[44] He himself blamed this on the
Swiss, but even if they had shown more of their old fighting spirit, it is
unlikely that they could have altered the outcome of the battle, for it was
as good as lost by the time most of them arrived on the field.[45]

The king's captivity

Immediately after the battle, Francis was taken to Pavia, where he was
given a meal, served by the viceroy of Naples and the duc de Bourbon.
Rumours that he had been wounded were soon dispelled: a medical
examination revealed that he had suffered only a bruise on one leg and a
scratch between the fingers of one hand.[46] Francis attributed his escape
from more serious injury to the excellent suit of armour which he had
been wearing. In order to prove to his mother that he had not been badly
hurt, he wrote to her in his own hand. 'All that is left to me', he
announced, 'is my honour and my life, which is safe.'[47] He appealed to her
customary prudence and recommended his children to her. Francis also
wrote to the emperor, appealing to his magnanimity. 'You may be sure',
he said, 'if it is your pleasure mercifully to offer the ransom which the
imprisonment of a king of France deserves, that, instead of acquiring a
useless prisoner, you will turn a king into your slave for ever.'[48]

Charles received news of his victory on 10 March in Madrid. With
characteristic reticence he forbade noisy celebrations, arranged services
of thanksgiving and retired to his private oratory. At the same time he
instructed the viceroy of Naples to take good care of Francis's health and
to ensure that his mother received frequent news of him. The king was, in
fact, well treated by his captors. From Pavia he was taken to the castle of
Pizzighettone on the Adda, some twenty kilometres west of Cremona,
where he remained for nearly three months in the custody of a Spanish
captain called Fernando de Alarçon, who allowed him companions,
visitors and physical exercise. On 4 March, Jean de La Barre, who shared
the king's captivity, wrote to Louise of Savoy. Her son, he said, was in
good health and hoped to be released soon; but he needed money and
silver plate. La Barre was also worried about Francis's fasting. 'He will
not eat eggs', he explained, 'or anything other than fish, which does not

---

[44]   Monluc possibly had this in mind when he wrote: 'the business was not well carried out
       in several places on our side, which occasioned their ruin who behaved themselves best
       upon that occasion'. *Blaise de Monluc*, ed. I. Roy (London, 1971), p. 49. F. L. Taylor in
       The Art of War in Italy, 1494–1529, p. 101, writes: 'The imperialists . . . owed their
       victory on both occasions [i.e. Pavia and La Bicocca] chiefly to their bold use of the
       improved infantry firearms.'

[45]   *L.P.*, iv. 1175.   [46]   *Ibid.*, iv. 1164; *C.S.P. Span.*, 1525–26, p. 57.
[47]   Champollion-Figeac, p. 129.   [48]   *Ibid.*, pp. 130–1.

suit him, and wishes to fast a few days each week.'[49] Anne de Mont-morency, another of the king's companions at Pizzighettone, kept Mar-guerite d'Angoulême informed about her brother's condition. He assured her, on 22 March, that Francis's health was good and that he was being well treated. He asked her to send Francis frequent news of herself and Louise, which was 'the only thing which gives him the utmost pleasure'.[50]

News of Francis's defeat and his letter, written immediately after the battle, were received by his mother at Saint-Just near Lyons on 1 March. She immediately replied, thanking God for having spared his honour, life and health and allowing him to fall into the hands of an honourable man. She also urged him to accept whatever God had in store for him, promis-ing to take good care of his children and kingdom.[51] Marguerite, for her part, did as much as she could to console her brother; she urged him to stop fasting and sent him the epistles of St Paul to read. But the king did not spend all his time in pious devotions; he also played ball games with his companions and captors. He played billiards with Florange, the count of Egmont and Charles de Bourbon.[52]

An interesting glimpse of Francis in captivity is provided by a letter from a papal nuncio who saw him at Pizzighettone on 27 March. He spoke to the king as he was about to go to church, but, owing to the presence of many Spaniards, he was able only to make a few tactful remarks. Francis wore an ash-coloured garment trimmed with marten skins of little value, which he had not changed since his capture. At the reading of the Gospel he stood up and rubbed his head with his right hand; otherwise the nuncio noted no sign of anxiety in his behaviour. After the service Alarçon allowed him to speak to Francis in private. The king asked eagerly for news of Albany and was astonished to learn that he had fled from Italy; he then enquired about Giovanni de' Medici and was told that he would soon ride again. As the nuncio remarked that all was lost, Francis seemed much moved and replied that nothing else could be expected. At breakfast, during which Alarçon held the king's napkin and drank his health, Francis was asked by the nuncio if he had any message for the pope. 'I have no other', he replied; 'recommend me to our lord, fortune.' He then left the room without looking at his visitor. 'It was a pitiable sight', wrote the nuncio, 'for he does not seem a prisoner of the emperor and his captains, so much as of his guards, who all claim a right in him. He behaves courteously and liberally and jokes with them, think-ing it no less virtue to accommodate himself to fortune than to command a kingdom. Montmorency is his only comfort.'[53]

---

[49] *Ibid.*, p. 133.   [50] *Ibid.*, p. 141.   [51] *Ibid.*, p. 134.   [52] Florange, ii. 256.
[53] *St.P.*, vi. 409–11 (*L.P.*, iv. 1219). 'Non altro, raccomandatemi a nostro signor la fortuna.'

The Spanish captivity

Francis remained at Pizzighettone until 18 May 1525, when he was taken
to the castle at Genoa. The imperial authorities had decided, probably for
reasons of security, to send him to a prison in Naples, but Francis was
much alarmed at the prospect of being taken so far from his kingdom and
to a notoriously unhealthy place at that. He begged Lannoy to take him to
Spain instead, and the viceroy agreed on condition that six French galleys
were placed at his disposal, presumably as a guarantee against molesta-
tion by the fleet based at Marseilles. His request, which was carried to
France by Montmorency, was conceded, although it caused certain misgivings among the regent's councillors.[54] On 31 May, after Montmorency's return, Francis was taken down to the harbour at Genoa,
where fifteen Spanish galleys lay at anchor. He was welcomed aboard the
largest, the *Capitana of Castile*, by Admiral Portundo. She had been
magnificently decorated for the occasion, upwards of 1,000 ducats having been spent on the flooring of the king's cabin alone. The fleet set sail at
the beginning of June, but, instead of heading for Spain, it proceeded
eastwards along the Italian coast as far as Portofino. Here it dropped
anchor and waited for the French galleys. These arrived on 8 June, after
taking on Spanish crews at Genoa.[55] The whole fleet then altered course
for Spain. As it passed close to the Iles d'Hyères, local people came out in
small boats to greet their king and offer him gifts. On 15 June the fleet was
sighted off Collioure; two days later, it reached Palamós, in Spain.[56]

Strange as it may seem, the decision to take Francis to Spain instead of
Naples had been taken by the viceroy alone. Bourbon was not told about
it until the eve of the king's departure, and wrote a strong protest to the
emperor on 10 June.[57] Not even Charles V knew of Lannoy's decision
until Francis had actually landed in Spain.[58] Far from being angry, however, he wrote to the viceroy, approving of his action and urging him to
show every hospitality to the king. By the same post he welcomed Francis
to Spain and expressed the hope that his coming would lead to a general
peace.[59]

Francis was given a truly royal welcome at Barcelona on 19 June. He

[54] Decrue, i. 55.
[55] *C.S.P. Span., 1525–26*, pp. 179–80; *L.P.*, iv. 1419; *C.S.P. Ven.*, iii. no. 1041.
[56] *C.S.P. Ven.*, iii. no. 1048.
[57] Champollion-Figeac, pp. 216–18; *L.P.*, iv. 1405.
[58] This is clear from a letter of 15 June written by Charles to Lannoy. He had not yet
      received Lannoy's message, sent from Villefranche on 11 June, announcing the change
      of plan. L. E. Halkin and G. Dansaert, *Charles de Lannoy* (Brussels, 1934), pp. 284–7;
      L.P., iv. 1407.
[59] *L.P.*, iv. 1442; Champollion-Figeac, p. 233.

attended mass at the cathedral amidst a pomp normally reserved for Spanish monarchs and touched a large number of sick people.[60] A few days later he was taken by sea to the castle at Tarragona, where he narrowly escaped being killed. A mutiny had broken out among the viceroy's troops, and, as Francis looked out of a window to see what was happening, a shot from an arquebus passed 'within a span of his head'.[61] Towards the end of June he was taken to Valencia, but was so hard-pressed by crowds of sightseers and sick people seeking his touch that Alarçon decided to take him to a pleasant country house a few miles away at Benisanó.[62] Montmorency, meanwhile, travelled to Toledo with three requests for the emperor: first, to issue a safe-conduct for the king's sister, Marguerite, so that she might come to Spain to negotiate a peace; secondly, to allow Francis to come nearer to the conference table so that he might be more easily consulted; and thirdly, to agree to a truce while the peace negotiations were in progress. All three requests were granted by Charles without difficulty, whereupon Montmorency returned to France to report to the regent and obtain the powers necessary to conclude a truce.[63]

At the end of July, Francis was taken to Madrid, and his journey, which lasted nearly three weeks, resembled a royal progress. At Guadalajara, he was lavishly entertained by the duke of Infantado, one of the principal Spanish grandees. Banquets, bullfights and other entertainments were staged in his honour, and among the gifts he received was a horse with trappings worth more than 5,000 ducats. Francis also visited the famous university of Alcalá de Henares, founded less than twenty years before, by Cardinal Jiménez de Cisneros. Wherever he went, we are told, he made an excellent impression. 'He bears his prison admirably', wrote a Venetian, 'and in all places through which he passes is so well greeted by reason of the extreme affability and courtesy evinced by him towards everybody, that he is well nigh adored in this country.'[64] Francis arrived in Madrid on 11 August and was given a room in the Alcazar, which stood on the site of the present royal palace.[65] He remained there till February 1526.

---

[60] Champollion-Figeac, pp. 253–4; M. Bloch, *Les rois thaumaturges* (1961), p. 313; C. Terrasse, *François Ier* (1945–70), i. 331.

[61] *C.S.P. Ven.*, iii. no. 1057.

[62] Champollion-Figeac, p. 236. I am much indebted to Dr J. Casey of the University of East Anglia for identifying 'Venyssolo' (the name given in some contemporary letters) with Benisanó.

[63] Le Glay, ii. 610–11.

[64] A theory that Francis stayed for a time in the tower of Los Lujanes has been disproved by A. Lopez de Meneses in *Anales del Instituto des Estudios madrileños*, vii (1971), 121–47.

[65] The Alcazar was destroyed by fire in 1734. Among the last persons to see the room traditionally occupied by Francis was the duc de Saint-Simon.

12

The regency of Louise of Savoy

(1525–6)

FRANCIS I's captivity lasted just over a year, from 24 February 1525 until 17 March 1526, during which time the responsibility of governing his kingdom was borne by his mother, Louise of Savoy, who resided throughout at Saint-Just, near Lyons. She was faced by a threefold task: first, to defend the kingdom against the threat of foreign invasion; secondly, to uphold the crown's authority in respect of bodies like the Parlement; and thirdly, to secure her son's release on terms that were not excessively harsh.

The defence of the kingdom

The emperor's victory at Pavia did not end the war. For several months afterwards France was threatened with invasion, particularly in the north. Henry VIII had been delighted by Francis's defeat. 'Now is the time', he declared, 'for the emperor and myself to devise means of getting full satisfaction from France. Not an hour is to be lost.'[1] He began to assemble an army, sought military aid in the Netherlands and set about raising a so-called Amicable Grant from his subjects. Henry also sent an embassy to Spain so as to enlist Charles V's support, which, he hoped, would enable him to mar ch on Paris, be crowned there and enter upon all that was his 'by just title of inheritance'. The proposals he sent to the emperor envisaged nothing less than the total dismemberment of France. He believed that it would be culpable folly to restore Francis, even to a smaller kingdom; rather should his line and succession be 'abolished, removed and utterly extinct'. At the very least, Henry hoped to acquire Normandy or Picardy in addition to Boulogne and some other towns.[2]

Fortunately for Louise, Charles received Henry's proposals coolly.

---

[1] C.S.P. Span., 1525–26, p. 82. 'My friend', he said to the messenger who brought him the news of Francis's defeat, 'you are like St. Gabriel who announced the coming of Christ.' J. J. Scarisbrick, Henry VIII (London, 1968), p. 136.
[2] St.P., vi. 412–36 (L.P., iv. 1212).

Henry had remained inactive earlier in the war when the emperor had wanted him to invade northern France, and it was also known to Charles that Wolsey had been secretly negotiating with Louise on the eve of the battle of Pavia. Furthermore, the imperial ambassador in England had been roughly treated by the cardinal.[3] There was, consequently, little love lost between the allies. Charles also had many pressing problems on his hands: his army in Italy was unpaid and mutinous, the Peasants' War had just broken out in Germany, and, in eastern Europe, the Turks were again restive. He therefore cold-shouldered Henry's plan, leaving him to invade France alone, if he so wished.

If Henry and Charles had invaded France in the spring of 1525, they would almost certainly have been victorious, for Francis had largely denuded his kingdom of troops, armaments and supplies in the interest of his Italian campaign. The commanders of garrison towns in northern France had been starved of funds to such an extent that they had had to dismiss many of their troops. These were now living off the countryside, which had little to offer them after a series of bad harvests; they were also terrorizing villages near Paris and even its suburbs. In the south of France the situation was less critical: remnants of the king's army were trickling back across the Alps and, in April, Albany's expeditionary force was brought back almost intact from central Italy by the French navy.[4] By May Louise had 4,000 *lances* at her disposal and a sizable infantry. To pay for this army, she anticipated the *taille*, demanded a *crue* of 1,200,000 *livres* and curtailed expenditure on the royal household.[5] Even so, she could not satisfy all the troops that came back from Italy, so that many drifted northwards to swell the number of disbanded troops already on the rampage near the capital.

In arranging for the defence of the kingdom Louise paid special attention to Burgundy, which Charles V was most anxious to recover. The province was all the more vulnerable in that some of its inhabitants at least regarded Charles as their lawful ruler: after rejoicing over his recent victory, they looked forward to being handed over to him soon. In order to ward off the threat of an imperial invasion from Franche-Comté, possibly aided by a Burgundian 'fifth column', Louise posted spies to watch the enemy's movements across the river Saône and sent the comte de Guise on a tour of inspection of Burgundy's fortresses. Their guns were overhauled, stocks of gunpowder replenished and captains duly paid. At the same time Louise was careful not to offend local feeling. Thus she

[3] *L.P.*, iv. 1093; G. Jacqueton, *La politique extérieure de Louise de Savoie* (1892), pp. 64–83.
[4] Doucet, ii. 73–7.
[5] *Ibid.*, 24–5.

dropped a proposal to put a garrison into Dijon after the inhabitants had claimed the right to defend themselves.[6]

But, if Louise acted decisively in the south and south-east of France, she relied almost entirely on assistance from the Parlement of Paris in providing for the defence of the north against a possible Anglo-imperial invasion. This being an unaccustomed role for the Parlement, it showed some reluctance at first to act alone. It invited the Chambre des Comptes, the municipal government of Paris (Bureau de la Ville) and local clergy to send representatives to a special assembly, which became known, after its meeting-place, as the Chambre de la Salle Verte. The authority of this body, however, was so ill-defined that its members soon began to quarrel among themselves, and many stayed away. Within a short time the assembly was dissolved, the Parlement being left to act on its own.[7]

Apart from the threat of invasion, a problem urgently in need of attention was that of the hordes of disbanded and unpaid troops converging on the capital. A strong military leadership was required, but the comte de Saint-Pol, who was governor of Paris and the Ile-de-France, had been taken prisoner at Pavia. His duties had automatically devolved on his lieutenant, Pierre Filhol, archbishop of Aix, but the latter's appointment in November 1522 had, for some unknown reason, been bitterly opposed by Jean Morin, an *échevin* of Paris. Morin had since become *prévôt des marchands* and now pressed for the archbishop's dismissal on the grounds that the emergency called for the services of a soldier, not a churchman. The Parisians looked to the elderly Guillaume de Montmorency to lead them, but Louise insisted on Filhol remaining at his post. At the same time, she sent the comte de Braisne to deal with the rampaging soldiery. This only created more confusion, for Braisne asked to be formally recognized as Saint-Pol's lieutenant, and the Parlement would not agree without Filhol's consent. The matter generated much ill feeling, and was only finally settled when Saint-Pol reappeared in the capital, in July 1525, after escaping from captivity.[8]

Another matter in which the Parlement was not given a completely free hand was that of providing supplies to the garrison towns of northern France. Although they were desperately short of food, arms and gunpowder, the government's victualler, Favier, showed no sense of urgency; he remained in Lyons, dealing with his own private affairs. After vainly trying to stir him into action, the Parlement felt in duty bound to act on its own: it obtained money directly from the *receveur-général*, Ruzé, and

[6] H. Hauser, 'Le traité de Madrid et la cession de la Bourgogne à Charles-Quint', *Revue bourguignonne*, xxii (1912).
[7] Doucet, ii. 36–45; M. Félibien, *Histoire de la ville de Paris* (1725), ii. 953.
[8] Félibien, ii. 946, 961, 964, 967–70.

persuaded the Chambre des Comptes to ratify this irregular transaction. It purchased grain for dispatch to various towns in Picardy, and persuaded the municipal authorities in Paris to send them arms and gunpowder from its arsenal. Louise sanctioned these measures retrospectively, but warned the Parlement against trespassing on the king's authority.[9]

The defence of royal authority

Louise was perfectly capable of administering the kingdom, but the idea of a female regent did not command universal acceptance among Frenchmen in 1525. Some adhered to the tradition that the regent ought to be the king's nearest male kinsman, who in that year was Charles de Bourbon, duc de Vendôme.

There is evidence that early in the captivity an attempt was made by a few *parlementaires* and members of the Bureau de la Ville of Paris to unseat Louise; they urged Vendôme, as he passed through Paris on his way from Picardy to Lyons, to take charge of the government, but he refused, saying that he did not wish to divide the nation in the midst of an emergency. Instead of opposing Louise, he became a leading member of her council, acting sometimes as its official spokesman.[10]

Otherwise Louise's authority as regent was not seriously challenged. In March 1525 the Parlement assured the king, his children and the regent of its loyalty and devotion; it also urged Frenchmen not to blame their rulers for the nation's misfortunes, but to look on the latter rather as a divine punishment on themselves.[11] Louise, for her part, was more tactful in dealing with the Parlement than her son had been. She flattered it, enlisted its co-operation in organizing the defence of northern France and enlarged her council at its suggestion. The Parlement's first president, Jean de Selve, was admitted to the council and served as a link between the court in Paris and the government in Lyons.

Louise also invited the Parlement to submit remonstrances, and the court duly responded in April. Normally, remonstrances were concerned with a particular piece of legislation; but on this occasion the Parlement, encouraged no doubt by the regent's forthcoming attitude, criticized a number of royal policies that had been pursued since the beginning of the reign. In particular, it complained of the leniency shown to heretics, the undermining of the Gallican liberties, the use of fiscal expedients and interference with the normal course of justice. Though not mentioned by

[9] Doucet, ii. 93.
[10] Du Bellay, ii. 2. Cf. Doucet, ii. 30 n. 4. Vendôme had been summoned to Lyons by the regent, not by the Parlement as stated in *J.B.P.*, p. 195. He was in Paris on 10 March.
[11] Doucet, ii. 30–2.

name, Francis was implicitly criticized, for who else had appointed bad prelates or shielded 'heretics'? Louise accepted the remonstrances without demur. They were, she said, 'to the honour of God, exaltation of the faith, and very useful and necessary for the good of the king and the commonwealth'.[12] But she continued to govern as if they had never existed; nor were they ever mentioned again.

Only in the matter of heresy did Louise go some way towards satisfying the Parlement, which had become much concerned about recent disturbances in the diocese of Meaux, principally between Bishop Briçonnet and the local Cordeliers. On 20 March the bishop of Paris was instructed by the Parlement to set up a special commission, consisting of two *parlementaires* and two theologians, to try heresy cases. Though at first limited to the diocese of Paris, the competence of the new tribunal was soon extended to all other dioceses (including Meaux) within the Parlement's *ressort*, or area of jurisdiction. This meant, in effect, that bishops lost their traditional right to deal with heresy cases. But the Parlement was also anxious that the commissioners should have the power to try bishops themselves (it clearly had Briçonnet in mind), if these were suspected of heresy. This could only be conferred by the pope. On 29 April, therefore, Louise wrote to Pope Clement VII asking for a rescript against Lutherans.[13] He duly obliged on 17 May by delegating apostolic powers to the four commissioners who had already been appointed by the Parlement; they accordingly became known as the *juges-délégués*.[14] They were empowered to judge heresy cases independently of the ecclesiastical courts and to act, if necessary, against bishops. An appeals procedure was established from them to the Parlement, which thus acquired an overriding control of heresy jurisdiction.

The creation of the *juges-délégués* enabled the Parlement to support the Sorbonne more effectively in its campaign against the Cercle de Meaux. On 27 August anyone possessing religious books in French was ordered to hand them over to the clerk of the court within a week. The Parlement was particularly anxious to seize copies of Lefèvre's *Epitre et évangiles des cinquante et deux dimanches*, which had just been published anonymously. This was condemned by the Sorbonne on 6 November, and Briçonnet, who was suspected of being its author, was ordered, in December, to appear before the Parlement, though it is not known whether he actually did so. On 5 February 1526 the Parlement issued a decree in which heresy was defined so broadly as to include any deviation, however slight, from orthodoxy.[15] Censorship was carried to greater lengths than ever before, printers and booksellers being forbidden to publish or even

[12] *Ibid.*, ii. 110.
[14] *Ordonnances*, iv. no. 387.
[13] *Ibid.*, ii. 160–4, 168–9.
[15] Doucet, ii. 188–90; *J.B.P.*, pp. 232–3.

stock translations of religious works. Bishops throughout the kingdom were instructed to preach against heresy and prosecute suspects.

Books were not the only victims of the persecution. In October 1525 eight artisans of Meaux were sent to Paris for trial on a heresy charge, but the Parlement was mainly concerned to silence the leaders of the Cercle de Meaux. The *juges-délégués* were ordered to prosecute Lefèvre, Caroli, Mazurier, Roussel and Mangin, while the regent was asked to hand over Michel d'Arande. This all-out attack on the Cercle de Meaux prompted Francis to make from captivity one of his rare interventions in the domestic affairs of his kingdom (he had presumably been informed of what was happening by his sister during her visit to Spain). On 12 November he wrote to the Parlement ordering it to suspend its proceedings against Lefèvre, Caroli and Roussel. They were, he said, being unfairly persecuted by the Sorbonne, and Lefèvre had already been cleared of heresy; any new complaints about the three men should be referred to his mother.[16]

The Parlement was profoundly irritated by the king's letter, particularly its insinuation that it was acting under orders from the Sorbonne. The king, it remonstrated, was being unfair: why was he protecting only three of the accused and the most guilty at that? When Louise, who had so far failed to hand over d'Arande, came out in support of her son's demand, she was accused by the Parlement of being inconsistent: having helped to set up the *juges délégués*, she was now trying to impede them in their task of suppressing heresy. 'The character of the times in which we live', it told her, 'makes it imperative that all offences and scandals committed directly against God and His Catholic church should be promptly ... punished and extirpated.' On 29 November the *juges-délégués* were instructed by the court to press on with their task regardless of the king's intervention.[17]

Thus the Cercle de Meaux continued to be harassed; but Lefèvre had already fled to Strassburg, where he was soon joined by Roussel and Caroli. Mazurier, however, was forced to recant. As for Briçonnet, he earned the contempt of reformers by rallying to the side of strict orthodoxy.[18] Roussel expressed his discouragement in a letter to Farel: 'si pergant saevire', he wrote, 'nescio quis tutus audebit annunciare Christum'.[19] Six months later no one dared to preach evangelism at Meaux.

Another victim of the persecution during the king's captivity was Louis de Berquin. He was arrested for the second time in January 1526, while his books were seized and condemned by the Sorbonne. Having

---

[16] Herminjard, i. 401–3.   [17] Doucet, ii. 192–3.
[18] Pierre Toussain described the bishop as a false prophet who tailored his views to circumstances. Herminjard, i. 446.   [19] *Ibid.*, i. 391.

previously recanted, Berquin was now liable to the death penalty as a relapsed heretic. The *juges-délégués* found him guilty and sent him to the Parlement for sentencing, but the court held back when it heard that the king was on his way home.[20]

If Louise was unable to prevent a more comprehensive religious persecution than she would have liked ideally, she did successfully resist pressure from the Parlement to revert to the system of ecclesiastical elections that had existed before the Concordat. In February 1525 she appointed her chancellor, Duprat, as archbishop of Sens and abbot of Saint-Benoît-sur-Loire.[21] At the same time she vetoed the election by the respective chapters of two rival candidates, Jean de Salazar at Sens and François de Poncher at Saint-Benoît.[22] The chapters appealed to the Parlement, but Louise revoked both suits to the Grand Conseil, while the chancellor sent a force of armed men, led by Jacques Groslot and P. Berruyer, to occupy the abbey of Saint-Benoît. On 5 May the Parlement began to examine the appeal of the chapter of Sens, cancelling an order of the Grand Conseil for the confiscation of its temporalities. It also made two unsuccessful attempts to dislodge Duprat's men from Saint-Benoît. On 11 May Louise wrote to Guillaume de Montmorency, complaining bitterly of the Parlement's actions, which, she claimed, were undermining the king's authority, playing into the hands of France's enemies and imperilling her efforts to save the kingdom from invasion. She denied that the Parlement had any right to interfere in beneficial disputes and threatened to set up a special commission to judge the two lawsuits. After debating the contents of the regent's letter, the Parlement adopted a more conciliatory line: while reaffirming the principle that the king should not interfere with the jurisdiction of the sovereign courts, it decided not to press for the abrogation of the Concordat in the king's absence. On 3 June, however, the Grand Conseil, acting on orders from the chancellor, annulled the Parlement's recent decrees concerning the Saint-Benoît dispute and summoned two members of the court, Nicole Hennequin and François Roger, to appear before it. But the Parlement forbade them to obey the summons and received appeals from them; it also reaffirmed its decrees concerning Saint-Benoît. On 24 June Louise ordered the Parlement and Grand Conseil to hand over the two lawsuits to a special commission appointed by herself. At the same time she rebuked the

---

[20] Doucet, ii. 199–202; *J.B.P.*, p. 234. Cf. Berquin's letter to Erasmus (17 April 1526) in Herminjard, i. 422–7.

[21] Sens and Saint-Benoît-sur-Loire were two of the richest benefices in France. The vacancies were caused by the death of Etienne de Poncher. *J.B.P.*, pp. 190–1.

[22] François de Poncher was the nephew of Etienne, whom he had succeeded as bishop of Paris.

Parlement for receiving the appeals of Hennequin and Roger and sent three companies of men-at-arms to Paris, presumably to intimidate the court. The Parlement nevertheless ordered its decrees to be put into effect, by force if necessary, and punished two of Duprat's agents for their activities at Saint-Benoît. On 30 June it reaffirmed its determination to administer justice impartially in both secular and ecclesiastical causes and issued summonses against two members of the Grand Conseil and some monks of Saint-Benoît who had come out in support of Duprat.[23]

The Parlement also unleashed an attack on the chancellor. Remonstrances, drawn up on 22 May, accused him of trying to 'abolish and confound, remove and pervert all the ordinary justices and jurisdictions of this kingdom', and, on 27 June, the Parlement asked Louise to send him to Paris to discuss certain unspecified matters. The regent was left in no doubt that, if Duprat failed to appear, he would be prosecuted. Meanwhile, five *parlementaires* were instructed to look into his misdeeds, and the *gens du roi* to draw up his indictment. Faced by this new challenge to her authority, Louise played for time by inviting the Parlement to send her three representatives with an elucidation of its intentions. Early in September the Parlement planned to call a meeting of the court of peers to try the chancellor, but Vendôme, whose support was necessary to such a course of action, refused to be drawn into the court's quarrel with Duprat. Louise, in the meantime, greatly strengthened her own hand in dealing with opposition at home by signing a separate peace with England and removing the threat of an invasion of northern France. Thus, when the Parlement's representatives eventually reached Lyons, she kept them waiting six days for an audience, and then put them firmly in their place. The Parlement, she said, would need to be reformed if it were to regain its reputation for fairness. She also suggested that the Parlement and Grand Conseil should debate their differences in front of her own council, and demanded to know why Duprat had been called to Paris. Her resolute attitude had the effect she had hoped for: the Parlement dropped its attack on the chancellor and offered to suspend its examination of the lawsuits concerning Sens and Saint-Benoît if the Grand Conseil would do likewise. This satisfied Louise, and matters rested there till the king's return from captivity.[24]

The treaties of the More (30 August 1525) and Madrid (14 January 1526)

Louise was most successful in her foreign policy. While negotiating directly with Charles V for her son's release from prison, she tried to make

[23] Doucet, ii. 120–8, 134–43.   [24] *Ibid.*, ii. 133, 146–54.

him more amenable by breaking up his alliance with England and stirring up trouble for him in Italy and elsewhere.

The terms which Charles initially laid down as the price of Francis's freedom were anything but generous. The king was to give up Burgundy and all the other territories that had been in the hands of Charles the Bold at the time of his death; he was also to surrender Thérouanne and Hesdin. Bourbon was to have his property restored; an independent kingdom, including Provence, was to be created for him, and his accomplices were to be pardoned. Henry VIII's French claims were to be satisfied, and Francis was to settle an indemnity owed by Charles to Henry. The prince of Orange, whom the French had taken prisoner, was to be released and his principality restored to him. The peace was to be sealed by a marriage between Charles's niece, Mary, and the Dauphin. Finally, the release of Francis was to be conditional on the preliminary ratification of the treaty by the French estates and parlements.[25]

These terms were submitted to Francis by Beaurain, the emperor's chamberlain, in mid-April, but the king refused to negotiate as a prisoner, and referred him to his mother.[26] On 28 April 1525 she appointed François de Tournon, archbishop of Embrun, to go to Spain as her ambassador and gave him instructions which clearly laid down that no part of France was to be ceded to the emperor while leaving room for compromise in respect of other territories. Tournon was soon joined in Spain by Jean de Selve.[27]

The two ambassadors met the emperor at Toledo on 17 July and were told plainly that he would not release the king of France for a ransom. When, three days later, they and a team of imperial commissioners began to examine the obstacles to a peace settlement, it soon became clear that the question of Burgundy was the principal one. While de Selve claimed that the duchy had escheated to the French crown on the death of Charles the Bold, Gattinara argued that it had been unlawfully annexed by Louis XI. A debate followed in which the French were left in no doubt as to the emperor's commitment to Burgundy's recovery: there would be no lasting peace, Gattinara declared, as long as the duchy remained in French hands.[28] Soon afterwards, Tournon and de Selve were joined in Spain by Philippe Chabot, who had been sent by the regent to arrange a truce. This was signed on 11 August, but it was only an 'abstinence of war' designed to facilitate the movement of ambassadors and messengers; normal trading relations between the belligerent powers were not restored.[29] Soon afterwards Tournon and Chabot went to Madrid to see Francis, who, on

[25] Champollion-Figeac, pp. 149–59.
[26] L.P., iv. 1283.
[27] Champollion-Figeac, pp. 174–7.
[28] Ibid., pp. 255–62.
[29] Ibid., pp. 244–9, 294; L.P., iv. 1557–8.

16 August, made a secret declaration in their presence to the effect that he would never willingly surrender Burgundy and that if he were ever forced to do so he would thereafter regard his action as null and void.[30] Francis thus fell into line with the policy followed consistently by his mother since the start of his captivity. When the talks at Toledo were resumed on 24 August, Alarçon announced that Francis had expressed a willingness to give up Burgundy forthwith, pending the result of arbitration on its lawful ownership. But he was promptly corrected by Tournon: the king, he explained, had offered to send Burgundian representatives to the French court of peers (i.e. the Parlement of Paris) so that the matter might be settled. Whereupon Gattinara rejected the implication that such a body had any right to decide Burgundy's fate, pointing out, not unreasonably, that an impartial verdict could hardly be expected of it.[31]

Louise, in the meantime, worked hard to isolate the emperor from his allies, particularly England, who by now had abandoned her warlike attitude. Fearing that the emperor was about to sign a separate peace with Francis, the English government invited the regent to resume the secret Anglo-French peace talks which the battle of Pavia had interrupted.[32] Jean Brinon and Jean-Joachim de Passano accordingly returned to London, and on 30 August the peace of the More was signed. This comprised five separate agreements. The first restored peace between the two countries and set up a defensive alliance, while Henry undertook to use his influence with Charles to secure Francis's release on reasonable terms. Under the second treaty, Francis promised to pay Henry 2 million *écus* in annual instalments of 100,000. These were to be halved in the event of Henry dying before final settlement. A third treaty provided for the settlement of maritime disputes between the two countries. The Scots were conditionally admitted to the peace under a fourth treaty; they were to stop armed incursions across the border, and Albany was to be barred from Scotland during James V's minority. Finally, the French government promised to compensate Louis XII's widow, Mary, now duchess of Suffolk, for losses incurred as a result of the war.[33]

Owing to the exceptional situation created by the king's captivity, the English government demanded a number of guarantees for the treaty's fulfilment. It was to be registered by the parlements and provincial estates of France, and financial securities were demanded from eight leading noblemen and nine major towns. The noblemen did what was expected of them, particularly as the regent promised to indemnify them for any losses

30   *Ibid.*, pp. 300–3.
31   M. François, *Le cardinal François de Tournon* (1951), pp. 39–40.
32   Scarisbrick, *Henry VIII*, p. 141.
33   Jacqueton, *La politique extérieure*, p. 119; *Ordonnances*, iv. nos. 394–5, 398–400.

they might incur, but the Parlement of Paris, the estates of Normandy and some towns were less co-operative. While the Parlement did not register the treaty till 20 October, the estates of Normandy failed to do so at all. Among the nine major towns the most troublesome were Paris, Rouen, Bordeaux, Tours and Orléans. In Paris the main stumbling-block was the refusal of the sovereign courts, university and local clergy to send representatives to an assembly of citizens called by the Bureau de la Ville. Fortunately for the regent, she managed to persuade the English government to postpone the deadline for the surrender of the securities and also to waive a clause in the treaty of the More whereby individual citizens, as distinct from corporations, had to engage their property. This concession, by removing the necessity for a representative gathering of Parisians, enabled the Bureau de la Ville to comply with the regent's wishes on 24 January 1526, and its example was soon followed by the other towns.[34]

In addition to breaking up the Anglo-imperial alliance, Louise tried to put pressure on the emperor in Italy by encouraging opposition to him wherever possible. But she carefully avoided attempts to draw her into an anti-imperial coalition for fear of prejudicing her chances of reaching an early settlement with Charles and involving herself in military expenditure she could ill afford. In June 1525 she proposed to the pope and Venice an alliance aimed at driving the imperialists out of Italy and forcing Charles to release her son. She offered them a monthly subsidy of 40,000 *écus* and renunciation of the French claim to Milan, but they wanted her also to send an army across the Alps.[35] In October the negotiations almost collapsed following the discovery of an anti-imperial plot in Milan. This was the brain-child of Hieronimo Morone, chancellor of Duke Francesco Sforza. Knowing that the marquis of Pescara, who commanded the imperial army in Lombardy, was for various reasons dissatisfied with the emperor, Morone tried to lure him into treason by offering him the crown of Naples. Pescara feigned interest, but informed his master of the plot. Morone was arrested, Sforza shut himself up in Milan castle and the duchy passed directly under imperial rule.[36]

These dramatic events shook the confidence of the Venetians and the pope, but early in November they received new proposals from Louise: she now offered to send 500 men-at-arms to Italy at her own expense in addition to the monthly subsidy of 40,000 *écus*. For her part, she asked the Italians to pay for 20,000 troops, claimed the county of Asti and demanded permanent annuities from the future rulers of Milan and Naples. On 18 November the Venetians agreed to join a league on the

[34] Jacqueton, *La politique extérieure*, pp. 155–98.
[35] *Ibid.*, pp. 204–11.
[36] F. Mignet, *La rivalité de François 1er et de Charles-Quint* (1875), pp. 135–8.

regent's terms, provided the pope would do so too. Clement seemed equally well disposed, though he laid down two difficult conditions: he asked Louise to deposit in advance three or four instalments of her subsidy, either in Venice or Rome, and invited Henry VIII to stand surety for her promises. Matters stood thus when, early in December, an imperial envoy persuaded the pope to sign an undertaking not to act against the emperor for two months. Although the Venetians were disappointed by the pope's action, they decided to act alone, while the English pressed for a Franco-Venetian alliance under Henry VIII's protection.[37]

Louise's diplomatic activity was not confined to western Europe. Immediately after Pavia, she sent an envoy to Constantinople, but he was murdered on the way. John Frangipani was then dispatched with letters for the sultan, Suleiman the Magnificent, from Francis and his mother begging him to come to the king's aid. The envoy reached Constantinople in December and duly conveyed his messages to the sultan, warning him that, unless he intervened, Francis would be obliged to treat with Charles, who would then become 'master of the world'. Suleiman promised to lead an expedition against the emperor, but his reply to Francis contained only florid expressions of encouragement.[38]

Despite Louise's diplomatic successes, Charles V resolutely adhered to his demand for the surrender of Burgundy as a *sine qua non* of peace with France. On 11 September, however, his calculations were gravely upset when Francis fell seriously ill. Within a week the king's condition became so critical that his doctors gave him up for lost, and the emperor, who so far had shown no desire to meet him, hurried to his bedside. Soon afterwards Marguerite d'Angoulême arrived, after travelling poste-haste from Barcelona. On 22 September Francis was reported to be on the point of death, but, later that day, an abscess was discovered in his head. This raised the hopes of his doctors, who previously had not been able to attribute his condition to any physical cause. The abscess then burst and Francis regained consciousness.[39]

De Selve described the king's recovery as follows in a letter to the Parlement, dated 1 October:

Eight days have passed since my lady the duchess [Marguerite] asked all the gentlemen of the king's household and her own, as well as the ladies, to pray to God. They all took communion and afterwards mass was said in the king's chamber. At the elevation of the Blessed Sacrament, my lord the archbishop of

---

[37] Jacqueton, *La politique extérieure*, pp. 229–39.
[38] E. Charrière (ed.), *Négociations de la France dans le Levant* (1848–60), i. 112–18.
[39] *C.S.P. Ven.*, iii. nos. 1112, 1115, 1119; P. Jourda, *Marguerite d'Angoulême* (1930), i. 116–17.

Embrun exhorted the king to look at it, and he, who had been unable to see or speak, looked at it and raised his hands. After the mass, my lady the duchess had the Blessed Sacrament presented to the king so that he might adore it, and he said: 'Here is my God, who will cure my soul and my body; I pray that I may receive Him.' When told that he would not be able to swallow the Host, he replied that he would manage to do so. My lady the duchess then had a piece broken off, which he received with so much humility and devotion that everyone wept. My lady the duchess received the rest of the Blessed Sacrament. From this time onwards he has improved steadily and, thanks to God, he is now rid of the fever that has gripped him for twenty-three days without respite. Nature has performed all its functions, as much by way of evacuation above and below as by sleeping, drinking and eating so that he is now out of danger.[40]

The king's recovery was followed by a resumption of the peace talks in Toledo; but none of the proposals Marguerite put before Charles and his council was acceptable. On 11 October, therefore, the talks were suspended, and the duchess returned to Madrid.[41] About this time an Italian captain called Emilio Cavriana formed a daring plan for the king's escape, but it was betrayed by Clément Champion, one of Francis's servants.[42] Despite this incident, Marguerite and other French negotiators were invited back to Toledo on 14 November. They offered Charles a ransom of 3 million gold *écus*, and again proposed a marriage between Francis and Eleanor of Portugal, who would receive Burgundy as her dowry. But they met with a flat refusal, and Marguerite decided that she might as well go home. She left Madrid on 27 November and returned to France in December, shortly before the truce expired. On her way home, she wrote several times to her brother, urging him not to despair, but his plight now seemed truly hopeless: he had offered Charles a large ransom and much else besides, yet the emperor continued to demand Burgundy.[43]

Deceit was the only course left to Francis other than capitulation. In November (the precise date is unknown) he drew up an edict relinquishing his throne to the Dauphin and appointing Louise as regent during the prince's minority. The edict, however, stipulated that the Dauphin should stand down in the event of Francis being able to resume his kingship. Almost certainly it was only a ploy aimed at frightening the emperor into a more reasonable attitude. Having failed to achieve this, it remained a dead letter.[44]

[40]   Champollion-Figeac, pp. 331–3. Writing to Henry VIII, Louise described her son's recovery as a near miracle. *L.P.*, iv. 1692.
[41]   Champollion-Figeac, pp. 359–69. Francis seems to have suffered a relapse in the interval. It was reported on 2 December that he had had a second sickness, more serious than the first, which had left him very weak and 'melancholy'. *L.P.*, iv. 1799.
[42]   G. Salles, 'Un traître au XVIe siècle: Clément Champion, valet de chambre de François Ier', *R.Q.H.*, n.s., xxiv (1900), 41–73.
[43]   Jourda, *Marguerite d'Angoulême*, i. 130–3.   [44]   Champollion-Figeac, pp. 416–25.

As the truce was about to expire, Louise of Savoy decided to yield to the emperor's conditions. In a memorandum addressed to Chabot, she argued that the surrender of Burgundy was a price worth paying for her son's liberation. The kingdom would suffer irreparable damage, she said, if he remained in prison, for the Dauphin was too young to rule and she herself could not carry the burden of regency for much longer. Far more had been given away by the peace treaty following the capture of King John at the battle of Poitiers. It seemed senseless, Louise concluded, to risk destroying a kingdom for the sake of a duchy.[45] Francis soon came round to the same opinion. Rather than remain in prison for the rest of his life, he decided to accept Charles's terms. Talks were, therefore, resumed, and a peace treaty thrashed out. A few difficulties cropped up, but Francis advised his representatives to deal 'graciously' with the imperialists. Under the treaty Francis abandoned Burgundy and its dependencies along with his claims in Italy and Artois. Henri d'Albret gave up Navarre; Bourbon and his accomplices were reinstated. In short, Francis threw away every principle his ambassadors had so strenuously defended for months. He also agreed to hand over the Dauphin and his second son as hostages, pending fulfilment of the treaty.[46]

Yet the treaty of Madrid, humiliating as it was, was not an unconditional surrender. Francis made two requests of the emperor. He asked, first, to be set free before the treaty was implemented on the ground that he alone could persuade his subjects to give up Burgundy, and, secondly, for the hand of Eleanor of Portugal. Both demands were highly dangerous for the emperor. The first carried the risk that the treaty might not be implemented at all; the second threatened Charles's friendship with Bourbon, who had been promised Eleanor. Gattinara saw these dangers clearly. He believed that the only sensible course open to Charles was either to release Francis unconditionally in the hope of winning his friendship or to keep him locked up. If the king's demands were granted, he feared that the emperor would be left holding two worthless hostages. History has proved Gattinara right, but the emperor preferred the advice of Lannoy, who thought the king should be trusted.[47]

Francis never intended to keep the peace of Madrid. On 14 January 1526, shortly before the imperial commissioners came for his signature, he made another secret declaration, nullifying in advance his surrender of Burgundy. Having thus salved his conscience, he took a solemn oath to observe the treaty and promised as a knight to return voluntarily to prison if he should break his word.

Francis was not released from prison immediately after the peace of

[45] *Ibid.*, pp. 408–15.   [46] *Ordonnances*, iv. no. 412.
[47] L. E. Halkin and G. Dansaert, *Charles de Lannoy* (Brussels, 1934), p. 91.

Madrid had been signed. He remained at the Alcazar in Madrid until mid-February, possibly for reasons of health.[48] He was still unwell on 20 January, when he was betrothed by proxy to Eleanor, and Bishop Tunstall found him weak and pale on the 28th.[49] On the following day, however, he was able to attend vespers at the church of Nuestra Señora de Atocha. He was carried there in a litter, but returned on a mule and declared himself fit enough to hunt a stag. On 30 January the king was entertained to lunch by a Spanish countess; afterwards he visited a convent and touched thirty scrofulous nuns.[50] Charles V came to Madrid on 13 February and spent three days in the king's company. He then took Francis to Illescas and introduced him to his sister, Eleanor. She tried to kiss the king's hand, but he insisted on embracing her as a husband. Next day she performed a Spanish dance for his benefit. On 19 February the two sovereigns, who had stayed together at Torrejon, parted company: while Charles left for Seville to marry Isabella of Portugal, Francis returned to Madrid on the first stage of his journey home.[51] This took him to Burgos, Vittoria and San Sebastian. Though still under guard, he was allowed to go hunting on the way, but more serious matters also held his attention. At Aranda, on 26 February, he and the viceroy of Naples worked out the details of the exchange between himself and his children. It was agreed that this would take place on 17 March on the river Bidassoa near Fuenterrabía. All troops were banned from the area as well as ships and boats, gatherings of local people were forbidden, and no member of the king's household was allowed south of Bayonne. Before leaving Spain, Francis distributed gifts to his gaolers, including Alarçon, who had followed him everywhere since he had been at Pizzighettone. He also wrote to Charles asking him to send Eleanor to him before Holy Week.[52]

Montmorency, meanwhile, carried news of the peace to France. He arrived at Lyons on 29 January and was able to reassure Louise, who had received no news from Spain for more than a month. She promptly informed the Parlement of the king's impending return and ordered prayers and processions for his safe deliverance.[53] On 1 February she left Saint-Just for Blois. Dr Taylor, the English ambassador, complained bitterly of the hardships of the journey. The Loire near Blois had burst its banks and 'the wind was so ragious that no one might pass over it without

[48]   Francis later complained that he was forbidden to leave the Alcazar, even when a fire partially destroyed it, and that guards continued to peer into his bed at night. These allegations should be treated with caution. They were made after the king's release and served as an excuse for his refusal to honour the treaty of Madrid. Champollion-Figeac, pp. 506–7.

[49]   L.P., iv. 1933.

[50]   Champollion-Figeac, p. 488.

[51]   Ibid., pp. 503–4, 508–9.

[52]   Ibid., pp. 504, 510–12, 516–18.

[53]   Ibid., p. 484.

great danger'. Louise also had to contend with gout, yet she pressed on regardless. From Blois she travelled to Amboise, where she picked up the Dauphin and the duc d'Orléans, who were needed as hostages. On 25 February the bishop of Tarbes brought her good news from Spain: her son was well and expected to be at Bayonne on 10 March. Louise made a great effort to make the rendezvous in time, but she got there only on the 15th.[54] She was presumably relieved to find that her son was still on his way.

Early on 17 March, two rowing boats faced each other across the Bidassoa: one carried the king of France, the viceroy of Naples and Alarçon; the other, the Dauphin, the duc d'Orléans, their two governesses and Marshal Lautrec. At an agreed signal the two boats moved towards a pontoon moored in the middle of the river, where they exchanged passengers. With tears in his eyes, Francis urged his sons to look after themselves, promised to send for them soon and made the sign of the cross over them. The boats then returned to their original moorings and Francis set foot on French soil. Escorted by Lautrec and a few servants, he travelled in haste to Saint-Jean-de-Luz, where he stopped for lunch, then to Bayonne, where his mother, sister, ministers and friends were waiting for him. His arrival about 3 p.m. was greeted by a salvo of ordnance, but public rejoicing had to be postponed because of Lent. On 20 March Francis and Louise attended a thanksgiving service at the cathedral.[55] The king's ordeal was over; it remained to be seen whether he had learnt anything from it.

[54] *L.P.*, iv. 1999, 2009, 2032.
[55] *Ibid.*, iv. 1938; Champollion-Figeac, pp. 522–3.

13

The king's return

(1526–8)

AFTER HIS RELEASE from prison Francis spent several months travelling in a leisurely fashion through south-west and central France. Among the more important places he visited were Bordeaux (9–23 April), Cognac (27 April–28 May), Angoulême (30 May–4 July) and Amboise (30 July–13 September). During this progress he had much business to deal with, but also found time to go hunting (he broke his left arm in a riding accident on 9 June) and indulge in other pastimes.[1]

It was probably at this time that he first met Anne d'Heilly, who took the place in his affections formerly occupied by Françoise de Foix. On the evidence of certain anonymous poems which have been ascribed to her and the king, it has been claimed that their liaison antedated the Pavia campaign, but the weight of contemporary evidence contradicts this. Tradition has it that they first met at Mont-de-Marsan at the end of March 1526. Anne was eighteen at the time and a maid-of-honour of Louise of Savoy.[2] By 1527 she had become one of the 'band' of ladies the king liked to have about him on hunting expeditions. The aftermath of a royal hunt near Amiens in August of that year was described by Sir Anthony Browne in a letter to Henry VIII as follows:

Furthermore, the king's bed is always carried with him, when he hunts; and anon, after that the deer is killed, he repairs to some house near at hand, where the same is set up, and there reposes himself three or four hours, and against his return there is provided for him a supper by some nobleman, as by Monsr. de Vendôme, Monsr. de Guise or other; whereunto a great number of ladies and gentlewomen, used to be in his company be sent for, and there he passes his time until ten or eleven o'clock, among whom above others, as the report is, he favours a maiden of Madame de Vendôme, called Hely whose beauty, after my mind, is not highly to be praised.[3]

Browne was probably prejudiced, for Anne was widely praised for her beauty (she was fair, unlike Françoise de Foix), intelligence and vivacious-

---

[1] C.A.F., viii. 450–1; L.P., iv (pt 1), 2243; J.B.P., pp. 241–2.
[2] P. Paris, *Etudes sur François premier* (1885), ii. 208–9, 231–4.
[3] St.P., vi. 58. I have modernized the spelling.

ness. She was the daughter of Guillaume d'Heilly, seigneur de Pisseleu, a nobleman from Picardy, who married three times and had thirty children. After the death of Louise of Savoy, in September 1531, Anne became the governess of the king's daughters, Madeleine and Marguerite. About 1534 the king married her off to Jean de Brosse, seigneur de Penthièvre, and on 23 June he gave them both the county of Etampes, raising it two years later to ducal status. Thus did Anne d'Heilly become the duchesse d'Etampes, the title by which she is best remembered. In spite of her marriage she remained at court and continued to exercise a powerful influence on the king and his entourage till the end of the reign.[4]

Other important events concerning the royal family also occurred soon after the king's return home. At the end of October the bodies of Queen Claude and her six-year-old daughter Louise, whose funerals had to be postponed because of the war, were carried in procession from Blois to the abbey of Saint-Denis, where they were duly buried on 7 November.[5] And on 30 January 1527 Francis's sister, Marguerite, took as her second husband Henri d'Albret, king of Navarre, who had become something of a hero after escaping from the castle at Pavia. The marriage, which prompted eight days of continual festivities and tournaments, had obvious political implications, since Henri's claim to Spanish Navarre had yet to be satisfied. Although Marguerite visited her small kingdom, she soon returned to the French court and was present, in June 1528, at the marriage of Princess Renée with Ercole d'Este, son of the duke of Ferrara. On 16 November Marguerite gave birth to a daughter, Jeanne, who was to become the mother of Henri IV of France.[6]

New administrative appointments

The king's homecoming has been fairly described as a 'second accession', for it was accompanied by a distribution of honours comparable to that in 1515.[7] This was partly due to necessity, partly to gratitude. The treason of the duc de Bourbon and the slaughter of so many French noblemen at Pavia had created vacancies in the royal administration which needed filling, while Francis was naturally anxious to reward courtiers who had demonstrated their loyalty to him during his captivity. Foremost among the new appointments were Anne de Montmorency and Philippe

[4] Paris, ii. 204–323; E. Desgardins, *Anne de Pisseleu duchesse d'Etampes et François Ier* (1904), passim; *C.A.F.*, ii. 7189, 7256; iii. 8768. See also below, ch. 26.
[5] *J.B.P.*, pp. 248–51.
[6] *Ibid.*, pp. 253, 304–5; P. Jourda, *Marguerite d'Angoulême* (1930), i. 145–53.
[7] C. Terrasse, *François Ier* (1945–70), ii. 21.

Chabot, who had both been captured with the king at Pavia and had since helped to secure his release.

Montmorency was thirty-three years old and a member of one of the oldest and richest noble families in France. He had been brought up with the king and, since 1515, had participated in several military campaigns. In August 1522 he had become a marshal of France, a knight of St Michael and a king's councillor. Now, on 23 March 1526, he became grand master (in place of René of Savoy) and governor of Languedoc (in place of Bourbon). As the official head of the king's household, Montmorency soon became one of Francis's chief advisers, though the influence on policy-making of the king's mother and other experienced councillors, like Duprat and Robertet, was not eclipsed overnight; Montmorency served an initial period of ministerial apprenticeship. Even so, his principles were already formed: as one would expect of a strict, even brutal, disciplinarian, he believed in a strong monarchy and was a conservative in religion. On 10 January 1527 he became related to the royal family by marrying Madeleine of Savoy, daughter of the king's deceased uncle, René, and was henceforth addressed as 'my nephew' by the king's mother and her daughter, Marguerite. Madeleine brought her husband a sizable dowry, which helped to swell his already considerable fortune.[8]

The career of Philippe Chabot, seigneur de Brion, who was appointed Admiral of France in succession to Bonnivet, the king's deceased favourite, on 23 March 1526, was in many ways remarkably similar to Montmorency's. He was roughly of the same age and had also been brought up with the king. Within a few years of Francis's accession, he had become a gentleman of the king's chamber, captain of a company of forty *lances*, a knight of St Michael and mayor of Bordeaux. Among his military exploits was his successful defence of Marseilles in 1524 against Bourbon. For his many services, including his contribution to the peace of Madrid, Chabot was well rewarded: in addition to the admiralship of France, he was appointed captain of Honfleur and of Dijon and governor of Burgundy and of Valois. He also received many gifts of land and money, though he never became as wealthy as Montmorency. In January 1527 Chabot also joined the king's family circle by marrying Françoise de Longwy, daughter of Francis's bastard sister.[9]

Other notable appointments made by Francis in 1526 were the following: Galiot de Genouillac became Master of the Horse (*Grand Ecuyer*) in place of Galeazzo da San Severino. Robert de La Marck, seigneur de Florange, who had served his imprisonment in Flanders, was made a marshal of France. Jean de La Barre became comte d'Etampes and *prévôt*

8   Decrue, i. 28, 67, 70–1, 75–8; C.A.F., i. 2307–8.
9   D.B.F., viii. 134–5; C.A.F., i. 2305, 2086, 2408, 2861; v. 18592, 18661; viii. 32430.

of Paris, and François de Tournon was promoted to the archbishopric of Bourges.[10]

The fall of Semblançay (January–August 1527)

On 13 January 1527 Semblançay was arrested and thrown into the Bastille, his goods being seized.[11] The only reason for his arrest, it seems, was to rid the king of a tiresome creditor. For, although the former minister had not been completely excluded from public affairs during the captivity, he had transacted no important business for the crown since 1525. His energies had been mainly absorbed by his private affairs, especially the recovery of his debts.[12] This was perhaps his greatest mistake, for he made many influential enemies by his importunity. He pleaded poverty when foreign bankers asked him to repay loans he had guaranteed, yet he was still a very rich man with much property in and around Tours.[13] This being so, he would have been wise to leave his creditors in peace. It was particularly foolish of him to seek reimbursement by the crown at a time of national crisis. Tact was evidently not his forte.

Semblançay's trial in 1527 is sometimes described as a retrial, but this is incorrect, for hitherto he had been required only to submit his accounts for examination; no criminal charges had been levelled against him. Now he faced a formidable indictment amounting to *lèse-majesté*. He was accused *inter alia* of appropriating to himself important sums belonging to the crown, obliging the king to borrow when he himself owed Francis money, taking bribes, corruptly manipulating taxes and fraudulently concealing the extent of his private fortune.[14] How much truth did these charges contain? By modern standards Semblançay's bookkeeping was certainly not impeccable; but the discrepancies in his accounts were due to the complexities of sixteenth-century fiscal practice rather than to dishonesty on his part. His situation was further complicated by the fact that he was a banker in his own right as well as a public servant. He tried to keep the two roles separate by using business associates in London and Lyons as intermediaries, but the deviousness of his operations caused misunderstandings and exposed him to the charge of misappropriating royal funds.

[10] C.A.F., i. 2313; ii. 6169; v. 18548; vii. 23873; Versoris, pp. 91–2; M. François, *Le cardinal François de Tournon* (1951), p. 47.

[11] J.B.P., pp. 253–4. Others arrested at the same time were Roberto Albizzi, a Lyons banker, and Jean Prévost, *trésorier des finances*. Albizzi was one of Semblançay's business associates, but Prévost was a protégé of Louise of Savoy. His arrest was widely seen as a move by the government to create an illusion of fairness.

[12] Doucet, ii. 225–6.

[13] A. Spont, *Semblançay* (1895), pp. 239–42.

[14] Doucet, ii. 228–30.

Semblançay's trial was nothing short of a travesty. He was at first given the same judges as those who had examined his accounts in 1523, but they were soon dismissed, presumably because they had shown their impartiality, and replaced by the government's creatures or his personal enemies. Thereafter the verdict was never in doubt. Though Semblançay produced documentary evidence refuting the charges against him, he was found guilty on 9 August and sentenced to death.[15] The verdict was unusually terse: none of the charges was discussed in detail and no reason given for setting aside the decree of 1523.

The baron appealed to the Parlement, but the validity of his appeal was challenged on the ground that his judges had been drawn from the Parlement and other sovereign courts, so that their judgment could be taken as final. The matter was referred to the king, who had gone to Amiens for his meeting with Wolsey. Semblançay wrote to him, in the meantime, reminding him of his past services and pleading for mercy.[16] But Francis was unmoved: he ordered the baron's immediate execution. On 11 August, therefore, Semblançay was removed from the Bastille and taken to the famous gibbet at Montfaucon. The old man (he was about eighty) was escorted through Paris by Gilles Maillart, *lieutenant-criminel* of the Châtelet, and some troops. He seemed calm and acknowledged friends in the crowd that had come to watch him pass.[17] It was not a hostile crowd. Although the *gens des finances* were not popular, Semblançay attracted sympathy on account of his age and dignity. 'He was much pitied and mourned by the people', wrote a chronicler, 'who would have been pleased if the king had seen fit to spare him.'[18] Their sympathy may have been connected with their hatred of Duprat, who was known to be Semblançay's enemy. A well-known 'Epigramme' by Marot expressed their feelings:

> Lorsque Maillart, juge d'enfer, menoit
> A Montfaulcon Semblançay l'âme rendre
> A vostre advis, lequel des deux tenoit
> Meilleur maintien? Pour le vous faire entendre,
> Maillart sembloit homme que mort va prendre,
> Et Semblançay fut si ferme vieillart
> Que l'on cuidoit, pour vray qu'il menast pendre
> A Montfaulcon le lieutenant Maillart.[19]

[15] *J.B.P.*, p. 255.   [16] B.N., MS. fr. 2981, fol. 68.
[17] Spont, p. 262.   [18] Versoris, p. 106.
[19] C. Marot, *Les épigrammes*, ed. C. A. Mayer (London, 1970), p. 129. 'When Maillart, judge of hell, led Semblançay to Montfaucon to render up his soul, which of the two, in your opinion, had the better bearing? You should know that Maillart looked like a man whom death was about to carry off, whereas Semblançay was such a strong old man that it seemed as if he was leading the lieutenant Maillart to Montfaucon to be hanged.'

Twice on the way to Montfaucon and once at the foot of the gibbet Semblançay had to listen to a public recital of his crimes. Outside the convent of the Filles-Dieu, his bonnet was removed and he was handed a wooden cross after receiving the customary gifts of bread and wine. He was taken along the rue Saint-Denis to the place of execution, where he was kept waiting six hours before he was hanged. Thus ended the career of the man who had once been described as 'quasi king in France'.[20] A few days later his body vanished mysteriously, and Duprat, who never missed a chance of being vindictive, ordered a search so that it might be strung up again. It was eventually found dismembered in a graveyard near Pantin by one of Semblançay's servants: he gathered up the remains and carried them to Paris, where they were decently buried in the church of Sainte-Catherine-des-Ecoliers.[21]

This, however, was not the end of the Semblançay affair. For his widow, Jeanne Ruzé, and her son, Guillaume de Beaune, *général des finances*, appealed against his sentence. It is unlikely that they expected it to be reversed. Their aim was more probably to focus public attention on a miscarriage of justice for which they held the chancellor chiefly responsible. They said that they would press their appeal until justice had been restored in France. Such a challenge could not be ignored by the crown. A high-powered commission, comprising two presidents from every parlement in the kingdom, was set up to examine the appeal. How seriously it performed its task is not known, but its verdict was predictable. On 11 February 1529 it confirmed Semblançay's sentence and condemned the appellants. Jeanne Ruzé had her property confiscated, and her son, who had fled to Germany, was sentenced to death. Two lawyers on whose advice the appeal had been lodged were suspended. Eventually, however, the sentences were revised in exchange for substantial damages: Jeanne Ruzé recovered part of her property, her son was pardoned and the two lawyers were reinstated.[22]

But the hunting-down of allegedly corrupt financiers by the Commission de la Tour Carrée continued until 1536. Among its victims were many of Semblançay's relatives, notably his nephew, Gilles Berthelot, who had to repay 29,399 *livres* in addition to paying a fine of 20,000 *livres*, his daughter, Marie de Beaune, the widow of Raoul Hurault, who was fined 100,000 *livres*, and his grandnephew, Antoine Bohier, who was

[20] Versoris, p. 106.
[21] Spont, pp. 263–4. According to P. de Bourdeille, abbé de Brantôme, many people thought Francis should have pardoned Semblançay because of his venerable age, his services to four kings and because he, Francis, used to call him 'father'. Brantôme, *Oeuvres complètes*, ed. L. Lalanne (1864–82), iii. 90.
[22] Doucet, ii. 238–9; *J.B.P.*, pp. 262, 422–3; *C.A.F.*, i. 3316, 3646.

fined 190,000 *livres*. Nor was Semblançay the only financier to die for his alleged malpractices: Jean de Poncher, *trésorier-général* of Languedoc, was executed in September 1535.[23]

Francis and the Parisians

Francis had good cause to feel displeased with the Parisians in March 1526. Not only had they imperilled the success of his mother's foreign policy, and consequently the security of the kingdom, by opposing the demand for an obligation under the treaty of the More, but some had also behaved in a disloyal way on other occasions. When, for example, news of the king's recovery from his serious illness in Spain had reached the capital, some practical jokers, disguised as royal messengers, had ridden through the streets shouting that he was really dead and that the government was concealing the truth from the people.[24] On another occasion, there had been a masquerade from the cloister of Notre-Dame in which a woman had appeared riding a horse drawn by devils and surrounded with doctors of theology bearing Luther's name on their fronts and backs – clearly a reference to the widely held belief in the capital that heresy flourished at court.[25]

It is possible, though not certain, that Francis deliberately delayed his return to the capital as a demonstration of his displeasure. When eventually he did reappear, on 14 April 1527, he gave the authorities such short notice that little of the customary ceremonial – not even the canopy under which the king traditionally made his entry – could be prepared. His entry, moreover, was immediately preceded by the arrest of eight citizens who had led the opposition to the guarantees required under the treaty of the More. It was reported at the time that as many as sixty arrests had been planned by the government. The eight arrested were a canon of Notre-Dame, Jacques Merlin; three *avocats* of the Parlement, Jean Bouchard, Jean Dugué and François Boileau; a notary of the Châtelet, Jean de Thamereau; and three merchants, Jean Godefroy, Jean Le Riche and Jean de Gastine. The notary and the merchants were released almost at once, but the others were left to languish in prison for two years, and they would almost certainly have stayed there longer but for the timely intervention of the Bureau de la Ville when the king asked for another subsidy from the capital. The sentences they eventually received were not severe: Merlin was banished to Nantes for a year, while Bouchard was

---

23   Spont, pp. 274–7; *J.B.P.*, pp. 393–4; Guiffrey, p. 139.
24   Champollion-Figeac, pp. 379–80; M. Félibien, *Histoire de la ville de Paris* (1725), ii. 973.
25   Félibien, ii. 978.

fined 400 *livres*, suspended from his practice for one year and banned for life from holding municipal office. The rest had only to pay costs.[26]

Francis and the Parlement of Paris

Soon after his return from Spain, Francis vindicated the authority of his mother and chancellor in respect of ecclesiastical appointments. On 9 April 1526 he allowed Duprat to take possession of the abbey of Saint-Benoît-sur-Loire, and a few weeks later gave effect to the decree of the Grand Conseil which had conferred upon him the archbishopric of Sens. But the king also wanted to humiliate the *parlementaires*, who had dared to challenge his own authority by their attack upon the chancellor. In December 1526, therefore, he acted on the proposal, originally made by his mother, that the Parlement and Grand Conseil should debate their differences in front of his council. On 4 December four representatives of the Parlement and three of the Grand Conseil duly appeared before fifteen members of the king's council, of whom only two – de Selve and Robertet – were known to be sympathetic to the Parlement. After the representatives of the Grand Conseil had presented their case, the chancellor explained why the government had become involved in the dispute at Saint-Benoît: the Parlement, he said, had defied the regent's authority and issued decrees harmful to the king. The four *parlementaires* who had been directly concerned with the dispute tried to justify themselves but failed to get the support of their colleagues. On 10 December the king's council decided that the Parlement had acted illegally and in a manner likely to encourage the enemies of the kingdom. It declared, furthermore, that the Parlement's decrees, including those directed against members of the Grand Conseil, were null and void. The four *parlementaires* were forbidden to resume their normal duties until further notice.[27]

On 10 January 1527 Francis took another step to vindicate the chancellor. He ordered the clerk of the Parlement to bring him the record of its debates during his captivity. At first the court would send him only transcripts, but eventually it complied, after deleting certain passages concerning Duprat. This must have given the chancellor much satisfaction; the deletions were an eloquent testimony to his power and to the Parlement's humiliation.[28]

Among the churchmen who had been involved in the Saint-Benoît affair, the most severely punished was Duprat's rival, François de Poncher, bishop of Paris. He was accused of sedition, and on 14 January 1527

---

[26] G. Jacqueton, *La politique extérieure de Louise de Savoie* (1892), pp. 188–9; *J.B.P.*, pp. 266–7; Versoris, p. 102.

[27] Doucet, ii. 220–3; *C.A.F.*, i. 2504; v. 18563. [28] Doucet, ii. 223–4.

the Grand Conseil was ordered to investigate his activities. The bishop was imprisoned at Vincennes in August 1531 and died there in September 1532.[29]

The dispute between the king and the Parlement was finally settled at a *lit-de-justice* on 24 July 1527. The meeting began with a speech by the first president, Charles Guillart, in which he tried to justify the Parlement's past actions. While admitting that the king ruled by the grace of God, he said that his authority also rested on the obedience of his subjects, which in turn depended on his use of good ministers and laws. 'We do not wish to challenge your authority', Guillart continued, 'for this would be a sort of sacrilege and we are well aware that you are above the law and that no laws or ordinances can constrain you . . . but we wish to say that you . . . should not wish to do all that lies within your power but only that which is reasonable and just.' The king, Guillart said, should observe the laws of his predecessors, who had ruled well; but he went even further. The Parlement, he claimed (without any historical justification), held its power not from the king, but from the people, for it had originally been a popular assembly, a sort of 'convention of estates'. Finally, he denounced royal policies which had produced friction between the Parlement and the crown, such as the protection of heretics and the use of *évocations*. He voiced his indignation at the way in which the Grand Conseil had been absolved, and even praised, for its illegal acts concerning the benefices at Sens and Saint-Benoît, while the Parlement's representatives had been 'condemned ignominiously'.[30]

Remarkable as it was for its courage and frankness, Guillart's speech did nothing to mollify the king; rather the reverse. That afternoon Francis held a council meeting at which an edict was drawn up defining the Parlement's authority. In accordance with royal policy before the captivity, the court was forbidden to meddle in affairs of state and confined to its judicial role. Even this was so narrowly defined as to exclude cognizance of beneficial disputes. While the Parlement was allowed to submit remonstrances, it was forbidden to amend any piece of royal legislation at the time of its registration. It was also required to obtain from the king each year formal confirmation of its delegated powers; any action by the Parlement in excess of these powers was annulled retrospectively and for the future. While the Parlement was forbidden to restrict Louise of Savoy's powers as regent, all her past decisions were confirmed and all contradictory ones by the Parlement revoked. The edict also confirmed the chancellor's independence of the court. Finally, it announced the setting up of a royal commission to reform the judicial administration.

Justice, it claimed, was suffering because a few families of venal office-holders dominated the judiciary.[31]

The presentation of the edict was as humiliating to the Parlement as its contents. Once the council had finished its business, representatives of the Parlement were called before the king in the Salle Verte and Robertet read the edict out to them. Normally, they would have been given a chance to reply, but on this occasion the king and his councillors swept out of the room before they could utter a word. Francis then added a further insult by insisting that the edict be registered not only by the Parlement but also by his own council and by the Grand Conseil. Though deeply hurt by the king's action, the Parlement no longer had the heart to resist; it merely showed its contempt for the edict by registering it without the customary formalities. It was nevertheless a watershed in the relations between crown and Parlement: the king had successfully checked the tendency towards a more limited monarchy, which his recent incapacity had encouraged. Although the Parlement continued to remonstrate about certain royal policies till the end of the reign, it never again seriously encroached on the king's authority. Having made his point, Francis could afford to be generous: on 26 July he pardoned the four *parlementaires* who had been suspended for their parts in the Sens and Saint-Benoît affairs.[32]

The condemnation of Bourbon

Another loose knot that needed to be tied following the king's return from captivity was the case of Charles, duc de Bourbon, and his accomplices.

In 1525, as we have seen, Francis had been angered by the lenient sentences the Parlement had passed on some of the duke's accomplices and had forbidden their release. During his captivity he appears to have had second thoughts, perhaps in line with his mother's concern to achieve a *modus vivendi* with the Parlement. De Prie and d'Escars had been released accordingly. By March 1526 only three of Bourbon's principal accomplices remained in captivity, namely, Jean de Poitiers, seigneur de Saint-Vallier, Jacques Hurault, bishop of Autun, and Antoine de Chabannes, bishop of Le Puy. Saint-Vallier was released in July and recovered his property and dignities in the following year; Hurault was pardoned in 1527; and Chabannes's fate is unknown.[33] But, if Francis was prepared to treat these men leniently, he showed no inclination to reinstate Bourbon, as he had promised to do in the peace of Madrid. No legal action, however, was taken against him until after his death in the sack of Rome.

[31] *Ordonnances*, v. no. 463, pp. 81–3.   [32] Doucet, ii. 256–7.
[33] *Ibid.*, ii. 243–6; J.B.P., p. 206; C.A.F., i. 2415, 2745, 2929; vii. 23855.

In July 1527 the *procureur-général* presented two documents to a special commission set up by the king to try the duke posthumously: the first repeated some wild accusations levelled at him in 1523 and subsequently disproved, while the second concentrated on his more recent 'crimes', notably the invasion of Provence and the sack of Rome. Only four days were needed to complete the preliminary investigation, and on 26 July the duke's trial by the court of peers began in the king's presence. Although the peers numbered only five, the scene did not lack solemnity, as the whole Parlement was present. The proceedings began with an usher summoning the dead duke to appear; when no one responded, the court got down to business. The *procureur-général* demanded that Bourbon's memory be condemned, his coat-of-arms effaced and his property sequestered. A purely formal debate ensued, after which the court drew up its verdict, which was announced on the following day. This second session was even more solemn than the first: a large concourse of distinguished spectators, including foreign ambassadors, marshals of France, gentlemen of the household and officers of the king's guard listened to the chancellor as he read out the sentence. This declared Bourbon guilty of '*lèse-majesté*, rebellion and felony' and conceded all the chief prosecutor's demands: the duke lost his coat-of-arms and title; his fiefs were formally annexed to the royal demesne; and all his personal property was confiscated.[34]

The growth of 'Lutheranism'

During the captivity a vigorous attempt had been made by the Parlement, aided and abetted by the Sorbonne, to check the progress of heresy. With the help of new powers obtained by the regent from the pope, a campaign had been mounted against the Cercle de Meaux, forcing its members either to recant or go into exile. Berquin had been arrested for the second time and tried as a relapsed heretic; but he still awaited sentence when the king returned.

Francis, who had been kept informed of these events by his sister during her visit to Spain, very soon expressed his disapproval of certain aspects of the persecution. On 1 April 1526 he rebuked the Parlement for its disobedience in respect of Berquin's trial, forbade it to pass sentence and threatened to call its judges to account. The Parlement, while offering

---

[34] Doucet, ii. 246–50. Some of this property was restored to Bourbon's heirs under the peace of Cambrai (see ch. 14), but only after protracted litigation: e.g. in August 1538 the constable's aunt, Louise, princesse de La Roche-sur-Yon, received the county of Montpensier, the *dauphiné* of Auvergne and three lordships (*C.A.F.*, iii. 10231). Final settlement was not achieved till the reign of Charles IX.

excuses for its actions, duly obeyed. In July, however, Francis ordered Berquin's release within Paris or at least that he be allowed unrestricted access to the courtyard (*préau*) of the Conciergerie. But the Parlement would only permit him to use the courtyard for two hours each day and in silence. Soon afterwards Berquin fell ill, and the king ordered his transfer to the Louvre, but again the Parlement refused on the ground that the Louvre was unsafe. It did, however, allow La Barre, *bailli* of Paris, to see the prisoner, who seemed well treated and in good health. In October, the Parlement sent two representatives to the king to explain why Berquin could not be released, but, after following the king from place to place for a fortnight, they failed to get a hearing. On 19 November Francis sent La Barre to the Parlement with another demand for Berquin's release. The court again refused, but it offered no opposition to the *bailli* when he removed the prisoner from the Conciergerie. Berquin's life had again been saved by the king.[35]

Francis also extended his protection to members of the Cercle de Meaux. Lefèvre, Roussel and Caroli, who had gone into exile during the captivity, were now able to come home: Lefèvre took charge of the royal library at Blois, Roussel became Marguerite de Navarre's almoner and Caroli resumed preaching in Paris. But the Sorbonne did not readily submit to this state of affairs. On 16 May it condemned the *Colloquies* of Erasmus, and, soon afterwards, Béda published his *Annotationes*, in which Erasmus and Lefèvre were accused of every kind of heresy. Erasmus was sufficiently frightened by the offensive to appeal directly to the king and Parlement; he even tried to dissociate himself from the cause of Lefèvre.[36] The Parlement indicated in reply that it could take no action against the faculty, but Francis rose to the defence of both Erasmus and Lefèvre. He ordered the Parlement to ban the publication of any work by the Sorbonne which had not been previously examined and approved by the court. Béda and other members of the faculty were invited by the Parlement to expound their views, which they did without sparing the king.[37] But, in the end, the Parlement was not prepared to fight the king on their behalf. It banned the sale of Béda's work and forbade the faculty to publish anything without its permission. On 14 December 1526 the Sorbonne censured Lefèvre and, almost exactly a year later, did the same to Erasmus. But the faculty could do little without the Parlement's backing. Early in 1527 Francis scored another victory against the religious reactionaries by abolishing the *juges délégués*.[38]

[35] *Ibid.*, ii. 210–13. The king's letters to the Parlement are in A.N., X[1a] 1529, fols. 198–9, 316, 442–3.

[36] Herminjard, i. 435–8; A.N., X[1a] 1529, fols. 307–8.   [37] Doucet, ii. 217.

[38] *Ibid.*, ii. 219; J. Fraikin (ed.), *Nonciatures de France: Clément VII* (1906), i. 428–33.

The king's actions naturally created the impression abroad that he was veering towards the Reformation. 'The king favours the Word', Capito wrote to Zwingli on 1 January 1527.[39] This, however, was an illusion. Francis was simply reasserting his authority after a concerted attempt by the Parlement and Sorbonne to deal with heresy as they thought fit. He may have 'favoured the Word' to the extent of not understanding how a faith more firmly rooted in Scripture could be heretical, but he continued to be firmly opposed to any form of religious dissent which offended orthodoxy as he envisaged it, particularly if it disturbed the peace. Thus in December 1527 he answered a demand from the clergy for the extirpation of 'the damned and insufferable Lutheran sect' by promising to show his subjects that he was the 'Most Christian King' in deed as well as in name. He was at this moment anxiously seeking money from the clergy to help pay his sons' ransom, and his antiheretical professions may have been, at least in part, a *quid pro quo* for the clergy's decision, on 16 December, to grant him 1.3 million *écus*.[40] In June 1528, Francis reacted strongly to the mutilation by persons unknown of a statue of the Virgin and Child in Paris: he offered a substantial reward for information about the culprits, took part in a procession to the scene of the sacrilege and ordered a statue of solid silver to replace the damaged one.[41]

Early in 1528 Duprat, acting in his capacity as archbishop of Sens, outlined a programme of draconian penalties for heresy, and in July a revolting device for putting heretics to death called *l'estrapade* was first used at Meaux. Instead of being burned at the stake, the victim was suspended by means of iron chains over the flames, into which he was alternately lowered and raised so as to prolong his agony.[42]

But if Francis sanctioned these various measures, he would still not allow the Parlement and Sorbonne to impose their narrow standard of orthodoxy upon his court. His attitude was authoritarian rather than liberal: he viewed any outside interference with the day-to-day life of his court as an insult to his dignity. He may even have believed that his court could safely digest a larger dose of evangelism than the kingdom at large. Thus, in spite of his official denunciation of the 'damned Lutheran sect', he continued to protect certain evangelical preachers and scholars from persecution. His protection, however, was not foolproof. His frequent

[39]   Herminjard, ii. 4.
[40]   See below, ch. 14. N. M. Sutherland (*The Huguenot Struggle for Recognition* (New Haven and London, 1980), pp. 19–20) suggests that the king's necessity was deliberately exploited by the Parlement and clergy 'to augment the religious persecution'.
[41]   Imbart de La Tour, iii. 262; *J.B.P.*, pp. 290–3.
[42]   Imbart de La Tour, iii. 262–7; A. Buisson, *Le chancelier Antoine Duprat* (1935), pp. 293–5; V.-L. Bourrilly and N. Weiss, 'Jean du Bellay, les Protestants et la Sorbonne', *B.S.H.P.F.*, liii (1904), 114.

and often prolonged absences from the capital meant that he could be outstripped by events there, while international events might also inhibit him. Both factors contributed to Berquin's final undoing.

In March 1528 Berquin's trial was resumed before a commission of twelve laymen specially appointed by the pope at the king's request. These judges, however, were soon denounced as 'Lutherans' by the Sorbonne, and the ever-vacillating Clement was persuaded to revoke their powers. Francis protested vehemently to the papal legate, but soon afterwards he received bad news from Italy. Lautrec's army, with which he had hoped to overawe the pope, had surrendered, leaving him with no option but to accept Clement's decision. Berquin consequently had to face the same hostile judges as in 1525. On 15 April he was found guilty and sentenced to life imprisonment. Instead of accepting this verdict, he decided against the advice of his friends to appeal to the Parlement. Two days later, while the king was away from the capital, the appeal was rejected and Berquin was burnt on the Place de Grève. How Francis reacted to this event is not known, but the fact that no one responsible for it was subsequently punished suggests that Berquin had already been written off by the king.[43]

[43] M. Mann, *Erasme et les débuts de la réforme française* (1934), pp. 144–8; *J.B.P.*, pp. 317–22, 423–7.

14

From Cognac to Cambrai

(1526–9)

THERE WAS MUCH scepticism and foreboding in Europe at large when the peace of Madrid was first announced. Cardinal Wolsey could not believe that the king of France had accepted such harsh terms. He and his master feared the enormous extension of the emperor's power if he should gain Burgundy and his sister become queen of France. The Franco-imperial marriage, Henry VIII said, carried a heavy risk, for, if Charles and his brother died without issue, their sister Eleanor would acquire their entire inheritance.[1] Pope Clement VII doubted whether Francis would honour the treaty in full. It was likely, he thought, that the king would fulfil only those terms that were necessary for him to regain his freedom and would then ignore the rest.[2]

The first clear indication of Francis's real intentions was his refusal to ratify the treaty immediately after his return to France. The imperial ambassador, de Praet, who had come to fetch the ratification, was told that his powers were insufficient and sent home empty-handed. Yet at the same time Francis ratified the treaty of the More with England. On 2 April he complained that a garbled text of the treaty of Madrid had been published prematurely in Antwerp, Rome and Florence, thereby making it difficult for him to surrender Burgundy. His subjects were angry, he said, and were asking to be heard before the treaty was ratified.[3] Was this an excuse, or did the king genuinely intend to consult his subjects about the treaty? Historians once believed that Francis's decision to repudiate it was taken only after he had called the Estates General to Cognac in May 1526 and the Burgundian representatives had proudly refused to be separated from the French crown. But, as Hauser has shown, no such assembly was called.[4] Nor were the Burgundians as loyal to the French

---

[1] G. Jacqueton, *La politique extérieure de Louise de Savoie* (1892), pp. 256–8; *L.P.*, iv. 1963.   [2] *L.P.*, iv. 1956.

[3] H. Hauser, 'Le traité de Madrid et la cession de la Bourgogne à Charles-Quint', *Revue bourguignonne*, xxii (1912), 150–3; Le Glay, ii. 656–8.

[4] The story of the Estates-General of Cognac was invented by G. Paradin (*Memoriae nostrae libri quatuor* (Lyons, 1548), iv. 47) and repeated by all eighteenth-century historians. See Hauser, 'Traité de Madrid', pp. 1–4.

crown as was once supposed. A Burgundian deputation did call on Francis at Cognac in April 1526, but it seems to have exerted no significant influence on the king's policy. The delegates said they could do nothing on their own and suggested that Francis should call the provincial estates and send some important person to represent him.[5] This, in fact, was done in June. But the decision to break the treaty of Madrid had already been taken by the king's council more than a month before. Thus one is forced to the conclusion that the king merely invoked popular consultation as a means of gaining time during which to cement his relations with England, Venice and the papacy.

Early in May Charles de Lannoy, viceroy of Naples, visited Cognac in the hope of persuading Francis to ratify the treaty. He was warmly received, but the king did not allow gratitude to the man who had saved his life at Pavia and on whose advice he had recently been released from captivity to deflect him from his political aims.[6] On 10 May the viceroy was told by the king's council that Francis could not hand over Burgundy because his subjects would not tolerate such a diminution of his patrimony. The king explained that the promises extorted from him in prison had no binding force. He added, however, that he wished to remain friendly with the emperor and was ready to honour those clauses of the treaty which were acceptable to him, leaving the rest to be adjusted according to reason and honesty. In place of Burgundy, he suggested a ransom in cash.[7]

On 4 June the estates of Burgundy met at Dijon in the presence of Philippe Chabot, the king's representative, and endorsed the decision already taken by the king's council. Denouncing the treaty of Madrid as 'contrary to all reason and equity', the delegates affirmed their wish to remain under the French crown for ever. A similar pronouncement was made four days later by the estates of Auxonne. The fact that both estates used exactly the same words suggests that they had been well briefed by the government.[8]

In July a royal apologia intended for international consumption was published. In addition to stressing the 'fundamental law' which forbade

---

[5] Hauser doubted whether any Burgundian deputies had come to Cognac (*ibid.*, p. 83). But see M. François, *Le cardinal François de Tournon* (1951), p. 52 n. 2. On 21 April English ambassadors reported the presence in Cognac of 'a gentleman from Burgundy, who had remonstrated with the king against delivering Burgundy into the Emperor's hands without their own consent, and rather than they would be so delivered they will refuse obedience either to the King or the Emperor'. *L.P.*, iv. 2115.

[6] Hauser, 'Traité de Madrid', pp. 158–9; L.-E. Halkin and G. Dansaert, *Charles de Lannoy* (Brussels, 1934), p. 101; *C.S.P. Ven.*, iii. 1270, 1272–3, 1285.

[7] Halkin and Dansaert, pp. 102–3; Le Glay, ii. 660–1.

[8] Hauser, 'Traité de Madrid', pp. 78–81.

the king to alienate any part of his demesne, it laid down the principle that no province or town could change its ownership without the consent of the inhabitants. But Valdés, replying on the emperor's behalf, denied that popular consent was necessary for the restitution of a territory to its lawful ruler. He thought it strange that Francis, who had always boasted of his absolute authority, should now be championing the principle of 'popular consultation'.[9]

In addition to justifying his breach of faith on theoretical grounds, Francis took steps to prevent the emperor taking Burgundy by force. Chabot was instructed to inspect the fortresses of the province, receive an oath of loyalty from the inhabitants, draw up an inventory of available victuals and munitions, pass the musters, punish looters and set up a sort of espionage centre at Dijon. In carrying out these tasks, Chabot carefully avoided giving offence to local feeling: Burgundian officials were paid punctually, and regions like Charolais that had been heavily taxed in the past were given relief.

These precautions, however, proved unnecessary, for the emperor was too poor and had too many problems on his hands to attempt a forceful annexation of Burgundy. His army in Franche-Comté was unpaid, and no help was forthcoming either from his aunt, Margaret of Savoy, or his brother Ferdinand. An attempt by imperial troops to capture Auxonne failed miserably: it merely exposed Franche-Comté, which had been declared neutral, to a possible reprisal attack, and strengthened the inhabitants' desire to live at peace with their neighbours. In July they voted supplies to enable the prince of Orange, who commanded the imperial army in their territory, to withdraw his troops. Soon afterwards Charles ordered him to disband them; the emperor's dream of reuniting the two Burgundies had vanished for ever.[10]

The League of Cognac (22 May 1526)

Francis's policy towards the emperor in the first half of 1526 is clear: despite his repudiation of the peace of Madrid, he did not want to go to war with Charles immediately. He wanted to recover his sons, who were now serving as hostages in Spain, by peaceful means if possible. But he had to put pressure on Charles by strengthening his own relations with England, the Venetians and the pope, and very soon found himself caught up in a new war.

Francis repeatedly expressed his gratitude to Henry VIII for not having attacked France during his captivity and also for having aided his release.

---

[9] *Ibid.*, pp. 90–6.   [10] *Ibid.*, pp. 74, 85–9.

Francis of Angoulême, duc de Valois, at the age of ten (1504)
Marguerite d'Angoulême, sister of Francis I

Louise of Savoy, comtesse d'Angoulême, mother of Francis I
Francis of Angoulême, duc de Valois, in 1512

Francis I hunting with his huntsman Perot. Miniature by Godefroy le Batave in *Commentaires de la guerre gallique*, vol. 2

Château of Blois: Façade of the loggias, from an engraving by J. Androuet du Cerceau in *Les plus excellents bastiments de France* (1576–1607)

Château of Blois: Façade of the loggias, from a modern photograph

Château of Blois: Francis I staircase

The Battle of Pavia. Detail of a tapestry (design attributed to B. van Orley) in the Galleria Nazionale di Capodimonte, Naples. The king (with the fleur-de-lis) is charging at the head of his *gendarmerie* while Pescara's arquebusiers prepare to fire in the background

Francis I. Portrait attributed to Jean Clouet. Musée du Louvre, Paris

Rosso: Mars disarmed by Cupid and Venus disrobed by the Graces. Pen and ink drawing. Musée du Louvre, Paris

Château of Fontainebleau: Galerie François Ier

Château of Fontainebleau: Detail of the decoration by Rosso in the Galerie François Ier, showing the *éléphant fleurdelysé*

Articles veritables sur les horribles/grandz et importables abuz de la Messe papalle: inuentee directement contre la saincte Cene de Iesus Christ.

Ie inuocque le ciel et la terre/ en tesmoignage de Verite...

Premierement/ a tout fidele chrestien/ est a doibt estre trescertain que nostre Seigneur et seul sauueur Iesus Christ...

Secondement/ en ceste malheureuse messe on a prouocque quasi tout le monde a idolatrie publicque...

Tiercement/ ceulx paoures sacrificateurs pour adiouster erreur sur erreur...

Quartement/ le fruict de la messe est bien contraire au fruict de la saincte Cene de Iesus Christ...

The Placard against the mass of October 1534, written by Antoine Marcourt and printed at Neuchâtel by Pierre de Vingle

Antoine Duprat,
chancellor
of France and
cardinal-archbishop of Sens.
Drawing by
Jean Clouet.
Musée Condé,
Chantilly

Anne de Montmorency,
grand master
(1526) and
constable of
France (1538).
Drawing by
Jean Clouet.
Musée Condé,
Chantilly

Andrea del Sarto: *Charity* (1518). The only Italian painting surviving from Francis's collection which is known to have been painted in France for the king. Musée du Louvre, Paris

Benvenuto Cellini: *Juno*. Drawing for one of the twelve life-size candelabra commissioned by Francis, of which only the *Jupiter* was completed. Musée du Louvre, Paris

Francis I portrayed on a medal in lead designed by Benvenuto Cellini. Fitzwilliam Museum, Cambridge

Back view of a casket decorated with crystal panels, engraved by Valerio Belli and showing scenes from the life of Christ. The casket was given to Francis by Pope Clement VII on the occasion of the marriage between Henri, duc d'Orléans, and Catherine de' Medici

Guillaume Budé, the humanist scholar. Tempera and oil on wood, by Jean Clouet. The Greek inscription on the book reads 'It may seem a great thing to realize one's desires, but truly the greatest thing is not to desire what one shouldn't.' Metropolitan Museum of Art, New York

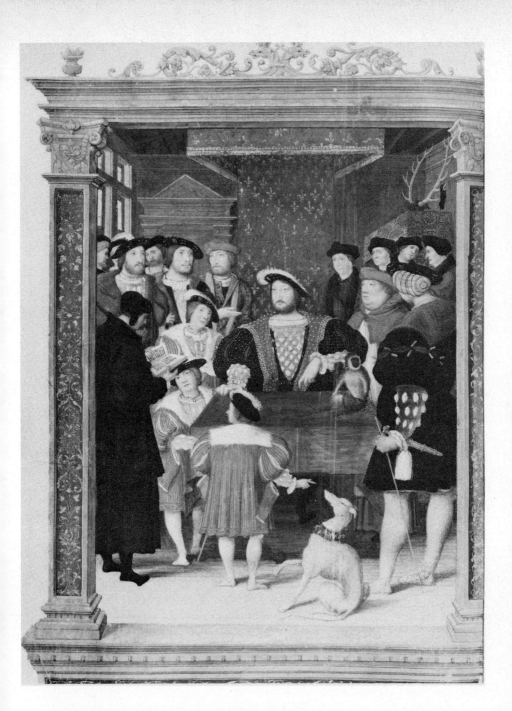

Francis and his courtiers listen to Antoine Macault reading from his translation of Diodorus Siculus, from an anonymous miniature of *c.* 1530. Among the king's entourage are his three sons (on his right), Cardinal Duprat (on his left) and the king's pet monkey. Musée Condé, Chantilly

The tomb of Francis I and of his first queen, Claude de France, designed by Philibert de l'Orme. The *priants* of the king and queen are by François Carmoy and François Marchand; those of the Dauphin François, Princess Charlotte and Charles d'Orléans are by Pierre Bontemps, who also carved the bas-reliefs depicting the battles of Marignano and Ceresole

As a mark of special favour, he invited Sir Thomas Cheyney, the English ambassador, to enter his privy chamber as freely as his own master's.[11] An incident which took place during Francis's entry into Bordeaux gave him another opportunity to show his high regard for England. He ordered the Portuguese ambassador, who had placed himself ahead of Cheyney in the procession, to fall back or withdraw. 'What!' he exclaimed, 'an apothecary's orator would presume to go before the king of England's orator! Let him go to Calicut and there make laws among his spiceries, for here he should make none!'[12] On 15 April Francis ratified the treaty of the More and declared his willingness to meet Henry whenever he should wish to cross the Channel. On 8 August England and France signed a new treaty, binding themselves not to treat separately with the emperor.[13]

At the end of March 1526 two envoys, representing Venice and the papacy respectively, arrived at the French court with a view to drawing Francis into an anti-imperial coalition. Much to their relief, they found the king prepared to join such a league, even if this meant leaving his sons in Spain for three or four years. He professed not to be worried about them. They would be well looked after, he said, and, being children, would learn Spanish and make friendships useful in the future. On 20 April Francis told the Venetian envoy that he would join a league not so much for his own advantage as in the interest of Italian liberty.[14]

The so-called Holy League of Cognac among France, the papacy, Venice, Florence and Francesco Sforza was concluded on 22 May.[15] Though Henry VIII was called its 'protector', he was not yet included in it. The emperor, ironically, was invited to join the league on four conditions: he was to release Francis's sons in exchange for a reasonable cash ransom, restore Sforza to the duchy of Milan, limit the size of the retinue he intended taking to Italy and pay his debts to Henry within three months. Since it was confidently expected that these terms would not be acceptable to Charles, the treaty provided for a future war against him, the contribution of each confederate being carefully specified. Francis promised to send 500 *lances* across the Alps and pay a monthly subsidy of 40,000 *écus* to the pope and the Venetians for the hire of Swiss troops. He also undertook to send an army across the Pyrenees. A powerful fleet, including twelve French galleys, was to be assembled with a view to capturing Genoa; later it was to join a combined land and sea attack on the kingdom

[11] *L.P.*, iv. 2087, 2092. Cheyney was a gentleman of Henry's privy chamber. His embassy was intended as a mark of special esteem for Francis, who reciprocated by sending the seigneur de Morette, a gentleman of his own chamber, to Henry VIII. *L.P.*, iv. 2104.

[12] *Ibid.*, iv. 2091.   [13] *Ibid.*, iv. 2135; *Ordonnances*, iv. no. 428.

[14] Jacqueton, *La politique extérieure*, pp. 262–3, 269; *C.S.P. Ven.*, iii. 1236, 1253.

[15] *Ordonnances*, iv. no. 418.

of Naples, which, once captured, was to be disposed of by the pope with
the consent of his allies. Francis gave up his claims to Milan and Naples,
but was promised handsome compensation: namely, an annuity of
50,000 ducats and the county of Asti from Sforza along with Genoa, and
another annuity of 75,000 ducats from the eventual recipient of Naples.

The treaty of Cognac shattered the emperor's plans. Having made
peace with France and married Isabella of Portugal, he had planned to go
first to Italy for his coronation by the pope, then to Germany, where the
Reformation was continuing to threaten his authority. Despite the edict
of Worms, Luther was as active as ever, and his followers among the
princes had banded together to defend themselves. In March Charles had
informed the Catholic princes of his intentions to come to their aid. He
hoped to leave Spain on 24 June, but long before this date he learnt of
Francis's breach of faith. Injured in his pride as much as in his policy, he
became morose. 'He is full of dumps', reported an English envoy, 'and
solitary, musing sometimes alone three or four hours together. There is no
mirth or comfort with him.'[16] Charles should not have listened to Lannoy
and released Francis before gaining possession of Burgundy. Now he had
to pay the price: instead of going to Italy in triumph, he had to remain in
Spain and prepare for a new struggle in the peninsula. Pavia might as well
not have happened.

The Italian powers prepared for war even before news of the League of
Cognac had reached them. They confidently believed that the hour of
their independence had struck, for the imperial army in north Italy was
penniless and disorganized. After capturing Lodi on 24 June, the League's
army under the duke of Urbino prepared to attack Milan, but it was
forced to retire after Bourbon had introduced money and troops into the
city.[17] As the tide of war began to turn against the League, Francis came
under heavy criticism from his allies for his failure so far to help them. He
had sent no troops to Italy, his fleet was still at Marseilles, and there was
still no sign of the subsidies he had promised.[18] He was, in fact, still hoping
that the emperor would agree to release his sons for a cash ransom. As
long as this remained a possibility, he was not prepared to declare war on
Charles. The League of Cognac was to him simply a useful means of
putting pressure on the emperor. He had no objection to the Italians going
to war, but he did not wish to become involved himself, for the time being
at least.

[16] *L.P.*, iv. 2094.
[17] J. Hook, *The Sack of Rome* (London, 1972), pp. 77ff.
[18] Clement VII suspected that he was being blackmailed by Francis, who wanted a red hat
      for Duprat and the see of Riez for François de Dinteville. V.-L. Bourrilly, *Guillaume du
      Bellay, seigneur de Langey* (1905), p. 20.

On 18 July Francis sent Guillaume du Bellay, seigneur de Langey, to Italy with words of reassurance for his allies.[19] Soon afterwards, however, the League suffered two more blows: Sforza, who had been defending Milan castle, surrendered on 25 July, and an attempt by a papal army to capture Siena was repulsed. Clement VII nearly went out of his mind blaming Francis for these misfortunes. The French became exceedingly unpopular at the curia. 'You have no idea', wrote the secretary of the French embassy in Rome, 'what things are said about us by persons of high standing in the Curia on account of our delays and our behaviour hitherto. The language is so frightful that I dare not write it!'[20] By mid-August, Clement had become thoroughly disenchanted with the League. He told du Bellay that he could no longer carry the main burden of paying for the war. Francis, he said, must pull his weight without delay. But du Bellay was unable to give him anything more than promises. On 21 September, therefore, Clement signed a four months' truce with the emperor.[21]

Charles, meanwhile, rejected the terms of membership offered him by the League. After the French ambassador, Jean de Calvimont, had tact-lessly 'summoned' him (as if he were calling on a beleaguered city to surrender) to release Francis's sons for a reasonable ransom, Charles hit out as follows:

I will not deliver them for money. I refused money for the father: I will much less take money for the sons. I am content to render them upon reasonable treaty, but not for money, nor will I trust any more the king's promise, for he has deceived me, and that like no noble prince. And where he excuses that he cannot fulfil some things without grudge of his subjects, let him fulfil that that is in his power, which he promised by the honour of a prince to fulfil; that is to say, that if he could not bring all his promise to pass he would return again hither into prison.

Charles declared that he would resist to the bitter end any attempt by Francis to recover his sons by force. 'Would to God', he added, 'that he were content, in the avoiding of Christian blood, to try the right with me, hand for hand, I would, upon confidence of my right take it on me, which I trust in the righteousness of God should defend me.'[22] Yet, even at this stage, Charles did not rule out the possibility of a peaceful settlement of his quarrel with Francis. He soon regretted his intemperate outburst and offered to negotiate about the release of the king's sons.

[19] *Ibid.*, pp. 20–2.
[20] L. von Pastor, *The History of the Popes*, tr. F. I. Antrobus and R. F. Kerr (London, 1891–1933), ix. 323–4.
[21] Bourrilly, *Guillaume du Bellay*, pp. 26–30.
[22] *L.P.*, iv. 2470. Cf. F. Mignet, *La rivalité de François Ier et de Charles-Quint* (1875), ii. 228–31.

By the autumn of 1526 Francis had come to appreciate the need to bring more pressure to bear on the emperor by supporting the League more effectively in Italy and turning the Anglo-French peace into an alliance. He promised to send Renzo da Ceri, leader of the Orsini faction, to Rome with a subsidy and to assemble an army at Lyons, whither he proposed to go himself before Christmas. This revived the pope's courage: he anathematized the Colonna and sent an army to destroy their towns, fortresses and villages. But his ardour soon cooled, for by late November no help had yet reached him from France. He was being threatened in several quarters: while, in the south, the Colonna invaded the States of the Church, in the north, Frundsberg's landsknechts reached Mantuan territory. The crisis was aggravated by the decision of the duke of Ferrara to throw in his lot with the emperor. The last straw for Clement was the arrival in a Tuscan port of an imperial fleet carrying Lannoy and 9,000 troops. On 28 November it was reported that he looked 'like a sick man whom the doctors have given up'.[23]

Francis undoubtedly looked to his friendship with England rather than to military involvement in Italy as the most economical way of bringing the emperor to heel. But England's friendship had to be bought, and Wolsey knew how to drive a hard bargain. Although the cardinal had helped to create the League of Cognac, he had so far refused to join it on the ground that England could mediate between France and the empire more effectively by remaining outside. Nor did he ever miss a chance of playing one off against the other. Thus in October 1526 he greatly embarrassed Francis by proposing that he should marry Henry VIII's daughter, Mary. Francis explained that he was already engaged to the emperor's sister. 'I must do things', he said, 'as near as I can without displeasure of God and reproach of the world.'[24] Yet the English government continued to press for a marriage alliance. If Francis would take Mary, it said, Henry would join the League and Charles would be forced to release Francis's sons.[25]

In Italy, meanwhile, the pope continued to vacillate. At the start of 1527 he seemed ready to carry on the war, but, when Renzo da Ceri arrived in Rome without the subsidy promised by Francis, Clement agreed to a short truce. This infuriated Francis, who promptly gave the nuncio Acciauoli a piece of his mind. 'I hope to act in such a way', he declared, 'that the emperor will not succeed in his aim of subordinating everything to his tyranny, but I will leave those who have fallen into servitude through their own baseness and fear.'[26] But no sooner had he uttered these words than news reached him that the pope had broken his

[23] Pastor, ix. 345.   [24] L.P., iv. 2606.
[25] Ibid., iv. 2728.   [26] Mignet, ii. 289–90; Desjardins, ii. 900ff.

agreement with the imperial viceroy and launched a campaign against Naples. This time Francis expressed his satisfaction to the papal nuncio. He informed him that an Anglo-French alliance was imminent and gave him details of the help Clement would soon receive.[27] By mid-March, however, the pope was again in desperate straits: Lannoy had invaded the States of the Church, and another imperial army under Bourbon and Frundsberg was preparing to descend into central Italy from the north. On 15 March Clement concluded an eight months' truce with the viceroy of Naples.

The League's failure in Italy had the effect of bringing France and England closer together in opposition to the emperor, who no longer seemed prepared to compromise. On 30 April the treaty of Westminster was signed: Francis and Henry agreed to send a joint embassy to Charles to negotiate for the release of Francis's sons and for the payment of the emperor's debts to Henry.[28] If Charles refused their terms, they would declare war on him. Princess Mary would marry either Francis or his second son, the duc d'Orléans. The treaty also provided for another meeting between Francis and Henry, albeit a less costly one than the Field of Cloth of Gold.

From the pope's point of view, the Anglo-French treaty came too late, for Bourbon continued to march on Rome, despite the truce Clement had signed with Lannoy. Cold and hungry, his troops intended to get the loot they had been promised. Bypassing Florence, which was covered by the League's army, they advanced towards Rome at an incredible speed. On 25 April Clement, realizing that he had been duped, rejoined the League; but his allies could not save him. On 6 May the sack of Rome began.[29] Bourbon was killed as he scaled the city wall, but his troops poured into the city like a torrent in flood, destroying all in their path. Clement and some cardinals took refuge in the castle of Sant'Angelo. On 5 June the pope signed a humiliating treaty with the viceroy of Naples which left him virtually a prisoner in imperial hands.

An immediate consequence of the sack of Rome was an even closer understanding between England and France, for Henry VIII was afraid that the pope's plight would seriously prejudice his own chances of divorcing Catherine of Aragon, who was the emperor's aunt. A new sense of urgency animated Wolsey's foreign policy; peace remained its objective, but now he wanted it not only for reasons of national and personal prestige, but also to free the pope. It was primarily with this end in view

---

27 Bourrilly, *Guillaume du Bellay*, p. 38. Francis had sent Rabodanges with 50,000 *écus* to the pope in February.
28 *Ordonnances*, v. no. 452; *L.P.*, iv. 3080.
29 *L.P.*, iv. 3114–16, 3136. See also Hook, pp. 156ff.

that he met Francis at Amiens early in August.[30] On 16 August the
cardinal informed his master that he had finished his business with the
king, save for one thing: he had not yet told him about Henry's intended
divorce. This he proposed to do in 'so cloudy and dark a sort' that Francis
would not realize Henry's 'utter determination'.[31] On 18 August the
treaty of Amiens was signed: Mary was promised to the duc d'Orléans,
and Henry waived his objection to the marriage between Francis and
Eleanor (which was far less dangerous to England now that Charles had a
son). In the event of war with the emperor, English merchants would have
the same privileges in France as they had previously enjoyed in the
Netherlands. Neither France nor England would obey a summons to a
general council as long as the pope remained a prisoner.[32] The meeting at
Amiens was followed by a conference at Compiègne at which measures
for the government of the church during Clement's captivity were discussed. The Anglo-French talks were rounded off with an exchange of
honours: Montmorency went to England to confer the order of St
Michael on Henry VIII, who reciprocated by sending the Garter to
Francis. Louise of Savoy was delighted. Now that the two kings were
'under one clothing', she hoped they would continue 'in one mind and
heart'.[33]

Francis did not confine his diplomatic activities to western Europe. The
disputed succession to the Hungarian throne, which followed the death of
King Louis II on the battlefield of Mohács, offered him an excellent
opportunity of undermining Habsburg interests in central Europe. In
February 1527 he sent Antonio Rincon, a Spanish renegade, to offer
French support to John Zápolyai, voivode of Transylvania, who had been
elected king in opposition to Charles V's brother, Ferdinand. Rincon also
went to Poland in an attempt to win the support of King Sigismund for
Zápolyai's cause. By the end of the year, however, the voivode had been
defeated and had lost his throne to Ferdinand. He did not, however, give
up the struggle, and in the autumn of 1528 a Hungarian bishop called
John Stafileo came to Paris and signed an alliance with Francis. In return
for a promise of financial aid, Zápolyai agreed to bequeath his kingdom,
in the event of his dying childless, to the duc d'Orléans. This alliance had
far-reaching consequences, for Zápolyai was also allied to the Turkish

---

[30] On 23 June Francis explained that he could not leave Saint-Denis because of a tertian
     fever. But on 2 July he was said to be out of danger. His health, however, remained
     troublesome. When Wolsey saw him on 5 August, he was 'lying on a couch with a white
     sheet made for the easement of his leg, which was so swelled he could not stand'. *L.P.*,
     iv. 3193, 3225, 3309, 3337.
[31] *Ibid.*, iv. 3350.
[32] *Ibid.*, iv. 3356; *Ordonnances*, v. no. 466.
[33] *L.P.*, iv. 3574; Decrue, i. 97–9.

sultan, who, in 1529, confirmed him as king as he overran Hungary on his way to besiege Vienna.[34]

Francis, in the meantime, committed himself to armed intervention in Italy. In August 1527 a French army commanded by Marshal Lautrec crossed the Alps and overran the whole of Lombardy, except Milan, while Andrea Doria, who had entered the service of France, captured Genoa. In the autumn, following a decision taken at Compiègne, Lautrec was ordered to march on Naples instead of completing the conquest of Milan. He moved accordingly to Parma, remaining there from 7 November until 14 December. Meanwhile, Alfonso d'Este, duke of Ferrara, agreed to join the League in exchange for substantial concessions. He was given Modena and Reggio by a group of cardinals acting for the pope and was promised the hand of Princess Renée for his son Ercole, along with the county of Chartres. Alfonso, for his part, undertook to pay 6,000 ducats a month to Lautrec for half a year.[35] This must have been welcome to the marshal, who had complained repeatedly of not receiving enough money from France to pay his army.[36]

On 16 December Francis held an 'assembly of notables' in Paris with a view to gaining financial support for his foreign policy. It consisted of 200 delegates drawn from the nobility, the clergy, the parlements and the people of Paris. In his opening speech the king tried to justify his policy since the start of his reign.[37] His aim, he explained, had always been peace; he had been forced into war by his enemies, including Bourbon, and it was to protect France from further attacks that he had again invaded Italy. As for the treaty of Madrid, it had been negotiated by his mother and his ambassadors; he did not feel bound to honour it or his oath, as both had been extorted under duress. Turning to recent events, Francis explained that he had simply used the League of Cognac as a threat with which to force the emperor to waive his demand for Burgundy, while he himself concluded an alliance with England. He and Henry VIII, he said, had submitted reasonable terms to the emperor and were awaiting a reply. But, whatever this might be, the sum of 2 million *écus* would be needed either for the ransom of his sons or to invade Flanders. In conclusion, the king asked the delegates for their views on the validity of the peace of Madrid; on whether or not, having broken his oath, he was bound to return to prison; and on his demand for

---

[34] V.-L. Bourrilly, 'Antonio Rincon et la politique orientale de François Ier', *R.H.*, cxiii (1913), 76–83.

[35] *L.P.*, iv. 3578; *C.A.F.*, i. 2822. The marriage between Ercole and Renée was concluded on 10 February 1528, when the county of Chartres was turned into a duchy. See *Ordonnances*, v. p. 36n.

[36] Decrue, i. 101–3; B. de Chantérac, *Odet de Foix, vicomte de Lautrec* (1930), p. 100.

[37] T. Godefroy, *Le cérémonial françois* (1649), ii. 478; Doucet, ii. 288–96.

money. He made it abundantly plain, however, that he was consulting them simply to 'honour' them, not because he was under any compulsion to do so.

The king's speech, however tendentious, was apparently well received; each group of delegates then met separately to consider its reply. On 20 December they unanimously gave Francis all he wanted: the treaty of Madrid was declared null and void, as was the king's oath, so that he was released from the obligation to return to prison. All four groups, moreover, agreed to contribute to the sum demanded by Francis, the clergy's share being fixed at 1.3 million *écus*.[38]

Charles, in the meantime, refused to release Francis's sons at any price unless Lautrec's army were first recalled from Italy and its conquests restored. This condition being unacceptable to the king of France and his English ally, war became inevitable. On 22 January 1528 the heralds Guyenne and Clarencieux, who had accompanied the Anglo-French negotiators to Spain in the event of the talks breaking down, bade the emperor defiance in the names of their respective masters. They justified their action by reciting Charles's alleged misdeeds, including the pope's imprisonment. Replying to the French herald, the emperor expressed surprise that Francis should now feel it necessary to declare war, considering that he had been fighting him for six or seven years without such a formality. As for the pope, his royal champions could set their minds at rest: Clement was now a free man.[39] The pope had indeed escaped to Orvieto on 6 December with the emperor's connivance.

Among the first to feel the effects of the declaration of war were the Dauphin and the duc d'Orléans. So far, they had been treated quite well, but in February 1528 the emperor ordered them to be moved to a castle near Segovia and dismissed nearly all their French attendants. This apparently upset Eleanor of Portugal so much that she retired to a monastery for a time. On 16 May Louise complained to Wolsey of the emperor's inhumane treatment of her grandchildren; she claimed that he had not only deprived them of their servants, but intended to send these to the galleys. She may, however, have been exaggerating in order to stir the cardinal's conscience; for England did not, as yet, show much enthusiasm for the war.[40]

Even after war had been declared, Francis and Charles engaged in a strangely archaic ritual. On 18 March the emperor repeated the challenge to a duel he had already made in 1526. This time, however, he put it in

---

[38]   François, *François de Tournon*, p. 62.
[39]   *L.P.*, iv. 3453, 3455, 3597, 3826; K. Brandi, *The Emperor Charles V*, tr. C. V. Wedgwood (London, 1939), p. 265.
[40]   *L.P.*, iv. 3982, 4266.

writing so as to ensure its proper delivery. Ten days later Francis accepted the challenge. Charles proposed that the duel should be fought on the Bidassoa, but a herald he sent to France to arrange it was kept waiting by Francis for more than a month at the Franco-Spanish border for a safe-conduct. When eventually he did reach the French court, the king would not allow him to carry out his instructions. The herald therefore returned to Spain, his mission unfulfilled. The Council of Castile declared that Francis by refusing the emperor's challenge, had again demonstrated that he was no gentleman.[41]

In the end, it was in Italy, not on the Bidassoa, that the king and the emperor fought out their quarrel. On 9 February Lautrec, after overrunning the Romagna, invaded the kingdom of Naples. He was greeted as a liberator by the towns of the Abruzzi and soon gained control of Apulia as well. Towards the end of April he reached the outskirts of Naples, which was being blockaded on the seaward side by a fleet commanded by Andrea Doria's nephew, Filippino. An attempt by Moncada to break the blockade ended in disaster on 28 April, when he was killed and his fleet wiped out.[42] No one expected Naples to hold out much longer. On 28 July Francis wrote of his joy to Montmorency. How astonished his enemies would be, he said, to see their forces diminishing each day as his own grew in proportion.[43] But, unbeknown to the king, the situation in Italy had already changed radically. One reason for this was Andrea Doria's dissatisfaction with his French employer.

As a Genoese, Doria backed the claim of his compatriots to the Ligurian port of Savona, which Francis, after investigating the matter, decided to keep in his own hands. What is more, he fortified the town and turned it into a centre for the distribution of salt from Provence to north Italy. He instituted a *gabelle* from which he expected to obtain substantial revenues. This naturally angered the Genoese, who tried by every means in their power to disrupt Savona's trade. But Doria also had personal grievances. He complained that he had received no reward from Francis for capturing the prince of Orange in July 1527, nor had he received his expenses for his part in the reconquest of Genoa and in an abortive expedition to Sardinia. The last straw came when Francis appointed a Frenchman to lead a fleet that was being sent to Naples. In June 1528 Doria withdrew to a castle near La Spezia, and ordered his nephew Filippino to join him. Only then did Francis begin to give the Genoese serious attention. He ordered Savona to be restored to them, but Doria

[41] Mignet, *La rivalité de François 1er et de Charles-Quint*, ii. 394–408; Granvelle, *Papiers d'état*, i. 360–424.

[42] Chantérac, pp. 99–107.

[43] Mignet, ii. 430.

had already decided to transfer his services to the emperor.[44] Francis was to pay dearly for his earlier insouciance.

On 4 July Filippino Doria, acting on his uncle's instruction, removed his fleet from the bay of Naples, so that supplies were soon able to reach the city. This was followed by an outbreak of plague or cholera in Lautrec's camp outside Naples. Though urged by his captains to retire to the purer air of neighbouring hill-towns, the marshal preferred to remain in his sun-baked camp amidst a fast-growing heap of rotting corpses. On 17 August he himself was carried off.[45] By then his army had been reduced to a third of its original size. Lautrec's successor, the marquis of Saluzzo, ordered a retreat, but he capitulated soon afterwards at Aversa. On 9 September the prince of Orange informed Charles V that the war in south Italy was virtually at an end; only a few pockets of resistance remained in Apulia and Calabria. These disasters were soon followed by others in north Italy. On 12 September Genoa regained its independence with the help of Andrea Doria, and, on 21 October, the French garrison in Savona surrendered. The whole Ligurian coast thus passed into enemy hands. But there was worse to come. In 1529 the comte de Saint-Pol, hearing that Doria had left for Spain, attempted to recapture Genoa, only to be defeated and captured on 21 June at Landriano.

The French collapse finally convinced the pope that he stood to gain nothing by remaining neutral. Only the emperor could provide him with the military support needed to restore his Medici kinsmen to power in Florence; only he could halt the progress of Lutheranism in Germany or the westward expansion of the Turks. So for once Clement came to a decision. 'I have quite made up my mind', he announced, 'to become an Imperialist, and to live and die as such.'[46] On 29 June he and Charles signed the treaty of Barcelona. This provided for the restoration of Medici rule in Florence and the return of Ravenna, Cervia, Modena and Reggio to the pope. Clement, on his part, promised to crown Charles emperor and absolve all those responsible for the sack of Rome. A marriage was arranged between his nephew, Alessandro de' Medici, and Charles's illegitimate daughter Margaret.[47] A direct consequence of the treaty was Clement's decision, on 16 July, to revoke Henry VIII's divorce suit to Rome, which precipitated Wolsey's fall and led ultimately to England's breach with Rome.

---

[44] V.-L. Bourrilly, *Jacques Colin, abbé de Saint-Ambroise* (1905), pp. 14–35; *Ordonnances*, v. no. 489.
[45] Chantérac, pp. 111–14; *L.P.*, iv. 4663.
[46] *C.S.P. Span.*, iv. 73.
[47] Pastor, *History of the Popes*, x. 56–7.

The 'Peace of the Ladies' (3 August 1529)

By December 1528 Francis was anxiously seeking an opportunity to reopen peace negotiations with the emperor. This was provided by a truce which England and France had recently signed with Margaret of Savoy, regent of the Netherlands. She was not only the emperor's aunt but also the sister-in-law of Louise of Savoy, who put out peace feelers when Margaret's secretary visited Paris in connexion with ratification of the truce. Margaret's reaction was guarded at first, but when it became clear that the emperor would also welcome a respite from war, she sent ambassadors to Paris and eventually agreed to meet Louise at Cambrai.[48] As news of these negotiations leaked out, Francis's Italian allies, notably the Venetians, Sforza, Alfonso d'Este and the Florentines, became fearful that he was about to desert them. But the king solemnly assured them of his loyalty. 'I protest', he said, 'that I would rather sacrifice my life and those of my children than abandon the confederates.'[49] Louise gave similar assurances to the League's ambassadors on the eve of her departure for Cambrai. By negotiating through his mother, rather than directly, Francis avoided the embarrassment of bringing his Italian and English allies into the talks; he also retained the freedom to reject any result which failed to satisfy him.

The talks at Cambrai began on 5 July and lasted nearly a month. Louise was accompanied by leading members of the king's council. Francis did not take part. He went hunting with Admiral Chabot at La Fère and Coucy, but was kept fully informed of the progress of the negotiations by a continual stream of messengers. The talks proved far more gruelling and protracted than he had expected. Only the intervention of the papal nuncio averted a breakdown after Margaret had asked for certain border towns as securities.[50] Thereafter, progress was rapid, and, on 3 August, the treaty, which became known as the Peace of the Ladies, was signed. Two days later, it was celebrated in Cambrai cathedral in the presence of the king of France.

In all essentials, the treaty of Cambrai was a revision of the peace of Madrid. In place of Burgundy the emperor accepted a ransom of 2 million gold *écus*, of which 1.2 million were to be paid in a single lump sum. The balance was to be settled, first, by settling the emperor's debts to Henry VIII (estimated at 290,000 *écus*) and, secondly, by disposing of lands held by the duchesse de Vendôme in Brabant, Hainault, Artois and Flanders. Francis gave up all his Italian claims, as well as the towns of Hesdin,

[48] Mignet, ii. 457–9.
[49] C. Terrasse, *François Ier* (1948), ii. 116.
[50] Bourrilly, *Guillaume du Bellay*, pp. 72–4.

Arras, Lille and Tournai and his suzerainty over Flanders and Artois. He agreed to lend Charles twelve galleys for six months and guaranteed the rights of Bourbon's heirs. Finally, he deserted his Italian allies by allowing them to be left out of the treaty; England was only accommodated at the eleventh hour. The emperor, for his part, promised, on fulfilment of Francis's obligations, to send his sister Eleanor to France along with the Dauphin and the duc d'Orléans.[51]

The peace of Cambrai has been described as 'wholly favourable to Charles'.[52] This is an exaggeration. It certainly contained humiliating terms for the king of France, but in two important respects it marked a triumph for his diplomacy since 1526: he retained Burgundy and re-covered his sons for a cash ransom.[53] From the emperor's point of view, the peace was of enormous value in that it enabled him to settle the affairs of Italy peacefully before attending to those of Germany. Having been deserted by France, the Italian powers were unlikely to offer much resistance to his plans. Early in November Charles met the pope in Bologna, and for the next four months they discussed the international situation against a background of civic revelry. The emperor's main fear was that Francis would break the peace as soon as he had recovered his sons. To avert this danger a league of Italian states was formed on 23 December.[54] The Venetians agreed to restore Ravenna and Cervia to the pope, and Sforza was restored to Milan. A clause in the agreement provided for the eventual admission of the duke of Ferrara. Only Florence had to be left out because of its refusal to restore the Medici. Charles accordingly placed his army at the pope's disposal, and an eight months' siege ensued. On 12 August 1530 Florence surrendered, and, eighteen months later, Clement's nephew Alessandro became its hereditary duke. In the meantime, Charles attained his highest ambition: on 24 February, the anniversary of his birth and of the victory at Pavia, he was crowned Holy Roman Emperor in San Petronio at Bologna. A month later he left for Germany to preside at the diet of Augsburg.

[51] *Ordonnances*, v. no. 507.
[52] Brandi, *Charles V*, p. 279.
[53] J. Jacquart, *François Ier* (1981), p. 219.
[54] *L.P.*, iv. 6101.

15

The hollow peace

(1530–4)

THERE WAS AS much scepticism in Europe about the fulfilment of the peace of Cambrai as there had been three years earlier about that of Madrid. It was widely believed that Francis would again break his word once his sons had been returned to him. This time, however, he could not claim that he had acted under duress. He therefore ratified the new treaty on 20 October 1529 and, in accordance with the emperor's wishes, instructed the parlements and local estates to do likewise.[1] On 21 February 1530 he appointed Anne de Montmorency and François de Tournon to supervise arrangements for the return of his sons.[2] They arrived in Bayonne on 22 March and, during the next three months, worked closely together, helped by a large team of financial experts. While the grand master dealt mainly with diplomatic business, Tournon (who had become a cardinal on 10 March) supervised the collection and counting of the ransom for the king's sons.[3]

The treaty of Cambrai had laid down three ways in which the ransom of 2 million gold *écus au soleil* was to be paid: first, the payment of a single lump sum of 1.2 million *écus*; secondly, the reimbursement of Charles's debts to Henry VIII, estimated at 290,000 *écus*; and thirdly, the payment of an annuity of 25,500 *écus* to be raised from lands held by Marie de Luxembourg, duchesse de Vendôme, in the Netherlands. Francis could expect no leniency from the emperor, but he was able to obtain some relief from Henry VIII. On 6 August he promised to pay Henry 185,000 *écus* in half-yearly instalments of 50,000 *écus*. The agreement, however, did not allow for the redemption of a rich Burgundian jewel called the 'Fleur-de-lis', which the Emperor Maximilian had pawned in England in 1508 for 50,000 crowns; nor did it deal with the so-called Windsor indemnity, which Charles had promised Henry in 1522 as compensation for the loss of his French pension. On 16 August, therefore, Francis sent

---

[1] C.A.F., i. 3514.
[2] Ibid., i. 3624.
[3] M. François, Le cardinal François de Tournon (1951), p. 77.

du Bellay, seigneur de Langey, to England to secure further alleviation of his financial obligations.[4]

Henry would not at first consider any financial concessions to the king of France until he had received the full text of the Cambrai treaty. On 31 August, however, his attitude suddenly changed when he agreed not only to remit the redemption money for the 'Fleur-de-lis', but also to return the jewel itself. As an additional concession, he remitted an instalment of his French pension for 1529, provided this was spent on the French princes' ransom.[5] In return for his generosity he looked to Francis for help in obtaining his divorce from Catherine of Aragon.

In spite of the alleviation of the English debt, Francis still had great difficulty raising the huge lump sum needed to recover his sons. The kingdom had been bled white by earlier demands for money, and although the nobility and clergy had promised contributions, they proved far less amenable when they were actually asked to pay up. The king was also hampered by corruption and inefficiency within his own financial administration. As the gold crowns began to arrive in Bayonne, their weight and alloy were found to be inferior to the standards laid down in the treaty. An enquiry was set up, following which the mints of Dauphiné and Provence were temporarily closed down. Meanwhile, additional gold crowns had to be found to make up the deficiency in the amount so far collected. By 9 April, however, there were no more *écus au soleil* to be found, so that it became necessary to gather up foreign coins that were circulating in France. But these were of inferior alloy, and the imperial commissioners insisted on their being melted down and reissued at the king's expense as *écus au soleil*. Another source of delay was the slowness of the collectors of the *taille* in sending their revenues to Bayonne. As late as 2 April one of them had still not sent money due from the October quarter. Nor did the imperial commissioners help: they quibbled over every transaction and demanded concessions not mentioned in the treaty. In each case Francis instructed his own commissioners to give way.[6]

Because of these and other complications too numerous and petty to mention here, the date of 1 March, originally fixed for the release of the

4   V.-L. Bourrilly, *Guillaume du Bellay, seigneur de Langey* (1905), pp. 75–80; *L.P.*, iv. 5871, 5911.
5   The jewel was carefully examined by an expert sent by Margaret of Savoy to ensure that it was identical in all respects to that originally pawned. It was carefully wrapped up, placed in a sealed box and entrusted to Sir Francis Bryan and Langey for transportation to Bayonne. Under an agreement of 18 February 1530 it was to be handed over to the emperor within six months; otherwise it was to be returned to Henry. *L.P.*, iv. 6227; Bourrilly, *Guillaume du Bellay*, pp. 88–9; *Ordonnances*, vi. nos. 524–5.
6   François, *Francois de Tournon*, pp. 76–82; Decrue, i. 141–53; *Correspondance du cardinal François de Tournon*, ed. M. François (1946), p. 62.

king's sons, repeatedly had to be postponed. It was only on 10 June that Don Alvares de Lugo, one of the emperor's agents, formally acknowledged receipt of the ransom money, and only on 1 July that it was actually exchanged for the king's sons and Eleanor of Portugal at a point on the river Bidassoa halfway between Fuenterrabía and Hendaye. On 3 July Eleanor met Francis at Roquefort-de-Marsan. Although they had already been married by proxy, a second ceremony in the presence of both partners was evidently felt to be desirable, if only to underline Francis's sincerity. This took place on 7 July in a chapel adjoining the monastery of Beyries.[7] Thus was the peace of Cambrai sealed: Francis was now the brother-in-law of his chief rival and enemy, and for the next six years he remained at peace with him, at least on the surface.

The peace entailed no fundamental change of direction in Francis's foreign policy, which continued to be aimed at the recovery of Milan. It merely provided him with a breathing space in which to replenish his treasury, rebuild his forces and consolidate his alliances. Between 1530 and 1534 Francis stirred up trouble for the emperor in Germany and in the Mediterranean without, however, openly contravening the peace treaty. At the same time, he built up a coalition of anti-Habsburg powers, comprising the German princes, the king of England, the pope and the Turks. But the Protestant Reformation, which divided Germany into two great religious camps, and Henry VIII's divorce, which incurred the pope's condemnation, were serious obstacles in the path of a unified opposition to the Habsburgs. They obliged Francis to assume the part of a religious peacemaker while he was imperilling his reputation as a Christian monarch by secretly intriguing with the Infidel.

Francis and the German princes

The election of Charles V's brother Ferdinand as King of the Romans in January 1531 had the effect of widening the rift between the emperor and many German princes. No constitutional warrant existed for such a choice during the emperor's lifetime, and Protestant princes were naturally alarmed by the election of a Catholic ruler dedicated to the preservation of his faith. On 16 February they appealed for help to the king of France, and eleven days later six Protestant princes and ten cities formed a league at Schmalkalden to defend their interests.[8]

Although Francis had undertaken at Cambrai not to meddle in German affairs, he found it impossible to resist the appeal of the Protestant

[7] François, *François du Tournon*, pp. 85–7; Decrue, i. 159–62.
[8] *Corpus Reformatorum*, ed. C. G. Bretschneider (18 vols., Halle, 1834), ii. cols. 472–7, 478–80.

princes. In May 1531 he sent Gervais Wain to Germany to investigate the situation.[9] This, as Wain soon discovered, was anything but clear-cut. The elector of Saxony, for example, though opposed to Ferdinand's election, was fundamentally loyal to the Habsburgs, whereas the landgrave of Hesse and the two dukes of Bavaria were prepared to fight them. Another controversial issue was the duchy of Württemberg, which the Habsburgs had seized in 1519. Philip of Hesse wanted to restore Duke Ulrich, but the dukes of Bavaria were opposed to this. They hated Ulrich, who was their brother-in-law and, as Catholics, were afraid that the landgrave would use Ulrich's restoration to introduce Lutheranism into Württemberg.

As a first step, therefore, towards creating an effective opposition to the Habsburgs, Wain had to mediate between the Bavarian dukes and the Schmalkaldic League, and he succeeded so well that they signed an alliance at Saalfeld on 26 October.[10] This was the foundation-stone of Francis's future policy in Germany: an anti-Habsburg coalition of Catholic and Protestant princes had been formed, ostensibly to defend German liberties. Though Francis and Henry VIII were invited to join the confederates, they did not, in fact, do so. Francis helped them diplomatically in Switzerland, but refused to send them money until Henry had agreed to do so as well.[11] In March 1532, however, Francis promised them financial aid on condition that it was used strictly for defensive purposes. He then changed his mind and gave his blessing to the idea of a war for the reconquest of Württemberg. As a sop to the dukes of Bavaria, he suggested that it might be fought in the name of Ulrich's son, Christopher. On 26 May an alliance was signed at Scheyern among France, Saxony, Hesse and Bavaria, Francis promising to contribute 100,000 écus towards the cost of the forthcoming war. But, before this could be declared, the Turks invaded central Europe.

Francis and the Turks

Although Francis had celebrated the withdrawal of the Turks from Vienna in October 1529, he had not given up his intrigues with them. In July 1530 Antonio Rincon was sent to Constantinople for the purpose, so the imperialists claimed, of persuading Sultan Suleiman to attack Charles V in Italy, and, in March 1531, Giorgio Gritti, a Venetian in the service of

---

[9] C.A.F., ii. 4042.   [10] Bourrilly, *Guillaume du Bellay*, p. 126.
[11] Francis helped to bring about the peace of Bremgarten (20 November) between the Catholic and Protestant cantons. E. Rott, *Histoire de la représentation diplomatique de la France auprès des cantons suisses*, i. (1900–35), 281, 383–5; A. Hyrvoix, 'François 1er et la première guerre de religion en Suisse, 1529–1531', *R.Q.H.*, lxxi (1902), 465.

the Turks, came to Paris, ostensibly on business but probably with a more sinister purpose in mind.[12] As Thomas Cromwell once remarked, no Christian scruple would deter the king of France from bringing the Turk and the devil into the heart of Christendom if this could help him recover Milan.[13] Francis admitted almost as much himself to the Venetian envoy, Giustinian: 'I cannot deny', he declared, 'that I keenly desire the Turk powerful and ready for war, not for himself, because he is an infidel and we are Christians, but to undermine the emperor's power, to force heavy expenses upon him and to reassure all other governments against so powerful an enemy.'[14]

But, even as the ally of the Turks, Francis could not determine their strategy, and this could work to his disadvantage. Nothing, for example, was as likely to harm French interests in Germany as a Turkish attack on central Europe; it was the surest way of rallying support behind the emperor and his brother. From Francis's point of view an attack by the sultan on Italy was far preferable, since it might provide him with a pretext for invading the peninsula as the champion of Christendom. Thus in March 1532 Francis sent Rincon to the sultan, who was preparing a new offensive against the west, in an effort to persuade him to attack Italy rather than Hungary. But, after being delayed by illness, Rincon arrived at the sultan's camp too late to influence his strategy.[15] The Turks, after sweeping through the Balkans, pushed towards the valley of the Danube. Rincon's presence in their midst only served to lend substance to imperial allegations of collusion between the king of France and the Infidel. In the end, the Turkish offensive failed. The sultan, after being held up for three weeks by the heroic defenders of Güns, retreated across the Drava, and, on 23 September, Charles V entered Vienna in triumph.

Clement VII and Henry VIII

The widening rift between England and the Holy See caused by Henry VIII's repudiation of the emperor's aunt, Catherine of Aragon, was a matter of serious concern to Francis, who wanted both to be his friends. At the same time, he was anxious to harness Clement VII to the French cause by means of a marriage between the houses of Valois and Medici. In April 1531, therefore, he sent Cardinal Gramont to Rome in an attempt

---

[12] J. Ursu, *La politique orientale de François Ier* (1908), pp. 58, 60–1.
[13] *C.S.P. Span.*, v. no. 157, p. 455.
[14] *Relations des ambassadeurs vénitiens sur les affaires de France*, ed. N. Tommaseo (1838), i. 67.
[15] Ursu, pp. 66–72; *C.S.P. Span.*, iv. 456–7; V.-L. Bourrilly, 'Antonio Rincon et la politique orientale de François Ier', *R.H.*, cxiii (1913), 276–7.

to solve the problem of Henry's divorce and to propose a marriage between his own second son, Henri, duc d'Orléans, and the pope's niece, Catherine de' Medici. The cardinal was sufficiently encouraged by his mission to advise Francis, on his return in July, to establish regular contacts with Clement at the highest level. The king accordingly appointed Cardinal Tournon, who was distantly related to Catherine de' Medici, as ambassador extraordinary to the Holy See. Illness, however, prevented Tournon's departure until the end of 1532.[16] Meanwhile, Francis and Henry VIII met for the second time.

Although ostensibly directed against the Turks, the real purpose of the meeting between the two kings was to co-ordinate their actions in Germany and Rome. While Francis wanted Henry to share the burden of subsidizing the League of Scheyern, Henry needed French support for his divorce. Having recently got rid of Cardinal Wolsey, he was ill-equipped to manipulate the curia. He had tried in vain to obtain red hats for other Englishmen sympathetic to his cause, and now had only French cardinals to lean on.[17]

The Anglo-French meeting of 1532 was a much less elaborate affair than the Field of Cloth of Gold: it lasted only eight days (21–9 October); it took place half in Calais, half in Boulogne; and the expenses were shared by the two kings.[18] At the invitation of Francis, Henry was accompanied by Anne Boleyn, while Queen Eleanor stayed away. The entertainments provided included a bear-baiting, a wrestling match between Englishmen and French priests and dancing in which Francis partnered Anne. At the end, gifts and honours were exchanged: Anne received a diamond worth 15,000 écus from Francis, while Henry remitted 300,000 écus owed to him by the king of France. As a further sign of friendship, Henry sent his natural son, the duke of Richmond, to be brought up at the French court with Francis's sons. Finally, the dukes of Norfolk and Suffolk were admitted to the order of St Michael, while Montmorency and Chabot became knights of the Garter.[19]

On 28 October the kings signed an alliance directed against the Turks, but this was only a smoke-screen; their real concern was the emperor's avowed intention of returning shortly to Italy.[20] Francis was afraid that the peninsula would be closed to him once Pope Clement had fallen under Charles's domination, while Henry dreaded a formal condemnation of

[16] François, *François de Tournon*, pp. 94–7.
[17] J. J. Scarisbrick, *Henry VIII* (London, 1968), p. 305.
[18] Le P. Hamy, *Entrevue de François 1er avec Henri VIII à Boulogne-sur-Mer en 1532* (1898), passim.
[19] *L.P.*, v. 1484–5.
[20] *Ordonnances*, vi. no. 605; *C.S.P. Ven.*, iv. nos. 820–5.

his divorce, which would force him to choose between surrender and schism. Both monarchs consequently decided to send Cardinals Gramont and Tournon to the pope with a message combining promises with threats. The two cardinals were also instructed to arrange a meeting between the pope and the king of France.[21]

The most potent threat which could be held over Clement VII was that of calling a general council of the church. Many Christians, including the emperor and the German Protestants, believed that it was the only practical answer to the troubles of the church. But the pope was afraid that a council would follow the example set by the fifteenth-century councils of Basle and Constance by seeking to depose him. He could not, however, refuse to call one for fear of being accused of hindering the religious pacification of Christendom. So he procrastinated: while recognizing the need for a council, he made its summoning depend on other powers, notably the king of France.[22]

Francis did not want a council any more than did the pope, for he believed that it would simply be used by the emperor to restore order in Germany, obtain help against the Turks and increase his own power. For two decades, therefore, he thwarted every attempt to call a council, mainly by raising procedural difficulties or objecting to whichever venue was proposed. Outwardly, however, he professed to be in favour of it and, in 1533, used the idea to put pressure on the pope.[23]

Gramont and Tournon arrived in Bologna on 3 January 1533, several weeks after the emperor. They were nevertheless well received by Clement and were soon able to report progress: before the end of the month Clement had agreed to a meeting with Francis provided this was kept secret until the emperor's departure from Italy; he had also given his consent to the marriage between his niece and the duc d'Orléans.[24] Some headway was even made with respect to Henry VIII's divorce: although under heavy imperialist pressure to condemn the king, Clement issued the bulls required by Cranmer to become archbishop of Canterbury.

But Francis's efforts on Henry's behalf were frustrated by the latter's impatience. On 25 January he married Anne Boleyn in secret, and in March sent her brother, Lord Rochford, across the Channel to put Francis in the picture. The marriage was not officially announced till May, but long before that date it had become common knowledge, if only because Anne's pregnancy could not be concealed. Henry subsequently

[21] François, *François de Tournon*, pp. 99–100.
[22] H. Jedin, *A History of the Council of Trent*, tr. E. Graf (London, 1957–61), i. 264–7.
[23] *Ibid.*, i. 270–1; *C.S.P. Span.*, iv. no. 505; L. von Pastor, *The History of the Popes*, tr. F. I. Antrobus and R. Kerr (London, 1891–1933), x. 154–6.
[24] François, *François de Tournon*, pp. 101–5; *L.P.*, vi. 38, 64, 92.

claimed that he had married her with Francis's encouragement, which may have been true.[25] The king of France certainly stood to gain from a match which inevitably drove a deep wedge between Henry and the emperor. Yet he was not prepared to defend Henry's action at the cost of sacrificing his own good relations with the pope. Thus, when Rochford suggested that he might increase pressure on Clement to grant Henry's divorce by threatening to break off his own son's marriage to Catherine de' Medici, he flatly refused. Such a move, he said, would merely drive the pope into the emperor's arms.[26] All he was prepared to do at this stage was to try to persuade Clement not to punish Henry immediately.

The fate of the English monarch depended to some extent on the outcome of Francis's meeting with the pope. This had to be postponed for several reasons: notably, the refusal of the duke of Savoy to allow Nice to be used for the meeting, the activities of Turkish pirates off the Italian coast, the pope's gout, bad weather in August and the intrigues of France's enemies. The delay was a serious matter for Henry, as he wanted his second marriage to be legalized before the birth of Anne Boleyn's child, which was due in September. On 23 May, therefore, Cranmer, usurping the pope's jurisdiction, declared the king's marriage lawful and, on 1 June, crowned Anne queen. This was more than the pope could tolerate: on 11 July he condemned Henry's remarriage, giving him till September to take back Catherine under pain of excommunication. Henry, in the meantime, sent the duke of Norfolk to France in an effort to dissuade Francis from meeting the pope, but the king of France would not call off the interview. He told the duke that he did not think the pope's sentence was final or a sufficient cause to cancel the interview. Matters might still be put right, he said, if only Henry would send a representative to the meeting, equipped with powers to negotiate. He urged Norfolk to stay, but the duke preferred to obey his master, who had recalled him to England.[27] In September, as the pope waited near Pisa to embark for Marseilles, Tournon persuaded him to extend the deadline for Henry's excommunication, but the latter was now bent on a policy that could lead only to schism.[28]

The murder of Maraviglia (7 July 1533)

In the treaty of Cambrai Francis had reluctantly recognized Sforza as duke of Milan. He had not, however, given up hope of eventually regaining the duchy and needed only a pretext to withdraw his recognition. This was now presented to him, as it were, on a plate. In August 1533, as

[25] L.P., vi. 230.
[27] Ibid., vi. 954, 1038, 1070.
[26] Ibid., vi. 254.
[28] Ibid., vi. 1155.

Francis prepared to meet the pope, he was informed that Giovan-Alberto Maraviglia had been murdered in Milan.

Maraviglia, known in France as 'Merveilles', was a Milanese who had entered the service of Louis XII about 1506 as a stable groom (*écuyer d'écurie*). He had continued to serve Francis in France and on various occasions in Italy. In September 1532 he was sent to Milan on a secret mission, possibly to spy on the emperor. On arrival, he found that Sforza had gone to Bologna and thought of following him there, but he was persuaded by Taverna, the Milanese chancellor, to await the duke's return. Even then, however, he failed to see Sforza, who put him off, presumably to avoid giving offence to the emperor. On 4 July 1533 Maraviglia was arrested following a street brawl in which a Milanese nobleman had been killed; three days later his decapitated body was found in a market square of Milan.

On receiving the news of Maraviglia's murder, Francis protested strongly to Sforza and demanded reparation, whereupon the duke sent his chancellor to France with excuses. Taverna explained that Maraviglia had been punished as a Milanese subject for a crime he had committed, but the king's council insisted that Sforza must have known that he was Francis's envoy. Unless the duke offered reparation, it continued, Francis would compel him to do so. But even this threat failed to produce a result satisfactory to the king, who accordingly revived his own claim to Milan.[29]

Francis and Clement VII meet in Marseilles
(October–November 1533)

By 1 September 1533 the various obstacles in the way of Francis's meeting with the pope had been cleared. Catherine de' Medici accordingly sailed from La Spezia to Villefranche, where she was joined a few weeks later by her uncle the pope. Early on 11 October the papal fleet – sixty ships in all – arrived at Marseilles to be greeted by a great roar of welcome from the shore batteries. Next day, Clement made his entry into the city, accompanied by fourteen cardinals riding their mules. Francis arrived on 13 October and prostrated himself at the feet of the Holy Father. On 28 October the marriage of Henri, duc d'Orléans, and Catherine was celebrated with much pomp; the bridegroom was fifteen years old and his bride only twelve. On 7 November Clement created four French cardinals: Jean Le Veneur, Philippe de La Chambre, Odet de Coligny and

---

[29] V.-L. Bourrilly, 'Les diplomates de François Ier: Maraviglia à Milan (1532–1533)', *Bulletin italien*, vi. (1906), 133–46; E. Picot, 'Les italiens en France au XVIe siècle', *ibid.*, i (1901), 284–5; du Bellay, ii. 206–25; C.S.P. Ven., iv. no. 947.

Claude de Longwy. Among other concessions obtained by Francis was
the permission to levy another clerical tenth. The meeting ended on 12
November, when the pope left Marseilles for Italy and Francis travelled to
Avignon.[30]

The marriage of Henri d'Orléans and Catherine de' Medici was but the
outward sign of a Franco-papal alliance. This, however, was never formalized in a treaty, and no one knows what Francis and Clement actually
decided at Marseilles, though a clue may be found in a draft agreement
written in the king's hand. This anticipates an offensive alliance for the
conquest of Milan as well as the cession of Parma and Piacenza to the
pope.[31] Clement was subsequently accused by his enemies of acquiescing
in Francis's alliance with the German Protestants and the Turks, but this
cannot be proved. What is certain is that the pope subsequently betrayed
to Charles some of Francis's confidences. 'Not only will I not oppose the
invasion of Christendom by the Turk', Francis allegedly declared, 'but I
will favour him as much as I can, in order the more easily to recover that
which plainly belongs to me and my children, and has been usurped by the
emperor.'[32]

Three topics certainly discussed at Marseilles were the spread of heresy
in France, the calling of a general council and Henry VIII's divorce.
Francis allegedly promised to root out heresy in his own kingdom, but
refused to take any action hostile to the German Protestants. Be this as it
may, Clement issued a bull against French Lutherans on 10 November.[33]
As regards a general council, Francis argued that it could serve no useful
purpose as long as he was on bad terms with the emperor, and Clement
was only too glad to postpone it indefinitely.[34] Henry VIII's divorce
proved more troublesome. Francis asked for a further delay of six months
before Henry's excommunication was given effect, but Clement would
concede only one. In the meantime, Stephen Gardiner, bishop of Win-
chester, acting on Henry's behalf, asked the pope to lift the sentence of
excommunication and give his approval to his master's divorce. Both
demands were politely refused, but, at Francis's request, Clement offered

[30] Du Bellay, ii. 225–31; le P. Hamy, *Entrevue de François Ier avec Clément VII à
      Marseille, 1533* (1900), passim.
[31] R. Reumont and A. Baschet, *La jeunesse de Catherine de Médicis* (1866), pp. 325ff.
[32] *C.S.P. Span.*, v. no. 131, p. 396.
[33] Decrue, i. 212; Pastor, x. 304. See also below, p. 245.
[34] This decision caused great bitterness among German Catholics. Writing to Vergerio,
      Duke George of Saxony complained that the pope had allowed himself to be fooled by
      Francis. If the Roman church lost 10,000 ducats, he said, excommunications would be
      hurled, swords drawn and all Christendom asked for aid; but if 100,000 souls were
      lost, the pope listened only to him who was bent on injuring and enslaving Christen-
      dom. *C.S.P. Span.*, iv. no. 1136, p. 825; Pastor, x. 321–2.

to submit Henry's suit to a Franco-papal commission at Avignon. On 7 November Dr Edmund Bonner delivered Henry's reply. Forcing his way into the pope's chamber, he 'intimated' his master's appeal to a future general council. This angered Francis almost as much as the pope, for Henry, without having consulted him, had insulted his guest. 'As fast as I study to win the pope,' he told Gardiner, 'ye study to lose him.'[35] At the end of November he sent Jean du Bellay to Henry to complain that his agents had undone one week's work in an hour and to warn him that he had better act less strangely and suspiciously if he valued the friendship of 'the most powerful king and best friend in Christendom'. But Henry no longer trusted Francis: he kept du Bellay waiting four days, then complained that his master had behaved dishonourably by treating with his worst enemy.[36] On 23 March 1534 Clement fulminated his anathema against the king of England, whereupon Henry completed England's breach with Rome.

The reconquest of Württemberg

By the autumn of 1533 the German princes who had signed the treaty of Scheyern were determined to wrest Württemberg from the Habsburgs, but first they wanted to be sure of receiving the subsidy promised by Francis. They also wanted to secure the dissolution of the Swabian League, which was due for renewal shortly, or at least Württemberg's exclusion from it.

On 16 November, shortly after the pope's departure for Italy, Francis received an appeal for help from Christopher of Württemberg, who had been invited to submit his case to the next diet of the Swabian League at Augsburg. Francis, who needed no prompting to fish in the troubled waters of the empire, accordingly instructed Langey, his principal agent in Germany, to attend the diet in support of Christopher.[37] In a speech to the diet on 10 December Langey claimed that his master wanted only fair play. Francis, he explained, had long been torn between the desire to help Christopher, a weak, unfortunate and innocent prince, and fear of offending the emperor, his brother and the Swabian League. He had now decided to intervene only because Ferdinand had called the diet. Then, after praising the King of the Romans and the estates for their 'sacred council and just deliberation', Langey urged them to restore the towns of Tübingen and Neyff to Christopher and to temper justice with clemency

---

[35] *L.P.*, vi. 1403, 1425–6; Scarisbrick, *Henry VIII*, pp. 319–20.
[36] *L.P.*, vi.1558, 1572; *Correspondance du cardinal Jean du Bellay*, ed. R. Scheurer (1969–73), i. 323–32.
[37] Du Bellay, ii. 236.

in respect of the rest of Württemberg. He then withdrew from the assembly as a demonstration of his disinterestedness. Outside the diet, however, the envoy was anything but disinterested: he encouraged Christopher to lay down conditions unacceptable to the Habsburgs and carefully fostered separatist tendencies within the Swabian League. His activities alarmed Ferdinand's agents. 'The Frenchman', one of them reported, 'is up to his neck in this affair; he acts as if he would like to see war break out, and if he is not offering help openly, he is distributing cash by the fistful so as to create discord in our midst.'[38]

Langey's intrigues culminated on 28 January 1534 in a secret treaty in which Francis undertook to pay one-third (i.e. 100,000 *écus*) of the cost of a war in defence of German liberties. Three days later Langey spoke to the diet again, this time more truthfully. He accused the Habsburg representatives of deceit and warned the delegates of the grave consequences that would follow any refusal on their part to grant redress to Ulrich of Württemberg and his son. He also urged them not to renew the Swabian League, or at least to exclude Württemberg from it so that Christopher might the more easily recover his property. Such was the impact of Langey's words that on 1 February the diet adjourned indefinitely without renewing the League.[39]

Francis, in the meantime, met and signed a treaty with Philip of Hesse at Bar-le-Duc (20 January 1534). While the landgrave promised to declare war on the King of the Romans within three months, Francis undertook to pay Ulrich of Württemberg a subsidy of 125,000 *écus*. This, however, was disguised so as to protect Francis from the charge of breaking the treaty of Cambrai: Ulrich sold him the county of Montbéliard for the amount of the subsidy with the option of buying it back.[40] Soon afterwards Philip overran Württemberg and restored Ulrich to power. On 29 June he made peace with Ferdinand, and the dukes of Bavaria soon did the same.

The attempt to reunify the churches

One of the main obstacles to the formation of a large coalition against the Habsburgs in Germany was the religious schism dividing the princes of that country. Hence Francis's decision in 1534 to become a religious peacemaker. His agent once again was Langey, who returned to Germany by way of Switzerland in May.

The main purpose of this new mission was to persuade both the Swiss and the German reformers that Francis's recent meeting with the pope

---

[38] Bourrilly, *Guillaume du Bellay*, pp. 160–1.
[39] *Ibid.*, pp. 150–62.   [40] *Ordonnances*, vii. no. 651.

had created a climate favourable to a reunion of the churches. Langey told the delegates at the diet of Baden that Clement had shown not only a desire to change institutions which had become anachronisms, but also to accept 'some of the views of those in Germany who call themselves evangelicals'. This being so, he invited the Swiss and German reformers to submit statements indicating how far, in their view, it was possible to achieve a doctrinal compromise with the Catholics.[41] Although suspicious of Francis's motives, the reformers were sufficiently won over by Langey's eloquence to comply with his request. Among the first to respond was Philip Melanchthon, Luther's lieutenant, whose submission reached Paris in the summer of 1534. It could not have been more conciliatory. Melanchthon showed that the churches could agree, given mutual good will. He denied that he and his fellow reformers had ever aimed at the overthrow of the Roman church and acknowledged the necessity for episcopal authority, even for papal supremacy. Melanchthon was also sure that a mutually acceptable definition of justification could be achieved provided the preponderant role of faith was recognized by all. The mass, he admitted, was a more difficult problem, but he did not see it as insurmountable; a synod, he thought, should be able to solve it. Although he himself was in favour of abolishing the cult of saints, he thought it might be reprieved if a formula could be found safeguarding God's prerogative. Monasteries, too, might be retained as colleges or schools. This matter as well as that of clerical celibacy, he felt, could be left to the pope's decision. On 17 August two other German reformers, Bucer and Hedio, replied to Langey's questionnaire in more or less the same spirit.[42] Nothing could have been more encouraging to Francis; it seemed as if a settlement of the religious schism, the essential prerequisite for a united opposition to the Habsburgs in Germany, was about to be achieved.

Khair ad-Din Barbarossa

Francis's intrigues against the Habsburgs also extended to the Mediterranean area. In July 1533 an envoy from Khair ad-Din Barbarossa, the famous Algerian corsair, had met him at Le Puy, bringing a number of French captives whom his master had released as a goodwill gesture. The purpose of his mission, it seems, was to pave the way for an ambassador from the sultan, who arrived soon afterwards with words of encouragement for Francis in his struggle with the emperor and with offers of military help.[43] But Suleiman was too busy fighting the Persians in 1534 to

[41] Bourrilly, *Guillaume du Bellay*, pp. 173–7.
[42] *Ibid.*, pp. 179–83.   [43] Ursu, *La politique orientale*, pp. 77–8.

attack the Habsburgs. He relied instead on Barbarossa, who, after building a fleet at Constantinople, raided the coasts of Italy and Sardinia. In August he captured Tunis, expelling its ruler, Mulcy Hassan, the emperor's ally, and in November sent another envoy to the king of France, ostensibly to sign a commercial truce, but more probably to agree on joint military action in the future.[44]

By the end of 1534 Barbarossa's activities had become so damaging to Spanish shipping that the emperor decided to mount an expedition against his base in north Africa. But first he needed to free himself from entanglements elsewhere; hence his philosophical acceptance of the loss of Württemberg. 'We must take things as they are', he wrote to his brother; and the same attitude characterized his dealings with France and England. He gave both governments fair words and instructed his ambassadors to be as flexible in their negotiations with them as his honour would allow.[45]

Two important embassies

In October 1534 Charles sent Henry, count of Nassau, to France with two proposals. First, he suggested that Sforza might settle a pension on the duc d'Orléans in exchange for French acceptance of his dukedom, but Montmorency immediately rejected this proposal. On 20 October he gave Nassau a written statement reaffirming Francis's claims to Milan and Genoa. Nassau's second proposal was for a marriage between Mary, Henry VIII's daughter by Catherine of Aragon, and Francis's third son, the duc d'Angoulême. This was doubtless intended to help Mary, who had recently been bastardized by her father, but it may also have had a mischievous intent, for, if adopted by Francis, it was bound to damage Anglo-French relations. Charles was confident that the king of France would rise to the bait, for Mary had been recognized by the pope as Henry's lawful heir and was therefore a most desirable match for Francis's youngest son. Indeed, Montmorency's response to this proposal was sufficiently encouraging for the emperor to instruct his resident ambassador in France to press it further.[46]

By the autumn of 1534 Anglo-French relations had become strangely ambiguous. Henry was more than ever dependent on France now that he had broken with Rome, yet he was not sure how far he could trust Francis now that he had become the pope's kinsman and ally. Francis, for his

---

[44] The bourgeois of Paris naïvely reported that the envoy had come to seek a marriage alliance and baptism for the sultan and his son. *J.B.P.*, p. 357.

[45] K. Brandi, *The Emperor Charles V*, tr. C. V. Wedgwood (London, 1939), p. 360.

[46] Decrue, i. 230–1; Granvelle, *Papiers d'état*, ii. 224.

part, played on Henry's feeling of insecurity to get more financial aid from him; hence his decision to send Admiral Chabot to England armed with Nassau's proposal.

A magnificent reception awaited the French admiral in London. He was given accommodation at Henry's own palace of Bridewell, special pains being taken to fill the court with beautiful women. When, however, Chabot requested Mary's hand for the duc d'Angoulême, Henry refused to discuss the matter, saying that the admiral must be joking. After Chabot had produced his instructions proving that he was in earnest, Henry made a counter-proposal: he would give Mary to Angoulême, he said, if they would both renounce all claim to the English throne; alternatively, he would give Elizabeth, his daughter by Anne Boleyn, to the duke and would renounce his own claim to the French throne if Francis would persuade the pope to lift his excommunication. But Chabot showed no enthusiasm for either scheme and soon afterwards returned to France apparently much disgruntled.[47]

By the late summer of 1534 Francis could feel reasonably satisfied with his foreign policy over the past four years. Without resorting to arms or openly contravening the peace of Cambrai, he had successfully undermined the emperor's power in several quarters. He had won the pope over to his side and tied him down by a family compact. In Germany the emperor and his brother were being harassed by a coalition of Catholic and Protestant princes who had wrested from them the duchy of Württemberg. Furthermore, it seemed as if the religious schism in Germany, which had so far hindered the formation of a large-scale movement of opposition to the Habsburgs, was about to be healed. In the Mediterranean the foundations had been laid of a useful partnership between the king and the Turks. Only in respect of England could Francis feel less than satisfied. He had worked hard to avert a schism between Henry VIII and the papacy but had been frustrated by Henry's lack of self-control. Even so, the Anglo-French alliance had survived.

Before the year was out, however, two unexpected events radically altered the international scene: the death of Clement VII on 25 September cut away the basis of the new Franco-papal entente, reducing the marriage of the duc d'Orléans with Catherine de' Medici to the status of a *mésalliance*. If Clement had been succeeded by another member of the Medici family all would have been well, but on 12 October Alessandro Farnese was chosen to occupy the throne of St Peter. He took the name of Paul III and announced that his pontificate would be dedicated mainly to

---

[47] *C.S.P. Span.*, v. nos. 111–12, 114, 118.

three tasks: the pacification of Christendom, the calling of a general council and a new crusade against the Turks. Although Francis paid lip-service to all three, he was in reality opposed to them. Paul's accession consequently necessitated a revision of French policy towards the Holy See. The second event, which had a profound effect on the king's foreign policy, was the Affair of the Placards on 18 October. This act of defiance by a group of French Protestant radicals provoked a campaign of religious persecution in France more savage than any since the start of Francis's reign. This shocked Protestant opinion throughout Europe and called into question the king's sincerity as a religious peacemaker. The imperialists made capital out of the situation by pointing to the contrast between Francis's friendly reception of the Infidel's ambassadors and his cruel treatment of French Protestants.

16

Domestic problems

(1530–4)

THE SUCCESSFUL outcome of the Bayonne talks in July 1530 greatly enhanced Montmorency's standing at court. Congratulations reached him from all parts, and his enemies, notably Chabot, were silenced. As the court travelled back slowly to Paris from the south, the grand master retired to his château at Chantilly. Already a very rich man, he became even more so following the death of his old and much respected father, Guillaume, in May 1531. Anne acquired two-thirds of the paternal inheritance, leaving the rest to his brother, François.[1]

Early in 1531 Montmorency supervised arrangements for the coronation of Queen Eleanor. This took place at Saint-Denis on 5 March and was followed two days later by the queen's entry into Paris. The grand master's feelings for Eleanor were nothing short of a cult. Frenchmen, he thought, ought to thank God for giving them 'so beautiful and virtuous a lady'.[2] Francis was less enthusiastic. In March Sir Francis Bryan told Henry VIII that he did not think all was well between the royal couple. His reasons were as follows:

For the first, being both in one house they lie not together once in four nights; another he speaks very seldom unto her openly; another, he is never out of my lady's chamber, and all for Hely's sake, his old lover; another is, there has been no feast or banquet yet, since the beginning of the triumph, but, the table furnished, he has come and sat in the midst of the board, where Hely has sat, and the Cardinal of Lorraine and the Admiral likewise with their lovers. He has also divers times ridden six or seven miles from the Queen and lain out four or five days together, as it is said, at the houses of his old lovers; and the same day she should make her entry into Paris, he, having knowledge where Hely and divers other ladies and gentlewomen stood, took with him the Admiral and Cardinal of Lorraine; and they, finding these gentlewomen in the said house, the French king took Hely and set her before him in an open window and there stood devising with her two long hours in the sight and face of all the people, which was not a little marvelled at of the beholders.[3]

---

[1] Decrue, i. 166–7, 170–1.
[2] *Ibid.*, i. 164.
[3] *St.P.*, vii. 291. I have modernized the spelling.

Two years later, Marguerite de Navarre told the duke of Norfolk that no man could be less satisfied with his wife than her brother; for the past seven months 'he neither lay with her, nor yet meddled with her'. Norfolk asked her why. 'Purce quil ne le trouve plesaunt a son apetyde', she replied, 'nor when he doth lie with her, he cannot sleep; and when he lieth fro her no man sleepeth better.' Again Norfolk pressed for an explanation. 'She is very hot in bed', replied Marguerite, 'and desireth to be too much embraced'; whereupon she 'fell upon a great laughter, saying, "I would not for all the good in Paris that the king of Navarre were no better pleased to be in my bed than my brother is to be in hers."'[4]

Eleanor, it seems, also failed to get on with her mother-in-law, but at least she did not have to put up with her for long. Louise, who had been riddled with gout for many years, died at Grez-sur-Loing on 22 September 1531. Her 'Caesar' was not at her bedside, being with Montmorency at Chantilly. But he gave her a splendid funeral. Her body was taken first to the abbey of Saint-Maur-des-Fossés, where her effigy in wax was displayed, then to Paris for the funeral service at Notre-Dame, and finally to the abbey of Saint-Denis for burial on 19 October. Louise's inheritance was even larger than her avarice had led people to expect: her movables were valued at 150,000 écus, while her lands included Angoumois, Anjou and Maine (given to her by Francis) and Bourbonnais, Beaujolais, Auvergne, Châtellerault, Forez, Marche, Montpensier and Clermont (taken from the constable of Bourbon). All were now absorbed into the royal demesne.[5]

The *lecteurs royaux* (March 1530)

The return of peace in 1529 enabled Francis to give more attention to the patronage of scholars. Spurred on by Guillaume Budé and other humanists, who reminded him of his promise to found a college for the study of classical languages, Francis set up four regius professorships, the so-called *lecteurs royaux*, in March 1530. Pierre Danès and Jacques Toussaint were appointed to teach Greek, François Vatable and Agathias Guidacerius to teach Hebrew. All may have been recommended by Budé.

Humanists everywhere acclaimed the king's action. 'The river which the king is about to let flow', wrote a Flemish scholar, 'will water many lands and make them fertile.' Erasmus urged the teachers at Louvain to redouble their efforts in face of the new competition from France. She was more fortunate, he thought, as a result of the appointment of the *lecteurs royaux* 'than if the whole of Italy lay under her domination'. The founda-

---

[4] *L.P.*, vi. 682.   [5] C. Terrasse, *François Ier* (1945–70), ii. 150–2.

tion of the lectureships from which the Collège de France takes its origin was certainly an important stage in the history of French education. Students from far and wide were attracted by the free and independent courses they provided, and soon additional lectureships were created. Oronce Finé was appointed to teach mathematics, a subject recently neglected in France, and in 1531 a third professor of Hebrew was appointed in the person of Paul Canossa, *alias* Paradis, a converted Venetian Jew. At first no provision was made for the teaching of Latin, which was regarded as the university's responsibility. Many people, however, believed that this needed to be brought up to date, and it was doubtless with this end in view that, in 1534, Barthélemy Le Masson *alias* Latomus, a dedicated Ciceronian, was appointed by the king.

Important as it was, the foundation of the *lecteurs royaux* was a modest achievement by comparison with the college originally envisaged by the king. For the *lecteurs* were given no building of their own: they had to lecture either in existing colleges or in the open, and were sometimes forced to interrupt their teaching owing to obtrusive street smells and noises. The method of their payment was also unsatisfactory. Their salary, which the *trésorier de l'Epargne* was supposed to pay, seldom materialized, so that they had to give up valuable teaching time to press their claims at court. Eventually, they were put on to the payroll of the king's household, but trouble over their remuneration lasted till the end of the reign.[6]

Troubles with the Sorbonne

In spite of its reactionary teaching, the faculty of theology of the university of Paris still ranked as the most prestigious body of its kind in Christendom. It was, therefore, natural that Henry VIII should wish to obtain its blessing for his divorce from Catherine of Aragon when he decided to consult the continental universities after the revocation of his lawsuit to Rome. He expected Francis, in return for certain financial concessions, to bring pressure to bear on the French universities and was assured of support by Guillaume du Bellay, seigneur de Langey, during his embassy to England.

But the Sorbonne, at least its more reactionary wing led by Noël Béda, did not readily submit to outside intimidation. Even after he had been rebuked by the grand master for opposing Henry's cause, Béda persuaded fifteen of his colleagues to sign a statement endorsing the validity of the

[6]   A. Lefranc, *Histoire du Collège de France* (1893), pp. 101–23.

king's marriage to Catherine. Langey, for his part, worked hard to win the faculty over to the opposite point of view, even by means of bribery. On 7 June 1530 Henry's 'great matter' was debated by the Sorbonne, which had been deliberately 'packed' for the occasion. Langey presented the king's case in the most persuasive terms. Henry, he said, was only asking for advice, not a judgment. But Béda argued that true doctrine was being sacrificed for the sake of the Anglo-French alliance. A debate then followed among the doctors of the faculty as to whether or not the pope should be consulted before any decision was reached, but it ended in uproar with Béda and his supporters claiming victory.

On 17 June Francis ordered the first president of the Parlement to warn Béda that any consultation of the pope would constitute a breach of the kingdom's rights and privileges. This left the Sorbonne in no doubt as to where its duty lay: on 2 July it decided in Henry's favour, albeit by a slender majority. Béda tried to get the vote rescinded but only managed to prevent some absentees from adding their signatures to the faculty's pronouncement.[7]

After this defeat, the Bédaistes tried to get their own back by spreading a report that Jean du Bellay, bishop of Bayonne, the brother of Guillaume, had been charged with heresy in the Parlement. The bishop complained to the king, who asked for an explanation. The Parlement denied that any such charge had been made, but the bishop requested an opportunity to clear his name. Francis accordingly referred the matter to the Grand Conseil, which presumably found du Bellay innocent, since he was appointed ambassador to England in October 1531 and bishop of Paris in September 1532.[8]

Fiscal reform: the second stage (February 1532)

The enormous financial burden imposed on Francis by the peace of Cambrai delayed the reorganization of his fiscal administration. On 7 February 1532, however, after he had paid the first instalment of the ransom due to the emperor, he issued the ordinance of Rouen, regulating the duties and functions of the *Epargne*.[9] This laid down that the coffers in which the *trésorier de l'Epargne* kept his cash would no longer follow the court but be fixed at the Louvre, in Paris, and that all the king's revenues except the *parties casuelles* would be paid into them. The idea behind these arrangements was evidently to build a large reserve of ready cash.

[7]   V.-L. Bourrilly, *Guillaume du Bellay, seigneur de Langey* (1905), pp. 92–107.
[8]   V.-L. Bourrilly and N. Weiss, 'Jean du Bellay, les Protestants et la Sorbonne', *B.S.H.P.F.*, lii (1903), 114–20.
[9]   *Ordonnances*, vi. 584.

The same ordinance also laid down regulations for the safekeeping of the coffers. In addition to the *trésorier de l'Epargne* and two auditors, a committee was set up consisting of the first and second presidents of the Chambre des Comptes. Its powers, however, were purely supervisory: the commissioners had to be present whenever the coffers were opened or closed; but only the *trésorier* controlled the *Epargne*'s receipts and expenses. He was not obliged, however, to reside at the Louvre; in fact, he continued to follow the king so as to provide for his day-to-day expenses and to assist him and his council in dealing with financial matters. He was also allowed to delegate the task of cashing and disbursing revenues, provided he always signed the warrants given to the receivers. In order to open the coffers at the Louvre or even to reach them, the collaboration of the three bodies which together constituted the *Epargne* was essential, for each coffer had three locks and as many keys. One of these was kept by the *présidents*, another by the *contrôleurs* and the last by the *trésorier* himself and his assistants. The door of the tower containing the coffers was guarded by two archers of the king's guard.

The ordinance of Rouen did not affect the *trésoriers de France* and *généraux des finances*, but it was the first of a series of measures taken against the *changeur du Trésor* and *receveurs-généraux*. These officials were accused of not handing over their revenues to the *Epargne*, as they had been instructed to do in 1523. Pending an investigation of their accounts, they were suspended and replaced by officials known as *commis à l'exercice*. In the following year three commissioners were assigned to each *recette-générale* to collect all the king's revenues, including those from the demesne. This meant, in effect, the suppression of the *change du Trésor*. In 1539 the three commissioners were replaced by a single *commis*, and this arrangement was apparently maintained until the creation of the *recettes-générales* in 1543.

More is known about the functioning of the *Epargne* after the reform of 1532 than before, thanks to the survival of six of its registers for the period 1532–5.[10] These show that the wages of the sovereign courts, *mortes-payes* and *gendarmerie* were paid out of the coffers at the Louvre in spite of the ordinance of 1532, which had exempted revenues destined for such uses from transfer to the *Epargne*. The registers also show that important sums of money in the hands of the *receveurs-généraux* never reached the Louvre. They were levied instead by the *trésorier de l'Epargne* wherever he might be and used to pay the king's day-to-day expenses. From 1532 to 1535 the *trésorier* received a total of 1,275,000 *livres* in this way. During the same period Preudomme also paid out 150,000 *livres* by

10   B.N., MSS. fr. 15628–33.

means of warrants assigned on local tax collectors. Thus a total of 1,425,000 *livres* never reached the coffers at the Louvre.[11]

The annexation of Brittany (August 1532)

It is often assumed that the duchy of Brittany became part of France in 1491 as a result of the marriage between King Charles VIII and the Duchess Anne. Actually it was in 1532 that the duchy was formally annexed to the kingdom of France. In April 1515 Francis had persuaded his first queen, Claude, who had inherited the duchy from her mother, to give him its administration during her lifetime, and, in June, her grant had been turned into a perpetual gift. Thus ever since 1515 Brittany had been administered by the king of France in the right of his wife. Then, in 1524, shortly before her death, Claude had made a will bequeathing the duchy to her eldest son, François, but, as he was a minor, the king had continued to administer it. When François came of age in 1532 it became necessary to regularize the duchy's status, for Claude's will had been endorsed only by the Breton parlement (called Grands Jours till 1554) and a case could be made out for his younger brother, Henri, under an arrangement of 1499 which the Breton estates had ratified. If Brittany's permanent union to France was to be guaranteed, it was necessary to establish the Dauphin's right to it beyond dispute.

As a first step towards achieving this, the French chancellor, Duprat, who had also been chancellor of Brittany since 1518, invited a number of influential Bretons to Paris. They included Louis des Désers, president of the Grands Jours of Rennes, who suggested that the demand for permanent union with France should come from the Breton estates themselves, and that it was only necessary to bribe three or four nobles and a few members of the clergy and third estate to secure this. The advice was well taken, and in 1532 many bribes and favours were distributed by the king of France to influential Bretons. Then, in August, Francis took up residence at the castle of Suscinio, near Vannes, where the Breton estates met to discuss the proposed union with France.

Ardent patriots among the deputies argued that union with France would drag the duchy into foreign wars and subject it to heavy taxation, but their opponents pointed to all the hardships that had befallen Brittany in the late fifteenth century when it had been independent. Even the partisans of union, however, wanted certain conditions laid down. On 4 August, therefore, the estates sent four demands to the king: the Dauphin

---

[11]   G. Jacqueton, 'Le Trésor de l'Epargne sous François Ier, 1523–1547', *R.H.*, lvi (1894), 1–13. See also M. Wolfe, *The Fiscal System of Renaissance France* (New Haven and London, 1972), pp. 86–9.

was to be sent to Rennes as duke and owner of the duchy; its administration and usufruct were to be reserved to the king; its rights and privileges were to be respected in spite of its union with France; and the Dauphin was to take an oath to this effect.

Francis immediately agreed to these demands and issued an edict whereby Brittany was irrevocably annexed to France. On 12 August the Dauphin made his entry into Rennes; two days later, he was crowned as Duke Francis III. He was the last to hold the ducal title; when he died in 1536 Brittany became an ordinary French province. By completing the process initiated by Charles VIII forty-five years earlier, Francis had made a notable contribution to French unification. A small, independent, yet vassal, state, which in the past had often called in the foreigner to defend its independence, was no more. From Calais to the Pyrenees the Atlantic seaboard now belonged to France.[12]

More troubles with the Sorbonne (1531–3)

In Lent 1531 Gérard Roussel, a former member of the Cercle de Meaux and now Marguerite de Navarre's almoner, was accused by the Sorbonne of preaching heresy in her presence at the Louvre. He was called by the king and ordered to give advance notice in future of whatever he intended to say in his sermons. This ended the touble for the time being, but in 1533 Roussel was again accused of preaching heresy at the Louvre. The Sorbonne instructed six bachelors of theology, who had been chosen to preach Lenten sermons in the capital, to denounce Lutheran errors, albeit without mentioning any names. But the bachelors soon forgot their brief and began to denounce not only Roussel but also his protectors, the king and queen of Navarre. Such was the stir created by them in the capital that Francis was again forced to intervene. He set up a commission under the chancellor to look into the Lenten sermons and invited the Sorbonne to submit its complaints to it. This seems to have frightened the faculty, for it sent a deputation to Fontainebleau to tell the king that he had been misinformed. Francis was nevertheless determined to restore order in the capital before leaving for the south of France to meet the pope. Both Roussel and his critics were ordered to hold their tongues, and their movements were controlled. But whereas the almoner was confined to Marguerite's household, his accusers, including Béda, were banished from the capital. This seemingly partisan decision caused a furore within the university, where Béda commanded much respect on account of his advanced age, great learning and courage. As he prepared to leave his

[12] J. de La Martinière, 'Les Etats de 1532 et l'Union de la Bretagne à la France', *Bulletin de la Société polymathique du Morbihan* (Vannes, 1911), pp. 177–93.

college, a large crowd of sympathizers gathered outside. Posters also appeared in the streets of Paris attacking Roussel and calling for the violent suppression of heresy. Some of the university's resentment was directed against the king's sister, who was held to be largely responsible for the troubles.

Early in October 1533, while Francis was in the south of France, students of the Collège de Navarre put on a satirical play in which Marguerite was shown preaching heresy at the instigation of a fury called Mégère (a pun on Gérard Roussel's name) and tormenting anyone who would not listen to her. The play came to Marguerite's notice, and the college was soon afterwards raided by the *prévôt de Paris*. The author, however, was not discovered, though two senior members of the college were detained. It is not known how the affair ended.

Later in the month Marguerite again came under fire when the *Miroir de l'âme pécheresse* (*Mirror of the Sinful Soul*), a poem she had published anonymously, appeared in a black list drawn up by the university of Paris. The king asked for an explanation, whereupon Nicolas Cop, the university's rector, called a meeting of all the faculties. He blamed a handful of theologians for what had happened and called on his other colleagues to dissociate themselves from their action. The theologian responsible for blacklisting the poem explained that no offence had been intended to Marguerite. Her work, he said, had been listed because it had been published without the Sorbonne's *imprimatur*, which was essential for all writings touching the faith. Cop then moved that Marguerite's poem be removed from the black list and an apology sent to the king. Finding itself alone among the faculties, the Sorbonne had to back down. On 8 October fifty-eight theologians signed a statement to the effect that they had never read the poem and, therefore, had neither condemned it nor given it their approval. This apparently satisfied the king.[13]

Cop's sermon (November 1533)

It was the custom for a newly elected rector of the university of Paris to preach a sermon on the feast of All Saints in the church of the Mathurins, but the sermon preached by Nicolas Cop on 1 November 1533 was not quite what the audience had come to expect. Drawing heavily on works by Erasmus and Luther, he denounced the 'Sophists', who were turning theology into a hair-splitting science, and ended with the following words: 'Blessed are the persecuted! Let us not be afraid of confessing the Gospel. Should we strive to please man rather than God? Should we fear

---

[13] Bourrilly and Weiss, pp. 120–2, 193–213; C. Schmidt, *Gérard Roussel prédicateur de la reine Marguerite de Navarre* (Strasbourg, 1845), pp. 85–99.

those who can kill the body yet are powerless over the soul?'[14] The sermon was brought to the notice of the Parlement, but before the court could take any action, Cop called a meeting of the whole university. Claiming that his words had been misrepresented and the university's privileges impugned, he demanded that his critics be called to account. But the rector failed to get the support of all the faculties. Then, just as he seemed about to obey a summons from the Parlement, he vanished, taking with him the university's seal. Three months later he turned up in Basle. His flight was soon followed by that of his friend John Calvin, who was once regarded, wrongly it seems, as the author of Cop's sermon.[15]

At the end of November the Parlement made a number of arrests. Precisely how many is not certain: some authorities say 50, others about 300. The Sorbonne, too, was very active: it set up a commission to co-operate with the Parlement in matters of faith and began to investigate its own members. At the same time both bodies wrote to the king warning him about the growth of heresy in the capital. Replying from Lyons, Francis expressed his concern. 'We are angry and displeased', he wrote, 'to learn that . . . this damned heretical Lutheran sect is flourishing in our good town of Paris.'[16] He ordered three counter-measures: the appointment of two *parlementaires* to judge appeals in heresy cases, the publication of two recent papal bulls against heresy and the appointment by the bishop of Paris of two commissioners to be chosen by the Parlement to try heretics in the diocese. This last measure, however, was strongly resisted by René du Bellay, one of the bishop's two vicars-general. It was, he said, both unnecessary and an infringement of the bishop's authority. He claimed that the danger of heresy in the capital had been much exaggerated and rejected the implication that his brother, the bishop, had been negligent in hunting down heretics. If it were true that heresy had grown in Paris, René continued, the Parlement and the Sorbonne had only themselves to blame, for they had prevented the registration of royal letters patent intended to strengthen episcopal control of preaching in the diocese. The Sorbonne's own preachers also had much to answer for: instead of preaching the word of God, they had given Luther widespread publicity by denouncing his errors. Finally, du Bellay rejected the allegations that heresy suspects had been released from the bishop's prison without trial after only a few days.[17]

Friends of René du Bellay were afraid that his resistance would bring him into serious trouble with the king. This, however, did not happen.

[14] M. Mann, *Erasme et les débuts de la réforme française, 1517–1536* (1934), p. 165.
[15] F. Wendel, *Calvin* (London, 1965), pp. 40–2; T. H. L. Parker, *John Calvin* (London, 1975), p. 30.
[16] Herminjard, iii. 114–18.   [17] Bourrilly and Weiss, pp. 219–24.

Francis returned to Paris in February 1534, and almost at once the persecution petered out. Roussel was cleared of the charges that had been hanging over him and set free, while Béda, who had been rash enough in January to lead an attack in the Parlement on the *lecteurs royaux*, was tried on a charge of *lèse-majesté* and banished for life to Mont-Saint-Michel.[18] What was the reason for this change in the king's attitude? Two explanations are usually offered: first, at Lyons the king had been dominated by Montmorency and Duprat, both of them staunchly orthodox ministers, whereas now he was in the company of his sister and Jean du Bellay, who sympathized with the reform movement. Secondly, in the winter of 1533 Francis had been keen to demonstrate his zeal for the faith to Pope Clement VII, whereas now he was more interested in improving his relations with the German Protestants. Both explanations are plausible, but another may be nearer the truth. The persecution, one should remember, had begun in the king's absence; it had been instigated by the Parlement and the Sorbonne. The king had merely condoned it until such time as he could judge the situation in the capital for himself. It is likely that he found this to be less serious than he had been led to believe, and therefore decided to return to the more liberal regime that had existed before his departure for the south.

Military reform: the provincial legions (July 1534)

A most difficult problem facing the king of France in the early sixteenth century was that of finding a large force of infantry that was efficient and reliable, yet cheap. The Swiss were efficient but not always reliable and anything but cheap. Francis could not dispense with them for fear that the emperor might use them, but wanted to lessen his dependence on them: hence, his decision to set up seven legions of foot-soldiers recruited within his own kingdom.

Under an ordinance of 24 July 1534 Normandy, Brittany, Picardy, Languedoc and Guyenne were each to raise one legion.[19] The sixth was to be provided jointly by Burgundy, Champagne and Nivernais and the seventh by Dauphiné, Provence, Lyonnais and Auvergne. Everyone serving in a legion was to be a native of the province that raised it, perhaps to stimulate competition among the legions. The ordinance is silent about the method of recruitment, but this was almost certainly voluntary enlistment. Noblemen who enlisted were promised exemption from the *ban et arrière-ban*, and commoners exemption from the *taille*.

---

[18] *Ibid.*, p. 228. The charge against Béda arose out of a pamphlet he and two others had addressed to the king during their recent exile. Herminjard, iii. 158–9.

[19] *Ordonnances*, vii. no. 666.

Each legion was divided into six *bandes* of a thousand men each under a captain, who had to be a nobleman chosen by the king. One of the six captains was also the colonel commanding the whole legion. Each captain was free to appoint his own subordinates, who comprised two lieutenants, two ensigns, ten *centeniers*, forty corporals, four quartermasters, six sergeants, four drummers and four fifers. A captain was to be paid 50 *livres* per month in peacetime and 100 *livres* in wartime, proportional amounts being laid down for his subordinates. The rank and file were to be paid only in wartime. Those who were wounded or fell sick on service were to be paid as usual; those permanently disabled were exempted from the *taille* and given the chance to serve in garrisons as *mortes-payes*.

Legionaries were armed with pikes, halberds and arquebuses, the distribution of weapons varying with each legion. There were relatively more arquebusiers in the southern legions than in those from the north. Altogether there were meant to be 12,000 arquebusiers as against 42,000 pikemen and halberdiers. The defensive armour of the legionaries consisted of a gorget of mail and a light helmet. Musters were to be held twice a year and were intended partly as training exercises; false musters were subject to severe penalties.

The ordinance of 1534 laid down a strict code of discipline. No legionary below the rank of officer was to talk loudly or shout on pain of having his tongue pierced. Each was to swear an oath to protect sick and pregnant women. A legionary who stole from a church in peacetime was to be hanged and strangled; one who blasphemed was to wear a heavy iron collar (*carcan*) for six hours. If he repeated the offence a third time his tongue was to be pierced and he was to be banished from the legion. Mutiny, desertion, arson, pillage and theft all carried the death penalty. No legionary could switch legions or be accompanied by a woman. But the ordinance also offered rewards. In imitation of the ancient Romans, a gold ring was to be awarded for outstanding valour, and a legionary who had achieved this distinction was to be allowed to rise through the ranks. On becoming a lieutenant he was to be ennobled. This, at least, was the theory.

The ordinance of 1534 was swiftly put into practice. The Normandy legion was inspected by the king at Rouen in April 1535 and the Picardy legion at Amiens in June. On 6 August Francis reviewed the Champagne legion near Rheims and soon afterwards used it to bring to heel the seigneur de Lumes, who had been disloyal. Other legions were in the meantime being raised in the south.[20] But the ordinance was not carried out in every particular. For some unknown reason the Breton legion was

[20] Du Bellay, ii. 288–92; *C.A.F.*, iii. 7802–3, 7814, 1941.

never formed, and the rule governing the provenance of legionaries was interpreted flexibly. Monluc tells us that many of the troops serving in the Languedoc legion had actually been raised in Guyenne.[21]

Despite all the contemporary publicity given to the legions, they proved a disappointment. Their discipline left much to be desired, and they showed up badly in action. The main weakness was their lack of regular training. 'Sixteenth-century wars', John Hale has written, 'were not to be won by clapping civilians into uniform and giving them a Roman name.'[22] The legions were soon relegated to the secondary role of garrisoning border towns and fortresses, and the king had to fall back on foreign mercenaries whenever he required a first-class infantry force.

The Affair of the Placards (October 1534)

For nearly two decades the Protestant Reformation in France offered no clear-cut confessions of faith; its adherents felt free to switch from one doctrine to another in their search for the truth. Guillaume Farel, for example, after belonging to the Cercle de Meaux, turned to Lutheranism. Then, in the mid-twenties, he adopted the more radical ideas of Karlstadt and Zwingli. Yet he would have been called a 'Lutheran' by the French authorities, for this was the label affixed by them to all religious dissenters, whatever their beliefs. In 1534, however, an event took place which clearly indicated how far certain French reformers had moved from Lutheranism in a radical direction.

On the morning of Sunday 18 October Parisians going to church were startled to find that Protestant placards or broadsheets had been put up in several public places during the night. Each placard consisted of a single sheet of paper, 37 by 25 centimetres, printed in Gothic type. It was entitled 'Articles véritables sur les horribles, grands & importables abuz de la Messe papalle' (True articles on the horrible, great and insufferable abuses of the papal mass), and the text was made up of a preamble and four paragraphs. The mass was attacked on four grounds: first, there had been only one sacrifice, that of Christ on the Cross, which, being perfect, could not be repeated; secondly, the mass implied the real presence of Christ in the host, yet Scripture tells us that He is with God the Father till the Day of Judgment; thirdly, transubstantiation was a human invention contrary to Scripture; and lastly, the communion service was a memorial service, not a miracle.[23] Here, in short, was a brief, clear statement of the

[21] B. de Monluc, *Commentaires*, ed. P. Courteault (1911–25), i. 102.
[22] J. R. Hale, in *The New Cambridge Modern History*, ii, *The Reformation*, ed. G. R. Elton (Cambridge, 1958), p. 491.
[23] R. Hari, 'Les placards de 1534', in *Aspects de la propagande religieuse*, ed. G. Berthoud *et al.* (Geneva, 1957), pp. 114, 119–20.

Zwinglian or sacramentarian position on the mass, not the Lutheran one. Neither Luther nor Zwingli accepted the Catholic view of the mass as a sacrifice, but Luther continued to believe in the real presence of Christ in the communion, whereas Zwingli rejected this absolutely.

The authorship of the 'Articles véritables' was for a long time in doubt. Farel was suspected by many, but we now know that the author was Antoine Marcourt, a Frenchman exiled in Switzerland, who in 1530 had become the first pastor of Neuchâtel. In November 1534 he also published a pamphlet, entitled *Petit traicté . . . de la Sainte Eucharistie* (Small treatise . . . on the Holy Eucharist) in whose preface he states quite explicitly that he alone had written the 'Articles véritables' so as to expose publicly the 'seducers' who were holding the people in ignorance. But Marcourt alone could not have distributed the placards. It seems that these were smuggled into France by Guillaume Féret, a servant of the king's apothecary, and put up in Paris by a group of radical dissenters possibly intent on demonstrating their implacable hostility to the mass at a time when certain Protestant reformers were leaning towards some sort of compromise with Rome.[24]

The effect of the placards on the Parisians was shattering. A wave of hysteria swept through the capital as it was rumoured that the reformers were planning to sack the Louvre, burn down all the churches and massacre the faithful at mass. Foreigners came under suspicion, and a Flemish merchant was lynched by a crowd shouting 'He is a German! His death will gain us indulgences!' Soon the fears of Parisians were heightened by reports that placards had also been found in about five provincial towns (Orléans, Amboise, Blois, Tours and Rouen) and even at the château of Amboise, where the king was in residence.[25]

Within twenty-four hours of the discovery of the placards, the Parlement ordered a general procession in Paris and began a search for the culprits. Soon the prisons began to fill up, and on 13 November a shoemaker's son, known as 'the paralytic', was burnt; next day it was the turn of Jean du Bourg, a rich draper. By the end of the month four more dissenters had been executed. Francis, in the meantime, left Amboise and travelled slowly back to the capital, arriving there early in January. On 9 December he wrote to the chancellor giving his approval to the police measures so far taken and asking that they be continued.[26] On 16 December Duprat sent to the king a list of persons who were not to be allowed to

[24] G. Berthoud, *Antoine Marcourt* (Geneva, 1973), pp. 174–6.
[25] The well-known story of the placard found on the king's bedchamber door rests on more or less contemporary evidence, but this is not unanimous as to details. See my 'Francis I, "Defender of the Faith"?', in *Wealth and Power in Tudor England*, ed. E. W. Ives, R. J. Knecht and J. J. Scarisbrick (London, 1978), p. 122.
[26] Bourrilly and Weiss, p. 117.

escape. Francis then set up a special commission of twelve *parlementaires* to judge heresy cases, along with a subcommission to deal with suspects within the Parlement's own ranks. On 13 January, soon after the king's return to the capital, the Protestants struck again. This time they left copies of Marcourt's *Petit traité*, an elaboration of the doctrine of the placards, in the streets of Paris. This 'second' affair was almost worse than the 'first', since it cocked a snook at the authorities just as they were congratulating themselves on having crushed the 'October plot'. Francis reacted on the same day by banning the publication of all new books till further notice and ordering a general procession for 21 January.[27]

This turned out to be one of the most spectacular demonstrations of orthodoxy ever seen in the capital. It brought together the royal court and all the main corporate bodies in Paris: sovereign courts, university, religious orders, municipal government and trade guilds. A notable feature was the large number of shrines and relics brought out of the churches for the occasion. The most precious came from the Sainte-Chapelle and included the Crown of Thorns, at the sight of which, we are told, the 'people's hair stood on end'. But the central feature of the procession was the Blessed Sacrament, which the placards had outraged: it was carried most reverently by the bishop of Paris beneath a canopy borne aloft by the king's three sons and the duc de Vendôme. Immediately behind walked Francis, bareheaded, dressed in black and holding a lighted torch. To the sound of church bells, hymn-singing and instrumental music, the huge cortège wound its way from Saint-Germain-l'Auxerrois to Notre-Dame. Every now and again it came to a halt and the host was placed on a temporary altar. An anthem was sung and the king lost himself in prayer. Occasionally someone in the crowd shouted: 'Sire, do good justice!' and the king would reply with a sign indicating that he could be relied upon.[28]

---

[27] *Ibid.*, p. 118. This ban on printing was not registered by the Parlement and was lifted on 26 February 1535. A.N., X^{1a} 1538, fol. 113. The evidence for this second 'affair' is an unsigned letter written from Paris to John Longland, bishop of Lincoln. It was transcribed into his register, and E. Peacock published it in *Athenaeum*, no. 2761 (25 Sept. 1880), 401. It contains the following passage: 'Ther was within thise fewe dayes by the stretes of parrys scatoryd books which was Intitled Parantiphrasyn scilicet a right prouffitable Intreatise concernynge the Sacrament of the aulter. wherin as they say were scarsely soo many sentences as blasphemyes contrary to the said sacrament wherewith the Kynge was highely offended.'

[28] There are several contemporary accounts of this procession. One of the fullest is in *Cronique du roy Françoys premier*, ed. G. Guiffrey (1960). See also *Athenaeum*, no. 2761 (25 Sept. 1880), 401. The best modern account is in Berthoud, *Antoine Marcourt*, pp. 190–5. For a discussion of comparable processions in Rouen see P. Benedict, *Rouen during the Wars of Religion* (Cambridge, 1981), pp. 62–4. The author shows how such processions 'served as a rite of purification for a city soiled by heresy, thereby conveying very clearly to the onlooking crowds the message that the Protestants formed a force within society whose polluting actions required community atonement'.

After high mass at Notre-Dame, Francis and the queen were entertained to lunch at the bishop's palace. Then, in the presence of a large and
distinguished crowd, the king made a speech in which he urged his
subjects to denounce all heretics, even close relatives and friends. The day
ended with six more burnings, but the king did not light the faggots
himself, as was once thought. He did not even watch the burnings, but left
Paris as soon as the victims had done public penance. This, alas, was not
the end of the persecution. Many more burnings took place before it
ended in May. Meanwhile, other measures of repression were taken: on
24 January a royal proclamation called on seventy-three 'Lutherans' who
had gone into hiding to give themselves up. They included some famous
names, notably Pierre Caroli, Clément Marot, Mathurin Cordier and
Simon du Bois. On the twenty-ninth an edict made harbourers of heretics
liable to the same penalties as the heretics themselves and offered
informers a quarter share of their victims' property.[29]

Why was the persecution so prolonged and savage? It is usually said
that it was the king's answer to a placard found on his bedchamber door.
But it seems strange that an incident at Amboise should have provoked
such a violent reaction as far away as Paris. What is more, the persecution
in the capital began immediately after the discovery of the placards on 18
October, and it is unlikely that an order from the king could have reached
Paris so quickly.[30] When the municipal government met on 19 October it
was in response to a call from the Parlement, not the king.[31] Nor does
Francis's behaviour immediately after the affair suggest a great outburst
of rage on his part. He left Amboise, it is true, but he travelled back to the
capital very slowly, and it was only on 9 December, nearly two months
after the affair, that he wrote to the chancellor giving his approval to the
persecution. Furthermore, it may be doubted if the discovery of a placard
within the royal apartments was an incident of sufficient gravity to justify
such a sweeping persecution. In January 1533 three armed strangers
had been found in the king's chamber at the Louvre, yet his reaction on
this occasion had been simply to ask the Parlement to exercise more
vigilance in the streets of Paris at night.[32]

[29] *Ibid.*, p. 196; Hari, pp. 104–6; Bourrilly and Weiss, p. 129. A letter written by Andrew
Baynton to Thomas Cromwell from Paris on 1 February 1535 contains an interesting
account of these momentous events. Paris, he states, is full of heretics of both sexes:
twenty have already been burned, thousands are in hiding and about a hundred have
fled. He alleges that Francis in his speech asked for God's pardon for his own slackness
in persecuting heretics over the previous two years and swore henceforth to burn all
who fell into his hands. To do this, Baynton suggests, the king would need to shut the
gates of Paris and set fire to the city. Public Record Office, London: SP 1/89/136–7.
[30] The journey from Amboise to Paris normally took three days. A royal messenger could
probably have covered the distance in twenty-four hours.
[31] R.D.B.V.P., ii. 194.   [32] A.N., X^{la} 1536, fol. 68v.

All the available evidence suggests that the persecution which followed the Affair of the Placards was initiated not by the king, but by the Parlement acting in his name. But why did Francis condone it instead of checking it as he had done in 1534 after Cop's sermon? The answer is, surely, that the Protestant challenge this time was of a very different kind. Cop's sermon had been an essentially moderate statement addressed to a learned audience;[33] the placards were a violent and abusive attack on the mass and the priesthood directed at all the king's subjects. Even if the king had wanted to stop the persecution, he would have found it difficult to do so, given the popular hysteria unleashed by the placards. His credibility as the Most Christian King would have suffered irreparable damage. He therefore chose the only sensible course of action: that of identifying himself with the persecution and giving it his full encouragement.

The Affair of the Placards has been rightly regarded as a watershed in the history of the French Reformation, but usually for the wrong reason. It did not mark a sudden change in royal policy from toleration to persecution.[34] Francis had never tolerated heresy: he had only intervened from time to time to protect certain scholars and preachers connected with the court. They had been helped by the fact that in the past heresy had not been easily defined. The boundary between it and Christian humanism had often been blurred. Now the situation was entirely different. Nothing could be clearer than the doctrine of the placards. It was sacramentarianism in its most militant form, which neither the king nor the Parlement was prepared to tolerate. For years the Parlement and the Sorbonne had been obstructed by the king in their efforts to silence the voice of reform. Now there could be no argument as to the seriousness of the Protestant challenge. French Protestantism, it has been said, was transformed by the Affair of the Placards into a 'religion for rebels'; as such, it had to be stamped out.[35]

---

[33] I am aware of no justification for J. Jacquart's statement (*François 1ᵉʳ* (1981), p. 269) that Cop's sermon contained ideas 'close to those of the sacramentarians'.

[34] N. M. Sutherland (*The Huguenot Struggle for Recognition* (New Haven and London, 1980), pp. 14–18) argues that Francis's 'definitive attitude towards heresy . . . was quite clearly adopted and annunciated [*sic*] in, or by, April 1526'. She attaches some importance to Zwingli's dedication of his *Traité de la vrai et fausse religion* to the king in March 1525 and claims that, as from April 1526, Francis was determined 'to permit no interference with the Sacrament of the Eucharist'. I believe, however, that such interference antedated 1526 and that the king's motivation was less precise in its doctrinal commitment in the period between 1526 and 1534. The implications of the affair are discussed by D. R. Kelley, *The Beginning of Ideology: Consciousness and Society in the French Reformation* (Cambridge, 1981), pp. 13–19. Arguing that the affair was 'pivotal' for a variety of reasons, the author shows that 'the fundamental issue was not merely doctrinal disagreement but obedience to established authority'.

[35] Berthoud, *Antoine Marcourt*, p. 219.

17

Patron of the arts and 'father of letters'

IN MARCH 1528, two years after his return from captivity, Francis informed the municipal authorities in Paris of his intention 'henceforth to reside for most of the time in and around his good town of Paris rather than elsewhere in the kingdom'.[1] In fact, he continued to travel about his kingdom as much and as widely as before; nor did he abandon the Loire valley, as is sometimes claimed. But he did shift the centre of his building activities from the Loire valley to Paris and the Ile-de-France. It was then that he began rebuilding the Louvre, erected the château of Madrid in the Bois de Boulogne, remodelled Saint-Germain-en-Laye to the west of the capital, built Villers-Cotterêts to the north of it, and to the south-east embarked on the transformation of Fontainebleau into one of the most magnificent royal palaces in Europe.

Why did Francis shift his building activities in this way? It is possible, though unlikely, that the disloyalty shown by certain Parisians during his captivity had convinced him of the need to overawe them. Strategic reasons, too, may have influenced him: the highly vulnerable frontiers of northern and eastern France were more easily reached from the Paris area than from the Loire valley. But probably a more important reason than either of these was the political ascendancy of Anne de Montmorency, which lasted from 1528 until 1541. Montmorency's principal estates – Chantilly, Ecouen, Fère-en-Tardenois – lay near the capital, and he for one would have welcomed an arrangement which would enable him to keep an eye on his own châteaux while continuing to attend the court. Francis was frequently Montmorency's guest during the same period.

The reason why Francis built so many châteaux around Paris was the lack of any suitable building which he might use within the capital itself. The Louvre was a decrepit medieval fortress, and the demolition of its keep in 1528 could not transform it overnight into a satisfactory residence

---

[1] *R.D.B.V.P.*, ii. 17.

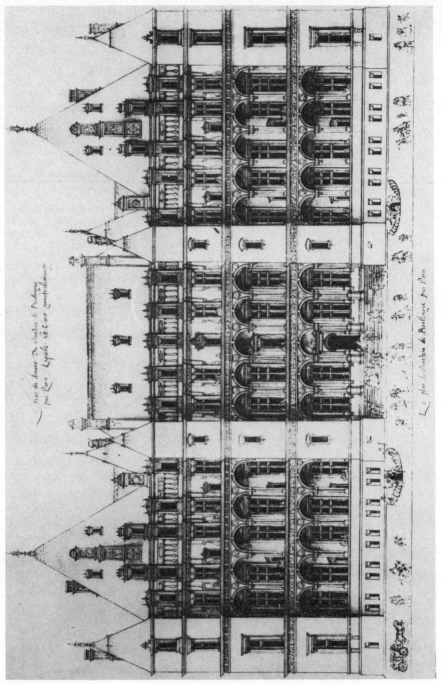

Plan du dessus De iardin de Boullongne pres Paris Lequelle est tout quarellement

Le plan du iardin de Boullongne pres Paris

8   Elevation of the château of Madrid.

for the court.[2] Until the construction of the new Louvre Paris lacked a courtyard suitable for the kind of entertainment favoured by Renaissance princes. This need had been underlined early in the reign, when the courtyard of the Bastille had been used for a banquet in honour of a distinguished English embassy.[3] When the Emperor Charles V visited Paris in the winter of 1539–40 the Louvre was given a hasty face-lift, but the great hall of the Palais – headquarters of the Parlement – had to be used for a banquet.[4] All this must have convinced Francis of the need to rebuild the Louvre, but this could not be achieved quickly; there were many physical difficulties in the way. Thus it was only in 1546, shortly before the king's death, that Pierre Lescot was given the task.[5] Meanwhile, the king had to make do with other châteaux outside Paris where there was more room to build and also where he could more easily indulge his taste for hunting.

Nothing remains of the château built by Francis in the Bois de Boulogne outside Paris, but its plan and elevation are recorded in du Cerceau's engravings and in such eyewitness accounts as that in John Evelyn's *Diary*.[6] Three men were concerned with the building of Madrid, as the château came to be called, two Frenchmen and one Italian: Girolamo della Robbia, a member of the famous Florentine family of ceramists. He arrived in France about 1528 and set up a ceramics factory at Suresnes, near Paris. But Girolamo was more than a ceramist; he is repeatedly described as a master mason in documents related to the building of Madrid, and it is likely that he had a large share of responsibility for the château's Italianate features, notably the horizontal emphasis of the galleries, the treatment of the pillars, the triangular pediments over the dormers, the central flight of steps, and above all the lavish use of terracotta ornamentation both inside and outside the building.[7]

How did the château get its nickname? The problem has caused much speculation over the centuries. The anonymous bourgeois of Paris tells us

---

[2] *J.B.P.*, p. 274. Other parts of the Louvre were repaired at this time and some buildings added, including the kitchen court to the west, two tennis courts to the east and lists to the south. See A. Chastel, 'La demeure royale au XVIᵉ siècle et le nouveau Louvre', in *Studies in Renaissance and Baroque Art Presented to Anthony Blunt* (London, 1967), pp. 78–82.

[3] E. Hall, *Henry VIII*, ed. C. Whibley (London, 1904), i. 173.

[4] *Fêtes et cérémonies au temps de Charles Quint*, ed. J. Jacquot (1960), p. 438.

[5] L. de Laborde, *Les comptes des bâtiments du roi, 1528–71* (1878–80), i. 249–51.

[6] J. A. du Cerceau, *Les plus excellents bastiments de France (1576–1607)* (facsimile repr., Farnborough, 1972), i. 4; *The Diary of John Evelyn*, ed. E. S. De Beer (London 1959), p. 284.

[7] F. Gébelin, *Les châteaux de la Renaissance* (1927), p. 146. The Italianate character of Madrid has been disputed. Cf. A. Blunt, *Art and Architecture in France, 1500–1700* (Harmondsworth, 1957), p. 23.

that the king called it 'Madrid' because it resembled the building where he had been held a prisoner in Spain.[8] But this cannot be right, for the Alcazar was quite different. Evelyn, along with many others, has a different explanation. The king, he writes, christened the château Madrid 'to absolve him of his oath that he would not go from Madrid (in which he was a prisoner) in Spain, but from whence he made his escape'.[9] Another explanation is given by Sauval in his *Antiquités de la ville de Paris*. Francis, he writes, never wanted to be troubled with affairs of state when he vanished into the Bois de Boulogne, so much so that his courtiers complained that they saw as little of him as when he was in Madrid. They called the new château 'his Madrid' and the name stuck.[10]

Madrid broke away from French tradition by having neither a central courtyard nor a water-filled moat; yet it had a high-pitched roof and spiral staircases. In plan, it was a solid rectangular mass surrounded by a dry moat and divided into three parts: in the middle was the great hall flanked by two open loggias, and at each end stood a square pavilion containing *appartements*. These were reached by six spiral staircases situated in the angles of the great hall and at each end of the building. The elevation comprised two superimposed exterior galleries running round the entire building and interrupted at regular intervals by the staircase turrets and square corner towers. The dormer windows, instead of bearing complicated open-work designs, as at Blois and Chambord, were mostly covered by straight pediments. But the château's most unusual feature was its decoration, both interior and exterior, of brightly coloured terracotta. Work on the château went on almost continuously from 1528 until 1570, but the bulk of it was finished under Francis, when more than 174,000 *livres* were spent on the masonry alone.[11]

According to du Cerceau, Francis was so knowledgeable (*ententif*) about architecture that one could almost say that he alone was the architect of Saint-Germain-en-Laye.[12] This suggests at least a close collaboration between the king and the Parisian master mason Pierre Chambige, who began rebuilding the château in September 1539. Keeping as much as he could of the medieval château, Chambige added two storeys and completely renovated the inner façades. His chief innovation, which may have been suggested by the king, was the terraced roof, constructed of large, superimposed stone slabs. This proved of such a weight that the supporting edifice had to be reinforced with large buttresses and held together by long iron tie-bars.[13]

[8] *J.B.P.*, p. 274.   [9] *Diary of John Evelyn*, p. 64.
[10] H. Sauval, *Histoire et recherches des antiquités de la ville de Paris* (1724), ii. 309.
[11] Gébelin, pp. 145–9; Blunt, pp. 23–6.
[12] Du Cerceau, p. 5b.   [13] Gébelin, pp. 161–6.

In March 1542 Francis commissioned Chambige to build another château in the forest of Saint-Germain at a spot, called La Muette, where he liked to watch the deer retire 'exhausted from the labours of the chase'. Though this château, too, had a terraced roof and stone walls decorated with brick, it differed from Saint-Germain in plan and was also much smaller.[14]

From 1532 onwards Francis was a frequent visitor to the château of Villers-Cotterêts, situated eighty-five kilometres north-east of Paris. Work on the château began about 1533 and was largely completed in Francis's lifetime. It was carried out by two Parisian master masons, Guillaume and Jacques Le Breton. The château was built around two rectangular courtyards, one of which served as a tennis court. In its present state the main feature at Villers-Cotterêts is the wing that divides the courtyards. This contains a chapel (now the Salle des Etats) and two straight staircases of which the larger has a coffered vault decorated with scenes from Colonna's *Il sogno di Polifilo*.[15]

Fontainebleau

By far the most important château built by Francis in the last twenty years of his life was Fontainebleau. In December 1529 he announced his intention to spend more time there on account of the pleasure he derived from hunting red deer and wild boar in the neighbouring forest.[16] Fontainebleau did, in fact, become Francis's favourite residence. He 'liked it so much', writes du Cerceau, 'that he spent most of his time there . . . all that he could find of excellence was for his Fontainebleau of which he was so fond that whenever he went there he would say that he was going home'.[17] This is confirmed by the king's itinerary: he spent more time at Fontainebleau after 1528 than anywhere else save Paris.[18]

A castle, oval in shape with flanking towers and a square keep, had existed at Fontainebleau since the twelfth century. By the sixteenth century, however, it could no longer serve the needs of a large, sophisticated court. In April 1528, therefore, a Parisian master mason called Gilles Le Breton was commissioned by the king to carry out alterations and additions. These included a new entrance (Porte Dorée) to the courtyard, a long gallery (Galerie François 1er) behind the keep and two short blocks

---

[14] Laborde, *Les comptes des bâtiments*, i. 222–4.
[15] Gébelin, pp. 181–4. Other châteaux built by Francis after 1528 included Challuau and Folembray. See du Cerceau, i. 4–5; ii. 6–7; C.A.F., vi. 23044, 23120.
[16] P. Guilbert (Abbé), *Description historique des château, bourg et forest de Fontaine-bleau* (2 vols., 1731), ii. 262.
[17] Du Cerceau, ii. 3.
[18] C.A.F., viii. pp. 455–533, 541–8.

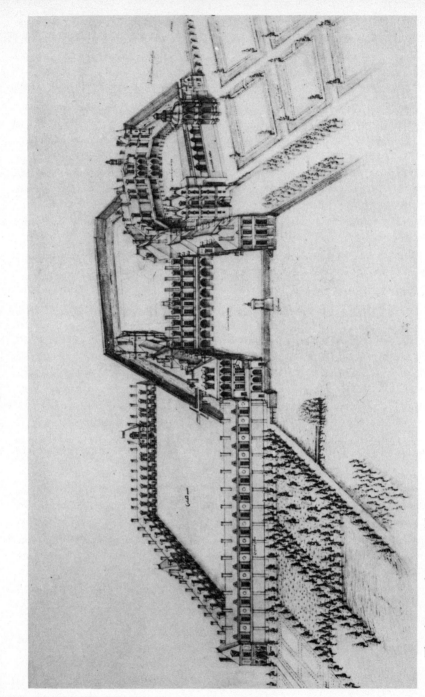

9   The château of Fontainebleau.

linking the new entrance to the keep.[19] Le Breton may also have been responsible for the great courtyard, subsequently called Cour du Cheval Blanc, built on the site of a monastery which the king had acquired for this purpose. Simplicity is the keynote of Le Breton's style as exemplified by the Porte Dorée with its flat pilasters and straight pediments over the windows. But this may be due to functional necessity rather than aesthetic judgment, for the local stone or *grès*, which Le Breton used, is too coarse in texture to allow of fine carving. Le Breton has been dismissed as a mere craftsman devoid of originality, but he must have been rather better than that if, as has been claimed, he designed the monumental staircase in the Cour Ovale. The remains of this staircase point to a more classical style of decoration widely adopted in France in the 1530s.[20]

The same staircase was once attributed to the Italian architect Sebastiano Serlio, who came to Fontainebleau in 1541, but his contribution to the château remains an enigma. About 1537 he dedicated to Francis a copy of Book 4 of his famous treatise on architecture and asked to be taken into his service, but he received only a promise of money. Three years later, however, he dedicated the third book of his treatise to the king and soon afterwards was invited to Fontainebleau. Yet no part of the château can be attributed to him; it seems that he acted simply as an adviser, while continuing to write his treatise.[21]

Today the visitor to Fontainebleau enters the château through the Cour des Adieux (formerly Cour du Cheval Blanc), but in the sixteenth century he would have used the Porte Dorée. The courtyard was not an integral part of the château, save for its east wing, which was incomplete at the end of Francis's reign. It is important to realize that Fontainebleau was built in a piecemeal fashion over a long period. Francis did not live to see it finished. During much of his reign it must have been a noisy and dirty place, full of scaffolding and workmen. Much of what was built under Francis has also been destroyed. Only the north wing of the Cour du Cheval Blanc is more or less in its original state, though it was shortened in 1565 to make way for a moat. The west wing was destroyed by Napoleon I, and the south wing was rebuilt by Louis XV. This involved the destruction of the famous Galerie d'Ulysse with its decorations by Primaticcio.

In the early seventeenth century the Cour du Cheval Blanc (named after a plaster copy of the Capitoline statue of Marcus Aurelius, which

[19] Laborde, i. 25–50.
[20] Blunt, *Art and Architecture*, p. 27. Cf. A. Chastel, 'L'escalier de la Cour Ovale à Fontainebleau', in *Essays . . . to Rudolf Wittkower*, ed. D. Fraser, H. Hibbard and M. J. Lewine (London, 1967), pp. 74–80.
[21] Blunt, p. 39.

Catherine de' Medici set up in the middle) was used for equestrian displays, and it may already have been used for this purpose by Francis, for his stables occupied the ground floor of the south wing till 1537. The horses were then moved to Monceau and the ground floor placed at the disposal of privileged merchants and artisans attached to the court. Originally, the south wing was probably similar to the northern one, but about 1537 an additional floor was added containing the Galerie d'Ulysse.

The Cour du Cheval Blanc was entered through the centre pavilion of the west wing, which was traditionally occupied by a company of the *Cent-Suisses*. What the other pavilions were used for is uncertain. That at the north end of the west wing may have housed the foundry used to cast bronzes of ancient statues from casts brought back from Rome by Primaticcio in 1541; later it became a tapestry workshop. Only two of the five pavilions of the east wing were built under Francis. The ground floor of the Pavillon des Armes, which has since been rebuilt, was where the king stored his ancient statues; the first floor contained the constable's apartment, and the second the king's armoury. According to a contemporary chronicler, the other pavilion, called Pavillon aux Poesles, was built in 1539 specifically for the visit of the Emperor Charles V, but this is unlikely. It was probably built some four years earlier, and, as its name indicates, the ground floor housed stoves, which heated the floors above.[22] The only part of the original south wing still surviving is the Grotte des Pins with its giants emerging from a rocky background. This was for a long time one of the château's most controversial features. In fact, it was built about 1543 and was obviously intended as a summerhouse. The notion that it was used as a bathroom and that James V of Scotland saw his future bride, Madeleine de France, bathing there naked is a figment of eighteenth-century imagination.[23]

Today the most important survival of Renaissance Fontainebleau is the Galerie François 1er, which occupies the first floor of the wing that was added to the keep. In the early sixteenth century it served as a passage from the royal apartments to the church of the Mathurins, which stood on the site of the present Chapelle de la Sainte-Trinité. It is important to realize that the present building is twice the width of the original, so that, instead of having windows on both sides, it is now lit from one side only. Other differences should also be noted. At first there was no terrace on the side facing the Cour de la Fontaine. This was added in 1535 to accommodate six kitchens and larders. A passage beneath the gallery which the local townspeople had used to reach a pond and the Porte Dorée was

22   F. Herbet, *Le château de Fontainebleau* (1937), pp. 3–127.
23   L. Golson, 'Serlio, Primaticcio and the Architectural Grotto', *G.B.A.*, 6th ser., lxxvii (1971), 95–108.

blocked, and Francis was thus able to turn the ground floor into an *appartement des bains*, comprising a bathroom and sweating-rooms (*étuves*). According to an Italian visitor of the early seventeenth century, the bath was square and about five feet deep. It was reached by a flight of wooden steps, and two spouts provided hot and cold water. The bath was surrounded by a wooden balustrade, painted to look like bronze, around which people could walk two abreast. The vault and lunettes were decorated with paintings and stucco. But the decoration was not confined to murals, for it was here, in the hot and humid atmosphere of the *appartement des bains*, that Francis chose to display his unique collection of paintings. The modern mind boggles, but a cultivated Renaissance man would have seen nothing incongruous in the dedication of a building simultaneously to the care of the body and pleasures of the mind.[24]

Much admired as they were by contemporaries, Francis's baths were outshone by the Galerie François Ier on the floor immediately above. It was here, in the earliest surviving example of a long gallery north of the Alps, that Giovanni Battista Rosso evolved a distinctive style of interior decoration. Rosso was a Florentine artist who had come under the influence of Michelangelo and Raphael while working in Rome. About 1529 he moved to Venice and did a drawing of *Mars and Venus* for Pietro Aretino. This drawing, which was an allegory of the peace of Cambrai (for 'Mars' read 'Francis' and for 'Venus', 'Eleanor of Portugal'), was presented to Francis and doubtless paved the way for Rosso's invitation to France. He arrived in 1531, and, being not only a good painter but also a cultivated man, he immediately made a good impression on the king, who appointed him his First Painter.[25] A year later, Rosso was followed to Fontainebleau by Francesco Primaticcio, a pupil of Giulio Romano, who came recommended by the Duke of Mantua.[26] He was, it seems, particularly skilled in the art of stucco. Indeed, Vasari gives him credit for introducing it to Fontainebleau, but this is doubtful, for the style of the Galerie François Ier, which contains the earliest stucco work in the château, is unmistakably Rosso's.[27] Between them, Rosso and Primaticcio decorated many parts of Fontainebleau. Sometimes they collaborated, but more often they worked independently, each with a large team of

[24] Herbet, pp. 153–6. The king's baths clearly did not do his pictures much good. Some had been damaged beyond repair by the seventeenth century, when Henri IV moved them to another part of the château. They eventually formed the nucleus of the collection of paintings at the Louvre.

[25] K. Kusenberg, *Le Rosso* (1931), passim; J. Adhémar, 'Aretino: Artistic Adviser to Francis I', *J.W.C.I.*, xvii (1954), 311–18.

[26] L. Dimier, *Le Primatice* (1900), passim.

[27] G. Vasari, *Lives of the Painters, Sculptors and Architects*, ed. W. Gaunt (London, 1963), iv. 193; Blunt, *Art and Architecture*, p. 31.

assistants. Unfortunately, much of their work has been destroyed. It is known thanks to preliminary drawings which have survived, and a large number of contemporary etchings and engravings copied from or inspired by their designs.[28]

All that remains of Rosso's work at Fontainebleau is contained in the Galerie François 1er, which remains impressive in spite of drastic alterations and clumsy restoration over the centuries.[29] The walls are divided into two roughly equal parts, the lower containing carved wood panelling by Scibec de Carpi, and the upper a combination of stucco and painting. Each space between the windows has a painted panel in the middle, flanked by varied decorations in stucco, including nudes, herms, putti, garlands of fruit and strap-work (i.e. stucco made to look like rolls of leather cut into fantastic shapes). All of this represents stylistically a rejection of High Renaissance classicism in favour of Mannerism. The meaning of the decoration of the Galerie François 1er has baffled many generations of art historians. One eminent authority has argued that it forms 'a coherent and, on its own complex premises, consistent system' aiming at the glorification of the monarch through mythological references to various moments in his life.[30] This view, however, has been seriously undermined by the recent restoration of the gallery. Much more is now known about the chronology of Rosso's decorations. The frescoes, it seems, were executed by four men of varying skill between 1534 and 1538 *after* the stucco had been completed. Thus some of the ingenious references to moments in the king's life, which have been read into the frescoes on the assumption of a piecemeal execution over a longer period, are no longer acceptable. Much haste was apparently applied to finishing the gallery for the emperor's visit in 1539.[31]

The art of Primaticcio is even less well represented at Fontainebleau than Rosso's. All that survives of his work before 1540 is the upper part of a fireplace in the Chambre de la Reine, but his drawings for decorations in the Chambre du Roi and elsewhere show that until then he was still much under the influence of his master, Giulio Romano. In 1540, however, he was sent to Rome to collect works of art for the king and came into contact with ancient sculpture and the art of Parmigianino. Following his return to Fontainebleau, he developed a style of figure-drawing well exemplified by the caryatids of the Chambre de la Duchesse d'Etampes

[28] H. Zerner, *The School of Fontainebleau* (London, 1969), passim.
[29] The most up-to-date account of this gallery is now to be found in the *Revue de l'Art*, special no. 16–17 (1972).
[30] D. Panofsky and E. Panofsky, 'The Iconography of the Galerie François 1er at Fontainebleau', *G.B.A.*, 6th ser., lii (1958), 113–90.
[31] *Revue de l'Art*, special no. 16–17.

with their long, tapering limbs, thin necks and small heads with exaggeratedly classical profiles.[32] Primaticcio's main work after 1540 was done in the Salle de Bal and the Galerie d'Ulysse, but most of it dates from after Francis's reign. He was, however, responsible for the decoration of the king's baths, which were, alas, destroyed by Louis XIV.

Francis's pride in Fontainebleau is well attested by Sir John Wallop, the English ambassador to France, in 1540. The king told the ambassador that he had heard that Henry VIII used much gilding in his houses, whereas he himself used little or none. He preferred 'timber finely wrought with divers colours of wood natural, as ebony, brazil and certain others', which he reckoned were richer than gilding and also more durable. Soon afterwards, Wallop was able to see all this for himself at Fontainebleau. He found the royal bedchamber 'very singular, as well with antique borders, as costly ceiling and a chimney right well made'. After helping the ambassador to stand on a bench so that he might touch the 'said matter and stuff', Francis led him to his gallery, the key of which he kept on his person. This impressed Wallop so much that he urged his master to copy it at St James's palace. Francis then took Wallop to see his baths. 'These', the ambassador continues, 'being warm and reeked so much, like it had been a mist, that the king went before to guide me.'[33]

On the south side of the wing housing the Galerie François 1er lay the Cour de la Fontaine, where in 1539 a tall column, spouting fire, water and wine, was erected for the emperor's benefit. The fountain itself was added about 1541, its main feature being a colossal statue of Hercules by Michelangelo, which was eventually moved to an island in the middle of the Etang aux Carpes. This pond was much used for aquatic displays in the mid-sixteenth century and may already have been used in this way by Francis.[34]

The main royal apartments were situated, as they had always been, within the old castle, whose courtyard, the Cour Ovale, was given a face-lift under Francis, in addition to the monumental staircase already referred to and two superimposed chapels. The courtyard was used from time to time for festivities, as in 1546 on the occasion of the baptism of Catherine de' Medici's daughter, when it served for an exhibition of royal treasures assembled from all corners of the kingdom. An awning of blue silk was stretched across the courtyard and supported in the middle by a tall mast. At the foot of this mast was a pyramid with nine shelves on which the king's plate was displayed along with many vases

---

[32] Blunt, p. 58. See also *L'Ecole de Fontainebleau* (catalogue of exhibition at Grand Palais, Paris 1972–3), pp. 130–72.

[33] *St.P.*, viii (pt v), 482–4. I have modernized the spelling.

[34] Herbet, *Fontainebleau*, pp. 110–12, 131–40; Guiffrey, p. 290.

and antique pieces. Specially appointed guides told visitors where all these precious objects had come from: some, they explained, had been brought to France by Charlemagne; others were the gifts of foreign potentates.[35]

Patron of the arts

Francis I was not the first French monarch to collect pictures, but the royal collection was heterogeneous and of variable quality until he took it over.[36] The art of painting in France was at a low ebb about 1500, the only French artists of any significance being Jean Bourdichon and Jean Pérréal; Italian painters seldom troubled to visit France. In 1515, however, an important change came about as a result of Francis's conquest of Milan. He was able to see some of the masterpieces of the Italian Renaissance, including Leonardo da Vinci's *Last Supper*, which apparently impressed him so much that he invited the artist to settle in his kingdom.

Leonardo was sixty-five years old in March 1516, when he accepted the king's invitation. He was given the manor of Cloux, near Amboise, and an annuity of 500 *livres*. What the king expected in return is not known. Leonardo's sketches and notes show that he was interested in canal-building, town-planning and architecture; he may have been commissioned by the king to carry out some work at Romorantin, but nothing came of this. Nor is there any evidence that he painted any pictures in France. Leonardo died at Cloux on 2 May 1519, but not in the arms of the king, as Vasari would have us believe; on the day in question Francis was at Saint-Germain-en-Laye. His esteem for Leonardo was nevertheless high; twenty years later he told Cellini that Leonardo had been 'a great philosopher' who knew more than any other man about painting, sculpture and architecture. By 1545 the royal collection at Fontainebleau included several major works by Leonardo.[37]

Another Italian artist of the first rank who visited France early in Francis's reign was Andrea del Sarto. He painted a portrait of the infant Dauphin for the king and also a *Charity*, now in the Louvre. But he soon

---

[35] Herbet, pp. 240–1.
[36] J. Cox-Rearick, *La collection de François Ier* (1972), p. 7; J. Adhémar, 'The Collection of Francis the First', *G.B.A.*, 6th ser., xxx (1946), 5–16.
[37] See above pp. 99–100. *The Travel Journal of Antonio De Beatis: Germany, Switzerland, the Low Countries, France and Italy, 1517–1518*, ed. J. R. Hale (London, 1979), p. 132; C. Pedretti, 'Leonardo da Vinci: Manuscripts and Drawings of the French Period, 1517–18', *G.B.A.*, 6th ser., lxxvi (1970), 285–318; Cox-Rearick, pp. 14–21. De Beatis assumed that Leonardo could no longer paint because he had become paralysed in his right hand. He was evidently unaware that the artist was left-handed.

returned to Florence, where he allegedly misused funds given to him by Francis to purchase works of art on his behalf.[38]

Francis's artistic interests were not exclusively Italian. For portraiture he turned mainly to Jean Clouet, an artist who hailed almost certainly from the Netherlands. Portraiture became very popular during the reign, and many chalk drawings have survived of the king, members of his family and entourage. Some are of high quality and are usually attributed to Clouet; others are contemporary copies of variable quality. These were put to different uses: they might be sent to friends and relatives of the sitter, as are photographs today, or gathered into albums containing fifty or sixty drawings each. Although Clouet was almost certainly French-trained, his use of parallel diagonal hatching strokes to obtain a three-dimensional effect was of Italian origin. For this reason he has been described as 'one of the first artists in France to comprehend the principles of the Italian High Renaissance'.[39] He died in 1540 and was succeeded as Painter to the King by his son, François, who continued the series of French court portraits.

By 1525 Francis's collection of works of art comprised a significant number of paintings by Florentine and Roman artists of the High Renaissance.[40] Thereafter its scope was enlarged. Agents were employed by the king to find him paintings, statues, books and other rare and valuable items. Some were French diplomats like Guillaume du Bellay, who was paid 2,050 *livres* in 1526 for sending certain 'articules' to the king from Rome; others were Italians, like Battista della Palla and Pietro Aretino.[41] According to Vasari, della Palla ransacked Florence for the king of France, but the works which he is known to have sent him are few. The paintings included a *Resurrection of Lazarus* by Pontormo and a *St Sebastian* by Fra Bartolommeo, both of which have disappeared. Unscrupulous as he was, della Palla was not always able to satisfy the king. During the siege of Florence, for example, he tried unsuccessfully to seize some famous wood panels and paintings belonging to the Borgherini family. His usefulness as an artistic agent ended in 1530, when he was

38　J. Shearman, *Andrea del Sarto* (Oxford, 1965), i. 3–4, 77, 314; S. J. Freedberg, *Andrea del Sarto* (Cambridge, Mass., 1963), i. 47.

39　P. Mellen, *Jean Clouet* (London, 1971), p. 29. See also R. de Broglie, 'Les Clouet de Chantilly: catalogue illustré', *G.B.A.*, 6th ser., lxxvii (1971), 257–336. Francis also looked to the Netherlands for tapestries. See S. Schneebalg-Perelman, 'Richesses du garde-meuble parisien de François Ier: inventaire inédits de 1542 et 1551', *G.B.A.*, 6th ser., lxxviii (1971), 253–304.

40　Viz. Leonardo's *Virgin of the Rocks, A Lady of the Court of Milan, Mona Lisa*, the *Bacchus–St John*, the *Virgin and St Anne* and *St John the Baptist*, Andrea del Sarto's *Charity* and Raphael's *Belle Jardinière* and *St Michael*.

41　V.-L. Bourrilly, *Guillaume du Bellay* (1905), p. 36 n. 5.

imprisoned by the Medici.[42] Even so, Francis continued to add Florentine works to his collection, including Michelangelo's *Leda and the Swan* (now lost) and, possibly, Bronzino's *Allegory of Passion* (now in the National Gallery, London).[43]

Though most of the artists represented in the royal collection at Fontainebleau were Florentine, Venetians were not overlooked. In 1538 Aretino sent two pictures to Francis, 'one magnifying the honour of man, the other magnifying the glory of God'. The first was Titian's portrait of the king, now in the Louvre, which was painted not from life, but from a medal; the other has not been identified, but was obviously a religious work, possibly also by Titian. It was presumably on the evidence of these works that Titian was invited to France by the king, but the artist declined, allegedly because he 'never wanted to abandon Venice'.

Aretino's artistic services to the king of France began in 1529, when he attached himself to the circle of scholars and artists formed by Lazare de Baïf, the French ambassador in Venice. In the following year he was promised a gold chain by the king, but he received it only three years later. It consisted of overlapping enamelled gold tongues, weighed eight pounds and was worth 500 crowns. Aretino wore it with pride, as may be seen in the engraved portrait serving as the frontispiece to his works. But he failed to receive an annuity which the king had promised him and warned Francis that 'the furnace of Murano', burning in his honour, would grow cold unless he kept his word. About 1539 Aretino sent two portraits, one of Plato, the other of Aristotle, to the cardinal of Lorraine, who gave them to the king. After looking at them for a long time and praising their colour, Francis said that he already had a bust of Aristotle and recognized him perfectly, but that he did not remember having seen a portrait of Plato before. He ordered both pictures to be taken to the room at Fontainebleau where he kept his favourite possessions. Rossi, to whom we owe these details, adds that Francis commended Titian highly; his portrait of the cardinal, he said, was so perfect that it needed only movement and speech to be the real man.[44]

Sculpture entered the royal collection later than painting. In 1520 Cardinal Bibbiena reported that it contained no statues, ancient or modern. This prompted Cardinal Medici to order for the king a copy by Bandinelli of the recently discovered *Laocoön*. But it was never sent, perhaps because it was not thought good enough; other ancient statues,

[42] M. G. de La Coste-Messelière, 'Battista della Palla conspirateur, marchand ou homme de cour?', *L'œil*, cxxix (1965), 19–24, 34.

[43] Cox-Rearick, *La collection de François Ier*, pp. 39–41.

[44] Adhémar, 'Aretino', pp. 311–18. See also H. Tietze, 'Titian's Portrait of King Francis I', *Connoisseur*, cxxvi (Oct. 1950), 83–5.

so far unidentified, were sent to the king instead. His main supplier of statues in the 1520s was della Palla, but the only one to survive is Tribolo's *Cibele*, which was given a place of honour at Fontainebleau. Della Palla sent Francis at least two other statues by contemporary artists: one was Bandinelli's *Mercury Holding a Flute* and the other Michelangelo's *Hercules*. This early work by the artist was purchased in 1529 and used at Fontainebleau as part of the fountain after which the Cour de la Fontaine was named. It was later removed to the Jardin de l'Etang, where it remained until the reign of Louis XIV, when it disappeared along with the garden. Francis twice invited Michelangelo to France, but the artist never made the journey. He promised, if he should live long enough, to execute for the king 'a work in marble, one in bronze, one in painting'; ironically, it was the king who died first.[45]

Francis was also interested in ancient sculpture. In February 1540 he sent Primaticcio to Rome to buy and copy antiquities, and the artist returned in the following year with a number of plaster casts of ancient statues, mostly from the papal collection at the Belvedere. These included the *Ariadne*, *Laocoön*, *Apollo Belvedere*, *Cnidian Venus*, *Hercules Commodus*, *Tiber*, two sphinxes and two satyrs. They were turned into bronzes by Vignola, the future architect, who set up a foundry at Fontainebleau in 1541. The bronzes, however, were not exact replicas. For example, the attitude of the Fontainebleau *Ariadne* is different from that of her Roman counterpart. Such discrepancies were due in part to repairs necessitated by damage to the plaster casts while in transit from Rome or by faults in casting, partly to a conscious attempt to improve on the originals.[46] The bronzes were displayed initially in the Galerie François Ier and were much admired by the king and his entourage. The sight of Venus inspired Francis to flatter the duchesse d'Etampes: her body, he said, was no less perfect than that of the goddess.[47] Not all the bronzes in Francis's collection were acquired by Primaticcio in Rome. Sansovino's *Boy Drawing Out a Thorn*, for instance, was given to the king in 1540 by the cardinal of Ferrara. Nor were bronzes made from all the casts brought back by Primaticcio: Michelangelo's *Pietà*, reliefs from Trajan's column, and a horse (possibly that of Marcus Aurelius on the Capitol) were reproduced in plaster only.

Francis's art collection contained many works other than paintings and

[45] Cox-Rearick, p. 44.
[46] S. Pressouyre, 'Les fontes de Primatice', *Bulletin monumental*, cxxvii, 3 (1969), 223–39.
[47] Five of the bronzes (the *Tiber*, sphinxes and satyrs) were melted down during the French Revolution; the rest were sent to the Louvre. They have recently been returned to Fontainebleau.

statues. They included a perfume-burner designed by Raphael and probably given to the king about 1520. Unfortunately, this is another lost work, known only from an engraving. Another important item in the collection was a jewel casket decorated with crystal panels showing scenes from the life of Christ. It was made by Valerio Belli and given to the king by Pope Clement VII on the occasion of Catherine de' Medici's marriage. It is now at the Pitti museum in Florence.[48]

Fontainebleau became not only Francis I's favourite residence in the latter part of his reign, but also something of a great European cultural centre to which people flocked from different corners of Europe; Vasari described it as 'a kind of new Rome'.[49]

Benvenuto Cellini

Some of the most valuable objects in Francis's collection were made by Benvenuto Cellini, the Florentine goldsmith and sculptor. He visited France twice, in 1537 and 1540. The first visit was a disappointment to him: war between France and the empire had just started again, and Francis had other preoccupations than art. Thus Cellini failed to secure any royal commission. But he did gain the patronage of Ippolito d'Este, the future cardinal of Ferrara, who paved the way for his return in 1540.[50]

Cellini's second visit lasted five years. He began to follow the court on its travels, but soon became restless, as he needed a fixed residence in which to carry on his work. The cardinal of Ferrara advised him to appear as often as possible at the king's table. 'This I did then', writes Cellini in his autobiography, 'and one morning at his dinner the King called me. He began to talk to me in Italian, saying that he had it in his mind to execute several great works, and that he would soon give orders where I was to labour, and provide me with all necessaries.'[51] The artist was eventually given accommodation in Paris at the Petit Nesle, a building on the left bank of the Seine opposite the Louvre.

With the help of a cosmopolitan team of assistants Cellini undertook several works for the king during his stay in France. The first was a statue of Jupiter in silver. Francis asked for twelve such statues to serve as candlesticks for his table; they were 'to represent six gods and six goddesses, and to have exactly the same height as his Majesty, which was a trifle

---

[48] Cox-Rearick, p. 51. It is not certain that Raphael's perfume-burner was ever actually made.

[49] 'quasi una nuova Roma'. G. Vasari, Le vite de' più eccellenti pittori, scultori ed architettori, ed. G. Milanesi (Florence, 1878–85), vii. 408.

[50] The Life of Benvenuto Cellini Written by Himself, tr. J. A. Symonds, ed. J. Pope-Hennessy (London, 1949), pp. 187–8.

[51] Ibid., p. 264.

under four cubits'. Cellini made small wax models of Jupiter, Juno, Apollo and Vulcan for the king's inspection, but he was commissioned to proceed only with Jupiter and given 300 pounds of silver for the purpose. Cellini's drawing of Juno is all that survives of this project. Of the works for Francis actually completed by Cellini only two survive: a gold salt-cellar, now in Vienna, and a bronze relief, the *Nymph of Fontainebleau*, now in the Louvre. The artist had already started work on his Jupiter when Francis asked for the salt-cellar. Without delay, Cellini submitted a model which he had made some time before in Rome for the cardinal of Ferrara. The king was delighted with this and ordered that 1,000 gold *écus* be given to Cellini so that the work might proceed. When he saw it for the first time, Francis allegedly 'uttered a loud cry of astonishment and could not satiate his eyes with gazing at it'. The *Nymph of Fontainebleau* is only part of a decorative scheme designed by Cellini for the Porte Dorée at Fontainebleau. In a model which he submitted to the king he corrected the proportions of Le Breton's doorway, and, instead of columns, he fashioned two satyrs. Each supported the cornice with one hand whilst holding a club or a lash in the other. The lunette above contained the reclining nymph, her left arm resting on a stag's neck. Out of this composition only the nymph was actually cast in bronze, and she never did adorn the Porte Dorée. She was eventually given by Henri II to his mistress, Diane de Poitiers, and placed over the entrance to her château at Anet.[52]

Cellini also designed a fountain for Fontainebleau shaped 'in a perfect square, with handsome steps all round'. On a pedestal in the middle stood a nude male figure, holding up a broken lance in the right hand and resting the left on a scimitar. His right foot rested on a richly decorated helmet. At each angle of the fountain sat a figure 'accompanied by many beautiful and appropriate emblems'. Though Francis was pleased by the design, he was baffled by its symbolism until Cellini explained that the central figure was the king himself in the guise of Mars and the seated figures represented the arts and sciences which he so generously patronized.[53]

Cellini's testimony should always be taken with a pinch of salt, yet his autobiography does throw valuable light on Francis's artistic patronage. The close personal interest which he took in the arts is clearly revealed, as, for example, when he visited Cellini's studio.[54] But the artist also shows that the king delegated much of his patronage to subordinates, who were not always punctilious in carrying out his wishes. If Cellini is to be believed, he did not always get the rich rewards promised by Francis;

[52] The symbolism of the salt-cellar and *Nymph of Fontainebleau* is fully described by Cellini. *Ibid.*, pp. 283, 305–6.

[53] *Ibid.*, pp. 284–5.   [54] *Ibid.*, pp. 272–3.

yet his labours did not go unrewarded: in addition to cash payments, he received letters of naturalization free of charge and was given possession of the Petit Nesle.[55]

Cellini's stay in France was anything but peaceful: attempts were made to dislodge him from the Petit Nesle, and he was attacked in the streets and in the courts. For many of his troubles, however, he had only himself to blame: his arrogance, bombast and violent temper earned him many enemies, the most important of whom was the king's mistress, the duchesse d'Etampes. She allegedly did everything possible to poison the king's mind against him and even tried to sabotage the presentation of his Jupiter. Cellini was ordered to bring the statue to the Galerie François Ier, where Primaticcio's bronzes were already on display. The duchess hoped that their proximity would detract from Cellini's work; she also delayed the king's appearance till nightfall so as to darken the gallery for the presentation. But Cellini's ingenuity overcame her malice. He had mounted his statue on a movable plinth and introduced a wax torch among the flames of Jupiter's thunderbolt. As the king entered the gallery, Cellini lit the torch and his apprentice pushed the statue forward. This made it seem alive, and Primaticcio's bronzes were eclipsed. But the duchess was not through yet: as Francis praised the Jupiter, she said that it would show to less advantage in daylight and pointed to a veil which, she claimed, was hiding its faults. This threw the artist into a rage. He pulled off and tore the veil, which he had intended only for modesty. The duchess was outraged by his impertinence, and only Francis's timely intervention averted an ugly scene.[56]

Patron of letters

Among the marvels to be seen at Fontainebleau in the last years of Francis's reign, not the least remarkable was the library situated on the floor above the Galerie François Ier.

At the beginning of the reign the king's library was at the château of Blois, where it was seen in 1517 by Antonio De Beatis, who described it as follows:

in the castle, or rather palace, we saw a library consisting of a sizeable room not only furnished with shelves from end to end but also lined with book-cases from floor to ceiling, and literally packed with books – to say nothing of those put away in chests in an inner room. These books are all of parchment, handwritten in beautiful lettering and bound in silk of various colours, with elaborate locks and clasps of silver gilt.[57]

[55] *Ibid.*, pp. 269, 280–1; C.A.F., iv. 12681; vi. 22859.
[56] *Life of Cellini*, pp. 271, 275–7, 285–6, 289–92, 312–14.
[57] *Travel Journal of Antonio De Beatis*, p. 133.

According to an inventory drawn up in 1518 the library contained 1,626 volumes including 41 in Greek, 4 in Hebrew and 2 in Arabic. Some of these books had been acquired by Francis's royal predecessors; others had come from his parents. In 1515 the keeper of the library at Blois was Adam Laigre, almoner to Queen Claude. He was succeeded by Guillaume Petit, Jacques Lefèvre d'Etaples, Jean de La Barre and Mellin de Saint-Gelais, in that order.[58]

In 1522 the new post of Master of the King's Library was created for Guillaume Budé, and it was probably under his influence that Francis began a search for rare manuscripts, especially in Greek, in Italy and the Near East. His move was probably part and parcel of the scheme to set up a college in France for the study of ancient languages.[59] The first person sent abroad by the king to look for manuscripts was allegedly the Dauphin's tutor, Girolamo Fondulo of Cremona. He returned with sixty which had cost him 1,200 *écus*. Among the most assiduous collectors of rare books for the king were his ambassadors in Rome and in Venice, who were instructed to buy all the Greek manuscripts they could find or to copy those that could not be bought. Georges d'Armagnac, bishop of Rodez, employed a German to copy fourteen Greek manuscripts during the four years of his embassy in Rome, while Guillaume Pellicier employed twelve copyists continually during his embassy to Venice (1539–42). Other notable contributors to the king's collection of rare books were Antonios Eparchos, a refugee from Corfu who had settled in Venice, and Giovanni Francesco d'Asola, brother-in-law of Aldo Manuzio, the famous Venetian printer.[60]

With the help of men such as these, and under Budé's general supervision, Francis gradually built up a second library at Fontainebleau, to which the books from the duc de Bourbon's library were added after 1523. A third library followed the court on its travels. For Francis was not content simply to collect books; he liked to read them or at least to have them read aloud to him at mealtimes. This was the role of the *lecteur du roi*, a post held in 1529 by Jacques Colin, the translator of Castiglione's *Il Cortegiano*, and in 1537 by Pierre du Chastel.[61] In 1536 the king's mobile library consisted of two chests the contents of which tell us something about his taste in reading. Though not a classical scholar, he

---

[58] E. Quentin-Bauchart, *La bibliothèque de Fontainebleau, 1515–89* (1891), pp. 6–7; A. Franklin, *Précis de l'histoire de la Bibliothèque du Roi* (2nd edn, 1875), pp. 63–70.

[59] Franklin, pp. 65–6; Quentin-Bauchart, p. 42. See also above ch. 9.

[60] Quentin-Bauchart, pp. 13–17; A. Hobson, *Great Libraries* (London, 1970), p. 126. Odet de Selve tried during his English embassy (November 1546) to obtain a Plotinus from Oxford for Francis. *L.P.*, xxi (pt 2), 346.

[61] V.-L. Bourrilly, *Jacques Colin, abbé de Saint-Ambroise* (1905; repr. Geneva, 1970), pp. 36–41.

was evidently fond of Roman history and the heroic exploits of antiquity. For the chests contained works by Justinus, Thucydides, Appian and Diodorus Siculus as well as the *Destruction de Troie la Grant*, the *Roman de la Rose* and other romances.[62] There is evidence, too, that Francis not only knew his library but could also direct someone to the contents of a particular book on his shelves. Thus in 1531 Germain Brice [de Brie ?] reported a conversation at the king's table in a letter to the Italian poet Vida. During the discussion Francis turned to Brice and asked him if he had read Vida's *Eclogues*. Brice replied that he had read some of his poems, but not the *Eclogues*, whereupon the king indicated to Colin in which volume they were to be found and where in his library.[63]

The king's library, though rich in manuscripts, contained relatively few printed books, and it was with a view to remedying this weakness that the famous ordinance of Montpellier, generally regarded as the first law of legal deposit in any country, was issued on 28 December 1537. This required all printers and booksellers to deliver a copy of every new book in any language by any author, ancient or modern, to the keeper of the library at Blois. Foreign books imported for sale were to be deposited for examination and purchase if considered suitable. In this way, the ordinance explained, contemporary works would be assembled at Blois as a monument to the literary glory of the reign, the king's successors would acquire a taste for study and be more inclined to continue his patronage of letters, and posterity would find texts in their original purity which might otherwise become corrupt and disappear. Unfortunately, it seems that this ordinance was a dead letter, for an inventory of the library at Blois drawn up in 1544 lists only 109 printed books.[64]

By this time Francis thought it expedient to gather all his books in one place. On 22 May, therefore, he ordered the library at Blois to be moved to Fontainebleau, which thus acquired 1,894 volumes, a terrestrial globe and a crocodile's head in a leather case.[65] At about the same time the king ordered many of his books to be rebound, an undertaking which was continued on a more lavish scale by his successor. In 1567 Pierre Ramus, one of the *lecteurs royaux*, petitioned Catherine de' Medici for the king's library to be brought to Paris, where it would be more accessible to scholars. He was successful, and two years later the library – now consisting of 3,650 titles – was moved to an unidentified building in the capital.[66] It became eventually the nucleus of the Bibliothèque Nationale.

[62] Quentin-Bauchart, pp. 8–9.   [63] Bourrilly, *Jacques Colin*, pp. 40–1.
[64] *Ordonnances*, viii. no. 828, pp. 494–500; Quentin-Bauchart, pp. 21–2.
[65] C.A.F., iv. 13866. The inventory drawn up on this occasion is now B.N., MS. fr. 5660; Hobson, *Great Libraries*, p. 128.
[66] Quentin-Bauchart, pp. 36–7, 46–9; Franklin, *Bibliothèque du Roi*, pp. 77–9, 85–6.

But Francis had already wanted his collection of books to be available to scholars; hence the great interest which he took in printing. Robert Estienne, who was appointed in 1539 as the king's printer in Hebrew and Latin and in 1542 as his printer in Greek explained Francis's intentions in the preface to one of his publications as follows: 'Far from grudging to anyone the records of ancient writers which he at great and truly royal cost has procured from Italy and Greece, he intends to put them at the disposal of and service of all men.'[67] Thus three special founts of Greek type (the *grecs du roi*), cut by Claude Garamond and modelled on the writing of Angelos Vergecios, a Cretan employed in the royal library, were financed by grants from the king. The first work to be published with the new type was Eusebius's *Ecclesiastical History* (1544), and the most influential was an edition of the New Testament (1550) based on nine manuscripts in the royal library. It is said that Francis himself chose the Roman history of Dionysius of Halicarnassus for publication in 1546–7 and suggested the small Greek type used for a pocket New Testament in 1546.[68]

[67] Hobson, p. 126; E. Armstrong, *Robert Estienne, Royal Printer* (Cambridge, 1954), pp. 63, 117.
[68] Armstrong, p. 52; Hobson, p. 128.

18

Triumph and stalemate

(1535–7)

WAR IN WESTERN Europe was imminent at the beginning of 1535. The emperor was arming with a view to attacking the Barbary corsairs in north Africa, who had become a serious menace to Spanish shipping in the western Mediterranean, and this provided Francis with a pretext to prepare his next war with the emperor. The court of France was gripped by a war fever. 'The engagements entered into with me', the king declared to the imperial ambassador, 'are not kept at all. If the emperor arms, I cannot but do the same.'[1] The papal nuncio noted the king's belligerency with concern. His hatred, he wrote, had grown to such an extent 'that he seems to make it his business to provoke the emperor'.[2]

In the late spring of 1535, as we have seen, Francis toured the provinces of northern France reviewing his new legions.[3] Meanwhile his diplomats were active in every corner of Europe. Two were particularly important: Jean de La Forêt and Cardinal Jean du Bellay. La Forêt was sent to the Ottoman court in February in the hope of obtaining a subsidy from the sultan and his military co-operation in a future war against the emperor. Stopping in north Africa on the way, he offered Khair ad-Din-Barbarossa fifty ships as well as victuals and munitions in return for help against the Genoese.[4] The most obvious result of La Forêt's mission to Constantinople was a commercial treaty, signed in February 1536, called the *Capitulations*. This has long been regarded as the foundation of the influence exerted by the French in the Levant till the nineteenth century, but the existence of the treaty has recently been called into question, for the original text has not been found either in France or Turkey. The earliest version that survives is only a draft. All that is certain is that negotiations took place between La Forêt and Ibrahim, the sultan's chief

---

[1] C.S.P. Span., v (pt 1), no. 130.
[2] H. Jedin, *A History of the Council of Trent*, tr. E. Graf (London, 1957–61), i. 300.
[3] See above, ch. 16.
[4] E. Charrière (ed.), *Négociations de la France dans le Levant* (1848–60), i. 255–63; V.-L. Bourrilly, 'L'ambassade de La Forest et de Marillac à Constantinople (1535–38)', *R.H.*, lxxvi (1901), 297–328.

minister, and it is probable in the light of subsequent events that an agreement to co-operate in the military field was reached. No formal alliance, however, appears to have been concluded. If a commercial treaty was discussed at all at this stage, it appears to have been shelved.[5]

Cardinal Jean du Bellay was sent to Italy in June 1535 primarily to win over the new pope, Paul III, to Francis's side and to dissuade him from calling a general council, which, Francis believed, would only help to increase the emperor's power. On his way south, the cardinal visited Ferrara and tried to patch up the quarrel between its duke, Ercole, and his French wife, Renée, Francis's sister-in-law. He promised to obtain the recall of Madame de Soubise, Renée's ex-governess, who, in the duke's judgment, was exerting too much influence on his wife. The cardinal also made contact with a number of Italian *condottieri*. It would have been impossible for him to accept all their offers of service, but he persuaded Francis to employ Stefano Colonna, John of Turin and Gian-Paolo Orsini. In Rome, du Bellay collaborated with Filippo Strozzi, leader of the Florentine *fuorusciti*, who were plotting to liberate their city from the rule of the emperor's son-in-law, Alessandro de' Medici. As far as the main object of his mission was concerned, the cardinal was only moderately successful. Pope Paul listened to all he had to say with interest but reserved his position. He did not altogether trust Francis's professions of devotion to the Holy See.[6] In particular, he was puzzled by the king's attitude towards Henry VIII. When speaking to the papal nuncio, Francis professed to be shocked by Henry's religious policy, yet, when asked by the pope to help depose Henry, he would say that it was up to the emperor to avenge his aunt Catherine.[7]

In Germany and Switzerland French diplomacy was signally unsuccessful. Francis's dealings with the Turks, his persecution of Protestants after the Affair of the Placards and his opposition to a general council had made him extremely unpopular even among enemies of the house of Habsburg. The king defended his policies in a memorandum addressed to the imperial estates on 1 February. He accused the Habsburgs of slanders aimed at undermining his friendship with the Germans, which stood in the way of their ambitions. In another message to the estates, dated 25 February, Francis denied that he was opposed to a general council.[8] He also tried to salvage something from Langey's negotiations of 1534 with the German reformers in June 1535 by inviting Melanchthon to France

[5] *Ordonnances*, viii. pp. 503–74.
[6] V.-L. Bourrilly, 'Le cardinal Jean du Bellay en Italie', *Revue des études rabelaisiennes*, v (1907), 246–53, 262–74.
[7] *L.P.*, viii. 837; ix. 148.
[8] V.-L. Bourrilly, *Guillaume du Bellay* (1905), pp. 191–2; Herminjard, iii. 249–54.

and, in July, by offering a conditional amnesty to religious exiles and prisoners in the edict of Coucy. But the elector of Saxony forbade Melanchthon's journey to France.[9] As for the Swiss reformers, no number of goodwill gestures could win them round to the idea of a reunion of the churches sponsored by the king of France. The papacy, Bullinger said, was as likely to reform itself as an Ethiopian was to change his skin, and the French were not to be trusted; treating with them was 'like holding an eel'.[10]

In spite of the warlike noises coming from the court of France and the intrigues of French diplomats everywhere, Charles V pressed on with his own war plan, and on 10 June sailed out of Barcelona at the head of a large expeditionary force. On 14 July he captured La Goletta, a fortress guarding the entrance to the bay of Tunis, and among the large quantity of booty which fell into his hands were several French cannon, identifiable by the Fleur-de-lis on their barrels. Tunis fell soon afterwards, though Barbarossa himself escaped to Algiers with part of his fleet. On 22 August Charles landed in Sicily at the start of a triumphal progress which was to take him up the entire length of the Italian peninsula.[11]

Francis, in the meantime, did nothing, much to the chagrin of the war-party at his court led by Admiral Chabot. Montmorency, who had given his word to the imperial ambassador that Francis would take no unfair advantage of Charles during his absence, came in for much bitter criticism and, in July, left the court and retired to Chantilly. Chabot became effectively the king's chief minister, but it would be wrong to suppose that Montmorency's withdrawal from the court amounted to a disgrace: although he ceased for a time to attend the council, he remained at the head of the royal household and retained all his titles, offices and pensions. In October he presided over the estates of Languedoc as governor of the province, mustered its legion and inspected the fortifications at Narbonne.[12]

Montmorency, in fact, may not have been responsible for Francis's inertia in the summer of 1535. Other reasons for it can be suggested. The king, as yet, had no *casus belli*. Doubtless he could have found one in his bottom drawer of age-old grievances, but he would have damaged his international reputation seriously if he had stabbed the emperor in the back while he was busy fighting the Infidel. On a more practical level,

9   Bourrilly *Guillaume du Bellay*, pp. 193–7, 201; Herminjard, iii. 300–1.
10 J. V. Pollet, *Martin Bucer* (1962), ii. 503.
11 K. Brandi, *The Emperor Charles V*, tr. C. V. Wedgwood (London, 1939), pp. 365–8.
12 Decrue, i. 241–4.

Francis was not ready for war; in July 1535 he was still mustering his legions. By the time he was ready to move south the fighting season was already far advanced, and, in the autumn, he was detained at Dijon by an illness so serious that processions for his recovery were held throughout France.[13] He left Dijon on 23 November and reached Lyons only about mid-January.

The invasion of Savoy

The principal aim of Francis's foreign policy since his accession had been to establish his rule in the duchy of Milan, which he regarded as his by right of inheritance. He had achieved this aim in 1515 as a result of the battle of Marignano, but had been expelled from the duchy in 1522. His attempt to regain it by force in 1525 had been defeated at Pavia. Since then the duchy had been ruled by Francesco Sforza, and Francis had been forced to give up his claim to it in the treaty of Cambrai. On 1 November 1535 the question of Milan was reopened when Sforza died leaving no male heir. Francis at once proposed that the duchy be given to his second son, Henri, duc d'Orléans, but the emperor, who, as suzerain of Milan, had its investiture in his gift, viewed this as a preposterous suggestion. Henri was too close to the French throne to be acceptable to him. Furthermore, as the husband of Catherine de' Medici, Henri had a claim to the duchy of Urbino; if he were given Milan, he would need only Naples to become effectively the master of Italy. But the emperor did not rule out the possibility of giving the duchy to Francis's third son, Charles, duc d'Angoulême.

Matters stood thus in January 1536, when Francis suddenly invaded the duchy of Savoy. His relations with his uncle, Charles III of Savoy, had long been strained. Francis claimed that the duke was clinging to territories which had belonged to his own mother, Louise of Savoy; and he had not yet forgiven Charles's refusal to let him use Nice for his meeting, two years before, with Pope Clement VII. In December 1535 Francis took advantage of a war between the duke and the city of Geneva to assert his claims. Meanwhile, some French cavalry were captured as they attempted to relieve Geneva. Disclaiming all responsibility for their action, Francis nonetheless demanded their release. Duke Charles promptly complied, but this did not satisfy the king. In January he sent Guillaume Poyet to Savoy with an ultimatum containing sweeping territorial demands. At this juncture, the Bernese threw in their lot with the Genevans, and,

[13] Francis's illness was described as 'a fever, flux of the belly and stomach pain'. M. François, *Le cardinal François de Tournon* (1951), p. 126 n. 3; *C.S.P. Span.*, v (pt 1), no. 226; *R.D.B.V.P.*, ii. 209.

ironically, the duke asked Francis for assistance. The king sent an envoy to the Bernese camp ostensibly to offer his mediation, but in reality to reveal his own plan for the conquest of Savoy. The Bernese accordingly called off their campaign, leaving Francis a free hand. On 11 February he ordered his army to invade the duchy. Two legions under Saint-Pol overran Bresse and Bugey. Being hopelessly outnumbered, the ducal forces offered little resistance. On 24 February Bourg-en-Bresse fell to the French, and, five days later, Chambéry. The conquest of the duchy was completed in March, when Chabot pushed eastward into Piedmont, capturing the capital, Turin. He then laid siege to Vercelli near the Milanese border, but was careful not to cross it. If there was to be war with the emperor, Francis wanted to be able to say that it was Charles V, not himself, who had started it.[14]

Francis claimed that his attack on Savoy was an act of self-defence, since he was only trying to recover territories that were lawfully his. The fact that the duke had been included in the treaty of Cambrai did not, he argued, dispense him from fulfilling his obligations. These, however, were transparent excuses for what was, in reality, naked aggression aimed at providing Francis with a territory that might serve as a bargaining counter in his negotiations with the emperor over the future of Milan or as a springboard for a new invasion of Milan should these negotiations fail.[15] But it is arguable that the attack on Savoy was a serious blunder in that it caused great offence to the emperor, for Charles III was his brother-in-law and ally. At the time of the invasion, however, the emperor was still in southern Italy, too far away to come to the duke's aid. He also needed to reorganize his army after his north African campaign and to establish his authority in south and central Italy. The emperor, therefore, played for time: he kept the question of the Milanese succession open to discussion and even offered to consider the candidature of the duc d'Orléans. Privately, however, he made it quite clear that he would never entertain it.[16] On 17 April, two days after arriving in Rome, he denounced the French invasion in a speech before the pope and the college of cardinals. He gave Francis the choice between accepting Milan on certain conditions for his youngest son or meeting him, the emperor, in single combat, the prize being Burgundy on the one side and Milan on the other. The essential prerequisite for any talks, he emphasized, was the withdrawal of all French forces from Piedmont. Paul III, for his part, said that he could not allow a duel between the two monarchs, whose lives were far too precious to be thus put at risk. He promised to make every effort to reconcile them

---

[14] Du Bellay, ii. 302ff.
[15] Decrue, i. 253.
[16] C.S.P. Span., v (pt 2), no. 26, p. 48.

and to declare against the one that would oppose a reasonable settlement.[17]

On 24 April the cardinal of Lorraine met the emperor at Siena and tried to bring him to accept a demand from Francis for the life reversion of the duchy of Milan, which would be given immediately to Orléans. But Charles no longer needed to temporize now that he was within reach of the Lombard plain. He therefore repeated his offer to cede the duchy to the king's third son, but emphatically refused to give Francis its life reversion. The cardinal then proceeded to Rome to test the pope's attitude. He found Paul angry with both monarchs, but willing to make a last effort to avert a war between them.[18] On 11 May Francis replied to the emperor's speech of 17 April. 'I cannot understand', he said, 'how the Emperor can claim that in making war upon the duke [of Savoy] I contravene any treaty made with him, for nothing belonging to the Empire has been touched by my troops; on the contrary, both the generals and captains of my army have received instructions not to attempt anything against the Emperor's territory.' He was willing to submit his claims to Savoy to the pope's arbitration, feeling sure that they would be found indisputable. As for the emperor's challenge to a duel, Francis accepted it while making it clear that, in his view, Charles had no injury to avenge. 'Should war break out', he concluded, 'it will not be through any fault of mine.'[19]

In north Italy, meanwhile, an undeclared state of war already existed between the French and the imperialists. In April Chabot was ordered to plant garrisons in Pinerolo, Turin, Fossano and Coni and to bring the rest of his army back to France. He was replaced as lieutenant-general in Piedmont by Francis, marquis of Saluzzo. The reason for Chabot's recall is not clear. The king, it has been suggested, was dissatisfied with him because of his failure to conquer the Milanese, but this is unlikely. The admiral's recall was probably a consequence of Montmorency's return to power; by 7 May the latter was again playing his full part in the government. Nor is this surprising, for he was generally regarded as France's best general.[20]

A strong hand was certainly needed to take charge of military operations. Early in May de Leyva advanced into Piedmont, threatening the garrisons left behind by Chabot; Turin could withstand a siege, but other

---

[17] L. von Pastor, *The History of the Popes*, tr. F. I. Antrobus and R. F. Kerr (London, 1891–1933), xi. 247–52; du Bellay, ii. 354–70.

[18] Du Bellay, ii. 383–4, 393–8; iii. 12–26; *C.S.P. Span.*, v (pt 2), nos. 45–6.

[19] Du Bellay, ii. 402–12; *C.S.P. Span.*, v (pt 2), no. 52. The king's reply was written by Guillaume du Bellay and circulated widely. See Bourrilly, *Guillaume du Bellay*, pp. 215–16.

[20] Decrue, i. 257; *C.S.P. Span.*, v (pt 2), no. 50, p. 111; du Bellay, ii. 399–401; iii. 64–6.

towns were more vulnerable. The marquis of Saluzzo suggested that the whole province, except Turin, should be evacuated; but his captains objected that this would open the way to an imperial descent on Provence. Reluctantly the marquis agreed to defend Fossano and Coni, but his extraordinary slowness aroused the suspicions of his subordinates. He was, in fact, secretly in league with the enemy. Although he had been generously treated by Francis, he coveted the county of Montferrat and believed that he stood a better chance of getting it by siding with the emperor. Eventually all became clear. On 17 May, after surrendering Coni, he returned his insignia of the order of St Michael to Francis. His defection nearly caused the collapse of the French defences in Piedmont, but the garrison at Fossano held out for almost a month, allowing Francis more time to prepare the defence of south-east France.[21] He decided to gather as many troops as possible around himself at Lyons and to send them wherever the emperor's attack might fall. Jean de Humières, who was appointed lieutenant-general in Dauphiné, Savoy and Piedmont, concentrated supplies at Grenoble and distributed troops and munitions among the castles guarding the Alpine passes. Work was also begun on fortifications at Marseilles.[22]

By now it was idle to pretend that peace still existed between France and the empire. Neither had declared war, as neither would admit to being the aggressor. Yet war had become a reality, and on 11 June Francis dismissed the imperial ambassador from his court. The pope, meanwhile, convened a general council for the following May, and appointed two cardinal-legates, Caracciolo and Trivulzio, to announce this to Francis and Charles and to mediate between them. The emperor, however, would not listen to them when they visited his camp at Savigliano: ever since he had left Rome, he said, Francis had continued to provoke him; now he could only defend himself. On 13 July he decided to invade Provence rather than attempt to dislodge the French garrisons left in Piedmont.[23]

The campaign of 1536 marked a turning point in Francis's military thinking: instead of rushing into Italy as in the past, he waited patiently in his own kingdom for the enemy to attack. Credit for this strategy should probably be given to Montmorency, who, on 14 July, was appointed lieutenant-general 'on either side of the mountains' with powers to assemble troops, direct military operations, appoint officers and, if necessary, engage talks with the enemy.[24] His rival, Chabot, retired quietly to his *gouvernement* of Burgundy. Francis himself took no part in the

21   Du Bellay, iii. 9–12, 66–86, 94–108.
22   *Ibid.*, iii. 33–44.
23   *Ibid.*, iii. 116–30; C.S.P. *Span.*, v (pt 2), nos. 62, 73, 74, 75; Decrue, i. 259.
24   C.A.F., iii. 8563.

fighting. On the advice of his council he kept well behind the front line so as not to compromise the defensive strategy; otherwise he would have been in honour bound to respond to a personal challenge by the emperor. He nevertheless took an active part in the military preparations and was kept continually informed of developments in the fighting. On 13 July Jean du Bellay reported that Francis had decided to 'act rather as captain than as soldier'.[25]

Once it became clear that the emperor would bypass the Alps and advance into Provence along the coast road through Nice, the king's army was directed to Avignon, which the French had recently occupied. Some 30,000 men had gathered there by 25 July, when Montmorency took up his command; by the end of August they had roughly doubled in number. The emperor, for his part, would have been well advised to expel the French from Piedmont before attacking France itself, but he preferred to revive the plan Bourbon had failed to carry out in 1524: namely, to invade Provence and, at the same time, launch an attack on northern France, thereby obliging Francis to divide his forces. Charles had several advantages over Bourbon: his army was larger and more experienced, he had better naval support and, above all, he did not have to count on the king of England to create the diversion in northern France. Henry of Nassau could be relied upon to invade at the right moment. The emperor was warned that the fighting season was already well advanced, that he lacked the cash necessary for a lengthy campaign and that Francis was only waiting for him to invade to stir up trouble for him in Italy. But he was confident that the French could be defeated before the winter, and, on 24 July he crossed the Var into Provence.[26]

Montmorency could either go forward and engage the enemy or wait for him in carefully selected and strongly fortified positions. Though some of his captains wanted to defend Aix, he preferred to remain near Avignon, his purpose being 'not to join battle or play for high stakes unless compelled by extreme necessity or a sure opportunity offered itself'.[27] This was consistent with the strategy which the king had outlined in June: he would not offer the emperor battle, he said, but would harass him with continual skirmishes and force him to waste time and money.[28] Before committing himself finally, however, Montmorency went on a tour of inspection of Aix and Marseilles. On 1 August he reported to Francis that the defence of Aix was impracticable: a month would be needed to repair its fortifications, nor were there enough supplies available to support the garrison of 6,000 men that would be needed to defend it. He therefore

[25] *Correspondance du cardinal Jean du Bellay*, ed. R. Scheurer (1969–73), ii. 378.
[26] Du Bellay, iii. 140; *C.S.P. Span.*, v (pt 2), no. 74.
[27] Du Bellay, iii. 285.   [28] *C.S.P. Span.*, v (pt 2), no. 59.

ordered the town's evacuation. The inhabitants were given six days in which to destroy or remove everything of value to the enemy.[29]

The decision to leave Aix to its fate was part of a comprehensive strategy aimed at creating a vacuum in front of the advancing enemy. Lower Provence was turned into a veritable desert by a systematic policy of 'scorched earth', or *gast*, carried out by a company of men-at-arms under the deputy governor, Bonneval. Throughout the area mills were destroyed, wells filled up, stocks of wood and grain burnt, wine barrels smashed open, supplies of salt spoiled and farm animals let loose. Only fruit trees and vines were spared in the hope that they would encourage dysentery among the enemy. Here and there the local peasants offered resistance, notably at Brignoles, but in general they co-operated before taking shelter in woods and caves.[30] The *gast* was not, of course, applied to Marseilles, which had contributed so decisively to Bourbon's defeat in 1524. Since May its fortifications had been strengthened and its garrison reinforced. A large fleet under Saint-Blancard was stationed in the harbour.[31]

An important part of Montmorency's strategy was to prevent the emperor from crossing the Rhône into Languedoc in case he should link up with a possible invading army from Spain. Thus, while Lower Provence was evacuated, the towns guarding the Rhône – Arles, Tarascon and Beaucaire – were heavily fortified. The hub of the French defensive system was Montmorency's camp situated south-east of Avignon, near the junction of the Rhône and Durance. It was easily accessible to supplies and reinforcements coming down the Rhône from the north, and the heights of Caumont and Noves provided useful vantage points nearby. The camp, which may have been consciously inspired by the ancient Roman model, was enclosed by a ditch twenty-four feet wide and an earthen rampart carrying artillery platforms. A watercourse running through the middle and linked to a network of channels ensured an unusually high standard of hygiene. Strict discipline was maintained by segregating the various nationalities in the army, each being allotted a compartment formed by the grid of water channels. Montmorency's tent occupied a central mound from which the whole camp could be surveyed. 'No camp', he wrote, 'was ever seen in our time which was stronger, more beautiful, more free from disease or as well supplied with victuals.'[32]

[29] Du Bellay, iii. 181–2; Decrue, i. 270–1.
[30] Du Bellay, iii. 183, 188, 191; G. Procacci, 'La Provence à la veille des Guerres de Religion: une période décisive, 1535–45', *Rev. d'hist. mod. et contemp.*, v (1958), 249–50.
[31] Du Bellay, iii. 178–80.
[32] *Ibid.*, iii. 193–4, 208–11; Decrue, i. 271–3, 275, 279.

While the grand master was organizing the defence of the Rhône valley, Francis moved from Lyons to Valence, which served as his headquarters from 8 August until 10 September.[33] He would have liked to join Montmorency, but was urged to stay put so as to guard against a possible northward thrust by the emperor. Under the king's direction Valence became an important assembly point for troops, artillery and supplies destined for the camp at Avignon. It was also a useful centre from which to co-ordinate the defence of northern France with that of the south. Francis kept in constant touch not only with Montmorency and his own council at Lyons but also with the authorities responsible for the defence of the north.

The emperor's invasion of Provence had been timed to coincide with an attack on the north by Henry of Nassau. He captured the town of Guise without difficulty, but failed to take Saint-Quentin. On 12 August he laid siege to Péronne.[34] The defence of northern France was entrusted mainly to three men: Charles, duc de Vendôme, governor of Picardy; Claude, duc de Guise, governor of Champagne; and Cardinal Jean du Bellay, governor of Paris and the Ile-de-France. Their task was made difficult by the fact that the flower of the French army – the *gendarmerie* – was in the south and that they had very little money to pay their troops. Nothing is as revealing of the hand-to-mouth way in which the defence of the north was provided for than the correspondence between Vendôme and Cardinal du Bellay. Vendôme was utterly contemptuous of the legionaries and *aventuriers* under his command. He felt sure that in the absence of the *gendarmerie*, which alone could enforce discipline, they would mutiny unless they were paid punctually. Yet the king had left him without adequate funds; hence his desperate appeals for assistance to du Bellay, who, as governor of Paris, could tap the wealth of its inhabitants. But the cardinal had been instructed by the king to undertake a massive and costly programme of fortification in the capital. The clash of priorities caused much tension between him and Vendôme, but, in the end, the cardinal's ingenuity prevailed: without sacrificing his fortification programme he raised a loan of 140,000 *livres* from the Parisians and persuaded them to pay for 6,000 additional infantry for service in Picardy.[35] Vendôme's troops also proved more dependable than he had supposed, so that Nassau was eventually forced to lift the siege of Péronne and retire into Flanders.

Meanwhile, in Provence, Montmorency's defensive strategy yielded rich dividends. The emperor, after capturing Aix on 13 August, pitched camp a few miles south-west of the town. He could advance either north

---

[33] Du Bellay, iii. 211–12. [34] *Ibid.*, iii. 212–14; *C.S.P. Span.*, v (pt 2), no. 96.
[35] *Correspondance du cardinal Jean du Bellay*, ii. nos. 387, 389, 395, 401, 402.

into Dauphiné or west into Languedoc. But, whichever way he turned, his path was barred by French troops, and in the south he had to contend with Marseilles, which had been such a thorn in the side of Bourbon twelve years earlier. After carrying out reconnaissances in all three directions, Charles decided to stay put, but conditions in his camp very soon became intolerable, owing to the hot weather, poor sanitation and inadequate supplies. Convoys reaching the camp from the coast were regularly plundered by the local peasantry, while soldiers who strayed from the camp in search of food were set upon and butchered. On 2 September Montmorency reported that the emperor had already lost 7,000 or 8,000 men from famine or dysentery.[36] Five days later de Leyva, Charles's principal lieutenant, died.

But Francis also suffered a great loss at this time. On 10 August his eldest son, the Dauphin François, died suddenly at Tournus. Natural causes were almost certainly responsible, but poison was immediately suspected, and one of the Dauphin's squires, Sebastiano de Montecuculli, a native of Ferrara, was accused of his murder. Incriminating documents were found in his possession, including a treatise on poisons and a safe-conduct from de Leyva. Montecuculli confessed his guilt under torture, but subsequently retracted. He was none the less executed with appalling cruelty at Lyons on 7 October. Meanwhile, the French government accused the emperor and Ferrante Gonzaga, governor of Milan, of having instigated the Dauphin's murder, a charge they vigorously denied. Equally unfairly they accused the Dauphin's brother, Henri, and his sister-in-law, Catherine de' Medici.[37] Such charges and countercharges did nothing to mend Franco-imperial relations. But the papal legate, Cardinal Trivulzio, tried to persuade Francis that the Dauphin's death was a divine admonition to peace. He pointed out that the main obstacle to a peaceful settlement of the Milanese question had been removed; now that the duc d'Orléans stood too close to the throne to be a suitable candidate for the duchy, only Charles d'Angoulême could be considered, and the emperor had already indicated his willingness to accept him. Francis, however, wanted to lay hands on Milan immediately, and Charles was less favourably inclined to Angoulême now that he stood second, instead of third, in line of succession to the French throne. He told the nuncio that Francis would have to choose between the submission of realistic peace terms and the trial of strength which he had so far avoided.[38] So the war continued, but winter was approaching and the emperor was still hopelessly immobilized at Aix.

[36] Du Bellay, iii. 195–204, 241–8; Decrue, i. 276–9; *C.S.P. Span.*, v (pt 2), no. 97.
[37] François, *François de Tournon*, p. 132; Bourrilly, *Guillaume du Bellay*, pp. 229, 233; Guiffrey, pp. 188–9.   [38] *C.S.P. Span.*, v (pt 2), no. 92.

On 11 September Charles began to retreat towards Fréjus, having already sent his heavy guns down to the coast; yet Francis, who joined Montmorency at Avignon on the twelfth, resisted the temptation to rush off in pursuit of the enemy. News of Nassau's retreat from Péronne had not yet reached him; therefore, he could not be certain that his army would not be needed in the north. He was also desperately short of cash. The first year of the war had virtually wiped out his savings. He had started out with only 1,500,000 *livres*, and the war had so far cost him more than 4,500,000 *livres*.[39] He had other resources, of course, but needed every *sou* to prepare the next season's offensive. So he did not try to cut off the emperor's retreat by a quick dash across the Alps; he merely sent his light cavalry to harass the imperial rearguard. Mocking the king's timidity, Charles boasted that his retreat had been accomplished in perfect order and without serious loss. But it was a sadly depleted army which he brought back to Italy on 23 September. Soon afterwards he embarked at Genoa for Spain.[40]

Francis, in the meantime, went on a tour of inspection of Provence. He visited several towns, including Marseilles, but stayed away from Aix, where plague was reported. He was able to see for himself something of the devastation in the province, but refused to compensate the inhabitants as long as the war lasted, thereby prompting a Marseillais chronicler to comment: 'the donkey always carries the saddle'.[41] The task of disbanding the army that was no longer needed in Provence was given to Cardinal Tournon, who, on 10 October, was appointed lieutenant-general in south-east France. Using money borrowed from the bankers of Lyons, he paid off the foreign mercenaries and thereby saved Vienne from being sacked. But the cardinal was unable to find enough money for the garrisons in Piedmont. 'I could not send you a single *écu*', he wrote to Humières, 'even if the army were dying of hunger.'[42]

In about mid-October Francis left Lyons and travelled back to Paris by way of the Loire valley. Meeting James V of Scotland on the way, he gave him the hand of his daughter Madeleine. The marriage took place in Paris on 1 January 1537 and prompted the usual round of banquets, dancing and tournaments.[43] Then, on 15 January, at a *lit-de-justice*, Francis proclaimed the confiscation of Flanders, Artois and Charolais, whose suzerainty he had surrendered in the peace of Cambrai. His intention,

[39] G. Jacqueton, 'Le Trésor de l'Epargne sous François Ier, 1523–1547', *R.H.*, lvi (1894), 20–1.

[40] Decrue, i. 286.

[41] Bourrilly, *Guillaume du Bellay*, pp. 230–1; Procacci, 'Provence', p. 251.

[42] François, *François de Tournon*, pp. 133–7.

[43] G. Donaldson, *Scottish Kings* (London, 1967), pp. 155–9; du Bellay, iii. 338, 342. The long sea journey to Scotland proved too much for the princess, who died on 7 July.

however, was not to annex a large part of the Netherlands so much as to consolidate the northern border of France by bringing Thérouanne into his kingdom. The obvious person to accomplish this task was Montmorency, whose prestige had been much enhanced by his recent triumph in Provence. On 10 March he was reappointed as lieutenant-general with the immediate object of recovering the counties of Artois and Saint-Pol.[44]

Early in March Montmorency and the king marched north from Amiens. After capturing Auxy-le-Château, the grand master laid siege to Hesdin, while Francis pitched his camp further south at Pernes. On 6 May, however, after the county of Saint-Pol had been reconquered, the king suddenly stopped the offensive so as to assist his army in Piedmont. Montmorency informed Humières that he was being sent 10,000 landsknechts and that the king would soon be leaving for Lyons. Francis knew that the Turks were planning a descent on the kingdom of Naples. But the prospect of a joint Franco-Turkish invasion of the peninsula vanished when Charles V launched a counter-offensive in northern France. After capturing Saint-Pol and Montreuil, he laid siege to Thérouanne. Montmorency was immediately sent back to Artois, and all the troops intended for Piedmont, except the landsknechts, were recalled. As the flow of money, which had started to trickle through to Piedmont, dried up, Pinerolo was sacked by Italian troops serving in the French army. Fortunately for Humières, the campaign in the north ended abruptly. Montmorency and the Dauphin were about to march to the relief of Thérouanne when the regent of the Netherlands applied for a truce. This was signed at Bomy on 30 July and the siege of Thérouanne lifted. Francis was allowed to fortify the towns he had captured in the spring; only Saint-Pol remained in enemy hands.[45]

Thanks to the truce, Francis was able to go to the rescue of his army in Piedmont, but it was now too late for him to co-ordinate his action with the Turks, who, after landing in Apulia, had turned their attention to Corfu.[46] Early in October Francis arrived in Lyons to supervise preparations for a new invasion of Italy, and on 8 October the bulk of the army set off for the Alps under Montmorency. After crossing the Mont-Genèvre, the grand master forced his way along the Val di Susa and relieved the garrisons of Savigliano, Pinerolo and Turin. The king, who followed with the rest of the army, ordered prayers and processions of thanksgiving throughout France.[47] Within a few days the French had occupied the whole of Piedmont as far as Montferrat.

[44] Decrue, i. 294, 297–302.
[45] Ibid., i. 305, 307, 310; Bourrilly, Guillaume du Bellay, p. 244; J. Ursu, La politique orientale de François Ier (1908), p. 100.
[46] Ursu, pp. 103–4.   [47] Decrue, i. 326.

By now, however, both sides were worn out. The campaign of 1537 had cost Francis 5,500,000 *livres*, even more than that of 1536, which had emptied his war-chests at the Louvre.[48] The emperor, too, was bankrupt. A three months' truce was, therefore, signed at Monzon, in Spain, on 16 November, and soon afterwards it was followed by peace talks at Leucate, near Narbonne. Francis was represented by Montmorency and the cardinal of Lorraine, Charles by Granvelle and Cobos. Representatives of the king of Navarre and duke of Savoy also attended. It was now agreed that Milan should eventually be given to Charles d'Angoulême and that he should marry the daughter of the King of the Romans. But both sides put forward mutually unacceptable demands concerning the interim administration of the duchy: Francis wanted to be given it for five years, while Charles asked to keep it for as long. Other difficulties proved equally insuperable, with the result that after three weeks the talks collapsed, leaving only the truce, which was extended till 1 June.[49]

This was disappointing for Montmorency, who still hoped for a lasting reconciliation between his master and the emperor, but it did not detract from his martial achievement. On 10 February 1538 he was rewarded with the office of constable of France, which had been vacant since the treason of Bourbon. It was, symbolically, at Moulins, Bourbon's old capital, that Montmorency received the king's sword in the presence of the whole court. Two new marshals of France, Claude d'Annebault and René de Montjehan, were created at the same time.[50]

The war had ended triumphantly for Montmorency, but had it accomplished anything for the kingdom at large? The campaign of 1536 had not only rescued France from foreign invasion but had shown that Francis could, with Montmorency's advice, pursue an effective defensive strategy. While leaving much to chance in the north, he had shown foresight and prudence in the south. The year 1536 has been justly acclaimed as the most glorious year in his reign after 1515; its Fabian tactics stood in sharp contrast to the foolhardiness that had marked the Pavia campaign.[51] Yet the war had achieved little else, because it had outlasted the king's capacity to pay for it. Within a year he had spent all that had been set aside since 1532. If he had had the means he might have pursued the emperor from Provence into Italy and defeated him decisively. But, as he could not afford a war on two fronts, he had been

---

[48] Jacqueton, 'Le Trésor de l'Epargne', p. 21.
[49] Decrue, i. 332–5.
[50] *Ibid.*, i. 337–41. Annebault succeeded Robert de La Marck, better known as Florange, who had died on 21 December 1536.
[51] H. Martin, *Histoire de France*, 4th edn (17 vols., 1858–60), viii. 244.

obliged to turn his attention to northern France and, as a result, had missed an opportunity of joint action with the Turks in Italy. Fortunately for Francis, the enemy, too, was bankrupt. The war thus ended in stalemate. If Charles had been humiliated, Francis had gained little: he still had a foothold in Italy, but in northern France he had actually lost ground. Provence lay impoverished, and the succession to Milan, over which the war had been fought, remained as doubtful as ever.

19

Fruitless entente

(1538–42)

FRANCIS I'S FOREIGN policy underwent a remarkable change in 1538: after years of bitter hostility towards the emperor, he suddenly chose to become his friend. The two monarchs met in July at Aigues-Mortes and astonished the world by exchanging tokens of friendship and agreeing to sink their differences. In the following year Charles passed through France on his way to the Netherlands and contemporaries marvelled that he should thus put himself at the mercy of his former prisoner.[1] But the alteration in Francis's policy was one of method, not purpose: this continued to be the recovery of Milan. The only difference from the past was that, instead of using force, Francis was now prepared to try conciliation.

The minister responsible for this change of method was the constable, Anne de Montmorency, who largely controlled the king's foreign policy between 1538 and 1540. No French ambassador wrote to the king without also writing to the constable; conversely, a letter from the king to an ambassador was invariably accompanied by another from Montmorency. 'The Constable', wrote a Venetian, 'has a great influence over the king's mind. He does all that he wishes in France, and sees that only peace can preserve for him this great authority.'[2] But Montmorency also appreciated the value of negotiating from a position of strength. He therefore used the truce of January 1538 to consolidate the French occupation of Savoy and Piedmont. Each region was given a parlement

---

[1]   In March 1652 the Parlement of Paris made the following comment in remonstrances attacking Mazarin's Machiavellianism: 'Francis I, one of your predecessors, when advised to order the arrest of the Emperor Charles V, who was travelling through France with a safe-conduct, replied to his evil counsellors that kings, who are not subject to human laws and retribution, should be restrained by their promises, which they must keep even if the rest of the world does otherwise' (Archives des Affaires Etrangères, Paris, Mémoires et Documents, France 882, fols. 99v–100r). Was Francis feeling guilty about the treaty of Madrid and trying to put the record straight? I owe this interesting reference to the kindness of Dr Richard Bonney.

[2]   *Relations des ambassadeurs vénitiens sur les affaires de France*, ed. N. Tommaseo (1838), i. 181.

and a Chambre des Comptes, and Turin was fortified.[3] Within France the truce was used to strengthen the frontiers. Montmorency urged his brother, La Rochepot, to complete the fortifications of towns in Picardy and Champagne, and to retaliate vigorously against any infringement of the truce by imperial troops based in the Netherlands.[4]

Francis also tried, as far as possible, to maintain his existing alliances. He was accused by Henry VIII of breaking his word by negotiating separately with the emperor, and reproached for granting the hand of the duchesse de Longueville to the king of Scotland. But, as Francis pointed out, his promise to Henry had been conditional on his receiving English aid, which had never materialized; as for the duchess, she had been promised to James V long before Henry had shown an interest in her. Neither excuse satisfied the English monarch, yet Anglo-French relations were not broken off.[5] In Germany the landgrave of Hesse and the elector of Saxony, alarmed by signs of a Catholic revival and by the pope's plan for a general council, sought a new agreement with Francis. Their ambassadors were assured by the king that he would never desert his German allies nor agree to a general council being held in Italy.[6] As for the Turks, they remained on good terms with Francis despite the truce.[7]

Thus, early in 1538, the international situation appeared virtually unchanged; a renewal of war between Francis and Charles seemed only a matter of time. The king of Navarre did not think his brother-in-law would improve on the offers he had made at Leucate, and Francis himself was said to be pessimistic about the prospects of peace.[8] How, then, did the change in French policy come about? The answer is to be found in Rome. No one wanted peace more fervently than Pope Paul III, for without it there could be neither general council nor crusade against the Infidel. In December 1537, therefore, he appointed two legates, one for France, the other for Spain, with the purpose of turning the truce into a lasting peace. Rodolfo Pio, cardinal of Carpi, who was sent to France, was not a happy choice for he was suspected at the French court of being an imperialist, yet he was well received by Francis at Montpellier in January 1538 and managed to persuade him to meet the emperor and the pope in the summer.[9]

[3] Decrue, i. 343; V.-L. Bourrilly, *Guillaume du Bellay* (1905), p. 264.
[4] Decrue, i. 344.   [5] *L.P.*, xiii (pt 1), 386, 994.
[6] J.-Y. Mariotte, 'François 1er et la Ligue de Smalkalde', *Revue suisse d'histoire*, xvi (1966), 215; see also below, ch. 23.
[7] J. Ursu, *La politique orientale de François 1er* (1908), p. 108.
[8] *C.S.P. Span.*, v (pt 2), no. 196; Decrue, i. 344.
[9] L. von Pastor, *The History of the Popes*, tr. F. I. Antrobus and R. F. Kerr (London, 1891–1933), xi. 274–5; M. François, *Le cardinal François de Tournon* (1951), p. 163.

But Francis soon changed his mind. On 8 February a Holy League was formed between the emperor, the pope, the King of the Romans and the Venetians. Although it was ostensibly directed against the Turks and a place was reserved among its members for Francis, he interpreted it as a hostile move and protested vehemently to the legate. He was also angered to learn that the pope was trying to marry his grandson to the daughter of the King of the Romans.[10] By mid-February he had decided against papal mediation and suggested an extension of the truce till September.[11] The emperor concluded that Francis had no serious desire for peace and only wanted to delay the general council and crusade. Charles was probably correct: Francis was anxious not to be identified with papal policies which would damage his relations with the German Protestants and the Turks. He had no objection, however, to resuming peace talks directly with the emperor, and early in March sent de Vély to Spain to bring this about. But Charles, having decided to meet the pope in Nice, refused to be side-tracked. This forced Francis's hand: rather than be left out in the cold, he agreed reluctantly to attend the meeting.[12]

The interview at Nice (May–June 1538)

The meeting at Nice lasted from 15 May until 20 June. As the duke of Savoy refused to place the castle at the pope's disposal, Paul put up at a Franciscan monastery outside the town. Charles, meanwhile, stayed on board his galley at Villefranche, and Francis resided at Villeneuve. The interview consisted principally of four meetings between the pope and the emperor, and two between the pope and the king of France. At his first meeting with Paul, on 2 June, Francis assured him of his total obedience, yet he refused to meet Charles in the pope's presence or to promise aid against the Turks unless Milan were restored to him immediately.[13] Since Francis and Charles could not be brought together, the pope appointed three cardinals to negotiate with each in turn, but nothing came of this. On 9 June Paul put forward the following peace plan: the daughter of the King of the Romans would marry the duc d'Orléans, and after three years the couple would receive Milan, which, in the meantime, would be held in trust for them by Ferdinand. But Francis rejected this idea on 13 June.[14] So Paul had to fall back on a truce, but even this proved difficult to arrange, as Francis wanted it to last fifteen or twenty years and Charles only five or less. Eventually, a ten-year truce was signed, based on the *status quo*. This

---

[10] Pastor, xi. 276–7; C.S.P. Span., v (pt 2), nos. 187, 192.
[11] Ibid., p. 456 and no. 184.
[12] Ibid., nos. 190, 191, 193.
[13] Pastor, xi. 287–8.
[14] Ibid., pp. 289–90.

fell far short of what the pope had wanted, yet he claimed that the truce made him happier than he had been on the day of his election.[15]

Although Francis and Charles did not meet at Nice, there were frequent contacts between their courts, and on 1 June Montmorency persuaded the emperor to meet his master after the pope's departure.[16] Ten days later, Queen Eleanor and several ladies of the French court travelled by sea to meet the emperor. As they disembarked, a wooden pier, specially erected for the occasion, collapsed, pitching the queen, the emperor and many others into the sea, but no one suffered any harm other than a drenching. On 19 June Eleanor paid a second visit to her brother and begged him to meet her husband soon.[17]

Pope Paul left Nice on 20 June and travelled to Genoa, where he had further talks with the emperor before returning to Rome. Charles, for his part, sailed to Aigues-Mortes, in Languedoc, where, on 14 July, he was greeted on board his galley by Francis. Next day he returned the compliment by stepping ashore. The warmest greetings and tokens of brotherly love were exchanged by the two monarchs. 'It seems', wrote an eyewitness, 'that what we are seeing is but a dream, considering all that we have seen in the past. God is letting us know that he governs the hearts of men as he pleases.'[18] Important matters were discussed at Aigues-Mortes, but only in a general way: the king and the emperor agreed to co-operate in defending Christendom and bringing heretics back into the church. Yet Montmorency regarded the meeting as a triumph; the two monarchs, he wrote, could henceforth regard each other's affairs as identical.[19]

In October there was a further demonstration of friendship between the two royal houses when Francis met his sister-in-law, Mary of Hungary, regent of the Netherlands, in northern France. They spent most of their time hunting, feasting and dancing. On 23 October they signed an agreement at Compiègne in which Francis promised not to aid the emperor's rebels in the Netherlands, while Mary undertook to satisfy certain French noblemen whose lands in the Netherlands had been confiscated during the war. On the eve of her departure Mary was given a superb diamond by Francis.[20]

The meetings at Aigues-Mortes and Compiègne were only the prelude to serious peace talks. In December two French ambassadors, the bishop of Tarbes and the seigneur de Brissac, submitted the following proposals

[15] *Ibid.*, pp. 290–1. The truce was signed on 18 June. A.N., X^{1a} 1541, fols. 484a–b, 485a.
[16] Decrue, i. 352.
[17] *C.S.P. Span.*, v (pt 2), nos. 206, 226, 227.
[18] Terrasse, *François Ier: le roi et le règne* (1945–70), ii. 293.
[19] Decrue, i. 356.
[20] *L.P.*, xiii (pt 1), 690, 749; Decrue, i. 362–3; *C.A.F.*, iii. no. 10386.

to the emperor in Spain: the duc d'Orléans would marry Charles's daughter or niece, and his son Philip would marry Francis's daughter Marguerite. Francis, for his part, would sever relations with England and join a crusade against the Turks; he would also collaborate with the emperor in matters of general concern to Christendom. To the great satisfaction of the French, Charles accepted these proposals on 22 December and ratified his acceptance in the presence of the two ambassadors on 1 February 1539. His action was interpreted in France as almost the equivalent of a treaty of peace and alliance.[21]

Not everyone, however, believed that the entente would last. Pope Paul thought that it was worthless and that Francis would try to prevent a crusade, which, if successful, would only serve to enhance the emperor's reputation. The emperor, too, had doubts about the king's sincerity, but was reassured by his ambassador in France. 'I can certify to Your Majesty', the latter wrote, 'under pain of being reproached as the lowest wretch in the world, that any promise made here will be completely fulfilled.'[22] There was also distrust of the other side at the French court, but Montmorency maintained that the truce had become a peace which would last for the lives of Francis and Charles, even if the surrender of Milan were delayed.[23]

There is no doubt that, under Montmorency's direction, the French government did honour the spirit of the Aigues-Mortes entente, in the expectation that Charles would eventually hand over Milan. Francis scrupulously abstained from any new involvement in Germany's domestic affairs. He informed the Schmalkaldic League that it could no longer count on his support and by remaining neutral facilitated the signing of the truce of Frankfurt (April 1539) between the League and the emperor. The German princes were so convinced that the king's attitude towards them had changed that they turned to England for aid; hence the marriage alliance between the duke of Cleves and Henry VIII.[24]

Yet Francis did not abandon his friends completely. He replied evasively, in December 1538, when the pope urged him to act against the German Protestants, and was equally cautious in his attitude to England.[25] Henry VIII feared that the Franco-imperial entente was the opening shot in a Catholic offensive aimed at deposing him and bringing his kingdom back into the papal fold. There were signs pointing that way.

[21] Decrue, i. 364–5; *L.P.*, xiv (pt 1), 198; *C.S.P. Span.*, vi (pt 1), no. 252.
[22] *C.S.P. Span.*, vi (pt 1), no. 35 (p. 101).
[23] *Ibid.*, no. 77.
[24] Mariotte, 'François 1er', pp. 219–21.
[25] *Correspondance des nonces . . . Carpi et Ferrerio, 1535–40*, ed. J. Lestocquoy (Rome and Paris, 1961), p. 428.

In December 1538, for example, Paul III, angered by Henry's desecration
of Becket's shrine, confirmed Henry's excommunication, which had been
suspended for three years; he also sent Cardinal Pole to Spain and France
in an attempt to gain secular backing for the bull.[26] Early in 1539 rumours
of an imminent Franco-imperial offensive against England caused Henry
to make frantic preparations to defend his realm. His apprehension
turned almost to hysteria in February, when the French and imperial
ambassadors in England were simultaneously recalled.[27]

But Henry had nothing to fear: Charles was preoccupied with the
Turks, and Francis had no intention of breaking with England simply to
please the pope. The simultaneous recall of their ambassadors was a mere
coincidence. Public opinion in France was generally hostile to Henry, and
Francis, in his private dealings with the papacy, seemed to favour some
sort of action against him, but he still insisted on the emperor making
the first move.[28] When Pole, after being disappointed in Spain, looked
for support to the king of France, he met with such a cool response
that he decided he might as well return to Italy.[29] Francis, meanwhile,
demonstrated his peaceful intentions towards Henry by appointing
a new resident ambassador to England in the person of Charles de
Marillac.[30]

Francis found it more difficult to reconcile his endorsement of the
emperor's crusade with the preservation of French interests in the Levant.
But the outbreak of a serious revolt in Ghent in April 1538 forced Charles
to shelve his plan, whereupon Francis offered his mediation between the
emperor and the sultan. With Charles's consent he instructed Rincon, his
resident in Turkey, to seek a general truce between Christendom and the
Infidel, but the sultan would only consider a settlement with the Venetians. Francis trimmed his mediation accordingly, but this did not suit the
emperor; failing a general truce, Charles wanted the Venetians to continue fighting the Turks until he was free to launch his crusade. He began
to suspect Francis of being a dishonest broker and, in order to test his
sincerity, suggested a joint Franco-imperial embassy to dissuade the
Venetians from making a separate peace. Francis had to agree, and, in
December, del Vasto and Annebault, representing the empire and France
respectively, arrived in Venice. The doge and senate, however, refused to
alter their policy, and eventually came to terms with the Turks. It has been

[26] L.P., xiii (pt 2), 1087, 1110; xiv (pt 1), 13.
[27] Ibid., xiv (pt 1), 337, 398, 418.
[28] Ibid., xiv (pt 1), 36–7, 115, 371.
[29] Ibid., xiv (pt 1), 536, 602–3, 723, 1110, 1277; W. Schenk, Reginald Pole (London,
       1950), p. 80.
[30] L.P., xiv (pt 1), 669, 670, 907–8.

suggested that they were secretly encouraged by Annebault, but this is only conjecture. What is certain is that, in spite of his understanding with Charles, Francis did retain the sultan's friendship. In September 1539 Suleiman even invited him to attend the celebrations for his son's circumcision.[31]

The emperor visits France (November 1539–January 1540)

The climax of the entente forged at Aigues-Mortes was the emperor's visit to France in the winter of 1539–40. It was originally suggested by Charles, who needed to reach the Netherlands from Spain as quickly as possible. The English Channel was dangerous in winter, and the alternative routes through Italy were far too long. By crossing France as the guest of her king, Charles would also save money. Only one factor was open to doubt: the emperor had to convince his council that he would be safe in France and that no attempt would be made to extort concessions from him. Nor was it enough for Francis to guarantee the emperor's safety; the king's health seemed so fragile that it was felt necessary also to obtain an invitation from the Dauphin and the king's chief ministers just in case the king died during the emperor's stay in France.[32]

All this was done. Montmorency avidly took up the idea of the emperor's visit to France as a means of persuading him to give up Milan. There was no question, however, of pressing for this during Charles's stay for fear that he might subsequently repudiate any concession on the ground that it had been extorted under duress, exactly as Francis had done after the peace of Madrid. Charles had to be treated fairly and honourably in the hope that he would respond in kind. Although it was reported in the spring that the king was pressing the emperor to go to Flanders through his kingdom, Francis did not issue an official invitation to Charles until 5 August. The latter accepted in principle, but explained that he could not fix the date of his coming until he knew more about Turkish intentions in the Mediterranean.[33] By the autumn, however, he had decided to leave, and, on 7 October, Francis wrote to him in the most friendly terms: he was anxious, he said, to spare him the hazards of sea travel and help solve his problems in the Netherlands; Charles could be assured of the most honourable reception in France; he had only to say the word and Francis and his children would come and meet him in Spain. Charles also received letters urging him to accept the king's invitation

---

[31] Ursu, *La politique orientale*, pp. 110–15; *L.P.*, xiv (pt 1), 849, 884, 1229.

[32] L.-P. Gachard, *Relations des troubles de Gand sous Charles-Quint, par un anonyme* (Brussels, 1846), pp. 249–53.

[33] *L.P.*, xiv (pt 1), 451, 550, 767, 810; (pt 2), 16.

from the Dauphin, the duc d'Orléans, Montmorency and other leading figures at the French court.[34]

On 22 October Charles formally accepted Francis's invitation and prepared to leave Spain. His decision caused much satisfaction in France, particularly as he asked for no hostages or other guarantees for his safety; he even asked Francis to lend him his own cooks. As the French chancellor pointed out to the municipality of Paris, such a demonstration of trust deserved a truly munificent welcome.[35] Francis only regretted that he was too weak to go as far as he would have liked to meet his guest. Having only just recovered from a serious illness, he could not ride.[36] He did, however, manage to go as far as Loches in a litter, while the Dauphin, the duc d'Orléans and the constable travelled to the south of France, issuing instructions on the way to towns and local noblemen as to how they should welcome the emperor.[37]

From the time of his arrival near Bayonne on 27 November, Charles and his small retinue were magnificently entertained. The emperor was given an entry at Bordeaux, Poitiers, Orléans and Paris, and the privilege of setting prisoners free. In each town he was given costly presents. At Poitiers, for example, he was given a piece of silver representing an eagle and a lily on a rock, while the Parisians offered him a life-size statue of Hercules holding two pillars, also in silver. Each entry offered scope for appropriate symbolism, 'Peace' and 'Concord' being the dominant themes of the street decorations for Charles's entry into Paris on 1 January.[38]

The emperor's itinerary from Loches northwards had evidently been devised to show him the principal artistic achievements of the reign. He visited Chenonceaux (which the king had recently acquired from the heirs of Thomas Bohier), Chambord, Fontainebleau, Madrid, the Louvre, Villers-Cotterêts and Chantilly. At Fontainebleau, where Christmas was celebrated, Charles was given accommodation in the Pavillon des Poesles, which Rosso and Primaticcio had decorated specially for him. From its windows he could look into the Cour de la Fontaine, where a tall pillar had been erected. This had a flame at the top burning night and day and wine and water flowing from its sides.[39] In Paris, too, the emperor saw much to admire. The hall of the Palais, where a banquet and a ball were held on the evening of his entry, had been decorated with beautiful

[34] Granvelle, *Papiers d'état*, ii. 540–2; Decrue, i. 372.
[35] *R.D.B.V.P.*, iii. 1–7.
[36] *C.S.P. Span.*, vi (pt 1), 92. On the king's illness, see *L.P.*, xiv (pt 2), 353, 492; Kaulek, pp. 136–7.
[37] Decrue, i. 374.
[38] *Fêtes et cérémonies au temps de Charles Quint*, ed. J. Jacquot (1960), pp. 433–9.
[39] F. Herbet, *Le château de Fontainebleau* (1937), pp. 109, 132.

tapestries depicting scenes from the *Iliad* and the Acts of the Apostles, while the courtyard of the Louvre, where Charles resided during his visit to the capital, was dominated by a huge statue of Vulcan.[40] In short, no expense had been spared to make his stay memorable.

The emperor's visit to France was naturally watched with keen interest by other European rulers, the most anxious perhaps being Henry VIII, who sent Sir Thomas Wyatt to France to find out what lay behind it. The ambassador was soon able to reassure his master. He reported on 21 December that no sign was visible of an impending Franco-imperial treaty. Charles and his suite seemed to be biding their time until they had 'wound themselves honestly out of France'. The emperor, he believed, had been forced to go there by the urgency of the crisis in the Netherlands; he and Francis did not seem to be plotting to divide the world between themselves despite 'all those entries, joining of arms, knitting of crowns and such like ceremonies'.[41]

The entente collapses

Before Charles left France for the Netherlands, he and Francis discussed the Turks and matters touching the faith, but they did not talk about their own affairs; the emperor merely promised to attend to them after meeting his brother, Ferdinand, in Brussels.[42] He took leave of Francis at Saint-Quentin on 20 January, and was escorted as far as Valenciennes by the king's two sons and Montmorency. They returned four days later, carrying gifts from the emperor, and it was generally assumed at the French court that the constable and the cardinal of Lorraine would soon be invited to Brussels to conclude a peace settlement. For two months, however, Montmorency waited in vain while the emperor put down the Ghent revolt. Meanwhile, rumours began to circulate to the effect that the Franco-imperial entente had broken down and that another war between Francis and Charles was imminent. Such talk, Montmorency declared, stemmed from malice and jealousy; the entente was as firm as ever, but, of course, important matters could not be settled overnight.[43]

The constable's valiant efforts to keep up appearances were soon frustrated by the emperor. In March he recalled his ambassador from France and, a few days later, sent him back with the peace proposals. Charles's daughter Mary would marry the duc d'Orléans, and both would eventually inherit the Netherlands, Burgundy and Charolais. They would administer these territories during the emperor's lifetime, albeit

[40] *Fêtes et cérémonies*, p. 438.   [41] *L.P.*, xiv (pt 2), 628, 741.

[42] *C.S.P. Span.*, vi (pt 1), 102.   [43] Decrue, i. 380, 388–9.

under his supervision. If Mary died without issue, her lands would revert to Charles's heirs in the male line. The emperor also proposed two other marriages: one between Francis's daughter Marguerite and the eldest son of the King of the Romans; the other between his own son Philip and Jeanne d'Albret, heiress to Navarre. Francis, for his part, would surrender his claim to Milan as well as Hesdin and the lands he had taken from the duke of Savoy. Furthermore, he would ratify the treaties of Madrid and Cambrai and join a league for the defence of Christendom.[44]

On receiving these proposals Francis, the Dauphin and Montmorency shut themselves in a room for an hour and a half; the constable then took to his bed for two or three days. On 4 April Francis delivered his reply. The Netherlands, he explained, were not an adequate substitute for Milan, which was his by right of inheritance and by virtue of the investiture sold at a high price to Louis XII by the Emperor Maximilian. The future enjoyment of the Netherlands was also a poor exchange for the immediate possession of Milan, which had been promised to the duc d'Orléans on condition that he married the Infanta. As for Marguerite, Francis preferred to delay her marriage; he was, however, ready to accept the match proposed for his niece, Jeanne d'Albret. He was willing to exchange Hesdin for Tournai, Mortagne and Saint-Omer, but refused to ratify the treaties of Madrid and Cambrai. If it could be proven that he held parts of Savoy unlawfully, he would return them in exchange for what the duke held, without valid title, of his. As for the league, this was no problem.[45]

On 24 April Francis modified his terms in response to new proposals from Charles. He now agreed, for the sake of peace, to suspend his claim to Milan if Charles would immediately hand over the Netherlands to the duc d'Orléans. He would also agree to their reverting to Charles in the event of Mary dying childless, but only if his own claim to Milan were recognized. He still refused to ratify the treaties of Madrid and Cambrai, but offered to sign a new agreement covering those concessions he could legitimately make.[46]

The two rulers continued to exchange proposals for several weeks, but their fundamental positions remained unchanged, Milan, as usual, being the stumbling-block; Francis wanted nothing else, while Charles was as determined as ever to prevent it passing into French hands. On 15 May he complained that the tone of Francis's last message was not what he had come to expect after the interviews of Aigues-Mortes and Paris: the king had spoken as if Charles held Milan unlawfully and had asked that the

[44] L.P., xv. 373; K. Brandi, The Emperor Charles V, tr. C. V. Wedgwood (London 1939), pp. 430–1.

[45] L.P., xv. 457.   [46] Ibid., xv. 573; Ribier, i. 509.

Netherlands be given unconditionally to his son. Charles was ready to let Orléans and his wife exercise 'just and reasonable authority' after the consummation of their marriage and under his own paternal guidance; but he insisted that Francis must first give up his claim to Milan and agree to his daughter's marriage to Ferdinand's son.[47]

Yet the last thing Charles wanted at this stage was a conflict with France, for he needed time to restore law and order to the Netherlands, heal the religious schism in Germany and prepare his crusade. He therefore instructed his ambassadors, if all else failed, to arrange another interview with Francis. If the king definitely refused the Netherlands, then he, Charles, was ready to stand by the promise he had made to Tarbes and Brissac; if, on the other hand, Francis so preferred, Charles was ready to leave things as they were and remain his friend.[48] The ambassadors, however, were not given a chance to show their instructions to Francis. They were told bluntly by the cardinal of Lorraine that Francis felt he should be given Milan freely and without fuss.[49] By June the talks had finally collapsed.

The fall of Montmorency

The failure of the Franco-imperial entente played into the hands of Montmorency's enemies at the French court, who had longed for such an opportunity to topple him. Prominent among them was the duchesse d'Etampes, who denounced him in no uncertain terms. 'He is a great scoundrel', she declared, 'for he has deceived the king by saying that the emperor would give him Milan at once when he knew that the opposite was true.'[50] But Montmorency did not immediately fall from favour; though his diplomacy had been discredited, Francis continued to value his companionship and his qualities as a military leader. 'I can see only one fault in you', he said to him, 'and that is that you do not love those whom I love.'[51] Montmorency continued to sit in the king's council, but as early as April 1540 he ceased to have any say in the direction of foreign policy. Whereas in the past Francis had turned to him and the cardinal of Lorraine for advice, he now began to consult Cardinals Tournon, du Bellay and Mâcon as well as the bishop of Soissons.[52] In August it was noted that the king was attending council meetings more regularly than in the past; he was also having long consultations with Chancellor Poyet and Cardinal Tournon, who, together with Madame d'Etampes, were continually in his company. The imperial envoy described the duchess as

[47] *C.S.P. Span.*, vi (pt 1), 108.   [48] *Ibid.*
[49] *Ibid.*, 117.   [50] François, *François de Tournon*, p. 179 n. 1.
[51] Decrue, i. 401.   [52] *L.P.*, xv. 574.

'the real president of the king's most private and intimate council'. This was not likely to lead to any improvement of Franco-imperial relations. 'I hear from a good quarter', the same ambassador wrote to Charles, 'that the reason for her angry feelings is that when Your Majesty passed through the kingdom you did not make so much of her as she expected which has hardened her heart in such a way that it will be very difficult, nay, almost impossible, to appease her.'[53]

On 11 October the emperor invested his own son, Philip, with the duchy of Milan, thereby precipitating Montmorency's fall.[54] Within a month the king's secretaries were forbidden to use the diplomatic ciphers he had given to them; princes and ambassadors ceased to write to him, and Poyet took charge of the department Montmorency had previously run. Believing that he was already in disgrace, the constable asked for permission to leave court, but Francis assured him that he still needed his services. In February 1541 Montmorency staged something of a come-back. 'The Constable', wrote the imperial ambassador, 'is beginning to recover his breath and to take part in affairs of state'; but not for long.[55] In April, Mary of Hungary received the following report from the French court: 'As for the government of the court, Madame d'Etampes has more credit than ever. The constable . . . is paying court to her; his credit is diminishing each day. He has had angry words with the chancellor.'[56] Soon Montmorency was no longer free to correspond even with his friends. He advised Langey, the king's lieutenant in Piedmont, to send his reports in future to Marshal d'Annebault. On 14 June he attended the marriage between the duke of Cleves and Jeanne d'Albret at Châtellerault.

The Cleves marriage (14 June 1541)

Henri d'Albret had for a long time been dissatisfied with his brother-in-law's policy, which had failed to secure imperial recognition of his claim to Spanish Navarre. In 1537, therefore, he had entered secretly into direct talks with Charles, but had obtained only vague words of encouragement. The talks had then lapsed until March 1538, when they had been revived, following the collapse of the peace talks at Leucate. How far Marguerite had been a party to her husband's secret intrigues is anyone's guess. According to one of Henri's councillors, she, too, had felt disenchanted with her brother's policy in respect of Navarre, and it had been with her encouragement that Henri had first approached Charles.[57] Be this as it

[53] C.S.P. Span., vi (pt 1), 117.   [54] Decrue, i. 400.   [55] Ibid., i. 402.   [56] Ibid.
[57] P. Jourda, Marguerite d'Angoulême (1930), i. 215–17, 222–4, 228–30; C.S.P. Span., v (pt 2), 196–7.

may, her position became difficult early in 1540, when Francis accepted a request from William, duke of Cleves, for the hand of her daughter, Jeanne. Marguerite was appalled at the prospect of a twelve-year-old girl marrying a man twice her age: she wrote to William in April 1541, begging him not to hasten a match, which was premature 'in the eyes of God and nature'. The duke nevertheless came to France soon afterwards at Francis's invitation. At this juncture, however, Jeanne, who had originally agreed to marry Duke William, changed her mind. This angered the king, and Tournon threatened her with imprisonment if she continued to disobey her uncle. Eventually Jeanne yielded and, on 14 June, she and the duke were married.[58] But the princess had to be carried to the altar by Montmorency by order of the king. This, as far as the constable was concerned, was the final indignity; next day he left the court, never to return during Francis's reign.[59]

The return to war

Francis's alliance with the duke of Cleves, though theoretically defensive, was the first clear sign of a reorientation of French foreign policy, for the duke was no friend of the emperor: he was currently in dispute with him over the succession to Guelders and was the brother-in-law of the elector of Saxony, one of the leaders of the anti-Habsburg opposition in Germany.[60] Another sign of change in French policy was a sharp increase of secret diplomatic activity at the French court, which led the imperial ambassador to suspect that a new league was being mooted among France, England, Venice and possibly the German Protestants. Publicly, Francis continued to speak of his friendship with Charles; privately, however, he spoke a different language: he boasted of his preparations for war against Charles and of the troubles he could stir up for him in central Europe and the Mediterranean with the help of the Turks.[61]

The change in French policy was most clearly manifested in those highly sensitive areas, Germany and the Levant. In May 1540 Francis sent Lazare de Baïf to Haguenau in search of an alliance with the Schmalkaldic League. Baïf was soon followed by other French agents, who had been instructed to tell the Protestant princes of Francis's friendly feelings towards them. But the leaders of the League were divided in their attitude

---

[58] A. de Ruble, *Le mariage de Jeanne d'Albret* (1877). Also Jourda, i. 251–67; N. L. Roelker, *Queen of Navarre, Jeanne d'Albret* (Cambridge, Mass., 1968), pp. 46–59.

[59] P. de Bourdeille, abbé de Brantôme, *Oeuvres complètes*, ed. L. Lalanne (1864–81), viii. 117; Decrue, i. 403.

[60] Mariotte, 'François Ier', pp. 223–5.

[61] *C.S.P. Span.*, vi (pt 1), 120.

to the king, while the rank and file distrusted him because of the persecution of Protestants in France. They suspected that his change of policy was a direct consequence of his recent disappointment over Milan. 'French advances . . .', the chancellor of Hesse declared, 'are taking place because the king has not been able to agree with the emperor; if they had been able to agree, these advances might not have taken place.'[62] Francis consequently failed to make any headway in Germany. Only the elector of Saxony was prepared to be his ally, but the elector failed to win general support for his policy at the diet of Naumburg in December 1540. Instead of agreeing to send an embassy to the king, the diet merely sent him a petition in support of his Protestant subjects. The emperor, on the other hand, signed a treaty with the landgrave of Hesse in June 1541 in which the latter promised not to ally with Francis or allow him to recruit troops within his territories. Charles was less successful in his dealings with the elector of Saxony, yet he did manage to neutralize him. The elector was unwilling to ally with France on his own; early in 1542, therefore, he came to terms with the King of the Romans.[63]

Francis was much more successful in the Levant, despite the resentment which the emperor's visit to France had aroused there. The sultan even threatened to execute Rincon, the French ambassador, for having lied to him in the past. By February 1540 Rincon had managed to regain Suleiman's confidence, so that Francis was able to send an envoy to Constantinople with a view to renewing the Franco-Turkish alliance. The king was helped by the situation in Hungary, where the death of John Zápolyai in July was followed by a disputed succession between Zápolyai's infant son and the King of the Romans. Suleiman took Zápolyai's son under his protection and, later in the summer, invaded Hungary. In order to prevent the emperor from coming to the aid of his brother, he encouraged Francis to stir up trouble for Charles further west. On 5 March 1541 Rincon, who had left Constantinople in November, arrived at the French court loaded with gifts from the sultan.[64] He had several conversations with Francis in the presence of a Turkish representative, and in May set off on the return journey to Constantinople, accompanied by Cesare Fregoso, a Genoese employed by the French, who was on a mission to Venice. Instead of travelling across Switzerland, the two envoys preferred to pass through Lombardy, which was, of course, under imperial occupation. They left Turin on 2 July, and two days later, as they were sailing down the Po near Pavia, they were murdered by imperial troops. Although the emperor disclaimed all responsibility for this crime and ordered an enquiry, the French government claimed that he had broken the truce, and retaliated

[62] Mariotte, p. 226.   [63] Ibid., pp. 227–32.
[64] Ursu, La politique orientale, pp. 116–17, 123–30.

by arresting the archbishop of Valencia, the Emperor Maximilian's natural son, as he was passing through Lyons.[65]

Rincon's death was a mixed blessing for the emperor: it rid him of a dangerous traitor and deprived Francis of a skilled diplomat with a rare expertise in Turkish affairs, but it could not have happened at a worse time. Charles was trying to disentangle himself in Europe so as to be free to lead another expedition against the Infidel in north Africa. But Francis was not aware of this: he interpreted Rincon's murder and the emperor's descent into Italy soon afterwards as the opening moves of a campaign aimed at ousting the French from Piedmont. From July onwards, therefore, he prepared for war. Annebault returned to Piedmont with powers to raise troops, and he was soon followed by important reinforcements of infantry and artillery. Before going to war, however, Francis wanted to demonstrate to the world that he was not to blame for the collapse of the truce. He therefore asked the pope to arbitrate in the Rincon affair. The pope agreed, and Charles welcomed his intervention, if only to gain time for his African campaign.[66]

On 28 September Charles sailed to Majorca, where he was joined by his expeditionary force. Meanwhile, Francis, seeing that the emperor was not, after all, bent on attacking Piedmont, promised not to declare war on him while he was fighting the Infidel. This, in addition to being good propaganda, gave Francis more time to raise money and gain allies. But the emperor's campaign soon met with disaster. After his fleet had been battered in a storm, he called off the siege of Algiers. At the end of November he returned to Spain, leaving behind his horses and guns. Francis found himself under pressure to open hostilities at once, but as yet he had few allies. Neither Henry VIII nor the German princes were willing to join him. He was more successful in his dealings with lesser powers: thus he signed a treaty with Denmark on 19 November and another with Sweden on 1 July 1542.[67] On 8 March, however, Baron de La Garde, often known as Captain Polin, Rincon's successor as French resident at the Porte, returned home from Constantinople with a promise of massive Turkish support by land and sea.[68] This was the signal Francis had been waiting for. Two days later he left Paris and, on 12 July, at Ligny-en-Barrois, declared war on Charles. In a proclamation that was read out throughout his kingdom, he listed all the injuries which he had received

---

[65] The best account of this famous affair is in Bourrilly, *Guillaume du Bellay*, pp. 327–41. See also *C.S.P. Span.*, vi (pt 1), 188.

[66] Bourrilly, *Guillaume du Bellay*, pp. 339–40.

[67] E. Lavisse (ed.), *Histoire de France depuis les origines jusqu'à la Révolution* (9 vols., 1910), v. 110; *C.A.F.*, iv. 12615.

[68] Ursu, p. 138; Bourrilly, *Guillaume du Bellay*, p. 348.

from Charles, including the murder of Rincon and Fregoso, 'an injury so great, so detestable and so strange to those who bear the title and quality of prince that it cannot in any way be forgiven, suffered or endured'.[69]

[69] Guiffrey, p. 392; *C.A.F.*, iv. 12628; Granvelle, *Papiers d'état*, ii. 628.

20

The kingdom's wealth

HOW PROSPEROUS was France under Francis I? De Beatis, writing in 1517, found much to praise, but described the peasants as 'in complete subjection, more ill-treated and oppressed than dogs or slaves'.[1] The earl of Surrey reported in September 1522 that poverty in France was universal.[2] Yet Marino Cavalli, writing in 1546, commented on the richness of the kingdom. 'This country', he wrote, 'thanks to its size, has a great variety of soil and products. These are of such high quality and so abundant that there are enough for France and even for foreign countries.'[3] How far is it possible to reconcile these seemingly contradictory statements?

The countryside

Peasant unrest, which became so notable a feature of French history in the late sixteenth and early seventeenth centuries, was virtually absent during the reign of Francis I. This is all the more surprising if one considers that the main direct tax, the *taille*, rose under Francis to its highest level since Louis XI and that the peasantry had to bear the heaviest burden. But two mitigating factors need to be taken into account: first, the relative prosperity of the peasantry after 1450; secondly, the fall in the real value of money during the same period.

The reign of Francis overlapped with the completion in many parts of France of the rural recovery from the devastation left by the Black Death and the Hundred Years' War. The misfortunes that had hit the peasantry between 1340 and 1450 did not disappear completely, but they were more widely spaced and, in general, less severe. Outbreaks of plague still occurred from time to time, but there were no pandemics of the kind that had swept across France between 1348 and 1440. Epidemics were limited

[1] *The Travel Journal of Antonio De Beatis*, ed. J. R. Hale (London, 1979), p. 165.
[2] *L.P.*, iii. 2549.
[3] *Relations des ambassadeurs vénitiens sur les affaires de France*, ed. N. Tommaseo (1838), i. 253.

now to one or two provinces at most, and destructive ones were less frequent. The decline in the virulence of plague may have been due to partial immunity acquired through natural selection, an improved diet and preventive measures taken by many towns in the 1520s.

Another scourge from which the French countryside was largely freed after 1450 was war. Except for certain border areas, like Picardy, Artois and Provence, little fighting took place within the kingdom between the Hundred Years' War and the Wars of Religion. True, large companies of disbanded troops and brigands did terrorize certain areas from time to time, but, in general, the fear and uncertainty which had discouraged agricultural enterprise before 1450 were removed. Another stimulus to rural prosperity was the absence of any major grain famine between 1440 and 1520.

Fewer epidemics, famines and wars naturally served to foster a rise in the population of France after 1450. This was of crucial importance to the economic life of the kingdom. Having been cut by a half between 1330 and 1450, it seems that the population of France doubled between 1450 and 1560. The rise was not uniform throughout the kingdom: certain villages, even regions, maintained a high annual growth rate over a long period, while others made more modest advances. In Languedoc and Provence, the rise began later than in Cambrésis, Artois, the Paris area and, to a lesser extent, the pays de Caux and Bordelais: it reached its peak in the early sixteenth century, when the rise in the north slowed down. Even within a province, there could be sharp local differences. Nor was the rise in population necessarily continuous: in the pays de Caux there were two peaks, before 1500 and after 1530, with a standstill in between. Despite these variations, however, the population of France had by 1560 returned to the same level as before the Black Death, though its distribution was not necessarily identical. Thus in Provence a sharp rise in the population of the lowlands was not matched by a corresponding rise in the uplands.

The need to feed more mouths and the presence of a large labour force on the land fostered a rise in agricultural production after 1450. This, however, was achieved as a consequence of land clearance and reclamation rather than improved agricultural techniques. In certain areas, such as Cambrésis, where long-term fallow was an anomaly, attention was concentrated on hitherto neglected marginal lands. But, in most cases, the agricultural revival took the form of a reclamation of arable that had been allowed to go to waste. This process, like the resettlement of the countryside, was subject to many regional variations. It began sooner, for example, in the Paris region and the south-west than in the Midi. Even in the north there were local differences in timing: whereas in most of the Paris region the land had been reclaimed by 1500, in some areas of thin or heavy soil the process continued till about 1520. In Provence and Languedoc it took up virtually the entire first quarter of the century.

The reconquest of the land was followed by a spectacular rise in grain production, albeit an uneven one. In general, there was a return to the levels of the early fourteenth century, but almost everywhere the movement ran out of steam in the early sixteenth century. In the Ile-de-France, for instance, there was a slowing down of production after 1500, which lasted till 1540, when a new rise took place. In the Midi grain production reached a peak in the 1540s, then declined. Some areas witnessed an expansion of crops other than grain: for example, the chestnut in the Massif Central and the olive in Languedoc. Another feature of the agricultural renaissance was the development in certain regions of specialized crops in response to market demands at home and abroad. Such products were woad from Toulouse, hemp from Le Mans and wine from Burgundy, the Ile-de-France, the Atlantic seaboard and Languedoc.

The land clearance and reclamation which underpinned the agricultural revival of the period after 1450 was not accomplished without some damage to pastoral farming. Many village communities, anxious to maximize their arable, tried to limit grazing as much as possible. Access to pastures was restricted to transhumant animals, and peasants were forbidden to own more than a fixed number of animals. But the necessity for manure precluded a complete ban on livestock. In certain areas, moreover, such as mountains, where arable farming was less important, steps were taken to protect pastures from excessive land clearance. Thus, in spite of the demographic pressure and resulting land-hunger, pastoral farming held its own.

All in all, French agriculture was prosperous in the first decade of Francis's reign. But about 1520 it began to show signs of strain. The most serious was the imbalance between the rise in population and agricultural productivity. While the population continued to rise, agricultural production suddenly slowed down and levelled off. In Languedoc there was even a recession after 1545. The reason for this was technical backwardness: agricultural tools remained primitive, and fallow was usually left bare. The agricultural expansion consequently ceased once the land had been reclaimed. The imbalance between the demographic rise and the level of agricultural production helped to push up grain prices after 1510 and to create grain shortages, some of which caused *mortalités*. In the Nantes region, for example, grain famines occurred in 1528–32, 1538 and 1543–5. The two longest were accompanied by *mortalités* (1531–2, 1544–6). These crises, however, were localized and not sufficiently severe to halt the overall rise in population. A number of mitigating factors also helped the peasantry to overcome the difficulties of the mid-sixteenth century. Speculative crops, for example, were less susceptible than grain to the fall in production after 1520. The vineyards continued to produce more in response to the stimulus of international trade. Another asset was the spread of buckwheat, a crop of high, albeit variable, yield, undemanding in terms of soil and climate.

Another problem that developed under Francis was the fragmentation of peasant holdings. As the ratio of births to deaths increased, the limited arable pertaining to a village community was progressively subdivided through the normal process of inheritance. Thus at Bessan, in Languedoc, where this was particularly marked, the number of peasant proprietors sharing the arable fields doubled and in some cases trebled between 1502 and 1559. A consequence of this fragmentation was the growth of distrust among the villagers towards outsiders. By 1500 immigration, which had played a vital role in the agricultural revival, had lost its impetus; under Francis it ceased to be significant. The village community had enough people of its own to accommodate; it did not need to attract more from outside. The reduction in the size of holdings inevitably undermined the self-sufficiency of the peasantry. By 1547 most peasants had not enough land to serve the needs of their families, the essential minimum of five hectares being seldom achieved. In Hurepoix, 94 per cent of holdings in seven parishes fell below this figure. But the peasant could often supplement his income in various ways. In many parts of France there was an active cottage industry, producing various kinds of cloth. The peasants were generally paid piece-rates by a merchant who provided the raw material and sometimes the tools and collected the finished article for distribution. Peasants might also add to their income by taking up seasonal employment on large estates.

Socially, the reign of Francis saw the culmination of three important trends in the countryside: a reduction in the wealth and authority of the seigneurie, the rise of a village aristocracy and the proletarianization of the lower strata of the peasantry. During the agricultural renaissance the seigneur had been forced to make concessions to his tenants: new leases had laid down precisely, and in writing, the services owed by them, so that they were protected from arbitrary exactions in the future. By 1500 serfdom had virtually disappeared. In the sixteenth century, however, as the demographic rise created land-hunger, the seigneur tried to backtrack on concessions. Sometimes he was successful, but usually he failed. The new customs were already held to be 'immemorial', and, even when the law decided in the seigneur's favour, it could not always be enforced. His authority, moreover, was being eroded by the crown. A long series of royal edicts and ordinances stretching back to Charles VII rode roughshod over local customs in respect of many rural matters. The king's judges heard appeals against decisions taken by the seigneurial courts; in cases involving bloodshed pardons were frequently granted by the crown. Another blow to the seigneur's prestige was the responsibility assigned by the crown to the village community in most of the kingdom to share out and collect the *taille*. In addition to losing some of his authority, the seigneur also suffered a loss of income. He had been forced in the fifteenth century to accept a reduction of the *cens* and to convert dues in kind into cash payments. As these were fixed by custom, they inevitably suffered a devaluation as a result of the sixteenth-century price rise. In these circumstances, he relied for the bulk of his income on his demesne; he tried to increase the rent paid by his tenant farmers. Yet if the seigneurie lost something of its wealth and authority, it retained its social pre-eminence in the countryside.

The peasantry, too, underwent a significant social transformation in the century after 1450. At the top of their social scale were the *fermiers* or *coqs de village*, who frequently acted as intermediaries between the seigneur and the rest of the peasantry. With thirty hectares at least at their disposal, the *fermiers* could produce more in a year than they needed to feed their families and pay their seigneurial dues. The surplus enabled them to set up as grain merchants or cattle-breeders. They lent tools, seed and money to less fortunate peasants and offered them seasonal work and artisanal commissions. At the same time, they collected leases, levied seigneurial dues and monopolized positions of influence in the village or parish. The rise of this village aristocracy did not affect the whole of France or even a majority of communities. The west was hardly touched by it. It was none the less a development of great significance for the future: in the late sixteenth and early seventeenth centuries there were few peasant revolts in areas that had seen the rise of the *fermier*.

Parallel to the emergence of a village aristocracy was the proletarianization of the lower orders of the peasantry. Until about 1450 agricultural workers had been well paid on account of their scarcity; thereafter, the real value of their wages had declined steadily. In the Paris region, for example, wages remained more or less static till 1530, while grain prices rose sharply. The price of the best wheat on the Paris market rose from 1.04 *livres* in 1440–60 to 1.56 *livres* in 1510–20, yet the abbeys of Saint-Denis and Saint-Germain-des-Prés paid their vineyard workers no more in 1510 than they had done in 1440. It has been estimated that the purchasing power of rural workers in the Paris region fell by as much as 50 per cent between 1450 and 1550. In Languedoc, where wages were normally in kind, the peasantry suffered less from inflation. Where the real value of wages did fall dramatically, small peasant proprietors were driven to borrow money in order to buy food. Those who could not repay the interest might have to sell their holdings. The next step might be to lapse into vagabondage.[4]

Trade and industry

The reign of Francis I has been called 'the springtime of French trade'.[5] The rise in population, the corresponding growth of urbanization and a general rise in the standard of living were mainly responsible for a boom which, having begun in the 1460s, lasted till about 1520. This was followed by thirty years of slower growth interrupted by a few peaks and troughs.

France was fortunate in being largely self-sufficient in respect of the basic necessities of life – grain, wine, salt and textiles. In terms of value and tonnage, grain was her most important commodity. Foreign grain sometimes had to be imported in times of famine, but normally the kingdom produced enough for its needs and was even able to export it. Paris drew its supplies from a large area comprising Beauce, Brie, the Ile-de-France, Picardy and Vexin. In difficult years it made demands on more remote provinces, such as Champagne. Lyons's main supplier was Burgundy, but in times of dearth it turned to Languedoc, Provence, Xaintois, Lorraine, the Ile-de-France, Picardy and Beauce.

The failure of grain production to keep pace with urban needs made for a precariousness of supplies encouraging to speculators. Seeing that the price of grain rose at the mere prospect of a shortage, merchants were tempted to hoard it until the price reached a maximum. Such malpractices caused distress and, sometimes, social unrest. Local authorities therefore tried to limit speculation by controlling the grain trade in various ways: weekly checks were kept of the prices charged on the local market, and attempts were made to fix a fair ratio between grain and bread prices. Sometimes municipal authorities tried to provide for emergencies by purchasing large quantities of grain in times of plenty and storing it in municipal granaries. Interprovincial problems, however, necessitated royal intervention. The Parisian authorities, for example, complained of having to allow the transportation of grain down the Seine to Rouen, whence it might be exported regardless of the capital's own needs. Royal ordinances tried as far as possible to meet Parisian requirements by alternately allowing and forbidding grain exports. The crown also inter-

[4]   G. Duby and A. Wallon (eds.), *Histoire de la France rurale*, ii (1975), 108–65; J. Jacquart, *La crise rurale en Ile-de-France 1550–1670* (1974), pp. 41–50.
[5]   P. Chaunu and R. Gascon, *Histoire économique et sociale de la France*, i (1450–1660), pt 1, *L'état et la ville* (1977), p. 236.

vened occasionally to persuade a province to release grain for the benefit of a town. In 1520 and 1528 Lyons was able to get grain from Burgundy only after such an intervention.[6]

Wine consumption increased enormously during the sixteenth century, as is shown by the rapid expansion of vineyards around Paris, Orléans, Rheims and Lyons, the yield from duties on wine and the multiplication of taverns. In Lyons the number of taverns increased five times between 1515 and 1545. Then, as now, wine was produced not only for the home market but also for export. Thus several major vineyards were developed along the Atlantic coast, around Bordeaux, La Rochelle and in the Basse-Loire. England and the Netherlands were the best customers: in 1543 wine accounted for a third of the cash value of all French imports into the Netherlands.[7]

Salt was, like wine, produced for both the home and foreign markets. Salt from marshes along the Mediterranean coast (at Peccais in Languedoc and at Marseilles, Saint-Victor and Hyères in Provence) was sent up the Rhône and Saône to south-east France, Burgundy and ultimately to the Swiss cantons and Savoy. Another group of salt marshes along the Atlantic coast (from Guérande to the bay of Bourgneuf, at Brouage and the isles of Ré and Oléron) supplied a much wider area. Their salt travelled up the Loire to Orléans and Chartres or by sea to Rouen and the towns of northern France. England, the Netherlands and the Baltic states all imported French salt, mainly from Nantes and La Rochelle. The salt tax or *gabelle* was, of course, an important source of royal revenue.[8]

The principal cloth-producing areas of France were Normandy, Picardy, Paris, Champagne, Berry, Poitou and Languedoc. Although usually called after towns, the various kinds of cloth were mainly produced in the countryside, the towns being merely the centres from which the cloth merchants operated. Generally speaking, French cloth was of ordinary quality and cheap; it served the day-to-day needs of the lower orders of society. Some of it was exported abroad, to Italy, the Barbary coast and the Levant, and until the sixties it competed successfully with English woollen cloth. But even the best French cloth (from Rouen and Paris) could not compete with certain foreign imports, such as Florentine serges. The finest wool also had to be imported from Spain, England, the Barbary coast and the Levant. Nor could France alone satisfy the increasingly sophisticated taste in textiles at court and among the nobility. For the finest linen she looked to the Netherlands and south Germany, and for silks to Italy. These comprised velvet from Genoa, damask

6   *Ibid.*, pp. 256–60.
7   *Ibid.*, pp. 260–1; R. Boutruche, *Bordeaux de 1453 à 1715* (Bordeaux, 1966), p. 101.
8   Chaunu and Gascon, pp. 263–4.

and satin from Florence and Lucca, and cloth of gold and silver from Milan.

Metalware, especially of iron or steel, was not widely used in early-sixteenth-century France. Agricultural and industrial tools were still largely made of wood. Apart from a few basic iron pots, the greatest demand in peacetime was for nails and pins. War, however, stimulated the metallurgical industry. As the Emperor Charles V controlled all the best European arsenals, including Milan after 1525, France had to manu-facture her own arms. There was, consequently, a rapid development of French iron production under Francis. In about 1542 there were allegedly more than 460 iron forges in France, of which more than 400 had been set up in the previous fifty years. They were situated mainly in Nivernais, Champagne, Burgundy, Berry and Dauphiné. In 1540 Francis set up a great forge at Breteuil for the manufacture of iron cannon. He also promoted the firearms industry in Forez, the only province where coal was used in the furnaces as early as the sixteenth century. Elsewhere, hydraulic power was used (hence most forges were set up along rivers). For non-ferruginous metals France continued to depend to some extent on foreign imports: she imported copper, brass and tinplate from Ger-many, pewter and lead from England and steel from Italy.[9]

The towns

The rapid growth of towns in France, which had begun at the end of the fifteenth century, was maintained under Francis. Although evidence for this is often selective (e.g. tax returns) or incomplete (e.g. parish registers), all of it points in the same direction. Thus Paris, which was by far the largest town in France, more than recovered its population (c. 200,000) of before the Black Death and the Hundred Years' War. Navagero estimated it as 400,000 in 1528, and Cavalli as 500,000 in 1546. These figures are probably exaggerated, but Paris may have had a population of around 400,000 in the mid-century. Lyons's population rose from 20,000 in the mid-fifteenth century to 80,000 in the 1550s. Rouen, Bordeaux and Toulouse went up from 20,000 at the end of the fifteenth century to 60,000, 50,000 and 40,000 respectively by the mid-sixteenth. Lesser towns showed a comparable growth. At Bourg-en-Bresse, for example, the number of hearths (feux) went up from 670 in 1491 to 1,069 in 1525.

The rise in urban population was due not only to natural growth but also to immigration from the countryside and other towns. Evidence of this may be found in apprenticeship or marriage contracts and registers of

⁹   Ibid., pp. 264–5; C.A.F., iv. 11639, 11676; viii. 32916.

admissions to hospitals. Out of 15,101 patients admitted to the Hôtel-Dieu at Lyons between 1520 and 1563, 39.55 per cent were natives of the city; the rest were outsiders, mainly from neighbouring provinces. They included a large number of apprentices, journeymen and servants, who were attracted to the city because of its freedom from gild controls.

Three towns – Paris, Lyons and Rouen – ranked with some of the largest in western Europe. Below them were about ten (Amiens, Nantes, La Rochelle, Bordeaux, Toulouse, Marseilles, Orléans, Tours, Rheims) with about 20,000 inhabitants each. Then there were some thirty towns (e.g. Le Puy, Blois, Châlons, Poitiers and Beauvais) of about 10,000 inhabitants each, and, lastly, a large number of small towns of a few thousand inhabitants. The character of each town was determined by its main activity. Trade was important to all of them, but some were administrative, intellectual and ecclesiastical centres as well. Eight towns (Paris, Toulouse, Grenoble, Bordeaux, Dijon, Rouen, Aix and Rennes) had parlements, about 90 were the capitals of *bailliages* and *sénéchaussées*, 15 (Paris, Toulouse, Montpellier, Orléans, Cahors, Angers, Aix, Poitiers, Valence, Caen, Nantes, Bourges, Bordeaux, Angoulême and Issoire) had universities, and about 150 were archiepiscopal or episcopal sees. Virtually the only industrial towns were Amiens, where the manufacture of cloth kept half the population employed, and Tours, where silk was important.[10]

Contemporaries tended to divide urban society into three groups: the *aisés* or well-to-do, the *menu peuple* or proletariat, and the poor. The reality, however, was more complex. Apart from the nobility and the clergy, which were not specifically urban categories (they were exempt from urban taxes and service in the militia), the upper end of the social scale comprised merchants and office-holders. In towns like Bordeaux and Toulouse, which had a parlement yet were important in international trade, the two groups were fairly evenly balanced, but in others like Lyons, where trade was all-important, the merchants were pre-eminent. They owned comfortable town houses and to the profits of their trade added revenues from their estates in the neighbouring countryside. In towns which were primarily administrative centres, office-holders were the dominant social group. They were often as rich as the merchants, from whose ranks many of them had risen. The core of urban society consisted of artisans and small to middling merchants. They worked for themselves, served in the urban militia, paid taxes, participated in general assemblies of the commune and owned enough property to guarantee their future security. Although not immune to the indirect effects of food

[10] Chaunu and Gascon, pp. 396–410.

shortages, they could count on having their own daily bread at least. Artisans were mainly of two types: those who employed large numbers of workmen and those who employed no labour other than their own families.

The lowest stratum of urban society – the *menu peuple* – consisted of manual workers (*gens vils et mécaniques*), who were excluded from any share in local government and lived from day to day in constant fear of hunger. They included journeymen, who were paid in money or money and kind, *manœuvres* (paid by the day) and *gagne-deniers* (paid by the piece). Typical of the average member of the *menu-peuple* was the building worker, who in Paris received 35 *deniers* per working day (there were only about 260 such days in a year, the rest being feast days). This had to pay for his daily food, rent, clothing and fuel. If he had a large family, his resources were stretched to the limit. A sudden rise in the cost of living, sickness, an accident or unemployment could easily drive him into poverty.

The reign of Francis I saw the beginning of a serious decline in the living standards of the urban proletariat. The first five years marked the end of a 'golden age' of cheap bread, which had begun at the end of the fifteenth century. As from 1520, nominal wages began to lag behind grain prices. By the end of the century the purchasing power of the working man was 40 per cent less than at the beginning. Rents and the cost of fuel and candles also went up sharply during the same period; only prices of manufactured goods, such as shoes and cloth, rose more slowly. As a result of this situation many of the *menu-peuple* joined the ranks of the poor.[11]

The growth of poverty

The activities of large gangs of vagabonds, who overran the countryside committing acts of pillage and terror, loom large in contemporary chronicles. Not all were dispossessed peasants; many were troops disbanded after a campaign. Their activities brought the poor generally into disrepute. They were commonly regarded as carriers of disease and as criminals. A public disaster invariably implicated them. In 1524, for example, after a large part of Troyes had been destroyed by fire, many vagabonds were suspected of arson and imprisoned.[12]

The most serious outbreak of popular disorder under Francis was the *Grande Rebeine* of Lyons. In April 1529 placards were put up in the city calling on the people to rise against the speculators, who were blamed for

[11] *Ibid.*, pp. 410–20.
[12] J. P. Gutton, *La société et les pauvres en Europe (XVIe–XVIIIe siècles)* (1974), p. 98.

the high price of bread. A mob, mainly of poor people, ransacked the Franciscan monastery and the homes of notables. The municipal granaries were broken into as well as that of the abbey of l'Ile Barbe. The municipal government, or Consulate, promised concessions so as to restore order, but a few weeks later it was busier hanging and whipping the leaders of the revolt than reducing the price of bread.[13]

Royal concern with vagabondage was reflected in a large number of edicts and ordinances. Several forbade soldiers to acknowledge vagabonds as their 'servants', while others ordered vagabonds to move only in small groups on pain of being 'cut to pieces'. These measures, however, proved ineffective. Vagabondage in the wake of armies remained a serious problem throughout the century. Royal legislation tried to improve policing methods. In January 1536 responsibility for arresting and punishing vagabonds was transferred from the *baillis* and *sénéchaux*, who were accused of lethargy, to the *prévôts des maréchaux*. In May 1537 the king empowered anyone to kill vagabonds as rebels against his authority.

Coercion, however, was not the only method used to deal with poverty in the sixteenth century. In the Middle Ages poor relief other than private almsgiving had been of two kinds: public handouts and hospitalization. No attempt had been made to discriminate between the impotent poor and sturdy beggars. All hospitals had been either ecclesiastical or private foundations; neither the state nor the municipal authorities had been responsible for them. In the early sixteenth century, however, methods of poor relief underwent a radical change. This began in Flanders and was marked by state intervention. The theory behind the reform was propounded by Juan Luis Vives in *De subventione pauperum* (Bruges, 1526), a work which was to prove successful in France.

Two notable developments concerning poor relief took place in France under Francis I: the reform and laicization of hospitals and the creation of municipal relief organizations, called Bureaux des Pauvres or Aumônes-Générales. As from 1519, the king set about reforming the hospitals and leper houses. His grand almoner was instructed to see that they carried out their duties and to inspect their accounts. A zealous reformer of hospitals was Pierre du Chastel.[14] The laicization of hospitals was also encouraged: in December 1543 the financial administration of leper

[13] J. P. Gutton, *La société et les pauvres: l'exemple de la généralité de Lyon, 1534–1789,* (1971), pp. 229–30; R. Gascon, *Grand commerce et vie urbaine au XVIᵉ siècle: Lyon et ses marchands* (1971), ii. 768–74. The riot was not religious in motivation, as H. Hauser once suggested (*Etudes sur la réforme française* (1909), p. 180). On this see N. Z. Davis, *Society and Culture in Early Modern France* (London, 1975), p. 9.

[14] R. Doucet, 'Pierre du Chastel, grand aumônier de France', *R.H.*, cxxxiv (1920), 38–45.

houses was entrusted to 'bourgeois'. But such measures were not applied universally owing to strong clerical resistance.

Sixteenth-century legislation insisted on the need for each town or village to care for its own poor. The existing hospitals, however, were for the most part inadequate. So the municipal authorities set up organizations designed to bring relief to the poor in their own homes and funded out of taxes on the well-to-do (*aisés*). In Paris, poor relief was traditionally administered by the Parlement, but in November 1544 Francis transferred this responsibility to the Bureau de la Ville. A Bureau des Pauvres of sixteen notables and sixteen commissioners was set up, the latter's task being to receive donations and collect the poor tax. The impotent poor were allowed to share in public handouts and to receive medical treatment in their own homes. At the same time, the Bureau employed sergeants to hunt down sturdy beggars and assign them to public works.

The most perfect French example of the institutional response to the new ideas on welfare was the Aumône-Générale, founded in Lyons after a grave famine in 1531. It was a temporary measure at first, but in 1534 a permanent Aumône was established. It consisted of eight commissioners (later called 'rectors') and a treasurer with wide discretionary powers to deal with the poor. Unlike medieval hospitals, the Aumône had no endowment: its income was made up of police fines, legacies, collections in churches and inns, and especially a tax, voluntary in theory but compulsory in practice, on a wide cross-section of Lyonnais society. The two main aspects of the Aumône's work were the care of orphans and foundlings, and the public distribution of bread.[15]

Royal control of trade

In the early sixteenth century it was generally believed that a nation's power lay in its stock of bullion and, therefore, that every effort should be made to conserve and enlarge it. Francis shared this view and, in March 1517, put forward a far-reaching programme of economic reform. Realizing, however, that 'many things profitable to one area may be harmful to others', he decided to consult the 'good towns' of his kingdom before finally drawing up an ordinance. Fifty-two delegates representing nineteen towns met in Paris on 25 March, when, in the king's presence, Chancellor Duprat delivered a long speech. France, he declared, was so rich in life's necessities as to be virtually self-sufficient, whereas her less fortunate neighbours could not do without her. It was necessary to stop money leaving the kingdom in exchange for goods 'tending to volup-

¹⁵ Gutton, *La société et les pauvres: Lyon*, pp. 256–7, 266–79.

tuousness rather than necessity' and to attract foreign money into the kingdom; hence the programme suggested by the king. This consisted of nine main proposals: a ban on imports of spices and drugs, except through the kingdom's seaports; a ban on imports of woollen cloth from England, Italy and Spain; the obligation on French merchants to pay for two-thirds of foreign purchases with French goods and on foreign merchants to accept such goods in exchange for two-thirds of their imports; a revaluation of the coinage; the unification of weights and measures; a ban on imports of luxury fabrics and furs; the regulation of inns and innkeepers; and a ban on gold and silver exports to the Holy See.[16]

The government's economic thinking, however, was too national for the towns. Their representatives felt unable to comment on the king's proposals without first consulting the people they represented. They were accordingly sent home after three days and ordered to send their replies in writing. Nine of these are known, and they show the parochialism of each town. Thus Bordeaux rejected any move designed to give control of the spice trade to Frenchmen; it opposed a ban on imports of English cloth for fear of retaliation against its own wine exports. Rouen pointed to its profits from trade with Flanders and Portugal and to the impossibility of trading direct with Calicut without the permission of the Portuguese crown. As a cloth-producer, it opposed silk imports, but, fearing reprisals, was against banning foreign cloth. Limoges pressed for a ban on all foreign wool and woollen cloth. Yet Bourges, which needed foreign wool for its own cloth industry, wanted its importation to be free. On the other hand, it advocated a ban on imports of foreign cloth likely to compete with its own. Only in respect of one of the government's proposals did the towns rise above local particularism: namely, the unification of weights and measures.[17]

The government, it seems, chose to ignore the replies from the towns. According to Barrillon, they were dropped unopened into a large leather sack and quietly forgotten. But if the reform programme of March 1517 was never embodied in a single ordinance, its principles were not abandoned. Many ordinances regulating imports and exports were issued during the reign, and various attempts were made by the crown to lessen dependence on foreign imports by encouraging home industries. In April 1540 Francis instituted a single unit of measurement, *l'aune du roi*, for textiles, but this attempt to bring some degree of standardization to the existing chaotic system of weights and measures was unsuccessful. So too was the long series of edicts aimed at clearing France's rivers of

---

[16] E. Coornaert, 'La politique économique de la France au début du règne de François Ier', *Annales de l'Université de Paris*, viii (1933), 414–27.

[17] Chaunu and Gascon, *Histoire économique et sociale*, i. 320–1.

seigneurial obstacles such as tolls and mills.[18] As many as 120 illicit tolls still punctuated the course of the Loire in 1567. Other royal measures for the encouragement of trade were more successful, notably the creation or restoration of a large number of fairs.[19]

Many royal ordinances attempted to regulate trade for a variety of reasons. The traditional fear of famine, coupled with the desire occasionally to dispose of harvest surpluses, prompted a long series of regulations authorizing, restricting or banning grain exports. In the winter of 1520–1, for example, Francis allowed grain to be exported to England, where it was scarce. Conversely, in October 1535, he banned its export from Dauphiné.[20] Another series of regulations sought to prevent gold and silver leaving the kingdom.[21]

Francis I's reign marked an important stage in the development of customs duties. These had originally been levied on exports only, but Louis XI had introduced a 5 per cent duty on silk imports, obliging them to enter the kingdom through Lyons only. In 1517 Francis extended this duty to imports of cloth of gold and silver and, later, goldsmiths' work and jewellery. In 1543 he revived a duty on alum, which Louis XII had created and abandoned. A year later, he extended it to all spices and drugs. Meanwhile, Francis undertook an ambitious reform of duties on exports. In 1540, following abuses by tax farmers, he decided that the *imposition foraine*, a duty of one *sou* per *livre* of the declared value of goods, would henceforth be collected by royal agents. In 1541 merchants who were not leaving the kingdom were spared the declaration; the complicated system of *acquit-à-caution* (whereby a merchant was reimbursed the duty paid at the point of dispatch on goods sold in provinces where the *aides* were in force) was also relaxed and in certain cases even abolished. In 1542 a tariff for goods subject to the *foraine* was published: it comprised no fewer than 450 items, but the values were exceedingly moderate. In 1544 the first *douane* in France was set up. This was a duty of six *deniers* per *livre* on all goods entering Lyons. It was discontinued in 1545 but was revived ten years later. Also in 1544 Francis appointed a *contrôleur-général des traites* to supervise the customs system.[22]

Among state activities with a direct bearing on the economy the most important was control of the coinage. In France the right to mint coins

---

[18] C.A.F., iv. 11483, 11687; E. Levasseur, *Histoire du commerce de la France* (1911), i. 185.

[19] Levasseur, i. 187, 189–92.

[20] L.P., iii. 1092, 1157; C.A.F., iii. 8153.

[21] E. Coornaert, *Les Français et le commerce international à Anvers* (1961), i. 73.

[22] Ibid., i. 76; G. Zeller, 'Aux origines de notre système douanier: les premières taxes à l'importation (XVIe siècle)', *Mélanges 1945*, Faculté des lettres de Strasbourg, Etudes historiques, vol. iii (1947).

had been regalian for a long time; jurists saw in it a sign of absolute sovereignty. But the coinage was not as yet national: foreign coins circulated freely within the realm and were accepted as legal tender unless the crown pronounced otherwise. Further complication was caused by the fact that prices were generally stated in money of account (*livre tournois*, subdivided into *sols* and *deniers*), whereas payments were made in real money. The principal coins under Francis were of three kinds: gold (*écu au soleil*), silver (*teston*) and billon (a mixture of copper and silver) (*douzains, dizains, sizains*). The value of coins was determined in relation to a fixed weight – the mark of gold or silver – and to the *livre tournois*, but this dual relationship was subject to frequent fluctuations.

The large number of monetary ordinances issued by Francis were concerned mainly with regulating the mints themselves and upholding the value of the *livre tournois*. Minting was farmed out to rich merchants whose workshops were subject to occasional visits by royal commissioners. Samples of their coins were sent in boxes to the Chambre des Monnaies in Paris for testing. In June 1515, Francis closed all French mints except four: Paris, Lyons, Rouen and Bayonne. But the number soon increased, and measures had to be taken to eradicate and discourage malpractices by their masters. In July 1536 coin-clippers were made liable to the same harsh penalties as counterfeiters. In 1540 several measures were taken to safeguard the quality of the coinage, and in March 1541 an important step was taken towards a more unified system of minting, when Burgundy, Dauphiné and Provence were forbidden to encroach on the jurisdiction of the Chambre des Monnaies.

The government tried to prevent depreciation of the *livre tournois* by fixing the relative values of gold and silver. As far as possible, it tried to adhere to the traditional ratio of one to twelve, but inflationary pressures at home and abroad forced periodic adjustments of the official rates. Gold as compared with silver was relatively plentiful in France in 1515. The market price of silver consequently rose to 13 *livres* 10 *sols* per mark, while the official rate remained fixed at 11 *livres*. Two years later the gold *écu* was fixed at 40 *sols*, while the silver *teston* was held at 10 *sols*. In May 1519 Francis ordered two mints (Paris and Lyons) to issue gold coins of inferior quality for two months only, but this debasement was ephemeral; in July it was decided to mint gold coins of 23 carats and of $71\frac{1}{6}$ to the mark, while the minting of *testons* was suspended. In May 1521, however, the crown, finding itself short of silver to pay for its war against Charles V, reversed its monetary policy: the price of a mark of silver was raised to 13 *livres* 5 *sols*, that of gold remaining unchanged. Much silver plate was melted down and turned into *testons*. This inevitably pushed up the market price of gold. Mints, which bought it at the official rate, ran short, and the gold famine became acute after Francis had been obliged to pay his sons' ransom in that metal. The *écu* was accordingly revalued in March 1533 at 45 *sols* and the *teston* at 10 *sols* 6 *deniers*. But the effect of this reorientation of royal policy was to drive silver out of the kingdom and open the way to billon from France's smaller neighbours, such as Béarn. In March 1541 an important ordinance reflected yet another change in official policy, this time in favour of silver: while the *écu* was kept at its 1533 value, the *teston* rose to 10 *sols* 8 *deniers*. This move, however, failed to check the *teston*'s disappearance from circulation. In July 1543 Francis complained that money from taxation was reaching him in billon, which was not easily transportable to the Epargne. Consequently, he encouraged the minting of *testons* by raising the value to 11 *sols*. The mark of silver was raised soon afterwards to 14 *livres* 10 *sols*. This caused a devaluation of gold: in January 1545 *écus* weighing only 2 *deniers* 15 *grains* were allowed to circulate alongside those of 2 *deniers* 16 *grains*. Yet there was no alleviation of the silver coins: while *testons* left the kingdom, billon entered it, mainly from Lorraine.[23]

In addition to controlling the coinage, the crown regulated bills of exchange. Italian merchants had made use of them for a long time, but it was only under Francis that the French monarchy regulated them, in a series of ordinances between 1537 and 1541. This legislation bore witness to the growth of credit and the problems this posed for the government, notably the question of interest on loans. Public opinion viewed this as normal, even if unjustified, but governments took a different view. While the imperial government fixed a rate of 8.333 per cent as lawful, the French crown continued to condemn all interest as usury.[24]

Can Francis I's economic policy be described as 'mercantilist'? Many historians have argued that the doctrine of national self-sufficiency, as enunciated by Duprat in March 1517, anticipated the views of Colbert. Indeed, the phrase 'Colbertism before Colbert' has become a cliché among French economic historians. But mercantilism, in the seventeenth-century sense, was a more sophisticated doctrine than that which inspired Francis's policy. He and his ministers may have vaguely understood that the yield from indirect taxes would rise and fall in response to national prosperity and depression, but the farming of such taxes inevitably restricted such fluctuations. Consequently, an essential aspect of mercantilism – namely the encouragement of trade and industry as a means of

[23] F. C. Spooner, *L'économie mondiale et les frappes monétaires en France, 1493–1680* (1956), pp. 108–36.
[24] Coornaert, *Les Français et le commerce*, i. 65–6.

boosting the king's revenues – was missing from Francis's policy, which is more correctly described as 'bullionist'.[25]

Three areas of economic growth

Three aspects of French economic growth under Francis I deserve special mention: the rise of Lyons, the expansion of trade in the Mediterranean and the opening up of the Atlantic ports. In each, the king made a contribution.

Lyons's prosperity rested on textiles, which accounted for more than 75 per cent of its imports in 1522–3. They comprised a wide variety of fabrics, ranging from the finest Italian silks to coarse cloth from central France. Among the city's other chief imports were spices, which Italian merchants brought from the Levant, either by sea through Marseilles or overland across the Alps. In the twenties and thirties, Portuguese spices began to arrive in Lyons, mainly from Antwerp, but in January 1540 Francis ensured the triumph of the Mediterranean spice trade by banning the import of spices except through Lyons, Marseilles and Rouen. Like silk, most spices sold at Lyons were for the home market, Paris being the largest single consumer.

In addition to being one of Europe's most important money markets, Lyons was noted for its printing and silk industries. The fact that it was a city of 'free work' – that is, one in which no fee or masterpiece or guild membership was required by artisan or entrepreneur – encouraged industrial enterprise. All that was needed to open a printing shop was capital. Lyons's first press was set up in 1473; forty years later it had more than a hundred. Most books sold in Lyons were also printed there, and each year large consignments were sent to the Frankfurt fair.

The introduction of the silk industry to Lyons was closely related to the policy of conserving the kingdom's bullion stock; if silk could be produced at home, there would be no need to use cash for its purchase abroad. In 1466 Louis XI had ordered the Consulate to set up a silk industry in the city; he had authorized it to levy a tax in order to cover its costs and had conferred privileges on the new industry so as to attract foreign workers. But the merchants of Lyons had not wanted to give up their profitable trade in Italian silk for the sake of an experiment of uncertain future. After only three years, therefore, Lyons had sent its silk-workers and looms to Tours, where a similar experiment had borne fruit.

Under Francis the attitude of the Lyonnais changed. The home demand

[25] M. Wolfe, 'French Views on Wealth and Taxes from the Middle Ages to the Old Régime', *Journal of Economic History*, xxvi (1966), 466–83.

for luxury cloth had grown to such an extent that it was now possible to envisage a native industry coexisting with foreign imports. Italian silk was, in any case, far superior to anything France could yet produce. Italian merchants, moreover, saw profits to be gained from a venture which would make demands on their capital, technical expertise and business contacts. At the same time, the Grande Rebeine of 1529 alerted the Consulate to the danger of harbouring a large number of unemployed poor in the city. Charity alone could not solve the problem; additional employment was needed. The silk industry could be the answer. By 1536, therefore, Lyons was prepared to accept a new royal initiative.

Francis's decision to revive Louis XI's experiment was a direct response to Genoa's so-called treason in 1528, when Andrea Doria sealed the fate of the French army in Naples by transferring his services to the emperor. Francis retaliated in 1530 by banning imports of Genoese velvet. This, however, caused resentment in Lyons, where the Consulate feared a boycott of the city's fairs. Cardinal Tournon, who was trying to raise a loan for the king from the city's Italian bankers, secured a compromise: the ban on Genoese velvet was lifted in January 1537 in exchange for a duty of two *écus* per piece. But Francis did not as yet forgive the Genoese: in October 1536 he exempted all Lyons's silk-workers from municipal taxes in the hope of bringing 'total ruin' to the Genoese 'rebels'. In March 1538, two months before the king's letters were published in Lyons, a merchant called Etienne Turquet asked the Consulate for a subsidy to set up looms for the manufacture of velvet. He was granted 500 *écus* over five years. Other local merchants contributed funds to the venture, and a company was formed, soon to be followed by others. By 1554 Lyons's silk industry was employing 12,000 workers. Four years later Italian merchants were importing less than a third or a quarter of the silks they had previously imported from Italy; instead, they were buying Lyons silk at far less cost.[26]

For much of the Middle Ages, France's window on the Mediterranean had been restricted to the coast of Languedoc. But in 1481 she had acquired Provence and some excellent ports, notably Marseilles. The rise of Lyons as an international market offered them a useful outlet for their imports and a precious source of capital.

The development of Marseilles can be traced in notarial acts and port books. For example, the yield from harbour dues rose from about 400 *livres* around 1500 to 1,300 in 1519–20 and to more than 3,000 in 1542. In the forties the annual average was 8,000 *livres*. The population of

---

[26] Gascon, *Grand commerce et vie urbaine*, i. 308–12.

Marseilles shows a parallel rise: from 15,000 inhabitants in 1520 to 30,000 in 1554. These figures reflect an expansion of Marseilles's trade along existing routes (to Languedoc, Catalonia, Corsica, Liguria, Tuscany, the States of the Church and Sicily) and the opening up of new ones. From the start of Francis's reign there were Marseillais at Alexandria. In 1528 the sultan confirmed privileges formerly given to French merchants in Egypt by the Mameluk sultans. He also gave them permission to go to Cairo. Francis's friendship with the Ottoman empire favoured the establishment of French trading posts at Beirut and Tripoli. Closer ties were also established with the Barbary coast. But penetration of the eastern market by the Marseillais did not seriously challenge the Italian spice monopoly. The Italians were superior in navigation, wealth and business expertise; their spices were cheaper and of better quality than the French imports. A large colony of Italian merchants in Marseilles reflected their dominance of Mediterranean trade. But if the Marseillais as yet played only a subordinate role, they could learn from their masters and might eventually displace them.[27]

The early sixteenth century witnessed a remarkable expansion of trade in the Atlantic as a consequence of Europe's overseas discoveries. The Portuguese and the Spaniards, who pioneered that movement, were, naturally enough, the first to benefit from it. But their principal ports, Lisbon and Seville, were not ideally suited to distribute goods to the rest of Europe. Antwerp offered better prospects, as the Portuguese recognized when they established their spice staple there in 1502. This marked the beginning of Antwerp's rapid rise to international pre-eminence as a market.

France, too, benefited from the growth of Atlantic trade, albeit in a more limited way. By now she had recovered all the coastline that had once been under English occupation. Since 1491 Brittany, too, had virtually passed under her control. Among the most important Atlantic ports were Rouen, Nantes, La Rochelle and Bordeaux. Rouen was the principal market for north-west France. In addition to distributing local produce, it served as a market for goods from all over France and overseas. Its imports far exceeded in quantity and variety its own needs or even those of its province. A significant proportion of the trade between Antwerp and Lyons passed through Rouen. Though not comparable to Antwerp as an international market, Rouen was nonetheless important: its sailors and merchants travelled widely in Europe and beyond; many foreign merchants were to be found among its inhabitants. 'Rouen', said Francis,

[27]   R. Collier and J. Billioud, *Histoire du commerce de Marseille*, iii (1480–1599), (1951), 179–85; Chaunu and Gascon, pp. 240–4.

'is the first town of France, for Paris is more than a town, it is a province.'
Nantes served not only as a port of call for ships plying between Bilbao
and the Netherlands, but also as an outlet for produce from the Loire
region. Among foreign merchants established in the town, the most
important was the Spanish family of Ruiz. Further south economic life
was dominated by two local products: salt and wine. The principal port
south of Nantes was La Rochelle, which exported wine, paper, linen cloth
and cheese and imported a wide variety of goods ranging from spices and
herrings to varnish and mercury. Bordeaux's prosperity in the sixteenth
century was due to the revival of the local vineyards, the rapid development of woad cultivation in the Toulouse region and the extraordinary
upsurge of inland water traffic. In an average year it exported between
20,000 and 30,000 barrels of wine.[28]

Francis's main contribution to the development of France's Atlantic
seaboard was the foundation of Le Havre. This was a response to pressure
from the community bordering the Seine estuary. The ports of Honfleur
and Leure were so silted up that a new harbour was urgently required. A
deep-water inlet at Grasse was already being used by ships, but it was
undefended, and there was a real danger that it might be seized by the
English in wartime. By 1517 the transformation of the inlet into a
properly fortified harbour had become a defensive necessity. Francis also
needed a good base from which to send a fleet to his ally James V of
Scotland. Thus the creation of Le Havre can be explained on other than
purely commercial grounds.[29]

The task of building the new harbour at Grasse was given to Admiral
Bonnivet on 7 February 1517, but he was too busy at court to attend to it
personally, so he commissioned Guyon Le Roy, seigneur du Chillou, to
act in his stead. He was empowered to force the inhabitants of a number
of places near Grasse to contribute one day's work each month on the
new harbour. The king was kept regularly informed of how the work was
progressing by Jacques d'Estimauville, who visited the court seven times
between May 1517 and May 1518. In October 1517 Francis granted
exemption from the *taille* and *droit de franc-salé* to anyone who came to
build and live at Grasse. This privilege was confirmed by the king when he
visited the new town in August 1520. By then work was so far advanced
that ships were able to use the harbour 'without danger or
inconvenience'.[30] Three years later it had fortifications and a shipbuilding

[28] Coornaert, *Les Français et le commerce*, i. 217–25, 311–12, 318–21, 324–7;
    P. Benedict, *Rouen during the Wars of Religion* (Cambridge, 1981), pp. 1–45.
[29] A. E. Borély, 'Origines de la ville du Havre', *R.H.*, xiv (1880), 286–311.
[30] S. de Merval (ed.), *Documents relatifs à la fondation du Havre* (Rouen, 1875),
    pp. 9–13, 24, 28, 59, 115–20, 257–61, 266.

yard, where a large vessel of 1,200 tons, called *Grande Françoise*, was under construction for the king. She was completed in 1524 but never sailed; her draught was so deep that she could not leave the harbour and had to be dismantled.[31]

Six years after visiting Le Havre for the second time in 1535, Francis commissioned Girolamo Bellarmato, a Sienese military engineer, to add a new district, called Quartier Saint-François, to the town. Unlike the town built by Le Guyon, which had been purely a speculative venture without aesthetic pretensions, this one conformed with the new ideas of Renaissance town planning: it was to comprise four blocks divided by two wide and straight streets crossing at right angles. All future houses were to conform to certain rules of alignment and decoration. Indeed, Bellarmato's commission (18 June 1541) has been called 'the first great document in the history of urban architecture in France'.[32]

The French economy, then, under Francis I was in general healthy: agriculture had recovered from the fourteenth-century crisis, urbanization was growing apace, new industries were being set up, and trade, both domestic and international, was thriving. All of this doubtless helps to explain the relative absence of popular unrest during the reign, in spite of an increasingly burdensome royal fiscality. Yet all was not well. The failure of agricultural production to keep pace with the needs of a fast-growing population was forcing a large number of people on to the breadline. Likewise, inflation was reducing the real wages and living standards of the lower orders of society. Unemployment and vagabondage were serious problems, and the state had been forced to intervene to solve or at best contain them. The seemingly contradictory comments of contemporary observers are not, therefore, irreconcilable: from about 1520 France's prosperity was under attack; it did not collapse, however, until the second half of the century.

[31] *J.B.P.*, p. 125; C. de La Roncière, *Histoire de la marine française* (1899–1932), ii. 473; iii. 176.

[32] P. Lavedan, *Histoire de l'urbanisme* (1941), pp. 93–100. Another example of town planning by Francis I is Vitry-le-François; see below, p. 368n.

21

France overseas

FRANCE TOOK no official part in the great movement of European expansion overseas until the reign of Francis I, yet she had as many advantages as Portugal and Spain, who had pioneered that movement: she had an extensive Atlantic coastline, many ports, good sailors and a sound economy. She also had as much interest as other Atlantic powers in breaking the Venetian monopoly of spices from the Far East. What she lacked until the early sixteenth century was a royal interest in overseas expansion.

The three immediate predecessors of Francis I were interested mainly in reviving and developing trade along traditional routes, particularly with the Levant, which had been disrupted by the Hundred Years' War. Louis XI reopened Bordeaux to English ships, gave the spice monopoly to the ports of the Languedoc and developed the port of Marseilles. Charles VIII was too preoccupied with Italy to be interested in the discovery of America or to object to Alexander VI's bull *Inter caetera*, which had allowed the Catholic Kings to claim all territories beyond a line drawn 100 leagues west of the Azores and Cape Verde islands. In November 1511 the Mameluk sultan offered Louis XII freedom to trade in Syria and Egypt along with pilgrimage facilities. He expected that, in return, Louis would put pressure on the Grand Master of Rhodes to release captured Egyptian ships, but the king failed to achieve this. Consequently the Venetians had their privileges confirmed, while France had to be content with a treaty guaranteeing freedom of trade.[1]

Under Francis spices continued to reach France via the Levant in spite of the alternative route to the East Indies recently opened up by the Portuguese. The French government was aware of this competition. In March 1517 Chancellor Duprat, speaking to a gathering of representatives of the 'good towns', alluded to the Portuguese spice trade. If it were true, he said, that the Portuguese were now getting cheaper spices, he hoped Frenchmen would soon emulate them. His chief concern, however,

[1] C.-A. Julien, *Les voyages de découverte et les premiers établissements* (1948), pp. 1, 47–52.

was not to facilitate this so much as to restrict the import of spices, which drained the kingdom of gold and silver.[2] Meanwhile, French merchants established depots at Constantinople, Beirut, Damascus and Nicosia of Smyrna. In 1528 the concessions previously accorded to them in Egypt were confirmed by the Ottoman sultan, and early in 1534 Francis concluded with him a commercial truce of three years. Whether further concessions were obtained from the sultan in February 1536 is a matter of controversy. There is no evidence that the French ambassador, La Forêt, was instructed to negotiate a new trade agreement with the sultan at this time, and, if such a treaty was signed, it is difficult to understand why it should have been kept a secret and why other powers, notably the Venetians, should not have reacted to it.[3] Be that as it may, French merchants certainly occupied a privileged position in the Levant, which inevitably undermined any incentive to look for alternative markets.

But, if the French monarchy was for long content to look no further than the Mediterranean in promoting overseas trade, its subjects were more enterprising. From the mid-fifteenth century onwards, seamen from France's Atlantic and Channel ports showed a considerable interest in the profits to be made in West Africa and Central and South America. As early as 1457 the king of Portugal was so concerned about French interlopers along the coast of Guinea that he planned to send a fleet of twenty ships to drive them away. The first Frenchman who can certainly be said to have gone to Brazil was Paulmier de Gonneville, a captain of Honfleur. He went there in 1504 and, after a stay of six months, returned to France with Essomericq, the son of an Indian ruler. Gonneville affirmed that other Frenchmen had preceded him to Brazil in search of dyewood, raw cotton, monkeys, parrots and other local products. The French got on well with the natives, and some stayed behind to learn their language and to organize resistance against the Portuguese.[4]

French pirates were also active from an early date. They attacked Portuguese ships carrying spices from the Indies and wood from Brazil, and Spanish treasure ships from America. The outbreak of war between Francis and the emperor in 1521 turned them into corsairs, among whom Jean Fleury of Honfleur was outstanding. In 1522 he caused a great stir by intercepting the ships sent by Cortés to Charles V with the treasures he had found in Mexico and sinking two of them near Cape St Vincent.[5]

2 E. Coornaert, 'La politique économique de la France au début du règne de François Iᵉʳ', *Annales de l'Université de Paris*, viii (1933), 418–19.
3 *Ordonnances*, viii. 560–7.
4 Julien, pp. 18–21, 70.
5 *Ibid.*, p. 72; C. de La Roncière, *Histoire de la marine française* (1899–1932), iii. 249–51.

Knowledge of French activities in the North Atlantic in the early sixteenth century is vague. According to a testimony of 1539, two Frenchmen, Jean Denys of Honfleur and Thomas Aubert of Dieppe, methodically explored the coast of Newfoundland in 1506 and 1508 respectively. It was almost certainly Aubert who, in 1509, brought back to Rouen seven natives with their clothes, weapons and canoe. These were described by Henri Estienne in a work published in 1512. Bretons went to Newfoundland to fish as early as 1504. In September 1510 a ship of Pléneuf sold Newfoundland fish at Rouen, and in December 1514 the inhabitants of Bréhat were paying tithe for fish caught off Newfoundland, Iceland and Brittany. When Queen Juana of Castile commissioned Juan de Agramonte to discover the 'secret of Newfoundland' in 1511, she allowed him to take two Bretons as pilots. It is, in fact, possible that French fishermen had been going to Newfoundland since the fifteenth century, but no documentary proof of this has yet been produced.[6]

A most important figure in all this private maritime activity was Jean Ango of Dieppe (1480–1551), a shipowner, banker and entrepreneur, who fitted out a fleet of twenty to thirty ships, entrusted them to captains well trained in navigation and sent them to Newfoundland, Guinea, Brazil and Indonesia. Despite his manifold activities, Ango also found time to lead a cultivated life. He built a handsome house overlooking the harbour at Dieppe and a summer residence a few miles outside the town, at Varengeville, of which some traces remain. In 1535 he entertained the king, who, in return, ennobled him and appointed him governor of Dieppe. On several occasions Ango was asked to lend the king money and ships; indeed, it was he who had to shoulder the heavy burden of victualling the forces sent to invade England in 1544. Such demands outstretched his means; he ran into debt and his last years were spent fighting off creditors.[7]

Giovanni da Verrazzano

When exactly Francis I first became interested in overseas exploration is not known, but he certainly became involved in it in 1522, when John III of Portugal was warned by Portuguese merchants in France of a French project likely to damage his interests. The king promptly sent João da Silveira to the French court with a request that Francis should forbid his subjects to attack Portuguese subjects and their property. The ambassador was well received, but Francis 'answered him vaguely, and with

6 Julien, pp. 21–8; H. P. Biggar, *The Precursors of Jacques Cartier 1497–1534* (Ottawa, 1911), p. 107.
7 E. Guénin, *Ango et ses pilotes* (1901), passim.

remarks more of appearance than of resolution, which seemed to have been uttered not so much to complete the business of which it was a question, but rather to put it off, and make time pass'.[8]

The project which so alarmed the Portuguese monarch was almost certainly the first voyage of Giovanni da Verrazzano, which was apparently initiated not by the French government, but by a syndicate of Florentine merchants resident in Lyons. No royal commission in respect of the voyage has survived, but it must have been issued, for it was to the king that Verrazzano reported on 8 July 1524 immediately after his return. 'I have not written to tell Your Majesty', he wrote, 'of what happened to the four ships which you sent out over the Ocean to explore new lands . . . [or how] we continued the original voyage with only the *Dauphine*; now on our return from this voyage, I will tell Your Majesty of what we found.' Later in the report he states that the voyage had been made by the king's command, and this was confirmed by his brother, Gerolamo, on a map of 1529. Nor was the king's role limited to granting a commission: the *Dauphine* was a royal ship, and her captain was paid by the king during the expedition.[9]

It is tempting to see a connexion between Verrazzano's first voyage and the first circumnavigation of the world, which Sebastiano Elcano completed on 7 September 1522. Not only was this achievement given wide publicity in January 1523 by Maximilian of Transylvania in *De Moluccis insulis*, but Antonio Pigafetta, a Venetian who had accompanied Elcano, visited the French court soon afterwards and made 'a gift of certain things from the other hemisphere' to Louise of Savoy.[10] It is likely, therefore, that Verrazzano's aim was to find an easier and more direct route across the American continent to Cathay than the Strait of Magellan. He set off about 1 January 1524 in four ships, but lost two of them in a storm. Eventually, he took only one, the *Dauphine*, and, after crossing the Atlantic, made landfall near Cape Fear. Instead of landing, however, he sailed southward along the coast for about 160 miles in an unsuccessful search for a port. Then, turning back, he returned to his original landfall and set foot for the first time on American soil. A few days later he set out on a long north-easterly coastal voyage. On 25 March he sighted 'an isthmus one mile wide and about two hundred miles long' and, beyond it, water which he identified with the Pacific. In fact, the 'isthmus'

[8]   L. C. Wroth, *The Voyages of Giovanni da Verrazzano, 1524–1528* (New Haven, 1970), p. 67.

[9]   *Ibid.*, p. 65. Three versions exist of Verrazzano's letter to Francis. The most authoritative is the *Cèllere Codex* in the Pierpont Morgan Library, New York. For a facsimile reproduction, transcription, English translation and editorial commentary see Wroth, pp. 96–152.

[10] Wroth, p. 220.

was the barrier-island chain of the Carolina Outer Banks, and the 'Pacific' consisted of the three sounds of Pamlico, Roanoke and Albemarle. Verrazzano's error was to vex geographers, cartographers and explorers for more than a century.

Verrazzano gave the name of Arcadia to the coast of Virginia and Maryland 'on account of the beauty of the trees'. Landing there, he and his men spent three days exploring the interior, during which they kidnapped an Indian boy. From Arcadia, Verrazzano sailed north-eastwards along a coast 'very green and forested but without harbours', calling it Lorraine after the cardinal of that name. Other topographical features were named after the duc d'Alençon, the seigneur de Bonnivet, the duc de Vendôme and the comte de Saint-Pol. Eventually, he came to the bay of New York, which he called Santa Margarita after Francis's sister, 'who surpasses all other matrons in modesty and intellect'. As for the land around the bay, Verrazzano called it Angoulême. He described Manhattan island as 'a very agreeable place between two small but prominent hills; between them a very wide river, deep at its mouth, flowed into the sea'. This was, of course, the Hudson, which was not to be rediscovered till 1609. Taking a small boat for a short distance upstream, Verrazzano found himself in a densely populated area. 'The people', he wrote, 'were dressed in birds' feathers of various colours, and they came toward us joyfully uttering loud cries of wonderment.'

After this brief glimpse of New York Bay, Verrazzano continued to sail north-eastward. After noting Block Island, which he called Aloysia in honour of Francis's mother, he proceeded to Newport, Rhode Island, where he spent a fortnight recuperating. Here he was visited by many Indians, who proved most friendly. 'These people', he wrote, 'are the most beautiful and have the most civil customs that we have found on this voyage. They are taller than we are; they are a bronze colour, some tending towards whiteness, others to a tawny colour; the face is clear-cut, the hair is long and black.' After rounding Cape Cod, Verrazzano followed the coasts of Massachusetts and Maine. He then sailed northwards until, on reaching the latitude of Cape Breton, he turned east and sighted Newfoundland. Finally, his stores almost gone, he recrossed the Atlantic and, on 8 July 1524, arrived at Dieppe.[11]

Although Verrazzano had failed to discover a northern passage to Cathay, his achievement was none the less remarkable. By exploring, describing and mapping out the east coast of North America from Florida to Cape Breton, he had closed an important gap in contemporary geographical knowledge. The report he sent to Francis on his return is 'the

[11] Ibid., pp. 71–90; D. B. Quinn, North America from Earliest Discovery to First Settlements (New York, 1978), pp. 154–9.

most accurate and the most valuable of all the early coastal voyages that has come down to us'.[12] About a third of it is devoted to the physical appearance, manner of life, customs and character of the American Indians. Verrazzano also showed an appreciation of the American land-scape, praising its beauty, its vegetation and, in places, its climate. He knew that it was not Asia, describing it as a 'new land which had never been seen before by any man, either ancient or modern', and called it Francesca in honour of his royal patron. Francis thus acquired a claim, albeit one without papal support, to territorial dominion in the New World.

Unfortunately for Verrazzano, his return coincided with the invasion of Provence by Bourbon. Francis had already left Blois and was travelling south to take charge of his army. He may not have found time to read Verrazzano's report or to meet him in Lyons in August, but the explorer was commissioned by the king about this time to undertake another voyage to the Indies. He was given four ships, but, just as they were about to sail, they were requisitioned to help defend the French Channel coast.[13] Verrazzano's next moves are obscure: he may have looked for a new patron in England and Portugal. But in April 1526 he obtained the backing of Admiral Chabot and Jean Ango, who formed a joint-stock company with a view to fitting out three ships to do 'the voyage to the Spice islands in the Indies'. This time the expedition managed to get away, but where did it go? There is evidence that Verrazzano tried to round the Cape of Good Hope but was forced by bad weather to go to Brazil. By 18 September 1527 he had returned to France.[14] Three months later the Portuguese ambassador reported to his master that Verrazzano had been ordered by Chabot to go with five ships to 'a great river on the coast of Brazil'. 'I think', he added, 'that they are going to establish a base there and thereafter, that they will push still further their exploration.' In April 1528 Verrazzano made an agreement with the crew of the *Flamengue* of Fécamp for a voyage of trade and exploration to the Indies sponsored by a group of merchants. There is evidence that he looked for a strait leading to the Pacific somewhere in Central America, but he did not survive to tell the tale. The *Flamengue* returned to France before 26 March 1529 with a small cargo of Brazil-wood, but without Verrazzano. It was reported that he had been killed and eaten by cannibals on an island in the Caribbean.[15]

[12] B. Penrose, *Travel and Discovery in the Renaissance, 1420–1620* (Cambridge, Mass., 1952), p. 146.

[13] Wroth, pp. 160–2; *C.A.F.*, viii. 31508.

[14] One of the three ships did apparently manage to round the Cape and reach Sumatra, where part of her crew were massacred. The survivors recrossed the Indian Ocean westward and were shipwrecked off Mozambique. Wroth, pp. 219–35.

[15] *Ibid.*, pp. 236–62.

Franco-Portuguese rivalry

The last two voyages of Verrazzano, whatever their exploratory purpose may have been, can be fitted into the context of the long and bitter commercial rivalry between France and Portugal, which was fought out mainly in Brazil and along the West African coast. Although John III professed to be concerned only with the suppression of French piracy, he was, in fact, hostile to all French shipping in what he regarded as Brazilian waters and gave orders for its destruction. At the same time, he tried to get restitution of all the Portuguese ships and cargoes that had been seized by the French, as well as guarantees for the future. Francis had good reason to be conciliatory towards John, whose support he needed against the emperor. But such a policy ran counter to the interests not only of French shipowners like Ango but also of the French admiralty, which could claim a share of all prizes. Thus the assurances given by Francis to the king of Portugal were seldom implemented. In September 1522 Bonnivet even granted a letter of marque to one of Ango's associates, allowing him to intercept Portuguese subjects and their merchandise.

Five years later the situation took a dangerous turn when Christovão Jaques, acting on orders from John III, captured and executed some Breton merchants as they were loading wood at Bahia in Brazil. The governor of Brittany complained to the king of France. But Francis was more concerned at this time to raise money for the ransom of his two sons, whom the emperor was holding hostage, than to champion the interests of French seamen. So, at the same time as he asked for compensation for the relatives of the victims of the Bahia massacre, he requested a loan of 400,000 cruzados. In reply the king of Portugal offered only a quarter of this sum. The rest, he said, would have to be levied by the French courts as compensation for the 300 Portuguese ships captured by the French over the previous thirty years. Francis, however, managed to pay his sons' ransom without Portuguese help, and thereafter was more inclined to listen to Chabot, who had consistently championed the cause of French shipowners. In July 1530, after Portuguese coastguards had seized the *Marie* of Dieppe near Lisbon, Francis issued a letter of marque to Ango, allowing him to recoup his loss at the expense of Portuguese ships. In April 1531 John was dismayed to learn that Ango had placed an embargo on all Portuguese vessels entering French ports on their way to Flanders and decided to get Ango's letter of marque revoked. After using diplomacy in vain, he resorted to corruption successfully: in return for a gift of 10,000 cruzados and a beautiful tapestry, Chabot, who was always susceptible to bribery, agreed to mediate in the dispute and to ban all French ships going to Brazil or Guinea. In July 1531, after French and

Portuguese negotiators had reached an agreement, Ango surrendered his letter of marque. But even with the backing of the French admiralty, Portugal could not totally exclude French interlopers from her dependencies. Thus in about 1531 Bertrand d'Ornesan, baron de Saint-Blancard, attempted to establish a French trading post at Pernambuco. In the autumn of the same year more than ten ships at Harfleur and six at Rouen were preparing to set off for Guinea and Brazil. Ango, too, continued to trade with both places, and Chabot himself secretly encouraged such ventures in return for a share of the profits.

John III was uncompromising in his attitude to the rights of discoverers. 'The seas', he declared, 'where everyone must and can navigate, are those which have always been known to all and common to all, but the others, which were not known and did not seem navigable and which were discovered at the cost of much effort on our part, are excluded from them.' Francis disagreed, believing that the seas were open to all, but his doctrine conflicted with Alexander VI's bull of 1493, which had divided the world between Castile and Portugal without taking effective occupation into account. This was an impediment to French overseas enterprise, but in October 1533 Clement VII was persuaded, apparently by the king's grand almoner, Jean Le Veneur, to reinterpret the bull: it applied, he said, only to 'known continents, not to territories subsequently discovered by other powers'. Francis was thus able to challenge the monopoly claimed by the Iberian powers without fear of incurring spiritual sanctions.[16]

The French in Canada: Cartier and Roberval

Le Veneur, in addition to being the king's grand almoner, was bishop of Lisieux and abbot of Mont-Saint-Michel. In May 1532 he entertained the king of France at his abbey and, being very much interested in maritime affairs, suggested that an expedition of discovery be sent beyond Newfoundland. He offered to contribute to its cost and to supply chaplains, if Francis would accept as its leader Jacques Cartier, a sea captain related to the abbey's treasurer.[17] The king agreed, and, in March 1534, after the pope had given his new ruling on the rights of discoverers, he commissioned Cartier 'to voyage and go to the New Lands and to pass the Strait of the Bay of the Castles [i.e. Strait of Belle Isle]'. Here, he was to discover 'certain islands and lands, where it is said he should find rich quantities of gold and other rich things'.[18]

[16] Julien, *Les voyages de découverte*, pp. 92–9, 105–17.
[17] Baron de La Chapelle, 'Jean Le Veneur et le Canada', *Nova Francia*, vi (1931), 341–3.
[18] *A Collection of Documents Relating to Jacques Cartier and the Sieur de Roberval*, ed. H. P. Biggar (Ottawa, 1930), pp. 42–3.

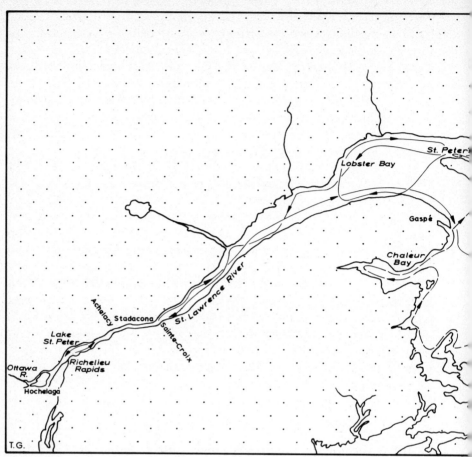

10   Map of the voyages of Jacques Cartier.

Little is known about Cartier's early life except that he was born in
Saint-Malo in 1491. He was an experienced seaman who had first-hand
knowledge of the Newfoundland fisheries and was well informed about
Brazil. Nothing associates him with Verrazzano's voyage to North America, but he was apparently aware of its results. His main objective in 1534
was probably to find the passage to Asia Verrazzano had failed to discover. He set sail from Saint-Malo with two sixty-ton ships in April and,
after crossing the Atlantic in twenty days, made landfall at Bonavista in
eastern Newfoundland. On 27 May he tried to enter the Strait of Belle
Isle, but because of icebergs was unable to do so till June. He then
explored its northern shore and came across a fishing vessel from La
Rochelle, proof that he was not the first Frenchman to reach this area. On
15 June Cartier began the first known exploration of the west coast of

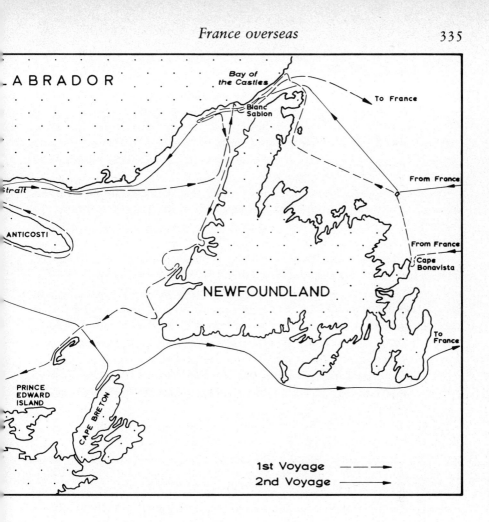

Newfoundland. He then made for Prince Edward Island, sighting it on 1 July, and two days later began to inspect Chaleur Bay, only to find that it did not lead to the interior. The bay was full of Indians, who had come to fish. They invited Cartier to come ashore, 'holding up to us some furs on sticks'. At first Cartier tried to frighten them off by firing several shots, but eventually mutual confidence was established, and the French bartered trinkets and weapons for furs. On 12 July, Cartier began to explore the coast of the Gaspé peninsula. He set up a cross at the entrance to Gaspé harbour and came across another large group of Indians who had come from afar to fish. These, however, had no furs to trade and wore little clothing. With the consent of their chief, Donnaconna, Cartier decided to take two young Indians back to France. He planned to teach them French and to learn more about their country from them. Their names were Dom

Agaya and Taignoagny. From Gaspé, Cartier sailed north-eastward to Anticosti, thereby missing the entrance to the St Lawrence river. He followed the island to its eastern extremity, then its north shore until it became clear that a strait separated it from the mainland. This he called St Peter's Strait, but, the season being late, he decided to postpone its exploration till the following year. He then returned to Blanc Sablon in the Strait of Belle Isle and, on 15 August, set sail for France. He returned to Saint-Malo on 5 September.[19]

Although he had found no gold, Cartier had collected much valuable information about climate, anchorages, good and bad terrain and the local flora and fauna. He now knew that there was a passage north and south of Anticosti leading to the west, which might prove to be a passage to Asia. On evidence supplied by the two captured Indians it seemed that a great kingdom, called Saguenay, lay far inland from their own Canada.

Francis was sufficiently impressed by these results to order a new expedition without delay. On 30 October Cartier was empowered to take three ships, each victualled for fifteen months, 'beyond the New Lands' which he had discovered.[20] The *Grande Hermine, Petite Hermine* and *Emerillon* were fitted out at once, but an outbreak of plague delayed the expedition's departure from Saint-Malo till 19 May 1535. Cartier's company included the two Indians, who by now had learnt enough French to serve as interpreters and guides.

After being dispersed in the Atlantic, Cartier's three ships met up at Blanc Sablon on 26 July. They then followed the coast of Labrador westward and passed through St Peter's Strait into the mouth of the St Lawrence river. Early in September, as Cartier made his way up river, Donnaconna met him bearing gifts. He welcomed back Dom Agaya and Taignoagny, who were now allowed to return to their tribe. Their village, Stadacona, near the site of modern Quebec, was pleasantly situated, but Cartier was not yet prepared to settle down for the winter. He was anxious to explore the kingdom of Hochelaga, further up the St Lawrence. The two Indians, after promising to lead him there, now refused. They even tried to deter him by sending a canoe downstream with three Indians disguised as devils, who warned him of hazards ahead. On 19 September, however, Cartier set off from Sainte-Croix with the *Emerillon* and two ships' boats. At Achelacy, he was warned by Indians of the dangers of the Richelieu rapids, but the rich woods, the loaded grapevines and the abundance of bird life beckoned him on. After crossing Lake St Peter, he left the *Emerillon* and her crew behind, and with a small party

---

19   *Les Français en Amérique pendant la première moitié du XVIe siècle*, ed. C.-A. Julien, R. Herval and T. Beauchesne (1946), pp. 79–112; Quinn, *North America*, pp. 169–75.
20   *Documents re. Cartier and Roberval*, pp. 44–5.

made his way to Hochelaga, where more than a thousand men, women and children came out to greet him. Neither Cartier nor the Indians showed any fear of each other; the women even had him touch their babies. In exchange for gifts of fish and corn, the French handed out knives and beads to the Indians.

On 3 October Cartier led twenty-three of his men to Hochelaga, near a mountain. The village, encircled by a triple palisade, contained about fifty longhouses, and Cartier's men noted down what the Indians ate and how it was cooked, how they slept and dressed and how they specially prized white wampum beads. From the top of the mountain, which he called Mont Réal, Cartier was shown the Ottawa river, which, the Indians believed, flowed past the kingdom of Saguenay. 'And without our putting any question or making any sign', the French reported, 'our Indian guides took the silver chain of the Captain's whistle and the handle of a dagger hanging at the side of one of our sailors, which was of brass as yellow as gold, and made signs that such things came from up the said river.' But Cartier was unable to find out how far Saguenay was. Rather than go further at this stage, he decided to return to Sainte-Croix, where the men he had left behind had built a fort 'enclosed on all sides with large wooden logs, planted upright, with artillery pointing every way.' This was now strengthened with deep, wide ditches, a gate and a drawbridge.

For five months, from mid-November 1535 till 13 April 1536, Cartier and his men were frozen in and snowed up at Sainte-Croix. Their fuel and supplies ran short, and many died of scurvy. The death toll would doubtless have been higher if Dom Agaya had not shown Cartier how to extract a healing mixture from the branches of a local tree (probably the Eastern White Cedar). As other Indians came to barter fresh meat and fish for goods, the Frenchmen regained their health. Yet in April Cartier decided to return to France without attempting further exploration. But first he kidnapped eight Indians, including Donnaconna, and, with two Indian children given to him by another chief further up the St Lawrence, set sail for France in two vessels (the third had been broken up) on 6 May after setting up a cross and taking formal possession for France. He reached Saint-Malo safely on 16 July, having passed out into the Atlantic by way of the Cabot Strait to the south of Newfoundland.[21]

What had Cartier achieved in the course of his second voyage? He had established the insularity of Anticosti as well as that of Newfoundland. More important still, he had determined the course of the St Lawrence as far as the Lachine rapids and discovered a territory beyond which lay the kingdom of Saguenay, where, according to Donnaconna, 'immense quantities of gold, rubies and other rich things were to be found' and the men were white and wore clothes like those worn by Frenchmen. But, apart from a few quills containing gold dust, Cartier brought back none of the riches he had been sent to find, so that, in the eyes of Francis and Chabot, his expedition must have seemed a failure. The time, in any case, was not ripe for a new expedition to North America, for war had broken out again between France and the empire. Not until the truce of Nice (18 June 1538) did Francis's interest in North America revive. In September he ordered two payments to Cartier: one for his past voyages, the other for feeding and looking after the Indians he had brought back.[22] During the same month Cartier submitted a long memorandum to the king setting out his needs for a successful voyage to Saguenay. He asked for six vessels of at least 100 tons each and two barques of about 50 tons, all furnished with provisions for two years. In addition to 120 sailors, Cartier required about 154 artisans and soldiers, including 2 goldsmiths 'skilled in handling precious stones' and 6 priests.

According to the memorandum's preamble, Francis, in spite of the exhaustion of his finances, was anxious to establish Christianity 'in a land of savages far removed from France, at the other end of the world, knowing full well that it offered neither mines of gold or silver nor any other hope of gain, save the conquest of an infinite number of souls for God'.[23] But this manifesto is not easily reconciled with the rest of the document or with Cartier's own ideas and behaviour. Though doubtless a devout Christian, he never showed a strong missionary zeal. His first two voyages produced no baptisms, and the Indians he brought back to France had to wait a long time for theirs. Nor does the king's alleged renunciation of mineral wealth accord well with Cartier's request for two goldsmiths. His manifesto was probably intended to satisfy the new pope, Paul III, who had not yet declared himself on French activities overseas. By claiming exclusively religious intentions, Cartier may have hoped to obtain for his royal patron privileges similar to those given by the papacy to the Portuguese and Spanish monarchs.[24]

A clear indication of the true motives underlying Cartier's third voyage is contained in the report of a conversation between the king of France and a Portuguese pilot called João Lagarto. After the latter had shown Francis two marine charts and an astrolabe, the king spoke to him 'with understanding and intelligence' for more than an hour. Next evening he

[22] *Documents re. Cartier and Roberval*, pp. 69–70. The sums were 3,499*l*. 4*s*. 6*d*. and 50 *écus soleil* respectively. Donnaconna and all his adult companions died before Cartier's third voyage.

[23] *Ibid.*, pp. 70–4.

[24] Julien, *Les voyages de découverte*, pp. 137–8, 147.

showed Lagarto two charts of his own 'well painted and illuminated, but not very accurate'. He pointed to 'a river in the land of Cod marked out and set down at his request'. 'He has sent there twice', writes Lagarto, 'and he has in this matter a great desire and longing, as was clearly shown, and what he says and wishes to do in the matter would make men marvel. And he spoke of this to me many times until I seemed to see it with his eyes.' Francis spoke of Cartier's two voyages and their results. He said that the river he had sent him to discover was allegedly 800 leagues long. Well up the river there were two falls, and he planned to send with the ships two brigantines which might be taken overland. 'Beyond the falls', Lagarto continues, 'the King of France says the Indian King told him there is a large city called Sagana, where there are many mines of gold and silver in great abundance, and men who dress and wear shoes like we do; and that there is abundance of clove, nutmeg and pepper. And thus I believe he will again decide to send there a third time seeing his great desire.' Francis told Lagarto that he wished a fort to be built well up the river whence the brigantines might be sent to pass the falls. The summer was short in that country, he explained, and the winter long and exceedingly harsh, but there were plenty of fish in the river as well as oranges and pomegranates at its mouth. There were animals with hides worth ten cruzados each and men with 'wings on their arms like bats', who flew 'but little, from the ground to a tree, and from tree to tree to the ground'. Cartier had brought him some goose quills containing fine gold from Saguenay. He used to believe that the river would lead to a passage into the southern sea but now knew that none existed. Lagarto expressed scepticism about the precious metals and spices, insinuating that Donnaconna had mentioned them so as to return to his country, but Francis brushed this suggestion aside with a laugh; the Indian king, he said, was an honest man who would be true to his promises.[25] Never in the course of this conversation was the conversion of the Indians so much as mentioned. Clearly the king's intention was to emulate the rulers of the Iberian peninsula by having Indies of his own; the religious motive was mere propaganda.

A report that Francis had commissioned Cartier and others to go to the Indies and settle the New Lands reached the emperor in the Netherlands in August 1540. Treating the French challenge as a serious breach of the truce of Nice, Charles sent a spy to keep a watch on shipping along the French Atlantic coast. Despite an assurance from Francis that Cartier would not be going to imperial territories, Charles took no chances: fearing that the French might establish a base from which to invade the Indies and control the Bahamas channel, he ordered all French ships

[25] *Documents re. Cartier and Roberval*, pp. 75–81.

bound for the Indies to be intercepted and their crews without exception thrown into the sea 'as a warning against similar expeditions'.[26]

Charles also tried to enlist the support of the king of Portugal and the pope in opposing Francis's overseas venture. But John III was prepared to defend only his own immediate interests. He refused to close Portuguese ports to French ships and sent an agent to Fontainebleau, who apparently won the favour of the duchesse d'Etampes and an assurance that neither Brazil nor Guinea would be encroached upon. As for Paul III, he received the emperor's entreaties with sympathy, but times had changed, and he was not prepared to uphold *Inter caetera* at the cost of alienating France. Francis would not accept the doctrine enshrined in that document, as he made clear to the imperial ambassador in December 1540. Popes, he said, held spiritual jurisdiction, but they had no power to distribute lands among kings; neither the king of France nor other Christian rulers had been consulted when the partition had taken place. He rejected, therefore, any Portuguese or Spanish privileges which failed to take his own interests into account. 'He said', the cardinal of Toledo reported, 'that he did not send these ships to make war nor to contravene the peace and friendship [with the Emperor] . . . but that the sun gave warmth to him as well as to others, and he much desired to see Adam's will to learn how he had partitioned the world.'[27] Yet, if Francis was determined to defend his rights, he was also willing to respect the emperor's wherever the latter was in effective occupation of a territory. He promised that his subjects would not go to the emperor's 'lands and ports' or to 'the parts not discovered by his predecessors, and belonging to his crown more than thirty years before the ships of Spain and Portugal sailed to the new Indies'. The imperial ambassador had no doubts as to Francis's meaning. 'In truth', he explained, 'I think he has in mind the populated and defended places, because he said that passing by and discovering with the eye was not taking possession.'[28]

No amount of foreign pressure could persuade Francis to abandon or modify his plans. On 17 October 1540 he commissioned Cartier to go to Canada and Hochelaga 'forming an extremity of Asia on the western side' and, if possible, Saguenay in order to convert its people.[29] Soon afterwards, however, he radically altered his plan. Instead of an expedition with an ostensibly proseletizing purpose, he now envisaged one that would lead to the establishment of a French province overseas. For such an ambitious expedition a leader capable of assuming the full responsibilities of a royal lieutenant-general was required. Cartier, though talented enough, was a mere commoner. The king also wanted someone rich

[26] *Ibid.*, pp. 104–27, 140–3, 259–66.   [27] *Ibid.*, pp. 189–92.
[28] *Ibid.*, pp. 169–71.   [29] *Ibid.*, pp. 128–31.

enough to shoulder some of the expense of the enterprise. His choice fell on Jean-François de La Roque, seigneur de Roberval, a Protestant nobleman from Languedoc. He was a soldier and allegedly an expert in fortification. Having lost money living at court, he hoped to rebuild his fortune by investing what was left in the Canadian enterprise.

In the king's letters patent of 15 January 1541 Roberval was instructed to go to the 'lands of Canada, Hochelaga and others circumjacent' and to organize them in the king's name provided none was occupied by the emperor, the king of Portugal or any other Christian prince. Although the religious aims of the expedition were restated, no particulars were given of any ecclesiastical personnel or institutions, a significant omission from a document otherwise rich in constitutional provisions. What the king had in mind was an occupation by peaceful means if possible, or by force if necessary. Once the country had been taken over, it was to be settled and organized; towns and forts were to be built, as well as temples and churches. As the king's lieutenant-general, Roberval was to exercise legislative and judicial powers, appoint to all offices and distribute lands as fiefs or lordships to noblemen ready to defend the country or as leasehold to persons of lower social status in return for annual rents. The profits of the expedition were to be divided into three parts: the first for the settlers, the second for Roberval and the third for the crown. It was intended that Roberval should be accompanied by noblemen, merchants and 'subjects of goodwill and of all qualities, arts and industry'.[30]

Cartier, in his commission, had been allowed to take fifty prisoners, except those convicted of heresy, *lèse-majesté* and false-coining, in addition to other 'subjects of goodwill'. But his efforts to recruit crews at Saint-Malo and other Breton ports met with stiff resistance, perhaps because word had passed around of the appalling hardships suffered by his men in the winter of 1536. By February 1541, however, after the king had intervened, preparations had reached an advanced stage. Roberval, too, was allowed to take prisoners under sentence of death, who were required to pay for their own transportation to Canada and their upkeep over two years.[31]

Cartier, who served under Roberval, left Saint-Malo first, on 23 May 1541, with five ships carrying several hundred men and enough supplies for two years. After a difficult crossing of the Atlantic, he rallied his fleet at Newfoundland and, on 23 August, returned to his old anchorage at Sainte-Croix. This, however, was unsuitable for Cartier's new fleet and numerous company; he moved, therefore, to a better site nine miles further up the St Lawrence. Here he established a settlement, called

30 *Ibid.*, pp. 178–85.
31 *Ibid.*, pp. 131–2, 153–4, 193, 199–202, 212–14, 228–30, 289–92.

Charles-Bourg-Royal (after the king's third son), and two forts. Meanwhile, two ships were sent back to France with reports for the king. The new settlement seemed all that the colonists could have wished for: as they set to work, they discovered iron, and, as they thought, gold and diamonds. Fruit trees abounded and vegetables prospered. But Cartier was anxious to reach Saguenay. On 7 September he made his way upriver in two boats to the island of Montreal. He managed to bypass two rapids, but before he could reach the third he was informed by Indians that the Ottawa was unnavigable. He then returned to Charles-Bourg, only to find that relations between his men and the Indians had become strained. Blame for this lay with the French, who, instead of returning the Indians' friendship, had exploited them and treated them cruelly. Consequently, the small French garrison found itself under attack almost daily. In May 1542 Cartier and his men left for France.[32]

Roberval, meanwhile, completed his preparations, but he was seriously delayed by lack of money. On 16 April he set sail from La Rochelle with three ships carrying about 200 men and women. At Newfoundland, on 8 June, they were surprised to see Cartier's ships heading for France. Roberval ordered him to return, but Cartier slipped away in the night, taking with him his valuable experience and help. Roberval pressed on none the less and, at the end of July, arrived at Charles-Bourg, which he rechristened France-Roy. He built two forts (the others having presumably been destroyed by the Indians) and, on 14 September, sent two ships home. As winter approached, Roberval tried to eke out his dwindling supplies by a system of rations; he also imposed a harsh discipline on his followers. For a time the Indians brought the colonists quantities of shad, but in the end they were overcome by scurvy, and at least fifty died before April 1543. By 5 June Roberval had only about a hundred men left. Taking seventy with him, he went upriver in eight boats. His objective, like Cartier's, was Saguenay. The journey proved hazardous. One boat overturned, drowning eight men, and the others failed to get past the Lachine rapids. Otherwise nothing is known about the expedition. It probably got no further than the Ottawa river. By the end of June Roberval had returned to his base.[33]

Meanwhile, Cartier's return to France had produced a bitter disappointment. The diamonds and gold he had brought back were tested and found to be worthless. Francis, who was again at war with the emperor, lost interest in the Canadian enterprise. He cut his losses by sending two ships to repatriate Roberval and the remnants of his colony in the autumn of 1543. Neither Cartier nor Roberval made any profit out

[32] *Les Français en Amérique*, pp. 187–97.   [33] *Ibid.*, pp. 201–7.

of their expeditions. Cartier let it be known that in addition to the king's subsidy he had spent 8,638 *livres* out of his own pocket; Roberval lost whatever fortune he had left.[34] But, if contemporaries viewed the Cartier–Roberval expeditions as a failure, modern opinion is more charitable. They were genuine pioneering attempts to settle Europeans well inside North America, and they yielded an important residue of experience and knowledge.[35] A tradition had also been created that not only the coastline sketched out by Verrazzano but also the interior explored by Cartier constituted a New France, which could still be occupied by France whenever she wished. As such, the Cartier–Roberval expeditions represented 'a standing challenge to the Spanish claim to a monopoly of rights to North America as a whole'.[36] If Cartier had failed to achieve any of the fundamental objectives he had set himself, he had nevertheless taken possession in Francis's name of a new territory and shown the way, which was to be followed successfully by Champlain in the seventeenth century.

[34] *Documents re. Cartier and Roberval*, pp. 480–4.
[35] Ramusio published accounts in Italian of the first two Cartier voyages (1556). A published map associated with Sebastian Cabot (1544) was the first to record something of the St Lawrence discoveries.
[36] Quinn, *North America*, p. 190.

22

The crown and the provinces

HOW ABSOLUTE was the monarchy of Francis I? Two sharply contrasted schools of thought exist on the question. 'Francis I and Henri II',
according to Pagès 'were as powerful as any other kings of France; it was
at the beginning of the sixteenth century that the absolute monarchy
triumphed.'[1] Imbart de La Tour believed that in 1519 'the whole nation
abdicated into the king's hands'. In his view the destruction of provincial
autonomy had begun under Louis XII and been completed by Francis.[2]
For Doucet, it was under Francis that 'a new system of government' was
set up, which, 'starting from the traditional and still feudal monarchy of
Louis XII, foreshadowed the absolute and centralized monarchy of the
following centuries'.[3] But Dognon warns us against confusing Francis's
reign with that of Louis XIV, 'for the old traditions did not give way so
easily to the new rules'.[4] Prentout is more emphatic still: 'absolute monarchy', he writes, 'if one must use this label, begins only with Louis XIV'.
Historians, he suggests, who take it back to Francis and beyond fail to
distinguish between the absorption of the great fiefs into the royal demesne and monarchical centralization; the two processes were separated
by several centuries, not merely forty years, as the partisans of an early
absolutism imply. They fail to see 'how long the kings had been obliged to
abstain from touching the form of the provinces, how long they had been
forced to respect the privileges of each estate and pays'. Prentout thinks a
more suitable label for the monarchy between 1285 and 1589 would be
'contractual'.[5] More recently, the American scholar J. Russell Major has
described it as 'popular and consultative'. It stressed legitimacy because of
its 'feudal-dynastic structure' and tolerated decentralization because of
the limitations on its power. Ultimately it depended more on popular

---

[1]   G. Pagès, *La monarchie d'Ancien Régime en France* (1946), p. 3.
[2]   Imbart de La Tour, i. 199–205.
[3]   Doucet, i. 3.
[4]   P. Dognon, *Les institutions politiques et administratives du Pays de Languedoc du
      XIIIe siècle aux Guerres de Religion* (Toulouse, 1895), p. 491.
[5]   H. Prentout, *Les Etats Provinciaux de Normandie* (Caen, 1925), ii. 469–74.

support than on military power and promoted the growth of representative institutions. Even under Francis, Major argues, 'the popular, consultative nature of the monarchy continued unmodified for the first third of the period and was only mildly altered thereafter'.[6] How far does an examination of the principal organs of provincial government support this view? We need to look at the governors, parlements and estates.

The governors

Of all the king's agents, the provincial governors were those whose character and functions were the least precisely defined.[7] There was much scope for confusion not only in respect of their titles but also of their actual number. In the early sixteenth century there were eleven governorships (*gouvernements*), corresponding roughly to the kingdom's border provinces. This was taken to mean that they had been set up originally to defend the kingdom, not to administer it. But this was wrong, for there had once been governorships in central France. Their disappearance may have been due to the creation of apanages that would have precluded royal representatives.[8] Be that as it may, Francis did not at first regard only the eleven border governorships as legitimate, for he created governors in Anjou (1516), Bourbonnais and Auvergne (1523) and La Rochelle and Poitou (1528).

Francis's governors were normally recruited from princes of the blood and members of the high nobility. They included his sons, François, Henri and Charles; his brothers-in-law, Charles d'Alençon and Henri d'Albret; his uncle, René of Savoy; his favourites, Bonnivet, Chabot and Montmorency. Jean de Laval, seigneur de Châteaubriant, and Jean de Brosse, duc d'Etampes, the husbands of Francis's two principal mistresses, succeeded each other as governors of Brittany. Odet de Foix, Jacques de Chabannes and Teodoro Trivulzio were marshals of France. The house of Bourbon was represented by Charles, the third duke; Charles and Antoine, ducs de Vendôme; and François I and II, comtes de Saint-Pol; and that of Guise by Claude, first duke of that name. Other well-known

---

[6] J. Russell Major, *Representative Institutions in Renaissance France, 1421–1559* (Madison, 1960), pp. 3–20, 126–44. In his *Representative Government in Early Modern France* (New Haven and London, 1980), Major argues (p. 179) that 'the liberal assumption that the kings and the estates were natural adversaries' must be abandoned. Their roles, he suggests, can be 'more aptly compared with those of the president and Congress of the United States. Disagreements between the two are frequent and at times one tries to dominate, but each accepts the existence of the other and makes no effort to destroy it.'

[7] Doucet, *Institutions*, i. 229–41.

[8] G. Zeller, 'Gouverneurs de provinces au XVIe siècle', *R.H.*, clxxxv (1939), p. 242.

names in the list are Artus Gouffier, the king's administrator during his minority, and Galiot de Genouillac, grand master of the artillery.[9] Francis, in short, ruled France through a network of 'viceroys' recruited among his relatives and close friends.

'Viceroy' is not too grand a term for a royal agent who, in the view of contemporaries, was closely identified with the monarch's own person and authority. Though never more than a commissioner appointed by the king and revocable at his pleasure, a governor was commonly accorded quasi regalian honours – for example, a canopy when he entered a town in his province for the first time. Local authorities were sometimes in doubt as to whether such a high honour should be accorded a governor, but Francis encouraged the practice: in 1531 he ordered the town council of Rouen to provide a canopy for the new governor (who was, admittedly, the Dauphin), and, in 1537, he requested one even for the governor's lieutenant.[10]

A governor was so often busy at court or fighting for the king that he seldom resided in his province. His local duties were performed by a lieutenant – usually a lesser nobleman or prelate – who was often appointed by the king. But the governor could do much for his province at a distance. He could, for example, ensure that the demands (*doléances*) of the local estates were given a favourable hearing by the king's council; hence the substantial gifts made by the estates of Languedoc (not usually noted for their generosity) to Montmorency that he might be 'all the more assiduous in recommending their affairs to the king'. A sort of contract, in fact, existed between the estates and the governor, which found expression in the annual gift he received from them and in the conditions attached to it.[11] In spite of his onerous ministerial duties, Montmorency never neglected his governorship. He kept up a regular correspondence with his lieutenant, Clermont, sent a trustworthy representative to each general assembly of the estates and received a duplicate of their *doléances*. The estates were dissuaded by Montmorency from incurring the expense of sending deputations to the king: they had only to write to him, he said, and they would find him as ready to answer their requests as 'a father would be to his children'. Nor was this a vain promise. Languedoc under his rule never had to support as many troops as other parts of the kingdom. But, of course, his influence was a two-edged weapon: it could also be used to promote royal centralization. Montmorency persuaded the estates to accept general legislation which he could not spare them. He frequently asked them to concede the king's demands 'liberally'. Refer-

[9]   R. R. Harding, *Anatomy of a Power Elite: The Provincial Governors of Early Modern France* (New Haven and London, 1978), pp. 221–7.
[10] *Ibid.*, pp. 11–13.   [11] Dognon, pp. 453–4.

ring to a subsidy for fortifications, he wrote: 'I will ensure that it is so well used that you will have no cause, as I hope, to regret its grant.' The king, as a result of Montmorency's tact and influence, invariably got his way. At the same time, the governor ensured that the affairs of Languedoc did receive attention in the king's council.[12]

The governor's presence at court also gave him unique opportunities of patronage which he might use to build up a powerful clientele within his province. This was made up of three main elements: the *compagnies d'ordonnances*, household officers and servants, and local gentlemen. No law stipulated that a governor had to be a captain of the *gendarmerie*, but all Francis's governors save one were captains. Though officially in the king's service and paid out of his treasury, the companies were tied to their captains, who controlled their recruitment and promotion within their ranks. The governor would also have a large private household capable of providing jobs for members of the local nobility and an education for their children. In time, their sons might serve in the governor's company. Most military offices in a province, such as the captaincies of forts, castles and towns, were in his gift.

A governor's powers as stated in his 'letters of provision' or commission were seldom clearly defined. While it was the custom for the commission to stress his military responsibilities (e.g. the security of the fortresses and frontiers, the supplying and disciplining of troops etc.), it also frequently contained a clause open to wider interpretation. In 1515, for example, Odet de Foix, governor of Guyenne, was instructed 'generally to do . . . in other things all that we would see and recognize as necessary to the good of ourselves and our affairs and useful to the commonwealth.'[13] This was tantamount to a general delegation of royal authority. But governors' commissions lacked uniformity. In drafting them, the king was more concerned, it seems, with particular circumstances than in maintaining a functional harmony among his senior provincial representatives.

A distinction needs to be drawn between a *gouverneur* and a *lieutenant-général*. Both titles were commonly given to the same person, but a *lieutenant-général* was not necessarily a *gouverneur*. The crown sometimes conferred exceptional powers on a great personage in an emergency. Such an appointment carried the title of *lieutenant-général*; it was always temporary, and the authority conveyed by it could extend over several provinces. In July 1536, for example, Cardinal du Bellay was appointed *lieutenant-général* of Paris and the Ile-de-France, in the absence of the governor, with powers to organize the defence of the

---

[12] *Ibid.*, pp. 454–6.   [13] *Ordonnances*, i. no. 5.

capital and other towns in the province. Contemporary chroniclers refer to him as *gouverneur*, but he quite clearly held a distinct commission, which had lapsed by the end of December.[14] In October of that same year, Cardinal Tournon was appointed *lieutenant-général* in Lyonnais, Auvergne, Dauphiné and five other provinces, covering in all not less than a third of the kingdom. He was empowered to pay the army, alienate royal lands up to a certain value and borrow in the king's name.[15] Two other examples of *lieutenants-généraux* are Henri d'Albret, appointed in 1543 in Guyenne, Poitou, Languedoc and Provence, and the Dauphin Henri, appointed in 1544 in the whole kingdom.

The governor was obviously a potentially dangerous institution. He might use his personal following within a province to undermine the crown's authority. With this danger in mind, Louis XII had attempted to restrict the powers of governors, but his law had not been strictly enforced. In May 1542 Francis annulled the powers of governors and lieutenants-general on the ground that they had become excessive, but his ordinance was nothing more than a polite means of depriving Anne de Montmorency of his governorship of Languedoc, for two days after its publication letters of confirmation were sent out to the other governors. Francis, it seems, was unwilling to inflict a public humiliation on his former chief minister: having excluded him from his court and council, he still needed to strip him of his provincial powers. By suspending all the governors and then restoring them, save Montmorency, he achieved his object with a minimum of offence to the constable's pride.[16]

A second ordinance in May 1545 limited the number of *lieutenants-généraux* and for the first time distinguished between border provinces and the rest. Provincial governors since the fifteenth century had assumed the title of *gouverneur et lieutenant-général* so as to be more easily distinguished from the *baillis* and *sénéchaux* who had usurped the title of *gouverneur*. This was clearly an abuse, since the title of *lieutenant-général* was sometimes conferred, as we have seen, on eminent persons charged temporarily with the administration of a province or group of provinces. The 1545 edict laid down that in future only the governors of border provinces would be entitled to call themselves *lieutenants-généraux*, but this rule was very soon broken.[17]

The provincial parlements

The provincial parlements developed out of the courts that had existed in

[14] *Ibid.*, viii. no. 750 and p. 134 n. 1.   [15] *Ibid.*, viii. nos. 756, 758.
[16] Isambert, xii. 779–80; Zeller, 'Gouverneurs', pp. 243–5.
[17] Isambert, xii. 892–3; Zeller, pp. 245–7.

the great fiefs before their absorption into the kingdom. Modelled on the Paris Parlement, they exercised a similar jurisdiction within their respective areas. At Francis's accession there were five provincial parlements: Toulouse, Bordeaux, Grenoble, Dijon and Aix. Normandy had a high court that had developed out of the old Exchequer, but it was Francis who turned it into a parlement in February 1515.[18] Brittany had Grands Jours, which met annually at fixed dates. This became permanent only in 1554. Two other provincial parlements were set up under Francis: at Dombes in 1523 and Chambéry in 1537. The principality of Dombes, situated within the Holy Roman Empire, was annexed by Francis in 1523 following the treason of the duc de Bourbon. It was never actually incorporated into the kingdom, and its parlement sat at Lyons. The parlement at Chambéry lasted till 1559, as long, that is, as the French occupation of Savoy.[19]

All these parlements claimed equality of authority and jurisdiction with that of Paris, but the latter had certain privileges not shared by the rest: it could admit office-holders, judge crimes committed by princes and turn itself into a court of peers. Each parlement was sovereign within its own territory in respect of the registration and publication of royal ordinances. Thus many laws which were applied in Paris were never registered by the parlement of Toulouse and were therefore not applied in Languedoc. Francis claimed absolute sovereignty over all the parlements: their role, he affirmed, was to administer justice, not to question royal decisions. But members of the parlements regarded themselves not only as supreme judges under the king but also as defenders of provincial rights and privileges. They consequently opposed the creation of offices and the imposition of extraordinary taxes. Often they were more successful in their opposition to the crown than the Parlement of Paris because of their distance from the centre of government. This caused delays in the sending of *lettres de jussion* and made the holding of *lits-de-justice* difficult, if not impossible. Yet the king could make life very difficult for a provincial parlement if he set his mind to it, as the parlement of Rouen discovered in 1540.

The magistrates of Rouen had an unsavoury reputation under Francis. It was said that they wore beards and dressed in a 'dissolute' manner, arrived late in court or suffering from hangovers, spent too much time playing tennis, cards or at dice, frequented bawdy houses, associated with people of low station, committed grave indiscretions, took bribes and allowed other improper considerations to affect their conduct as judges. The first president, Marcillac, complained in November 1539 that 'female suitors who lacked physical beauty were advised to bring with

---

[18]   C.A.F., v. 15756.   [19]   *Ibid.*, i. 1934; vi. 23138.

them beautiful girls or chambermaids when they called on magistrates concerned with their cases'. He warned his colleagues to mend their ways; otherwise, he said, 'the king, our sovereign lord, will be forced to intervene'.[20]

Having set up the parlement of Rouen, Francis was all the more put out by the reports of its disreputable activities. At a meeting of his council in 1527 he proposed that the councillors of Rouen be distributed among the other courts of the kingdom and replaced by members of other parlements. This was not followed up, but the parlement received a message from the king which it described as 'rough and strange'. No further action was taken until the chancellorship of Guillaume Poyet, who clashed with the court over several matters. One was its attempt to recover part of the inheritance of a certain Le Bailly, who had been condemned for forgery by the king's council; another was the parlement's opposition to the famous ordinance of Villers-Cotterêts. Whereas in Paris it had been registered within a month, at Rouen it met with innumerable delays and difficulties. More serious still was the parlement's deceitful omission of sixteen clauses, which it found unpalatable, from the ordinance when eventually it was registered on 16 June 1540.

On 4 August the parlement received a sinister command from the king. He forbade it to go into recess, saying that he would soon be coming to Rouen and would have important things to say to the court. The parlement accordingly remained in session and, fearing the worst, sent a deputation on 20 August to the chancellor, who had come ahead of the king. After reminding the representatives that the sovereign courts had been created as 'an example and a light to others', Poyet harshly criticized the conduct of the magistrates, both within and outside their court. Marcillac begged him not to listen to slanders and to placate the king's wrath. On 26 August, in a last-minute attempt to ward off disaster, the parlement hurriedly registered the whole of the Villers-Cotterêts ordinance. Nine days later it sent a deputation to the king at the palace of Saint-Ouen, but his message to them was hardly reassuring. 'I will go, Messieurs', he said, 'to see my parlement; the worthy (*gens de bien*) will be pleased and the unworthy displeased.' Next day the parlement gathered expecting a *lit-de-justice*, but the chancellor came instead of the king and delivered a speech lasting four hours in which he denounced the court's misdeeds. 'The king', he said, 'had planted a vineyard with choice plants; he had built a winepress nearby in anticipation of the harvest; but the vines had produced only wild and sour grapes.' On 10 September the magistrates were peremptorily summoned to the king's presence. With a

---

[20] A. Floquet, *Histoire du parlement de Normandie* (Rouen, 1840), i. 505–22.

stern countenance he declared that he was cancelling several of their recent *arrêts* and closing down the parlement till further notice. That same day the parlement surrendered its seal to the king, while letters patent announcing its suspension were posted up in Rouen.[21]

There was, however, too much crime in Normandy to allow a complete suspension of royal justice. The king consequently commissioned some of the Rouen magistrates – presumably the least objectionable ones – to continue judging criminal cases in the town, and others to hold Grands Jours at Bayeux. Grands Jours were commissions of *parlementaires* sent out from time to time to various parts of the kingdom so as to buttress the administration of justice and relieve the parlements of part of their heavy load of work. They usually comprised two chambers – one civil, the other criminal – and their venue, which was chosen by the king, varied according to circumstances.[22] The strengths and weaknesses of the system are well illustrated by the Grands Jours held at Bayeux in September 1540. The magistrates were given ample powers to deal with criminal matters, including heresy, and they got through an enormous amount of business in less than three months. The main causes of disorder they encountered were, in Pasquier's phrase, 'the unruly insolence of the nobility and the connivance of the local judges'. The situation was indeed so bad that the commissioners had to seek military backing from the governor's lieutenant, the archbishop of Rouen. Even so, their jurisdiction made only a limited impact, as many offenders had deserted the area as soon as the Grands Jours had been announced. Many executions consequently had to be carried out in effigy only: a life-size dummy of the condemned man, dressed in his own clothes, was hanged, beheaded or broken on the wheel. But the Grands Jours were not always so helpless: for example, they reformed religious houses and hospitals in the Cotentin and Bessin, where disorder was rife, and punished many royal officials guilty of corruption or negligence. The effects of the Grands Jours, however, were short-lived: by 1548 when they returned to Bayeux, Lower Normandy had reverted to the near anarchy of before 1540.[23]

The two commissions set up by Francis in September 1540 gave the Rouen *parlementaires* a chance to redeem themselves. On 7 January 1541 they got their reward. At a meeting in the palace at Rouen, the archbishop announced the king's decision to reopen the parlement in the light of their good work. Nine councillors, however, were excluded from the reprieve and examined by a royal commission. All save one were subsequently reinstated. The only exception, Antoine Le Marchant, was

---

21 B.N., MS. Dupuy 17, fol. 168b; Floquet, i. 522–35; ii. 1–15.
22 Doucet, *Institutions*, i. 217–20.
23 Floquet, ii. 16–42.

banished from the kingdom after a long imprisonment. The other magistrates were warned by the archbishop to perform their judicial duties diligently and fairly and to carry out the king's ordinances. He forbade them, in future, to allow the *procureur* of the provincial estates to 'contradict, discuss, deduce or allege anything against verification of the edicts'. The king, he added, would be keeping a close watch on them; those found wanting would be punished and the rest exalted.[24]

The provincial estates

The fact that Francis I never called a meeting of the Estates-General, the principal representative institution in France under the Ancien Régime, is itself a matter of considerable interest. It shows that he regarded them as both useless and dangerous and never found himself in a sufficiently weak position to be compelled to call them. The only time a meeting of the Estates-General was seriously considered during his reign was in 1525 during his captivity.[25] It was discussed by the Parlement, but fear was expressed that the people's representatives might be tempted to take the regent's place or control her actions too closely. The idea was consequently dropped, and the estates remained in abeyance till 1560, when a combination of religious unrest and royal bankruptcy forced Francis's grandson to call them.

In the absence of the Estates-General, the only national body remotely comparable to them which Francis summoned was the Assembly of Notables of 1527. This was officially described as a *lit-de-justice*, but it was unusual in several respects. Though it met in the Palais within the context of the Parlement, its membership was much wider than customary for a *lit-de-justice*. In addition to the normal attendance, Francis had summoned many churchmen, representatives of the provincial parlements and *baillis* and *sénéchaux*. Even the Parlement's barristers were allowed to attend. The assembly was thus a compromise between a *lit-de-justice* and the Estates-General. Its procedure was also tailored to circumstances. In no sense was it a truly representative body, for, unlike the Estates-General, it was not preceded by general elections. The important matters submitted to the notables would, in normal circumstances, have been decided by the king's council. The assembly was, in fact, a sort of enlarged royal council designed to give an appearance of national consultation.[26]

At the provincial level, of course, representative estates did exist in

---

[24] *Ibid.*, ii. 42–80.   [25] Doucet, ii. 98–9.
[26] Doucet, *Institutions*, i. 329–30. See also above, p. 215.

France in a large part of the kingdom. The principal *pays d'états* were Normandy, Languedoc, Dauphiné, Burgundy, Provence and Brittany. In most of them the three estates were represented, but they were not always chosen in the same way; nor was their role identical from one province to another. The clergy sat as landowners, not as representatives of the church, so as to avoid binding it to decisions taken by the estates. The nobles represented not only themselves but the rural population in general. As for the third estate, it consisted of urban representatives only. There were numerous local variations. In Normandy, for example, a complicated electoral system gave the third estate a numerical preponderance in the general assembly; in Languedoc a high proportion of nobles and clergy failed to attend, while the third estate was made up of representatives of municipal oligarchies; in Brittany and Provence the nobility tended to dominate the estates, the upper clergy seldom attended and the third estate was again restricted to urban oligarchs. None of the estates was democratic: the majority of the people, both rural and urban, had no voice.[27]

The estates depended for their existence on the king. He called them, fixed the date and place of their meeting, appointed their president and determined their agenda. His commissioners put forward his demands, negotiated with the delegates and met some of their requests. Usually the estates met once a year, but they could meet more often. In Normandy, for example, there were nearly always two under Francis and sometimes three meetings a year until 1528; thereafter there was only one each year except in 1544. The frequency of meetings was determined by the crown's fiscal needs.[28] In theory the voting of a subsidy was conditional: this at least was the theory in Languedoc before 1538. The royal commissioners were supposed to attend to the estates' 'very humble supplications' before supply (*octroi*) was granted. But the estates expected little of the commissioners; they knew that the only decisions that mattered were those taken by the king and his council, which invariably followed a grant by several months. In 1538 Francis refused to accept even the theory: he ordered his commissioners at the estates of Albi not to reply to their *doléances* before the *octroi* had been granted. The estates protested, then accepted a compromise. They drafted their *doléances* on the eve of the vote and sent them direct to the king, bypassing his commissioners. In September 1541 the estates of Montpellier were not allowed to send a deputy to the king until they had given their verbal consent to his demand for a subsidy. Even then he rejected six out of their seven demands.[29]

[27] Doucet, *Institutions*, i. 337–59.
[28] Prentout, *Les Etats Provinciaux de Normandie*, i. 256.
[29] Dognon, *Institutions du Languedoc*, pp. 574–5.

It has been argued that Francis, far from being absolute, treated the estates of Normandy 'in the same good-natured way as had his predecessors'.[30] It is true that in a formulary laying down the terms of their convocation he instructed his commissioners to ask them 'freely to grant' (*libérallement octroier*) the sum demanded by him. But what did this freedom amount to? Certainly not the freedom to refuse the *taille* or even to demand a reduction of the amount. The estates could only argue over demands for supplementary taxes or *crues*, usually to no effect. In 1516 a delegate said that nothing should be voted save in return for the abolition of all 'the innovations created since the start of the reign'. The 'innovations', however, remained and each year the estates voted for ever larger *crues*. In Languedoc the situation was much the same. The estates were sometimes able to delay a *crue*, but they were never able to avoid it completely or to reduce the amount. So predictable indeed was their compliance that the king and *généraux des finances* commonly assigned funds on a *crue* still to be voted by the estates.[31]

The estates frequently complained of some of the king's fiscal expedients, but seldom persuaded him to abandon them. In 1517, for example, he planned to extend the salt tax to the whole of Normandy. The estates protested, whereupon their spokesman, Arthur Fillou, was prosecuted for using words disparaging to the king. Francis dropped his proposal, it is true, but only for a time: in June 1546 the salt tax was restored. The same tax also caused trouble in Languedoc, where the estates claimed that in 1488 they had been promised that no such tax would be imposed without their consent. Francis acknowledged their privilege but violated it at the same time. In 1537 the *crue* on salt became permanent in Languedoc. Its purpose was allegedly to pay the wages of the sovereign courts, but, as the estates pointed out, they had already voted the *octroi* for this purpose. Francis, however, chose to ignore them.[32]

The creation of offices was a frequent source of trouble between the king and the estates. In 1543 Francis created a Chambre des Comptes at Rouen. The members were to buy their offices and receive their wages out

---

[30]　Prentout, ii. 473.

[31]　*Ibid.*, i. 257; Dognon, p. 504. In Dauphiné an extension of the administrative jurisdiction granted to the estates by Francis in 1537 and confirmed in 1542 did not result in a resurgence of provincial autonomy. As L. S. Van Doren shows ('War Taxation, Institutional Change and Social Conflict in Provincial France – The Royal *Taille* in Dauphiné, 1494–1559', *Proceedings of the American Philosophical Society*, cxxi, 1 (Feb. 1977), 94), 'the weight of the war levies during the 1540s and 1550s deepened divisions among and within the communities in ways that prevented the Estates from consolidating an effective defense of provincial liberties'.

[32]　Prentout, ii. 266–9; iii. 141–64; Dognon, pp. 519–20.

of a local tax on goods. The people of Rouen demanded a meeting of the estates, which the king conceded – one of the rare instances when the initiative came from them. On 5 April the royal commissioners announced that Francis was ready to drop the new chamber in exchange for a composition of 220,000 *livres* (100,000 more than he had expected to get from the sale of the offices concerned). In the end, they paid 246,875 *livres* for the chamber's suppression. In Languedoc, too, the estates found that the only way they could obtain the abolition of new offices harmful to existing local interests was by buying them up. They could not always be sure, however, that an office suppressed in this way would not reappear. Indeed, this often happened.[33]

It is a mistake to imagine that the king could not raise taxes within a *pays d'états* except with the consent of the people's representatives. In Languedoc the towns, clergy and nobility were all subjected to impositions quite regardless of the estates. Most towns were liable to taxation like the countryside: only Carcassonne was totally exempt and Toulouse and Narbonne partially so. Yet Francis imposed an additional tax on them called *solde des gens de pied*. The estates claimed exemption from it, whereupon the king accepted a composition from them in return for recognition of their privilege. Toulouse, however, was asked for a subsidy. Again the estates protested on the ground that it was not a 'ville franche', but the king would not give way. 'Where there is a profit to be made in Languedoc', he said, 'the people of Toulouse are always there; but where there is an obligation, they declare themselves exempt.' The *solde*, in fact, became a heavy burden on the town. The church, too, was roughly handled by Francis in spite of the estates' attempt to prevent it becoming 'taxable'. The king raised a whole series of tenths without the consent of either the estates or the assembly of the French church. Bishops were ordered to obtain the money direct from their clergy. As for the nobility, they had to suffer the feudal levy or *ban et arrière-ban*. They might be called up four or five times in a single year and kept under arms at their own expense for several months. The estates asked for the length of service to be restricted to forty days: in January 1544 it was fixed at three months within the kingdom and forty days outside. Commoners who owned noble fiefs, even very small ones, had to compound for military service.[34]

The burden of supporting military garrisons or troops passing through the province was a standing grievance with the estates of Languedoc. In 1522 Francis promised to reimburse the province what it had spent on his army, but he never kept his word. A year later, at the request of the

[33] Prentout, i. 275–8; Dognon, pp. 521–2.
[34] Dognon, pp. 524–32.

estates, he fixed a tariff for supplies bought by his troops. It was low enough, yet no attempt was made to enforce it. The estates did manage to obtain a reduction of the garrisons in the province, but their number rose again as soon as Montmorency had fallen from power. Attempts made by them to ensure a fair distribution of the burden of supporting the armies proved unworkable. Languedoc had to disburse considerable sums in 1536 for the camp at Avignon and in 1542 for the army besieging Perpignan. In neither case were the estates even consulted.

The amount of taxes actually voted by the estates is no sure guide as to the amount of money actually raised by the king within a province. On the basis of the accounts of a single *diocèse* in Languedoc it has been estimated that no less than two-fifths of the taxes raised were unknown to the estates.[35]

An examination of the relations between the crown and the estates purely in terms of fiscality could easily lead to the conclusion that the latter no longer had any significant role to play in the state. This, however, would be an overstatement. The *doléances* they submitted to the king's commissioners were not concerned exclusively with the defence of local privileges; they dealt with many administrative and economic matters about which no fundamental disagreement necessarily existed between them and the crown. It was, for example, mutually advantageous for corruption or negligence among royal officials to be brought to the notice of the central administration and punished. The estates might also have some useful suggestions to make regarding trade. The seriousness with which the government viewed such suggestions is attested by comments such as 'reasonable', 'granted', or 'they will have letters on this' to be found in the margins of the *doléances*. Yet it has to be said that under Francis the effectiveness of the estates was limited to matters of secondary importance to the crown; where its financial interest was at stake, they were virtually powerless.[36]

---

[35] *Ibid.*, pp. 534–44.

[36] *Ibid.*, pp. 577–80. While conceding that Francis was a 'strong' monarch who occasionally imposed his will on the estates, particularly in fiscal matters, Major argues that the reign failed to check the revival of the estates which, in his view, spanned the late fifteenth and sixteenth centuries. Francis, he writes (*Representative Government in Early Modern France*, p. 55), 'accepted the existence of the provincial and local estates, recognized their right to give consent to taxation and generally respected their privileges'. This is strictly true, but the king's official pronouncements cannot always be taken at their face value. His authoritarianism was widely recognized by contemporary observers, e.g. Prince Philip, writing to Charles V (25 Jan. 1547), states that Francis I ruled like a despot rather than a natural overlord, following his whim rather than his reason, and that the French people were willing to put up with anything. *C.S.P. Span.*, viii. no. 384, p. 552.

Royal legislation: the forest laws and the ordinance of
Villers-Cotterêts

An important test of royal absolutism is the effectiveness of royal legislation. All too often this is dealt with only in terms of acceptance or
resistance by the parlements; but one should also consider how far the
law, once accepted, was actually enforced. This, of course, is a more
difficult question to answer, owing to the infinite number of variables
involved. Two sets of royal legislation under Francis offer some scope for
a brief excursus into the murky waters of enforcement: the forest laws
and the ordinance of Villers-Cotterêts of August 1539.

Francis was passionately interested in the forests of his kingdom. As a
keen sportsman, he wanted to conserve the natural habitat of the deer,
wild boar and lesser game which he and the nobility so loved to slaughter.
Thus his first forest ordinance of March 1516 was principally aimed at
suppressing the hunting rights of commoners. It laid down draconian
penalties, including death, for various sorts of poaching in the royal
forests, renewed the ban on hunting by commoners and authorized nobles
to adopt its provisions in respect of their own forests. The parlements
were displeased: they held up the ordinance, but eventually had to give
way. It came into force, but offences against the game laws continued, so
that the king had to tighten up supervision of the forests themselves. In
1538 he transferred the responsibility for enforcing the game laws from
the Grand Maître des Eaux et Forêts and his staff to the *prévôts des
maréchaux*. At the same time, he tried to unify the game laws throughout
his kingdom. On discovering in August 1533, during his progress in the
Midi, that an ancient privilege of Languedoc allowed commoners to hunt,
he promptly abolished it, but this provoked such opposition from the
parlement of Toulouse that the privilege was restored in October 1535
except in respect of deer, boar, herons, pheasants and quail.[37]

Hunting apart, the 1516 ordinance did little to protect the forests from
the erosion which caused many people at the time to fear for their
survival. Two new ordinances, in March 1517 and January 1519, tried to
redress the situation: the first regulated sales of wood and the second
defined and rationalized penalties against the forest laws. At the same
time royal commissioners were sent out with a view to recovering parts of
the royal forests that had been usurped and restricting their privileges.
They imposed heavy fines for offences against the forest laws, bringing a
significant income into the royal treasury, and helped increase the revenue
from the forests themselves by resuming land they had lost. Such was the

---

[37] *Ordonnances*, i. no. 80; M. Devèze, *La vie de la forêt française au XVIᵉ siècle* (1961), i.
64–8, 70–1.

profitability to the crown of the forest eyres that, after 1535, many
seigneurs invited the royal commissioners to extend their operations to
their own forests. In this way the forest laws came to be widely applied in
the kingdom, displacing the old variegated customs.

The eyres were but one aspect of Francis's forest administration. As in
other areas of government, his reign was marked by a sizable increase in
the number of office-holders, particularly after 1535. The motive for this
change was, as usual, fiscal, but it was also beneficial to the forests, where
the increase in the number of royal foresters led to a distinct improvement
in conservation, which, in turn, was reflected in a rise in the crown's forest
revenues. In spite of local resistance, the forest laws were certainly
applied: it was largely thanks to the crown's timely intervention that
several forests were saved from destruction and others reinstated.[38]

Probably the most important royal ordinance issued by Francis was
that of Villers-Cotterêts of 30 August 1539, for which Chancellor Guillaume Poyet was mainly responsible.[39] It is best remembered for 4 of its
192 clauses: that French instead of Latin be used in legal documents, that
registers of births and deaths be kept by all parish priests, that in a
criminal case the accused be denied counsel and that all confraternities be
abolished. The main purpose of the act, as stated in its preamble, was the
reform of the judicial system. The use of French in legal documents was
aimed at avoiding retrials by eradicating from judgments all 'ambiguity,
uncertainty or reason to demand an interpretation'. Likewise, the registration of births and deaths was intended to facilitate the verification of
the rights of parties to a lawsuit. The denial of counsel and retention of the
use of torture – measures much criticized even at the time – were intended
'to shorten proceedings' rather than merely to harass the accused and
render him defenceless.[40] But how generally was the ordinance applied? A
full reply to this question would require a detailed investigation of the
judicial process in the period after 1539. All that can be suggested here are
some doubts in respect of three of its provisions: the registration of births
and burials, the use of French in legal documents and the abolition of
confraternities.

Clause 50 of the ordinance demanded that registers be kept of all
benefice-holders, and, so that the age of their majority might be established, clause 51 prescribed the registration of all baptisms with an
indication of the date and time of birth. The accuracy of the information

38 *Ordonnances*, ii. nos. 108, 181; Devèze, i. 75–171.
39 Isambert, xii. 592–640.
40 J. H. Langbein, *Prosecuting Crime in the Renaissance* (Cambridge, Mass., 1974),
    pp. 246–7. Cf. A. Esmein, *A History of Continental Criminal Procedure*, tr.
    J. Simpson (London, 1914), pp. 148–74.

provided was to be guaranteed (clause 53) by the signatures of a notary and parish priest or his vicar-general. Each year the registers were to be submitted to the *greffe* of the nearest court of the *bailli* or *sénéchal*. In the Nantes region such registers had been kept since the early fifteenth century at the instance of the local ecclesiastical authorities. As for the detailed provisions of the ordinance, they seem to have been ignored. No evidence exists of the registers having been submitted to the *greffe* of the *bailliage*. Only within Nantes itself were they signed by a notary, and this was mainly in the second half of the century. As for the date and time of birth, they went unrecorded. In short, the ordinance was followed only in so far as it endorsed existing routine.[41]

As for the use of French in legal documents (clause 111), the evidence of parish registers in the Nantes area again suggests a local response to royal legislation that was less than immediate or comprehensive. In both urban and rural parishes the use of Latin actually increased from the end of the fifteenth century till about 1550, perhaps as a consequence of an overall improvement in clerical education. Thereafter French took precedence in the urban parishes, but Latin survived in the rural ones till the early seventeenth century. It cannot be assumed, therefore, that the ordinance of Villers-Cotterêts led to the immediate adoption of French for legal records throughout the kingdom.[42]

The ordinance appears to have been even less effective in regard to the confraternities (clause 185). These were associations of masters, apprentices and journeymen formed principally for religious and charitable purposes: they arranged masses and memorial services, provided aid for their less fortunate members and threw banquets which sometimes gave offence to the ecclesiastical authorities by turning into orgies. Confraternities, especially those limited to journeymen, were also frowned upon by the state, as they provided a focus for political and religious dissent. Indeed, the decision to ban them was almost certainly prompted by a strike of journeyman printers in Lyons in April 1539, which had caused the local *sénéchal* to ban all gatherings of more than five journeymen. This decision was endorsed by the king on 21 August, ten days before the Villers-Cotterêts ordinance was issued. Neither measure succeeded in restoring good industrial relations in Lyons. As for the confraternities, they too survived. Although in Paris their property was seized by the *prévôt*, some reappeared soon afterwards. The Parisian clothworkers, for example, had their confraternity reprieved in April 1541, and other trades subsequently obtained similar concessions. In 1561 confraternities were reminded by the government that their funds should

[41] A. Croix, *Nantes et le Pays nantais au XVIe siècle* (1974), p. 24.
[42] *Ibid.*, pp. 30–1.

be used only for charitable and religious purposes, a clear enough indication of their survival.[43]

Historians who have attempted to characterize the monarchy of Francis I fall into two camps: those whose standpoint has been from the centre of the kingdom, looking outwards, and those who have approached it from the periphery. The first have seen it as 'absolute', and the second as 'contractual' or 'popular and consultative'. Both views deserve serious consideration. Francis's monarchy was limited by the substructure of medieval privilege on which it was built. Royal legislation was subject to ratification by the parlements, and, in the *pays d'états*, royal taxation was subject, in theory at least, to the consent of the people's representatives. The enforcement of the law depended on a willingness to obey not always evinced by local authorities. The testimony of the Grands Jours of Bayeux shows that even in an area fairly near Paris law and order had largely broken down by 1540. However ineffective the provincial estates may have been in resisting the crown's fiscal pressure, they nevertheless managed to survive. Clearly, a monarchy whose effectiveness was subject to so many practical limitations cannot be called 'absolute'. But can it be called 'contractual' if local privileges are repeatedly flouted, or 'popular and consultative' if the bulk of the population is unrepresented and consultation is nothing more than a sham designed to give respectability to preordained policies?

If constitutional labels are to mean anything at all, they ought surely to take into account not only the realities of power but also the intentions of the ruler. Did Francis I show respect for local autonomy, or did he work for administrative uniformity throughout his kingdom? Many of his statements, notably the angry outbursts he addressed to the parlements, reveal an uncompromisingly authoritarian disposition, bent on centralization. When the estates of Languedoc claimed the right of exemption from the garrisoning of troops, he replied: 'this kingdom is one body and monarchy'. All his subjects, he said, should be treated alike, since he esteemed and loved them all equally; the exemption of some would mean that others would have to carry a proportionately heavier burden. On another occasion he declared: 'in times of necessity all privileges cease, and not only privileges but common laws as well, for necessity knows no law'. The estates certainly did not see him as a 'contractual' monarch: they complained in 1522 that he was treating them 'as if they had never had nor acquired the said privileges'.[44] True, he did sometimes bargain

---

43   H. Hauser, *Ouvriers du temps passé* (1927), pp. 161–7, 177–234; N. Z. Davis, 'A Trade Union in Sixteenth-Century France', *Econ. H.R.*, xix (1966), 48–69.
44   Dognon, *Institutions du Languedoc*, pp. 576–7.

with them, but only over the means to raise a sum, not over the sum itself. He did not mind suppressing offices as long as he received as much money in compensation for their suppression as he would have got from their sale. In all matters other than fiscal, his policy was less systematic. The estates could always hope for a reversal in their favour, but in the long term royal policy seriously undermined provincial autonomy. Francis's political philosophy is best summed up by Poyet's words to the parlement of Rouen in 1540: 'The king is not asking for advice as to whether or not they [his laws] are to be observed; once the prince has decreed them one must proceed; no one has the right to interpret, adjust or diminish them.'[45] Can a monarchy holding such views be deemed 'contractual' or 'popular and consultative'? 'Absolutism' in the seventeenth-century sense of the word cannot be said to have been achieved in Francis's reign, but his actions and some of his pronouncements certainly pointed in that direction.[46]

[45] Floquet, *Parlement de Normandie*, ii. 9.
[46] The total number of fiscal and judicial office-holders under Francis has been estimated at 5,000: i.e. one per 115 square kilometres or per 3,000 inhabitants (assuming a total population of 15 million). Louis XIV had eleven times as many servants to impose his will on his 20 million subjects. J. Jacquart, *François 1er* (1981), pp. 282–3.

23

The last war

(1542–6)

AFTER DECLARING war on the emperor in July 1542 Francis launched
an offensive on two fronts simultaneously: in the north an army officially
led by his younger son, Charles d'Orléans, captured Luxemburg, while in
the south a much larger one, under the Dauphin and Marshal d'Annebault, laid siege to Perpignan. Francis himself took no part in the fighting.
He went to Lyons early in August; then, leaving his council behind,
travelled down the Rhône to Avignon. On 22 August he arrived at
Montpellier, and on the following day the Dauphin launched an assault
on Perpignan, but the town was too well defended. The French assault
was beaten off by a fierce artillery barrage, and the king ordered his army
to retreat. Meanwhile, in the north Luxemburg was recaptured by the
imperialists after Orléans had gone south to join his brother. Thus on
both fronts the French offensive had failed miserably.[1] As winter
approached Francis gathered up his forces in the south and sent them to
reinforce the French garrisons in Piedmont, while he himself went to La
Rochelle to put down the revolt over the *gabelle*.[2] Early in January he
began to travel back to Fontainebleau, hunting all the way. Serious
business, however, was not neglected. It was at this time that the French
government took a large number of steps to raise revenue for another
military campaign in the summer.[3] Meanwhile, a new coalition was being
formed between the king of England and the emperor.

Relations between France and England had been deteriorating for some
time. Henry VIII was annoyed by Francis's failure to keep up payments of
his pension and other obligations under past treaties. Maritime disputes
between the two countries were another source of friction, as was Scotland, where the defeat of James V at Solway Moss and his death soon
afterwards paved the way for a bitter struggle for power between the
pro-French faction, led by Cardinal Beaton, and the pro-English one, led
by the earl of Angus. For James's successor, Mary Stuart, was an infant,
and the earl of Arran, who was governor of the realm, was weak. In July

---

[1] *L.P.*, xvii. 755, 838; du Bellay, iv. 63–6, 73, 75, 79–81.
[2] See below, ch. 24.   [3] *Ibid.*

Henry scored a notable success by persuading the Scots to sign the treaties of Greenwich, which provided for the betrothal of their young queen to his own son, Prince Edward. Before the end of the year, however, the Scots had repudiated the treaties and renewed their league with France.[4]

On 11 February Henry made a secret alliance with the emperor, which provided for a joint invasion of France within two years, and soon afterwards he recalled his ambassador, William Paget, from the French court.[5] Francis was appalled. He tried to detain Paget and urged him to intercede with Henry on his behalf. Maritime disputes, he said, were but trifles which could easily be overcome. 'If my good brother will join with me', he told Paget, 'tell him I will stick upon no money matters, he shall rule me as he list.'[6] The last thing Francis wanted was an English invasion of northern France just as he was preparing to deal the emperor another blow. But Henry was determined: at the end of May he and the emperor sent heralds to the king of France with an ultimatum threatening war within twenty days unless impossible conditions were met. Francis, however, refused a safe-conduct to the imperial herald. The ultimatum therefore had to be delivered to the French ambassador in England. On 22 June, as the deadline expired, England and the empire declared war on France, and soon afterwards an English expeditionary force under Sir John Wallop entered the Boulonnais from Calais, destroying villages in its path.[7]

By this time fighting had flared up along the borders of Artois and Hainault. The moment seemed opportune for a French offensive, as many imperial troops had been withdrawn from the area to fight France's ally, William, duke of Cleves, who, after capturing Guelders, had invaded Brabant. In April the duc de Vendôme, who commanded the French army in Picardy, revictualled Thérouanne and captured Lillers, but Francis did not launch his main offensive until June, when an army under Annebault captured Landrecies. But instead of pushing forward vigorously to help the duke of Cleves, Francis withdrew to the neighbourhood of Rheims, where he went hunting while thinking about his next move.[8] This lull in the French offensive left the duke in an extremely perilous situation, for the emperor had been mustering an army in the Rhineland. In August Charles invaded the duchy of Jülich, capturing Düren after a brief siege. Francis decided that the best way to help his ally was to recapture

[4] L.P., xvii. 185, 1144, 1159, 1220, 1236; L.P., xviii (pt 1), 804; (pt 2), 481, 499; C.A.F., iv. 13490.
[5] L.P., xviii (pt 1), 144, 182.
[6] Ibid., 217.   [7] Ibid., 622, 707, 754.
[8] Du Bellay, iv. 124–32, 134–44. Twice during April Francis reported to the Parlement victories by the duke of Cleves. A.N., X^{1a} 1550, fols. 355b–356a, 397b–398a.

Luxemburg, but his timing was at fault. Three days before Luxemburg fell to the duc d'Orléans and Annebault (10 September), the duke of Cleves had been forced to submit to the emperor at Venloo. In return for the emperor's pardon he had given up Zutphen and Guelders, renounced his allies and reverted to the Catholic faith.[9] His capitulation inevitably destroyed the political *raison d'être* of his marriage to Francis's niece, Jeanne d'Albret, and Marguerite de Navarre promptly urged her brother to break it off. The marriage was, in fact, annulled by the pope in April 1545 after some prickly negotiations, and Duke William fittingly remarried the emperor's niece.[10]

Though strongly advised to withdraw from Luxemburg, as it was inaccessible to supplies, Francis refused on the ground that it formed part of his inheritance. He ordered Philibert Babou to mobilize supplies for the town and went there himself to celebrate the feast of St Michael on 28 September.[11] But he soon had to face up to realities, for news reached him that the emperor was marching on Landrecies. After returning to Coucy with the bulk of his army, Francis advanced on 28 October to the outskirts of Landrecies, which was already under siege and being pounded by the enemy's guns. That night Francis fired his own artillery to let the enemy know of his approach. This had the desired effect: the emperor drew back, and Saint-Pol and Annebault were able to relieve the beleaguered garrison, an event that caused much jubilation in France. The emperor then tried to engage Francis in battle, but on the night of 4 November the king slipped away quietly; soon afterwards he put his army into winter quarters at Saint-Quentin. Charles, for his part, retreated northwards and rounded off the unification of the Netherlands by seizing Cambrai. As for the English expeditionary force under Wallop, it returned to Calais in November after taking part in the siege of Landrecies.[12]

The Franco-Turkish alliance

Meanwhile, unusual events had been taking place in the Mediterranean area. In April, following two missions to the Porte by Baron de La Garde, the sultan informed Francis that he was placing Barbarossa's fleet at his disposal for the coming season. The fleet, including 110 galleys, left the Dardanelles with the French ambassador on board, and after raiding the coasts of Sicily and Italy (but not the States of the Church, allegedly at

9   *L.P.* xviii (pt 2), 143.
10 P. Jourda, *Marguerite d'Angoulême* (1930), i. 281–2.
11 Du Bellay, iv. 158–61.
12 *L.P.*, xviii (pt 2), 341, 346; du Bellay, iv. 185–7.

Francis's request) it appeared off Marseilles in early July, to a warm welcome by François de Bourbon, comte d'Enghien, who commanded the French Mediterranean fleet. Having recently suffered a rebuff at the hands of Andrea Doria during a surprise attack on Nice, he eagerly grasped the opportunity of adding the Turkish fleet to his own in order to accomplish his purpose. On 6 August the two fleets appeared off Nice, and, on the following day, the Turks landed troops and artillery at Villefranche. For the next two weeks Nice was bombarded from land and sea, and repulsed three assaults. On 22 August the town surrendered, but its castle held out until 8 September, when the besiegers, hearing that an army under the duke of Savoy and the marquis del Vasto was approaching, lifted the siege. Before retiring to Antibes, however, they set fire to half the town.[13]

The sight of Christians fighting Christians with the help of Infidels was shocking enough to many people at the time, but there was worse to come. On 6 September Barbarossa threatened to leave unless Francis gave him the means to refit and revictual his fleet. Rather than lose his naval superiority, the king placed the port of Toulon at the disposal of his ally. All the inhabitants, except 'heads of households', were ordered to leave with their belongings on pain of death so as to make way for Barbarossa's men. By way of compensation they were given ten years' exemption from the *taille*.[14] Toulon consequently became a Turkish colony for eight months, each of Barbarossa's captains being given a house for himself, his servants and slaves. Turks who could not be accommodated within the town (they numbered about 30,000 altogether) were allowed to pitch tents outside. Neighbouring villages provided them with food. The transformation of a Christian town into a Moslem one, complete with mosque and slave market, did not fail to amaze those who witnessed it. They were also unanimous in their praise of the strict discipline of the Turks, which contrasted favourably with the manners commonly displayed by Christian armies.[15]

On the surface, relations between the French and the Turks were amicable enough. Barbarossa received a gift of silver plate and a clock from the king of France, and his captains also benefited from the king's largesse. But Francis suspected Barbarossa of having a secret understanding with Doria and instructed La Garde to keep him under close watch.

[13] Du Bellay, iv. 132–4; C. de La Roncière, *Histoire de la marine française* (1899–1932), iii. 376–84.
[14] J. J. Champollion-Figeac, *Documents historiques inédits sur l'histoire de France tirés des collections manuscrites de la Bibliothèque Royale* (4 vols., 1841–8), iii. 559; C.A.F., iv. 13481.
[15] La Roncière, iii. 386–7.

He also began to find the Turkish presence on French soil embarrassing, since it earned him universal opprobrium and many complaints from his Provençal subjects. He was much relieved, therefore, to regain possession of Toulon in May 1544, but this was at a price. Before departing, Barbarossa asked for all Turkish and Barbary corsairs serving on French galleys to be handed over to him so that he might relieve his own crews. He also revictualled his fleet by ransacking five French ships in Toulon harbour.[16]

Barbarossa left Toulon on 23 May accompanied by six French galleys under La Garde and Leone Strozzi, who had to witness some harrowing scenes as the Turks ravaged islands and coastal towns in the kingdom of Naples, carrying off their inhabitants into slavery. Eventually the small French squadron broke free, but, instead of returning to Provence, it proceeded eastwards, calling at Delos, Troy and other ancient sites in Greece and Asia Minor. On 10 August it sailed triumphantly into the Bosphorus and was treated to a most cordial reception by the sultan.[17]

The Anglo-imperial invasion of France (1544)

In November 1543 Pope Paul III sent Cardinal Farnese on a peace mission to the French and imperial courts. But, if Francis seemed willing to listen to the nuncio, Charles told him bluntly that he was unwelcome and rejected all his proposals.[18] On 31 December the emperor and Henry VIII signed a treaty in which they agreed to invade France in person before 20 June. Charles was to invade Champagne, and Henry, Picardy; and the two armies, each consisting of 35,000 foot and 7,000 horse, were then to converge on Paris.[19] But before the treaty could be put into effect Henry had to ensure that the Scots would not invade his kingdom while his back was turned. He therefore dispatched a force under Hertford to Scotland with instructions to burn down Edinburgh, sack Leith and turn St Andrews upside down so that 'the upper stone might be the nether, and not one stick stand by another'. By 15 May Hertford was able to assure his master that the Scots would never recover from the mischief done to them nor be able to raise an army that year.[20] Meanwhile, the emperor presided over a meeting of the imperial diet at Speyer and persuaded the German princes to give him military and financial aid against the Turks and the French. Francis had hoped to defend his policy at the diet, but his

[16] *Ibid.*, iii. 390; J. Ursu, *La politique orientale de François Ier* (1908), p. 150.
[17] La Roncière, iii. 390–5.
[18] *L.P.*, xix (pt 1), 20, 31, 64.
[19] *L.P.*, xviii (pt 2), 526.
[20] *L.P.*, xix (pt 1), 314, 508, 510.

ambassadors were refused a safe-conduct. A French herald who dared to go to Speyer without one was unable to accomplish his mission and was sent home after being told that he deserved to be hanged.[21]

Meanwhile, in Piedmont the French scored a notable victory, though not a particularly significant one in the long term. In January Enghien, after becoming lieutenant-general in Piedmont, had laid siege to Carignano. As del Vasto marched to its relief, Enghien sent a messenger to Francis with a request for permission to engage the enemy in battle. According to Blaise de Monluc, he himself was the messenger and it was thanks to his Gascon eloquence that the battle was fought. Francis's councillors had grave misgivings about risking a battle in Italy when northern France was threatened with invasion. But an impassioned plea by Monluc won the king over to the opposite view; throwing his bonnet on the table, he exclaimed: 'Let them fight! let them fight!' As news of the king's decision filtered through the court, many young noblemen set off for Italy in search of military glory. True or false, Monluc's account offers a unique glimpse of the king's council in session, with the Dauphin standing behind the king's chair, laughing and egging on the messenger.[22]

The battle, which was fought at Ceresole (in French, Cérisoles) on 14 April, began so badly for the French that Enghien allegedly tried to commit suicide, but the tide suddenly turned in their favour, and in the end victory was theirs. Enghien, however, failed to follow it up (partly because some of his best troops were recalled to France), and its effect was to a large extent cancelled out by the defeat inflicted by the prince of Salerno at Serravalle on 4 June on Piero Strozzi and the count of Pitigliano, who had been commissioned by Francis to raise troops in Italy.[23]

By this time preparations for the Anglo-imperial invasion of northern France were complete. In May 1544 the emperor had two armies ready: the first under Ferrante Gonzaga, viceroy of Sicily, lay to the north of Luxemburg; the other, under Charles himself, waited in the Palatinate. On 25 May Gonzaga easily recaptured Luxemburg, which had run out of supplies. He then advanced swiftly southwards, taking Commercy and Ligny, and on 1 July issued a proclamation to the effect that the emperor was making war not to dismember France but to rid her of a tyrant who was the ally of the Turks. On 8 July Gonzaga laid siege to Saint-Dizier, where the emperor joined him a few days later with the rest of the imperial army.[24]

[21] *Ibid.*, 132, 137, 160, 167.
[22] B. de Monluc, *Commentaires*, ed. P. Courteault (1911–25), i. 239–50; P. Courteault, *Blaise de Monluc historien* (1908), pp. 152–5.
[23] Courteault, pp. 155–71. Cf. du Bellay, iv. 196–235.
[24] C. Paillard, *L'invasion allemande en 1544* (1884), pp. 32–119.

Henry VIII, in the meantime, sent a huge army to Calais under the dukes of Norfolk and Suffolk. After penetrating France, it divided into two parts: the first, under Norfolk, laid siege to Montreuil, while the second, under Suffolk, besieged Boulogne. On 14 July Henry himself crossed the Channel and assumed command of the latter. The imperialists complained that the king, by allowing himself to get bogged down in two sieges near the Channel coast, was breaking his agreement with Charles and that he should have marched straight on Paris. Henry retorted that, unless Montreuil and Boulogne were taken, an advancing army could not be supplied. This, however, was an excuse: Henry was only interested in seizing a piece of French soil near Calais. He was not sorry to see his imperial ally held up at Saint-Dizier, for this gave him an excuse to stay put.[25]

Until the first week of July all had gone well for the emperor. But Saint-Dizier proved a tougher nut to crack than any he had so far encountered. It had been fortified by Girolamo Marini, one of the best military engineers of the time, and was bravely defended by a garrison under the comte de Sancerre and Captain Lalande. On 24 July an imperial force managed to capture Vitry, whence the French had been harassing the besiegers of Saint-Dizier, but this failed to break the spirit of its defenders.[26] On 8 August, however, as their ammunition began to run out, they sought honourable terms from the emperor. It was agreed that unless they received help within seven days they would be allowed to leave with banners unfurled and two guns of their choice. The seven days passed without help reaching them; on 17 August, therefore, they capitulated.[27]

The siege of Saint-Dizier, which had lasted forty-one days, broke the impetus of the imperial invasion. On 21 August the emperor held a council of war to decide whether to march on Paris or to retreat. Some of

---

[25]   J. J. Scarisbrick, *Henry VIII* (London, 1968), pp. 446–8.

[26]   Vitry-en-Perthois occupied an important strategic position near the junction of the rivers Saux and Marne. It was destroyed by Charles V's army on 27 July 1544. Francis decided to rebuild it on another site further south better suited to contemporary military conditions. Special privileges granted to the settlers included twenty years' exemption from the *taille*, three annual fairs and a market each week. *C.A.F.*, iv. 14422, 14465. The plan of Vitry-le-François, as the new town was called, was the work of Girolamo Marini, a Bolognese engineer. It consisted of a square of 612 metres per side, divided into sixteen compartments by six main roads, three in each direction crossing at right angles. Each compartment was subdivided by a smaller street. A large square in the centre of the town offered scope for military displays. P. Lavedan, *Histoire de l'urbanisme* (1941), pp. 76–81.

[27]   Paillard, pp. 119–260; A. Rozet, and J.-F. Lembey, *L'invasion de la France et le siège de Saint-Dizier par Charles-Quint en 1544* (1910), pp. 60–156. For the king's reports to the Parlement on the siege, see A.N., X^{1a} 1553, fols. 249b, 328a.

his captains advised retreat, for the fighting season was well advanced and the army was short of provisions, but politically there was much to be said in favour of pressing on. Charles wanted to show Henry that he at least was sticking to his side of the invasion plan. He also wanted to frighten Francis into accepting a peace on his own terms, and thought a retreat at this stage would harm his prestige internationally At the end of August, therefore, the imperial army advanced to the neighbourhood of Châlons. But Charles was deterred from crossing the Marne by the French army, which had taken up a strong position at Jâlons, on the left bank. Nor did he try to capture Châlons, which might have held him up even more than Saint-Dizier had done. Instead, he captured Epernay, where the French had gathered a large stock of provisions. As the imperialists marched on through Champagne, capturing Châtillon-sur-Marne, Château-Thierry and Soissons, foreign observers were astonished at the inactivity of the French king. 'Who ever would have thought', exclaimed the Venetian ambassador, 'that the French would allow the invaders free passage and let them devastate their country!'[28]

There was panic in the capital as the imperial army drew closer. On 1 September all the religious houses in Paris and its suburbs were ordered by the Parlement to hold processions and celebrate masses for the peace of Christendom. Nine days later three presidents of the court called on Francis at the Louvre. He assured them that, as Paris was the capital of his kingdom and he was its head, he had come to defend it himself, being resolved to live and die there. In spite of the emperor's advance, he said, Parisians had nothing to fear. He ordered the Parlement to administer justice as usual, adding that within a few days he hoped to inflict shame and confusion on the enemy. Francis also commanded that the city's gates and shops, which had been shut, should be reopened. He then left the room before the presidents could reply. Turning to Tournon, they asked him to explain to the king that justice could not be administered as usual, since many barristers and solicitors had already fled from the capital. Tournon replied that he did not think Francis expected the impossible from them; he would be satisfied if they did their best so as to avoid panic among the proletariat (*petit peuple*).[29]

Francis, in fact, did almost nothing to hamper the imperial advance or even its retreat after Charles had decided, on 11 September, to abandon his march on Paris. But for a cavalry skirmish near Soissons in which more than a hundred Spaniards were taken prisoner, the French made no move against the imperialists after the fall of Saint-Dizier; they were content simply to cover their movements from the left bank of the Meuse.

[28] Rozet and Lembey, p. 178.
[29] A.N., X¹ᵃ 1553, fols. 447b, 487a–b.

Francis's strategy, perplexing as it may have been to contemporaries, was sensible: he was fighting a war on two fronts; if he had lost a battle in Champagne the consequences for his kingdom could have been disastrous. By holding his main army in reserve for the defence of the capital, he kept the allies apart and even split them up.

Ever since the invasion began Francis had been putting out unofficial peace feelers in the hope of detaching at least one of the parties to the Anglo-imperial coalition. Henry would listen to no overtures until he had captured Boulogne, an objective which was not achieved until 13 September. The emperor, on the other hand, had shot his bolt. Having captured Saint-Dizier, an achievement which fell far short of his original aim, his one idea was to pull out of the war in order to tackle the religious situation in Germany. A formula for the pacification of that country had been advanced at the diet of Speyer, but the Catholics had rejected it at the eleventh hour and the whole matter had been postponed until another diet, due to meet at Regensburg in October. The emperor was also short of money. On 20 June he had informed his sister that his means would not last beyond 25 September.[30] It was Charles, therefore, not Henry, who first wavered in response to Francis's overtures. The opening moves were made, early in August, by Gabriel Guzman, a Dominican in the service of Queen Eleanor, who visited the imperial camp several times. Then, on 29 August, plenipotentiaries from both sides met for the first of a series of meetings. Soon afterwards, the emperor sent the bishop of Arras to Henry with a request that the king must either help him by marching at once into France or allow him to come to terms with the French. But Charles did not even wait for the bishop's return to conclude with Francis. On 18 September the treaty of Crépy-en-Laonnais was signed.[31]

This consisted of two agreements: one open, the other secret. The open instrument of peace laid down that Francis should help fight the Turks, that the territorial *status quo* at the time of the truce of Nice (1538) be restored and that the duc d'Orléans should marry either Charles's daughter Mary or Ferdinand's second daughter, Anne. In the first case, he was to receive the Netherlands and Franche-Comté as dowry; in the second, Milan. The final decision as to which of the two marriages should take place was left to the emperor, who was given four months to make up his mind. Francis, for his part, was to give Orléans the duchies of Bourbon, Châtellerault and Angoulême. He also gave up his claims to Savoy and Piedmont, while Charles did the same in respect of Burgundy. In the second, secret, agreement, Francis promised to help the emperor reform the church, to further the meeting of a general council and to bring back

---

[30]   K. Brandi, *The Emperor Charles V*, tr. C. V. Wedgwood (London, 1939), p. 522.
[31]   Rozet and Lembey, pp. 164–9, 186–8; *L.P.*, xix (pt 2), 198–9, 205, 213, 249, 291.

the German Protestants into the Catholic fold. If these could only be reduced by force, he agreed to give Charles as much assistance as he had already promised against the Turks.

Among the first to be delighted with the peace was Queen Eleanor, who had tried to avert a conflict between her husband and her brother through the intercession of her sister, Mary of Hungary. On 22 September she left Paris, accompanied by Madame d'Etampes, and travelled to Brussels, where she was joined by the duc d'Orléans. The queen's entry into Brussels on 22 October was followed by several days of festivities, hunts, jousts and balls, culminating in a tournament on the Grand' Place.[32] However, not everyone in France was pleased with the peace. The Dauphin protested against it formally on 12 December, his example being soon followed by the parlement of Toulouse. The Parlement of Paris registered the treaty only at the second request from the king.[33] Abroad, the peace aroused mixed feelings. The pope professed to be pleased, but the king of England felt that he had been deserted by his ally. As for the sultan, he was so incensed by Francis's betrayal that he nearly had the French ambassador impaled.[34]

But the treaty of Crépy proved little more than a dead letter. Francis did fulfil some of its terms: he asked the pope to summon a general council and returned Stenay, a fortified town in Lorraine, to Charles. These, however, were minor concessions; at the core of the treaty were the alternative marriages proposed for the duc d'Orléans. Charles hesitated about these for a long time, and Francis did not press him, since he was not especially keen to implement his main territorial obligations under the treaty. Eventually, the emperor came down in favour of the duke's marriage to Ferdinand's daughter; but on 9 September 1545 Charles d'Orléans died of a brief and mysterious illness. Francis was heartbroken. He had lost not only a much-loved son, but, as he himself said, 'he by whom Christianity might have remained in perpetual repose and quietude; he would have nourished peace and tranquillity among the princes'.[35] Orléans's death destroyed the foundations of the peace, and a change in French foreign policy became immediately apparent. Negotiations with the emperor continued, and there was widespread support for a proposed marriage between Francis's daughter Marguerite and Prince Philip, but mutual suspicion prevented any positive achievement.[36] Yet, if

[32] C. Terrasse, *François Ier* (1945–70), iii. 132–3; *L.P.*, xix (pt 2), 568, 570.
[33] *C.A.F.*, iv. 14267, 14306; *L.P.*, xix (pt 2), 597, 740.
[34] Rozet and Lembey, pp. 201–2; *L.P.*, xix (pt 2), 304; E. Charrière (ed.), *Négociations de la France dans le Levant* (1848–60), i. 593n.
[35] M. François, *Le cardinal François de Tournon* (1951), p. 213; *L.P.*, xix (pt 2), 642.
[36] François, *François de Tournon*, pp. 213–14.

an early resumption of war between Francis and Charles seemed likely, neither wanted to precipitate it; Charles needed to set his German house in order, while Francis still had to defeat Henry VIII.

The war against England

In the autumn of 1544 peace talks between England and France took place at Calais, but they made no headway on account of Henry's refusal to hand back Boulogne and his insistence on France abandoning the Scots.[37] Since a negotiated settlement seemed impossible, the French decided to force Henry into a more reasonable attitude by an attack on the south coast of England, to be coupled, if possible, with a Scottish invasion of the north. It is unlikely that a full-scale invasion of England was contemplated. The French plan was probably limited to the disruption of communications between England and Boulogne so as to facilitate the latter's recapture by the Dauphin's army in Picardy.

On 31 May a French expeditionary force landed in Scotland, and in response to this show of friendship the Scots decided, on 26 June, to raise an army for the invasion of northern England.[38] Francis, in the meantime, assembled an army of 30,000 men in Normandy and seven *compagnies d'ordonnances* in Picardy. He also gathered at Le Havre a fleet of more than 200 ships, including galleys of the Mediterranean fleet under Baron de La Garde. On 27 June command of this fleet was given to Admiral d'Annebault, who, in spite of his title, had no experience of war at sea.[39]

Early in July the English admiral, Lord Lisle, planned to attack the French fleet in its anchorage but was frustrated by bad weather. Some of his ships, however, did manage to frighten Francis as he surveyed his fleet from the clifftop at Sainte-Adresse. Their cannon shots passed dangerously close to the beautiful tent of foliage beneath which he sheltered from the sun. But the only serious damage suffered by the French fleet at this stage was self-inflicted: on 12 July Annebault's flagship, *Le Philippe*, was destroyed by fire, and, on the following day, his new flagship, the *Grande Maistresse*, ran aground. Despite these mishaps, however, the fleet sailed out of Le Havre on 16 July, and, a few days later, entered the Solent as Henry VIII was dining on board his flagship, *Great Harry*. An engagement ensued during which the *Mary Rose* sank with the loss of 500 men. She sank, however, not as a result of French action, but after a breeze had

---

[37] L.P., xix (pt 2), 382, 392, 455–6.
[38] L.P., xx (pt 1), p. xxxii, nos. 513, 767, 1049.
[39] L.-H. Labande (ed.), *Correspondance de Joachim de Matignon, lieutenant-général du roi en Normandie (1516–1548)* (Monaco, 1914), pp. 116–24; La Roncière, *La marine française*, pp. 412–17; C.A.F., vii. 25203.

sprung up and water had poured through her open gun-ports. On 21 July the French landed on the Isle of Wight and burned a few villages before they were driven back to their ships. Four days later they landed at Seaford, but again withdrew, this time to Dover. The French admiral then crossed the strait and jettisoned his troops so as to strengthen the French camp outside Boulogne. On 15 August he came out to sea again and encountered the English fleet. A brief skirmish took place near Beachy Head, but Annebault, instead of taking advantage of his numerical superiority, retired to Le Havre.[40] Meanwhile, in the north, the Scots, after drawing close to the border, also withdrew without doing any damage, leaving the way clear for Hertford to carry out another destructive raid in the Lowlands.

By the beginning of September the war had evidently reached a stalemate, and both sides looked to the German Protestants for help. The English attempted to draw French troops away from Boulogne by mounting a diversionary campaign in Champagne under the Hessian captain, Friedrich von Reiffenberg; but French agents in Germany skilfully frustrated this move in the course of their own quest for mercenaries. Neither side, however, was able to gain the wholehearted support of the Protestant princes, whose personal interest lay in bringing the war to an end. As the emperor prepared to impose a religious settlement in Germany, the Schmalkaldic League desperately looked for French and English support. This, however, could not be obtained as long as the two countries were at war; hence the League's decision to offer its mediation. As a basis for a settlement, the League's envoys suggested that Boulogne be handed over to themselves in trust, pending settlement of Francis's debts to Henry. But the League's efforts, culminating in a conference near Calais in November, failed, largely because of mutual distrust between the English and French. Each side was negotiating with the emperor and believed the other to be preparing an alliance with him. There was also strong opposition on the part of certain members of the French government, notably Cardinal Tournon, to the Protestant mediators. In the end they did not even secure a truce.[41]

Following the breakdown of the peace talks, both sides began to rearm, but neither was keen to resume hostilities in earnest. Henry VIII's only concern was to keep Boulogne, while Francis could not afford a large-scale military enterprise. Within a short time, therefore, another peace initiative was under way. This time it was taken by Francesco Bernardo, a

[40] La Roncière, pp. 417–28; Scarisbrick, *Henry VIII*, p. 455.
[41] D. L. Potter, 'Diplomacy in the Mid-16th Century: England and France, 1536–1550' (unpublished Ph.D. thesis, Cambridge University, 1973), pp. 83–136; François, *François de Tournon*, p. 201.

Venetian merchant resident in London, who visited France with a commission from Lord Lisle. His message was sufficiently encouraging for Francis to appoint three commissioners (Annebault, Bochetel and Rémon) on 21 April to discuss peace terms with English commissioners. The principal matters for discussion were the sum of money Henry was prepared to accept for the return of Boulogne, the territory he was to retain until settlement of this sum, and the Scots. The talks, which began on 6 May, nearly broke down twice, but in the end, after much hard bargaining (the English began by demanding a war indemnity of 8 million *écus*), agreement was reached. Under the treaty of Ardres (7 June) France was to pay England 2 million *écus* in 1554 in exchange for Boulogne. In the meantime, Henry would retain the town and county of Boulogne, and neither side would begin any new fortification in the county. In addition to the 2 million *écus*, France would pay England all the pensions owed under former treaties, the first instalment falling due the following November. A claim for 512,022 *écus*, advanced by Henry on the basis of certain letters of Francis of January 1529, would be submitted to two commissioners on either side within three months. The Scots were comprehended in the treaty, and England was not to attack them without a new cause.[42]

The peace was proclaimed simultaneously in London and Paris on 13 June and was received with relief in both countries, yet it did not immediately remove all traces of distrust. Lord Lisle, acting on oral instructions from Henry, even destroyed fortifications the French had built near Boulogne. The incident could have had serious consequences if Francis had not reacted in a conciliatory way: he agreed to hold an enquiry and to pull down any fortification built since the treaty.[43] Another matter which could easily have impaired the peace was England's relations with Scotland.

Henry had not forgiven the Scots for their repudiation of the treaties of Greenwich, and now that Cardinal Beaton, the main obstacle to the English cause, had been murdered, the king was anxious to subdue the Scots finally. He welcomed the peace with France as an opportunity to aid the pro-English faction that was holding St Andrews castle against the Scottish government. Although he had reluctantly conceded the French demand for the comprehension of the Scots in the peace treaty, he was not inclined to stand by this agreement. When two Scottish ambassadors came to Henry to request its confirmation, he told them that they had broken the conditions on which it had been granted. In the winter of 1546–7 Odet de Selve, the French ambassador to England, reported naval

---

[42] *L.P.*, xxi (pt 1), 1014. The treaty is known also as the treaty of Camp.
[43] G. Lefèvre-Pontalis, *Correspondance politique de Odet de Selve* (1888), pp. 23, 27; *L.P.*, xxi (pt 2), 117, 149, 254.

and military preparations in England which seemed to be aimed at the Scots, though he could not be certain that the English were not also contemplating an attack on the French fort near Boulogne, Ardres or Normandy. As for the Scots themselves, they sent a formal appeal for help to Francis on 26 November, and he did send them some assistance, though not enough to bring the pro-English faction to heel.[44]

Meanwhile, in Germany the Schmalkaldic War broke out between the emperor and the German Protestants. At first, the odds seemed to favour the Protestant side, but by September the imperial army had occupied several important towns in the Danube valley. The Protestants, who had begun to seek aid from England and France as early as March 1546, stepped up their efforts. But Francis laid down conditions which were nothing short of absurd. Sturm reported, in October, that the king required the election of a new emperor, and, if the papal nuncio to France is to be believed, Francis was thinking of himself or the Dauphin as the obvious candidate. This was clearly an impossible condition; although the Protestants commanded a majority in the electoral college, it would have been difficult for them to depose the emperor. What is more, Francis insisted on Henry VIII's participation in any alliance with the Protestants and on the immediate surrender of Boulogne to them as guarantors of the treaty of Ardres.[45]

Yet Protestant appeals for French help did not go completely unanswered, for during the autumn Piero Strozzi visited the Protestant camp at Donauwörth. According to Sleidan, Piero had been instructed by Francis to arrange for payment of a subsidy by the bankers of Lyons to the Protestants, but the money was not handed over, owing to the opposition of Cardinal Tournon. It seems, however, that Sleidan got his facts wrong. Strozzi's mission never had Francis's official backing. Furthermore, large sums of money apparently did reach the Protestants from the bankers of Lyons. An anonymous report at the end of 1546 put the figure as high as 600,000 *écus*. But whatever help the French king may have given to the Protestants was carefully disguised, for he was anxious to remain at peace with the emperor so as to concentrate his efforts on the early recovery of Boulogne. The situation in Germany was, in any case, too finely balanced in the early stages of the Schmalkaldic War to justify open French support for the Protestant cause. As late as mid-November Annebault gave a French envoy to understand that the imperial alliance must be preserved at all cost, even at the expense of the Protestants.[46]

---

[44] *L.P.*, xxi (pt 2), 451, 515; Lefèvre-Pontalis, pp. 63, 83.
[45] D. L. Potter, 'Foreign Policy in the Age of the Reformation: French Involvement in the Schmalkaldic War, 1544–1547', *Historical Journal*, xx 3 (1977), 540.
[46] *Ibid.*, pp. 541–2; François, *François de Tournon*, pp. 223–4.

By January 1547, however, the military situation had become so ominous for the Protestants that Francis saw the need to strengthen their hand. He sent an envoy to the elector of Saxony with instructions 'to find means to keep the war going in Germany against the emperor'. At the end of his reign Francis was negotiating with envoys from Saxony and Hesse, though he remained reluctant about committing himself until he had recovered Boulogne. The Protestants, therefore, failed to get the support which might have helped to avert their final defeat by Charles at Mühlberg on 24 April.[47]

Francis's policy towards the German Protestants at the end of his reign has been called indecisive and has been explained on two grounds: first, his diplomats consistently underestimated the military threat facing the Protestants; secondly, the king was hampered by differences within his own circle of advisers and his own 'lack of credibility at home and abroad'.[48] There is much truth in this analysis. French agents in Germany did not at first believe that the emperor would go to war against the Protestants, and, when this happened, they overestimated Protestant strength. Within the French court opinion was sharply divided about the Protestants. While Madame d'Etampes, Marguerite de Navarre and Jean du Bellay favoured an anti-Habsburg policy, implying close links with the Protestant party, Tournon and Annebault were committed to upholding the peace of Crépy.[49] Francis's credibility among the German Protestants had also been damaged by his persecution of their co-religionists in France and his alliance with the Turks. All these factors affected French policy beyond the Rhine, but an even more important one was Francis's insolvency. Five years of war had emptied his coffers, yet he had to find another vast sum with which to redeem Boulogne. How, then, could he have intervened decisively in the Schmalkaldic War? His immediate interest, in any case, did not lie in bringing this war to a swift conclusion but in prolonging it for as long as possible so as to keep the emperor out of Piedmont. This inevitably made for a certain deviousness on his part, which could easily be mistaken for indecision. Francis's first priority at this stage was to recover Boulogne; everything else, even Milan, was subordinate to this objective. It is ironical that a monarch who had given so much attention and effort to extending his rule to Italy should have ended his reign striving unsuccessfully to regain an integral part of his own kingdom.

[47] Potter, 'Foreign Policy in the Age of the Reformation', pp. 542–3.
[48] Ibid., pp. 532, 543–4.
[49] Ibid., p. 530; François, François de Tournon, pp. 197–200.

24

Reform and resistance

FRANCIS I'S DECLARATION of war in July 1542 rested once again on an absurdly optimistic view of his capacity to pay for it. The reserves stored in his war-chests at the Louvre were very soon exhausted, for the war proved extremely expensive. The accounts of the war treasuries (*extraordinaires des guerres*) speak for themselves: in 1542, they paid out nearly 5 million *livres*, and the next two campaigns cost more than 6 million each. In 1545, after the peace of Crépy, when France had only England to fight, the war still absorbed more than 3 million *livres*, and in 1546 more than 2 million. Thus, altogether it cost the king about 23 million *livres*.[1] Expenditure on such a scale inevitably entailed a frantic search for money in which every known expedient was pushed to the limits. Francis sold offices galore, levied clerical tenths, alienated crown lands, borrowed from the merchants of Lyons, taxed walled towns and tried to improve the yield of the salt tax. At the same time, he completed the reform of the fiscal administration begun in 1523.

The *recettes-générales*

From the reign of Charles VII until 1542 the old royal demesne had been divided into four very large fiscal areas or *généralités*: viz. Languedoïl, Normandy, Languedoc and Outre-Seine-et-Yonne. In addition, there had been *recettes-générales* for Guyenne, Dauphiné, Provence and Burgundy. Now, under the edict of Cognac of 7 December 1542, the old *généralités* were subdivided into twelve areas of smaller size.[2] Languedoïl was split up into four units, Normandy into two, Outre-Seine-et-Yonne into three and Languedoc into three. The new units were known as *recettes-générales*, making a total of sixteen. Each district was under a *receveur-général*, who was empowered to collect all regular revenues, including those from the demesne. This meant the final fusion of what had once

---

[1]   G. Jacqueton, 'Le Trésor de l'Epargne sous François 1er, 1523–1547', *R.H.*, lvi (1894), 35.
[2]   Isambert, xii. 796–806.

been called the 'ordinary' and 'extraordinary' revenues. Since there was no longer any need for a special treasurer for domainial revenues, the post of *changeur du Trésor* disappeared. The *receveur-général* was also directed to collect many of the *deniers casuels*, including clerical tenths, forced loans and other levies on towns.

Another change initiated in December 1542 was the ending of the dual system in the higher fiscal administration created by the reforms of 1523–4. The *receveur-général des parties casuelles* was reduced to disbursing sums arising from the sale of offices. Jean Laguette protested vigorously at this diminution of his powers. He claimed responsibility for the collection and receipt of all the king's 'extraordinary' revenues, but an ordinance of January 1544 laid down that all the king's revenues, both 'ordinary' and 'extraordinary' should in future be paid to the *trésorier de l'Epargne*. This rule, however, was not strictly observed. As early as February 1544 Laguette was authorized to disburse cash out of receipts which had not been handed over to the *trésorier de l'Epargne*.

After 1542 Francis gave up the idea of making all or most royal payments in cash and from Paris. The *recettes-générales* were empowered to make regular local payments, such as salaries and pensions, but only on the authority of warrants from the *Epargne*. They were also authorized to meet 'unforeseeable' obligations if these could not be met from Paris, but again they needed a warrant (*mandement portant quittance*) from the *trésorier de l'Epargne*. Indeed, most emergency payments were made in this way.

A consequence of these changes was the enhanced importance of the *trésorier de l'Epargne*, who was not only at the head of all the *receveurs-généraux*, but also had charge of locating emergency funds. This meant, in effect, that he shared the authority formerly exercised by the *gens des finances*, but he was not allowed to tap local resources (i.e. the revenues of the *élections* and *bailliages*). Nor was he allowed to control policy, as the *gens des finances* had done. All the legislation of the period emphasizes the supremacy in fiscal matters of the king's council. The *trésorier de l'Epargne* was simply its executive officer or cashier. A list of February 1543 giving names of those whom the king wished to admit to his council (*Conseil pour le fait de ses finances*) is significant in this respect: the *trésorier* appears in the list, but right at the bottom, *after* the financial secretaries (*secrétaires des finances*), Bayard and Bochetel.

The creation of the *recettes-générales* rounded off a programme of fiscal reform that had lasted twenty years. The elimination of the old fiscal aristocracy of the *trésoriers, généraux* and *receveurs* had been the outcome not of blind resentment or unthinking jealousy, but of a broadly conceived plan to replace the old regime by a better one. This had admittedly been accomplished in a piecemeal fashion. The overwhelming fiscal pressure of recurrent wars had prevented the smooth application of the reform programme; there had been hesitations, even back-tracking. But the ultimate purpose Francis and his ministers had set themselves at the beginning was never forgotten. Each of its three components – centralization, uniformity and simplification – had been achieved by the end of the reign: centralization, by the suppression of the commission of the *gens des finances*, the transfer of their powers to the king's council and the subordination of all the royal receivers to a single accountant (*trésorier de l'Epargne*), who had to reside near the king; uniformity, by the fusion of the 'ordinary' and 'extraordinary' revenues and the absorption into the *Epargne* of the *parties casuelles*; and simplification, by the replacement of the slow and cumbersome system of *décharges* and *écrous* by more rapid and convenient methods of assignment and collection. Admittedly, the fiscal system at the end of Francis's reign still had gaps and inconsistencies, but the essential guidelines had been laid down; his successor needed only to add the finishing touches.[3]

Fiscal expedients

Among the fiscal expedients used by Francis during the war of 1542–6, three were particularly important: the alienation of crown lands, the sale of offices and loans from the bankers of Lyons.

In August 1543 the king ordered the sale of crown lands worth 600,000 *livres* 'in order to pay for military expenses necessitated by the threatening attitude of the emperor and the king of England', and, in September, he put up for sale several royal houses and lands in Paris.[4] In March 1544 a further alienation of crown lands worth 160,000 *écus* was decreed.[5]

At the same time, a very large number of offices were put up for sale. As the Venetian ambassador wrote in 1546, 'the offices are infinite in number and increase every day: *avocats du roi* in each small locality, *receveurs des tailles, trésoriers, conseillers, présidents des comptes et de justice, maîtres des requêtes, procureurs du fisc, prévôts, élus, baillis, vicomtes, généraux* [*des finances*] and so many others half of whom would suffice'.[6] This statement is fully supported by documentary evidence. Thus in March 1543 the king created eight *receveurs des tailles* and fifteen councillors in the parlement of Bordeaux, four at Dijon, four at Grenoble, fifteen at Rouen, twenty at Toulouse, four in the *bailliage* of Troyes and four in the

[3] Jacqueton, 'Le Trésor de l'Epargne', pp. 30–8.
[4] C.A.F., iv. 13297, 13355.
[5] *Ibid.*, iv. 13746.
[6] R. Mousnier, *La venalité des offices sous Henry IV et Louis XIII*, 2nd edn (1971), p. 41.

sénéchaussée of Auvergne.[7] In May he created a fourth *Chambre des enquêtes* in the Parlement of Paris under the name of *Chambre du domaine des eaux et forêts*, consisting of two presidents and eighteen councillors. The reason officially given for this creation was the need to relieve the existing magistrates of certain domainial lawsuits requiring a particular expertise, but the real reason was mercenary: offices, particularly in the parlements, fetched very high prices.[8] The cost of a councillorship in the Parlement of Paris was 3,000 *écus*, which was, of course, disguised as a 'loan' to the king.[9] The Venetian ambassador, Marino Cavalli, estimated that Francis received as much as 400,000 *écus* (or 900,000 *livres*) per annum from the creation of offices.[10]

Existing office-holders viewed with concern the multiplication of offices, which inevitably undermined the status and income of their own, and tried to limit the process. Sometimes they managed to obtain the suppression of a new office, but only by buying it themselves. In February 1544, for example, Francis agreed to revoke the creation of a third *enquêteur* in the *bailliage* of Amiens at the request of the other two, provided they reimbursed the sum which the third had paid to the king.[11] Resistance to the creation of offices could also take the form of dilatoriness by the parlements in registering the edict of creation or in admitting the king's nominees. On 9 October 1543, for example, Francis issued a *lettre de jussion* for the registration of an edict of the previous August creating two councillors at Fontenay-le-Comte in the *sénéchaussée* of Poitou, notwithstanding the opposition of the local *lieutenant-général*.[12] A particularly hard struggle was fought over the new *Chambre du domaine*. Francis became exceedingly impatient at the slowness of the Parlement of Paris in admitting councillors to the new court and demanded that it should start functioning, even with only ten members, the rest being provisionally supplied in rotation by the other chambers. He asked to be kept informed of any failures in the examinations for admissions, so that he might provide replacements. After barely two months' delay, the king demonstrated his displeasure to the *avocat-général*, Rémon, who had come to him on important business. Rémon was greeted 'with such bitter words that his hair stood on end as he heard the king threaten the court with the last extremities. But for the grace of God, it was surely

---

[7] C.A.F., iv. 12934, 12936–41, 12952.
[8] *Ibid.*, iv. 13120; A.N., X¹ᵃ 8613, fol. 473; E. Maugis, *Histoire du Parlement de Paris* (1913–16), i. 157–8.
[9] Maugis, i. 152, 177–9; Mousnier, *La vénalité des offices*, pp. 63–4; A.N., X¹ᵃ 1551, fol. 612a–b.
[10] Mousnier, *La vénalité des offices*, p. 68.
[11] C.A.F., iv. 13607.
[12] A.N., X¹ᵃ 1551, fols. 588b–589a.

faced by some disaster.' On 14 July the Parlement took steps to speed up the examination of the king's nominees. Thirteen were admitted within the next two months and four within six months. No sooner had this process been completed than the king created in three stages twenty-one new offices in the Parlement, including two presidents and twelve councillors in the Grand' Chambre, moves which again met with resistance.[13]

Loans raised with the bankers of Lyons were another major source of royal revenue in the last years of Francis's reign. Such loans had, of course, been raised before, but only exceptionally. As from 1542 they were regular and systematic: the loans were raised annually and renewed at each of the four Lyons fairs. The amount of interest paid was 4 per cent at each fair or 16 per cent over the year. One of the earliest contemporary references to the government's credit operations is to be found among Paget's dispatches. Writing from Lyons on 9 August 1542, he says: 'great means is daily made for money. For whereas here, in Lyons, and in other places, men that have gotten any sum of money, likewise widows and orphans, use to put the same in bank, some for five, some for eight in the hundred, the King desireth to have all, and to give ten in the hundred.'[14] But there is no corroborative evidence that this was actually done. The scheme mentioned by Paget cannot have been anything more than one discussed within the king's circle. All the royal loans for which documentary evidence exists were raised from the banks, not private capitalists, let alone widows and orphans.

The method of borrowing was as follows: the king appointed a number of commissioners to contract loans with the merchants and bankers of Lyons. The first commission was appointed on 13 April 1543 and was renewed at irregular intervals.[15] Then, as from 1545 a new commission, valid for one year, was appointed annually. The commissioners were mostly high-ranking members of the king's entourage, but there were also a number of local officials, who, being on the spot, played a leading part in actually negotiating the loans. Foremost among the commissioners was Cardinal Tournon, who, as governor of the south-east provinces, had a special interest in Lyons; but there is no truth in Bodin's allegation that loans were first introduced in France by him in 1543 or that he planned to set up a royal bank in Lyons.[16] Another important figure in the matter of royal loans, albeit an unofficial one, was Jean Cléberger, a German businessman who had settled in Lyons in 1530. As from 1543 he was constantly involved either as a lender or as intermediary between the French government and the German banks. Thus in 1545 he raised a loan

---

[13] *Ibid.*, fols. 527a–528a; Maugis, i. 159–61.
[14] *St.P.*, ix. 117.   [15] *C.A.F.*, vi. 22570.
[16] M. François, *Le cardinal François de Tournon* (1951), pp. 192–3, 478–82.

of 50,000 *écus* with the help of the Welsers of Nuremberg and Weikmann of Ulm, and in 1546 raised another loan to which he himself contributed 13,500 *livres*.[17]

Unfortunately, not enough precise information is available about the loans raised by Francis at the end of his reign. But they were certainly large and mostly drawn on Italian, Swiss and German banks. Such details as we have are as follows: in 1542 there was talk of a loan of 400,000 *livres*: viz. 200,000 from the Florentines, 100,000 from the Luccans, 50,000 from the Welsers of Augsburg and 50,000 from French bankers. In 1543 100,000 *écus* were borrowed. In 1544 the same amount was lent by the Italians and 50,000 by the Germans. These amounts, however, are but a small proportion of the total borrowed. Thereafter the pace of borrowing quickened: early in 1545 the Italian banks were asked for a loan of 100,000 *écus* and the Germans for 50,000. In 1546 a new loan of 300,000 *livres* was raised, and in September of that year negotiations were under way to find cash for the Schmalkaldic League. In spite of the peace of Crépy, Francis was anxious to keep the civil war going in Germany, and offered to reimburse 500,000 *écus* to his creditors so as to provide them with the necessary funds. Even after he had made peace with England, he continued to borrow, his policy being to use the peace in order to replenish his war-chests in anticipation of the next conflict.[18]

Not all the money borrowed by Francis was actually used. Much of it was stored in his war-chests at the Louvre. According to Bodin, the king had 500,000 *écus* in his chests 'and four times as much' (i.e. 2,500,000 *écus* or 5,625,000 *livres*).[19] What was the reasoning behind this policy of storing large sums of borrowed cash while paying off the interest at around 16 per cent per annum? Was it simply to provide for contingency needs, or did it have more subtle and far-reaching implications? Bodin tells us of a plan by Tournon to attract foreign capital to France so as to create a dearth on the European markets and prevent France's enemies from raising loans themselves. But if this did enter Francis's calculations, his policy was nonetheless dangerous: it paved the way for the *Grand Parti* under Henri II and the eventual bankruptcy of the French crown.[20]

New taxes

Two important innovations were brought into the French tax system

[17] R. Doucet, 'Le Grand Parti de Lyon au XVIᵉ siècle', *R.H.*, clxxi (1933), 474–82; A.N., X¹ᵃ 1555, fol. 143a–b; M. Vial, *L'histoire et la légende de Jean Cléberger dit 'le bon Allemand' (1485?–1546)* (Lyons, 1914).
[18] Doucet, 'Le Grand Parti', pp. 478–80.
[19] J. Bodin, *Les six livres de la République* (1577), p. 681.
[20] Doucet, 'Le Grand Parti', p. 482.

during the last years of Francis's reign: a tax on walled towns (*villes closes*), called the *solde des 50,000 hommes de pied* (the pay of 50,000 foot-soldiers), and the simplification of the *gabelle*.

A particularly unsatisfactory aspect of the tax system was the fact that the *taille* weighed so much more heavily on the rural population than on the urban one. This seemed particularly unfair at a time when a considerable amount of capital was accumulating in the towns. The government was, of course, well aware of this discrepancy, and, in the 1540s, tried to bring about a more even distribution of direct taxation by asking towns exempt from the *taille* to contribute to its military expenses. The *solde des 50,000 hommes*, however, was not a completely new tax. In 1522 Francis had asked the more important walled towns to pay for 1,000 infantry each and the less important ones 500. In 1538 a tax called the *solde des 20,000 hommes de pied* had been levied on all the towns. Then in 1543 it became the *solde des 50,000 hommes*. Its essential novelty was that it was henceforth levied annually, even in peacetime, so that, in effect, it was complementary to the *taille*.[21]

The impact of the new tax on municipal finances and on relations between the various social groups within a town could be far-reaching. Lyons's share of the *solde* in 1543, for example, was 60,000 *livres*. Strictly speaking, this was not a tax so much as a forced loan, for the government undertook to repay it over three years in four annual instalments, the debt being guaranteed against the revenues of Languedoc and the customs of Lyons. The loan was levied by the municipal government (the Consulate) by means of a levy on the chief inhabitants, who offered no resistance, since they were confident of being reimbursed. But the king broke his word: after two instalments the repayments ceased and the revenues of the customs of Lyons were granted to two Italian bankers in settlement of other royal debts. By 1546, when the loan should have been cleared, the government still owed Lyons 33,000 *livres*.

Such was the dissatisfaction created among the bourgeois of the town that the Consulate was no longer able to call upon them when the government renewed its demand for the *solde* in 1544 and in each succeeding year. The only way the town could raise the money was by borrowing at a high rate of interest from the Italian bankers and reimbursing itself by new indirect taxes. Thus in 1543 it created the *pied fourché*, a duty on cattle and meat imports and, in 1544, the *six deniers pour livre*, a duty on all imports other than foodstuffs. But indirect taxes of this kind were exceedingly unpopular, not only among the poor, who had to pay more for their food, clothing and fuel, but also among certain

---

[21] G. Zeller, *Les institutions de la France au XVIᵉ siècle* (1948), p. 259; C.A.F., iii. 9783; iv. 13039.

privileged groups, notably the clergy and foreign merchants. The clergy argued that they were being taxed twice, since they already paid clerical tenths; foreign merchants regarded the new taxes as in breach of the privileges granted to them by the crown, and they threatened to quit the town and disrupt its fairs. In the end, the Consulate had to give way. The *pied fourché* was abolished after three years and the *six deniers* after only thirteen months. As a result, Lyons was not able to recoup its loans to the government, not only for the *solde*, but also in response to a demand for 100,000 *livres* in respect of its fortifications. In 1547 it was left with a deficit of 107,000 *livres* and no revenues with which to clear it.[22]

In other towns, too, the *solde des 50,000 hommes* caused considerable problems. Paris repeatedly asked for a reduction of the sums demanded by the king, but to no avail; it was, therefore, obliged to resort to various foot-dragging procedures, which provoked royal threats of reprisal. In 1546 the municipal government (Bureau de la Ville) declared that the Parisians were among the king's most loyal subjects; they wanted to help him but could no longer do so because of the heavy burdens imposed upon them in the past. They were now utterly wretched, crushed by taxes and debts and at grips with the plague. It was the king's duty, the Bureau continued, to show them pity and to treat them as part of his family. In March 1547 the Bureau reminded Francis of the privileges enjoyed by Paris in the past. 'The capital of Christendom', it said, 'had never been subject to taxation and had once enjoyed a reputation for freedom equalling, perhaps even surpassing, that of Rome or any other city, but it had now fallen into extreme poverty.'[23] Was Francis moved by this appeal? We cannot tell, for he died before he could reply. His successor, Henri II, reduced the *solde* in 1547, but he did not abolish it. In 1555 he extended it, even to villages.

Resistance: the *gabelle* revolt

Instances of popular resistance to royal taxation during the reign of Francis I are remarkably few by comparison with the number later on, especially in the early seventeenth century. Francis's subjects had the reputation abroad of being extraordinarily docile. In 1546, for example, the Venetian ambassador wrote to his government as follows: 'The king has only to say I want such-and-such a sum, I order, I consent, and the

[22] R. Doucet, *Finances municipales et crédit public à Lyon au XVIᵉ siècle* (1937), pp. 24–8.
[23] *R.D.B.V.P.*, iii. 72, 74–5; P. Champion, *Paris au temps de la Renaissance: l'envers de la tapisserie* (1935), pp. 39–42. See also my 'Francis I and Paris', *History*, lxvi (Feb. 1981), 18–33.

thing is done as speedily as if it had been decided by the whole nation of its own volition. The situation has already gone so far that a few Frenchmen who can see a little more clearly than the rest say: our kings used to call themselves *Reges Francorum*, but at present they might as well be called *Reges servorum*. The king receives all that he asks for and the remainder is at his mercy.' This, however, is an exaggeration. Royal taxation was not always accepted without protest, and in 1542 it even met with open resistance in the west of France.[24]

At the start of Francis's reign, as we have seen, France was divided into three areas in respect of the salt tax or *gabelle*: the *pays de grandes gabelles* (the provinces of the old royal demesne), the *pays de petites gabelles* (viz. Languedoc, Burgundy, Dauphiné and Provence) and the *pays du quart de sel* (i.e., Guyenne, Saintonge, Aunis, Angoumois, Poitou, Périgord, Limousin and Marche). The area of *grandes gabelles* was subdivided into districts, called *greniers à sel*, each administered by a *grènetier* with a numerous staff. The salt merchants had to bring their salt to the *grenier*, where it was purchased by the *grenetier* and then sold to the public at a price fixed by the government. This took into account the costs of production and transport, and allowed a reasonable profit for the merchant (*droit du marchand*) and a share for the king (*droit du roi*). Under Francis the *droit du roi* trebled in twenty years: in 1515 it amounted to 15 *livres* per *muid* of salt, in 1535 to 30 *livres* and in 1537 to 45 *livres*. By comparison with the *pays de grandes gabelles*, the *pays du quart de sel* were lightly burdened. The absence of *greniers* meant, in practice, an almost complete lack of governmental control. The *quart* that was levied on the sale of the salt was a quarter of its value (in Angoumois it was only a fifth; hence the *quint*). This was increased by a half in 1537; hence, the *quart et demi-quart* (in Angoumois, the *quint et demi-quint*).[25]

In 1541, Francis attempted a radical reform of the salt tax. The edict of Châtellerault of 1 June introduced a single tax of 44 *livres* per *muid* to be

---

[24] S.-C. Gigon, *La révolte de la gabelle en Guyenne, 1548–1549* (1906), p. 18. For an account of discontent in Dauphiné caused by Francis I's taxation, see E. Le Roy Ladurie, *Carnival: A People's Uprising at Romans, 1579–1580* (London, 1980), pp. 49–51. 'The tax squeeze of 1535–1538 was so intense', the author writes, 'that it seemed to release all the repressed resentment in the kingdom.' This focused on the tax exemption enjoyed by the nobility, clergy and two towns, Montélimar and Gap. But country districts were in general hostile to all towns, particularly the larger ones, because of the purchase of so much rural land by the urban elite and also because they used their dominant influence in the estates to foist certain burdens, such as the billeting of troops, on to the villages. Royal loans, which in theory applied only to walled towns, were in fact spread out over entire districts, including rural areas.

[25] Gigon, pp. 20–2; G. Jacqueton, *Documents relatifs à l'administration financière en France de Charles VII à François Ier (1443–1523)* (1891), pp. vii–ix; M. Wolfe, *The Fiscal System of Renaissance France* (New Haven and London, 1972), pp. 330–42.

levied at the salt marsh.[26] Thereafter the salt was to circulate freely in the kingdom. This in effect abolished the *greniers* in the *pays de grandes gabelles* and shifted the whole apparatus of state control to the area of production, which thus lost its privileged status. Henceforth, the *pays du quart de sel* would have to pay the same tax as the *pays de grandes gabelles*. The edict, moreover, laid down severe penalties for fraud and smuggling: a first offence was to be punished by a fine and confiscation of the salt concerned and the means by which it was being transported, a second by corporal punishment, and a third by death. On 7 April 1542 another edict reduced the amount of tax to 24 *livres* per *muid*, but extended it to salt for export and fishing salt, which had hitherto been tax-free.[27] The purpose of this legislation was clearly to simplify the *gabelle* and thereby increase its yield to the royal treasury.

However reasonable these reforms may have been in terms of the government's needs, they were bitterly opposed by the people of the salt marshes, who felt that their livelihood was being threatened. According to a royal edict of 27 September 1542, the inhabitants of the 'isles' of Marennes, Oléron, Saint-Fort, Saint-Jean-d'Angély, Saint-Just, Bourg, Libourne, Bordeaux, Saint-Macaire, Langart and elsewhere had taken up arms and, in large numbers, had resisted two successive waves of royal commissioners sent to the salt marshes to enforce the legislation. Such had been the opposition that the commissioners had been unable to carry out their mission and the king had been forced to summon the *ban et arrière-ban* of Poitou. But the rebels, knowing that his army was engaged on several fronts at once and that he could not afford to put another in the field, had rebelled yet again. Ten thousand or more, equipped with artillery, had barred the way to the 'isles', forcing the royal commissioners to retire. On hearing of these events, Francis had summoned the salters to appear before him and his council at Chizé, and many had done so. Their crimes had been read out to them, and, without offering any excuses, they had asked for the king's pardon. Before passing final judgment, however, Francis wanted time to reflect. He therefore ordered the nobles and principal men of the rebellious 'isles' to come to La Rochelle for judgment on 31 December. In the meantime their salt marshes were confiscated.[28]

The choice of La Rochelle as the venue for the king's sentence was not fortuitous. The town stood in the midst of the salt marshes and had itself been the centre of unrest for years. This, however, had been caused not by the *gabelle* but by Francis's high-handed treatment of the local corporation. Traditionally, this consisted of an elected mayor and 100 *échevins*, but in July 1535 Francis had decreed that, in future, the mayor would be a

---

[26] Isambert, xii. 745–58; Gigon, pp. 22–3.
[27] Gigon, p. 23.   [28] Isambert, xii. 787–9.

royal appointment; he had also reduced the number of *échevins* to 20.[29] Thereafter, there had been nothing but trouble between the governor (who was also the mayor), Charles Chabot, seigneur de Jarnac, and the local community. Matters came to a head in August 1542, after the king had been told of a conspiracy in the town. He ordered Jarnac to round up suspects and to raise 200 or 300 infantry for the town's defence. But soon after these troops had entered La Rochelle a riot broke out between them and the townspeople, many on both sides being wounded. The troops had to be withdrawn, but Jarnac brought them back soon afterwards along with fifty men-at-arms. He also imposed a curfew on the town and disarmed its inhabitants. Meanwhile, representatives of the town called on the king at Cognac, but they were given no redress and forbidden to go home; instead, they were ordered to follow the court.[30]

On 30 December Francis arrived outside La Rochelle. At his own command none of the townspeople came out to meet him; no guns were fired in salute or church bells rung. The town waited in silence for the king, who was preceded by the captive rebels in chains. They were taken to the castle by the king's archers. Nor was the suspense broken for twenty-four hours, for Francis spent the morning of Sunday 31 December at mass and visiting the harbour and its fortifications. Not until Monday afternoon did he sit in judgment on the two groups of rebels. The setting was suitably awe-inspiring: the king sat on a dais four steps high, flanked, on his right, by the ducs de Vendôme and Orléans and other princes and, on his left, by the cardinals of Tournon, Lorraine and Ferrara. Members of his council stood behind his throne, and Montholon, the keeper of the seals, sat at his feet. As for the prisoners, they stood in two groups on the floor below with their respective counsel.

The formal proceedings began with a speech on behalf of the 'men of the islands' by Guillaume Le Blanc, a barrister of the parlement of Bordeaux. Offering no excuses for their actions, he expressed their remorse and begged the king to pardon them and return their marshes to them, without which they could not live. At this point, the prisoners, falling on their knees, cried 'Miséricorde!' in a loud voice. Next to speak was Etienne Noyau, the lieutenant of La Rochelle, who likewise asked for the king's pardon for his fellow citizens. In return for this favour, he said, they and their descendants would sing his praises for ever. Francis then replied. He began by reminding the rebels of the seriousness of their crime, which had been committed at a time when he and his sons were busy defending the kingdom. They deserved to lose their lives and property, yet, as a prince, he could not refuse his pardon to those who had

[29] C.A.F., vi. 20929, 20931.
[30] Guiffrey, pp. 396–406.

asked for it in a state of true repentance, nor did he wish to treat his subjects as the emperor had treated the people of Ghent. He therefore granted their request.

After Francis had finished speaking, sweet music was heard coming from the belfry of St Bartholomew's church. Its bells then rang out, and those of all the other churches in the town followed suit. Bonfires were lit everywhere and the guns of the castle thundered out. That evening the king was entertained to supper by the townspeople, and, as further proof of his trust, he allowed them to serve him at table, retaining only two of his own servants. Next morning he left La Rochelle amid the loud plaudits of its people. 'I believe', he told them, 'that I have won your hearts, and I assure you, *foi de gentilhomme*, that you will have mine.'[31]

Much has been made of Francis's magnanimity towards La Rochelle. It certainly compared favourably with the harsh treatment meted out by Henry VIII and Charles V to their own rebels. But three important qualifications have to be made. First, Francis's pardon was not uncondi-tional, at least in respect of the owners of the salt marshes of Guyenne and Saintonge, who were ordered to deliver 15,000 *muids* of salt to the *grenier* of Rouen.[32] This doubtless enabled Francis, in September 1543, to repay some of his creditors with salt. Secondly, Francis could not afford to be otherwise than magnanimous. He was in the middle of a war and, having just failed in one campaign, was getting ready for the next. To have put down the rebellion by force would have entailed a costly diver-sion of military effort; it would also have left much bitterness behind in an area vulnerable to English intervention at a time when Anglo-French relations were at a low ebb. A pardon, in short, was the only statesman-like course open to the king in the circumstances. Finally, Francis did not abandon his long-term plans for the *gabelle*. The ordinance of 1542 was revoked in May 1543 and the earlier system restored, but the idea of unifying the salt tax was not abandoned. Two ordinances issued in 1544 (1 July and 6 December) extended the system of *greniers à sel* to the whole kingdom except Languedoc, Dauphiné, Brittany and Provence. But the new regime was not set up overnight. It probably took the whole of 1545 to establish the new *greniers* and their staffs, and this may explain why Guyenne remained fairly quiet in spite of popular dissatisfaction; the only disturbances that year were in Périgord, and they elicited a fairly mild military repression by the prince of Melfi. In 1546, however, serious riots occurred in Saintonge. But the smuggling of salt on a large scale, which

[31] *Ibid.*, pp. 413–25. Cf. *Le voyage du roy François Iᵉʳ en sa ville de la Rochelle l'an 1542* etc. in L. Cimber and F. Danjou (eds.), *Archives curieuses de l'histoire de France depuis Louis XI jusqu'à Louis XVIII* (1834–49), iii. 35.
[32] C.A.F., i. 12865.

carried on regardless of the activities of a small force of archers, called *chevaucheurs du sel*, prevented the new system from yielding enough revenue. In March 1546, therefore, the government decided to farm out the *gabelle* for ten years, with the result that by 1548 the salt tax had become so oppressive as to ignite in July a new revolt, far more serious than that of 1542, in Angoumois and Saintonge. This was savagely put down by Henri II.[33]

Francis I's magnanimous treatment of La Rochelle in 1542 was neither disinterested nor necessarily characteristic of his attitude to rebellions elsewhere. In November 1544, following a rebellion at Lagny-sur-Marne two months earlier, he ordered the seigneur de Lorges to sack the town and forbade the inhabitants to prosecute de Lorges or his troops in any court of the realm for actions committed in pursuance of his own command, and any court to hear such a lawsuit. This drastic measure evidently worried the Parlement of Paris, for it was registered only in March 1545 after three letters of *jussion*.[34]

When Francis I died, several million *livres* were found in his coffers. According to de Thou, the king left 400,000 *écus* in cash after settlement of his debts and excluding a quarter's instalment of taxes yet to be levied. Bodin states that 1,800,000 *écus* were found in the *Epargne*. Such statements earned the king the posthumous reputation of having been a brilliant businessman who had managed to leave his son a surplus after many years of war. The truth, alas, is rather different. In 1547 Francis owed the Lyons bankers 6,860,844 *livres*, almost as much as his entire income for that year (7,183,271 *livres*). It was this loan, or part of it, which was found in his coffers at his death. His successor, Henri II, wisely repaid part of the loan within that same year, yet at the end of 1548 the debt to the Lyons bankers was still 2,421,846 *livres tournois*, which was presumably the backlog of Francis's debt to them. Thus, instead of a disposable surplus, the old king left a sizable debt.[35] 'The origin of all France's misfortunes', Bodin wrote, 'was when King Francis I began to borrow money at interest, having 1,800,000 *écus* in his coffers and peace in his kingdom. No well-advised prince shall ever do that, for by so doing he will destroy the foundation of his finances.'[36]

[33] Gigon, *La révolte de la gabelle*, pp. 24–7; Y.-M. Bercé, *Croquants et Nu-pieds* (1974), pp. 19–43.
[34] A.N., X^{1a} 1556, fol. 84a–b.
[35] Jacqueton, 'Le Trésor de l'Epargne', pp. 35–7.
[36] Bodin, *Les six livres*, p. 683.

25

The growth of persecution

THE AFFAIR OF the Placards of October 1534 was an important
turning point in the early French Reformation, not, as is sometimes
thought, because it marked the transition in royal policy from toleration
to persecution, but because it served to clarify an ideological situation
that had been volatile and confused. The appearance of an outspoken and
aggressive sacramentarianism within the French dissenting community
not only alerted the government to a threat which had so far escaped its
notice, but helped to polarize opinion. Dissent did not become cohesive
overnight. Calvinism began to make its mark only in 1541 and did not
become the predominant heresy in France till around 1550.[1] In the
meantime, the term 'Lutheran' covered a wide range of unorthodox views
ranging from evangelical mysticism at one end to militant sacramentarianism at the other.[2] But the battle lines were clearer after October 1534.
Some people were sufficiently committed to Protestantism in one form
or another to risk imprisonment, banishment or death; other, less
courageous spirits preferred to conform to the official faith. Some writers
even went to the trouble of deleting compromising words like 'Christ'
from their works.[3] Even Marguerite de Navarre became more reserved.
She continued to offer the protection of her court at Nérac to evangelicals,
but none of them, she assured her brother, was a sacramentarian.[4]

Francis's attitude to heresy definitely hardened after 1534, though he
continued to befriend Protestants abroad. After an attempt in 1535 and

[1] Imbart de La Tour, iv. 219–20.
[2] 'Men of the sects of Zwingli and Oecolampadius, whom the populace calls Lutherans'
(A. Fabrice, 23 Jan. 1535). Herminjard, iii. 252 n. 8. Saint-Mauris, the imperial
ambassador, reported (27 July 1545) that there were many Lutherans in France, chiefly
in Guyenne and Normandy, and that most of them were sacramentarians. B.L., Add.
MS. 28594, fol. 144.
[3] The usage 'Christ', as distinct from 'Jesus Christ', was distinctively Protestant.
[4] G. Berthoud, *Antoine Marcourt* (Geneva, 1973), pp. 216–20; P. Jourda, *Marguerite
d'Angoulême* (1930), ii. 1069–70. In a letter to her brother of December 1542 Marguerite wrote: 'Thank God, my lord, none of ours has been found to be a sacramentarian.' Herminjard, vii. 392; P. Jourda, *Repertoire analytique et chronologique de la
correspondance de Marguerite d'Angoulême* (1930), no. 903.

1536 to unwind the recent persecution, largely, it seems, to placate German opinion, he issued a series of edicts aimed at eradicating heresy from his kingdom. He identified it with sedition, a crime against the state, and placed the ecclesiastical courts, traditionally responsible for its suppression, under the authority of the lay courts. The men behind this policy were the king's ministers, Montmorency, Poyet and Tournon, but it was probably the king's policy as well. Such vacillations as may be discerned were not due to any lack of determination on his part but rather to the stresses of reconciling an anti-Protestant domestic policy with a pro-Protestant foreign policy.

The cruel aftermath of the Placards gravely damaged Francis's reputation among the German Protestants just as he was trying to draw closer to them. It was made worse by imperial agents, who made propaganda out of the situation. They pointed to the shameful contrast between the king's treatment of his fellow Christians and his friendly reception of the Infidel's envoys, claimed that he was the main obstacle to the calling of a general council, and spread stories about Parisian prisons being full of Germans.[5] In a manifesto to the imperial estates dated 1 February 1535 Francis denied these charges. The persecution in France, he claimed, had been political, not religious. He had punished sedition, as the imperial estates would have done in his place. He had done nothing wrong in negotiating with the Turks; the emperor's brother had done so too and Christendom needed peace. There were no Germans among the victims of the persecution. 'My court, my towns and my lands', he wrote, 'are open to all of your nation . . . they are as free in France as my own subjects and even my children.' It was not difficult to see, he concluded, why he had been slandered: it was to sow discord between the French and the Germans, whose friendship constituted a barrier to the fulfilment of Habsburg ambitions; if it were destroyed nothing would stop the emperor from building a universal monarchy on the ruins of the German liberties.[6] In another message to the estates, dated 25 February, Francis denied that he was hostile to a general council. A papal nuncio, he declared, had just arrived at his court, and he intended to keep him there until the place, date and agenda of a council had been settled.[7]

The king's manifestos by themselves could not counter the effects of

[5] V.-L. Bourrilly, *Guillaume du Bellay* (1905), pp. 188–9; Granvelle, *Papiers d'état*, ii. 283.

[6] Herminjard, iii. no. 492, pp. 249–54. As D. R. Kelley shows (*The Beginning of Ideology* (Cambridge, 1981), p. 19), 'official fears about the inseparability of heresy and sedition were not without foundation . . . To reject immanence, and thereby traditional authority, on grounds of private conscience was merely heretical; but to proclaim these views publicly was treasonable.'

[7] A.N., K. 1483, no. 61.

imperial propaganda; deeds were also needed. In June 1535, therefore, he asked the Parlement to be less severe in its treatment of heretics.[8] Then, on 16 July, he issued the famous edict of Coucy calling a halt to the persecution on the ground that heresy had been wiped out. It ordered all religious prisoners to be released and allowed religious exiles to come home, offering both categories a pardon. Yet it was not an edict of toleration, for sacramentarians were excluded from the pardon, and this was made conditional on the rest abjuring their faith within six months. If they relapsed thereafter, they were to be hanged.[9]

The edict of Coucy coincided with a reopening of negotiations with the German Protestants. In March, after Barnabé de Voré had praised Melanchthon's learning, moderation and intellect, Francis expressed the wish to meet him. An unofficial invitation from the king to Melanchthon was followed on 23 June by a formal one, which Voré himself carried to Germany. He left France on 16 July, the very day on which the edict of Coucy was issued, no mere coincidence, to be sure. Melanchthon was invited to take part in a conference with theologians of the Sorbonne; he was assured of a warm welcome whether he came on his own account or as the representative of the German Protestants as a whole.[10]

But it takes two sides at least to make a conference. In July Francis informed the Sorbonne that Melanchthon and 'certain Germans' had asked 'to be received in the church'. He invited the faculty to send ten or twelve doctors to a debate with Melanchthon. But the Sorbonne refused. A discussion among the doctors clearly showed where their sentiments lay. 'One must not listen to heretics', they declared, 'or have any dealings with them.' Confronted by such intransigence, Francis could only play for time: he thanked the Sorbonne for its 'good' advice and promised to let it know his decision in due course. Guillaume du Bellay, seigneur de Langey, meanwhile submitted to the faculty a set of twelve articles based on the replies to his questionnaire of 1534, which he had received from Melanchthon, Bucer and Hedio. He would await the Sorbonne's verdict on these articles, he said, before returning to Germany. On 30 August the faculty rejected them as a trap designed to seduce the people. It emphatically refused to take part in any debate with their authors. The king was

---

[8] He did so allegedly at the request of Pope Paul III. *J.B.P.*, p. 458.

[9] *Ordonnances*, vii. no. 701, pp. 248–51. For its effects see N. Weiss, 'Documents inédits pour servir à l'histoire de la réforme sous François Ier, 1536–1537', *B.S.H.P.F.*, xxxiv (1885), 164–77. Also *C.A.F.*, vi. 20990. For a provocative discussion of Francis I's edicts against heresy see N. M. Sutherland, *The Huguenot Struggle for Recognition* (New Haven and London, 1980), pp. 1–39, 333–40. She indicates that the edict of Coucy was 'the first regulation to introduce the death penalty for the propagation of heresy by any spoken or written means'.

[10] Herminjard, iii. no. 498, pp. 266–70; no. 512, pp. 300–1.

reminded that in Germany such debates had produced only division, strife and the loss of numberless souls. If the Lutherans wanted a settlement, the Sorbonne concluded, they had only to submit to the teaching of the church.[11]

In Germany, too, Francis's hopes were soon dashed. Johannes Sturm, the Strassburg reformer, urged Melanchthon to accept the king's invitation for the sake of his French co-religionists. His coming, he said, would be like a patch of blue in a stormy sky; he might even succeed in converting the king to the Gospel. 'He is quick-witted and sensible', Sturm wrote, 'and not stubborn; he submits readily to reasoned arguments.' Melanchthon found himself in a quandary: if he went to France, he might be trapped into conceding fundamental points of doctrine in exchange for trivial ones; if not, his friends would feel let down. In the end, his mind was made up for him: on 17 August his lord, the elector of Saxony, refused him permission to go to France.[12]

Yet Francis did not immediately give up hope of coming to an understanding with the German Protestants. He was encouraged by Bucer, who revived the idea of a debate between French and German divines. He advised the king to make a new approach to the German princes and the city of Strassburg, but stressed the need to keep politics out of religion.[13] Langey was accordingly dispatched to the diet of the Schmalkaldic League. On 19 December in a speech to the assembled delegates, he urged them to send representatives to a conference in France before accepting a papal invitation to the general council at Mantua. In the course of private conversations with Melanchthon, Bucer and Brück, the Saxon chancellor, Langey said that Francis shared their views on most points of doctrine. The king, he explained, regarded the papal primacy as a human institution; he held their views on the Eucharist, the intercession of saints, religious images and free will. He favoured mutual concessions on the mass. Only their attitude to Purgatory and good works was likely to cause difficulty, yet Francis believed that this was not insuperable. He wanted clerical celibacy maintained, but was in favour of exempting priests who were already married. Lastly, he hoped to gain concessions from the pope regarding communion in both kinds.

Was Francis really prepared to go so far in a Protestant direction? This is unlikely. He was always ready to listen to new ideas, but never showed any special interest in Protestantism. Langey had probably been instructed to exaggerate his master's willingness to compromise over religion in order to gain the political support of the Schmalkaldic League. In

---

11   Imbart de La Tour, iii. 575–8; Herminjard, iii. 341 n. 2; *C.S.P. Span.*, v (pt 1), no. 225.
12   Herminjard, iii. no. 515, pp. 306–12; Bourrilly, *Guillaume du Bellay*, pp. 193–4.
13   J. V. Pollet, *Martin Bucer* (1962), ii. 505; *L.P.*, ix. no. 544.

December 1535 Francis was preparing the conquest of Savoy. Sooner or later it was bound to bring him into conflict with the emperor. He therefore needed the support of the German Protestants, but he fell into the trap Bucer had warned him against: by intimating that he was prepared to join the Schmalkaldic League, he mixed politics with religion, thereby arousing the distrust of the delegates. They turned down the pope's invitation to Mantua, but at the same time evaded the issue of the theological debate in France. Nor would they admit Francis to their League. Instead, they undertook not to help his enemies in any quarrel that did not involve the emperor or his dominions.[14]

Distrust of France among the German Protestants was sustained by reports that their French co-religionists were still suffering persecution in spite of the edict of Coucy. In July 1535, for example, they received an appeal for help from the Vaudois or Waldenses of Provence.[15] These were a religious sect whose origins went back to the twelfth-century Poor Men of Lyons. They had since spread to various parts of central and southern Europe, notably Piedmont and Provence. The Vaudois of Provence in the early sixteenth century were mostly peasants who lived in villages and small towns spread out along the valley of the Durance between the Upper Alps and Aix-en-Provence. Their main centres were Mérindol in Provence and Cabrières in the Comtat-Venaissin, which belonged to the papacy. Substituting their own apostolic forms for the authority and practice of the Roman church, the Vaudois believed spiritual probity to be essential to the administration of the sacraments. They rejected the doctrine of purgatory, most prayers, the intercession of saints and almost all visible signs in ritual. They stressed the importance of baptism and of their own form of the Eucharist. Itinerant preachers, called *barbes*, attended to their spiritual needs. The Vaudois began to show an interest in the Reformation as early as 1526, and in September 1532, after making contact with leaders of the Swiss Reformation, they adopted a new confession of faith which included predestination. They formally repudiated the Roman church, accepted clerical marriage and ordered communal worship to be henceforth open and public. Even more important was their acceptance of the Zwinglian view of the Eucharist, which meant that, as sacramentarians, they were not eligible for the amnesty granted by the edict of Coucy.[16]

---

[14] Bourrilly, *Guillaume du Bellay*, pp. 206–11.

[15] Herminjard, iii. no. 521, pp. 327–32; no. 523, pp. 335–9.

[16] G. Leff, *Heresy in the Later Middle Ages* (Manchester, 1967), ii. 452–85; J. Marx, *L'Inquisition en Dauphiné: étude sur le développement et la répression de l'hérésie et de la sorcellerie du XIVᵉ siècle au début du règne de François Iᵉʳ* (1914), pp. 19–23; G. H. Williams, *The Radical Reformation* (London, 1962), pp. 519–29.

This edict, however, limited as it was, encouraged reformers to hope that Francis was still open to persuasion. They believed he had been deliberately misled by evil counsellors about the activities of his evangelical subjects. He had been told that they were trouble-makers bent on overthrowing church and state, and some reformers hoped that the king might still be prepared to listen to the truth. This hope was most eloquently expressed by John Calvin in the preface to his *Christianae religionis institutio*, which he addressed to Francis. It was completed in August 1535 and published in Basle in March 1536. Calvin's original purpose, he states, had been to write merely a work of pious instruction for those who hungered after Christ, but, after the terrible persecution which had been directed against them, he had decided to write instead a confession of faith for the king's information. The evangelicals, Calvin explained, had been falsely charged with sedition, and their cause, the very cause of Christ, was being torn and trampled upon. 'This has happened', he writes, 'as a result of the tyranny of certain Pharisees rather than by your will.' Not even those who sympathize with the evangelicals are prepared to rise in their defence; they talk merely of pardoning the error and imprudence of ignorant men. It is the king's duty to listen to what the evangelicals have to say in their own defence. A true king is one who rules as God's minister on earth; otherwise he is not a king but a robber. Replying to the objections commonly raised to evangelical teaching, Calvin argues that it is the fashionable theology of the late-medieval church that is new; the evangelicals are the true heirs of the primitive church. In a final appeal to the king he writes: 'although your heart is at present alienated from, even inflamed against, us, I trust that we may regain its favour, if you will only read our confession once without indignation or wrath'.[17]

It is not known whether Francis ever read Calvin's epistle, but reformers were further encouraged on 31 May 1536, when the king, allegedly in response to an appeal from the council of Berne, extended the pardon contained in the edict of Coucy to all heretics, including sacramentarians. But the condition attached to the pardon remained: a dissenter was required to abjure his faith within six months, and this continued seriously to disturb Protestant consciences.[18] In July the governments of Strassburg, Zürich, Basle and Berne appealed to Francis to waive the

---

[17] Herminjard, iv. no. 545, pp. 3–23. See also T. H. L. Parker, *John Calvin* (London, 1975), pp. 34–7.

[18] *Ordonnances*, viii. no. 741, pp. 93–6; Herminjard, iv. 71 n. 2. The poet Clément Marot, who had been in Italy in April 1535, returned to Lyons, where he abjured in December 1536. See C. A. Mayer, *La religion de Marot* (Geneva, 1960), pp. 35–9; M. François, *Le cardinal François de Tournon* (1951), p. 145 n. 1.

condition, but he did not reply. Doubtless he had more urgent matters to
attend to: the emperor had just invaded Provence, and Francis lost his
eldest son on 10 August. In November, therefore, the four cities decided
to send two envoys to the king. They were instructed *inter alia* to tell
Francis that it was unreasonable to expect Protestants to abjure their
faith. They were also to praise the 'good conversation and honesty' of the
French exiles they had seen: far from criticizing and cursing the king, they
had sung his praises and prayed for him. He had no cause, therefore, to
fear any 'tumult or rebellion' on their part; all they wanted was freedom
of conscience.[19]

The envoys saw Francis at Compiègne on 17 February 1537 and were
pleased by what he told them, but they had no sooner left for home than
Montmorency sent them a written reply from the king which satisfied
them less. They ought to be content, he said, with the extension of the
edict of Coucy, which had been conceded on their account alone; all
religious exiles were now free to return to France without danger to their
lives and property. As for heretics who were said to be still in prison, he
would order their release and pardon them like the rest. But the letter
made no mention of abjuration.[20] On 15 March the council of Berne
reported to the other cities on the mission of the two envoys. Apart from
Langey and Count Wilhelm von Fürstenberg, the mercenary captain, they
had come across few friends of the Gospel at the French court and
therefore had been less successful than they might have been in more
favourable circumstances. The queen of Navarre, however, had done all
in her power to assist them. The council was anxious to find out from
Fürstenberg whether the king's letter truly reflected his intentions, for he
had told the count that he had dismissed the Swiss envoys fully satisfied.[21]

We do not know whether Count Wilhelm was able to throw light on
the discrepancy between Francis's verbal and written statements to the
Swiss envoys, but in September he was again approached, this time by the
council of Geneva, in the interest of evangelical prisoners held at
Grenoble, Lyons and elsewhere. Fürstenberg obtained a promise that they
would be set free, but in November the Genevan pastors were dismayed
to learn of the burning of two Protestants at Nîmes. Believing that
Zürich had recently signed a treaty with Francis in which he had promised
to treat heretics more leniently, they asked the canton to protest to the
king without delay. What this treaty was is not clear: Zürich had consistently refused to allow its subjects to serve as mercenaries, and in the

[19] Herminjard, iv. no. 566, pp. 70–3; no. 577, pp. 95–8; no. 604, pp. 169–72.
[20] *Ibid.*, iv. no. 612, pp. 191–3.
[21] *Ibid.*, iv. no. 618, pp. 202–3. On Fürstenberg see *ibid.*, vi. 123 n. 9 and J. V. Wagner,
      Graf Wilhelm von Fürstenberg, 1491–1549 (Stuttgart, 1966).

summer of 1535 it had resisted French efforts to bring about a change in its policy. On 17 November Berne appealed to Francis to stop the persecution in his kingdom, but to no avail.[22] In short, what the king promised and did were quite different things: persecution in France continued in spite of the edicts of 1535 and 1536. As long as the war with the emperor lasted, Francis was content to string the Protestant powers along with 'fair words'.

In June 1538, however, the war was brought to an end by the truce of Nice, and in July Francis and Charles met at Aigues-Mortes. This meeting was followed by a genuine attempt to heal the differences between the two rulers, which culminated in the emperor's visit to France in the winter of 1539–40.[23] Inevitably, this *volte-face* in French foreign policy affected Francis's relations with the Protestant powers. In August an embassy from the Schmalkaldic League, which had come to France in the hope of concluding an alliance, left empty-handed but for a letter in which Francis assured the German Protestants of his friendship. Montmorency was more forthright: when the ambassadors reminded him of promises formerly given to them by Langey, he told them bluntly that 'times had changed'. Did this mean that Francis planned to desert them? The Germans were uncertain about this. The elector of Saxony suspected that the king's protestations of friendship were meant only to strengthen his hand in his negotiations with Charles; the Strassburgers, on the other hand, believed they were genuine. In fact, Francis's policy at this moment was one of strict neutrality in respect of German domestic affairs. He replied evasively, in December 1538, to a papal request that he should intervene against the German Protestants, but he was equally determined not to help them. In May 1539 he urged them to come to terms with Charles.[24]

The main impact of the change in French foreign policy on Protestants in France was to isolate them from their friends abroad at a time when they badly needed help. By 1538 it had become clear to the royal administration that only by giving the parlements more power to deal with heresy would its progress be checked. Thus on 16 December Francis urged the parlement of Toulouse to prosecute heretics vigorously and to punish them in an exemplary way.[25] On 24 June 1539 all judges, both secular and ecclesiastical, were instructed to co-operate in fighting heresy, but the procedure laid down by this edict was too complicated: it made for friction among the authorities concerned, thereby lessening their

---

[22] Herminjard, iv. no. 658, pp. 293–4; no. 668, pp. 315–19; no. 669, pp. 320–1.
[23] See above, ch. 19.
[24] J.-Y. Mariotte, 'François Iᵉʳ et la Ligue de Smalkalde', *Revue suisse d'histoire*, xvi (1966), 216–20; Herminjard, vi. 236 n. 14.
[25] C.A.F., iii. 10534.

effectiveness.[26] On 1 June 1540, therefore, a new edict – the famous edict of Fontainebleau – gave the parlements what they had long wanted: overall control of jurisdiction over heresy. The preamble recalled all the measures taken by the king in the past to extirpate 'evil errors' from his kingdom. He believed that it had been purged of these, but now they had reappeared. They were being spread partly by religious exiles who had come home, partly by heretics who had lain low during the persecution. Both sorts were being helped and sheltered by 'a number of important people'; hence the need for exceptional measures. The ordinance entrusted to all royal judges (i.e. members of the sovereign courts, *baillis, sénéchaux, prévôts* etc.), 'indifferently and concurrently', the right of enquiry (*inquisition*) in respect of all persons, lay and ecclesiastical, except clergy in major orders. After prosecution (*information*), suspects were to be sent immediately to the sovereign courts for sentencing, regardless of any privilege or franchise they might claim. All feudal lords (*hauts justiciers*) were enjoined on pain of deprivation of their jurisdiction to carry out searching enquiries within their respective areas and to refer suspects to the king's judges. The ecclesiastical courts retained their jurisdiction over clerks in major orders but were to be assisted by the secular arm. Finally, all the king's subjects were ordered, on pain of *lèse-majesté*, not to harbour or assist heretics but to denounce them and assist in their extirpation, 'just as each is bound to run in order to put out a public fire'. The king expressed the hope that thanks to these measures his people would remain instructed in the true faith.[27]

On 30 August 1542 Francis signed a new edict. Despite the measures so far taken, he admitted, heresy was growing. He urged the sovereign courts, therefore, to enquire 'diligently, secretly and thoroughly' into the 'assemblies, conventicles, intelligences and secret practices of the sectarians'. The ecclesiastical authorities were instructed to do likewise and to report their findings to the parlements within four months on pain of losing their temporalities.[28] But the clergy stood up for their privileges: they resented the encroachment of the secular courts on their jurisdiction in cases of heresy. Francis gave way, in theory at least. On 23 July 1543 he decided that the power of search and arrest would henceforth be shared by the secular and ecclesiastical authorities.[29] Thereafter royal decrees against heresy were issued almost without interruption till the end of the reign: they included admonitions to the parlements to stimulate their zeal, renewal of the powers of inquisitors of the faith, and commissions to

---

[26] Isambert, xii. 566; *C.A.F.*, iv. 11072.
[27] Isambert, xii. 676–81.
[28] *Ibid.*, xii. 785–7; A.N., X[1a] 1549, fol. 440b.
[29] Isambert, xii. 818; *C.A.F.*, iv. 13225; A.N., U. 2035, fol. 53a.

members of the sovereign courts to hunt down heretics in areas of special infestation.

The Sorbonne, meanwhile, took steps to provide the persecutors with clear doctrinal guidelines, for many people, even among the clergy, were still in some doubt as to what the doctrine of the church was. One preacher might say one thing, and another the opposite. To help people choose between them the faculty drew up a list of twenty-five articles, which all doctors and bachelors of the university were required to sign. Anyone who refused was to be expelled, for 'it is dangerous for wolves to be fed among one's flock'. The articles were a complete reaffirmation of Catholic dogma, worship and organization. They urged the faithful to speak of 'Jesus Christ', not just 'Christ', and of St Paul and St Matthew, not just Paul and Matthew without the honorific prefix. On 23 July Francis formally approved the articles and ordered their publication throughout the kingdom. Anyone preaching or teaching another doctrine was to be prosecuted.[30] The official adoption of the Sorbonne's confession of faith provided the campaign against heresy with a clearer sense of direction.

Books also came under fire in 1542. On 1 July a proclamation, read out at all the main crossroads in Paris 'to the sound of trumpets', called on every inhabitant to surrender to the clerk of the Parlement, within twenty-four hours and on pain of hanging, Calvin's *Institutes* and all other books banned by the court. This was followed by a series of measures aimed at clandestine presses and at controlling the book trade. Every master printer had to have his mark and was made personally responsible for the misdeeds of his journeymen. Also in 1542 the Sorbonne began to draw up the first index of forbidden books. It was published in the following year and included sixty-five titles, including works by Calvin, Luther, Melanchthon, Dolet and Marot and translations of Scripture published by Robert Estienne. This caused much alarm in the book trade. Twenty-four booksellers protested, but the index was revised and enlarged in 1545 and 1546. Soon the search for banned books by the Parlement's commissioners in shops, colleges, religious houses and private homes began to yield results. On 14 January 1544 Calvin's *Institutes* and fourteen works published by Etienne Dolet were ceremonially burnt outside Notre-Dame. Between 1541 and 1544 six Parisian booksellers or printers were prosecuted; one was tortured and two sent to the stake.[31] In the provinces, too, members of the book trade suffered persecution. The most vulnerable were the *colporteurs* or book-peddlars. Whereas booksellers or

---

[30] Isambert, xii. 820–7.
[31] N. Weiss, 'La Sorbonne, le Parlement de Paris et les livres hérétiques de 1542 à 1546', *B.S.H.P.F.*, xxxiv (1885), 19–28; A.N., U. 2035, fol. 60a; A.N., X^{1a} 1551, fol. 550b.

printers could sometimes save themselves by invoking the protection of some influential client or friend, the *colporteurs* had no such recourse: if caught, they were burnt along with their wares.

The persecution was, of course, directed at a much wider circle than just members of the book trade. During the thirties and forties heresy made deep inroads into French society, certain groups being more affected than others. Among the secular clergy, the bishops and cathedral chapters were largely immune, but the Reformation had much support among the lower clergy. The regular clergy, especially the mendicant orders, was seriously 'contaminated'. As yet the nobility and peasantry were largely untouched, but heresy was rife among the bourgeoisie and proletariat of certain towns. The last seven years of Francis's reign saw a steep rise in the number of prosecutions for heresy by the Parlement of Paris. A purge of the capital's religious houses, especially the Augustinians, was undertaken, and the Parlement's prisons began to fill up.[32] Parisians, who had seen few burnings since May 1535, had to witness a new round of grisly spectacles. Foremost among the victims was the printer-publisher Etienne Dolet, who had already been arrested in Lyons, tried and pardoned. But his unorthodox views again attracted the notice of the authorities, and, on 3 August 1546, he was burned in the Place Maubert as a relapsed heretic.[33]

Outside Paris, yet within the *ressort* of its Parlement, bishops were obliged to delegate their judicial powers (*bailler vicariat*) to members of the Parlement charged with the prosecution of heretics. In 1545 five commissioners were assigned to particular areas with full powers of search and punishment. One of the most active was Nicole Sanguin at Meaux, who arrested sixty people – three of them priests – in September 1546. Of these, fourteen were tortured and burnt, four banished and the rest given various penalties; only four were released. The Parlement's commissioners were also very active in the Loire valley and along the Atlantic coast. At Orléans and Beaugency, Pierre Hotman threw so many people into prison for no rhyme or reason that the bishop's official and the royal *bailli* had to intervene and get them released. At La Rochelle, where the authorities feared a link-up of religious and political unrest, 118 people were arrested and 25 sentenced to death.[34]

[32] Imbart de La Tour, iv. 219–65; A.N., X¹ᵃ 1553, fols. 109b–110a, 274b–275a.
[33] J. Viénot, *Histoire de la réforme française des origines à l'Edit de Nantes* (1926), i. 158; R. C. Christie, *Etienne Dolet, the Martyr of the Renaissance* (London, 1880), p. 456. Cf. L. Febvre, *Le problème de l'incroyance au XVIᵉ siècle: la religion de Rabelais* (1947), pp. 48–53. Herminjard, viii. 303 n. 22. D. R. Kelley, *The Beginning of Ideology: Consciousness and Society in the French Reformation* (Cambridge, 1981), pp. 215–20.
[34] Imbart de La Tour, iv. 322–31; Weiss, 'La Sorbonne', p. 26.

Elsewhere in France the actions of the parlements were uneven. In Dauphiné only eleven cases of heresy in seven years were reported and only light sentences given. Yet there were certainly Protestant groups in that province. In Normandy the parlement was so lethargic that the king suspended it in 1540 and appointed commissioners to hold the Grands Jours at Bayeux, specifically to deal with heresy. Even after the parlement had been reinstated it remained feeble. In May 1542 it was the scene of a remarkable squabble between the president and the archbishop's official, each blaming the other for a sharp rise in heresy in Rouen.[35] In Guyenne the parlement was also fairly easy-going. In 1542 it carried out a search, and four years later repeated the exercise rather more energetically. Even so, the king suspended the court after the revolt at La Rochelle, transferring its powers to a special commission which demonstrated far more zeal. But if four parlements were less than assiduous in tracking down and punishing heretics, the two parlements where Roman law was applied fell over themselves to do their duty. The court at Toulouse waged a fierce campaign against dissenters in Languedoc. Prosecutions between 1540 and 1549 numbered 200 at least, and 18 death sentences were passed. In Provence the parlement was even more militant: within fifteen months more than 60 people were arrested and sentenced. Persecution of the Vaudois was intensified.[36]

Intermittent persecution of the Vaudois had taken place since the fourteenth century. In 1487 Pope Innocent VIII had launched a crusade against them, but in France at least this had been stopped by Louis XII.[37] The persecution, however, was resumed under Francis. About 1528 Jean de Roma, the Dominican inquisitor of the faith, toured their villages extorting confessions under torture (his favourite method was to pour boiling fat into their boots). His activities, however, came to the king's notice. An enquiry commission was set up and a warrant issued for de Roma's arrest, but he managed to escape to Avignon, where he died.[38] Yet persecution of the Vaudois continued. In 1533 a teacher at Avignon reported that the Vaudois (whose number he estimated at 6,000) were being burned and their property seized.[39] In 1538, after they had complained of renewed persecution, the German Protestants began to agitate on their behalf. During the next two years the violence continued in spite of the lack of enthusiasm shown by Chasseneuz, president of the parlement of Provence, and Sadoleto, bishop of Carpentras. In May 1540

[35] Viénot, i. 151–3.   [36] Imbart de La Tour, iv. 331–6.

[37] Marx, *L'Inquisition en Dauphiné*, pp. 158–67, 178–98.

[38] Herminjard, vii. 465–88, 513; viii. 4 n. 6; E. Arnaud, *Histoire des Protestants de Provence, du Comtat-Venaissin et de la principauté d'Orange* (1884), i. 3–6.

[39] J. Bonnet, 'La tolérance du cardinal Sadolet', *B.S.H.P.F.*, xxxv (1886), 484.

Francis empowered the parlement to conduct on-the-spot prosecutions against the Vaudois, using torture if necessary, and to judge them in first instance.[40] On 18 November the parlement sentenced nineteen Vaudois of Mérindol who had failed to answer a summons to be burned, their families to be arrested or banished from the kingdom, their property to be confiscated and Mérindol itself to be destroyed. In December Francis ordered the decree, generally called the *arrêt de Mérindol*, to be carried out, but soon afterwards he changed his mind, perhaps in consequence of a report submitted by Guillaume du Bellay.[41] This showed that the Vaudois, for all their idiosyncratic religious practices, were hard-working, God-fearing and loyal subjects.[42]

In February 1541 Francis pardoned the Vaudois on condition that they abjured their faith within three months.[43] But they would not do this unless their error could be proved by reference to Scripture. In April they petitioned the parlement of Provence, enclosing their confession of faith. They explained that they had disobeyed the parlement's summons not in any spirit of rebellion, but in the light of the harsh punishments meted out to their brethren who, in the past, had obeyed the court. They begged to be allowed to live in peace.[44] The parlement, in reply, invited the Vaudois to come to Aix formally to abjure, but only one turned up with a demand for an unconditional pardon. The king, after receiving a complaint against them from the parlement, ordered the seigneur de Grignan, the provincial governor, to wipe them out.[45] But an appeal sent to Francis by the German Protestants assembled at Regensburg seems to have led to a temporary stay of execution.[46] In March 1542 the parlement sent commissioners to Mérindol in an attempt to persuade the inhabitants to abjure, but the mission failed miserably. Soon afterwards one of the commissioners, the bishop of Cavaillon, led an armed force against the Vaudois of Cabrières. This provoked an intervention in their favour by their neighbours at Mérindol, and in March 1543 Francis ordered the decree of November 1540 to be reactivated. Yet once again they were spared after they had sent a deputation to the king in Paris with a complaint that their persecutors were more interested in seizing their goods than in defending the faith. The king suspended the *arrêt* and set up

---

[40] Bourrilly, *Guillaume du Bellay*, pp. 314–15.
[41] Herminjard, vii. 17 n. 15; Isambert, xii. 698; Arnaud, i. 22.
[42] *C.A.F.*, iv. 11758; Bourrilly, *Guillaume du Bellay*, pp. 315–17. The original text of the report is missing, but it is summarized in J.-A. de Thou, *Histoire universelle* (London, 1734), i (bk vi), 416–17. It is sometimes claimed that the report was commissioned by Francis, but this is uncertain. Du Bellay may have acted on his own initiative or in response to the German Protestants.
[43] *C.A.F.*, iv. 11826.   [44] Herminjard, vii. 80–2.
[45] Arnaud, i. 42.   [46] *Ibid.*, i. 43–5; Herminjard, vii. no. 983, pp. 126–8.

a commission to discover the facts. Meanwhile, he revoked the affair to his own court and forbade the parlement to deal with it.[47]

The vacillations in the king's policy towards the Vaudois are symptomatic of the uncertainties, difficulties and pressures facing the authorities in their fight against heresy. The persecution, even where it was carried out with vigour, could not by its very nature be wholly successful. Judicial enquiries, especially in large towns, were slow and tentative; it was fairly easy for a heretic to escape notice by going into hiding or simply keeping his mouth shut. Investigations tended to be judicial rather than theological in method: magistrates would look for tangible offences rather than discuss ideas. Generally, torture was used only if and when a suspect refused to answer questions. There were many clashes over jurisdiction between secular and ecclesiastical courts, and parlements did not hesitate to revise or quash sentences passed by local magistrates or ecclesiastical judges if they detected some technical error or abuse.[48] The penalties imposed for heresy were not uniform: judges used a graduated scale that varied with the gravity of an offence and the status of the accused. Many convicted heretics were given light sentences, such as public penance or a fine. The more serious offenders were flogged. Only the incorrigible ones were normally banished or burnt. Burnings before 1550 were relatively few. In 1543, for example, the Parlement of Paris judged forty-three cases of heresy, yet not one resulted in an execution; fourteen ended in an acquittal.[49]

Given these facts and others, such as the immunity from prosecution enjoyed by many foreign Protestants in France – German and Swiss mercenaries, university students and teachers, merchants and artisans – and the reluctance of the more liberal prelates to apply the law harshly, it is not really surprising that heresy continued to thrive in France after 1538. Throughout the late thirties and forties 'Lutherans' (they were still called by this name though their views were often different or far more extreme than Luther's) continued to be reported from almost every part of the kingdom. In May 1542 the president of the parlement of Rouen claimed that the church had never been in so much danger since the days of the Arian heresy. Having contaminated the lower orders in Rouen, it had begun to win support among the 'chief families' in the city. The

---

[47] Arnaud, i. 45–54. See Francis's reply to the council of Basle (14 Oct. 1543). Herminjard, ix. no. 1293, pp. 68–70.

[48] On 1 August 1544 the Parlement of Paris forbade the *bailli* of Touraine to obstruct the *lieutenant-criminel* of the *sénéchaussée* of Anjou in his search for 'Lutherans' at Chinon on pain of a fine and loss of office. A.N., X^1a 1553, fols. 293b–294a.

[49] E. de Moreau, P. Jourda and P. Janelle, *La crise religieuse du XVIe siècle* (1950), pp. 273–4.

archbishop's official pointed to a sharp drop in the number of communicants as evidence of a loss of confidence in the Sacrament.[50] Every now and again an incident brought the peril home to the king. In 1542, for example, disturbances occurred in Paris as a result of the heretical sermons of François Landry, *curé* of Sainte-Croix-de-la-Cité. Francis himself questioned the preacher, who was so terrified that he lapsed into total silence. But others continued to preach in the same vein, notably François Perrucel, a Franciscan, at Saint-Germain-l'Auxerrois, provoking yet more disturbances.[51] All this was a matter of serious concern to the government, particularly now that heresy was officially regarded as a crime against the state. What is more, it was an international disease. The emperor, too, was worried about Protestantism undermining his authority in Germany. Inevitably, the topic came up for discussion in the Franco-imperial talks that produced the peace of Crépy. On 20 September 1544 Charles de Milly informed the Parlement of the peace. He added that Francis and the emperor were determined to rid their dominions completely of heretics and that the king wanted those already imprisoned to be tried expeditiously. The emperor had chosen Cardinal Tournon to go and discuss the matter with him. The first president, Lizet, thanked Milly for his good news and promised that the Parlement would do its best to scatter the 'sectarians'.[52] When Tournon returned from Flanders in November he had reason to hope that the friendship between Francis and Charles was firm enough to allow for more effective action in defence of the faith. But he may have felt the need for a demonstration of good intent by his master. This could be the explanation of the massacre of the Vaudois in April 1545 which historians have all too often regarded as an isolated episode in the history of the early French Reformation.[53] From Tournon's standpoint the massacre could not have occurred more opportunely. Yet there is strong evidence that local circumstances rather than a decision of the central government precipitated the massacre.

Local pressure for renewed persecution of the Vaudois arose naturally out of the appointment of Jean Meynier, baron d'Oppède, as first president of the parlement of Provence.[54] Oppède's hatred of the Vaudois was not merely religious: he had long wanted a pretext to seize the land of his

[50] Viénot, *Histoire de la réforme*, i. 151–2. See also D. Nicholls, 'Inertia and Reform in the Pre-Tridentine French Church: The Response to Protestantism in the Diocese of Rouen, 1520–1562', *Journal of Ecclesiastical History*, xxxii (1981), 185–97.

[51] T. de Bèze, *Histoire ecclésiastique* (Lille, 1841), pp. 19–20.

[52] A.N., X¹ᵃ 1553, fols. 490b–491a.

[53] François, *François de Tournon*, pp. 214–16.

[54] Jean Meynier became second president of the parlement of Provence in November 1541 and succeeded G. Garçonnet as first president in December 1543. *C.A.F.*, vii. 24741, 25047.

neighbour, the dame de Cental, who owned several Vaudois villages. Unfortunately for the Vaudois, Oppède's rise to power coincided with the disappearance of certain moderating influences. Guillaume du Bellay had died in January 1543, and Sadoleto returned to Italy in March 1545.[55] During the winter of 1544–5 alarming reports of Vaudois activities, deliberately coloured by Oppède to suggest sedition on their part, began to reach the ears of the king and his ministers. On 1 January 1545, therefore, Francis ordered the *arrêt de Mérindol* to be carried out.[56] In the absence of Grignan, who had gone to Germany on embassy, responsibility for this fell on Oppède, who succeeded, possibly with the king's approval, in securing the services of the so-called *bandes de Piémont*, veterans of the Italian wars under the command of 'Captain Polin', baron de La Garde, who were about to embark at Marseilles for service in the Anglo-French war around Boulogne.[57]

On 11 April Oppède and Polin held a council of war at Marseilles, and a week later operations against the Vaudois began. Five villages owned by the dame de Cental (who had allegedly refused her daughter's hand to one of Oppède's relatives) were the first to be pillaged and put to the sword. The male inhabitants were either butchered or sent to the galleys, and their womenfolk raped. Another five villages were then destroyed, though no massacres took place there, as the inhabitants had fled. Oppède and Polin then turned their attention to Mérindol, where they had expected the Vaudois to make a stand. Instead they found a young imbecile, who was interrogated and shot, and a crowd of women who had taken refuge in the church. These were dragged out and made to suffer every sort of cruelty and indignity. At Cabrières Oppède and Polin met with some resistance, so they bombarded the village. The defenders surrendered in exchange for their lives, but as they came into the open they were butchered or taken prisoner and sold as slaves.

The number of victims of the Vaudois massacre is not known exactly. Contemporary estimates vary widely: some say hundreds, others thousands. According to the emperor, between 6,000 and 8,000 were killed, including 700 women who were burnt in a church. Another report put the number of survivors sent to the galleys at Marseilles at 666, including young children and men in their eighties; of this total, about 200 died of hunger and exposure. On the other hand, a few years after the massacre, an eyewitness found the Vaudois villages prosperous and full of people, the fields well cultivated and the crops plentiful. This suggests that

---

[55] Bourrilly, *Guillaume du Bellay*, p. 365; Bonnet, 'La tolérance du cardinal Sadolet', *B.S.H.P.F.*, xxxvi (1887), 57, 115.

[56] Arnaud, i. 56.

[57] *C.S.P. Span.*, viii. no. 82, p. 148.

the scale of the massacre may have been exaggerated by Protestant or imperial propagandists. Even so, it was a monstrous crime, particularly as the victims had never been tried. Many people at the time were profoundly shocked by it, but the king was not amongst them. On 18 August he formally approved the action taken against the Vaudois. He also congratulated Oppède for his efficient enforcement of the law and, in the following year, allowed him to receive a papal knighthood.[58]

Protestants abroad were appalled by the massacre. The council of Strassburg protested to the king, only to be sharply rebuked by him. He had never meddled with their subjects, he said, and was therefore surprised that they should do so with his and question the punishments he decreed for them. The Vaudois, he continued, had interfered with the running of an important border province of his kingdom, and he could not see that, in so doing, they had been following the precepts of the Gospel. Their views, moreover, were such that no German prince or state would tolerate them. Finally, he asked the Strassburgers to avoid using such words as 'tyranny' and 'atrocious punishments' when they next wrote to him; otherwise he would have to answer them harshly. He was surprised, knowing their prudence, that they should write so carelessly. A protest by the Swiss cantons received the same reply.[59]

This was not the end of the story of the massacre. Under Henri II Oppède and his associates were brought to justice following a complaint from the dame de Cental, who had suffered heavy material damage as a result of the massacre. A special tribunal, called *chambre de la reine*, was set up at Melun, but it was soon dissolved because of the partiality to the accused shown by the judges. In March 1549 the case was transferred to the Parlement of Paris, where it took up fifty consecutive sessions of the court and became a *cause célèbre*. Comparing himself to Saul, to whom Jehovah had given the task of exterminating the Amalekites, Oppède claimed that he had only carried out the king's orders. He denied liability for the massacre at Cabrières, since the town lay outside his jurisdiction. Turning the tables on the dame de Cental, he accused her of having protected heretics and brought disaster on her vassals by her stubborn refusal to obey the parlement's decrees. In the end Oppède and all the other accused save one were acquitted. The exception was the *avocat-général* Guérin, who was hanged on account of crimes not directly concerned with the massacre.[60]

The massacre of the Vaudois was the last chapter in the grim story of mounting religious persecution under Francis I. But was the whole court

[58]   Arnaud, i. 60–76; P. Gaffarel, 'Les massacres de Cabrières et de Mérindol en 1545', *R.H.*, cvii (1911), 241–64; François, *François de Tournon*, p. 221 n. 2.
[59]   Arnaud, i. 82–4.   [60]   Gaffarel, pp. 264–71.

committed to it? What of those members of the king's entourage who were described as 'Lutherans' by foreign observers? Did they approve of the repression to which Francis set his seal? Foremost among such 'Lutherans' were the king's mistress, Madame d'Etampes, and his younger son, Charles d'Orléans. Another was Jean du Bellay, cardinal-bishop of Paris. In September 1543 Orléans wrote to the landgrave of Hesse saying that it was his wish that the Gospel be preached in France and that only respect for his father and brother had restrained him from introducing it into his duchy. He intended, however, to do so in Luxemburg, and for this reason asked to be admitted to the Schmalkaldic League.[61] At first this may seem an astonishing letter, but once it is placed in its political context it ceases to surprise. The duke had just conquered Luxemburg and was looking to the German Protestants for approval and support. His letter was, in brief, a piece of pure political expediency.

In October 1546 Madame d'Etampes apparently wanted Francis to break with Rome, a less extreme view being advocated by Cardinal du Bellay. He wanted to see an Anglo-French alliance in aid of the hard-pressed German Protestants and saw a repudiation of papal authority as the inescapable sequel of such a move.[62] In November the French court was said to be full of 'Lutherans', whom Madame d'Etampes described as her 'evangelical brothers'.[63] But these statements occur in the reports of foreign diplomats and again need to be interpreted politically rather than religiously. In 1546 there was a powerful anti-imperial lobby at the French court. The emperor was engaged in a war with the German Protestants. He was being helped by the pope and was far more successful than the French had expected at first. Rather than see the Protestants crushed, Madame d'Etampes and her friends wanted the formation of an Anglo-French alliance aimed at rescuing them. Not unnaturally, supporters of such a policy were described as 'Lutherans' by the imperial ambassador. This did not necessarily mean, however, that their personal faith was Protestant or that they favoured religious toleration at home. Be that as it may, the persecution in France continued into the next reign, when it acquired an even greater momentum following the creation of the notorious *Chambre Ardente*.

[61] Herminjard, ix. no. 1278, pp. 23–5.
[62] *L.P.*, xxi (pt 1), 248; xxi (pt 2), 457; *St.P.*, xi. 322, 353.
[63] *C.S.P. Span.*, viii. no. 347; *L.P.*, xxi (pt 2), 406.

26

The triumph of faction

FACTION LOOMED large in the political life of France during the last five years of Francis I's reign. This was reflected in the changing fortunes of certain high-ranking officials and in the comments of foreign observers. Three reasons may be suggested for this state of affairs: the king's failing health; the enmity between the Dauphin and his brother, the duc d'Orléans; and the baneful influence of the duchesse d'Etampes.

In January 1543 William Paget, the English ambassador to France, explained to Henry VIII that it would be difficult for him to discover Francis's designs in Scotland. 'This king', he wrote, 'never sojourns two nights in one place, disposing himself as the report of great harts is made to him, and continually removing at an hour's warning so that no man can tell where to find the Court.'[1] Similar complaints punctuate much of the diplomatic correspondence from France at this time.[2] Francis was continually dashing about the countryside, usually accompanied by a few gentlemen and his 'privy band' of ladies. These included the duchesse d'Etampes and other favourites, such as Mesdames de Canaples and Massy.[3] The queen was always left behind.

But, for all his remarkable energy, Francis was a desperately sick man. Ever since his almost fatal illness in Spain he had suffered relapses. The most serious had occurred in 1539, on the eve of the emperor's visit to France. In January 1545 he succumbed at Fontainebleau to an intermittent fever, provoked by an excruciatingly painful 'aposthume' or abscess 'in his lower parts'. Doctors and surgeons were called to his bedside from Paris and cauterized the abscess. They opened it up in three places, releasing a large quantity of pus. The king was then prescribed a course of 'Chinese wood' for twenty days. His doctors thought he was suffering from 'the French disease', but they also suspected an ulcerated bladder. By

---

[1] *L.P.*, xviii (pt 1), 29.
[2] E.g. *Correspondance des nonces en France: Capodiferro, Dandino et Guidiccione, 1541–1546*, ed. J. Lestocquoy (Rome, 1963), p. 65.
[3] Marie d'Acigné, wife of Jean de Créquy, seigneur de Canaples, and Marie de Montchenu, wife of Louis d'Harcourt, seigneur de Massy.

about 7 February Francis had recovered sufficiently to set off for the Loire valley in a litter.[4] He told the imperial envoy that he was fit again, 'albeit dead in respect of the ladies'. But in March his abscess had to be reopened. Some of his doctors thought his days were numbered, especially as he continued 'to indulge his appetite'; others were more hopeful. All, however, were agreed about the king's 'inside' being 'rotten'.[5] In July he ruptured a vein on which, according to his physician, the life of a man depends, yet he recovered.[6] In January 1546 his abscess gave further trouble, prompting the imperial envoy to remark: 'if the game lasts much longer, he may cease to play altogether'. But the abscess burst of its own accord, to the king's great relief. Early in February he was again hunting in a litter.[7] In July Sir Thomas Cheyney found him in much better shape than when he had last seen him, and later that month Lord Lisle saw him leap on his mule and kill a stag.[8] In November the king rose early each morning and covered seven or eight leagues a day, causing serious hardship to those who followed him on foot.[9]

In spite of all these fluctuations in his health, Francis remained firmly in charge of affairs of state; his relentless pursuit of pleasure entailed no surrender of authority. Decisions relating to peace or war were his alone. Each morning before he went hunting he would hear his councillors, and, in the evening, they would report to him on what had been done in his absence.[10] Foreign ambassadors describing their audiences with the king offer no evidence of the mental disorders commonly associated with syphilis in its tertiary stage. Francis continued to show a good grasp of international affairs, even if his judgment was sometimes at fault. His authoritarianism, too, was undimmed: he imposed a strict discipline on his courtiers. When Julien de Clermont murdered a fellow nobleman, no one save his sister dared to incur the king's displeasure by interceding on his behalf.[11] Yet everyone knew that Francis's days were numbered and that his demise would be followed by a palace revolution. For there was no love lost between the king and the Dauphin or between their respective mistresses, the duchesse d'Etampes and Diane de Poitiers. There was consequently much jockeying for position in anticipation of the next

---

4   C.S.P. Span., viii. no. 115; B.L., Add. MS. 28594, fol. 189a–b; L.P., xx (pt 1), 45.
5   B.L., Add. MS. 28594, fol. 103b.
6   C.S.P. Span., viii. no. 104; B.L., Add. MS. 28594, fol. 142.
7   C.S.P. Span., viii. nos. 187, 194; B.L., Add. MS. 28594, fols. 223–4.
8   L.P., xxi (pt 1), 1200, 1365, 1405.
9   C.S.P. Span., viii. no. 347.
10 L.P., xix (pt 1), 573.
11 Julien de Clermont, alias Tallard, was a friend of the Dauphin. His sister, Louise, married François du Bellay. He was executed in spite of an appeal by Henry VIII for clemency. St.P., xi. 270, 272, 301; C.A.F., v. 15322, vi. 22018, viii. 31004.

reign. 'Thus', wrote Wotton in August 1546, '. . . the Court everywhere is the Court, that is to say, a place where is used good shouldering and lifting at each other.'[12]

A powerful stimulus to faction was the rivalry between Francis's two sons, the Dauphin Henri and Charles, duc d'Orléans. This began in 1536 following the death of the Dauphin François, when Charles became the king's favourite son. The rift between the brothers widened in 1541 as a result of Montmorency's fall. Henri remained loyal to him throughout his disgrace, whereas Charles became the darling of Madame d'Etampes, the constable's implacable foe. Each prince thus became the focus of a party at court: while Montmorency's friends rallied round Henri, his enemies, including Admiral Chabot, Marguerite de Navarre and Madame d'Etampes, gathered round Charles. After the outbreak of war in 1542 the rivalry between the brothers was exacerbated by their military performance: whereas Charles added lustre to his exaggerated reputation as a soldier by his conquest of Luxemburg, Henri suffered the humiliation of having to retreat from Perpignan. His hopes of staging a comeback were dashed by the peace of Crépy, which was all the more galling to him in that it seemed devised to advance his brother's prospects. One of the aims of Francis's foreign policy in the early forties had been to create an Italian patrimony for his younger son, while Henri had to be satisfied for the present with Brittany. Under the terms of Crépy, Charles d'Orléans seemed set to marry the emperor's daughter and become duke of Milan. When he visited Antwerp in the autumn of 1544 he bore the arms of Milan quartered with those of France. Had the peace been implemented, Henri would have lost not only his rights in Italy but even perhaps much of his kingdom, for Charles had been promised four French duchies in apanage. This danger, however, was removed, in September 1545, by Charles's death. Thereafter Francis drew closer to the Dauphin: he admitted him to his council and tried to give him more administrative responsibility, but the old wounds were not so easily healed. Henri preferred to stay in the wings until the stage could be truly his.[13]

The third cause of faction was the influence of the king's mistress, the duchesse d'Etampes.[14] She was, as we have seen, the enemy of Montmorency and the Dauphin, and the friend of Admiral Chabot, Marguerite de Navarre and Charles d'Orléans. She also had favourites, notably Nicolas Bossu, seigneur de Longueval. Her political views were broadly consistent with her personal loyalties: thus, in foreign affairs, she leaned

---

[12]   St.P., xi. 277.
[13]   L. Romier, *Les origines politiques des Guerres de Religion* (1913), i. 1–11.
[14]   E. Desgardins, *Anne de Pisseleu duchesse d'Etampes et François 1er* (1904).

towards England rather than the empire, and, in religion, had Lutheran sympathies.[15] But she exercised her influence more to advance her relatives and friends than for some higher purpose, so that on this level she did not always appear consistent. She was also fickle in her personal relations and might easily abandon one favourite for another. In 1545, for example, she tried to get Admiral d'Annebault, who owed his advancement to her, dismissed so that Bossu might take his place. Having previously opposed the war with England, she now agreed to it in the hope that it would bring discredit on the admiral.[16] When Tournon tried to frustrate her intrigues, she turned against him too and tried to bring about his fall by instigating a charge of dishonesty during his administration of Lyons in 1536.[17] It has been suggested that the duchess had no political influence and that all the discreditable stories about her role in the war of 1536–42 and her responsibility for the peace of Crépy are the inventions of malevolent historians.[18] Some of these stories are probably untrue, but the importance of the duchess's political influence is amply attested by the diplomatic correspondence of the time. The papal nuncio Dandino, writing in May 1543, described it as follows: 'The king is more than ever addicted to his lascivious pleasures, being totally in the power of Madame d'Etampes, who, in order to appear wise always contradicts others and lets the king believe that he is God on earth, that no one can harm him and that those who deny this are moved by selfish interest.'[19]

In October 1542 Paget told Chabot that he was worried about the possible effects on Anglo-French relations of a schism within the French court. He identified two rival camps: on the one hand, the queen of Navarre, the duc d'Orléans, the duchesse d'Etampes and Chabot himself, and, on the other, the queen, the Dauphin, the constable and most of the cardinals. What would happen, he asked, if the papal legate, Sadoleto, were to win over the king with the help of Chabot's enemies? The admiral did not question the accuracy of Paget's assessment of the situation. 'No man', he replied, 'can serve in my place without many and great enemies and yet man must serve and abide to adventure.'[20] And this is exactly what he did. After his restoration to favour in March 1541 he had been reappointed to his various offices. A year later, he was cleared of *lèse-majesté* and, soon afterwards, of all other charges as well. On 10 October, however, he collapsed as he was talking to the king and had to be carried

15 *C.S.P. Span.*, viii. no. 347.
16 *C.S.P. Ven.*, v. no. 327.
17 M. François, *Le cardinal François de Tournon* (1951), pp. 208–10.
18 P. Paris, *Études sur François Premier* (1885), i. 253.
19 *Correspondance des nonces . . . Capodiferro* etc., p. 220.
20 *L.P.*, xvii. 935; *St.P.*, ix. 192.

to his lodging. He died on 1 June 1543, and, six days later, was given a magnificent funeral by the king.[21]

Chabot's rehabilitation led inevitably to the downfall of the chancellor, Guillaume Poyet, who had helped to bring him to trial. On 2 August 1542 he was arrested and sent to the Bastille. Various rumours circulated as to the reason for his detention, but he was evidently the victim of a court intrigue involving Madame d'Etampes.[22] With her help a certain La Renaudie had obtained the transfer of a lawsuit from the Parlement of Paris to that of Toulouse, but the chancellor had refused to seal the king's letters authorizing the transfer unless they were modified in some way. The duchess complained to the king, whereupon Poyet spoke disparagingly about women who meddle in affairs of state. His words reached the ears of the king; hence his arrest. Poyet begged the king to let him know his offence and wrote grovelling letters to his enemies. 'Madame', he wrote to the duchesse d'Etampes, 'your kindness to me had been so constant that I only became aware of it after I had lost it; and my first realization was that I was unworthy of it.' He also appealed to Chabot and Tournon, but his letters remained unanswered.[23]

Poyet's trial did not begin until April 1544, two years after his arrest. As chancellor, he was entitled to be tried by the whole Parlement, but Francis set aside this privilege on the ground that its implementation would disturb the normal course of justice. Instead, he appointed thirty-four special commissioners, who were mainly drawn from the Parlement. The chancellor was also denied counsel under a provision of the ordinance of Villers-Cotterêts, which he had promulgated. When he complained of this to his judges, they replied curtly: 'Patere legem quam ipse tulisti.' The king gave evidence against Poyet; he also suggested that the gens du roi should, contrary to normal usage, attend the rapport or final judicial review of the case and only withdraw for the judges' discussion. But he backed down in the face of strong opposition from the judges; it was agreed that the gens du roi would appear only to present his case.

Many were the charges levelled at Poyet. He was accused of fraud in respect of a royal gift arising out of the inheritance of Louise of Savoy, of cheating the comtesse de Brienne over the purchase of an estate, of corruptly misusing his privilege of judging counterfeiters of the king's seal, of evoking lawsuits from the Grand Conseil and giving personal judgments in the name of the court as a whole, of misappropriating fines,

---

[21] C.A.F., iv. 11862, 11987; St.P., ix. 200; A.N., U. 2035, fols. 20b–21b; A. Martineau, 'L'amiral Chabot, seigneur de Brion (1492?–1542)', in Positions de thèses de l'Ecole des Chartes (1883), p. 83.   [22] Ribier, i. 561.
[23] C. Porée, Un parlementaire sous François 1er: Guillaume Poyet, 1473–1548 (Angers, 1898), pp. 104–7; L.P., xvii. 567.

of modifying or altering decisions of the sovereign courts in exchange for bribes, of selling judicial offices for personal gain and of usurping the king's exclusive right of creating such offices. Poyet's role in Chabot's trial also came under attack: he was accused of having intimidated the judges, withheld evidence from the court and tampered with its verdict, making it harsher. It is impossible to say how justified these charges were, for the prosecution failed to produce any conclusive evidence and its witnesses frequently contradicted themselves.

Poyet, despite his physical debility, defended himself vigorously. He read out a long statement recalling his past services to the crown and his irreproachable parliamentary career. He tried to win over his judges by means of flattery and a display of humility curiously at variance with his former arrogance. The chancellor also tried to secure the removal of judges who were hostile to him or to sow doubts as to their impartiality by pretending to be in league with them. His judges were certainly impressed by his behaviour: they admired his burning sincerity and could not easily forget his former eminence; but they were also under heavy pressure from his enemies to convict. None showed more impatience than the king.[24] He complained of delays engineered by Poyet's relatives and ordered a suspension of the trial until his own return to Paris, presumably in the hope of ensuring a heavier sentence.

In the end, Poyet got off fairly lightly: he was fined 100,000 *livres*, deprived of the chancellorship, debarred from any royal office and sentenced to five years' imprisonment. The king was informed that two factors had mitigated the sentence: the prosecution's failure to produce any proof of the chancellor's guilt and the fact that he was in holy orders. But Francis was not mollified by these arguments: a chancellor who lost his office, he declared, should also lose his life. He complained that lawyers in general were inadequately punished, that Poyet's property should have been confiscated and that his own testimony had not been given sufficient weight. Finally, he told the court's representatives of the low opinion in which he held his own judiciary.

Poyet received his sentence before the whole Parlement on 23 April. He was then taken back to the Bastille. On 16 May he was required to pay his fine, but, as he did not possess 100,000 *livres* in cash, he persuaded the king to take some of his lands instead. Francis then relented to the extent of cutting Poyet's term of imprisonment. The ex-chancellor was released on 11 July 1545. In April 1548 he obtained leave from the Parlement to have a retrial at his own risk but died before this could be given effect.[25]

---

[24] A.N., X^(1a) 1554, fol. 1a–b.
[25] Porée, pp. 107–24. See also A.N., U. 797, 798 (seventeenth-century copies of the trial proceedings). Also X^(1a) 1555, fols. 19b, 21a–b; 1556, fol. 309a–b.

Poyet's fall and Chabot's death cleared the way for the ascendancy of two younger members of the king's council: Admiral Claude d'Annebault and Cardinal François de Tournon. They had been prominent in the administration since the thirties, but it was only after 1542 that they virtually ran it under the king. Annebault, who succeeded Chabot as admiral in February 1544, was undoubtedly the senior of the two. This was made clear in September 1543, when Tournon was left in charge of affairs in the admiral's absence.[26] In May 1544 an English observer reported: 'the admiral is the king's factor to whom he commands all things', and, in December, the Florentine ambassador wrote: 'the admiral rules everything; without him one cannot speak to the king or obtain anything'.[27] Two years later Cavalli reported that Francis entrusted everything to Annebault and Tournon and did only what they wanted or advised.[28] The king, however, did insist on being consulted about all important matters of state and any war plans. Indeed, if Dandino is to be believed, Annebault and Tournon were only yes-men: 'Tournon and Annebault, who govern at present', he wrote in May 1543, '– Annebault being more dead than alive – grope their way along and dare not say a word which might upset the king.'[29]

Annebault owed his position initially to his friendship with the duchesse d'Etampes. Early in 1545, however, she apparently turned against him, but not for long. The king, moreover, continued to employ the admiral in spite of his bungling of the attack on the south coast of England. In the autumn of 1545 Annebault led an embassy to the imperial court, and, in the following year, he was the chief French plenipotentiary at the peace talks at Ardres. In August he travelled to England in order to obtain Henry VIII's ratification of the peace treaty. And in January 1546 the king gave him the lordship of Compiègne as a reward for his services during the war and his management of the highest affairs of state.[30]

Although subordinate to the admiral, Tournon's political contribution was distinctive and important. His particular expertise was financial, and

[26] Du Bellay, iv. 160.

[27] *L.P.*, xix (pt 1), 573; Desjardins, iii. 140.

[28] E. Albèri (ed.), *Relazioni degli ambasciatori veneti al Senato* (Florence, 1839–63), i. 238.

[29] *Correspondance des nonces . . . Capodiferro* etc., p. 220. In January 1577, during the Estates-General of Blois, Catherine de' Medici recalled how Francis, after banishing the constable of Montmorency, had wanted to open dispatches (*les paquets*) and do everything himself, but all had remained undone, whereupon he had become angry and had taken on Admiral d'Annebault and the cardinal of Lorraine. C. J. Mayer, *Des Etats Généraux et autres assemblées nationales* (The Hague and Paris, 1788–9), xiii. 106. I owe this reference to the kindness of Dr Mark Greengrass.

[30] E. Dermenghem, 'Un ministre de François Ier: la grandeur et la disgrace de l'amiral Claude d'Annebault', *Rev. du XVIe siècle*, ix (1922), 34–50.

one of his main tasks in 1542, after he had been reappointed lieutenant-general in the Lyonnais and south-east France, was to secure funds for the war. In February 1543 his name figured at the head of a list of people the king wanted to admit to the financial committee of his council (*conseil pour le fait de ses finances*). An English agent noted in 1544 that this body met regularly at Tournon's house. But the cardinal was not concerned only with financial matters; the whole range of public affairs came within his competence as a royal councillor. He was the king's principal adviser in the admiral's absence and opened all letters addressed to the king. In September 1543, after the peace of Crépy, he was sent on an embassy to the imperial court. Like Montmorency before him, he worked for a closer understanding between the king of France and the emperor, hoping that they might eventually form a united front against Protestantism. But the cardinal did not always get his way. Ultimately it was Francis who determined foreign policy, and he was susceptible to contradictory influences among his entourage. Thus, in October 1545, Tournon vainly opposed the attempt by German Protestants to mediate between England and France, and it was against his wishes that the peace of Ardres was signed in the following year.

Despite the presence of faction at court, Tournon managed to retain the king's confidence. This is all the more surprising when one considers that his chief enemies were the king's sister and mistress. Both women disliked the cardinal's religious conservatism, but they also had other bones to pick with him. Marguerite blamed him for not having insisted on the restoration of Navarre to her husband as one of the conditions of the peace of Crépy, while Madame d'Etampes fell out with the cardinal after he had ordered the arrest of her protégé, the count of Anguillara, and opposed her efforts to oust Annebault from the admiralship in favour of Longueval. She tried to overthrow the cardinal by persuading one of his own servants to lodge an anonymous complaint about him with the king's council. Tournon managed to defuse the situation by withdrawing temporarily from the court on medical grounds. On his return the king treated him to a great show of friendship. 'Tournon has overcome everything', wrote the Florentine ambassador, 'and is now greater than ever.'[31] But the duchess had another card up her sleeve: at her instigation the cardinal was accused of having lined his own pockets during the war of 1536 by exploiting special fund-raising powers given to him by the king. The accusation was not groundless (Tournon had speculated over duties on Genoese imports through Lyons), and it caused the cardinal some embarrassment. But he extricated himself from it by offering the king a

<hr />

[31] Desjardins, iii. 160.

loan of 25,000 *écus*. On 8 June he received new powers to raise loans from the Lyons bankers. By the end of July Tournon had been reconciled to the duchess: they were often seen eating together, and they jointly pleaded with the king not to go to Picardy in time of plague. The cardinal's position in the government remained unchallenged thereafter till the end of the reign.[32]

The king's death (31 March 1547)

There was rejoicing at the French court when it heard that Henry VIII had died on 28 January 1547. True, Annebault told the English ambassador's servant of Francis's grief over the loss of his 'good and true friend', but the king was seen that same day at a ball 'laughing much and enjoying himself with his ladies'.[33] He became depressed, however, after he had allegedly received a message, sent by Henry on his death bed, reminding him that he too was mortal. About the same time he fell into a fever.[34] Yet about mid-February he left Saint-Germain and visited Villepreux, Dampierre and Limours. After hunting for three days at Rochefort-en-Yvelines, the king set off for the capital, where he planned a memorial service for Henry. But at the château of Rambouillet he became too ill to move.[35]

Many accounts exist of Francis's last days, but only a few are sufficiently contemporaneous to merit serious attention. One of the most informative was sent to the Parlement by Pierre du Chastel, bishop of Mâcon, who, as royal confessor, had attended to the king's last spiritual needs. On 20 March, he tells us, Francis began to prepare for death: after hearing mass, he made his confession and took communion. Then, after making a public confession, he admitted that he had broken the divine commandments frequently and variously. But he expressed confidence in God's mercy. Next, turning to the Dauphin, he urged him to look to the kingdom's defence, to honour justice and to bear in mind the divinely ordained obligation incumbent on all monarchs to govern well. That

32 François, *François de Tournon*, pp. 205–11.
33 A. Castan, 'La mort de François Iᵉʳ', *Mémoires de la Societé d'émulation du Doubs*, 5th ser., iii (1878), 441–2. According to Saint-Mauris, when the news of Henry VIII's death was received at the French court, the duchesse d'Etampes ran to the queen's bedchamber at an early hour shouting at the top of her voice: 'News! News! We have lost our chief enemy, and the King has commanded me to come and tell you of it!' This greatly upset the queen, who thought at first that the news referred to her brother (*C.S.P. Span.*, ix. 493).
34 *C.S.P. Span.*, ix. 62–4.
35 Castan, pp. 442–4; *C.A.F.*, viii. pp. 532–3; du Bellay, iv. 334–5. A memorial service for Henry VIII was celebrated at Notre-Dame on 21 March 1547 before a large crowd. An orator praised his magnanimity, liberality and prudence, and certain books published in his name (*C.S.P. Span.*, ix. 498–9).

same afternoon Princess Marguerite called on her father. 'Touchez-là', he said, holding out his hand, but his emotion was such that he could say no more and turned on his side. On 29 March, he asked for extreme unction and, repeating his earlier admonitions to the Dauphin, said that, as far as justice was concerned, his conscience was clear: he could think of no one whom he had treated unjustly. Shortly before midnight he fell into a rigor which reduced his attendants to despair. He received the last sacrament, took communion and blessed his son. Francis spoke of visions from which he was being shielded by Christ and talked of religion with his attendants. Next morning he recognized some of his servants and thanked them for all they had done. He embraced and blessed the Dauphin. Then, after hearing mass, the king expressed confidence in the glory that awaits the children of God. That evening, the Dauphin received his father's blessing for the third time. During the night the king was disturbed by more visions and recited various passages from Scripture. On Thursday 31 March, after hearing mass for the last time, he forgave his enemies and tried to comfort his attendants by speaking of the heavenly crown he was about to receive. He asked to hear a homily by Chrysostom, but was given one by Origen instead. Noticing the error, he asked if Origen was not suspect. That afternoon, as his speech grew indistinct, he clasped a crucifix and kissed it. He then recalled God's forgiveness of the good thief and said: 'In manus tuas, Domine, commendo spiritum meum.' His last word was 'Jesus'. Finally, having lost both speech and sight, he made the sign of the cross over his bed several times and breathed his last.[36]

Another account of the king's last moments, addressed to the regent of the Netherlands by the imperial ambassador, Saint-Mauris, suggests that the king's conscience may not have been quite so clear, after all. Francis, he says, admitted to his son that he had done harm to his subjects, especially by going to war on trifling pretexts. He expressed remorse for his 'great practices' against the good of Christendom (was he thinking of the Turks?) and urged his son to repair the injustices done to Charles III of Savoy, who had been deprived of his territories for eleven years. He also warned the Dauphin against allowing himself to be ruled by others, as he himself had been ruled by Madame d'Etampes. He asked Henri to settle certain debts he had contracted with merchants. Saint-Mauris provides some interesting details omitted by du Chastel. Francis allegedly recommended Madame d'Etampes to his son. 'She is a lady', he said. But he did not want her to witness his death: he waved her away as he was about to receive extreme unction. On the other hand, he asked Annebault, Tournon, Boisy and Sourdis to stay with him till the end 'lest he should lose his

[36] R. Doucet, 'La mort de François Ier', *R.H.*, cxiii (1913), 309–16.

reason and be less able to take care of his conscience'. During the night of 30 March the Dauphin fainted on his father's bed, and the king, half embracing him, would not let him go. Finally, Saint-Mauris confirms the story of the mistaken homily (though he cites a different one from du Chastel's). Francis, he notes, in spotting the error, showed his 'great memory in that he could distinguish one from the other'. In another dispatch, written on 9 April to Philip of Spain, the ambassador states that the king urged Henri to take care of his sister, Marguerite, and to marry her off fittingly. He advised him also to defend the faith, to abstain from burdening his subjects with taxes unnecessarily and to protect Queen Eleanor, knowing how badly he himself had treated her.[37]

Two notable absentees from the king's bedside were his queen and sister. News of his illness was apparently kept from Eleanor in the daily expectation that he would recover. That at least was the excuse given to her by Henri after Francis's death.[38] As for Marguerite, she was on a retreat at a monastery in Navarre. She knew of her brother's illness and offered up prayers for his recovery, but she was told of his death only long after the event. Her *Chansons spirituelles* – perhaps the most deeply felt of her poems – are an eloquent testimony to her anguish and the consolation which she found in religion:

> Je n'ay plus ny Père ny Mère
>   Ny Soeur ny Frère
> Sinon Dieu seul auquel j'espère.[39]

Francis died between 1 and 2 p.m. on Thursday 31 March. He was fifty-two years old. The exact cause of his death is unknown, though it was for a long time believed to be syphilis. Unfortunately, the record of the king's post-mortem has not survived, but two contemporary accounts

[37]   C. Paillard, 'La mort de François Ier et les premiers temps du règne de Henri II d'après les dépêches de Jean de Saint-Mauris (avril–juin 1547)', *R.H.*, v (1877), 84–120. Grief over the king's death was not universal in France. At Annecy, in Savoy, which the king had annexed in 1536, it set off a hostile demonstration. A shoemaker called Nicolas Vindret and others were prosecuted for putting up posters on 7 April 1547 insulting to the late king; they read simply: 'Le Roy est mort et allé atous les diables'. F. Mugnier and C. Duval, 'Procédures pour placards injurieux affichés à Annecy à la mort de François Ier, roi de France (1547)', *Mémoires et documents publiés par la Société Savoisienne d'histoire et d'archéologie*, xxxviii (1899), 1–44. I owe this reference to the kindness of Dr Mark Greengrass.
[38]   Castan, pp. 445–6.
[39]   P. Jourda, *Marguerite d'Angoulême* (1930), i. 313–17. Marguerite spent the rest of her life mainly in Navarre. Her pension was continued by Henri II, but she never regained any political influence. In September 1548 she witnessed Henri's entry into Lyons, and, in October, was at Moulins for the marriage of her daughter, Jeanne, to Antoine de Bourbon. She died at the château of Odos, near Tarbes, on 21 December 1549. *Ibid.*, i. 319–39.

suggest an extensive deterioration of his vital organs. The first, written by a Swiss doctor, indicates that his right lung was diseased.[40] The second, by Saint-Mauris, states that an 'aposthume' had been found in the king's stomach, that his kidneys were wasted, his entrails decayed, his throat cankered and a lung affected.[41] For more than a hundred years medical historians have argued the case for and against syphilis as the cause of Francis's death. No one doubts that he had been treated for this disease; what is less certain is that he actually died of it. Dr Cullerier, writing in 1856, argued that the symptoms described by historians in their accounts of Francis's death are not characteristic of syphilis. It was likely, in his view, that in the sixteenth century any disorder of the genital organs would have been identified with syphilis, and he concluded that the king's death was caused by a 'disease of the urinary ducts associated with an abscess in the region of the urethra'. Such a disease could have had a venereal origin without being syphilitic.[42] More recently, Dr Fraisse has reached a similar conclusion, namely that Francis died as a result of a urinary infection. His abscess was probably the result of a stricture of the urethra, possibly caused by gonorrhea, which at the time would have been mistaken for syphilis.[43]

On 31 March the new king, Henri II, gave instructions for the triple funeral of his father and two brothers, the Dauphin François and Charles, duc d'Orléans, whose bodies had remained since their deaths at Tournon and Beauvais respectively. At the same time, the artist François Clouet travelled to Rambouillet from Paris to make Francis's death mask and to draw and take measurements for his funeral effigy. This took a fortnight to make. That night some mendicant friars prayed and stood vigil over the king's body. On 1 April the royal physicians and surgeons carried out its examination. The king's heart and entrails were removed and placed in two caskets, while his body was embalmed and placed in a coffin. Next day the coffin and caskets were carried in procession to the priory of Haute-Bruyère, about six miles north of Rambouillet. For two days and nights the church bells rang continuously and services were held. On 6 April Francis's heart and entrails were buried in the priory church; five days later his body was taken to the palace of Saint-Cloud, belonging to the cardinal-bishop of Paris.

On 24 April the focus of the funeral ceremony shifted from the king's

[40] G. Dodu, 'Les amours et la mort de François Ier', *R.H.*, clxi (1929), 268, 273.
[41] Castan, p. 445; *C.S.P. Span.*, ix. 73.
[42] Dr Cullerier, 'De quelle maladie est mort François Ier?', *Gazette hebdomadaire de médecine*, xlix (1856), 865–76.
[43] M. Fraisse, 'Sur la maladie et la mort de François Ier' (unpublished medical thesis, University of Paris, 1962). I am most grateful to Professor René Pillorget for comments on this thesis and for photocopies of it and of Dr Cullerier's article.

body to his effigy, which lay, hands clasped, on a bed of state at the end of the great hall at Saint-Cloud. This had been lavishly decorated with hangings of blue velvet and cloth of gold. The effigy had been made as lifelike as possible. It wore the state robes, the collar of St Michael around its neck and, on its head, the imperial crown. On either side of it, on pillows, lay the sceptre and hand of justice. There was a canopy over the bed and, at its foot, a cross and holy water stoop. Nearby were two stools, where heralds kept watch night and day, and offered the aspergillum to those who came to throw holy water on the effigy. Four candles provided the only illumination for the hall. Along the walls were benches for the nobles and clerics, who attended the religious services and the dead king's meals. These were the strangest part of the entire ceremonial. For eleven days they were served as if Francis were still alive: the table was laid and the courses were brought in and sampled. The napkin used to wipe his hands was, as usual, presented by the steward to the most eminent person present, and wine was served to the king twice during each meal. At the end grace was said by a cardinal with the addition of two psalms appropriate to a funeral.

On 4 May the last meal was served and the effigy removed. Overnight the *salle d'honneur*, where it had been displayed, was turned into a *salle funèbre*, the blue and gold drapes being replaced by black ones. The king's coffin, which had been in an adjacent room, was now brought in and deposited in the centre of the hall. On it were placed the crown, sceptre and hand of justice. On 18 May Henri came to Saint-Cloud and aspersed his father's body; this was his only official public appearance between Francis's death and his own coronation. Had he appeared while the effigy was still on display, the illusion of his predecessor still being alive would have been destroyed. The simultaneous exposure of two kings of France was held to be inadmissible.

On 21 May the king's coffin was taken on a waggon drawn by six horses to Notre-Dame-des-Champs and placed in the choir alongside the coffins of his two sons, François and Charles. That evening a requiem service was held, and all that night vigil was kept by Francis's officers and servants. Next morning, after mass had been celebrated, the church was closed and the effigies of Francis and his sons were produced and attached to litters. The king's effigy now had a different pair of hands: instead of being clasped in prayer, one held the sceptre and the other the hand of justice. When everything was ready, the church was opened to admit the members of the Parlement, who had come in solemn procession from Paris.

At about 2 p.m. the funeral cortège set out for Notre-Dame-de-Paris. Its order was as follows: the parish clergy, 500 poor carrying torches, the archers of the guard, and the town criers and watch. Marching on either side of the road were the mendicant orders, followed by the students of the university and other collegiate clergy. Then came a group of royal officers followed by trumpeters and last the chariot bearing Francis's coffin. Immediately behind rode twelve pages and knights, carrying the king's gloves, helmet, shield and coat-of-arms. Thirty-three prelates, including Cardinal Jean du Bellay, came next; then the effigies of Francis's sons, each carried by gentlemen of their households, two knights carrying the king's spurs, his parade horse led by two grooms, and Boisy holding the sword of France. He preceded the king's effigy, which was carried by the *hanouars* or salt-carriers of Paris. Only their feet, however, were visible, for the litter bearing the effigy was covered with a golden drape which trailed almost to the ground. Alongside marched eight gentlemen of Francis's household, who were attached to the litter by a kind of halter. Behind the effigy rode the admiral with the banner of France, four princes in deep mourning and, finally, the papal legate, a group of cardinals and ambassadors and troops of the guard.

After a short service at Notre-Dame, the large company broke up, but it reassembled on the following day for the last rites. Each prince made an offering, and du Chastel delivered a long funeral oration. After a break for lunch, the company reassembled and, in the same order as before, set off with the effigies and coffins to the abbey of Saint-Denis, the traditional resting place of French kings. That evening vespers were celebrated, and next morning the last rites were repeated. The effigies were then removed and the coffins taken to a vault. The heralds deposited their coats-of-arms on a railing, the royal insignia were placed on the king's coffin, Boisy rested the point of the sword of France upon it, Francis's stewards threw their wands into the grave, and the admiral, sitting near its edge, dipped the banner of France until its tip touched the coffin. 'Le Roy est mort!' cried Normandy herald three times, but the admiral was too moved to shout 'Vive le Roy!', so the herald had to do so for him. Whereupon the sword and banner were raised and the various coats of arms retrieved. The company then retired to the refectory for supper, at the end of which Francis's chief steward, Mendoza, broke his wand to signify the dissolution of the king's household. He told his fellow officials that they no longer had a master and must provide for themselves, but added tactfully that they could rest their hopes on the new king's kindness.[44]

Although Henri's relations with his father had not always been good, he performed his filial duty punctiliously by commissioning a splendid tomb for him. It was designed by Philibert de L'Orme on the model of a

[44] R. E. Giesey, *The Royal Funeral Ceremony in Renaissance France* (Geneva, 1960), pp. 1–17, 193–5.

Roman triumphal arch, while at the same time conforming to the fifteenth-century convention of combining kneeling figures (*priants*) of the deceased and members of his family above the tomb with recumbent figures (*gisants*) on a sarcophagus in an arcaded enclosure below. The sculptor Pierre Bontemps, who had worked under Primaticcio at Fontainebleau in 1536, was responsible for the *gisants* and the bas-reliefs depicting the battles of Marignano and Ceresole round the base of the tomb. The *priants*, apart from the king and Queen Claude, are of the Dauphin François, Princess Charlotte and Charles d'Orléans. Henri had intended that his sister Louise and his grandmother, Louise of Savoy, should also be represented, but their statues were never installed. The *priants* of the king and queen are the work of two lesser sculptors, François Carmoy and François Marchand.[45] Bontemps also worked under de L'Orme on a monument for the heart of Francis. This was set up at Haute-Bruyère in 1556, but is now at Saint-Denis. It is of white marble and consists of an urn and tall pedestal. The urn is decorated with bas-reliefs representing Architecture, Sculpture, Painting and Geometry, and the pedestal with others depicting Astronomy, Instrumental Music, Song and Lyric Poetry.[46] Another testimony to Henri II's filial devotion – a full-length statue of Francis wearing his state robes and holding the sceptre and hand of justice – was set up in the Palais de Justice in 1556, but was, alas, destroyed in a fire in March 1618.[47]

The palace revolution

The death of Francis was followed, as expected, by a palace revolution.[48] The forces of faction which had been gathering momentum during the last years of the reign, but which the king had managed to some extent to contain, were now allowed free rein. Henri II had not forgiven his father's mistress and ministers for the peace of Crépy. As the close friend of Anne de Montmorency he was unwilling to tolerate the presence at court of the constable's enemies. His character, so different in many respects from his father's, predisposed him to a cleaning up of the court. He began by curbing its entertainments so as to devote more of his time to 'grave and virtuous thoughts' and cashiered Francis's 'fair band'. Some of the ladies sought refuge in the household of the long-suffering Queen Eleanor, but she would take only two of them – Madame de Massy and Françoise de

---

[45] A. Blunt, *Philibert de L'Orme* (London, 1958), pp. 69–70, 73; M. Roy, *Artistes et monuments de la Renaissance en France* (1929), pp. 157–92.
[46] P. S. Wingert, 'The Funerary Urn of Francis I', *Art Bulletin*, xxi (1939), 383–96.
[47] Roy, p. 170.
[48] Decrue, ii. 1–20; Romier, *Origines politiques*, pp. 34–57.

Longwy, Admiral Chabot's widow. Madame de Canaples was expelled from the court and repudiated by her husband on the ground that she had been the late king's concubine. Henri also tried to get rid of the duchesse de Montpensier but was prevented by his sister Marguerite, who refused to go to court without her.

No one stood to lose as much from Francis's death as Madame d'Etampes, for she had created many enemies by her arrogance and interested patronage. Saint-Mauris believed that, if she had appeared in public, she would have been stoned. Having retired to Limours shortly before Francis died, she tried early in April to reoccupy her apartment at Saint-Germain. But she was informed by Henri that Queen Eleanor would determine its allocation. This was only the first of a series of humiliations which the duchess had to endure. She was forced to disgorge jewels given to her by Francis; was sued by her husband, who claimed that she had cheated him of certain revenues in her sister's interest; and for a time she was even imprisoned. Yet Madame d'Etampes was not totally ruined. She retired to one of her châteaux and devoted her last years to good works. As for her friend (and lover?) the seigneur de Longueval, he was tried for high treason, but saved his head by giving up an estate near Laon to the cardinal of Lorraine.[49]

Queen Eleanor, who had suffered so much indignity at the hands of Madame d'Etampes, was invited by Henri to remain in France, but she preferred to go to the Netherlands. In October 1555 she witnessed in Brussels the abdication of her brother the emperor, and soon afterwards returned to Spain. She died at Talaveruela in February 1558.[50]

The person who triumphed as a result of Madame d'Etampes's overthrow was her arch-enemy, Diane de Poitiers. As Henri's mistress (she was forty-eight and he only twenty-seven) she now became the dominant woman at court and was soon receiving gifts and distributing favours to her favourites and kinsmen as unscrupulously as her predecessor had ever done.[51]

But the palace revolution of 1547 did not affect only the distaff side of the court. Its most significant feature was the return to power of the constable, Anne de Montmorency. He had been living on his estates since his fall in 1541, but he had not lost his principal offices. He had simply ceased to exercise them or to draw their wages. The Dauphin, who was grateful to Montmorency for having freed him from four and a half years as a hostage in Spain, had remained in close touch with him throughout his disgrace, and his first act after his accession was to call the constable to

---

[49] Castan, 'La mort de François Ier', p. 446; *C.S.P. Span.*, ix. 73–7.
[50] K. Brandi, *The Emperor Charles V*, tr. C. V. Wedgwood (London, 1939), pp. 633, 641.
[51] Decrue, ii. 14–20.

Saint-Germain. Here they talked in private for two hours, at the end of which Montmorency emerged as president of the king's council. On 12 April he took the oath of constable to the new king and, at the same time, was confirmed as grand master. His arrears of pay – amounting to 100,000 *écus* – were settled, and he recovered his governorship of Languedoc, while his brother, La Rochepot, was reappointed governor of Paris and the Ile-de-France. In July 1551 Montmorency was created a duke and a peer, an unprecedented elevation for a mere baron, placing him on a par with the highest in the land.[52]

The return to power of Montmorency automatically led to the disgrace of Annebault and Tournon, who had run the government in Francis's last years. Annebault was allowed to remain admiral, albeit without pay, but he had to give up his marshalship to Jacques d'Albon. He was also admitted to the new king's council, but only to its less important section. The admiral tried to link his fortunes to Montmorency's by suggesting a marriage between his son and one of the constable's seven daughters, but nothing came of this. He never regained his former political importance, which was probably as well for the kingdom, since many people thought him a bonehead. He died in 1552.[53]

Tournon's disgrace was, in the short term, more complete than the admiral's. He had allegedly tried to win the new king's trust by an extravagant display of grief over his late master's body, but the cardinal's tears and lamentations had evidently made no impression on Henri. Tournon's name was missing from the list of royal councillors published on 2 April, and he was given a cool reception by the king at Saint-Germain. He was forbidden to reside at court and replaced as chancellor of the order of St Michael by Charles de Lorraine. His nephews, Montrevel and Grignan, lost their governorships of Bresse and Provence respectively. After spending some time in his diocese of Auch, Tournon eventually went to Rome and participated in the conclave that elected Julius III. This gave him an opportunity to be of some use in Franco-papal diplomacy, and, in 1551, he became archbishop of Lyons. Two years later he and Montmorency were reconciled at Ecouen.[54]

The accession of Henri II was the signal for change not only at the highest ministerial level, but in other departments of state as well. Two of the king's secretaries of state, Bochetel and L'Aubespine, were retained, but Gilbert Bayard was dismissed, allegedly on account of a disparaging

---

[52] *Ibid.*, ii. 1–7.
[53] Dermenghem, 'Claude d'Annebault, pp. 44–6. 'I never talked in my life that I can remember', wrote Paget, 'with a man that should be wise and that hath so little reason.' *L.P.*, xviii (pt 1), 163.
[54] François, *François de Tournon*, pp. 228–35, 254, 276.

remark he had made about Diane de Poitiers's age and looks. He was replaced by Cosme Clausse, who had served the Dauphin. A fourth secretary was appointed in 1547 in the person of Jean du Thier.[55] Among new members of the royal council, two deserve particular notice: François, comte d'Aumale, and his brother Charles, archbishop of Rheims. They were the sons of Claude, the first duke of Guise, and the nephews of another royal councillor, Jean, cardinal of Lorraine. Within the fiscal administration, Jean Duval was replaced as *trésorier de l'Epargne* by Blondet, one of Diane de Poitiers's creatures.[56]

From the historical standpoint the most sinister aspect of the palace revolution of 1547 was the emergence of the house of Guise as a serious rival to those of Montmorency and Bourbon. A story to the effect that Francis, on his deathbed, had warned his son against its ambition is almost certainly an invention of historians inspired by the subsequent turn of events.[57] But the high favour enjoyed by the Guises at the start of Henri's reign is indisputable. Within a few months Charles de Lorraine had become a cardinal and François d'Aumale a duke. Both were in the flower of manhood, intelligent and immensely ambitious. They also had the backing of Diane de Poitiers, who needed a counterweight to the constable's influence. Thus the death of Francis was the signal for a struggle for power among the great nobles of France, which, capitalizing on the religious troubles of the age, was to find violent expression in the French civil wars later in the century.

[55] N. M. Sutherland, *The French Secretaries of State in the Age of Catherine de Medici* (London, 1962), pp. 17–19.
[56] Decrue, ii. 12–13.
[57] J.-A. de Thou, *Histoire universelle* (London, 1734), i (bk iii), 183.

Epilogue

IN THE MID-SIXTEENTH century Francis I was called 'le grand roy Françoys'. This, however, had little to do with his physical appearance. 'He was called great', writes Brantôme, 'not so much because of his very tall stature and presence or his very regal majesty as on account of his virtues, valour, great deeds and high merits, as were once Alexander, Pompey and others.'[1] De Thou in his *Histoire universelle* writes of the 'eulogies deserved by that great prince'.[2] By the late seventeenth century, however, Francis's reputation had slumped. 'Francis I', writes Bayle in his *Dictionnaire historique et critique* (1697), 'was one of those great princes in whom great qualities were mixed with many faults.' Only the blind, he continues, can fail to see clearly in Francis's reign 'a long series of errors and rash actions'. Bayle credits Francis with courage and that 'frank and open generosity that is so rare among persons of his condition', but criticizes him for allowing himself to be ruled by women and unworthy favourites. The king's greatest mistake, in his judgment, was to admit women to his court. This, he concedes, did not lead to the overthrow of the Salic law, but 'one may say that, from that time until more or less the end of the sixteenth century, France was ruled by women'.[3]

Francis's reputation reached its nadir in 1832, when Victor Hugo's play *Le roi s'amuse* received its première at the Comédie Française. It portrayed the king as a lecher who seduces the daughter of his fool, Triboulet, a hunchback. The latter hires an assassin to murder the king, only to be cruelly deceived. The story is better known today as the plot of Verdi's opera *Rigoletto*, which was originally called *Triboletto*. Only the location and identities have been changed in the opera to satisfy the Venetian censors. Why Verdi should have chosen in 1851 to turn an unsuccessful play into an opera is not our concern; but the failure of *Le roi s'amuse* is of interest. The audience on the first night was shocked by

---

[1] Pierre de Bourdeille, abbé de Brantôme, *Oeuvres complètes*, ed. L. Lalanne (1864–82), iii. 82.
[2] J.-A. de Thou, *Histoire universelle* (London, 1734), i (bk iii), 180.
[3] P. Bayle, *Dictionnaire historique et critique* (1820), vi. 558, 560.

its improbability and immorality; it was not revived till fifty years later.[4] Hugo's discomfiture, however, did not lead to the rehabilitation of Francis demanded by logic. The king's reputation suffered even worse damage at the hands of the great historian Jules Michelet, who, in 1840 to 1841, lectured at the Collège de France on the Renaissance and the Reformation. As a child of the French Revolution, Michelet viewed history as a long progression towards that supreme emancipation of the human spirit. For him, the Lutheran Reformation was an abortive attempt to achieve the same result two and a half centuries earlier. It failed in France because of the lack of understanding shown by the king and the persecution he initiated. For Michelet, Francis was anything but great: he was 'charm itself . . . a charming speaker, a fluent one, too fluent, for whom speech was not a serious matter'. The whole of Francis's upbringing, according to Michelet, can be summed up in two words: 'women' and 'war' – 'war to please women'. 'This dangerous object', he writes, 'who was to deceive everyone, was born, one might say, between two prostrate women, his mother and his sister, and thus they remained in this ecstasy of worship and devotion.'[5]

In 1885, thirty years after publication of Michelet's volumes on the Renaissance and Reformation in his *Histoire de France*, a serious attempt was made by Paulin Paris to rehabilitate Francis. In a two-volume work edited posthumously by his son, he argued that most of the scabrous stories told about the king were the deliberate invention of three writers closely related to the house of Bourbon: namely, François Beaucaire, the sieur de Marillac and Antoine de Laval. All three had served the traitor Charles, duc de Bourbon. To these writers Paris adds the names of Brantôme, who could never resist a good story, particularly a dirty one; an obscure doctor of Uzerche called Guyon; and Varillas, who, in 1686, published a two-volume history of Francis's reign containing many 'secret anecdotes'.[6]

The indictment drawn up by these authors either to vindicate Bourbon's treason or simply for effect is a long one. Francis had allegedly been dissolute since his earliest days; no beautiful woman had been safe from his lust. He had forced his attentions on Mary Tudor, Louis XII's widow, and only a warning that he might lose the throne to his own bastard had persuaded him to desist. He had contracted syphilis (invariably described as 'a shameful malady') in the arms of La Belle Ferronière and had passed it to his first wife, Claude de France, who had died of it. He had lured the

4   E. Biré, *Victor Hugo après 1830* (2 vols., 1891), i. 57–77; W. D. Pendell, *Victor Hugo's Acted Dramas and the Contemporary Press* (Baltimore, Md., 1947), pp. 61–71.
5   J. Michelet, *Histoire de France* (n.d.), ix, *La Renaissance*, pp. 344–6.
6   P. Paris, *Etudes sur François Premier* (1885), i. 1–25.

beautiful comtesse de Châteaubriant to his court by means of a cheap trick, and she, after becoming his mistress, had used her influence to have her three incompetent brothers appointed to high military commands, with disastrous results. For purely selfish reasons, she had allied with the queen mother and had forced treason on the duc de Bourbon. Having jilted Madame de Châteaubriant, who fell victim to her husband's cruel vengeance, Francis took as his mistress Anne de Pisseleu, one of his mother's ladies-in-waiting. But first he married her off to Jean de Brosse, comte d'Etampes, one of Bourbon's accomplices, who complied with the king's wish so as to recover his own confiscated lands. Madame d'Etampes now became the supreme dispenser of favours and disfavours. She also deceived the king by having affairs with the comte de Brissac, the constable of Montmorency, Admiral Chabot and the comte de Longueval. In 1539 she planned to take the emperor prisoner during his visit to the French court, but he won her over by dropping a large diamond at her feet. Thereafter she was an imperialist, and during the war of 1544 she and Longueval tricked the heroic garrison of Saint-Dizier into capitulating to Charles V. Yet she retained her credit with Francis, although he was aware of her treasonable intrigues. Turning to Michelet, we find another allegation about Francis: namely, that his love for his sister, Marguerite, was incestuous.

According to Paulin Paris, this long catalogue of Francis's vices is nothing but a pack of lies for which no contemporary evidence exists. Alas, this not strictly correct. Many of the stories can be disproved; others cannot be proved or disproved, as they rest on hearsay evidence only; others still, including the king's 'shameful malady', are almost certainly true. *Le roi s'amuse* may be a piece of republican propaganda, but its portrayal of the court of Francis is not altogether incredible; its morals left much to be desired. There are many contemporary references to the king's philandering, notably the journal of De Beatis, who visited France in 1517. 'The king . . .', he writes, 'is a great womaniser and readily breaks into others' gardens and drinks at many sources.'[7] The influence

---

[7]   *The Travel Journal of Antonio De Beatis: Germany, Switzerland, the Low Countries, France and Italy, 1517–1518*, ed. J. R. Hale (London, 1979), p. 107. The king's philandering appears to have got worse with age. Boisy wrote to Montmorency (18 Aug. 1543): 'our master's conduct is as you have always described it to me: the further he goes, the more he gets caught up with women, and he is quite shameless about it'. L. Romier, *Les origines politiques des Guerres de Religion* (1913–14), i. 22. Pope Paul III, on learning of the king's death, said that his morals had been those of Sardanapalus. *Ibid.*, i. 22 n. 2. Marshal Tavannes wrote in his memoirs: 'Alexander sees women when there is no business, Francis attends to business when there are no women.' *Collection complète des mémoires relatifs à l'histoire de France*, ed. C. B. Petitot (1819–26), xxiii. 217.

exerted by Madame d'Etampes for good or ill on the politics of the last decade of the reign was certainly great; foreign ambassadors confirm this.

Francis had many faults and made many mistakes. He was wilful (some writers have compared him, rightly, to a spoilt child), impetuous, grasping, profligate, licentious and fickle; but he had qualities: intelligence, eloquence, physical bravery and, by the standards of his age, humanity. According to Brantôme, the execution of Semblançay was his only serious crime. Among the king's mistakes were his short-sighted provocation of the emperor in 1521, his decision to campaign in the winter of 1524 and his handling of von Sickingen and Andrea Doria. He also did allow the duchesse d'Etampes too much influence. But the importance of his reign ought not to be judged simply in terms of the king's faults and errors. Nor should anachronistic criteria be applied. In the nineteenth century, for example, Francis's wars in Italy were deplored as a diversion of his subjects' energies away from their true destiny: the achievement of France's natural frontiers, especially in the east.[8] If territorial expansion is to be the only criterion, then Francis achieved little. He annexed parts of Savoy, but failed in his lifelong bid to extend his dominion beyond the Alps. His last years were overshadowed by the humiliation of losing Boulogne to the English. The king's main territorial success, apart from adding great fiefs to his demesne, was the purely negative one of holding on to Burgundy in the face of Charles V's determined efforts to recover the duchy.

A reign ought to be judged by its long-term impact on all aspects of national life. From this standpoint, that of Francis was of great significance, since it witnessed and, in varying degrees, promoted or fostered fundamental changes in France's political structure, economy, society, religion and cultural life. The king's obsession with war, reprehensible as it is on moral grounds, stimulated administrative change. By entailing an expenditure far in excess of what the crown's traditional resources could provide, it obliged him to look for new sources of wealth, to reorganize the ramshackle fiscal system handed down by Charles VII and to promote administrative centralization wherever possible. The creation of the *Trésor de l'Epargne* marked a radical break from medieval fiscal practice. But of course there were limits to the effectiveness of changes such as this. Francis never became as absolute as Louis XIV. To the end of his life, his kingdom contained many local privileges, exemptions and anomalies; his laws, even when registered by the parlements, were not always enforced. Yet, as Doucet has noted, Francis's reign marked the beginning of a new, more 'absolute', system of government. France was more unified at the

[8] G. Zeller, *La réunion de Metz à la France (1552–1648)*, i, *L'occupation* (1926), pp. 21–70.

end of his reign than it had been at the beginning. Among the king's fiscal expedients, the sale of offices, which he exploited more systematically than any of his predecessors, had the most far-reaching social and political effects. Though remunerative in the short term, it was highly dangerous to the future of the monarchy, for it created a sizeable class of royal officials, who, having bought their offices, quite naturally regarded them as their own property regardless of the public functions attached to them. Their loyalty or obedience had become so unreliable by the early seventeenth century that the crown had to bypass them by sending out commissioners – the famous *intendants de la justice, police et finances*, who became the chief agents of Louis XIV's absolutism. It may not be too far-fetched to argue that Francis promoted centralization by creating a problem for his successors.

Economically, his reign saw the completion of the agricultural reconstruction that had begun following the Hundred Years' War. While the land was being reclaimed, the population grew, town life flourished and trade, both at home and abroad, expanded. Parochialism was still too strongly entrenched among the king's subjects for them to understand, let alone endorse, the far-reaching programme of economic reform proposed by Duprat in 1517, but the government did adhere to that programme's principles in its subsequent legislation. A national awareness, which some economic historians have identified with the beginnings of Colbertism, certainly animated it, notably its reform of the customs system. New horizons were also opened up at this time: the ports of the Atlantic coast were developed, the east coast of North America was mapped out and Canada was settled for the first time. All, however, was not well with the economy. The failure of food production to keep pace with the needs of the rising population caused grain prices to increase, while inflation reduced the living standards of many peasants and artisans. The growth of poverty under Francis led to a reappraisal by the local authorities of existing methods of relief with results interesting for the future.

As the ruler who presided over the Renaissance and the Reformation in his kingdom, Francis has received a good deal of attention. Too much significance has perhaps been attached to the Concordat of Bologna, but it did clarify relations between the French crown and the Holy See, which the Pragmatic Sanction of Bourges had undermined, and by tightening and extending the king's hold on ecclesiastical appointments helped remove a possible incentive for breaking with Rome. Francis's ambiguous attitude to Protestantism in the period before 1534 has often been seen as an expression of his lack of seriousness or of his readiness to subordinate religious principle to diplomatic expediency. It may have been due rather to the ideological confusion of the age; but, whatever the cause, it did give the new faith a chance to strike roots in France. By the time sacramentarianism had alerted the king to the social and political dangers of Protestantism, it could no longer be eradicated. The burnings and massacres which disfigured the last years of the reign only served to inspire the dissenters by giving them martyrs. Only by appreciating the deep religious divisions under Francis can the French civil wars of the second half of the century be completely understood.

Francis's cultural patronage has always been widely acclaimed. The works of Budé and Marot, the handsome books printed by Robert Estienne, the portraits of Clouet and the châteaux built for the king and his nobles are all witnesses to the brilliant intellectual and artistic life of the court. Its impact on future generations is not easily measured, but few reigns have left a more notable cultural legacy. Francis's collection of works of art became the nucleus of the collection at the Louvre, and his library that of the Bibliothèque Nationale. By establishing the *lecteurs royaux* in 1530, he not only shattered the virtual monopoly of higher learning exercised by the Sorbonne, but also paved the way for the foundation of the Collège de France, where Michelet was to denigrate his memory in the 1840s.

Note on coinage

The sums of money mentioned in this book reflect the division between the two types of money which existed side by side in early modern France. These were *money of account*, which was the measure of value, and *actual coin*, which was the medium of exchange. Thus Francis I's accounts were kept in the former and actual transactions made in the latter. With a considerable variety of coins in circulation, the need for some yardstick and standard of value was necessary. This was provided by money of account. The two systems were as follows.

Money of account

The most common money of account in sixteenth-century France was the *livre tournois*. This was subdivided into *sous* (or *sols*) and *deniers*: i.e. 1 *livre tournois*=20 *sous*; 1 *sou*=12 *deniers*.

It was the French equivalent of the English system of pounds, shillings and pence sterling. There were about 10 *livres tournois* in 1 pound sterling; i.e. the *livre tournois* was worth about 2 shillings English.

The *livre parisis*, worth a quarter more than the *livre tournois*, was used hardly at all under Francis. But the *mercuriales* of the Halle of Paris were expressed in *livres parisis* till 1568.

Actual coin

Gold

Ecu au soleil. Issued from 1475. Worth 36 *sous* 3 *deniers* in 1515, 40 *sous* in 1516, 45 *sous* in 1533. Weight 3.357 gm.

In 1516 it was worth about 4 English shillings. The English *crown* (introduced in 1526) was worth 44 *sous tournois* in 1533 and 1549.

Ecu à la croisette. Essentially the same as *écu au soleil*.

Demi-écu. Half the weight and value of the *écu*.

Ecu à la couronne. Older than the *écu au soleil*. Worth 51 *sous*. Weight 3.819 gm.

Silver

Teston. Issued from 1514. The first French coin to carry, like certain Italian coins, the portrait bust of the king (hence its name). Worth 10 *sous tournois* in 1515; 10 *sous* 6 *deniers* in 1533; 10 *sous* 8 *deniers* in 1541; 11 *sous* in 1543. Weight 9.555 gm.

It remained the principal silver coin till Henri III introduced the *franc* in 1576. A gold *franc* existed in medieval France, but it had ceased to be struck by the early fifteenth century. Thereafter the *franc* was sometimes used as a sort of money of account equivalent to the *livre tournois*.

Demi-teston. Half the weight and value of the *teston*.

Billon

This was a mixture of silver with a high proportion of copper: it was divided into '*billon blanc*' and '*billon noir*'.

Douzain. Worth 12 *deniers* (hence its name). It was very common, as it represented the *sou tournois*, the principal unit of account in the retail trade.

Dizain.

Sizain.

There were about a dozen types of billon coins in circulation in 1515.

In addition to royal coins, provincial and foreign coins circulated in France. Provence had its own money of account, the *florin*, and coins: the *courronal*, worth ¾ of a *denier tournois*, and the *patac*.

Two kinds of foreign coins circulated: coins struck by French kings in Italy and coins struck by foreign rulers. In March 1541 Francis authorized the circulation of thirty-three foreign coins.

Manuscript sources

The list of sources which follows contains only those documents cited in the course of this book.

London: British Library
    Additional MS. 28594
    Harley MS. 3462

London: Public Record Office
    State Papers 89

Paris: Archives Nationales
    J. 942
    K. 1483
    KK. 98
    U. 797–8, 2035
    X^{1a} 1519–20, 1536, 1538, 1541, 1549–51, 1553–6, 8613

Paris: Bibliothèque Nationale
    MSS. français 143, 2200, 2794, 2953, 2981, 3897, 5109, 5660, 5709, 5770, 7853, 10383, 10390, 10900, 11495, 13429, 15628–33
    MSS. français, nouvelles acquisitions 8452
    MSS. Dupuy 17, 211

Select bibliography

This bibliography makes no pretence of being a comprehensive list of sources for the life and reign of Francis I. I have included only those works which I have found useful while working on this book. Unless otherwise indicated all books are published in Paris.

Primary works

Albèri, E. (ed.), *Relazioni degli ambasciatori veneti al Senato*, 14 vols. Florence, 1839–63.

Auton, Jean d', *Chronique de Louis XII*, ed. R. de Maulde La Clavière, 4 vols. Société de l'Histoire de France, 1889–95.

[Barrillon], *Journal de Jean Barrillon, secrétaire du chancelier Duprat, 1515–1521*, ed. P. de Vaissière, 2 vols. 1897–9.

Bèze, T. de, *Histoire ecclésiastique*. Lille, 1841.

Bodin, J., *Les six livres de la République*. 1577.

Bontems, C., Raybaud, L.-P., and Brancourt, J.-P. (eds.), *Le prince dans la France des XVIe et XVIIe siècles*. 1965.

Brantôme, P. de Bourdeille, abbé de, *Oeuvres complètes*, ed. L. Lalanne, 11 vols. 1864–82.

Briçonnet, G., and Marguerite d'Angoulême, *Correspondance (1521–1524)*, ed. C. Martineau and M. Veissière, 2 vols. Geneva, 1975–9.

Calendar of State Papers, Spanish, ed. G. Bergenroth, P. de Gayangos and M. A. S. Hume, 12 vols. London, 1862–95.

Calendar of State Papers, Venetian, ed. R. Brown, C. Bentinck and H. Brown, 9 vols. London, 1864–98.

Captivité du roi François Ier, ed. A. Champollion-Figeac. 1847.

Castiglione, B., *The Book of the Courtier*, tr. G. Bull. Harmondsworth, 1967.

Catalogue des actes de François Ier, 10 vols. 1887–1910.

[Catherine de' Medici], *Lettres de Catherine de Médicis*, ed. H. de La Ferrière-Percy, 10 vols. 1880–95.

[Cellini], *The Life of Benvenuto Cellini Written by Himself*, tr. J. A. Symonds, ed. J. Pope-Hennessy. London, 1949.

[Charles V], *Correspondenz des Kaisers Karl V*, ed. K. Lanz, 2 vols. Leipzig, 1844–5.

Charrière, E. (ed.), *Négociations de la France dans le Levant*, 4 vols. 1848–60.

Cimber, L., and Danjou, F. (eds.), *Archives curieuses de l'histoire de France depuis Louis XI jusqu'à Louis XVIII*, 30 vols. 1834–49.

Collection complète des mémoires relatifs à l'histoire de France, ed. C. B. Petitot, 52 vols. 1819–26.

Collection of Documents Relating to Jacques Cartier and the Sieur de Roberval, A, ed. H. P. Biggar. Ottawa, 1930.

Comptes de l'hôtel des rois de France aux XIVᵉ et XVᵉ siècles, ed. L. Douët-d'Arcq. 1865.

Comptes de Louise de Savoie et de Marguerite d'Angoulême (1512–39), ed. A. Lefranc and J. Boulenger. 1905.

Correspondance des nonces en France: Capodiferro, Dandino et Guidiccione, 1541–1546, ed. J. Lestocquoy. Rome, 1963.

Correspondance des nonces . . . Carpi et Ferrerio, 1535–40, ed. J. Lestocquoy. Rome and Paris, 1961.

Correspondance des réformateurs dans les pays de langue française, ed. A. Herminjard, 9 vols. Geneva, 1886–7.

Correspondance politique de MM. de Castillon et de Marillac, ambassadeurs de France en Angleterre 1537–42, ed. J. Kaulek. 1885.

De Beatis, A., *Voyage du cardinal d'Aragon (1517–18)*, tr. M. Havard de La Montagne. 1913.

   The Travel Journal of Antonio De Beatis: Germany, Switzerland, the Low Countries, France and Italy, 1517–1518, tr. J. R. Hale and J. M. A. Lindon, ed. J. R. Hale. London, 1979.

[du Bellay, Guillaume], *Fragments de la première Ogdoade de Guillaume du Bellay*, ed. V.-L. Bourrilly. 1905.

   Mémoires de Martin et Guillaume du Bellay, ed. V.-L. Bourrilly and F. Vindry, 4 vols. 1908–19.

du Bellay, Jean, *Ambassades en Angleterre. La première ambassade (sep. 1527–fév. 1529). Correspondance diplomatique*, ed. V.-L. Bourrilly and P. de Vaissière. 1905.

   Correspondance du cardinal Jean du Bellay, ed. R. Scheurer, 2 vols. 1969–73.

Erasmus, D., *Opus epistolarum*, ed. P. S. Allen and H. M. Allen, 8 vols. Oxford, 1906–34.

Estienne, C., *Le guide des chemins de France de 1553*, ed. J. Bonnerot, 2 vols. 1936.

[Evelyn], *The Diary of John Evelyn*, ed. E. S. De Beer. London, 1959.

[Florange], *Mémoires du maréchal de Florange dit le jeune adventureux*, ed. R. Goubaux and P. A. Lemoisne, 2 vols. 1913–24.

Fontanon, A. (ed.), *Les édicts et ordonnances des rois de France*, 3 vols. 1611.

Fourquevaux, Sieur de, *Instructions sur le Faict de la Guerre*, ed. G. Dickinson. London, 1954.

Fraikin, J. (ed.), *Nonciatures de France: Clément VII*, 2 vols. 1906.

Français en Amérique pendant la première moitié du XVIᵉ siècle, Les, ed. C.-A. Julien, R. Herval and T. Beauchesne. 1946.

[Francis I], *Cronique du roy Françoys Premier de ce nom*, ed. G. Guiffrey. 1860.

   Poésies de François Iᵉʳ, ed. A. Champollion-Figeac. 1847.

[Granvelle], *Papiers d'état du cardinal de Granvelle*, ed. C. Weiss, 9 vols. 1841–52.

Guicciardini, F., *The History of Italy*, tr. A. P. Goddard, 10 vols. London, 1763.

Guiffrey, G., *Procès criminel de Jehan de Poytiers, seigneur de Saint-Vallier*. 1867.

Hall, E., *Henry VIII*, ed. C. Whibley, 2 vols. London, 1904.

Isambert, F.-A., *Recueil général des anciennes lois françaises*, 29 vols. 1827–33.

Jacqueton, G., *Documents relatifs à l'administration financière en France de Charles VII à François Iᵉʳ (1443–1523)*. 1891.

Jourda, P., *Repertoire analytique et chronologique de la correspondance de Marguerite d'Angoulême*. 1930.

Journal d'un bourgeois de Paris sous le règne de François Ier *(1515–1536), Le*, ed. V.-L. Bourrilly. 1910.

Laborde, L. de, *Les comptes des bâtiments du roi (1528–1571)*, 2 vols. 1878–80.

Lefèvre-Pontalis, G., *Correspondance politique de Odet de Selve*. 1888.

Le Glay, A. J. C., *Négociations diplomatiques entre la France et l'Autriche*, 2 vols. 1845.

Letters and Papers, Foreign and Domestic, of the Reign of Henry VIII, ed. J. S. Brewer, J. Gairdner and R. H. Brodie, 21 vols. London, 1862–1910.

Louise de Savoie, *Journal*, in S. Guichenon, *Histoire généalogique de la royal maison de Savoie* (Lyons, 1660), vol. ii, p. 457. Also in Michaud et Poujoulat.

Loyal serviteur, Le, ed. J. Roman. 1878.

Marguerite d'Angoulême, *Heptaméron*, ed. M. François. 1942.

    Lettres de Marguerite d'Angoulême, ed. F. Génin. 1841.

    Nouvelles lettres de Marguerite d'Angoulême, ed. F. Génin. 1842.

Marot, C., *Les épigrammes*, ed. C. A. Mayer. London, 1970.

[Matignon], *Correspondance de Joachim de Matignon, lieutenant-général du roi en Normandie (1516–1548)*, ed. L.-H. Labande. Monaco, 1914.

Merval, S. de (ed.), *Documents relatifs à la fondation du Havre*. Rouen, 1875.

Monluc, B. de, *Commentaires*, ed. P. Courteault, 3 vols. 1911–25.

Négociations diplomatiques de la France avec la Toscane, ed. A. Desjardins, 6 vols. 1859–86.

Ordonnances des rois de France: règne de François Ier, 9 vols. 1902–75.

Paradin, G., *Histoire de nostre temps*. Lyons, 1556.

[Pellicier], *Correspondance politique de Guillaume Pellicier, ambassadeur de France à Venise, 1540–42*, ed. A. Tausserat-Radel, 2 vols. 1899.

Picot, E., *Chants historiques français du XVIe siècle*. 1903.

Procédures politiques du règne de Louis XII, ed. R. de Maulde La Clavière. 1885.

Registres des délibérations du Bureau de la Ville de Paris, i (1499–1526), ed. F. Bonnardot (1883); ii (1527–1539), ed. A. Tuetey (1886); iii (1539–1552), ed. P. Guérin (1886).

Relations des ambassadeurs vénitiens sur les affaires de France, ed. N. Tommaseo, 2 vols. 1838.

Ribier, G., *Lettres et mémoires d'Estat des roys, princes, ambassadeurs et autres ministres sous les règnes de François I*^{er}*, Henri II et François II*, 2 vols. 1666.

Ruble, A. de, 'La cour des enfants de France sous François Ier', *Notices et documents publiés pour la Société de l'Histoire de France*, 1884, pp. 323–30.

Sanuto, M., *Diarii*, 58 vols. Venice, 1879–1903.

Seyssel, C. de, *La monarchie de France*, ed. J. Poujol. 1961. English tr. *The Monarchy of France* by J. H. Hexter, ed. D. R. Kelley. New Haven, Conn., 1981.

State Papers of Henry VIII, 11 vols. London, 1830–52.

Teulet, A., *Relations politiques de la France et de l'Espagne avec l'Ecosse au XVIe siècle*, 5 vols. 1862.

[Tournon], *Correspondance du cardinal François de Tournon*, ed. M. François. 1946.

Vasari, G., *Le vite de' più eccellenti pittori, scultori ed architettori*, ed. G. Milanesi, 9 vols. Florence, 1878–85.

    Lives of the Painters, Sculptors and Architects, ed. W. Gaunt, 4 vols. London, 1963.

[Versoris], *Livre de raison de Me Nicolas Versoris, avocat au Parlement de Paris, 1519–1530*, ed. G. Fagniez. 1885.

Secondary works

Adhémar, J., 'The Collection of Francis the First', *G.B.A.*, 6th ser., xxx (1946), 5–16.
  'Aretino: Artistic Adviser to Francis I', *J.W.C.I.*, xvii (1954), 311–18.
Alvarez, M. F., *Charles V: Elected Emperor and Hereditary Ruler*. London, 1975.
Ambrière, F., *Le favori de François Ier, Gouffier de Bonnivet, amiral de France*. 1936.
Anglo, S., *Spectacle, Pageantry and Early Tudor Policy*. Oxford, 1969.
Armstrong, E., *Robert Estienne, Royal Printer*. Cambridge, 1954.
Arnaud, E., *Histoire des Protestants de Provence, du Comtat-Venaissin et de la principauté d'Orange*, 2 vols. 1884.
Aspects de la propagande religieuse, ed. G. Berthoud et al. Geneva, 1957.
Aubenas, R., and Ricard, R., *L'église et la Renaissance, 1449–1517*. 1951.
Ballaguy, P., *Bayard, 1476–1524*. 1935.
Bapst, E., *Les mariages de Jacques V*. 1889.
Baratier, E., *La démographie provençale du XIIIe au XVIe siècle*. 1961.
Baulant, M., and Meuvret, J., *Prix des céréales extraits de la mercuriale de Paris, 1520–1698*. 1960.
Béguin, S., *L'Ecole de Fontainebleau: le maniérisme à la cour de France*. 1960.
Béguin, S. et al., *La Galerie François Ier au château de Fontainebleau*, special no. 16–17, *Revue de l'art* (1972).
Benedict, P., *Rouen during the Wars of Religion*. Cambridge, 1981.
Bercé, Y.-M., *Croquants et Nu-pieds*. 1974.
Berthoud, G., 'La "Confession" de Maître Noël Béda et le problème de son auteur', *B.H.R.*, xxix (1967), 373–97.
  Antoine Marcourt. Geneva, 1973.
Bezard, Y., *La vie rurale dans le sud de la région parisienne de 1450 à 1560*. 1929.
Biggar, H. P., *The Precursors of Jacques Cartier 1497–1534*. Ottawa, 1911.
Bloch, J.-R., *L'anoblissement en France au temps de François Ier*. 1934.
Bloch, M., *Les rois thaumaturges*. 1961 edn. English tr. *The Royal Touch: Sacred Monarchy and Scrofula in England and France*. London, 1973.
  French Rural History. London, 1966.
Blunt, A., *Art and Architecture in France, 1500–1700*. Harmondsworth, 1957.
  Philibert de L'Orme. London, 1958.
Boissonnade, P., *Histoire de la réunion de la Navarre à la Castille*. 1893.
  'Le mouvement commercial entre la France et les îles britanniques au XVIe siècle', *R.H.*, cxxxiv (1920), 193–228; cxxxv (1920), 1–27.
Bonnet, J., 'La tolérance du cardinal Sadolet', *B.S.H.P.F.*, xxxv (1886), 481–95, 529–43; xxxvi (1887), 57–72, 113–26.
Borély, A. E., 'Origines de la ville du Havre', *R.H.*, xiv (1880), 286–311.
Bossuat, A., *Le bailliage royal de Montferrand, 1425–1556*. 1957.
Bourrilly, V.-L., 'François Ier et Henri VIII; l'intervention de la France dans l'affaire du divorce', *Rev. d'hist. mod. et contemp.*, i (1899), 271–84.
  'François Ier et les Protestants: les essais de concorde en 1535', *B.S.H.P.F.*, xlix (1900), 337–65, 477–95.
  'La première ambassade d'Antonio Rincon en Orient, 1522–23', *Rev. d'hist. mod. et contemp.*, ii (1900–1), 23–44.
  'L'ambassade de La Forest et de Marillac à Constantinople (1535–38)', *R.H.*, lxxvi (1901), 297–328.
  'Le règne de François Ier: état des travaux et questions à traiter', *Rev. d'hist. mod. et contemp.*, iv (1902–3), 513–31, 585–603.

Guillaume du Bellay, seigneur de Langey. 1905.

Jacques Colin, abbé de Saint-Ambroise. 1905; repr. Geneva, 1970.

'Les diplomates de François Ier: Maraviglia à Milan (1532–1533)', *Bulletin italien,* vi (Bordeaux, 1906), 133–46.

'Le cardinal Jean du Bellay en Italie', *Revue des études rabelaisiennes,* v (1907), 246–53, 262–74.

'Antonio Rincon et la politique orientale de François Ier', *R.H.,* cxiii (1913), 64–83, 268–308.

Bourrilly, V.-L., and Weiss, N., 'Jean du Bellay, les Protestants et la Sorbonne', *B.S.H.P.F.,* lii (1903), 97–127, 193–231, liii (1904), 97–143.

Boutruche, R., *Bordeaux de 1453 à 1715.* Bordeaux 1966.

Brandi, K., *The Emperor Charles V,* tr. C. V. Wedgwood. London, 1939.

Braudel, F., *The Mediterranean and the Mediterranean World in the Age of Philip II,* tr. S. Reynolds, 2 vols. London, 1972–3.

Capitalism and Material Life, 1400–1800, tr. M. Kochan. London, 1973.

Breen, Q., *John Calvin: A Study in French Humanism.* Grand Rapids, Mich., 1931.

Brésard, M., *Les foires à Lyon au XVe et au XVIe siècles.* Lyons, 1914.

Bridge, J. S. C., *History of France from the Death of Louis XI,* 5 vols. Oxford, 1921–36.

Buisson, A., *Le chancelier Antoine Duprat.* 1935.

Carrière, V., 'Guillaume Farel propagandiste de la Réformation', *R.H.E.F.,* xx (1934), 37–78.

Introduction aux études d'histoire ecclésiastique locales, 3 vols. 1934–40.

Castan, A., 'La mort de François Ier', *Mémoires de la Société d'émulation du Doubs,* 5th ser., iii (1878), 420–54.

Cauwès, P., 'Les commencements du crédit public en France: les rentes sur l'hôtel de ville au XVIe siècle', *Revue d'économie politique,* ix (1895), 97–123.

Cazeaux, I., *French Music in the Fifteenth and Sixteenth Centuries.* Oxford, 1975.

Champion, P., *Paris au temps de la Renaissance: l'envers de la tapisserie.* 1935.

Chantérac, B. de, *Odet de Foix, vicomte de Lautrec.* 1930.

Chartrou, J., *Les entrées solennelles et triomphales à la Renaissance (1484–1551).* 1928.

Chastel, A., 'L'escalier de la Cour Ovale à Fontainebleau', in *Essays . . . to Rudolf Wittkower,* ed. D. Fraser, H. Hibbard and M. J. Lewine (London, 1967), pp. 74–80.

'La demeure royale au XVIe siècle et le nouveau Louvre', in *Studies in Renaissance and Baroque Art Presented to Anthony Blunt* (London, 1967), pp. 78–82.

Chaunu, P., and Gascon, R., *Histoire économique et sociale de la France,* i (1450–1660), pt 1, *L'état et la ville.* 1977.

Christie, R. C., *Etienne Dolet, the Martyr of the Renaissance.* London, 1880.

Church, W. F., *Constitutional Thought in Sixteenth-Century France.* Cambridge, Mass., 1941.

Clamageran, J.-J., *Histoire de l'impôt en France,* 3 vols. 1867–76.

Clément-Simon, G., 'Un conseiller du roi François Ier, Jean de Selve', *R.Q.H.,* lxxiii (1903), 45–120.

Clough, C. H., 'Francis I and the Courtiers of Castiglione's *Courtier*', *E.S.R.,* viii (1978), 23–70.

Collier, R., and Billioud, J., *Histoire du commerce de Marseille,* iii. (1480–1599). 1951.

Contamine, P., 'L'artillerie royale française à la veille des guerres d'Italie', *Annales de Bretagne*, lxxi (1964), 221–61.

Guerre, état et société à la fin du Moyen Age. 1972.

Coornaert, E., 'La politique économique de la France au début du règne de François Ier', *Annales de l'Université de Paris*, viii (1933), 414–27.

Les Français et le commerce international à Anvers, 2 vols. 1961.

Les corporations en France avant 1789, 2nd edn. 1968.

Courteault, P., *Blaise de Monluc historien.* 1908.

Cox-Rearick, J., *La collection de François Ier.* 1972.

Croix, A., *Nantes et le Pays nantais au XVIe siècle.* 1974.

Cullerier, Dr, 'De quelle maladie est mort François Ier?', *Gazette hebdomadaire de médecine*, xlix (1856), 865–76.

Davis, N. Z., 'A Trade Union in Sixteenth-Century France', *Econ. H.R.*, xix (1966), 48–69.

Society and Culture in Early Modern France. London, 1975.

Decrue, F., *De consilio regis Francisci I.* 1885.

Anne de Montmorency, grand maître et connétable de France à la cour, aux armées et au conseil du roi François Ier. 1885.

Anne de Montmorency, connétable et pair de France sous les rois Henri II, François II et Charles IX. 1889.

Delaruelle, L., *Guillaume Budé.* 1907.

Denieul-Cormier, A., *La France de la Renaissance (1488–1559).* 1962.

Dermenghem, E., 'Un ministre de François Ier: la grandeur et la disgrace de l'amiral Claude d'Annebault', *Revue du XVIe siècle*, ix (1922), 34–50.

Desgardins, E., *Anne de Pisseleu duchesse d'Etampes et François Ier.* 1904.

Devèze, M., *La vie de la forêt française au XVIe siècle*, 2 vols. 1961.

Dictionnaire de biographie française.

Dimier, L., *Le Primatice.* 1900.

Les portraits peints de François Ier. 1910.

Histoire de la peinture française des origines au retour de Vouet 1300 à 1627. 1925.

Di Stefano, G., 'L'Hellénisme en France à l'orée de la Renaissance', in *Humanism in France at the End of the Middle Ages and in the Early Renaissance*, ed. A. H. T. Levi. Manchester, 1970.

Dodu, G., 'Les amours et la mort de François Ier', *R.H.*, clxi (1929), 237–77.

Dognon, P., 'La taille en Languedoc de Charles VIII à François Ier', *A. du M.*, iii (1891), 340.

Les institutions politiques et administratives du Pays de Languedoc du XIIIe siècle aux Guerres de Religion. Toulouse, 1895.

Doucet, R., 'La mort de François Ier', *R.H.*, cxiii (1913), 309–16.

'Pierre du Chastel, grand aumônier de France', *R.H.*, cxxxiii (1920), 212–57; cxxxiv (1920), 1–57.

Etude sur le gouvernement de François Ier dans ses rapports avec le Parlement de Paris, 2 vols. 1921–6.

L'état des finances de 1523. 1923.

'Le Grand Parti de Lyon au XVIe siècle', *R.H.*, clxxi (1933), 474–82.

Finances municipales et crédit public à Lyon au XVIe siècle. 1937.

Les institutions de la France au XVIe siècle, 2 vols. 1948.

'La banque en France au XVIe siècle', *Rev. d'hist. écon. et soc.*, xxix (1951), 115–23.

du Boulay, C.-E., *Historia Universitatis Parisiensis*, 6 vols. 1665–73.

Duby, G., and Wallon, A. (eds.), *Histoire de la France rurale*, ii. 1975.

du Cerceau, J. A., *Les plus excellents bastiments de France (1576–1607)*. Facsimile repr., Farnborough, 1972.

Dupont-Ferrier, G., *Les officiers royaux des bailliages et sénéchaussées*. 1902.

du Tillet, J., *Recueil des roys de France leurs couronne et maison*, 2 vols. 1602.

Ecole de Fontainebleau, L'., Catalogue of exhibition at Grand Palais, Paris, 1972–3.

Emerit, M. E., 'Les capitulations de 1535 ne sont pas une légende', *Annales E.S.C.*, xix (1964), 362–3.

Esmein, A., *A History of Continental Criminal Procedure*, tr. J. Simpson. London, 1914.

Febvre, L., *Autour de l'Heptaméron: amour sacré, amour profane*. 1944.
    'Dolet propagateur de l'évangile', *B.H.R.*, vi (1945), 98–170.
    Le problème de l'incroyance au XVIᵉ siècle: la religion de Rabelais. 1947.
    Au cœur religieux du XVIᵉ siècle. 1957.

Félibien, M., *Histoire de la ville de Paris*, 5 vols. 1725.

Fêtes et cérémonies au temps de Charles Quint, ed. J. Jacquot. 1960.

Floquet, A., *Histoire du parlement de Normandie*, 7 vols. Rouen, 1840.

Fraisse, M., 'Sur la maladie et la mort de François 1ᵉʳ'. Unpublished medical thesis, University of Paris, 1962.

François, M., *Le cardinal François de Tournon*. 1951.
    'L'idée d'empire en France à l'époque de Charles-Quint', *Charles-Quint et son temps*. 1959.

Franklin, A., *Précis de l'histoire de la Bibliothèque du Roi*, 2nd edn. 1875.

Freedberg, S. J., *Andrea del Sarto*, 2 vols. Cambridge, Mass., 1963.

French Humanism, 1470–1600, ed. W. L. Gundersheimer. London, 1969.

Freymond, J., *La politique de François 1ᵉʳ à l'égard de la Savoie*. Lausanne, 1939.

Gachard, L.-P., *La captivité de François 1ᵉʳ et le traité de Madrid*. Brussels, 1860.

Gaffarel, P., *Histoire du Brésil français au seizième siècle*. 1878.
    'Les massacres de Cabrières et de Mérindol en 1545', *R.H.*, cvii (1911), 241–71.

Gaillard, *Histoire de François premier*, 7 vols. 1766.

Gascon, R., *Grand commerce et vie urbaine au XVIᵉ siècle: Lyon et ses marchands*, 2 vols. 1971.

Gébelin, F., *Les châteaux de la Renaissance*. 1927.

Giesey, R. E., *The Royal Funeral Ceremony in Renaissance France*. Geneva, 1960.

Gigon, S.-C., *La révolte de la gabelle en Guyenne, 1548–1549*. 1906.

Giono, J., *Le désastre de Pavie*. 1963.

Godefroy, T., *Le cérémonial françois*, 2 vols. 1649.

Golson, L., 'Serlio, Primaticcio and the Architectural Grotto', *G.B.A.*, lxxvii (1971), 95–108.

Goubert, P., 'Recent Theories and Research on French Population between 1500–1700', in *Population in History*, ed. D. V. Glass and D. E. C. Eversley (London, 1965), pp. 456–73.

Guénée, B., *Tribunaux et gens de justice dans le bailliage de Senlis à la fin du Moyen Age*. Strasbourg, 1963.

Guénée, B., and Lehoux, F., *Les entrées royales françaises de 1328 à 1515*. 1968.

Guénin, E., *Ango et ses pilotes*. 1901.

Guillaume Farel, 1489–1565: biographie nouvelle écrite d'après les documents originaux par un groupe d'historiens, professeurs et pasteurs de Suisse, de France et d'Italie. Neuchâtel, 1930.

Guillaume, J., 'Léonard de Vinci, Dominique de Cortone et l'escalier du modèle en bois de Chambord', *G.B.A.*, i (1968), 93–108.

Gutton, J. P., *La société et les pauvres: l'exemple de la généralité de Lyon, 1534–1789*. 1971.

La société et les pauvres en Europe (XVIᵉ–XVIIIᵉ siècles). 1974.

Hale, J. R., 'Armies, Navies and the Art of War', in *The New Cambridge Modern History*, ii, *The Reformation*, ed. G. R. Elton. Cambridge, 1958.

Halkin, L. E., and Dansaert, G., *Charles de Lannoy*. Brussels, 1934.

Hamy, le P., *Entrevue de François Iᵉʳ avec Henri VIII à Boulogne-sur-Mer en 1532*. 1898.

Entrevue de François Iᵉʳ avec Clément VII à Marseille, 1533. 1900.

Harding, R. R., *Anatomy of a Power Elite: The Provincial Governors of Early Modern France*. New Haven, Conn. and London, 1978.

Hari, R., 'Les placards de 1534', in *Aspects de la propagande religieuse*, ed. G. Berthoud et al. Geneva, 1957.

Hauser, H., 'Sur la date exacte de la mort de Louis XII et de l'avènement de François Iᵉʳ', *Rev. d'hist. mod. et contemp.*, v (1903–4), 172–82.

Etudes sur la réforme française. 1909.

Les sources de l'histoire de France au XVIᵉ siècle, ii, *François Iᵉʳ et Henri II (1515–1559)*. 1909.

'Le traité de Madrid et la cession de la Bourgogne à Charles-Quint', *Revue bourguignonne*, xxii (1912).

Les débuts du capitalisme. 1924.

Ouvriers du temps passé. 1927.

Hempsall, D., 'The Languedoc 1520–1540: A Study of Pre-Calvinist Heresy in France', *A.R.*, lxii (1971), 225–44.

'Martin Luther and the Sorbonne, 1519–21', *B.I.H.R.*, xlvi (1973), 28–40.

'Measures to Suppress "La Peste Luthérienne" in France, 1521–2', *B.I.H.R.*, xlix (1976), 296–9.

Herbet, F., *Le château de Fontainebleau*. 1937.

Heubi, W., *François Iᵉʳ et le mouvement intellectuel en France, 1515–1547*. Lausanne, 1913.

Hexter, J. H., *The Vision of Politics on the Eve of the Reformation: More, Machiavelli and Seyssel*. London, 1973.

Heydenreich, L. H., 'Leonardo da Vinci, Architect of Francis I', *Burlington Magazine*, xciv (Oct. 1952), 277–85.

Hobson, A., *Great Libraries*. London, 1970.

Hook, J., *The Sack of Rome*. London, 1972.

Hyrvoix, A., 'François Iᵉʳ et la première guerre de religion en Suisse, 1529–1531', *R.Q.H.*, lxxi (1902), 465–537.

'Noël Bédier, d'après des documents inédits', *R.Q.H.*, lxxii (1902), 578–91.

Imbart de La Tour, P., *Les origines de la Réforme*, 4 vols. 1905–35.

Jacquart, J., *La crise rurale en Ile-de-France 1550–1670*. 1974.

François Iᵉʳ. 1981.

Jacqueton, G., *La politique extérieure de Louise de Savoie*. 1892.

'Le Trésor de l'Epargne sous François Iᵉʳ, 1523–1547', *R.H.*, lv (1894), 1–43; lvi (1894), 1–38.

Jedin, H., *A History of the Council of Trent*, tr. E. Graf, 2 vols. London, 1957–61.

Jourda, P., *Marguerite d'Angoulême*, 2 vols. 1930.

Julien, C. A., *Les voyages de découverte et les premiers établissements*. 1948.

Kane, J. E., 'Sur un poème du roi François Ier', *B.H.R.*, 38 (1976), 89–92.
'Edition critique de l'oeuvre du roi François Ier'. Unpublished Ph.D. thesis, University of Liverpool, 1977.

Kelley, D. R., *The Beginning of Ideology: Consciousness and Society in the French Reformation*. Cambridge, 1981.

Keohane, N. O., *Philosophy and the State in France: The Renaissance to the Enlightenment*. Princeton, N.J., 1980.

Knecht, R. J., 'The Concordat of 1516: A Re-assessment', *University of Birmingham Historical Journal*, ix (1963), 16–32. Repr. in *Government in Reformation Europe*, ed. H. J. Cohn (London, 1971), pp. 91–112.
Francis I and Absolute Monarchy. London, 1969.
'The Early Reformation in England and France: A Comparison', *History*, lvii (1972), 1–16.
'Francis I, Prince and Patron of the Northern Renaissance', in *The Courts of Europe*, ed. A. G. Dickens (London, 1977), pp. 99–119.
'The Court of Francis I', *E.S.R.*, viii (1978), 1–22.
'Francis I, "Defender of the Faith"?', in *Wealth and Power in Tudor England*, ed. E. W. Ives, R. J. Knecht and J. J. Scarisbrick. London, 1978.
'Francis I and Paris', *History*, lxvi (1981), 18–33.

Kusenberg, K., *Le Rosso*. 1931.

La Chapelle, Baron de, 'Jean Le Veneur et le Canada', *Nova Francia*, vi (1931), 341–3.

La Coste-Messelière, M. G. de, 'Battista della Palla conspirateur, marchand ou homme de cour?', *L'œil*, cxxix (1965), 19–24, 34.

La Martinière, J. de, 'Les Etats de 1532 et l'Union de la Bretagne à la France', *Bulletin de la Société polymathique du Morbihan*, Vannes, 1911, pp. 177–93.

Langbein, J. H., *Prosecuting Crime in the Renaissance*. Cambridge, Mass., 1974.

La Roncière, C. de, *Histoire de la marine française*, 6 vols. 1899–1932.

Lavedan, P., *Histoire de l'urbanisme*. 1941.

Lebey, A., *Le connétable de Bourbon*. 1904.

Lecoq, A.-M., 'La salamandre royale dans les entrées de François Ier', in *Les fêtes de la Renaissance*, iii, ed. J. Jacquot and E. Konigson (1975), pp. 93–104.

Leff, G., *Heresy in the Later Middle Ages*, 2 vols. Manchester, 1967.

Lefranc, A., *Histoire du Collège de France*. 1893.
La vie quotidienne au temps de la Renaissance. 1938.

Lemonnier, H., *Les guerres d'Italie: la France sous Charles VIII, Louis XII et François Ier (1492–1547)* (vol. v of *Histoire de France*, ed. E. Lavisse (1903)).

Léonard, E. G., *Le Protestant français*. 1953.
Histoire générale du Protestantisme, 2 vols. 1961.

Le Roy Ladurie, E., *Les paysans de Languedoc*, 2 vols. 1966.
Carnival: A People's Uprising at Romans, 1579–80, tr. M. Feeney (London, 1980).

Le Roy Ladurie, E., and Morineau, M., *Histoire économique et sociale de la France*, i (1450–1660), pt 2, *Paysannerie et croissance*. 1977.

Lesueur, F., and Lesueur, P., *Le château de Blois*. 1914–21.

Lesueur, P., *Dominique de Cortone, dit Le Boccador*. 1928.

Levasseur, E., 'Mémoire sur les monnaies du règne de François Ier', in *Ordonnances*, i, pp. xi–ccxxxvii.
Histoire du commerce de la France, 2 vols. 1911.

Lewis, P. S., *Later Medieval France*. London, 1968.

Loirette, G., 'La première application à Bordeaux du Concordat de 1516: Gabriel et Charles de Grammont (1529–30)', *A. du M.*, lxviii (1956).

Lot, F., *Recherches sur les effectifs des armées françaises des guerres d'Italie aux Guerres de Religion, 1494–1562*. 1962.

Loyseau, C., *Cinq livres du droit des offices*. 1610.

McNeil, D. O., *Guillaume Budé and Humanism in the Reign of Francis I*. Geneva, 1975.

Madelin, L., *François Ier le souverain politique*. 1937.

Major, J. Russell, *Representative Institutions in Renaissance France, 1421–1559*. Madison, Wisc., 1960.

'The Crown and the Aristocracy in Renaissance France', *American Historical Review*, lxix (1964), 631–45.

Representative Government in Early Modern France. New Haven, Conn. and London, 1980.

Mann, M., *Erasme et les débuts de la réforme française, 1517–1536*. 1934.

Mariotte, J.-Y., 'François Ier et la Ligue de Smalkalde', *Revue suisse d'histoire*, xvi (1966), 206–42.

Martin, V., *Les origines du Gallicanisme*, 2 vols. 1939.

Martineau, A., 'L'amiral Chabot, seigneur de Brion (1492?–1542)', in *Positions de thèses de l'Ecole des Chartes* (1883), pp. 77–83.

Marx, J., *L'Inquisition en Dauphiné: étude sur le développement et la répression de l'hérésie et de la sorcellerie du XIVe siècle au début du règne de François Ier*. 1914.

Maugis, E., *Histoire du Parlement de Paris*, 3 vols. 1913–16.

Maulde La Clavière, R. de, *Louise de Savoie et François Ier: trente ans de jeunesse, 1485–1515*. 1895.

Mayer, C. A., *La religion de Marot*. Geneva, 1960.

Mellen, P., *Jean Clouet*. London, 1971.

Merle, L., *La métairie et l'évolution agraire de la Gâtine poitevine de la fin du moyen âge à la Révolution*. 1958.

Michelet, J., *Histoire de France*, ix, *La Renaissance*; x, *La Réforme*. N.d.

Mignet, F., *La rivalité de François Ier et de Charles-Quint*, 2 vols. 1875.

Moore, W. G., *La réforme allemande et la littérature française*. Strasbourg, 1930.

'The Early French Reformation', *History*, xxv (1940), 48–53.

Moreau, E. de, Jourda, P., and Janelle, P., *La crise religieuse du XVIe siècle*. 1950.

Morgan, P., 'Un chroniqueur gallois à Calais', *Revue du Nord*, xlvii (1965), 195–202.

Mousnier, R., *Etudes sur la France de 1494 à 1559*. Cours de Sorbonne, 1964.

Etat et société sous François Ier et pendant le gouvernement personnel de Louis XIV. Cours de Sorbonne, 1966.

La vénalité des offices sous Henri IV et Louis XIII, 2nd edn. 1971.

Nicholls, D., 'Social Change and Early Protestantism in France: Normandy, 1520–62', *E.S.R.*, x (1980), 279–308.

'Inertia and Reform in the Pre-Tridentine French Church: The Response to Protestantism in the Diocese of Rouen, 1520–1562', *Journal of Ecclesiastical History*, xxxii (1981), 185–97.

Oman, C., *A History of the Art of War in the XVIth Century*. New York, 1937.

Pagès, G., *La monarchie d'Ancien Régime en France*. 1946.

Paillard, C., 'La mort de François Ier et les premiers temps du règne de Henri II d'après les dépêches de Jean de Saint-Mauris (avril–juin 1547)', *R.H.*, v (1877), 84–120.

'Documents relatifs aux projets d'évasion de François Ier ainsi qu'à la situation intérieure de la France', *R.H.*, viii (1878), 297–367.

L'invasion allemande en 1544. 1884.

Panofsky, D., and Panofsky, E., 'The Iconography of the Galerie François 1er at Fontainebleau', *G.B.A.*, 6th ser., lii (1958), 113–90.

Paris: fonctions d'une capitale, ed. G. Michaud. Colloques: Cahiers de civilisation, 1962.

Paris, P., *Etudes sur François Premier*, 2 vols. 1885.

Parker, T. H. L., *John Calvin*. London, 1975.

Pastor, L. von, *The History of the Popes*, tr. F. I. Antrobus and R. F. Kerr, 23 vols. London, 1891–1933.

Pedretti, C., 'Leonardo da Vinci: Manuscripts and Drawings of the French Period, 1517–18', *G.B.A.*, 6th ser., lxxvi (1970), 285–318.

   Leonardo da Vinci: The Royal Palace at Romorantin. Cambridge, Mass., 1972.

Penrose, B., *Travel and Discovery in the Renaissance, 1420–1620*. Cambridge, Mass., 1952.

Peronnet, M. C., 'Les évêques de l'ancienne France', 2 vols. Unpublished thesis, University of Lille, 1977.

Picot, E., 'Les italiens en France au XVIe siècle', *Bulletin italien*, i (Bordeaux, 1901), 92–137; iii (1903), 7–36.

Pieri, P., *Il Rinascimento e la crisi militare italiana*. Turin, 1952.

Pinvert, L., *Lazare de Baïf (1496?–1547)*. 1900.

Pollard, A. F., *Henry VIII*. London, 1913.

Pollet, J. V., *Martin Bucer*, 2 vols. 1962.

Porée, C., *Un parlementaire sous François 1er: Guillaume Poyet, 1473–1548*. Angers, 1898.

Potter, D. L., 'Diplomacy in the Mid-16th Century: England and France, 1536–1550'. Unpublished Ph.D. thesis, Cambridge University, 1973.

   'Foreign Policy in the Age of the Reformation: French Involvement in the Schmalkaldic War, 1544–1547', *Historical Journal*, xx, 3 (1977), 525–44.

Prentout, H., *Les Etats Provinciaux de Normandie*, 3 vols. Caen, 1925.

Pressouyre, S., 'Les fontes de Primatice', *Bulletin monumental*, 1969, pp. 223–39.

Procacci, G., 'La Provence à la veille des Guerres de Religion: une période décisive, 1535–45', *Rev. d'hist. mod. et contemp.*, v (1958), 249–50.

Quentin-Bauchart, E., *La bibliothèque de Fontainebleau, 1515–89*. 1891.

Quinn, D. B., *North America from Earliest Discovery to First Settlements*. New York, 1978.

Raveau, P., *La condition économique et l'état social du Poitou au XVIe siècle*. 1931.

Redlich, F., 'De Praeda Militari: looting and booty, 1500–1815', *Vierteljahrschrift für Sozial- und Wirtschaftsgeschichte*, no. 39 (1956).

Renaudet, A., *Préréforme et humanisme à Paris pendant les premières guerres d'Italie, 1494–1517*. 1953.

   Humanisme et Renaissance. Geneva, 1958.

Reumont, R., and Baschet, A., *La jeunesse de Catherine de Médicis*. 1866.

Reymond, M., and Reymond M.-R., 'Léonard de Vinci, architecte du château de Chambord', *G.B.A.*, i (1913), 337.

Rice, E. F., 'Humanist Aristotelianism in France', in *Humanism in France at the End of the Middle Ages and in the Early Renaissance*, ed. A. H. T. Levi. Manchester, 1970.

Roelker, N. L., *Queen of Navarre, Jeanne d'Albret*. Cambridge, Mass. 1968.

Romier, L., *Les origines politiques des Guerres de Religion*, 2 vols. 1913–14.

Rott, E., *Histoire de la représentation diplomatique de la France auprès des cantons suisses*, 10 vols. 1900–35.

Roy, M., *Artistes et monuments de la Renaissance en France*. 1929.

Rozet, A., and Lembey, J.-F., *L'invasion de la France et le siège de Saint-Dizier par Charles-Quint en 1544*. 1910.

Ruble, A. de, *Le mariage de Jeanne d'Albret*. 1877.

Russell, J. G., *The Field of Cloth of Gold*. London, 1969.
 'The Search for Universal Peace: The Conferences at Calais and Bruges in 1521', *B.I.H.R.*, xliv (Nov. 1971), 162–93.

Salles, G., 'Un traître au XVIᵉ siècle: Clément Champion, valet de chambre de François Iᵉʳ', *R.Q.H.*, n.s. xxiv (1900), 41–73.

Saulnier, V.-L., 'La mort du Dauphin François et son tombeau poétique (1536)', *B.H.R.*, vi (1945), 50–97.

Sauval, H., *Histoire et recherches des antiquités de la ville de Paris*, 2 vols. 1724.

Scarisbrick, J. J., *Henry VIII*. London, 1968.

Schenk, W., *Reginald Pole*. London, 1950.

Schick, L., *Un grand homme d'affaires au début du XVIᵉʳ siècle, Jacob Fugger*. 1957.

Schmidt, C., *Gérard Roussel prédicateur de la reine Marguerite de Navarre*. Strasbourg, 1845.

Schnapper, B., *Les rentes au XVIᵉ siècle*. 1957.

Schneebalg-Perelman, S., 'Richesses du garde-meuble parisien de François Iᵉʳ: inventaires inédits de 1542 et 1551', *G.B.A.*, 6th ser., lxxviii (1971), 253–304.

Seward, D., *Prince of the Renaissance: The Life of François I*. London, 1973.

Shearman, J., *Andrea del Sarto*, 2 vols. Oxford, 1965.
 Mannerism. Harmondsworth, 1967.

Shellabarger, S., *The Chevalier Bayard: A Study in Fading Chivalry*. London, n.d.

Shennan, J. H., *The Parlement of Paris*. London, 1968.
 The Origins of the Modern European State 1450–1725. London, 1974.

Simone, F., *Il Rinascimento francese*. Turin, 1961. Partially tr. H. G. Hall as *The French Renaissance*. London, 1969.

Smith, P. M., *The Anti-courtier Trend in Sixteenth Century French Literature*. Geneva, 1966.
 Clément Marot, Poet of the French Renaissance. London, 1970.

Spont, A., 'La taille en Languedoc, de 1450 à 1515', *A. du M.*, ii (1890).
 Semblançay (?–1527): la bourgeoisie financière au début du XVIᵉ siècle. 1895.
 'Marignan et l'organisation militaire sous François Iᵉʳ', *R.Q.H.*, n.s., xxii (1899), 59–77.

Spooner, F. C., *L'économie mondiale et les frappes monétaires en France, 1493–1680*. 1956.

Sutherland, N. M., *The French Secretaries of State in the Age of Catherine de Medici*. London, 1962.
 The Huguenot Struggle for Recognition. New Haven, Conn. and London, 1980.

Taylor, F. L., *The Art of War in Italy, 1494–1529*. Cambridge, 1921.

Terrasse, C., *François Iᵉʳ: le roi et le règne*, 3 vols. 1945–70.

Tervarent, G. de, 'La pensée de Rosso', *Les énigmes de l'art: l'Art Savant* (Bruges, 1952), pp. 28ff.

Thom, R., *Die Schlacht bei Pavia*. Berlin, 1907.

Thomas, J., *Le Concordat de 1516: ses origines, son histoire au XVIᵉ siècle*, 3 vols. 1910.

Thou, J.-A. de, *Histoire universelle*, 16 vols. London, 1734.

Tietze, H., 'Titian's Portrait of King Francis I', *Connoisseur*, cxxvi (Oct. 1950).

Toudouze, G.-G., *Françoise de Châteaubriant et François Iᵉʳ*. 1948.

Tietze, H., 'Titian's Portrait of King Francis I', *Connoisseur*, cxxvi (Oct. 1950).

Toudouze, G.-G., *Françoise de Châteaubriant et François Ier*. 1948.

Treccani degli Alfieri, G., *Storia di Milano*, 12 vols. and index. Milan, 1953–1966.

Trocmé, E., and Delafosse, M., *Le commerce rochelais de la fin du XVe siècle au début du XVIIe*. 1952.

Ursu, J., *La politique orientale de François Ier*. 1908.

Vaissière, P. de, *Charles de Marillac, ambassadeur et homme politique sous les règnes de François Ier, Henri II et François II (1510–1560)*. 1896.

Valois, N., *Histoire de la Sanction Pragmatique de Bourges sous Charles VII*. 1906.

Van Doren, L. Scott, 'War Taxation, Institutional Change and Social Conflict in Provincial France – The Royal *Taille* in Dauphiné, 1494–1559', *Proceedings of the American Philosophical Society*, cxxi, 1 (Feb. 1977), 70–96.

Varillas, A., *Histoire de François Ier*, 2 vols. 1685.

Veissière, M., 'Le groupe évangélique de Meaux (début du XVIe siècle) à la lumière de quelques travaux récents', *Bulletin de la Société d'histoire et d'art du diocèse de Meaux*, xxiv (1973), 1–9.

Vial, M., *L'histoire et la légende de Jean Cléberger dit 'le bon Allemand' (1485?–1546)*. Lyons, 1914.

Viénot, J., *Histoire de la réforme française des origines à l'Edit de Nantes*, 2 vols. 1926.

Vigne, M., *La banque à Lyon du XVe au XVIIIe siècle*. Lyons, 1903.

Viollet, P., *Le roi et ses ministres pendant les trois derniers siècles de la monarchie*. 1912.

Weiss, N., 'La Sorbonne, le Parlement de Paris et les livres hérétiques de 1542 à 1546', *B.S.H.P.F.*, xxxiv (1885), 19–28.

'Documents inédits pour servir à l'histoire de la réforme sous François Ier, 1536–1537', *B.S.H.P.F.*, xxxiv (1885), 164–77.

La Chambre Ardente: étude sur la liberté de conscience sous François Ier et Henri II, 1540–1550. 1889.

'Les premières professions de foi des Protestants français, 1532–47', *B.S.H.P.F.*, xliii (1894), 57–74.

Wendel, F., *Calvin*. London, 1965.

Williams, G. H., *The Radical Reformation*. London, 1962.

Wingert, P. S., 'The Funerary Urn of Francis I', *Art Bulletin*, xxi (1939), 383–396.

Wolfe, M., 'French Views on Wealth and Taxes from the Middle Ages to the Old Régime', *Journal of Economic History*, xxvi (1966), 466–83.

The Fiscal System of Renaissance France. New Haven, Conn. and London, 1972.

Wroth, L. C., *The Voyages of Giovanni da Verrazzano, 1524–1528*. New Haven, Conn., 1970.

Zeller, G., *La réunion de Metz à la France (1552–1648)*, i, *L'occupation*. 1926.

'Les rois de France candidats à l'Empire', *R.H.*, clxxiii (1934), 273–311, 497–534.

'Gouverneurs de provinces au XVIe siècle', *R.H.*, clxxxv (1939), 225–56.

'Aux origines de notre système douanier: les premières taxes à l'importation (XVIe siècle)', in *Mélanges 1945*. Faculté des lettres, Strasbourg, Etudes historiques, iii. 1947.

'Deux capitalistes strasbourgeois du XVIe siècle', *Etudes d'histoire moderne et contemporaine*, i (1947), 5–14.

'L'administration monarchique avant les intendants: parlements et gouverneurs',
  R.H., cxcvii (1947), 188–215.
Les institutions de la France au XVIe siècle. 1948.
'Une légende qui a la vie dure: les capitulations de 1535', *Rev. d'hist. mod. et
  contemp.*, ii (1955).
Zerner, H., *The School of Fontainebleau*. London, 1969.

Index